The Commonwealth Office

1925~68

The Commonwealth Office

1925~68

JOE GARNER

Former Permanent Under-Secretary in the Office

LONDON

HEINEMANN

IBADAN · NAIROBI · LUSAKA

Heinemann Educational Books Ltd
48 Charles Street, London WIX 8AH
P.M.B. 5205 Ibadan · P.O. Box 45314 Nairobi · P.O. Box 3966 Lusaka

EDINBURGH   MELBOURNE   TORONTO   AUCKLAND   SINGAPORE
HONG KONG   KUALA LUMPUR   NEW DELHI   KINGSTON

ISBN 0 435 32355 5

British Library Cataloguing in Publication Data

Garner, Joe
   The Commonwealth Office, 1925–68.
   1. Great Britain.   Commonwealth Office – History
   I. Title
   354′.41′00892   JN453.C/

   ISBN 0-435-32355-5

Set in 11 on 12pt Ehrhardt
Printed in Great Britain by
Richard Clay (The Chaucer Press) Ltd, Bungay, Suffolk

Contents

Contents

Foreword

By the Rt. Hon. Malcolm MacDonald, O.M.

When I was Secretary of State for Dominion Affairs in the mid-1930s my private secretary was Sir Edward Marsh. Tall, immaculately dressed and handsome, with a monocle stuck in one eye, he appeared much more like a Secretary of State than inelegant I did. An intellectual aesthete, he had many intimate friends in high and mighty places. He worked quite hard in his room alongside mine, but comparatively little of his toil was concerned with Dominion affairs. Much of the time he sat correcting the proofs of his friend Winston Churchill's latest book-to-be, studying the catalogues of exhibitions of paintings by up-and-coming artists of whom he was a patron, telephoning to theatrical stars like Noel Coward about forthcoming performances behind the footlights, and writing notes of thanks to duchesses and other eminent hostesses for grand social parties.

At a desk in the same room sat my assistant private secretary, a young man named Joe Garner. He in fact did almost all the day-to-day work of both the private secretary and the assistant private secretary. I depended on him a great deal not only in our normal, constantly busy official tasks, but now and then also through periods of crisis – such as King Edward VIII's abdication – which could seriously affect for good or ill Britain's relations with the Dominions. Hard-working, capable and unflappable, he was also intuitively wise. I therefore was not surprised to watch him through the next few decades rise from one important post to another, sometimes in Britain and at other times in countries overseas.

His official career coincided almost exactly with the 43 years' existence of the Commonwealth Office. He first entered it as a junior officer in 1930, five years after its creation (called then the Dominions Office); and he left it, having been for six years its Permanent Under Secretary, a few months before it was integrated with the Foreign Office in 1968. Among the other posts which he filled in the meantime were Deputy High Commissioner in Canada, Deputy High Commissioner in India and High Commissioner in Canada. He thus knew intimately the peoples of important nations in both the 'old' and the 'new' Commonwealth, a knowledge which was made ever more extensive by his frequent working visits to other lands throughout the Commonwealth.

During that era the Office played a vital role in making a notable piece of recent history. It helped to guide successfully the gradual transformation of most of Britain's old Colonial Empire into today's Commonwealth of Nations. When the Commonwealth was formally recognized by the 1926 Imperial Conference, its members consisted of only Great Britain and six independent Dominions, all of them ruled by governments of white men. By the time that the Office was joined with the Foreign Office, the number of free nations in the partnership had grown to 28; and it has since swelled to 36. They are distributed across all the continents and seas, their citizens constitute about a quarter of the total population of the world, and they represent almost every different race in the variegated human family. In these times when some of the most delicate, difficult and indeed dangerous problems that afflict mankind concern interracial relations, this unique multi-racial international partnership can play a distinctly valuable part in helping to solve them gradually, wisely and (it is to be hoped) peacefully.

Through most of its years the Office played a dual role. In addition to its primary task of being responsible for handling relations between the government in Britain and each of the governments of the Commonwealth nations overseas, it also acted as the unofficial 'secretariat' organizing Commonwealth Conferences and attempting to co-ordinate the views of all those governments on important international matters of common concern. It only ceased to perform the latter function when the official Commonwealth Secretariat was established in the 1960s. Its dual role sometimes produced uneasy problems. On the one hand some Ministries in Whitehall felt that the Office was less than whole-hearted in the defence of purely British interests in its dealings with our partners in the Commonwealth; and on the other hand some at least of the overseas governments and parliaments – touchy about their nations' sovereign independence – were suspicious that their old imperial master was still seeking to be their overlord. This called for exceptional tact, understanding and frankly honest diplomacy on the part of the officials as well as Ministers in the Office.

From its beginning the officials did their work in sensible, and sometimes rather novel, ways. Their contacts with Dominion High Commissioners, for instance, were much more informal, relaxed and indeed genial than those which the sometimes too pompous officials in more ancient and old-fashioned Ministries like the Foreign and Colonial Offices established with Foreign Ambassadors and Colonial eminences. This more friendly attitude was welcomed and reciprocated by the Ministers as well as the Diplomatic Representatives of the newly emerging Commonwealth nations. It helped to make cooperation between all the Commonwealth governments especially cordial.

Garner contributed considerably to this happy state of affairs. That was due largely to his personality. Informal and friendly, with a good sense of humour, he was sincere in everything that he did. He also possessed a shrewd understanding of what was practical in international affairs. Moreover, he always recognized the main principles involved in any problem that arose, and strove to ensure their maintenance in whatever policy was devised, without becoming (as more bureaucratic government officials do) unduly preoccupied with less important details. He believed deeply in the special value of the steadily expanding Commonwealth, and his increasingly worldwide diplomatic experience made him a sagacious counsellor to successive Secretaries of State regarding its growth.

It was his sense of realism that led him to favour in the mid-1960s the staffs of the Commonwealth Office and the Foreign Office being merged in a single Diplomatic Service. This was not an easy decision for the members of the Office to accept; and it was fortunate that they were led by a man whom they could trust to do his best for them, and to minimize the effect on their careers of being absorbed into a much larger organization. Garner himself became Head of the Diplomatic Service shortly after its inception, and guided it through its early years.

He was always greatly helped by his wife Peggy, who shared his attachment to the Office and his interest in Commonwealth affairs. Wherever they lived, in Britain or other lands, she worked to develop friendship and understanding among the women concerned with Commonwealth matters, especially the wives of the British and other Commonwealth officials. Hence, for instance, her creation of the CROWS described in this book.

No one is better qualified than Garner to write the narrative of the Commonwealth Office. He tells the whole story with great authority. He not only watched from close quarters a fine piece of history being made, but himself helped to make it.

Author's Preface

Chance plays a strange part in human affairs. In October 1930 I was assigned to the Dominions Office – a Department of whose existence up till that time I had been sublimely ignorant (my choice had been for the Board of Education, followed by the Air Ministry). The Dominions Office had been made a separate Department in 1925, but was only able to boast of a Secretary of State separate from the Colonial Office a few months before I arrived.

The name of the Office was changed to Commonwealth Relations Office in 1947 (a month before it absorbed the India Office) and to Commonwealth Office in 1966 (when it absorbed the Colonial Office). I retired in February 1968; two weeks later the Government announced the merger with the Foreign Office which came about in October of that year. By coincidence therefore I served in the Office for most of its existence as a separate Department.

All the important Departments of State have provided some public account of their stewardship, some on more than one occasion. Surprisingly, although the Office was concerned with events affecting the British people over a period of forty years, no full history of it has ever been written and the Office itself has long been conscious of this lack. After the Office ceased to have a separate existence I felt that, unless the task was undertaken soon while memories were still fresh, the story would never be written.

In my retirement the Institute of Commonwealth Studies in the University of London invited me to become Chairman of their Committee of Management. I found there great interest in the possibility of a book about the Commonwealth Office and was persuaded not unwillingly to undertake the job myself. I am grateful to Professor Morris-Jones the Director and to other members of the staff without whose support and encouragement the book would never have been written.

I have thought it convenient to tell the story chronologically and to divide it into four periods, each covering approximately a decade. Curiously 1947 marks a watershed in two ways. It divides the Dominions Office from the Commonwealth Relations Office. It is also the date up to which under the thirty-year rule the records are open. For the first two periods therefore I have been able to make use of new material from official sources and I acknowledge my gratitude to the Nuffield Foundation for a grant which made research in the Public Records Office possible. For the later periods, the records remain closed and I have not sought permission to refresh my memory by perusing the official papers; I have, however, here as elsewhere relied on the memory of myself and others and have also made use of biographical and diary material where it has seemed to throw light on matters.

I have been bold enough to attempt to give some impressions of both past and present members who played their part in the story as Ministers, High Commissioners or officials. Inevitably there are many more who are not specifically recorded in the book, for of necessity I have had to be selective and to choose examples to illustrate a general theme. I can only hope that I have given offence neither to those included nor to those omitted. All in their varied ways played their part and, if I were minded to make a dedication, it would be to all who served under the Commonwealth Office.

This is a book about an Office and, though I have sought to include sufficient information to describe the scene, I have tried to resist any temptation to stray into the wider field of developments in the Commonwealth as a whole, on which there already exists an authoritative and substantial literature. The story is not told at the request or on behalf of the Government; I am grateful to the FCO and particularly to the Librarian, Bernard Cheeseman, who kindly read the proofs and made some suggestions, but the book carries no sort of official endorsement. The views expressed are my own and I alone am responsible for them.

Finally it would be invidious to mention by name all those who have helped with advice, criticism and encouragement: the list would be a long one, but I believe that each of my friends knows how deeply felt is my appreciation. Nor perhaps is there any need to identify further the typist who for the last five years has tolerated and interpreted the vagaries of my handwriting as cheerfully as she has those of my style of living for forty years and to whom for this as for everything I remain always in debt.

List of Abbreviations

AG   Accountant General
AUS   Assistant Under Secretary

BCATP   British Commonwealth Air Training Plan
BIS   British Information Services
BOAC   British Overseas Airways Corporation

CENTO   Central Treaty Organization
CFB   Combined Food Board
CID   Committee of Imperial Defence
C in C   Commander in Chief
C.O.   Colonial Office
CORB   Children's Overseas Reception Board
COS   Chiefs of Staff
CPM   Commonwealth Prime Ministers
CPRB   Combined Production and Resources Board
CRO   Commonwealth Relations Office
CROWS   CRO Wives Society

DEA   Department of External Affairs
DHC   Deputy High Commission(er)
D.O.   Dominions Office
DTC   Department of Technical Cooperation
DUS   Deputy Under Secretary

EEC   European Economic Community
EFTA   European Free Trade Association
EMB   Empire Marketing Board

FCO   Foreign and Commonwealth Office
F.O.   Foreign Office
FSWA   Foreign Service Wives Association

GATT   General Agreement on Tariffs and Trade

HCO   High Commission Office
HMG   His (Her) Majesty's Government
HMOCS   His (Her) Majesty's Overseas Civil Service

HMSO	His (Her) Majesty's Stationery Office
H.O.	Home Office
ICS	Indian Civil Service
IEC	Imperial Economic Committee
IFS	Irish Free State
IMF	International Monetary Fund
I.O.	India Office
IRA	Irish Republican Army
MAP	Ministry of Aircraft Production
NATO	North Atlantic Treaty Organization
NIBMAR	No Independence Before Majority Rule
NSW	New South Wales
NZ	New Zealand
ODM	Overseas Development, Ministry of
OEEC	Organization for European Economic Cooperation
Parly US	Parliamentary Under Secretary
P.M.	Prime Minister
P.P.S.	Parliamentary Private Secretary
P.S.	Private Secretary
PSO	Principal Staff Officer
PUS	Permanent Under Secretary
RAF	Royal Air Force
RCAF	Royal Canadian Air Force
RN	Royal Navy
SEATO	South East Asia Treaty Organization
S. of S.	Secretary of State
UDI	Unilateral Declaration of Independence
UK	United Kingdom
UKIO	United Kingdom Information Office

Note on References

Unless otherwise stated, file numbers in the References to each chapter (pp. 442–57) refer to documents in the Public Record Office; an exception is that the initials 'R.A.' stand for 'Royal Archives' and designate correspondence preserved in the Round Tower at Windsor Castle. Of the private papers mentioned, the Machtig papers are in the custody of the FCO Library, as is also the letter from Rear-Admiral Searle about Admiral Evans, and the Inskip papers are at Churchill College, Cambridge.

The *Memoirs of Sir Charles William Dixon, KCMG, KCVO, OBE* with a Foreword by Sir Harry Batterbee, GCMG, KCVO were completed in 1969; cyclostyled copies were circulated by the author privately and presented, among others, to the FCO Library and the Royal Commonwealth Society.

In the References full details of works included in the List of Works Cited are not given, and the reader is directed to this List for details of any works not fully described in the References.

PART I

Before the War 1925–39

CHAPTER 1

Origins of the Dominions Office

The Empire between the Wars

The Dominions Office (D.O.), more than most other Departments, was the child of outside circumstances. Above all it was conditioned by the progress of the Empire; the Empire in turn reflected the changes taking place in the world as a whole. The 1920s were an age when Europe was still the centre of the world – though the massive industrial development of the USA and the growth of the Dominions were adding a new dimension. The USA stood aloof from the League of Nations which became an organization based on and dominated by the nations of Europe. Powerful currents were flowing in other parts of the world, with the growth of a nationalist spirit in India and the rapid modernization of Japan. But, in their own eyes, Europeans saw themselves as managing most of the world's business and still regarded large tracts of the rest of the world as their fief.

If the Englishman's attitude towards much of the rest of the world was contemptuous and arrogant, even when it was not simply ignorant, he felt differently towards the British Empire which he regarded with a proprietary air. Nevertheless there was something disturbing in the English attitude towards dependent peoples at that time. It is one of the mysteries of the British Empire that the British, a people with a deserved reputation for tolerance and liberalism, should have shown such insensitivity in personal relations with coloured people. To some extent they shared this prejudice with most other white people at the time, but the British arrogance had a peculiar edge to it and it cast long shadows.

During this period there were in effect three distinct parts of the Empire, each kept in a separate category and each the responsibility of a different Department of the British Government: the India Office (I.O.), the Colonial Office (C.O.) and the Dominions Office (D.O.). While these three parts were distinct, they were all comprised within the British Empire and each interacted with the others and in course of time they would virtually all be brought together again under the later title of Commonwealth. Curiously the nomenclature for the Empire was never authoritatively defined and there has been no legal definition of the term 'Commonwealth'. The term 'Commonwealth' was used at different times to describe Britain and the Dominions

3

only, and the term 'Empire' to describe only the dependent parts; the view favoured by the D.O. was that the terms are synonymous and that the term 'Commonwealth' describes the whole of what was formerly known as the Empire and is preferable.

The public viewed each part of the Empire in a different light. Towards the peoples of British stock in the Dominions there was unalloyed cordiality. Except in specialist circles the non-self-governing Colonies were not so well known; they were regarded largely in terms of advantage for British trade and investment and the idea hardly entered anyone's head that it would be possible to bring about large industrial development and create improved standards of living. The Indian Empire fell between the two categories and the public's attitude towards it was ambivalent. On the one hand, it was looked upon as the 'brightest jewel' and it was widely believed that Britain's prosperity depended on 'holding' India; on the other there was scant sympathy at the time for Gandhi and his strange antics. In its policies towards both India and the Colonies, Government policy was ahead of public opinion. Though intent on retaining ultimate control, successive steps marked constitutional progress in India – separate membership of the League of Nations (although India was not sovereign and did not conduct her own foreign policy), the Royal Commission of 1927,[1] the treatment of Gandhi as an equal by the Viceroy (Irwin), the Round Table Conference in 1931 (which was an important gesture and psychologically valuable) and the Government of India Act of 1935[2] with all that flowed from it, including virtual self-government in the Provinces, though not at the centre. Similarly in the Colonies, successive Governments paid increasing attention to the interests of the native inhabitants, developing the policies of trusteeship and indirect rule and making a beginning with economic development by the passage of the Colonial Development Act in 1929.[3]

Meanwhile in the self-governing part of the Empire, the Dominions had made rapid strides in their economies and were developing a growing sense of national consciousness. All the Dominions had taken part in the First World War; in this baptism of fire they had come to manhood; they emerged with an enhanced reputation and a growing self-confidence. Their importance had been recognized by the British Government in the Imperial War Conferences and simultaneous Imperial War Cabinet in 1917 and 1918 and, even more significantly, by the victorious Powers when the Dominions became signatories of the Peace Treaties and separate Members of the League of Nations. In all the Dominions there was a rapid increase in population; in the early 1920s they also provided a major outlet for emigration from Britain. Agriculture and mining became more efficient with mechanization, and industrialization got under way. The Dominions still looked to Britain for men, money and markets; above all they relied on Britain for their defence. At the Imperial Conference of 1923, they were joined by a new Member, the

Treaty of 1921 having recognized the independence of the Irish Free State (IFS) as a Member of the Commonwealth.

With a growing sense of nationalism and of strength, would the Dominions wish to break away on their own? Indeed might not the mother country herself seek to rid herself of such liabilities? Apart from the IFS and some few in the non-British minority groups in Canada, Australia and South Africa, there was no serious question of this. On the contrary, the Empire was thought to have proved itself in the war from which it had emerged victorious and the desire was strong that the association should continue. In addition to loyalty to the monarchy, sentiment, tradition and a common purpose and way of life – all of which were strong influences – there were the material benefits (of which both sides were equally aware) in finance, trade, defence and the free movement of ideas and people. Britain's commitment to defend the Dominions and her assumption that she could rely on the Dominions for support in the event of war were both equally important. The Royal Navy commitment to protect the Dominions from sea-borne attack remained throughout this period unquestioned and affected all appreciations of British strategy. It was the most striking benefit of the association to all the Dominions except Canada. The question therefore was not whether the Empire should continue, but in what form it should do so and how it could best operate to the advantage of its individual Members. This was the central question which engaged the D.O. throughout its existence.

The root question was whether the association should be a close federation, with a sense of unity and centralized control or whether it should be a voluntary partnership, resting on the agreement of the separate parts, with no element of compulsion. There were many variations on this theme and some elements of the controversy lingered even into the middle of the century. But by 1925 the decision in principle had been taken. The arguments in favour of the unitary theory had taken many forms at the beginning of the century, Joseph Chamberlain had powerfully urged the course of Tariff Reform in the hope of advancing economic unity; later there were those who saw in the establishment of the Committee of Imperial Defence a means of developing close defence cooperation; in 1917 an Imperial War Cabinet was established. The most persistent advocate of greater unity was Lionel Curtis who, in the Round Table and in other ways, urged the cause of greater cohesion and unity. But it was a forlorn cause – mainly no doubt because this was not the way the majority of the Dominions wanted things to go; they were insistent on their rights rather than obligations, they were determined to preserve their own freedom rather than accept automatic commitments, they wanted to develop their own personalities rather than a corporate sense. In other words they wanted to grow up – and after 1923 the IFS gave support to the forces opposed to federation, already strong in South Africa and Canada. Another reason was that the British Government themselves were never wholly converted to the imperial federation notion – partly because they saw in it a means of limiting their own authority.

It was clear that the federation idea was not acceptable to the majority at any Imperial Conference, yet the decision was never precise, nor clear-cut, nor complete. If the basic idea of some form of centralized control was not accepted, many forms of unity persisted and indeed would persist for many years to come – the most striking being the common allegiance of all to the Crown and the acceptance by all of the common status of British subject. Moreover various forms of imperial organization were preserved or even initiated – the Committee of Imperial Defence (1907), the Empire Marketing Board (1924), the Imperial Economic Committee (1925), the Imperial Shipping Committee (1920), and indeed the Imperial Conference itself, in concept if not in practice, and all were a manifestation of the Imperial idea.

Granted that the concept of federation was rejected, the question was at what point the claims of one impaired the unity of the whole. Throughout, the British Government, while genuinely seeking to make the new concept work, were vigilant to preserve what they felt to be the essentials of the partnership, since they feared – as proved to be the case in the middle of the century – that a weakening of the links in favour of one member would weaken the whole association. For the rest, the British Government had three main preoccupations with the Dominions: the first was to define the new partnership in legal and practical terms and to develop appropriate techniques of consultation; the second was to secure the greatest degree of economic cooperation; the third was to achieve broad support for British foreign policies and establish effective defence co-ordination in the event of war. In the first aim they were largely successful, in the second an advance in the reciprocal grant of preference was achieved at the Ottawa Economic Conference in 1932. In the third sphere there was an astonishing paradox; there was no single foreign policy, no agreed strategy or defence plan, not even a firm commitment of forces. And yet when war came, with the sole exception of Eire, the peoples of Britain and the Dominions stood together as one.

The Advent of the Dominions Office

Such in broad outline were the main factors in the world outside which influenced the life of the D.O. and shaped its policies. In retrospect it seems remarkable that there was no separate Department in the British Government responsible for relations with Dominion Governments until 1925 – nearly twenty years after the distinctness of the Dominions from the Colonies had been officially recognized. The Office took a long time coming. Its first recognizable ancestor is the Committee of the Privy Council 'for the Plantaçons' set up on the significant date of 4 July 1660. Later in the same year, Charles

II appointed a Council for Trade and a Council for Foreign Plantations. Instructions to the latter prophetically included the words: 'To use prudential means for rendering those dominions useful to England, and England helpful to them'.

The two Councils were united in 1672 and their work was subsequently carried out under a Secretary of State – first the S. of S. for the Southern Department (later the Home Secretary), then for a brief period from 1768 to 1784, its own S. of S. for the American or Colonial Department, and later still, after the loss of the thirteen Colonies, the S. of S. for War and the Colonies. As the war with Napoleon brought together the business of the C.O. and the War Office under a single S. of S., so the exigencies of the Crimean War separated them again and in 1854 a S. of S. for the Colonies was definitively appointed. There was subsequently an unbroken chain of command until 1966.

1867 is another date that plays its part in the title of the Office, since in that year the Confederation of Canada was formed with the formal title of 'Dominion of Canada' (overcoming some Canadian predilections in favour of a 'Kingdom' of Canada). And so for the first time, 'Dominion' was spelt with a capital letter and acquired an esoteric meaning almost the reverse of Dr Johnson's dictionary definition as 'territory considered as subject'. At the 1907 Colonial Conference, on the motion of the Canadian Government, it was agreed to adopt the term 'Dominion' as applying to all the self-governing units of the Empire, in distinction from the non-self-governing Colonies.

1907 marks an important stage in the development of the D.O. for another reason. At the Conference there was pressure from the Australians under their redoubtable leader, Deakin, supported to some extent by New Zealand and South Africa, for two innovations: first for a Department separate from the C.O. to handle Dominion affairs and secondly for a permanent Secretariat to organize Imperial Conferences and maintain consultation in the intervals between meetings. There was nothing revolutionary in these ideas; Deakin himself had castigated 'the natural *vis inertia* of the Office' as far back as the Colonial Conference of 1887. On the point of a Secretariat, Joseph Chamberlain had contemplated an 'Imperial Council' at the 1902 Conference and his successor (Lyttleton) had suggested setting up an advisory joint commission which would prepare material for an enlarged Colonial Conference to be termed in future 'Imperial Council'. The idea was torpedoed by Canada in a stand consistent with her opposition to anything that smacked of Imperial centralization. The Liberal Government that swept to power in Britain in 1906 also found little attraction in Chamberlain's dreams of Empire. At the 1907 Conference, the British knew in advance that they could count on the Canadian Prime Minister to resist any inordinate Australian demands and, in the event, Laurier almost rivalled the hyperbole in which later Mackenzie King, when fearful of any change, expressed his satisfaction with things as they were. The British certainly did not wish to have any Secretariat which would be outside their control and they had no desire to create a wholly separate new Department. In the event Elgin, the Colonial Secretary, had no great difficulty in resisting any major changes, but he gave a 'pledge' to the Conference to constitute a department to deal with the Dominions and to associate it with a permanent conference secretariat. Elgin always intended that this should be within the C.O., though he did not say so specifically. This was a compromise and one which, on the face of it, might have been expected to disappoint both sides and particularly the imperial reformers, the more so since, in the event, the change did not amount to as much as seemed to have been implied. In seeking Treasury approval for its proposals, the C.O. wrote that the S. of S. did not regard the creation of a separate department as either justifiable or necessary and was anxious, on financial as well as on other grounds, to retain the Imperial Secretariat as an integral part of the establishment of the C.O. The letter concluded that it was thought that the reorganization would 'be able to satisfy the pledge given by H.M.G. without making any further call upon the public purse'.[4] The language was no doubt designed to appeal to the Treasury; but the letter suggests that the C.O. itself wanted the minimum change that it could get away with. The C.O. got away with it for nearly twenty years! Elgin sent in due course a despatch[5] to the Dominions setting out the reorganization he had already carried out. There was added to the C.O. a Third Division called the 'Dominions Division' which handled relations with the Dominions (the nomenclature is confusing; the Dominions Division was organized in three Departments, but the whole was frequently also referred to as the 'Dominions Department'); an Imperial Conference Secretariat was also constituted which, though presented to the Dominions as 'linked to the Dominions Department without being entirely merged into it', was in practice an integral part of the Office. These arrangements were destined to survive substantially unchanged until 1925.

At the 1911 Conference, the New Zealand P.M. again raised the questions of an Imperial Council of State and of removing Dominions' business from the C.O.; in the absence of any stand by Australia, there was no support and the matter was not pressed. The S. of S. (Harcourt) had in fact been prepared to make concessions to what he imagined would be the attitude of the Dominions. He therefore put forward two proposals – bifurcation of the Office at the Permanent Under Secretary (PUS) level and a Standing Committee including Dominion representatives to maintain continuity between Conferences. But he did so half-heartedly, making the most of the objections, and he was under no pressure to accept these proposals, Laurier in particular stressing his 'ample' satisfaction with the existing arrangements.

What was the reason for this remarkably slow pace of development, at a time too when there was so much change and upheaval? In the first place the personalities changed; 1907 proved to be the last Conference for the formidable Deakin and no one fought the case with the same vigour, at least until W. M. Hughes appeared at the Imperial War Conference of 1918 to complain that the present method of administration through the C.O. had become an anachronism, and the functions of that Department were merely those of an 'unnecessary conduit pipe'.[6] But by 1918 the attitude of New Zealand had changed and her P.M. applauded the C.O. for having done 'well, thoroughly and enthusiastically'.[7] Secondly the 1914–18 War was a major factor; of necessity it forced the pace of consultation on all matters affecting the conduct of the war and encouraged the postponement of doctrinal disputes. Thirdly much of what Dominion Governments sought was achieved in other ways – increasing use was made of High Commissioners in London, there were in fact more frequent Ministerial meetings (especially at the end of the war and during the peace-making period); above all P.M.s met regularly and established a direct correspondence on the basis of personal knowledge.

Certain less worthy motives may have affected the attitude of the C.O. For the most part those concerned did not know the Dominions at first hand and did not understand them. One can detect a note of baffled incredulity in the comment of Sir G. Fiddes (who had in fact served in South Africa with Milner) on the arguments (which seem today entirely reasonable) by Deakin and Ward for a separation between Dominion and Colonial work: 'their views will best be stated in their own words, as the C.O. was quite unable to recognise itself in the description given of it.'[8] The attitude of the time is also revealingly illustrated by Elgin's resistance to a resolution by Deakin, inviting him to create opportunities for the permanent staff of the C.O. to acquire more intimate knowledge of the Colonies with whose business they had to deal. Elgin could see innumerable difficulties – local administration was the concern of the overseas government; the business that came to London depended more upon general principles than upon local characteristics; journeying over the world would be necessary as it would be no use visiting one colony only, etc.[9] It seems also that in this matter as in others the Treasury played a decisive role in controlling departmental administration and enforcing economies and that the need to contain expenditure was a factor never far from the minds of C.O. staff. Finally it is perhaps not unfair to suspect that in Whitehall there was some jealousy at the possibility of a separate Department seeking to justify its existence and therefore meddling unduly in Dominion affairs, instead of being content with the more laissez-faire policy imposed, almost of necessity, on an Office already burdened with all the problems of the Colonies.

Underlying all these factors was a more fundamental point, viz. that the proposals for a separate D.O. and a separate Secretariat were both parts of a wider question as to what sort of Commonwealth was envisaged and what machinery was required. Here there was inevitable conflict between the local nationalism and the wider imperialism, between individuality and unity, freedom and cooperation; in all this, pragmatic solutions were sought, but there was no unanimity and no clear path to follow. All these different considerations led to a situation where the British Government did not themselves positively wish for any major changes and where, among the Dominion Governments, there was not sufficient agreement between them or continuity of purpose to force Britain's hand.

And so from 1907 until 1925, the arrangements remained virtually unchanged – namely a Dominions Division within the C.O. and an Imperial Conference Secretariat which was in practice an integral part of the Office.

And then, suddenly, on 11 June 1925 came the announcement from the P.M. (Baldwin) that the conduct of affairs with the Dominions would be under a new S. of S. for Dominion Affairs. The change was made solely on the initiative of the British Government. It did not come in response to any external circumstances, nor, indeed, to any renewal of pressure from the Dominions. The creation of a separate Department was no doubt in the logic of events and was bound to come; but like its ending as a separate Department just over forty years later, the timing owed something to fortuitous ministerial changes in Britain. There seems no reason to doubt that the creation of the Dominions Office was due to the appointment as Colonial Secretary, in Baldwin's Government of 1924, of L. S. Amery whose lifetime ambition it had been to see this brought about. Indeed Amery was to be associated with the Empire and Commonwealth one way or another all his working life and was the only man to be in charge at different times of all three 'Imperial' Offices – C.O., I.O. and D.O. – there was therefore something fitting in his fathering the new Office.

Born in India, the son of a Conservator of Forests who subsequently tried farming in Ontario and died gold prospecting in British Guiana, he was married to the daughter of the Canadian, Hamar Greenwood. He had wide and varied experience, having been leader-writer on *The Times*, author of a history of the South African War, Member of Parliament and, during the First World War, recruiting agent, intelligence officer and Assistant Secretary to the War Cabinet. He came into close contact with all the personalities of Empire. His life ran in curious and contrasting parallel with that of Winston Churchill. At Harrow together, they were to meet again as newspaper reporters for the Boer War, to share more than thirty years as colleagues (and sometimes opponents) in Parliament, to serve in turn as Parliamentary Under Secretary (Parly US) and S. of S. in the C.O. and to work together in the Cabinet in the Second World War. Amery recounts two of his major differences with Churchill over Empire matters: the first was what Amery regarded for himself as the 'supreme issue', where Churchill's devotion to Free Trade made him out of sympathy with Amery's ideas on Imperial Preference and for economic unity:[10] the second was less predictable. Amery recalls that he advocated in 1907 some sort of Committee to keep the Colonies in touch with foreign affairs. He found Churchill (then Parliamentary Under Secretary at the C.O.) strongly opposed to any idea of consulting the Colonies on foreign affairs, seeing no point in doing so until they were military powers whose alliance could be useful. Amery added the illuminating comment: 'His one idea seemed to be that the Colonial P.M.s should be given a good time and sent away well-banqueted, but empty-handed.'[11]

As a youth, Amery had been inspired by Parkin, a Canadian and the Secretary of the Rhodes Trust of which Amery later became a Trustee. He was fired by enthusiasm for Joseph Chamberlain and his campaign for Tariff Reform. But the leader he followed without reservation was Milner, whose invitation to become one of the Kindergarten in 1905 he had to refuse (his place being taken by John Buchan) but whom he regarded as his 'spiritual chief for the rest of his days'.[12]

By the time he became Colonial Secretary in 1924, Amery's achievement in the Imperial sphere presented no mean record. He knew all the Dominions at first hand and was on close terms with the leading personalities in each; he had helped to launch the 'Round Table' in 1909; he had supported the founding of the Empire Parliamentary Association and went as a delegate to their very first Conference in Australia in 1912; he claims that the idea of inviting the Dominions to an Imperial War Conference with meetings of an Imperial War Cabinet interspersed was his, that, through Milner, it was accepted by the War Cabinet and that he himself drafted the appropriate telegrams; appointed Parly US at the C.O. in 1919, he extended his travels (Malta and Canada), immersed himself in economic development and introduced the Empire Settlement Bill.

Amery was also a man of quite remarkable tenacity and consistency and there was one matter affecting the Office on which he had repeatedly gone on record – his demand for the establishment of a separate Dominions Office. He had been urging this for over twenty years, in speeches, in articles, in representations to political leaders. Not surprisingly therefore, in accepting the appointment, he stipulated that he should be allowed to create a new and entirely separate office to deal with the Dominions.

Nevertheless despite the merits of the case which were never seriously in dispute and despite Amery's impassioned vigour, the new child still showed reluctance to enter the world. The Baldwin Administration came to power in November 1924 and the P.M.'s announcement was not made until June of the following year. There were various reasons for the delay: one was the absence of Amery himself on a visit to Iraq; another was the cumbersome movement of the Whitehall machine; but the most disturbing and, according to Amery, the main cause was the hostility of the Treasury.

The classic Whitehall response to the Amery proposal was to appoint a Committee of Enquiry. This was duly set up under Sir Russell Scott (at that time Director of Establishments at the Treasury) as Chairman, with Sir

Horace Hamilton (Board of Trade) and Sir Richard Hopkins (also Treasury).[13] All three were eminent civil servants in Whitehall. Their terms were to report on 'the best form of organisation for giving effect to the policy of creating a Secretary of Stateship for Dominion Relations separate from (but vested in the same person as holds) the office of Secretary of State for the Colonies'.

The Committee reached conclusions with the precision of a geometrical theorem, namely that there should be:

1. A single Minister who should combine both posts.
2. Two Parliamentary Under-Secretaries (i.e. one additional post).
3. A single PUS (they were emphatic that Ministers should have available the judgement and experience of a PUS 'whose writ runs over the whole office and who is thus able to deal authoritatively with such problems in their two-fold aspect').
4. An additional post of Deputy U.S. who could relieve the PUS of most of the work on the Colonial side, leaving him free to concentrate on the Dominions.

The Committee suggested 'that, in so far as the Dominions take an interest in the internal organisation of the Colonial Office, they are much more concerned with the Ministerial functions than with the arrangements of work between permanent officials.' Their scheme was plausible and ingenious; but it effectively killed the idea of a separate Department. Submitting their report to the P.M., Sir Warren Fisher (Head of the Treasury) minuted on 27 February 1925:[14]

I will confine myself to two remarks:
(a) On the one hand you have the opinion of the Colonial Secretary who started with his mind made up; on the other you have the conclusions, after impartial enquiry, of three of the most experienced and practical men of affairs in the Public Service.
(b) If, contrary to all business principles, the Colonial Secretary were nevertheless to succeed in getting what he seeks, it will be quite impossible to prevent any and every Department of State from having a similar duplication if demanded.

NFWF

The arrogance of this is almost breathtaking when one considers that this was essentially a political problem of how to handle relations with the Dominions, that Amery had formed his view in the light of direct experience over a period of twenty years and that the civil servants treated the problem solely as a matter of bureaucratic organization, without taking account of the political problem of relations with the Dominions.

The Treasury brought all their guns to bear. Earlier the Chancellor of the Exchequer had addressed a carefully argued letter to Amery.[15] Though the motive may have been financial, Churchill embellished the case with the wisdom of his own experience; he reminded Amery of his own long experience of Colonial affairs, recalled that when he himself was Colonial Secretary in 1921 he had suggested that the title should be altered to Secretary of State for Imperial Affairs. He was emphatic however that there was no sufficient case for the creation of a separate additional Secretaryship of State; he adduced two main reasons. It would not be popular in the Dominions since it would prejudice their dealing as heads of Government with the P.M. himself; it would certainly be criticized in the House of Commons as 'contrary to frugal administration; and if the work of these officers were decided on the basis of the number of papers dealt with compared to those handled by other Departments, the result of an examination would be an exposure.' Churchill concluded, with some lack of logic, that the suggestion that there should be two separate Secretaryships of State both vested in one single Minister 'is of course quite unobjectionable'.

Undeterred, Amery submitted a powerful and lucid memorandum[16] to the Cabinet arguing the case for a separate Office on broad grounds. He pointed to the long history of Dominion demands and was confident that the change would have a great effect on public opinion in the Dominions as a spontaneous recognition of their new status. He insisted that the work was 'essentially different in character' from that of the C.O., that work with the Dominions was entirely political and diplomatic and called for great insight and infinite tact; the work with the Colonies on the other hand was administrative and directive and called for initiative and drive. He also gave a careful analysis of the workload to show that the present staff were 'quite incapable of coping adequately with the two great fields of work'. He went on to make the interesting – and at that time almost novel – proposal that additional staff were required to meet the necessity for keeping the Office in direct personal touch both with the Dominions and also with the work in the Colonies and Protectorates.

The logic of all these arguments led to the concept of a completely separate Office, with a separate Minister and adequate staff. But Amery stopped short of this: in his paper he was willing to recognize the 'considerable practical objections to the creation, under present conditions at any rate, of an entirely separate D.O. with a separate S. of S. in a separate building or the combining of such a separate Office with some other Office, such as that of P.M., Foreign Secretary or President of the Council'. His proposal therefore was that the new Secretaryship should be vested in the same person as the Colonial Secretaryship and that the D.O. should be retained for internal administrative purposes as a part of the Colonial Office. He even went on to concede that the control of the C.O. as an Office would remain vested in the PUS for the Colonies and that the new PUS for Dominion Affairs would direct the work of his own subordinates 'but not be otherwise responsible for the conduct of the Office'. On the face of it, it seems astonishing that a man of Amery's determination should have been content with such half measures. Perhaps he realized that the full-blooded proposal stood no chance of approval – or did he possibly wish to make sure of continuing to hold the two posts himself?

The proposal was duly approved by the Cabinet, according to Amery who understood that it was accepted that the Dominions would in future deal with the Department of Dominion Affairs as an entity entirely distinct from the C.O. But his troubles were not over, for such was not the understanding of the Treasury. In a letter to Baldwin,[17] Amery complained bitterly that, after a talk and some correspondence with Fisher, it emerged that he 'wants to defeat the whole essence and purpose of the scheme' first of all by refusing to allow the senior official in the D.O. to have any higher pay than an ordinary Under Secretary and secondly by insisting that the PUS for the Colonies should exercise a control over his work. Amery concluded, not unjustly, 'Fisher's contention in fact really amounts to this: that the creation of the Secretaryship of State is merely the addition of a new fancy title to myself and does not imply the creation of a new department.'

Fortunately the Cabinet Secretary (Hankey) shared Amery's view as to the Cabinet conclusion and, with support from Baldwin, Amery gained his point on the main issue. But the Treasury had their way over the salary – they refused to pay the £3,000 a year salary of a PUS to the head of the D.O. or to recognize the no. 2 as formally having the rank of a Deputy Under Secretary (DUS).

By this time it was becoming urgent to make an announcement. The incident closed on a note that might have been taken from musical comedy. As Amery records: 'I suddenly discovered that, unless I kissed hands on acceptance of my new office ... within 48 hours, I should be faced with the necessity, as the law then stood, of a by-election. There was no time to make a new seal, but I sent my C.O. seal ahead of me by messenger and duly took it back, to His great amusement, at the King's hands.'[18]

The P.M.'s announcement of 11 June 1925[19] was followed by a further statement from Amery[20] in which he stressed the differences between Colonial and Dominion work on the lines of his Cabinet memorandum. The Dominions Office had arrived.

CHAPTER 2

Environment and Staff

Environment

The separate Dominions Office came about as a spontaneous gesture by the British Government. Dominion Governments were informed but not consulted in advance about the proposed change. They were no doubt gratified but showed no elation. Perhaps the continuance of the same Minister as Secretary of State of both Departments lessened the significance of the change, giving the impression of a reorganization at official level only. The D.O. came from the womb of the Colonial Office and many years passed before the umbilical cord was completely cut; for the new Department originally had its being under maternal protection, and it was not always clear where one Department ended and the other began. The D.O. occupied rooms in the C.O. building at the corner of Whitehall and Downing Street; it was destined to retain these for the whole of its existence as a separate Department. Shortage of space was a chronic preoccupation of Whitehall and, before many years had passed, the question of accommodation had become so acute that Passfield (in his dual capacity of Dominions Secretary and Colonial Secretary) felt it his duty to record, for the benefit of his Cabinet colleagues, his 'opinion that not only is the smooth working of the two departments already suffering, but also that their efficiency is in danger of being most seriously affected'.[1] Only a few months before the appointment of J. H. Thomas as a separate S. of S., he warned that, if a separate Dominions Secretary were appointed, 'it would be a matter of the greatest difficulty and inconvenience' to find suitable accommodation for him and his staff. Passfield drew a harrowing picture of the conditions under which officials had to work (deploring that 'the increasing use of shorthand-writers ... is naturally a source of annoyance to other occupants in the same room'), but little was done. What Passfield complained of as 'temporary makeshifts' continued to be the rule, mainly by outhousing sections. The problem was not solved until the lusty child ejected its mother from the home and the C.O. in 1946 left its offspring in sole possession, itself moving to Church House. A room for the separate Dominions Secretary was established on the Whitehall front; it lacked the splendour of the Colonial Secretary's room and was apt to be noisy. A partition was erected in the corridor of the first floor (but not on

15

others), though otherwise it was difficult to say where the boundary between the two Departments came.

The building is part of the block of public offices built between 1862–76. The story is well known that Sir Gilbert Scott the architect predictably prepared a Gothic design but was forced by Palmerston to make new designs of an Italianate character; to this day the buildings show both styles. There are some remarkable features; a façade of Portland stone, polished granite and marble which has been described as 'stately, elegant and symmetrical',[2] an inner quadrangle and an imposing group of statues crowning the summit facing Whitehall. Most remarkable of all is the profusion of decorative detail – Queen Victoria enthroned, the five continents, ample-bosomed female allegorical figures and historical characters (Kings of England, Raleigh, Livingstone) thought to be appropriate. The sculpture was largely the work of Henry Armstead and George Philip, who have left a remarkable memorial of the art of their time on the public face of Whitehall.[3] The outside was cleaned in 1971 and now shows the statuary in clear outline for the first time in living memory.

The Whitehall front overlooks the Cenotaph; No. 10 Downing Street is opposite; across Parliament Square lie the Houses of Parliament and Westminster Abbey; at the end of the Mall stands Buckingham Palace. The staff were thus brought close to all major events in the national life, both ceremonial State occasions and any public demonstrations. Inside, the building provided spaciousness rather than elegance or efficiency. The most impressive room was that of the Colonial Secretary (with a vast leather-topped walnut table, a magnificent walnut case of maps, a handsome pair of silver candlesticks* and an attractive eighteenth-century chimney-piece the mirror above which was said to have caught in its reflection Nelson and Wellington waiting to see the S. of S. – the only occasion on which they met). Although little modernization had been carried out and, with expansion of staff, conditions became cramped, the atmosphere in these years was characterized by cosiness.[4,5] Blazing coal fires remedied the deficiencies of the central heating system and the Resident Clerk was always able to make himself snug in his quarters where he was served a man-sized breakfast.

Staff

The Office owed its separate existence to Leo Amery and he was a powerful influence in the formative years. As we have seen, he had almost unrivalled knowledge of the Dominions and many of their leaders and had long cherished a vision of what the Empire could be. It was in fact given to him

---

* J. H. Thomas relished telling the story that on the day of his appointment in 1924 the candlesticks were removed by the Office Keeper when he learnt that the new Minister was a Socialist.

to see much of his dream fulfilled, but in one area he failed. He believed all his life that the strength of the Empire must be built on economic unity, but the elections of 1923 and 1924 and the Chancellor's (Churchill's) addiction to Free Trade told against any tariff changes while Amery was in office. Yet, in spite of his achievements, he left behind no legend that has lingered. Indeed, some harsh judgements were made about him; Austen Chamberlain's opinion was that 'Amery is a poor Parliamentarian, very unhandy so far in spite of his brains'.[6] Inevitably his pugnacity made him enemies; in spite of his vision, many of his ideas seemed to hark back rather than look forward. Somehow he did not appeal to the heart; but he had a real understanding of the Commonwealth, was ahead of his time and generally right in his ideas about its development. More than anyone else he can be saluted as the Founding Father of the D.O.

Lord Passfield (better known as Sidney Webb) succeeded Amery as the S. of S. for D.A. and for the Colonies when the Labour Party came to power in June 1929. He held the combined posts for a year only. This earnest and doctrinaire social reformer was seventy at the time of his appointment and showing signs of age. He found the Palestine problem alone a considerable burden and was in any case more attracted by the prospect of promoting welfare in the Colonies than by the problems of the settlers in the Dominions. He left therefore little mark on the Dominions side of the work. In 1930, while remaining Colonial Secretary, he was succeeded as Dominions Secretary by J. H. Thomas, who thus became the first Minister to hold the office separately. Thomas was a railwayman by origin and made his reputation as General Secretary of the NUR where he showed both doggedness (in the 1911 and 1921 strikes) and moderation (in the General Strike of 1926); at heart and in essentials he remained a Trade Unionist all his life. He had previously served as Colonial Secretary in the short-lived Labour Administration of 1924. When the Labour Party returned to power in 1929 he became Lord Privy Seal with responsibility (shared improbably with Oswald Mosley!) for dealing with unemployment. The title, he claimed, was a misnomer since he was neither a Lord, nor a Privy, nor a Seal. At that time with the onset of the Depression, it was a formidable task and Thomas was not equal to it. A move became necessary and he was appointed to the separate post of Dominions Secretary. The Treasury seem to have raised no difficulty on this occasion about the additional post, Snowden being no doubt willing to pay a price in order to have Thomas removed from dealing with unemployment. It was thus a political accident which first gave the new Department a S. of S. of its own. Thomas remained in the National Government and stayed on as Dominions Secretary until 1935 when he was transferred to the C.O. Shortly after he was involved in the notorious Budget Leakage which extinguished his political career.

Verdicts on Thomas have been harsh. Lloyd George called him 'the greatest blatherer living'.[7] One political commentator, after admitting that Thomas was the most picturesque figure in the Labour movement, described him as 'totally devoid of constructive ideas, intimate with the City and big business, the boon companion of half the House of Commons, the jingoistic upholder of imperial and national unity'.[8] Another referred to 'This painful but disarming personality ... He has created round him an atmosphere of vulgar cordiality and a hail-fellow-well-met manner which appears to have taken in the whole of the British Empire with the exception of about a dozen Communists'.[9] There was a basis of truth in all these shafts and his drinking, his gambling, his snobbery were all notorious. He relied heavily on bluff and was frequently crude – to the extent of unnecessarily offending Dominion visitors. At the time of the Silver Jubilee he had seen Lyons, Prime Minister of Australia, at various functions in frock coat, evening dress and court uniform; he gravely offended him by greeting him with the jest that Moss Bros must be making a fortune out of him. Yet he had considerable strengths; he remained throughout close to his leader, Ramsay MacDonald, and was regarded with affection, tinged with amusement, by many in the Conservative Party. He clearly appealed to King George V who enjoyed his jokes so hugely that, after his illness, he cracked a rib with laughter.[10] If Thomas lacked a sophisticated mental equipment, he had remarkable horse sense in gauging public opinion and his instincts were generally sound. Though he lacked eloquence, he enjoyed a ready gift of repartee and could often overcome an opponent with some monumental irrelevance that nevertheless gave him the last laugh. He was a tough bargainer, having learnt in a hard school, but was sufficiently pragmatic to be flexible. He was intensely human; he admired the domestic virtues, had a genuine love for his country and was capable of single-minded loyalty and warm affection.

Thomas did virtually all his work by discussion. He seldom read papers in the Office and virtually never wrote a minute beyond a pithy 'Discuss' or 'Approve'. The only letters he dictated were personal ones (and the English was always corrected by his P.S. before they were dispatched*). His favourite method of doing business was to summon the top officials concerned and to engage in a tough argument with them; this was the only way in which, as he said, he could get the subject firmly in his head. He received a variety of callers throughout the day, few of whom were concerned with the business of the Office. Nevertheless though he seldom brought himself to be concerned in any detail with the work of the Office, he exerted a decisive if not always happy influence on all major matters of policy.

Thomas was succeeded as Dominions Secretary by Malcolm MacDonald, the son of Ramsay MacDonald. In nearly every respect MacDonald formed

* Eddie Marsh, his private secretary, not only improved his English (as he was well qualified to do) but also signed with great skill his signature in all cases, with the exception only of submissions to the Palace and bank cheques.

a sharp contrast to his predecessor, with whom he nevertheless always enjoyed a close relationship. This was MacDonald's first Cabinet post at the early age of thirty-three. He was however no stranger to the Office since he had served as Parliamentary Private Secretary (P.P.S.) to Thomas and, after the formation of the National Government, had been Parliamentary Under-Secretary; as such he had more responsibility than most, partly perhaps because his father was Prime Minister, partly because Thomas had no desire to be involved in the ordinary running of the Office and partly because of his own remarkable capacity. He owed his appointment primarily to the facts that he was a member of the tiny National Labour Party in the coalition and that he was his father's son. He received Cabinet rank before many older men such as Anthony Eden, Harold Macmillan or Attlee: MacDonald's rapid promotion inevitably caused jealousies of which he could not fail to be aware and he was determined to justify his appointment on merit. He did so abundantly and went on to a distinguished career in a variety of posts overseas, making a powerful impact on the concept of the Commonwealth. In the early 1930s, however, he was still largely unknown; he applied himself to his task with industry and application – indeed with a sense of dedication. Though this gave an impression of serious-mindedness, he had a more light-hearted side and an agreeable sense of fun. Above all he was still young and his approach to problems was fresh. He was modest and unassuming and easily gained the confidence of older men. By nature he was moderate and always readily saw the point of view of the other side – though determined to reach his own conclusions. As his subsequent career suggests, his genius lay more in diplomacy than in administration. His arrival was like a breath of fresh air and gave the Office an invigorating sense of purpose which it had not enjoyed since Amery's day. He initiated new policies in relation to Ireland, gave deeper meaning to 'consultation' particularly by the range and frequency of his personal contacts with Dominion representatives and transformed the attitude of the staff in the D.O. by keeping in touch with many of them and giving the feeling that he valued their views. Above all he understood the Dominions, nearly all of which he had visited; he was in tune with the younger generation and, in all he did, showed a sympathetic and progressive spirit.

From 1930 onwards, the post of Dominions Secretary was normally held separately from that of Colonial Secretary, though there were occasions when the two were combined – for example in 1938 when MacDonald (by that time Colonial Secretary) combined them on the sudden death of Stanley who had been Dominions Secretary for a few months only. MacDonald continued as Dominions Secretary until 1939 when he was followed by Sir Thomas Inskip. Inskip returned to the Department in 1940 as Lord Caldecote, and his contribution is considered in a later chapter.

A new post of Parliamentary Under-Secretary for Dominion Affairs with duties confined to the D.O. was created at the outset: the incumbent served also as Chairman of the Overseas Settlement Board. The first Parly US was Lord Clarendon; he left within two years to become Chairman of the BBC (and later Governor-General of the Union). The rate of turn-over by Parly USs was rapid (there were over 30 in the 33 years of the existence of the Office); it was not easy in a short term to make a considerable impact, especially as most Secretaries of State reserved for themselves decisions on important questions of policy. For the most part, Ministers in charge of the D.O. were not of the front rank. Officials too were competent and conscientious rather than brilliant. None showed the ruthlessness of Warren Fisher, the panache of Vansittart or achieved the influence of Horace Wilson. The key advisers in the early days were Sir Charles Davis (PUS), Sir Edward Harding (AUS), with Sir Harry Batterbee (senior Assistant Secretary). Davis had been the Under-Secretary in charge of the old Dominions Department and was thus the obvious choice as the first PUS in the new D.O. That he was also selected on merit seems clear from Amery's warm references to him. Davis was an old college friend of Amery's; he had in fact defeated Amery (who does not appear to have borne any grudge) for the Classical Scholarship at Balliol. Amery referred to him later as 'one of the acutest minds in the whole Civil Service'[11] and, in preparation for the 1926 Conference, said that he 'owed much to the constitutional insight' of Davis. Dixon, his junior, who regarded Davis as 'one of the outstanding figures in the Civil Service' and felt that it was to him more than anyone else that he owed his knowledge of Commonwealth affairs, confirms that Amery relied heavily on Davis during the 1926 Conference.[12] He had a powerful intellect (he was a double first), and considerable experience in government. But he was intolerant and did not brook interference, even from Ministers. He was an individualist almost to the point of being eccentric. He could at times appear devious and he caused offence with his barbed shafts. Indeed it was the view of one of his contemporaries that he lacked the personal qualities to be really effective. These characteristics created at times a bad atmosphere in the Office; in particular there was jealousy between the D.O. and the C.O. Nevertheless Davis was quite unusually effective on paper and his qualities earned him the respect if not the affection of the staff. He suffered much ill health and was forced to retire in 1930.

He was succeeded by his deputy, Harding, who remained PUS until the outbreak of war. He was therefore in effective charge for nearly a decade, under five different Ministers, and left an indelible stamp on the Office in the pre-war years. Harding (invariably known from his initials as E.J.) was not without faults. His manner was cold, even distant: his eyes were steel grey and he could fix his interlocutor in an unblinking stare. He lacked warmth, a sense of humour and any social graces. His speech was curiously formal. He could be insensitive, even harsh. He did not shrink from controversy; indeed he relished it. What struck his subordinates most was his obsession with detail, often to the exclusion of wider considerations. He was a perfectionist and was congenitally incapable of accepting a draft without making some amendment of wording, if none of meaning.* But there were many admirable qualities: he had a rigid sense of duty and a stern conscience (legend had it that he returned to the Office after his wedding); he was a man of the utmost integrity and was completely straightforward. At least everyone knew where he stood with Harding – even if he did not relish the position. When Harding took charge, he transformed the atmosphere and the previous jealousies and antagonisms disappeared. He also showed great pertinacity – the Irish leader Michael Collins once said of him: 'E.J. could talk the hind legs off a donkey.'[13]

He earned high opinions from many in a good position to judge. Amery refers to his 'skill in draftmanship which proved invaluable during the (1926) Conference';[14] Hankey established what he described as 'such excellent relations' with him[15] (and also with Batterbee); Mackenzie King 'had formed the very highest opinion of his ability and judgement and would have welcomed him as the first British High Commissioner in Canada.'[16] Casey however took a less favourable view.[17] In short Harding never gained popularity and had no gift for getting on with people, but he defended unflinchingly the interests of the Office as he understood them.

By a coincidence, Harding's deputy was his own brother-in-law, Batterbee, who differed from him in nearly all respects and complemented him in many. Where Harding strove to achieve the classic virtues of order, neatness, precision and clarity, where he followed the path of prudence, Batterbee was a Romantic, throwing caution to the winds. He was an enthusiast and 'saw the Vision of the world, and all the wonder that would be'. When involved in some affair of State, he betrayed an excitement that could lead him into incoherence. A tall shambling figure with his long arms gesticulating in the air, it was not surprising that he was known as the White Knight. He had his foibles; but they were all harmless, and indeed likeable, ones. There was an element of intrigue which he enjoyed. He had a passion for anything to do with Royalty.† His contact with the Royal Family dated from a remarkable incident in 1918 which he relished recalling. At the opening of the Imperial

---

* There was some truth in the Office clerihew:
> Sir Edward Harding
> Once altered concerning to regarding
> But it gave him still greater satisfaction
> Slightly to amend the in LF action.

(LF is an abbreviation for Lithograph Form such as an acknowledgement or compliments slip.)

† His attentions at Buckingham Palace were so frequent that the staff used to enquire:
> Oh dear! What can the matter be?
> Here comes old Harry Batterbee.

War Conference it suddenly transpired that the traditional message from the King had not arrived. Rather than delay all proceedings by consulting the Palace, Batterbee, then P.S. to the S. of S., slipped next door and quickly drafted a message which he then read out. When the facts came to light, the S. of S. felt it necessary to send an explanation to the Palace and warned Batterbee that he was likely to receive a reprimand from the King, who attached great importance to his personal messages. A summons duly arrived and Batterbee presented himself, terror-struck. The gruff Monarch, however, promptly put him at his ease by commending him for his enterprise and for a 'damned good message'. He kept him in conversation for a long time and finally presented him with the C.V.O.! Batterbee claimed that thereafter King George V always took an interest in his career. In 1923–4 he was attached to the Special Squadron for its Empire Tour to arouse support for Naval Defence – a project close to the King's heart; and his association with the Royal Family received another fillip when he was appointed Political Secretary to the Duke of York on the tour to Australia and New Zealand in 1927. As a result he was rewarded with the K.C.V.O. – an unusual distinction for one of his rank at that time.

By his sense of the dramatic, his love of mystery and his temptation to exaggerate, Batterbee appeared to some in Whitehall as a figure of fun. But he supplied qualities that would otherwise have been missing – he had warmth of personality and he had charm; he therefore succeeded in getting on close terms with his opposite numbers in a way that Harding's stiffness would not have allowed; he was a zealous advocate of his cause and often showed skill in negotiation; he involved himself in a variety of matters not necessarily of direct concern to the Office; he saw himself as the honest broker and was always ready to promote a compromise if he thought it likely to lead to an acceptable solution. He made a special point of developing close personal relations with the Cabinet Office, Treasury and Foreign Office (F.O.); this stood the Office in good stead when conflicts developed and softened some of the acerbities of inter-departmental wrangling. He more than anyone else at the official level helped to put the D.O. on the map.

Harding and Batterbee were the main formative influences on the D.O. after the departure of Davis. A second Under Secretary post was added in 1931 which was filled by Sir Geoffrey Whiskard until his appointment as High Commissioner to Australia in 1936 when he was succeeded by Machtig. This post was mainly concerned with economic matters and will be considered in that context. It is of some interest that the first three Under Secretaries all carried out major Empire tours, Harding with Baldwin to Canada in 1927 (and he himself made an extensive tour to Australia and New Zealand in 1937), Batterbee on the two tours already mentioned, Whiskard as Amery's chief adviser on his Empire tour also in 1927; all were themselves later appointed as High Commissioners.

As to the staff as a whole, it is possible to distinguish three separate generations. At the top were men who had spent their working life in Whitehall, who for the most part had been exempt from military service, who were conscientious Civil Servants, devoted to maintaining the standards of the tradition in which they had grown up. They were men of honour and they had their virtues. All were intelligent, men of common sense and prudence, but they were cautious rather than courageous and flashes of imagination or of humour were rare. Their minds were analytical, the form appealed to them rather than the substance and they were not all at ease in society. In the middle ranks were men who had for the most part fought throughout the war; their education had either been interrupted or curtailed; but they had been submitted to the ordeal of Armageddon and had survived. They knew the world, they had learnt to command men and were impatient of the comfortable doctrines of an earlier generation. Far from being visionaries or rebels, they were essentially realists, but they had a compassion learned in a bitter experience. They were therefore men who wanted to get things done without being unduly concerned about the formalities.

The third generation was different again. They were too young to know the war other than as a childhood memory. They had completed their university education (frequently but not in all cases at Oxbridge), but had little experience otherwise. They tended to be more intellectual than the middle group (they contained more than one double first, including one in economics), but they lacked its practical wisdom. Until they later gained experience by serving in posts abroad, they appeared to be diffident and lacking the assurance to express ideas of great originality.

The staff, small though it was, covered a remarkable variation in types of men, running the gamut from bemonocled, aesthetic 'Eddie' Marsh (patron of poets, painters and writers and inveterate first-nighter) to the breezy quarter-deck rumbustiousness of Admiral Bromley who exuded the salty tang of the sea. In between it comprised a wide variety of characters, including Machtig, a gifted violinist, Sedgwick, a Fellow of Trinity (and distinguished history scholar), McSweeny, a writer of free verse (who later died tragically), Chadwick, who enterprisingly cycled to Persia, and Kimber, a yachtsman who was later to go with the little boats to Dunkirk.*

The smallness of the staff helped to create a degree of intimacy, well illustrated by the practice of the tea club. There was a single club in the D.O. but also mixing with clubs in the C.O. The clubs provided an easy opportunity to get to know senior staff, exchange gossip or seek advice. There was increasing use of Christian names particularly by the younger members, the older generation seeming to prefer a playful abbreviation of the surname or a nickname.

* With characteristic attention to detail Kimber put in a claim for one bowler hat and one umbrella lost at Dunkirk and duly received appropriate compensation from the Lords Commissioners of the Admiralty.

Discipline was seldom severe (though on one occasion a junior who had been seen hatless in St James's Park was reminded curtly by the PUS that 'gentlemen wear hats') and there was often some fun to be had. Clerihews were produced about other members of the staff with some ingenuity and there was some mild horse-play on occasion (though the organization of cricket matches in the wide corridors was merely a memory of the past).

CHAPTER 3

Functions and Organization

The main function of the D.O. was to act as the channel of communication between the British Government and the Governments of the Dominions.* In addition, the D.O. had responsibility for relations with the Australian States (with whom there was direct communication), for Southern Rhodesia (a self-governing Colony with certain powers reserved to the Crown), and for the High Commission Territories of Basutoland, Bechuanaland and Swaziland. (Both Rhodesia and the High Commission Territories had been the responsibility of the former Dominions Department in the C.O., because of the close connexion with South Africa, and this arrangement was continued when the D.O. became a separate Department). The D.O. was also the sponsoring Department for the Overseas Settlement Board (whose staff was later incorporated in the D.O.) and for the Empire Marketing Board.

The business of the D.O. is summed up, with a contemporary flavour, in the description (drafted in the D.O.)† in the report[1] of an inter-departmental Committee in 1937: 'The communications with Dominion Governments frequently raise issues of considerable importance and entail lengthy negotiations of a delicate character; it is therefore essential that the method of approach ... should be considered with great care and with due regard to the susceptibilities of the Dominion Governments ...' It concluded that the task of ensuring cooperation 'cannot, obviously, show concrete and positive results in many cases, but necessarily involves a considerable amount of labour on the part of Ministers and Officers in the Dominions Office'.

The first charge on the D.O. as a Department of the British Government was to further the interests of Britain; the D.O. was not the representative of the Dominions. Its aim was to secure the cooperation of the Dominions where necessary in carrying out British policies. It sought to present those policies in a manner likely to prove acceptable to Dominion Governments and at the same time to make known to British policy-makers any difficulties that Dominion Governments might see and to recommend ways of over-

* The Dominions (as later defined in the Statute of Westminster) were Canada, the Commonwealth of Australia, New Zealand, the Union of South Africa, the Irish Free State, Newfoundland. Newfoundland was to lose the status of Independent Dominion in 1934; it was then administered by a Commission under the supervision of the British Government; this lasted until 1949 when Newfoundland joined the Confederation of Canada as the 10th Province.
† The author was Secretary of the Committee.

coming these. Inevitably this led the D.O. into paths of compromise and, where differences could not be reconciled, the Office was in danger of being caught between two fires, exposed to complaints from each side that its case was not being sufficiently pressed.

The D.O. also remained the sole agency for co-ordinating matters in relation to the meetings of the Imperial Conference (and this remained the responsibility of the Office until the establishment of the Commonwealth Secretariat in 1965). The Conference of 1926 recognized the equality of status of the Dominions and the UK and the right of each Dominion to take its own decisions; the whole raison d'être of the D.O. was to make Commonwealth cooperation effective on this basis. Not all British politicians or Departments however were ready to accept the full implications of equal partnership and the D.O. often acted as the conscience of the British Government to ensure that they lived up to their part of the bargain. The basic problem lay in recon- ciling unity of purpose (which was the professed aim of all members of the Commonwealth) with diversity of interest. In effect the Empire rested on two conflicting principles – autonomy of the parts and unity of the whole.

In many respects the responsibilities of the D.O. both in kind and in degree differed significantly from those of the other Departments dealing with external matters and these differences resulted in the establishment of quite distinct traditions. The differences affected the character of the Office, its relationship with its agents overseas, the style it adopted and the degree of authority it possessed. The S. of S. for India had in the last resort complete authority and legally possessed the power to instruct the Viceroy to do his bidding. The authority of the Colonial Secretary was more circumscribed, since in many territories there were elected assemblies and the Governor, except in certain matters, could act only with the approval of his Council. The Foreign Secretary (with some exceptions) exercised no authority in a foreign country, but there existed ways of ensuring that his will prevailed (there were many variants of gunboat diplomacy). Only the Dominions Secretary had neither any authority nor any means of asserting his will – the Commonwealth partnership meant that the use of force was ruled out (the economic measures applied to the IFS in 1932 were a unique aberration) and the Dominions Secretary could achieve his aim solely by the exercise of diplomacy and by securing the willing consent of a Dominion Government. These differences were reflected in the organization of the various Services. In India the ICS had always been separate from the staff of the I.O. in London and had its distinct tradition; there was some antagonism, and jealousy, between the two and seldom a close personal understanding. In the Colonies, the Colonial Service was also separate from the C.O., but in order to improve understanding it was arranged in the inter-war period that men serving abroad should return for a spell of two years or so working in the C.O.

26

where they were known as 'beachcombers' and also that, in their early years in the C.O., recent entrants to the administrative grade should serve 'in the bush' for a period. In foreign countries, the diplomatic (as also the consular) service had been distinct from the staff of the F.O. up till 1920 and the services were not fully unified until after the Second World War. The overseas service of the D.O. began only in 1928 and remained very small; but the D.O. was the only Department to make no distinction from the start between the members of its staff at home and abroad. Broadly speaking, the functions of the I.O. and of the C.O. were administrative and regulatory; those of the D.O. and F.O. diplomatic and political.

The resultant of these various factors was that correspondence between the I.O. and the C.O. and their agents abroad tended to be direct, but impersonal, with the minimum of explanation of reasons and no flourishes; the I.O. style could be peremptory and that of the C.O. brusque. Certainly the C.O. would address a Governor in tones that the D.O. would not normally use to a High Commissioner. In the D.O. as in the F.O. the style was more expansive and was persuasive rather than peremptory; the F.O. with an ancient tradition behind it was often elegant, with an apposite literary allusion; the D.O., particularly when the correspondence was between individuals who knew each other personally (as often happened in so small a circle), was informal, did not disdain humour and was at times extremely frank in comment. Direct correspondence with Dominion Governments was courteous, even placatory in tone. In all these respects the D.O., though its members did not fully recognize it at the time, was far closer to the Department responsible for foreign affairs than it was to either of the other 'Empire' Departments.

An important feature of the Commonwealth partnership after the First World War was the greater frequency of opportunities for personal discussion between Ministers, facilitated by the growing introduction of air services. The Imperial Conference continued to hold regular meetings and brought both Ministers and officials in close contact for lengthy periods. In addition – apart from the unique Economic Conference at Ottawa in 1932 – there was a variety of *ad hoc* meetings between Ministers on trade and other matters. The series of international gatherings also provided regular opportunities for Ministers (including at times P.M.s) and officials to foregather and consult. International conferences had a further advantage for the D.O. as an official from the Office was normally included in the British delegation – this gave him the chance not only to get to know his Dominion opposite numbers but also to work closely with his colleagues in the F.O. Above all the traffic was now ceasing to be one-way: Baldwin was the first British P.M. in office to visit a Dominion when he went to Canada in 1927; but Ramsay MacDonald also visited Canada as P.M. in 1929; Amery made a tour of all the Dominions in 1927, Stanley visited Canada in 1938 and DeLaWarr (Lord Privy Seal) Australia in 1938; Malcolm MacDonald (1934) and Hartington

(1936) both visited Australia and New Zealand as Parliamentary Under Secretaries; Hankey visited all the Dominions in 1934 and Harding, Australia and New Zealand in 1937.

The channels used for communications by the D.O. varied and underwent changes as, with constitutional progress, the machinery for Commonwealth consultation developed. When the Office was set up in 1925, the official channel of communication between Britain and the Dominions was from the Dominions Secretary to the appropriate Governor-General. However in the following year it was agreed at the Imperial Conference of 1926 that the Governor-Generals should no longer be regarded as the agents of the British Government and that, in future, communication should be direct between Governments. As a result two changes were made: first the Minister for External Affairs replaced the Governor-General as the sender and recipient of messages (though New Zealand did not finally make the change until 1942); secondly the British Government began in 1928 the process of appointing High Commissioners in the Dominions. Thereafter messages might be exchanged either direct between Governments, or between the British High Commissioner and the Dominion Government, or between the Dominion High Commissioner in London and the British Government. At first the British Government found it convenient to continue to use the direct inter-governmental channel for most messages when it was a question of conveying information, but the practice of using the British High Commissioner as the channel steadily developed.

This system gave considerable flexibility; it enabled messages to be sent by mail or by telegraph and, in the latter case, in plain code or secret cypher; it covered both communications of the most formal kind and routine enquiries on individual matters and it also provided for personal and confidential messages to be exchanged direct between P.M.s or between other Ministers. Occasionally, too, officials in the two Governments corresponded with each other, but this never developed into a regular practice and in any case tended to disappear with the establishment of British High Commissioners in the Dominions.

If the D.O. was to achieve its object of bringing about the maximum co-operation, two things were necessary – first to establish an agreed concept of the Commonwealth association and the principles governing its operation and secondly to organize the machinery of the British Government required to ensure that cooperation. The first task is described in Chapter 5 dealing with constitutional matters. The second involved the establishment of a separate department at home and of a service overseas. Under Amery's inspiration, officials laboured with obstinacy and determination to achieve these objectives. Throughout they met strong opposition from the most powerful Departments of State – from the Treasury on grounds of expenditure and doctrines of Civil Service organization – from the F.O. who, in contra-distinction to the D.O., regarded foreign affairs as covering the whole world, including relations with the Dominions. Nevertheless though the 'separateness' of the early D.O. did not go as far as some had hoped, on each count Amery and his officials achieved their main points.

In accordance with the decision of the Cabinet, there were from the start limitations on the 'separateness' of the D.O. It was housed in the C.O. building and shared with them common facilities such as the Library, Legal Advisers, Accounts, printing, etc. More significantly, the S. of S. in both Departments was the same person, the staff was interchangeable (in spite of Amery's insistence on the very different qualities required) and the C.O. retained responsibility for all establishment questions.

As a consequence, the staff of the D.O. remained members of the Home Civil Service and were recruited by the Civil Service Commission in the same way as candidates for other Home Departments. Candidates appointed to the joint C.O.–D.O. staff were liable, as members of the C.O., to be seconded to a Colony for two years; later they were of course likely to be posted to a High Commissioner's Office in a Dominion; for these reasons entrants were required to give an undertaking to serve abroad if required. Although the term 'Commonwealth Service' was later frequently used, the staff in fact remained part of the Home Civil Service until the creation of the Diplomatic Service in 1965. There was considerable movement throughout the Home Civil Service and several who served in the D.O. transferred to other Departments, among them Bowyer, Pitblado and Flett all of whom later became PUSs elsewhere in Whitehall.

By any later standards the staff was minute. The permanent administrative staff consisted at the outset of 1 PUS, 1 Assistant Under Secretary (AUS), 3 Assistant Secretaries in charge of the three departments, 4 Principals and 4 Assistant Principals in these departments, making a total of 13 administrative staff; there were 18 in the clerical grades, thus – without counting those in the joint services shared with the C.O. – reaching a grand total of only 31 persons. The non-administrative staff covered confidential clerks, registry with despatch section and shorthand-writers and copy-typists. There was provision for class-to-class promotion but, unlike the C.O., no promotion was made in the D.O. before the war. Shorthand-writers were allocated to Ministers and Under Secretaries but the rest had to stand their chance by calling on the services of the pool.

The Office never closed and, to ensure a 24-hour service, particularly for messages to be sent to or received from all parts of the world, quarters were made available for a Resident Clerk (selected from a roster of juniors – who were invariably unmarried in those days); he acted for both Offices, normally serving for two weeks at a time. In times of crisis there was considerable business to be despatched, often late at night and frequently after a hard day's work; not all Resident Clerks showed the same high standard of skill in the somewhat mechanical but very exact skills of coding and cyphering.*

The organization of the Office followed the pattern in the old Dominions Department and the work was divided among three departments as shown in Appendix A, Table 1. The division of work was partly on a subject basis and partly on a geographical one. In the 1930s two substantial new responsibilities fell to the D.O. and two new departments were added (*see* Appendix A, Table 2). The first resulted from the establishment of a Commission Government in Newfoundland responsible to the British Government and the second from the D.O. taking over the work of the Oversea Settlement Committee. In 1932 it became clear that, with the decrease in migration, there was not sufficient work for the Vice-Chairman of the Oversea Settlement Committee; at the time Whiskard was filling this post and he was brought back to the D.O. as a second AUS to deal with the increasing work in the main Office. Compared with the distribution in 1925, the balance had shifted substantially in favour of the organization of business by subject rather than by area. This was in marked contrast to the continuing emphasis in the C.O. on a geographical distribution which was also largely the current trend in the F.O. In the case of the D.O., this shift was no doubt partly a reflexion in practical terms of the accepted philosophy of 'equality of status' between all Dominions and partly a matter of practical convenience; the arrangement ensured that, in any communication sent to all the Dominion Governments, a single focus of responsibility in the D.O. could be readily identified and that a single department had authority to act without the delay which might have been involved if it had been required to consult other departments in the Office. This speeded action and made for efficiency. On the other hand, the result was that there was no focus where all the aspects of a particular Dominion were considered together.

In 1937 with the additional work expected to fall to the Office on account of the Coronation and the subsequent Imperial Conference, approval was given for the temporary addition of a third AUS. This appointment was subsequently criticized in a report by the Select Committee on Estimates for 1937.[2] The Committee heard evidence from officials of the D.O., but found difficulty in grasping what appeared to be the complex processes of the D.O. and in accepting that such high-level staff was required for carrying them out. They were baffled by what they termed the 'triplication' of information – to the Dominion Governments direct, with copies to the Dominion High Commissioner in London and to the British High Commissioner in the Dominion capital. They were also concerned with what they regarded as

---

* A horrible example (probably apocryphal) used to be quoted of a Resident Clerk whose negligence in omitting the word 'not' had resulted in the hanging of some wretch whom the message was intended to reprieve. It is certainly the case that the Governor of Cyprus was frantically awaiting instructions during a crisis, that urgent messages were despatched to him in the small hours but owing to an over-zealous Resident Clerk (the author) they were received 'undecypherable' and all had to be repeated.

the duplication by departments in the D.O. of work already performed in the Office directly concerned (mainly the F.O. or the Board of Trade). In general their questions revealed that they were highly sceptical and were not satisfied that the D.O. was really anything more than a transmitter of information to the Dominions. They accordingly reported on the D.O. in somewhat scathing terms, concluding that there was undue concentration of work on the higher staff and that the staff seemed both numerous and highly graded in relation to the F.O. They did not feel that the high administrative posts had been kept to a minimum and recommended that the third Under Secretary post should be discontinued. They also felt that the Department should consider whether the methods adopted were as expeditious as possible, whether there was a full measure of devolution 'and whether the labour expended on different aspects of a problem is proportioned to their importance'.

The report was referred for examination to an inter-departmental Committee under the chairmanship of Howard Smith (Chief Clerk at the F.O.) with representatives from the Treasury and the D.O.[1] This Committee recommended that there was no call for the third Under Secretary post to be retained, but that there was full justification for the five departments. These recommendations were accepted without cavil by the D.O. and approved by the Treasury.

Methods of conducting business were inherited from the C.O. and conformed to the general Whitehall practice. Though minuting was regularized in the C.O. much earlier than elsewhere, the Office had nothing comparable to the F.O. Order Book[3] and no code of procedure existed until the middle 1930s. Minuting was formal and all official communications were sent in the name of the S. of S. Action was authorized by the magic signs 'at once' at the end of a minute or 'f.s.' (for signature) on a draft.

In general the work was conducted under more leisurely conditions than a more exacting age would later require and a high proportion of it was done on paper – in minuting to superiors, preparing memoranda or drafting communications. This work was performed with care and deliberation; the officer would study the matter in hand, consult the precedents and compose a well-balanced recommendation. He spent a far greater proportion of his time at his desk, compared with his successor of a later generation. In particular, he spent less time on the telephone or at inter-departmental meetings, calling on other officials, receiving visits from the staff of Commonwealth Missions, and far less attending a conference abroad or even in Britain outside Whitehall. A far longer proportion of an officer's time was spent in learning the job. An Assistant Principal had virtually no responsibility to take action on his own authority; this meant that for the first four years or so of his official life a man who had passed high in an honours degree was free to make any suggestions he liked to higher authority and these were no doubt frequently acted upon; but he was given no initiative on his own.

31

As war approached, the sense of crisis grew deeper and the volume of work increased steadily throughout the 1930s. Key members of the staff were hard pressed and departments were under strain for considerable periods at a time. Nevertheless until the war itself changed the old habits, the general pace in the Office remained unruffled and matters that were not urgent were treated in leisurely fashion. Hours of work were flexible and began very late by business standards at the time. Senior officers frequently did not arrive before 11 a.m. – but equally they would stay late and not leave before 7 p.m. as a normal rule, though sometimes even very much later. All staff below Under Secretary level were required to sign on and off. The holidays granted by the Civil Service at that time were certainly generous: six weeks for administrative staff and ten weeks after six years' service. In fact many often failed to take their full entitlement. On the other hand a five and a half day week was worked by all – and many stayed late on Saturday afternoon in the hope of leaving a clear desk. The shortness of the break therefore did not admit of lengthy travel at weekends; the 'cottage in the country' became a serious possibility only after the Second World War.

Though the Office was new in its independent existence, it inevitably inherited much from the C.O. and indeed in many ways continued a tradition that went back for a century. This tradition was cast in the mould of Victorian virtue; it had been based on an acceptance of the greatness of Britain and the idea of service for Empire; it embraced the doctrine of progress and was broadly humanitarian and libertarian. It had moved from the abolition of the slave trade and slavery to the concept of accountability under the Mandates system and to the doctrine of Trusteeship, with a responsibility to safeguard the interests of subject peoples. However erratically this tradition may have been applied in the past in administering coloured peoples, the significant fact for the D.O. was that the tradition, recognizing that there were no sanctions to compel obedience, accepted that those of British stock overseas had the right to be free and to run their own affairs.

Inside the Office there were certainly grumbles from time to time and some may have chafed at Harding's firm control on policy; but there were few rebels and there was normally good cooperation between all members of the staff. The atmosphere was congenial. Moreover the staff remained small and concentrated on broad political issues – indeed there were no large blocks of routine work which could be hived off to an executive branch. The work was never dull – on the contrary this relatively tiny Department was called upon to handle work of a high degree of interest and variety, since it was concerned with the whole gamut of governmental business – foreign affairs and defence, finance and trade, migration, citizenship, agriculture. All this provided a stimulating atmosphere and encouraged the development of fresh ideas. Together with the prospect of a posting overseas, this gave the Department something of the aura of an elite service and made it specially attractive.

CHAPTER 4

Representation Overseas

⋇⋇

The first British High Commissioner in a Dominion was appointed to Canada in 1928. Until that time in no Dominion did the British Government have their own servant charged with responsibility for all their affairs. The Imperial Conference of 1926, by establishing that the official channel of communication between the British and Dominion Governments should in future be between Government and Government direct (and no longer through the Governor-General), made some direct representation essential; but such a development might have been expected earlier. Many factors help to explain the delay. The Governor-General was not merely the formal channel of communication; up to that time he had always come from Britain; he had in fact been the agent of the British Government and was able to supply them with such confidential political reporting as they required. Secondly there was no call for any representative to cover some of the functions of a mission in a foreign country; a Trade Commissioner service had been established in the Dominions at the end of the nineteenth century; and for consular duties, owing to the acceptance of the common status of British subject, Dominion Governments carried out any services required.

The practice of appointing Commercial Attachés in foreign countries dates back to 1880 and a reorganized scheme was put into operation in 1906.[1] There was delay in following this example in the Dominions because the C.O. feared that Dominion Governments would resent the appointment of permanent officers to promote British trade. In 1907 all timidity was swept aside when the New Zealand Prime Minister proposed that Britain should have permanent trade officers in the Dominions. His resolution was adopted and in 1908 'Trade Commissioners' were appointed to the four major Dominions. The Royal Commission on Dominion Trade, set up by the Imperial Conference of 1911, investigated the work of the Trade Commissioners and recommended a large extension of the system. Accordingly, after the war the Service was reorganized and expanded: it came under the control of the Department of Overseas Trade, established in 1917. By the time the D.O. came into existence therefore, Trade Commission posts had been established in all the major cities in the Dominions.

There was also a curious technical reason why there had not been greater urgency over appointments of a diplomatic nature; it was argued that a full diplomatic representative could not be accredited in the normal way to the Head of State since the King could not appoint an ambassador to himself. However these factors do not wholly explain why, after the appointment of the first Dominion High Commissioner to London in 1880, nearly half a century elapsed before the British Government reciprocated and they do not explain at all why, after the 1926 decision, it was still fourteen years before Britain had a full mission in all the Dominions. The fact is that the British Government as a whole did not sufficiently recognize the independence of the Dominions or the need for an effort on their part to ensure cooperation; the Dominions were regarded as subordinate and expected to conform to British views. There were relics of the Colonial era, certainly in some British minds and sometimes also in Dominion attitudes. Something of Rhodes' 'Imperial factor' still persisted.

The title of High Commissioner had been established by the Canadian Government as long ago as 1878 – not without difficulty. Sir John Macdonald had first wanted the title 'Resident Minister'; but the British Government would not have this, arguing that the position was 'more analogous to that of an officer in the Home Service than to that of a Minister at a foreign court'. They suggested various pallid alternatives, exasperating Macdonald who finally declared 'It seems to me that it is a matter of no importance to the Imperial Government what title we may give our agent … Since the title of Resident Minister is objected to, I think we must adhere to that of High Commissioner.'[2] And so it was. Sir Alexander Galt arrived in 1880 and the title was established.

Nearly fifty years later, in 1928, Sir William Clark arrived in Ottawa as the first British High Commissioner in any Dominion. His journey also had taken a long time.

The Imperial Conference of 1926 had recorded that the 'delegates were impressed with the desirability of developing a system of personal contact, both in London and in the Dominion capitals.' But there was no general agreement on what form that personal contact should take. The British Government had entered the Conference hoping to revive the idea of a council of High Commissioners meeting in London regularly, with the aim of achieving some unity in foreign policy or, as Austen Chamberlain later minuted, 'of keeping the different Governments of the Empire in step'.[3] Predictably this was anathema to Mackenzie King; but, not so predictably, King, while making it clear – as he was to continue to do for twenty years – that he was not prepared to allow his High Commissioner in London to engage in consultations, nevertheless suggested a 'high commissioner' with diplomatic and consular powers to represent the British Government in Ottawa – an idea which he promoted with something bordering on enthusiasm. In some respects King became, uncharacteristically, the decisive factor in the matter and it is interesting to speculate why he expressed such strong views. His main object of course was to torpedo the idea of any Council in London and this he effectively did. It may be that he sought also to make amends for having destroyed the political position of the Governor-General. There was no doubt the further thought in his mind that, if Britain were going to send a representative to Canada, it was due to Canada (and important in relation to the USA) that the man should be worthy.

While the Cabinet readily accepted the Imperial Conference conclusion about the change in the channel of communications, there was opposition to the idea of appointing British Government representatives in the Dominions. As a first step Ministers decided to consult the four Governors-General privately both about their ceasing to be the channel and about the suggestion that, in some Dominions at least, there should be a British High Commissioner. In his message[4] Amery informed them of the discussions at the Conference and mentioned Mackenzie King's suggestion that in some Dominions at least there might be advantage in establishing, in effect, a British High Commissioner. He recognized that the position and functions of any British High Commissioner would need very careful thought and explained that the British Delegates at the Conference had reserved their position for discussion by the Cabinet; he added that the change in the channel of communication had received general support except from New Zealand and Newfoundland and that the appointment of a High Commissioner had also been received in principle 'with similar favour, though it did not appear as one on which early action was contemplated in all cases'.

The replies took startlingly different views. Willingdon from Canada agreed with Mackenzie King's views and felt that the appointment of a High Commissioner would make his own position as Governor-General more satisfactory. Indeed if the Governor-General was to cease being the channel of communication, then it would be essential that a High Commissioner should be appointed at the same time.[5]

Stonehaven from Australia accepted the need for the Governor-General to cease to be the channel, but thought the proposal to appoint a British High Commissioner 'open to grave objections'.[6] He felt it certain that the appointment of a High Commissioner would weaken the position of the Governor-General, 'accentuating artificial ceremonial and mechanical aspect of his office, abolition of which is already advocated by extreme Labour on grounds of expense and maintaining alleged useless anachronism'. Warming to his theme, he even feared that if Labour were returned to power and there were to be a bad season leading to drastic economies, it would be urged that 'representation of Britain' should be confined to a High Commissioner paid by the British taxpayer, thus saving the substantial expenditure borne by Australia in maintaining the Governor-General.

His colleague in New Zealand was hardly more restrained. 'I cannot too strongly emphasise my conviction,' cabled Fergusson,[7] 'that any departure from the procedure by which the Governor-General is the recognised channel will prove detrimental to the prestige of the Crown in the Dominions and will weaken the Imperial link.... If Mr. Mackenzie King's proposals are designed to eliminate the usefulness of the office of Governor-General and to lower the prestige of the occupant, then in my opinion they could hardly have been more admirably conceived.'

Athlone, from South Africa, however, shared Willingdon's view.[8] He felt that his usefulness would have been greater if he had not had responsibilities to the Imperial Government. He therefore offered no opposition and indeed thought that, if the changes came about, the Governor-General's powers would become more and not less effective. In an afterthought, he pointed out with percipience that, if Dominion Ministers were to submit their own selections for the post of Governor-General, the office might 'fall within the patronage of the party in power and in South Africa he would almost certainly be Dutch and a party man to all intents and purposes.'

The British Cabinet considered the matter on 10 November.[9] They raised 'no great objection in principle' to the proposed direct channel; Mackenzie King's proposal for a British High Commissioner was also 'felt to deserve most careful consideration' particularly as regards Canada. But the Cabinet was impressed by the strong arguments in the messages from the Governors-General of Australia and New Zealand. It is clear that Amery was most depressed at the upshot and particularly by the atmosphere shown. The immediate decision of the Cabinet however was merely to ask the P.M. and the Lord Chancellor to see the P.M. of Canada and, if they thought fit, the P.M. of Australia also 'with a view to finding a solution acceptable to all'.

Amery was depressed since he had long felt that representatives of the British Government were needed in the Dominions – to put across British policies, to ensure that the British Government knew Dominion intentions in good time and to watch over matters of concern to Britain; he was clear that the British Government could no longer look to the Governor-General for these services. He was however pessimistic about the chances of getting his colleagues to agree even to an appointment in Canada and confided in his diary that some of them were 'naturally behindhand ... with the developments of Empire relations'.[10] On 12 November[11] Amery put a new proposition to Chamberlain. (Chamberlain's reply[12] indicated that he too had been concerned at the line taken in the Cabinet for he told Amery that he 'gathered that the P.M. was less concerned by the Cabinet discussion than you and I were, attributing the opposition ... rather to their being taken by surprise by a novel proposition which they had imperfectly comprehended and not at all considered.') The plan which Amery sent to Chamberlain was a strange one. He said he had been thinking about the objections of their colleagues and thought that he had a way of meeting them. He suggested splitting the two functions of liaison on foreign affairs and defending British commercial and other interests. Instead of having one man big enough for both jobs, plus a high-sounding title, which might be thought to compete with the Governor-General's position, why not, he asked, have two rather smaller men with smaller titles to fulfil the two functions separately?

Not surprisingly Chamberlain did not think much of the idea. His reply expressed doubt about the proposal and restated his consistent view that what Mackenzie King wanted was liaison on foreign affairs and that the 'co-ordination of our scattered Trade Agents, the speaker who can at public banquets put in a word for the old country ... are minor objects put forward ... as inducements to us.'*

Baldwin made little headway in his talks with the P.M.s of Canada and Australia and no progress had been made before Amery left on his Empire tour when he took a further opportunity of sounding out views. In Australia he found that Bruce (the P.M.) had somewhat modified the view he had expressed to Amery in London that there was no need for anything in the nature of a High Commissioner or even for a liaison officer on foreign policy. In Canberra, Amery now found that, while Bruce was still opposed to anything ambitious or high-sounding, he felt that a liaison officer for general questions would be useful. He did not press for an immediate appointment, but suggested that the matter should be kept open. (Stonehaven apparently did not see the same objections to this more modest proposal.[14]) As soon as he returned to London, Amery took the matter up again with his colleagues.

In May of 1927, the three British Ministers mainly concerned – Balfour (Lord President), Chamberlain (Foreign Secretary) and Amery (Dominions Secretary) – put their names to a Cabinet memorandum which had been prepared in the D.O.[15] The memorandum made the case for representation in the Dominions in general terms and recommended a more detailed enquiry. This was approved; and a Committee of Five was appointed, Salisbury (Lord Privy Seal) and Cunliffe-Lister (President, Board of Trade) being added to the three signatories; the Committee worked in close consultation with the Treasury and the Chancellor of the Exchequer (Churchill).[16] Amery submitted detailed proposals. These were based on the need to adapt the arrangements to the different circumstances and standpoint in each Dominion and envisaged differential treatment. In Australia and New Zealand, the D.O. sought to place liaison officers in the first instance. In South Africa, a relatively junior official representative of the British Government was suggested. The appointment for the IFS was left open, depending on that Government's wishes. For Canada (which was the crux of the matter), Amery contemplated the appointment of a person corresponding to the

---

* There were lighter moments in the correspondence between the two Secretaries of State. Commenting on one of Amery's papers, Chamberlain began 'I have read with much interest and almost equal difficulty your memorandum ..., some thoughtful person in your office having taken the trouble to type it in nearly invisible ink.'[13]

Canadian High Commissioner in London.[17] In discussion in the Committee, Amery[18] recalled that the Governor-General and Prime Minister in Canada were hoping for a man of distinguished achievement who could be given considerable authority. He proposed that the representative should be responsible to the Dominions Secretary and be authorized to speak for the British Government in *all* matters, particularly foreign affairs, but also in any questions affecting inter-imperial relations including trade. The first occupant should preferably not be a diplomat and a diplomatic appointment with the appearance or title of 'minister' should be avoided, because it was highly undesirable to foster the impression in Canada that Anglo-Canadian relations were in any way similar to those between foreign countries. The unfolding of Amery's ideas led in the ensuing months to a prolonged clash between the D.O. and the F.O.

At bottom, the battle between the two Departments was for control; but it was much more than a question of a struggle for power or merely of selfish jealousy. There were profound differences between the two on what was in British interests, on the nature of the Commonwealth and on the ability of the other to carry the responsibility. The F.O. saw the matter inevitably as one primarily affecting foreign policy; the D.O. envisaged the representative covering all questions affecting the two Governments. The F.O. considered that a skilled diplomat was required; the D.O. looked for someone capable of conducting public relations and of explaining Britain to Canadians. The F.O., originally at least, hoped that the closer contact would lead to some degree of unity in foreign policy under British guidance; the D.O. recognized that, under the new concept of the Commonwealth, each Member had the right to decide its own policy. Finally, the F.O. viewed the new D.O. as inexperienced and only too prone to accommodate and coddle tiresome clients; the D.O. on the other hand felt that the diplomat's career might have given him a habit of mind unsuitable for work in the Dominions, where the special qualities developed in embassies and legations were not likely to be readily appreciated.

It was at this point that Amery enunciated, perhaps in extreme form, a doctrine that was to become the D.O. creed. Writing to Chamberlain he said 'I do see considerable dangers in having our first representative in Canada going there straight from the Diplomatic Service and with no training in the work of the Office with which he will primarily have to deal, or of the problems in other Dominions which are inevitably affected by anything which is done in any one Dominion.'[19]

Here in a nutshell was expressed the basic difference from the F.O. – the theory of the *inter se* relationship, the view that the Commonwealth was *sui generis*, that relations between Britain and the Dominions were special and different in kind from those between foreign countries.

Whatever the deeper motives, the F.O. reacted sharply to Amery's proposals. In revealing terms, the PUS (Sir William Tyrrell) minuted to Chamberlain:

> If our main object really be to respond to a desire of the Dominions for assistance in obtaining knowledge of foreign affairs, and thereby improving their eventual share in directing the policy of the Empire, all I can say is that Mr. Amery's scheme is a very poor attempt to meet such a demand ... even assuming that they (the Dominions) do not reject it, it will remain a sham nevertheless and I do not believe that we are promoting the unification of the Empire as regards foreign policy by such devices.[20]

Tyrrell went on to urge that, instead of 'parliamentary failures' whose work would amount to 'the production of imperial gas' and little else, a diplomat with the rank of Minister should be appointed to Canada.

As soon as Amery's proposals were tabled in detail, they also attracted the attention of the Treasury on the grounds of cost. Churchill in the Cabinet had already pointed out the desirability of avoiding increased expenditure without compensating economy. The F.O. were not averse from courting an unusual alliance with the Treasury in order to defeat what they regarded as the grandiose ideas of the D.O. The D.O. estimate for the Canadian operation amounted to £14,500 and the total for all Dominions was what today would seem the modest sum of £39,500. Nevertheless the F.O. wondered whether, when the other Dominions saw what was happening in Canada, they would not press for something similar; if so, the commitment could run to as much as £100,000 a year – a figure that was assumed to be unthinkable. The F.O. themselves prepared a revised estimate, reducing the Canadian operation and eliminating all other costs to achieve a figure of £10,000. In putting this forward, Sir Hubert Montgomery (an AUS in the F.O.) made a comment which showed how little he understood the emerging Commonwealth. He asked:

> ... most of these proposals really arise out of the fact that the Dominions are un-willing to have really responsible representatives in this country ... Is it quite fair that this country should, as a consequence, have such a severe financial burden imposed upon it?[21]

The unholy Alliance closed ranks: at a crucial meeting of the Cabinet Committee,[22] Chamberlain confirmed his conversion to the idea of British representation in Canada, emphasized the importance of the post for foreign policy and argued that the Government should be represented by an experienced diplomat. Churchill announced his support on the understanding that expenditure did not exceed £10,000 (though the Treasury, he said, would prefer to spend only half of this).

The sense of the meeting was clearly against Amery and in support of the Foreign Secretary. Fortunately for Amery, however, the Committee did not reach a final conclusion. Baldwin was to pay a visit to Canada in celebration of the Canadian Jubilee which happened to coincide with his own sixtieth birthday. It was suggested that he should take the opportunity to discuss the matter informally with the Governor-General and the Prime Minister. But the Cabinet stipulated that the representative to be appointed should not be regarded as being there to balance the United States Minister; any special title like 'High Commissioner' was frowned on and it was even suggested that the Canadian Government should be asked to provide accommodation.

Baldwin's visit to Canada brought no immediate solution, but it had its importance in this context since it was the Prime Minister who finally settled the matter. Meanwhile battle was joined in London. Amery and his staff fought their corner toughly. Chamberlain confessed himself 'reduced almost to despair' by their 'obstructionism'. A further F.O. memorandum[23] was launched; this rehearsed the special case of Canada and reached the predictable conclusion that an experienced diplomat should be appointed. Nevertheless the memorandum marked a distinct advance towards understanding the needs of consultation with the Dominions. It recognized that the essence of the matter was to establish machinery for rapid consultation; it accepted that foreign affairs were but one aspect of inter-imperial relations and it agreed on the undesirability of giving British representation in a Dominion any appearance of diplomatic status. On all these points the two Departments were in agreement. But the memorandum harked back to the earlier idea of a Council in London which it regarded as 'the best solution'. Canada therefore was to be treated as a special case; even so 'nothing should be done by setting up a grandiose and expensive representation in one Dominion, to impede that ultimate solution.' The memorandum dated 24 October 1927 was not shown to the D.O. for some months and was commented on tartly by officials on 7 March 1928.[24] They saw the memorandum as contemplating continuance of the pre-war system under which the 'Foreign Secretary carried on the foreign policy of the Empire,' whereas they interpreted the current conception as being that *each* Government carried on its foreign policy so far as necessary but doing so, of course, in consultation with the others. Nor did the paper find favour with Baldwin.

Early in the New Year, Amery was due to pay a visit to Canada. And here Mackenzie King provided all the evidence he wanted.[25] King reiterated the need for someone of exalted status (completely contrary to the British Cabinet's view); he insisted that he did not want a diplomat (and ventured that Harding – then an AUS in the D.O. – was the kind of man he had in mind). He even grew lyrical over the intimacy of the confidential exchanges to which he would look forward (though in the years to come the number of occasions on which he was to 'discuss freely all the issues affecting inter-imperial relations' hardly lived up to this promise). As to the title, the talk between the two sides reversed the rôles as they had been fifty years earlier over the London post. King doubted whether High Commissioner was important enough; Amery thought it was and indeed feared that it would be too high-sounding for his colleagues.

The F.O. were not converted by the report of the talks with King and their views and those of the D.O. were never reconciled. The matter was finally settled by a Cabinet Committee consisting of the Foreign Secretary, the Dominions Secretary and the Prime Minister. Baldwin therefore was in the key position and he threw his full weight behind Amery, virtually all of whose demands, including the title of High Commissioner, were met. It seems clear that Baldwin's visit to Canada made a deep impression on him; he was convinced of the need for Britain to hold her own in Canada; he was anxious to put a positive construction on the changes wrought by the 1926 Conference and to show that the old country was not played out. It may have helped too that one of his advisers throughout the tour was Harding.

Sir William Clark was appointed as High Commissioner and took up his post in April 1928. He proved a considerable success and seemed to meet the various requirements as well as any one man could. His name was suggested by Warren Fisher, Head of the Home Civil Service, and he was not strictly a diplomat. But he came close to having the requisite training to make him persona gratissima with the F.O. Appointed to the Board of Trade in 1899, he was Secretary to the Special Mission to negotiate a Commercial Treaty with China in 1901 and the following year was made an acting Secretary in the Diplomatic Service; he had been Private Secretary to Lloyd George and Churchill, Member for Commerce and Industry of the Council of the Viceroy of India (1910–16) and since 1917 had been Comptroller-General of the Department of Overseas Trade (which was jointly responsible to the F.O. and the Board of Trade). After his Ottawa assignment, he became High Commissioner in the Union of South Africa. The calibre of the High Commissioner, his personal quality and the manner in which he discharged his task largely reconciled the F.O. to the post. There continued to be difficulties. For example even the British Embassy in Washington expressed some nervousness: 'We are really a little anxious as to the ill-effects of the High Commissioner's activities ... No harm has been done so far, but it was impossible not to detect a certain nervousness on the part of the Canadian Legation at the establishment of direct communication between the High Commission and the Embassy.'[26] But the Foreign Secretary at least was placated. On seeing one of Clark's letters, Chamberlain minuted: 'Thank goodness that we have got Sir W. Clark in Ottawa. If Mackenzie King were not so weak' (presumably in standing up to his officials) 'we should have less difficulty.'[27]

This conflict in Whitehall illustrates graphically some of the problems besetting the D.O. in its infancy. It led to certain consequences which were to cast a long shadow. In the first place it reveals the struggle with the rest of Whitehall which the D.O. fought to be master in its own house. More seriously the incident, in the same way as the battle with the Treasury over setting up a separate D.O., shows the failure of other Departments in Whitehall to understand or to accept the new concept of the Commonwealth partnership. Lastly the affair left some scars on the harmony of the D.O.–F.O. relationship. The F.O. had seen the question as a matter of foreign policy and had taken the initiative in putting forward its own independent proposals. In the end, the bigger Department with the proud tradition suffered a defeat and the upstart D.O. was victorious. This may well have coloured the future patterns of mind, affecting the general attitude of the F.O. towards the D.O. and perhaps towards the Commonwealth in general, causing the D.O. to be ever on its guard against any encroachment of its authority and contributing to the violence of the confrontation in 1949.

The story of representation in the other Dominions can be told more briefly since no question of principle arose. Nevertheless another dozen years passed before the process was complete. In Australia and in South Africa the position was complicated by the fact that there already was political (and not merely trade) representation in each case. In Australia there had been a British Government Representative for Migration since 1925 and in South Africa the Governor-General had, since the inception of the post, also held the office of High Commissioner for the Territories and, in that capacity, had been advised by the Imperial Secretary, a servant of the British Government. Migration had come to a standstill and even turned into a reverse current during the Depression; in Australia therefore the Migration Representative (Crutchley) was in 1931 appointed 'Representative in the Commonwealth of Australia for H.M.G. in the U.K.', pending the arrival of a High Commissioner. He was instructed to carry out the duties of a High Commissioner: the Office was therefore a High Commissioner's Office in embryo. Accommodation was provided free by the Australian Government (in line with that for their Liaison Officer in the Cabinet Office). The opening of a full mission was delayed by the Treasury because of the continuing financial stringency and did not take place until 1936 when Whiskard became the first High Commissioner in Australia and the first D.O. officer to be appointed as High Commissioner.

In South Africa, Amery had discussed[28] the question of representation with Hertzog on his Empire tour in 1927. They agreed that, under the technical authority of the High Commissioner for South Africa (i.e. at that time the Governor-General), the Imperial Secretary should act as personal liaison with the British Government. Beyond the assistance of one official cognizant with foreign affairs, it was thought that this need involve no enlargement of the existing staff. Accordingly the Imperial Secretary (Capt. Clifford) was in 1928 appointed Representative in the Union of South Africa and an F.O. Secretary (Houston-Boswell) arrived to assist him. The first High Commissioner, Sir

Herbert Stanley (previously Governor of Ceylon and himself a former Imperial Secretary), was appointed in 1931 when he combined the two posts of High Commissioner in the Union and High Commissioner for the Territories, absorbing the staff of the Imperial Secretary.

The New Zealand Government had originally expressed a preference for a Liaison Officer from Britain. A member of the F.O. (P. B. B. Nichols) was accordingly seconded for attachment to the P.M.'s Department 'in an informative and consultative character, particularly in relation to foreign affairs'. The experiment was not repeated. The basic reason was no doubt that the New Zealand Government were not sufficiently interested in accepting responsibility for decisions affecting foreign affairs. Reporting on his tour in New Zealand in 1927, Whiskard had recorded: 'It is clear enough that neither the Ministry as a whole nor the Opposition have any real conception of the responsibilities which ought to attach to full Dominion status.'[29] And Nicholls certainly reported to the F.O. that the New Zealand Government were not at all interested in foreign affairs. They would probably have done better to follow the Australian example and appoint their own man in London. A permanent mission in New Zealand was first established in 1939 when Batterbee arrived as High Commissioner. With Harding appointed as High Commissioner in South Africa in 1939 three out of the four posts were, for a short period, held by members of the D.O.

In the IFS, there was no similar sense of urgency on either side about establishing a British presence; indeed both geography and history were obstacles to any appointment; physical propinquity made it less necessary for the British and the background of the past made the idea less welcome to the Irish. No post had therefore been set up when war broke out.

The staff of a High Commission consisted initially of a High Commissioner, normally two Secretaries with supporting staff of Registrar and Cypher Officer, Typists and Office Keeper. Of the two Secretaries, one came from the D.O. and one was seconded from the F.O.; the pattern of a secondment from the F.O. became normal though not invariable (it was more regularly adhered to in Canada and the Union than in Australia and New Zealand). Since candidates of British origin were readily available for all subordinate posts, the typing and clerical staff was generally recruited locally.

The Trade Commissioner Service remained a separate organization and reported direct to the Department of Overseas Trade. This had the incidental effect that neither at home nor overseas did D.O. staff have any direct experience of trade matters. The Senior Trade Commissioner was instructed to conform to any guidance laid down on policy matters by the High Commissioner; Clark recorded: 'They treat me in practice as if I were their chief [as of course he had been in London], informing me of all matters they are handling and submitting their proposed course of action for my approval.'[30]

But there were some initial difficulties in Australia and New Zealand, mainly because of incompatibility between individuals.

High Commissioners themselves were chosen from all branches of Government service – except significantly the Foreign Office. Before the war, two came from the D.O., one each from the Home Civil, Colonial and Consular Services, and Clark (who was High Commissioner in two posts) from a varied Government career. Like a Dominion High Commissioner in London, he was the representative of his Government and presented his letter of appointment to the Prime Minister. He also had the right of direct access to the Prime Minister (and indeed to any other Minister). He was not the representative of the Sovereign nor accredited to the Head of State; he was not therefore regarded as a member of the Diplomatic Corps and this resulted in the loss of some privileges and precedence. It was the High Commissioner's job to represent Britain throughout the country or, as Baldwin put it, in writing to the King: 'the need was to keep Britain and the British point of view constantly before the small political world in Ottawa and, from time to time, before the wider public.'[31]

His functions were broadly similar to those of an ambassador in a foreign country, but differed in some respects in degree, if not in kind. In his official contacts, the High Commissioner was conducting business with a friendly Government of the Commonwealth which shared the language, traditions and very often interests of his own country. Business was therefore carried on in a more informal manner and frequently in an intimate atmosphere. The informality was specially marked at a junior level between Secretaries and their opposite numbers who might have first met at Oxbridge and who behaved more as members of the same team than as representing different Governments. (None of this implies that there were not acute differences of interest and clashes of view from time to time; indeed frankness and, at times, toughness were all the greater because of the family relationship).

In the sphere of public relations, a High Commissioner was often seen as the representative of what most still regarded as their own Mother Country, and many too still felt emotionally drawn to Britain. He was therefore in constant demand to make personal contact with people in all walks of life – in Parliament, the Universities, the Churches, business – and to address gatherings of every description to explain the British point of view. He became involved in the life of the country and his contacts were made in considerable depth.

Given this favourable background, it is perhaps surprising that it took time before the posts could be regarded as firmly established; indeed some High Commissioners were strangely diffident about their achievements.

Clark composed some notes[32] after completing six years as High Commissioner in Canada. These – and the similar notes written by Stanley in South Africa and Crutchley in Australia – are largely concerned with questions of procedure and etiquette. Clark commented on the 'curious passion for listening to speeches' by the inhabitants of the North American continent, and since he was 'not only a new specimen, but a new specimen of a new species' had a strenuous time when he arrived. Crutchley asserted that the 'mania for listening to speeches' was just as marked in Australia.* In contrast to Clark's experience, Crutchley reported[33] that he had 'little personal touch with the Senior Trade Commissioner' (who was in Sydney), but that they frequently conferred and 'given goodwill and the desire to cooperate, there is no reason why it should not work smoothly.'

Clark also made the somewhat surprising comment that the Diplomatic Corps (there were in fact only five in all) 'treat me as one of themselves'. But in precedence the foreign diplomats ranked after the P.M. whereas the British High Commissioner was placed lower down and Clark felt that this was unsatisfactory.[34] He quoted an instance from a big government dinner where he was not even at the high table and commented that it did not look well at an international function for the British representative to be so conspicuously lower than those of foreign countries. The matter was taken up informally by the D.O. with the Canadian Government, but no change was made.

Four years later, Sir Francis Floud wrote more solemnly. He referred[35] to the 'almost complete failure on the part of United Kingdom visitors to Canada to realize the existence of the High Commissioner or of his Office'; to the 'failure, and that after some nine years of its establishment, of Canadians generally to appreciate the significance of the High Commissioner's appointment'; more seriously he found that 'the present P.M. [Mackenzie King] shows on the whole less of an inclination to [talk freely] than he did in the past' and that 'as regards personal discussion between the High Commissioner and Canadian Ministers, it cannot be said that experience has shown the original ideas entertained on this point to have been justified in practice.' He recorded the almost shattering conclusion: 'The idea that the Canadian Government would frequently wish to consult the High Commissioner has been entirely falsified.' His successor was equally frustrated: Campbell wrote to the D.O. in August 1939[36] that 'Mackenzie King made it perfectly clear to me that he finds oral communications at this time when peace and war are in the balance, most disquieting. He feels that he has no control over the use to what he or I say may be put and that ... he may be accused of committing Canada ... with nothing to show that this was actually groundless.'

---

*The after-dinner speech with amusement as well as instruction is something unique to the English-speaking wave-length and the representative of Britain is expected to be good at it. The Head of Mission in a Commonwealth country and especially in the old Dominions stands or falls in public reputation according to his ability as a public speaker.

The High Commissioners were perhaps unduly modest:* nevertheless there clearly were some gaps in British representation in the early days. They were after all feeling their way in a new and sensitive field and felt it prudent to proceed with circumspection. Moreover some P.M.s – especially Mackenzie King and Hertzog – were difficult men in any case and peculiarly so for a British High Commissioner. Clark was the outstanding British High Commissioner before the war and showed qualities of firmness and flexibility both in Canada and South Africa. The others all did a competent job, but most found it difficult to establish a close relationship with Ministers or make an impact on the country as a whole. Both Floud in Canada and Stanley in South Africa were trained and highly skilled civil servants, Stanley with a distinguished record as a Colonial Governor, Floud after a successful career in Whitehall which included being the official head of the Board of Customs and Excise, the Ministry of Agriculture and the Ministry of Labour. But both were new to diplomacy and set in their ways; there was a staidness and stiffness about the manner, Floud in particular being too little extrovert to appeal to the North American temperament. Nor did the performance of the early High Commissioners from the D.O. itself suggest that the transference from Whitehall to a High Commissionership was an easy one.

Whiskard, the first to be appointed from the D.O., had a varied career. After obtaining a double first at Oxford he joined the Home Office in 1911 and served throughout most of the war as Private Secretary to the Home Secretary. He was a relative late-comer to the D.O. which he entered via Dublin Castle and the Irish Office. He had accompanied Amery on his Empire tour in 1927; he was later attached to the Oversea Settlement Committee, becoming Vice-Chairman in 1929; he was fully absorbed in the D.O. when migration work declined, and became an AUS in 1931. On return from Australia he became PUS to the Ministry of Works (subsequently Town and Country Planning) until his retirement. In many ways he was an asset to the Office; he had a cultivated and incisive mind; he was a strictly disciplined person with an air of some distinction and, if aloof, had a more assured manner than his senior colleagues in the Office. But his ambition seemed to be limited, his zeal was not stoked by any remarkable industry and he suffered from an ill-concealed sense of superiority (which was strikingly revealed in the published *Letters to my Son* written during wartime in Australia). He was therefore not normally tempted into pastures other than

* Gerald Campbell struck a self-deprecatory note in his autobiography:[37] 'I am so glad that I had nearly a year ... in which to find myself before the war broke out, since I would otherwise have trodden all unwittingly on the toes of feet marching in the same direction as our own. To put it frankly, I had mighty little idea when I arrived, of what it means to a Dominion to be independent of all control from the country it once called Mother.' Incidentally he regarded his appointment 'in the nature of a venture, or gamble, since none of my Masters in the Dominions Office had even so much as set eyes on me before.'

his own economic interests and he made little impact on the outlook and development of the Office as a whole. In spite of his ability as shown in Whitehall, his term in Australia cannot be regarded as a success; he never really got to terms either with Ministers or with officials or with the public at large.* The reasons lay partly in his indolence (he never felt called upon to make a real effort himself) and partly in his air of disdain (he felt himself to be superior and was a snob; but more than that he genuinely if quite misguidedly held the view that a High Commissioner must set a standard and hold himself aloof in order to remain detached). His own correspondence best describes his attitude: a few months only after his appointment he wrote 'This is a most amusing job; but by God, I shall be tired of it before I've finished it';[38] and in 1941 he wrote 'There really is very little work for the H.C. to do here . . . It's the rarest thing in the world for me to go to the Office in the afternoon . . . The idleness has really been a heavy burden.'[39] Allowing for the effect of the tragic death of his wife in the previous year, and for his own ill-health, this was surely a strange comment to make in the middle of the campaign in Greece. He also revealed something of the nature of his relationship with the Australian P.M. as well as the quality of his political judgement when he wrote in 1940 '. . . Menzies has no more backbone than a jellyfish. It is regrettably true that Menzies would not last a day if there were any visible alternative, but there is none.'[40] Whiskard's aloofness was all the more marked in Australia since Crutchley, who had established the post, knew Australia well, was genial and approachable and universally popular.

It was perhaps easier at the official level to do an effective job and here younger members of the D.O. were already making their mark. Liesching had the unique task of setting up in turn the posts in Canada, South Africa and Australia; this gave him an unrivalled experience. There were many others who served in a variety of posts abroad (most in more than one), and increasingly added to the corpus of knowledge in the Office by their direct experience of life in the Dominions. The staff seconded from the F.O. were able to draw on their own tradition and in turn benefited from the experience of serving in a Commonwealth country.

Though performance by individuals was uneven and some High Commissioners were still feeling their way, the significant fact was that posts had been established in all Dominion capitals (except Dublin). By the time war broke out, machinery for cooperation existed and all posts had developed effective working relations with Dominion Governments.

---

* Harding who had received strong criticism of Whiskard from Mrs McFarlane, the wife of a former Official Secretary at Australia House, commented to Machtig 'it was I remember common gossip in the D.O. when Geoffrey was home in 1938 that he was rather suffering from swollen head' (Harding to Machtig, 27 October 1940, Machtig papers).

CHAPTER 5

Dominion Status
and its Consequences

The continuous task of the D.O. and historically its main achievement was
that of defining the constitutional status of the Dominions and, within an
agreed framework, developing the techniques for cooperation between the
nations of the Commonwealth. The task was made more difficult by the
attitudes adopted by the Dominions. These were scathingly described in a
surprising comment sent to Balfour by Hankey during the 1926 Conference:[1]
'There is always,' he wrote, 'some Dominion that gives trouble at an Imperial
Conference but it is hardly ever the same Dominion twice running. Before the
war on one occasion it was an Australian Labour Government – Australia is
now one of the most loyal. In 1921 it was Smuts who in 1923 was most
helpful. In 1923 it was Mackenzie King, who is now our staunch ally. This
time it is Hertzog – but what will his position be in 1929?' (In fact it was the
Irish who caused the most trouble at the next Conference in 1930!)

Attitudes among the Dominion Governments varied widely. At one
extreme were the Irish and South Africans who sought to clarify their rights
and safeguard their freedom of action in legal form. At the other stood New
Zealand where as Amery reported to the Cabinet, 'Imperial sentiment, ...
strong in Australia, ... is a passion, almost a religion.'[2] She accepted British
leadership (though this did not prevent her expressing her own view); she did
not want the trappings of autonomy and disliked the idea of any declaration
of status.

In between stood Canada and Australia both of whom rejected either
extreme and both of whom, while conscious of their own nationhood, sought
to preserve Empire unity and recognized that, in a major war involving
Britain, all would be involved. But they drew very different conclusions –
Canada rejecting any idea of Imperial centralization or of advance commitment, and therefore shying away from consultation; Australia seeking to make
consultation as early and effective as possible and to be fully informed about
the decision-making process. To this end a special arrangement was made
with the British Government in 1924 for the appointment of a Liaison Officer
who was accommodated in the Cabinet Office and largely, if not wholly, given
the run of the place.

48

The differing attitudes of Dominion Governments were not merely doctrinal; they derived from the realities of their different situations. South Africa and the IFS were in large part alien nationalities anxious to demonstrate the appearance as well as the substance of independence. Australia, strategically vulnerable, needed British protection and would have welcomed an 'alliance' with mutual obligations. Canada's position was quite different – strategically safe, anxious that there should be no obligations (she could not overlook her own alien nationality in Quebec), yet not wishing to cut adrift because of the fear of domination by the USA. New Zealand remained dependent on the UK, both strategically and economically, and was emotionally content to be seen as dependent.

The Imperial Conference 1926

The discussion of constitutional questions in the inter-war years covered a wide range of subjects. Some loomed large at the time and took up an apparently disproportionate amount of the time and energy of the D.O. Today the disputes recall those of the schoolmen in the Middle Ages. But matters of fundamental importance were involved; the dilemma was how to reconcile freedom of the individual members with the unity of the Empire as a whole. British Ministers and officials sought hard to avoid the dangers they foresaw if it were to be conceded that Dominion Ministers could offer advice to the Sovereign contrary to the advice of His British Ministers, could remain neutral in a situation where the King had declared war or even could secede from membership of the Commonwealth.

The Imperial Conference of 1926 was the main occasion for marking out the direction which the Commonwealth would follow and it determined the limits within which the newly formed D.O. would operate. The Conference decided on a separate Conference on the Operation of Dominion Legislation (1929);[3] this in turn led to the passage of the Statute of Westminster (1931).[4] There were also Imperial Conferences in 1930 (*see* below), and 1937 (*see* Chapter 7); an informal meeting of P.M.s at the time of the Silver Jubilee (1935) and the Ottawa Economic Conference of 1932 (*see* Chapter 9).

The preparations for the 1926 Conference by the British Government were thorough and substantial. The Permanent Secretaries of the Departments concerned held preliminary discussions together with Hankey (Cabinet Secretary) and Hurst (F.O. Legal Adviser). Davis attended for the D.O. and Harding and Batterbee were also involved. There seems no doubt that Davis' intellectual power was here of great value. The records show that he raised many penetrating questions on the drafts that were produced and kept a wary eye open for any dangerous implications. Amery pays tribute to him and contemporaries have confirmed that he was a tower of strength throughout the Conference and that Amery relied heavily on him. Dixon relates how it was necessary for the D.O. 'to press sometimes vigorously for the full recognition of the equal status of the Dominions, against the hesitations of the F.O. who were still wedded to the conceptions of a common policy for the Empire' and recalls how 'at one meeting the argumentation was so fierce that it ended with Harding and Hurst sitting glaring at each other and neither saying a word.'[5] Only the ingenuity of Batterbee in evolving an acceptable compromise succeeded in thawing the scene. The senior D.O. officials were fully engaged in the Conference itself, Harding acting as Deputy Secretary of the Conference, Batterbee serving with Hankey in the Secretariat and Dixon acting as one of the Secretaries of the Inter-Imperial Relations Committee. Amery records that, apart from the important passage written by Balfour himself, he and Harding wrote the rest of the Report[6] and Hankey, writing to congratulate Harding after the Conference was over, said: 'We have co-operated now for a good many years, but never more fruitfully than in the last six weeks.'[7]

The D.O. therefore played a full part in the preparations and discussions. But the leading style was played by Balfour, at that time Lord Privy Seal, who took the chair at the all-important Committee on Co-ordination of Imperial Relations. Balfour had been P.M. a quarter of a century earlier, had given his name to the Declaration about Palestine in 1917 and now became associated with definition of the Commonwealth. It seems that this happened almost by chance. Baldwin was suffering from lumbago and in preparation for the Conference wrote to Balfour that he would therefore be glad of his very active assistance at the meetings. Amery claims that he suggested to Baldwin that Balfour should take the Chair at the important Committee on Co-ordination of Imperial Relations and Hankey supported the idea. It was no doubt a wise choice – Baldwin himself was not deeply immersed in constitutional niceties and Amery's bent was pragmatic and his manner uncompromising. Amery had some hard things to say of Balfour; he referred to his 'ingenious inertia' and to his being a 'formula finder with no bent for action'; he described how in the Committee he often 'dozed off'. Yet in a final summing up he thought that 'of all the public men I have known who could claim to greatness Balfour had the keenest edge to his mind.' Clearly he also had an ingenious and fertile mind, some subtlety and great patience.

The attempt to define the constitutional status of the Dominions had a long history. In 1921 Smuts had sent Amery a document[8] urging the recognition of the equality of statehood of the Dominions, with direct access to the Sovereign, a distinctive flag and the removal of Dominion affairs from the C.O. Amery agreed with the views expressed and Hertzog, on succeeding Smuts, seized on this with relish;[9] he arrived at the 1926 meeting determined to make the running. Amery made clear that Hertzog was pushing at an open door, and claims that a dinner party which he gave on their arrival (when Baldwin, like Brer Rabbit, mostly 'lay low and said nuffin') 'settled the outcome of the Conference.'[10] The South Africans were strongly supported by the Irish who wished to eliminate all forms of subordination. The others were less keen – Mackenzie King was by nature averse to abstract definition and strongly objected to anything like a Declaration of Independence (but equally to any reference to the idea of a single and corporate Empire).[11] Neither Australia nor New Zealand felt any enthusiasm and Amery at first doubted the wisdom of attempting a general declaration.[12] Chamberlain shared this view and suggested to Amery that, in the past, Commonwealth members 'have felt, and surely they have felt rightly, that it is the very absence of precise definition which gives to our relationship its strength and its elasticity. Precise definitions and logical statements are dangerous. They are drawn up in the light of one set of conditions. They come in course of time to be applied in other conditions which no one has foreseen.'[13] There was therefore at the outset a clear majority opposed to the idea of a general declaration. But Hertzog persisted – and won.

There seems no reason to doubt the generally accepted story that, after much discussion, it was Balfour himself who produced the final version, resting on his bed, scribbling on sheets of loose-leaf notebook. But he merely fashioned into a new, elegant and acceptable form phrases that had been tossed around, sometimes for years. Amery, who was in any case Chairman of the drafting Committee for the Report as a whole, claimed a share of the credit and Hankey, in reply to a query by Harding, said he would not cavil at Amery's account.[14]

The formula itself – no doubt inevitably – maintained a skilful balance between the opposing views and introduced that antiphonal tone into Commonwealth public statements which, in an effort to satisfy all, were capable of different interpretations. The single sentence of the definition referred for example both to 'the British Empire' and 'the British Commonwealth of Nations' (admittedly in rather different senses); the description contained the antithesis that the UK and the Dominions were 'equal in status, in no way subordinate one to another, though' – and it is significant that the proviso was introduced with the word 'though' – united by a common allegiance to the Crown and freely associated as members of the British Commonwealth'. Even these last two qualifications begged some questions – was the common allegiance owed to a single Crown? and if the Members were 'freely' associated, were they equally free to dissociate? Nevertheless the Report[15]* made explicit the principles on which the British

* The irrepressible W. M. Hughes had an unkind word for the Report which he described as 'a wonderful document' – 'Every P.M. went away perfectly satisfied – Mr. Bruce because it altered nothing that affected Australia. Mr. Mackenzie King because it taught Lord Byng where he got off, and General Hertzog because he was able to assure the burghers that the King of England was no longer the king of South Africa, although it was true that the King of South Africa was also king of England.' (*See* Mansergh (ed.), Documents, vol. I: 21–7).

Commonwealth rested and did so in a way which was acceptable to all Commonwealth Members; it governed the relations between them for a quarter of a century and its central doctrine remained inviolate until adjustment was called for when India sought to remain a Member after becoming a Republic in 1949. The authors had no doubts about its significance. Balfour wrote that nothing new had been done but added 'We have been making, at first half-consciously, and now with full consciousness, the most novel and greatest experiment in Empire building which the world has ever seen.'[16] Hankey expressed a similar thought in a letter to Smuts when he said: '... I agree in your criticism that it really changed nothing. But what it did change was men's hearts, and that was important.'[17]

With the approval of the formula for Dominion status agreed, Amery set off for what he called a 'Pilgrimage of Empire'. This lasted six months and took him to each Dominion in turn in one single voyage. His purpose was to bring 'home to both sides the positive spirit and purpose of our conclusions'. In a letter to Baldwin, he added that it was essential to work away at removing the suspicion 'of an Empire governed, or at any rate bossed, from London', that there were various loose ends about consultation and liaison that needed tying up and a great deal of detail to settle about various matters. He also felt that the 1926 declaration was susceptible to a good many shades of interpretation which would undoubtedly tend to weaken the whole unity of the Empire. He told the P.M. 'I have sufficient faith in myself to believe that I could do a great deal in a few public speeches to ensure the prevalence of the right view on these matters, without at the same time creating any controversy.'[18] The results of the tour certainly pleased him[19] and indeed it seems to have been a remarkable success.* All the more remarkable that never before had such an extensive tour been undertaken by the Secretary of State – and, with the aid of air travel, never again would a Minister be absent for so long. Amery was rightly convinced at the end of his tour that what he had been doing would in future be an essential part of the duties of any Dominions Secretary.[20]

There was a discussion at the Conference about the position of Governors-General which was to have far-reaching consequences. As a result of the Byng controversy (*see* Chapter 6), Mackenzie King arrived in London determined to remove any remaining elements of insubordination and in particular to clarify the role of the Governor-General. When King raised the matter, Amery assured him that he would not meet with any opposition[21] and there was little difficulty in securing agreement in the Committee. They reported

---

* His report to the Cabinet was refreshingly uninhibited. In his notes, Amery described Hertzog as 'obsessed by his personal dislike of General Smuts whom he firmly believes to have hoofs inside his boots and a tail in the seat of his trousers'; while Smuts for his part regarded the P.M. as 'a muddle-headed and untrustworthy old ass, with whom it is hopeless to try and settle anything'. The coalition formed by this pair from 1933 to 1939 should have been a lively partnership![19]

that the Governor-General is the representative of the Crown and not the agent of the British Government and therefore that use of the Governor-General as the official channel of communication 'might be regarded as no longer wholly in accordance with the constitutional position'. Therefore the 'recognized channel should be in future between Government and Government direct'. Rather coyly the British representatives 'readily recognized that the existing procedure might be open to criticism and accepted the proposed change in principle'.[22]

The change in fact was brought about without any undue haste and did not take effect in New Zealand until as late as 1942. The natural corollary was the appointment of a British Government representative and Mackenzie King raised this at the same time (*see* Chapter 4).

The Statute of Westminster

Acceptance of the doctrine of equal status made necessary an amendment of the law so as to reflect the agreed position. The South Africans had set the pace for the Declaration; the Irish now took the lead in sweeping away anachronisms; not interested in pious declarations, they wanted to see positive progress.[23]

A sub-Committee under Amery's chairmanship investigated anomalies; the result was referred to the Conference held in 1929 on the Operation of Dominion Legislation. This consisted of representatives from Britain, the Dominions and India. The Chairman was the Secretary of State (Passfield) but he took little part and the lead for Britain was taken by the Attorney-General (Sir William Jowitt). The chief British official was Sir Maurice Gwyer (Treasury Solicitor, later Chief Justice of India). The D.O. team, under the supervision of Harding, consisted of Stephenson, Dixon and Bushe (Legal Adviser in the D.O.).

The Conference produced a lengthy report[24] recommending the form of legislation which could be passed recognizing the status of equality, while at the same time maintaining the unity of the Empire and the conception of a common Crown. The report was adopted by the Imperial Conference of 1930 and, in agreement with the Dominions, the necessary legislation was passed in Britain in the form of the Statute of Westminster, 1931. The conclusions of the Conference as a whole resulted from the collective wisdom of all the Commonwealth representatives, but the detailed form of the legislation owed most to the British experts, particularly Gwyer who is credited with the invention of the title, 'Statute of Westminster'. The D.O. team was highly skilled and on them fell the main responsibility for steering the legislation on to the Statute book.

These constitutional discussions brought two rising members of the staff into prominence – Stephenson and Dixon. Stephenson, a characteristic product of Winchester and New College, Oxford, was just old enough to serve throughout World War I after gaining 1st class honours. He had a singularly ingenious and fertile mind and, in the densest wood, could always hack his way through the trees to produce a workable solution. It may not have been ideal, but – in words that he used frequently and so aptly – 'it made sense'. The Wykehamist background left him with an amused scepticism that saved him from any excess either of enthusiasm or solemnity; but his gentle pessimism embraced a deep sense of human compassion and permitted an easy-going tolerance. He played a key part in the formulation of broad policy in the D.O. in the next decade and a half, and acted throughout as a bridge between the hierarchy and the junior staff, to whom he was invariably stimulating and considerate. He was essentially an adviser rather than a strong administrator. He was not personally ambitious; he had little desire to lead or to force his will on others; he never served abroad. But he was an ideal deputy at headquarters. Unfortunately he died in 1948 when DUS at the early age of fifty-five.

Dixon formed an effective partnership with Stephenson. He had an encyclopedic knowledge, an unfailing memory and an infinite capacity for never overlooking the minutest detail; he became the Office constitutional expert and his advice was heavily relied upon both by senior members of the Office and by Buckingham Palace. He was regarded as so indispensable that, when he retired in 1948, he was re-employed as Constitutional Adviser by successive PUSs until 1968 when he was nearly eighty. But he had the short-comings as well as all the virtues of the expert. His experience was very confined and his interests were limited; he never married and never travelled much outside Britain until after his retirement. He worked with a microscope rather than a broad brush; here was no extrovert, not one to take a long view. He shied from personal contacts and there was a certain aridity about him.* But for all his pedantry, he consistently gave sound advice, firmly grounded on a wealth of knowledge and for half a century he acted as the guardian of the conscience of the Office.

Bushe, the Legal Adviser, was in fact less in the popular image of a lawyer than Dixon. He always took a broad view and was unusual among Legal Advisers in using his remarkable ability, instead of raising objections, to find good reasons for following the policy which the Office favoured. He was later to serve with distinction as Governor of Barbados.

---

* As an unkind Office clerihew of the time had it:

> 'Our Mr. Dixon knows all there is to be known
> About Georgius Rex,
> But nothing at all
> About Sex.'

The Statute of Westminster Bill was introduced into Parliament late in 1931. In brief it provided that a Dominion Parliament could legislate without reference to the laws of the UK and that the British Parliament could not legislate for a Dominion without its consent. But at the request of certain of the Dominions, some restrictions remained on their own powers, particularly to safeguard the rights of the Canadian Provinces and Australian States. It was never adopted by Newfoundland (whose status as a Dominion was shortly to lapse); it was not adopted in Australia and New Zealand until 1942 and 1947 respectively. It was therefore only South Africa and the IFS (significantly both destined to leave the Commonwealth) who accepted the Statute without reservation; it can hardly be said to have aroused universal enthusiasm. The main responsibility for shepherding the Bill through the House of Commons fell on the newly appointed Dominions Secretary, J. H. Thomas. No one could pretend that constitutional law was his forte (and he habitually referred to the Bill as the 'Statue of Westminster'); but he won through with a combination of bluff and bonhomie. With his familiar hyperbole, he referred to the Bill on introduction as 'the most important and far-reaching that has been presented to this House for several generations'.[25] The only serious opposition came from Churchill and the right wing of the Conservative Party, partly on the ground that this would be a most undesirable precedent for India and partly because it would give the IFS the legal power to break the 1921 Treaty. The Bill was nevertheless passed by a decisive majority.[26]

The Imperial Conference 1930

The Conference of 1930 met in an atmosphere of considerable tension and its achievements were modest. Countries all over the world and especially all primary producers were suffering the effects of the Great Depression. In Britain itself, the minority Labour Government was torn with dissension and uncertain of its way. There was therefore no vigorous leadership, no country felt it could afford to be generous and some of the normal fare of an Imperial Conference must have seemed irrelevant to the grim realities of the day.

Preparations for the Conference had none the less been very thorough; Ramsay MacDonald set up a Cabinet Policy Committee under his own Chairmanship as early as February. This had a series of meetings throughout the summer; the Dominions Secretary was invariably present, accompanied by Harding and Batterbee. Hankey circulated a comprehensive survey of Imperial Defence Policy and D.O. officials were busy with preparing numerous memoranda on constitutional questions. Hankey was as usual Secretary to the Conference and Batterbee served as his deputy. But the opportunity was never taken to come to grips with the big issues and the attitude of the Chancellor of the Exchequer (Philip Snowden) put a brake on the British Government giving a lead. His rigid adherence to Free Trade principles ruled out any agreement on Imperial Preference and economic issues were postponed for a Conference planned to be held in the following year. In defence matters, the British insistence on economies at Singapore brought forth strong but ineffective protests from Australia and New Zealand, while Canada under R. B. Bennett drew back from any conceivable risk of a commitment. Hankey was 'bitterly disappointed that we failed at this Conference to get any progress in revising the Defence Resolutions or to discuss Defence adequately.'[27] In a letter to Hankey, Sankey summed up: 'At any rate there is one thing upon which we can congratulate ourselves – the Conference has come to an end but the Empire has not.'

The one area in which agreement could be reached without merely papering over the cracks was in constitutional matters and it was this that concerned the D.O. most directly. The Conference[28] set up a Committee on Inter-Imperial Relations at which the Chair was taken by the Lord Chancellor (Sankey); Dixon was one of the Assistant Secretaries. Most of its deliberations were devoted to the Report of the Committee on the Operation of Dominion Legislation; agreement was reached without difficulty on the terms of the UK legislation required. Agreement was also reached (not always without difficulty) on a number of other matters: the Ministers responsible for advising on the appointment of a Governor-General were declared to be those in the Dominion concerned. A vaguely worded passage on nationality was agreed which Stephenson commented could mean just what any particular party wished. The British Government would have liked to set up a Standing Commonwealth Court but this was not acceptable; it was agreed that any disputes could be referred to an *ad hoc* Tribunal. In fact this was never done. There was a running battle between the D.O. and the F.O. over the negotiation of international treaties; on one occasion Dixon recorded that he took fifty pages to argue that this was only one example of a tendency which if persisted in 'would mean the destruction of the Empire'.[29]

There was also controversy over the Great Seal. The British wanted a Commonwealth Seal which could be used by all. After the matter had been argued in Committee, Sankey asked Harding whether there was anything in the question. Harding replied that though it was not of any practical importance, 'the use of a single Seal might be a symbol which would help to check disruptive tendencies in the Commonwealth.' To which Sankey answered in his wisdom, 'My dear boy, if they want to break away, they'll break away, and you won't stop them with seals or anything else.'[30] Perhaps the conversation itself was a symbol of the faith of the D.O. in the forms, rather than the substance!

There were various matters on which it was not possible to reach agreement. The most important of those arose from the determination of the IFS to secure abolition of Appeals to the Judicial Committee of the Privy Council. They held that this had virtually been promised to them in 1926, but there was no proof since they claimed that Birkenhead had given the undertaking to Kevin O'Higgins and both were then dead. The Irish pressed hard for an agreement in order to forestall de Valera and the Fianna Fail opposition; the British refused since they were a minority Government and knew that any yielding on their part would be violently opposed by the Conservative Opposition as a breach of the Treaty undertakings. There were repercussions when de Valera came to power in the following year.

Particular Issues

A number of issues arose bilaterally between Britain and the Dominions which were not considered by the Commonwealth as a whole. The most important controversy was with the IFS (*see* Chapter 10). There were also difficulties with South Africa and a special problem with Australia arising over Western Australia's desire for secession.

South Africa

After the Irish, the South Africans were the pace-setters in nibbling away at constitutional reform in a manner which seemed dangerous to the orthodox. In the minds of D.O. officials, the two countries however came in separate categories. They regarded the Irish as in any case unreliable and incorrigible; and the Irish problem was seen more in the perspective of Anglo-Irish history than in the geographical dimension of an Empire over-seas. Ireland was therefore regarded as sui generis. There was a further consideration arising from the historical background – the British had rubbed shoulders with the Irish for centuries and knew how to get on with them. From Swift to Shaw, from Daniel O'Connell to Tim Healy and the long line of Irishmen known across the water, there was, behind the expressed contempt of the superior Englishman, a sneaking respect and a wealth of affection for the Irishman. No such emotions were felt for the Afrikaners in the Nationalist Party in South Africa. They were still regarded as Boers and alien – as indeed many of them were – with a strange language, a funda-mentalist religion and a rigid morality. With their obstinate refusal to be assimilated in the British way of life they were regarded as potentially hostile. There was an eloquent contrast in the treatment by D.O. officials of the official heads of the two External Affairs Departments. Walshe was regarded (as indeed he was) as cultured, charming, warm-hearted: he was 'Joe' to all who had dealings with him. Dr Bodenstein in Pretoria was considered (and no doubt was) pedantic, legalistic, inimical, cold: he was treated as a sinister figure and known as 'Bodie'.

In 1934 the Union of South Africa sought to follow in the Irish footsteps by introducing two Bills, 'the Status of the Union Bill' and 'the Royal Executive Functions and Seals Bill'. The first, after declaring that the Union possessed the status of a 'Sovereign and Independent State' added that the Executive Government was vested in the King 'acting on the advice of his Ministers of State for the Union' and could be administered either by H.M. in person, or by the Governor-General as his representative. The second Bill, described as being intended to 'regulate the King's acts as head of the Executive of the Union', contained a clause providing for the Governor-General to sign documents on the King's behalf if obtaining the signed manual of the King himself would, in the opinion of the P.M., retard the despatch of public business. These purposes sound innocuous enough today, but at the time they caused alarm both in the D.O. and at Buckingham Palace. Though the Bills were drafted with studied ingenuity and the language nowhere contained a direct challenge to the Crown, nevertheless they left the way open (by laying stress on independence in the Status Act) for possible secession from the Commonwealth and (by providing for a separate Seal and thus implying the divisibility of the Crown) for possible neutrality even when the King was at war. Mansergh put it plainly: 'In all this, Afrikaner legalism was seeking to find a way by which a separatist policy could – if or when the occasion arose – be legally carried through.'[31] Both the Palace and the D.O. through their separate channels (the Governor-General and the newly appointed High Commissioner) used every argument in an effort to avoid the dangerous consequences they foresaw. Nicolson reports that the King himself endeavoured tactfully to induce Hertzog at least to modify some of the expressions and was not without some minor successes.[32] Thus it was agreed that the word 'regularise' would be substituted for 'regulate' and that the Governor-General should not sign documents without first obtaining the King's approval. But Hertzog refused to accept the phrase 'sovereign and independent status' for the capitalized 'Sovereign and Independent State' and the two Bills were eventually passed, substantially in their original form.

There was another matter for argument between the South African and British Governments. This threatened to cause trouble at the 1937 Imperial Conference, but was in the end averted. The South African Government gave notice that they wished to bring up at the Conference the question of channels of communication. The D.O. immediately sniffed a rat and Batterbee asked Clark (the High Commissioner) to find out what lay behind it all. He noted that both the South African and Irish High Commissioners were constantly trying to establish the position that they alone should be the channel and observed sharply 'we must of course resist any such claim' (the British Government invariably used *their* High Commissioner for communications of importance). Clark duly took the matter up with Hertzog who 'obviously had never heard of it', but the sinister Bodenstein confessed that he was preparing a memorandum. Clark confirmed that the South Africans preferred the High Commissioner channel to the direct Government-to-Government channel and wished to assimilate High Commissioners with diplomatic representatives; but he himself sensibly did not see any objection to this.[33]

When the memorandum was eventually received, it transpired that the substantive proposal called for direct dealings between the F.O. and Commonwealth Governments and implied the disappearance of the D.O. In forwarding it Clark commented that 'the memorandum is neither very good English nor very good sense' and revealed that he had insisted on one paragraph being withdrawn. The offending paragraph reflected on 'the unsuitability of the officers of the D.O., in view of their origins in the C.O., to appreciate the principle of equality of status.'[34] Bodenstein was unwilling to omit this until Clark retorted that, if such suggestions were put forward, British Ministers might find it necessary to question whether the personnel of the DEA was entirely suited to conduct relations with the UK. (Stephenson commented that it was a pity the paragraph was not retained since the 'nigger in the woodpile' would then have been far more easily visible.) Reactions in the D.O. concentrated on the stupidity of the South African proposal and made all the obvious points viz. that Commonwealth relations covered more than foreign affairs; that Dominion Ministers and High Commissioners had direct dealings with the F.O. already; and that it was an advantage to the Dominions to have a separate Minister concerned with their affairs rather than that they should take their chance with the foreign countries. Harding considered that the essential points were that one Minister in the British Government should 'specialise' in relations with the Dominions. Incidentally he foreshadowed the change made in 1947 by suggesting that the title should be 'Secretary of State for Dominion Relations' (instead of 'Affairs') and that he should be assisted by a staff concerned with all aspects of relations with the Dominions.[35]

A brief for the British Government was produced by an inter-departmental committee.[36] This brought out that the main objection to the South African proposal was one of principle – because it failed to distinguish between foreign and inter-imperial relations and blurred the distinction between Britain's relationship with other Members of the Commonwealth and her relationship with foreign countries. The practical difficulties were also set out – it would not be possible for the Foreign Secretary to assume the added burden and any idea that the P.M. should be responsible, however attractive in constitutional theory, was quite impracticable. The memorandum referred to the practice of communications in the P.M.–to–P.M. channel and showed that the D.O. in practice handled the messages.

There seems to have been no difficulty in securing agreement in Whitehall; both Hankey and the F.O. concurred in the terms of the paper. At that time the F.O. seem to have shared the view that Commonwealth relations were different from relations with foreign countries and they did not relish the thought of taking over all the tedious business thrown up by the Dominions.

All the care that went into the preparation of the paper was not needed: the South Africans were persuaded not to bring the matter up formally at the Conference.

Australia

The Australian States continued uncritically as constitutional anomalies. Despite all the brave words about equality of status and the sovereign nationhood of Commonwealth Members, and hence the independence of the Commonwealth of Australia, the separate parts of that Commonwealth remained in some respects still subordinate, not to the Federal Government but to the metropolitan country. For example British Ministers were (and remained) formally responsible for the appointment of State Governors (though the custom of consulting State Governments in advance was increasingly followed). In most matters the Governor acted on the advice of his Executive Council; but there were certain occasions on which he was required to act on his own authority; he also had certain discretionary powers, notably in regard to the dissolution of Parliament. The Governor had no official relations with the Federal Government (indeed they frequently kept each other at arm's length) and singularly few even with the Governor-General. The State Governor reported to the Dominions Secretary in London and all necessary submissions (forwarding Bills, annual confidential reports on affairs, even recommendations for honours) were submitted direct to the British Government: only in the case of honours was a copy sent to the Governor-General for information. In the circumstances it is astonishing that these arrangements did not cause more strain than in fact proved to be the case. There were surely all the elements here for feelings of jealousy in Canberra, insubordination in the State capital and a sense of being imposed upon in London. There was a problem over the Governor's dismissal of his Ministers in New South Wales (*see* Chapter 6); otherwise the most critical issue affecting the States arose over the petition of Western Australia for secession.

In Western Australia there had been growing up an atmosphere of dissatisfaction with their place in the Australian Federation. This primarily reflected the economic distress resulting from the Depression; there were also complaints that the industrially dominated East did not pay sufficient attention to the farmers in the West and that Canberra was far away both in geography and in sentiment. In 1933 a referendum was organized which revealed an overwhelming vote against the Federation and the State organized petitions to Britain for secession; one was addressed to the King, one to the House of Lords and one to the House of Commons. The petitions asked for legislation severing Western Australia from the Commonwealth and constituting it a separate Dominion. It fell to the D.O. to advise on how these should be handled and it was decided to deal with the petition to the Commons first; in accordance with precedent, the question of receivability of the petition was referred to a Parliamentary Committee, of which Amery (now a backbencher) was Chairman. It reported in due course that the matter concerned not only the State, but also the Commonwealth of Australia and that, under the Statute of Westminster, such legislation would require the request and consent of the Commonwealth of Australia. As no such request and consent was forthcoming, the petition could not therefore be received. A formal reply in this sense was accordingly despatched – and that was virtually the end of the matter, acquiescence in Western Australia no doubt being assisted by the returning prosperity.

CHAPTER 6

The Crown

The new concept of the status of the Dominions had an obvious bearing on the relationship between the King and his Dominions overseas. Many of the forms were changed and different circumstances called for new procedures. In all these matters the D.O. and more particularly the officials concerned with constitutional questions – especially Batterbee and Dixon – were involved in giving advice to Buckingham Palace both formally and informally.

The Office of Governor-General

Two countries threw up delicate questions over the right of a Governor-General (or Governor) to decline to accept Ministerial advice.

In 1925 the general election in Canada had given no party a majority. Mackenzie King continued to govern, but after a minor defeat asked the Governor-General for a dissolution. Byng declined on the ground that Meighen (the Conservative Leader) could form an alternative government. Meighen agreed to do so, but was defeated when he faced the House and in turn asked for a dissolution which the Governor-General granted. King then fought the campaign virtually on the constitutional issue and claimed that Byng's action implied a derogation of Canada's status and relegated her to a position of colonial subordination. King won the election decisively. It is clear from a letter which Byng wrote to King George V that he acted throughout on his own initiative: Mackenzie King had 'requested' him to consult the Government in London but he 'flatly refused' – on the grounds that to do so would make the British Government open to criticism of participation in Canadian politics and that one person and one person alone had to be responsible for the decision.[1] Byng did not therefore consult the D.O. The merits of the case are still argued by the experts: there seems no doubt that Byng was fully justified by constitutional practice in exercising his own discretion though his judgement in this case may have been at fault; King on the other hand seems to have given an account that was not wholly in perspective but nevertheless proved his judgement as a political tactician.

Even before the constitutional crisis Davis had pointed out that Byng had sent very little information to the D.O. about political developments (though he sent reports to the King): he prompted Amery to ask Byng to send what information he thought would be useful – without in any way suggesting that he had been remiss in the past.[2] In fact Byng sent no reports to the D.O. before he made his decision, but he telegraphed the upshot of the crisis in messages to the D.O. on 30 June 1926. Amery circulated these on 6 July[3] to the Cabinet who duly took note on the following day.

Amery sent Byng a telegram on 1 July saying that he could not express any opinion on his action (refusal of dissolution to King) but added 'I unreservedly concur in the view which you took of the suggestion that you should refer to me before deciding.' He followed this up with a letter (undated) in which he again insisted that 'it is not for me from here to attempt to judge' and contented himself with describing the decision as 'courageous' and 'difficult'. He became more open in his comments on Mackenzie King describing him as having 'cut a contemptible figure in the whole business'. Amery could not imagine that his 'public denunciation of you, with its talk of Crown Colony Government etc., will do him anything but harm in the greater part of the country.'[4] In his autobiography, Amery records that he regarded Mackenzie King's request for consultation with London as an obvious trap, since if he supported King, Byng would be forced to give way; if he supported Byng, this would be regarded as Downing Street interference. Amery concluded that Byng therefore rightly declined and that, in refusing to grant a dissolution, he acted with perfect constitutional propriety.[5]

In New South Wales, the Governor (Sir Dudley de Chair) had, under pressure from his Premier (Lang, described by Amery as 'extremist Labour'), agreed in 1926 to pack the Upper House to the extent required to pass certain controversial legislation, but declined to swamp it entirely for the purpose of securing its abolition. Lang sought to force the Governor's hand and despatched his Attorney-General to urge Amery to instruct the Governor to give way. The Attorney contended that it was the Governor's duty to accept the advice of his Premier; Amery firmly retorted that this was not so, but declined to define the limits of the Governor's powers, insisting that no precise limits had been or could be fixed, that their exercise was a matter for the individual judgement of the King's representative and that it was certainly not for him (the Dominions Secretary) to give any instructions in a matter for which the Governor was responsible to the people of NSW.[6] The Governor's stand was supported by public opinion throughout Australia generally and was justified by the result of the election in NSW. Amery on his tour commented that 'The Governor's attitude ... has strengthened the sentiment in favour of retaining an impartial Governor from outside. It is clear that face to face with Ministers prepared to go to any length ... the reserve powers of the Crown as trustee for the constitution and the public interest may have to be exercised more frequently . . .'[7] Subsequently Lang returned to power when Sir Philip Game had succeeded de Chair. In 1931 he repeated his manoeuvre of demanding the appointment of a sufficient number of new members to the Legislative Council to ensure the prompt passage of Government measures. Game, like de Chair, refused and Lang again appealed to the British Government asking the Dominions Secretary to 'request' the Governor to act on the advice given. The matter was referred to the Law Officers and the Solicitor-General (Stafford Cripps) gave a lengthy opinion, the gist of which was that: the NSW Government must deal with the Governor alone and had no right to approach His Majesty direct; His Majesty had a right to give directions to the Governor; in doing so His Majesty would act on the advice of the Dominions Secretary. The opinion also suggested that the language used by Amery in 1926 went too far by implying that it would be impossible in any circumstances to intervene.[8]

Game was able to reach a temporary compromise with his Premier with whom, he reported, he continued to remain on good personal terms; but he was full of foreboding and reported 'a financial crash is imminent unless Commonwealth Bank finances the State. No legislation can avoid this in time available. I cannot forecast political result of the crash.'[9] The actions of the Lang Government scarcely appealed to the Commonwealth Bank and the situation deteriorated over the next few months with insistent popular demands that Game should dismiss his Ministers. The Governor refused, but in fact gave enough rope for Lang to hang himself. There were many developments which set the Lang Government at loggerheads with the banks and with the Commonwealth Government and many of the State Government's acts were of doubtful legality. On 23 April 1932 Game reported the complicated situation and concluded: 'I feel quite clear I cannot dismiss Ministers because their action offends my own and other people's sense of public integrity, however much warrant there may be for this opinion.' He added that he was reporting for information only and not for advice, but would of course be glad to receive any comments.[10] The D.O. drafted a reply which the Attorney-General approved. (The reply drew on precedents and previous opinions, was in general and inconclusive terms, but emphasized the difficulties of dismissal.[11]) However, before the reply could be sent, the Governor reported on 14 May that two days earlier it had come to his notice that the Cabinet had issued directions which appeared to conflict with Federal Law. Having satisfied himself that this was so, Game acted quickly and decisively. In a series of interviews with the Premier (all in the one day of 13 May), he pressed in turn for proof of legality, for the withdrawal of the instructions, for the resignation of the Cabinet. Lang refused all in turn; whereupon the Governor wrote to him that he could not retain Ministers in office and was seeking other advisers.[12] He asked the Leader of the Opposition to form a government; this he did and he won the ensuing election. Game himself returned to England in 1935 to become Commissioner of the Metropolitan Police.

There was therefore no effective intervention in either of these cases on the part of the D.O., in the case of Canada because they were not even told until after the event, in the case of NSW because they did not think it right to do so. In each case the King's representative acted on his own.

From time to time a number of matters affecting the Crown arose which concerned the D.O. In 1929, for example, Harding took the initiative in proposing that the procedure on the Demise of the Crown should be revised in order to take account of the changes since the last occasion in 1910. An inter-departmental committee was set up and recommended changes which were approved by King George V. These included a summons to the Commonwealth High Commissioners and were put into effect at the Accession and at the Coronation.[13]

A splendid alteration in the Royal Style was agreed upon by the 1930 Conference in deference to representations of the IFS, namely the substitution of a comma for the word 'and' between Great Britain and Ireland so that the Title read 'George V, by the Grace of God, of Great Britain, Ireland and the British Dominions beyond the Seas, King etc.' The King minuted, 'It is a bore having to change one's title' but though he had preferred an earlier alternative, he acquiesced.[14] He took a more serious view of the discussion about the Succession. 'I much regret,' he wrote to the P.M., 'that it has been found necessary for the Conference to deal with anything regarding legislation with respect to the Crown.' He would have preferred the Conference to break up, rather than to consent to the abolition of the Colonial Laws Validity Act, without any provision to ensure no tampering with the Settlement Act. He concluded, the triple negative emphasizing his gloom, 'After following the proceedings of the Conference and estimating the spirit in which the views of some of the Dominions have been expressed, I cannot look into the future without feelings of no little anxiety as to the continued unity of the Empire.'[15]

Lord Stamfordham, the King's Private Secretary, had been invited to attend a Session of the UK Government's Ministerial Committee preparing for the 1930 Conference.[16] An astonishing exchange took place. How, he asked, could Dominion Ministers claim the right to tender advice to the King and on what grounds could they claim to be H.M.'s Ministers? He pointed out that it would be physically unworkable for Dominion Ministers to advise the King, to whom they had no access. He hoped that Dominion Governments might be induced to agree that the channel by which their advice was tendered should be that of His Majesty's Ministers (i.e. in the UK). He added that, unfortunately, certain Dominions wished, so far as possible, to short-circuit Downing Street and communicate direct with Buckingham Palace.

Thomas at once took up the cudgels and put the practical point that, if the British were to claim that Dominion Ministers were *not* His Majesty's Ministers, then Dominion Ministers would certainly ask 'Whose Ministers then are we?' A reply that they were responsible only to the Governor-General would be quite inconsistent with the declaration regarding equal status. The Lord Chancellor (Sankey) gently observed that he would have found himself very much in agreement with Stamfordham before 1926, but that the whole position had been fundamentally altered by the Imperial Conference of that year. The Attorney-General drew attention to the statutory provisions in Dominion constitutions referring to 'King's' or 'Queen's Ministers'. At a later stage, Stamfordham actually asked who in future would be constitutionally responsible for the appointment when the King appointed a Governor-General; he received a firm answer from the P.M. that the responsibility would rest with the Dominion P.M. concerned. The more breath-taking of Stamfordham's comments may charitably be attributed to his advancing years (he was 80 and had but a few months to live), but the discussion throws a sharp searchlight on the difficulties experienced by the D.O. in gaining acceptance for effective equality of status, if the King's closest adviser could maintain such views four years after the 1926 decisions. As we have seen, the problem was unequivocally resolved at the Conference itself and not in the sense desired by Stamfordham.

One episode at the time of the 1930 Conference was to cause the King even more acute distress. In March 1930 Scullin, who had become P.M. of Australia in the previous year, intimated that he intended to advise the King to approve the appointment as the next Governor-General of Sir Isaac Isaacs, recently appointed Chief Justice. Although Isaacs was a man of some distinction and of long service in the law and politics, there were thought to be several counts against him; he was verging upon seventy-six years of age, the King had never seen him and had no personal knowledge of him and this was the first time that a native had been proposed as Governor-General in any Dominion (except the IFS). But the over-riding objection in the King's mind was, not to his being an Australian as such, but (according to Stamfordham) 'upon the principle that any local man ... must have local predilections ... whereas a nominee from England ... would ... stand aloof from all politics as much as the Sovereign does at home'.[17] Every device was therefore employed to avoid a clash. The King himself summoned the Dominions Secretary and told him that such an appointment could not be approved. The unhappy Passfield feared that for the King to act on his own initiative (since UK Ministers were now precluded from advising on a matter concerning a Dominion) would create an impossible situation and involve the Crown in political controversy. He therefore begged Scullin to wait for the Imperial Conference later in the year and, with some reluctance,

Scullin agreed. In the meantime the question of responsibility for advice was referred to the Law Officers of the Crown who contended somewhat unhelpfully that, as the Australian constitution did not permit Australian Ministers to advise the King and the 1926 resolutions did not permit British Ministers to tender advice on Dominion matters, there was nobody who could constitutionally advise the King! Before the constitutional problem was resolved at the Conference, both the P.M. (MacDonald) and Stamfordham in separate interviews with Scullin sought to dissuade him; he was not to be moved. After the Conference had ruled that, in making the appointment of a Governor-General, the King should act on the advice of Dominion Ministers, the King received Scullin and appealed to him to reconsider his recommendation. The King recorded the upshot laconically in his diary: 'Received Mr. Scullin ... He argued with me for some time ... and with great reluctance I had to approve of the appointment. I should think it would be very unpopular in Australia.'[18] Stamfordham added, with more asperity, that the King had pointed out to Scullin that he had departed from the time-honoured custom of informally suggesting names (and the Imperial Conference had also resolved that a formal submission should only be made after informal consultation) 'and moreover that in the history of this country there was no record of the King's wishes in such cases being ignored'. The final announcement icily proclaimed 'The King ... has appointed ...' instead of the traditional 'The King ... has been pleased to appoint ...' Nicolson records that, within weeks of being installed, the new Governor-General was bombarding the King with private letters of immense length.[19]

This now-forgotten incident is significant because it could have developed into a most damaging clash between Crown and people. That it did not is due to King George V, after he had resorted to every device, in the end agreeing not to press his objection. But, in his conscience, he did not feel the appointment to be right; it must have been an unkind blow for the ageing Stamfordham and a sad moment for the King himself.

The Abdication

Malcolm MacDonald has recalled that, one afternoon in the autumn of 1936, Baldwin summoned a half dozen senior Ministers to report on a conversation he had just held with King Edward VIII. Baldwin reported that he had felt it necessary to raise informally the question of the King's relations with Mrs Simpson and had advised on possible solutions. When he had finished, MacDonald remarked that Baldwin was 'not in a position to offer the King decisive advice, since the King's P.M.s of Canada, Australia and other independent Commonwealth nations were just as much concerned'.[20] The advice was sound, and indeed Baldwin himself had already, even before his talk with the King, written privately to Tweedsmuir (Governor-General) for his assessment of likely Canadian reactions and knew from earnest conversations with Bruce that the attitude of the Australian P.M. was unequivocal: 'If there was any question of marriage with Mrs Simpson, the King would have to go, so far as Australia was concerned.'[21]

Baldwin's first conversation with the King on the subject took place on 20 October; he had then spoken frankly about the dangers of a continued association with Mrs Simpson but, hoping that the warning would be heeded, had not pressed matters or even mentioned the question of marriage. He then waited. But the interval only served to strengthen the King in his determination to marry and this matter came to a head at the second meeting between the King and P.M. on 16 November. To the King's question whether the marriage would be approved, the P.M. replied bluntly that it would not; the King made it clear that he was determined to marry Mrs Simpson and for the first time mentioned that, in order to do so, he was ready to abdicate. Subsequently the idea of a morganatic marriage was mooted and at his third audience on 25 November, Baldwin was asked by the King whether he had considered this proposal. Baldwin replied that he was not able to give a considered judgement, but expressed the informal view that Parliament would never pass the necessary legislation. He went on to add that, as legislation was involved, he would have to communicate with the Dominion P.M.s. There had up to this point been no formal consultation with the Dominions (though Lyons of Australia had expressed his views through Bruce and Baldwin had an opportunity of discussion with Mackenzie King when the latter was passing through London). He therefore enquired whether the King really wished to set the procedure of consultation into motion. The King made it clear that such was his wish, but may not have fully understood all that was involved and that he would be bound to accept any formal advice tendered. (Beaverbrook saw this very clearly and commented: 'Sir, you have put your head on the execution block. All that Baldwin has to do now is to swing the execution axe.')[22]

The decision having been taken to bring the Dominions into consultation, there were two channels available. One was for the King to consult His Ministers in the Dominions through the Governor-General: the other for the British Government to consult Dominion Governments. The second course was chosen and was later the basis for a charge against Baldwin by Beaverbrook and others. Even Mansergh observes that the first course 'might have been expected'.[23] But the King himself ruled this out on the ground that 'the matter was much too personal, too delicate to be handled by the King himself.'[24] On all grounds this judgement seems right: there is the further point that the Government machinery was better able to handle all the messages, to co-ordinate action and to supply informally any supplementary information; undoubtedly too Dominion P.M.s felt more free to express themselves in a message to the British P.M. than they would have done in a formal submission to the Sovereign.

The D.O. was therefore given the responsibility for handling all the messages that were to be exchanged over the next few weeks. Elaborate security precautions were taken. MacDonald summoned his junior P.S.* and the P.S. to the PUS, told them that the P.M. wished to send messages of extreme secrecy to the Dominion P.M.s and instructed them to take sole charge of encyphering and decyphering any replies at any time of the day or night. (It is significant of the blanket of silence that had descended that neither of the two had up to that moment ever heard of Mrs Simpson!) The matter was therefore taken entirely out of the hands of the normal telegraph staff (in whom quite unfairly it implied a lack of confidence); book cyphering was a laborious and complicated process and many hours of the day and night were spent by the two novices until the messages became too numerous when additional members of the Administrative staff 'volunteered' to assist. The D.O. under Malcolm MacDonald had the responsibility not only for communications but also, in most cases, for drafting the outgoing messages, submitting them to No. 10 for approval, sometimes enlisting the help of the Chancellor (Neville Chamberlain) who took a keen interest, and consulting the Home Secretary (Sir John Simon) or the Attorney-General (Sir Donald Somervell) as legal points arose. The messages were all despatched in a special series through the British High Commissioners who transmitted the P.M.s' replies in the same way. The Duke of Windsor's account alleges that the messages were deliberately 'slanted': the records relating to the Abdication remain closed, but there is a wealth of evidence to refute the suggestion that any bias was shown.†

The gist of the Prime Ministers' replies has frequently been made known. Mackenzie King rejected a regular marriage as well as the proposal for a morganatic union. Lyons, the most forthright of all, spoke of 'wide-spread condemnation' if Mrs Simpson became Queen and of a morganatic marriage as 'running counter to the best traditions of the Monarchy'. Hertzog felt that abdication would be a lesser evil than marriage – 'The one would be a great shock, the other a permanent wound.' Savage of New Zealand, who had never heard of Mrs Simpson and had to ask the Governor-General who she was, sent a somewhat equivocal reply which Massey summarized unkindly as saying 'New Zealand characteristically would not quarrel with anything the King did nor with anything his government in the U.K. did to restrain him.'[25]

The IFS was an exception in the smooth-running procedure of consultation on this issue. There was no effective Governor-General and no British

---

*The author.

† *See* for example Eden, *facing the Dictators*, p. 410; Middlemas, *Baldwin*, p. 1000; Roskill, *Hankey*, vol. III, p. 252; and the recollection of Batterbee and others.

representative in Dublin so the mechanics of communication were more difficult; moreover, de Valera was a Republican at heart who had already sought to eliminate the role of the Crown. De Valera was therefore anxious to avoid any act which would commit him to positive approval of the monarchy. Accordingly MacDonald agreed with him on a procedure which would give him the maximum information on what was happening, whilst causing him the minimum of involvement. De Valera was kept informed, on the understanding that no formal expression of opinion would be sought from him unless this should be constitutionally necessary and that in the meantime it would be assumed that, unless he sent a message of disagreement, he would acquiesce in any decisions taken.[26] De Valera was therefore kept in touch normally by emissaries, including Batterbee (travelling incognito) and Dulanty.* There was no problem until the decision to abdicate was about to be taken since, for this to be effective, legislation would be required. De Valera sent a message to say that he could not at any time or in any circumstances be responsible for legislation recognizing a King in Ireland (though he appeared to agree that Edward VIII could no longer remain King). Batterbee was despatched to Dublin and instructed by MacDonald to make clear that, if the Parliament of Eire passed no legislation, then Edward VIII *would* remain King of Eire and, if he married Mrs Simpson, she would become Queen. Clearly this would have been intolerable and de Valera agreed to introduce legislation. But the legislation he brought in was a general statute dealing with Eire's status which he had had in mind for some time. This removed all reference to the Crown in the Constitution and, in the External Relations Act, defined the functions that might be discharged by the Crown in external matters. The form of the legislation (*see* Chapter 10) therefore made unnecessary any special reference to the Abdication. The Irish had a last victory; the passage of the legislation took two days. Similarly in South Africa the legislation was passed the day before the legislation at Westminster (which Dixon attributed unhesitatingly to the deliberate machinations of Bodenstein). King Edward therefore reigned one day less in South Africa and one day more in Southern Ireland than in the rest of the Commonwealth. This was of no practical importance, but the theory of the indivisibility of the Crown was blown sky high!†

Mansergh has described the Abdication as 'the first major test of the new

---

* IFS H.C. in London.

† Batterbee was acting PUS throughout as Harding was in Australia and N.Z. and carried with distinction the full responsibility in the office. He recalled that when he returned from Dublin and reported to Baldwin that de Valera was after all willing to acquiesce, the P.M. pronounced a heartfelt 'Thank you'. 'No', retorted Batterbee, 'Thank God. De Valera has always counted on winning any argument by towering over his adversary. As you know he is 6 feet 1. But the good God made me 6 feet 4!' Batterbee was also involved in some dramatic telephoning at all hours of the day and night. On one occasion he had to speak urgently to Walshe in Dublin about 'the cook giving notice and engaging someone to take his place'; on another he arranged for the Pretoria-Cape Town express to be stopped to enable him to talk to the Attorney-General of the Union at a wayside station.

constitutional arrangements'.[27] The Commonwealth survived the crisis on the whole with considerable credit and without any weakening of the association. One can too accept the verdict of Malcolm MacDonald that, with the exception of one important difference of opinion in the early stages – which was quickly resolved – 'our communications produced spontaneously and consistently unanimous counsel to the King at every stage of the difficult and in some ways dangerous affair.'[28] When one recalls that the Prime Ministers covered every political party – Conservative, Liberal, Labour; many religious sects – Church of England, Roman Catholic, Presbyterian, Methodist, Dutch Reformed, countries with different attitudes across the world; and moreover that two of them were Republican in sentiment, opposed in principle to the monarchy, this was surely a remarkable result.

The Coronation

The Coronation was essentially a Commonwealth occasion and the D.O. was heavily involved in the many preparations. Those more legalistically inclined in the various Dominion Governments enjoyed a field day in finding points to raise about the Coronation Oath, questions of precedence and protocol, the role of Dominion High Commissioners and Dominion P.M.s in the very changed circumstances since the previous Coronation in 1911. Although all this led to much discussion and correspondence, nothing of real substance was involved. The most important change in procedure was that, in addition to the usual Coronation Commission of the Privy Council, a separate Coronation Commission was set up, in the words of the Buckingham Palace communiqué, to recognize the equal interests of the King's several Governments and to harmonize 'ancient tradition with modern constitutional requirements'. The Commission was appointed on the advice of all the Governments (except Eire) and included the High Commissioners as representatives of the Dominions. Its business was largely formal. At the policy level, Batterbee and Dixon played the main role; at the operating level and on duty for the Coronation itself and all the social occasions which followed stood the Ceremonial and Reception Secretary, Rear-Admiral Arthur Bromley (awarded a KCMG in 1941 and a KCVO in 1952). Bromley had been Ceremonial and Reception Secretary at the C.O. and D.O. since 1931; he was also a Gentleman Usher of the Court. He was therefore well placed to ensure effective liaison between the Palace and Whitehall. By experience and character, he was admirably qualified for his post. His service training had given him the ability to take quick decisions, untroubled by any questions of precedent or regulations – and sometimes his decisions showed monstrous personal bias on his part. But he was always bluff, genial and heartily extrovert; he was never deferential but at the same time had a knack of appealing to every kind of individual – often characteristic of the Senior Service – and he invariably made himself most popular with visiting Dominion Ministers. In his way he made a unique contribution towards the smooth running of the most formal function; above all he acted like a tonic on people and, whatever the occasion was, made sure that they got the most out of it.

For the Coronation was an occasion for rejoicing, not least throughout the Commonwealth, where after the traumatic experience of the Abdication, it symbolized the readiness of its varied Members to bear witness again to the things they held in common.

CHAPTER 7

Foreign Affairs: The Triple Threat from Japan, Italy and Germany

Consultation

The problem in organizing consultation on foreign affairs derived from the contradictory assumptions on which the Commonwealth was based – that each Government was responsible for its own foreign policy, but was at the same time committed to maintain the essential unity of the Empire. Could freedom be reconciled with a single policy? This dilemma provided scope for widely diverging interpretations – there were disagreements between the British and Dominion Governments, differences among the Dominion Governments themselves, and there was conflict within individual Governments, not least in the British Government. The position is the more confused because politicians at the time exaggerated the unity in public and critics since have overstated the disharmony. Within the British Government, there was continuing conflict between the D.O. and the F.O. When Austen Chamberlain first became Foreign Secretary, he declared:

> The first thoughts of an Englishman on appointment to the office of Foreign Secretary must be that he speaks in the name, not of Great Britain only but of the British Dominions beyond the seas, and that it is his imperative duty to preserve in word and act the diplomatic unity of the British Empire. Our interests are one. Our intercourse must be intimate and constant and we must speak with one voice in the Councils of the world.[1]

Chamberlain expressed himself as 'anxious, eager rather, to meet as fully as possible the Dominion demand for both information and consultation' but added the important rider 'in a crisis the British Empire *must not be paralysed* because nowhere in that Empire has anyone the right to speak or act on its behalf.'[2] The form of consultation Chamberlain favoured was a Council in London at which British Ministers would discuss policies with qualified Dominion representatives. When this concept failed to be welcomed by the Dominions and was rejected decisively by Canada, he was reluctantly converted to the idea of British representation in the Dominions, at least in

73

Canada at first, on the assumption that the representative would be an experienced diplomat.

These ideas were not shared by the D.O. which regarded the F.O. attitude as based on a desire to carry on the foreign policy of the Empire as it had done before 1914. The D.O., on the contrary, supported the right of each Dominion to make its own decision and regarded foreign affairs as forming a part only of inter-Imperial consultation as a whole. It is interesting that Chamberlain in no way sought to hamper the establishment of a separate D.O., still less to take over its functions. In his memorandum he went on to state 'I think it highly inexpedient that the F.O., which is the mouth-piece of the Empire to foreign powers, should undertake the duty of being the representative or mouth-piece of the Imperial Government in its relations and consultation with the Dominion Governments. It cannot be the desire of Canada to assimilate the relations *inter se* of the seven self-governing nations of the Empire to the relations of these nations to the outer world.'[3]

Consultation was the magic word always invoked to describe the process of Commonwealth cooperation. It was never a precise term and meant different things to different people and at different times. The procedure had been spelt out at the Imperial Conference of 1923: 'a Government contemplating any negotiation should consider its effects upon the other Governments and keep them informed'; if no adverse comments were received it might proceed. The D.O. operated broadly on the basis that, while there was no attempt to operate a single foreign policy, the British Government were under an obligation to consult fully before engaging in any major undertaking, but recognized that no Dominion Government could be committed without their express consent. Sometimes there was formal concurrence as over the proposals submitted to the London Naval Conference of 1930;[4] sometimes consultation without commitment as over the Locarno Treaty; sometimes not even any consultation, as over the Polish Guarantee in 1939. Consultation took place in a number of different ways.

Supply of Information

During the First World War, when Dominion P.M.s were members of the Imperial War Cabinet, the practice had grown up of circulating to them copies of selected F.O. telegrams and of despatches received from H.M.'s representatives in foreign countries. This practice was later extended and, though not all telegrams and despatches were circulated to the Dominions, they received in this way information literally from all over the world. In addition, the practice developed over the years of telegraphing to Dominion Governments an account of important developments in the international situation. After the conclusion of the 1926 Conference Amery arranged that Dominion High

Commissioners in London should also be sent the F.O. print. This called down on his head a stern rebuke from Chamberlain who expostulated that he 'had made a great mistake',[5] but later apologized.[6]

In 1926 the F.O. set up a Dominions Information Department with the primary function of preparing information on foreign affairs for distribution to the Dominions by the D.O. It also acted as a watch-dog in the F.O. to alert other departments and Missions abroad to the new requirements imposed by the recognition of equality of status of the Dominions. On balance the Dominions Information Department performed a valuable task, but inevitably it carried out functions that the D.O. regarded as its own responsibility and it sometimes acted as a buffer between the D.O. and the department in the F.O. directly concerned. Therefore so far as foreign affairs were concerned it tended to make the D.O. appear even more of a Post Office. Nevertheless its service did provide a regular, comprehensive and authoritative survey of the international situation that could readily be obtained in no other way and this was greatly appreciated. With the worsening international situation in the 30s, the service was substantially stepped up and became even more important.

Conferences

Foreign affairs played an increasing part in the discussions at meetings of the Imperial Conference. In addition there were regular Commonwealth meetings at all sessions of the League of Nations Assembly. These discussions were particularly intense at the time of sanctions against Italy.

Personal contacts

The increasing frequency of Ministerial visits in both directions has already been described. In contacts on foreign affairs a new factor – and one which grew in importance and extent over the years – was the contact made by officials – and particularly by the younger members of the service. This provided something of a new style in diplomacy. This period saw the first posting of diplomats, in the normal sense of the term, between Commonwealth countries – from Britain to newly created posts in the Dominions, from the newly created Departments of External Affairs in the Dominions to the traditional High Commissions in London. Such men formed a new breed – they tended to be young, intelligent, curious, to feel completely at home in their new surroundings which they did not regard as foreign and where they made the widest possible contacts. They were frank and outspoken and made a break with 'old-school' diplomacy.

An early example of this new style was R. G. Casey, appointed Australian

Liaison Officer in 1924. Casey was succeeded by Keith Officer and he in turn by a line of able officers, all of whom achieved distinction if not the later fame of the first incumbent. At a much later date the New Zealand Government also appointed a Liaison Officer, largely for administrative reasons of their own; otherwise no other Government followed the Australian example. But the product of the new external affairs services was also beginning to arrive. The Political Secretary at Canada House during the 30s was a recent recruit without long experience by the name of L. B. Pearson. The young men from New Zealand and South Africa, though not achieving the international repute of a Casey or Pearson, were nevertheless cast in the same mould. Similarly there were young British officers establishing themselves in the capitals of the Dominions and quietly making effective contacts. These junior officers helped to promote understanding and provided a significant new strand in the texture of the Commonwealth fabric.*

Meetings with High Commissioners in London

Although, owing to Dominion opposition, nothing in the nature of an Empire Council developed, the practice of a British Minister meeting Dominion High Commissioners in London grew up and, as the international situation deteriorated, became more frequent and more significant. The basis of these meetings was that they were primarily an opportunity for British Ministers to furnish information and were not regarded as in any way committing Dominion Governments. Nevertheless they did enable High Commissioners to receive (and communicate to their Governments) a first-hand account of the British Government's thinking; they were able to ask questions and make comments.

Amery relates that in 1924,[8] he took up a suggestion of the Canadian High Commissioner (Mr Peter Larkin) to be 'at home' one morning every week for all the High Commissioners. This worked admirably, according to Amery, until Mackenzie King heard of the arrangement, when Larkin came to tell Amery that he was not allowed to see him except by himself. King knew Amery well and was always on his guard; when he heard of the 'at home' he described the idea in his diary as 'one of Amery's schemes to set up a round table council in London, and may create embarrassments. An effort to pull us into European affairs, Egypt, etc.'[9] Nevertheless in spite of his suspicions, he did not forbid the High Commissioner to attend. He cautioned Larkin and relied on his discretion to avoid any tacit commitments. He hoped that the meetings would be discontinued in as tactful a way as possible,

---

* Though Dominion political officers were welcome enough in London, the F.O. view in 1935 was 'The fewer Dominion Legations there are the happier we shall be': the D.O. succeeded in altering this, in a letter to the Embassy in Washington, to read 'We are not keen on the extension of the number of Dominion Legations.'[7]

but in fact, though Amery learnt to be cautious, they were held irregularly for the next two years. There were no difficulties with Australia or New Zealand who welcomed any confidences extended to their representatives.

After the 1926 Imperial Conference, Amery tried again to re-institute regular weekly meetings. This time, Larkin refused. When Amery sought to clear matters up with Mackenzie King, he was solemnly and firmly warned that the conferences were either official or they were not. If the latter, they should be avoided as liable to create 'an erroneous impression as to the obligations arising therefrom'. If the former, 'it would then appear that by continuing to countenance them, our Government would be helping to build up in London ... a sort of Cabinet ... the members of which will have had from their Governments no instructions of any kind and with respect to the doings of which their Governments, in the nature of things will have no knowledge.' Larkin reported later to King: 'The whole matter is settled now once and for all with the present Minister and any other who may succeed him.'[10] Amery was blocked and King would cling tenaciously to his view; but the matter was far from settled.

Malcolm MacDonald was instrumental in reviving meetings with High Commissioners as the situation in Europe deteriorated. Before Munich, meetings were held daily and throughout 1939 took place on an average of nearly once a week; the Dominions Secretary normally took the chair, but the Foreign Secretary addressed a number of meetings, as did Eden during the time that he was Minister for League of Nations Affairs. In 1935 Mackenzie King returned to power, and it was not long before King's old suspicions were aroused. On 1 May 1936, Massey (by then High Commissioner) received a cable referring to a press report of a meeting between the Foreign Secretary and Dominion representatives to consider the attitude to be adopted towards sanctions against Italy. The cable went on, with King firmly treading on familiar ground: Such 'meetings ... convey disturbing and erroneous impression in Canada ... Consultation between Foreign Secretary and all High Commissioners is liable to implication collective decision. We would not agree to development of an Imperial Council on foreign affairs sitting in London.'[11] Massey explained matters to his Government and Malcolm MacDonald wrote to reassure King that there was no attempt to reach or record conclusions and that there was 'no question, nor could there be, of any Dominion Government being committed to any line of policy by what takes place.'[12]

But King was not to be moved. In conversations with King, Massey was instructed not to attend any meetings in which the High Commissioners gathered informally with the Dominions Secretary or any other Minister. When he remonstrated that this would limit the amount of information Canada received, King replied that he could get this by seeing the Secretary of State alone. So Massey was placed in the same humiliating position as

Larkin ten years earlier and was forced to reveal his problem to MacDonald and seek a separate interview! However, his instructions did make an exception for 'special and unusual circumstances'.[13] When in 1938 with the war clouds gathering, the meetings became more frequent, Massey took full advantage of this proviso and attended all of them (though, if there were crowds about, he thought it prudent to use a back door).[14]

The value of these meetings can be exaggerated. They did not constitute full and effective consultation, nor did they lead to any understandings or agreements – this was not their purpose. Moreover the British Government did not at all times reveal the full facts and Dominion Governments (and not only Canada) did not put their representative in a position to participate fully or even to express views on their behalf. Nevertheless these meetings provided a useful piece of machinery for supplementing the mass of written material that was communicated and for filling in the gap left in the intervals between sessions of the Imperial Conference. The very informality not only suited all concerned (indeed the convention that they were not formal alone made them possible), but enhanced their value by permitting freedom in discussion. It was a service that was certainly appreciated by the High Commissioners themselves. On the day of the Munich Agreement the minutes of the meeting recorded that each of the Dominion representatives expressed his great satisfaction with the information which had been supplied to his Government from the D.O. throughout the crisis and with the help which had been given to him personally. They also paid a tribute to D.O. officials for their unremitting work.[15]

Some of this could have been politesse in a moment of euphoria. More convincing is the testimony of Massey (normally a severe critic of the D.O.); after confiding in his diary for 2 April 1936 'Meeting of H.C.s at D. Office on Rhineland crisis. These meetings are too formal and seem too far removed from the actual sources of knowledge,' he later added in his book: 'However many and perhaps a majority of our meetings were extremely informative.'[16] Elsewhere he commented with bitterness, 'Canada seems to have resolved to be silent and await the consequences on the ground that the affair [Nazi occupation of the Rhineland] is not hers', and added, 'It would be gratifying to be able to record that this episode was an unheroic exception ... Unfortunately it was not. Never during these years did our position err on the side of boldness.'[17] Massey concluded with some truth: 'The real obstacle to making the best use of these gatherings was not in London at all, but in Ottawa.'[18]

The Dominions Office Role

Before the 1930s, when the threats to peace first became serious, there was little occasion for individuals in the D.O. to play any major role in foreign affairs matters. Amery was responsible for initiating the procedures on consultation and was always keen on defence cooperation, but his major preoccupations were in the realms of economics and constitutional matters. Thomas made no pretence to master the subtler chequer-board moves of diplomacy;* in any case his personality was scarcely calculated to appeal to the consciously superior Foreign Secretaries during his term – Reading, Simon, Hoare. But in an international crisis he dutifully insisted on the importance of carrying the Dominions along with British policy. MacDonald was differently placed and approached any Foreign Secretary on an intellectual level. In particular he enjoyed a close and fruitful collaboration with Eden; they were of the same generation and shared similar progressive views. MacDonald was included as a member of the British Delegation to the League of Nations and in 1936 took charge after Eden and Halifax had left. With the Dominions he gave a new dimension to consultation by the forthcoming nature of his personal contacts. At the policy level the main official contacts were conducted by Harding, Batterbee and Stephenson; and Dixon had a close relationship with the Legal Advisers. At the working level – particularly in attendance at conferences abroad – those most prominent and effective in working with F.O. officials were Clutterbuck, Price and, at a later stage, Cockram.

The Triple Threat

The basic fact throughout the 1930s was that the combined forces of the British Empire alone were not capable of defending the whole in a war simultaneously against Germany, Japan and Italy. The crux of the matter lay in the necessity, in the event of trouble in the Far East, to hold Singapore and maintain a Fleet in the surrounding waters. This was the constant Australian anxiety and, in seeking to allay it, the British were not always frank.

Inevitably there were differences in the standpoints of the widely scattered parts of the Empire as to where the priority lay at any given moment. In

---

*Though he had little understanding of the finer points, he had a remarkable instinct and could be a faithful barometer of how public opinion would react. He returned from the Cabinet meeting which approved the Hoare–Laval Pact saying 'I cannot understand it, but to me it stinks!'

general towards Japan, South Africa was hostile, Australia (and New Zealand) anxious to avoid war and Canada wavering; against Italy, South Africa and New Zealand strongly supported sanctions, Australia was opposed to any provocation and Canada ambivalent; towards Germany all opposed British intervention by force, but with varying degrees of emphasis (South Africa showing sympathy for German claims, New Zealand, at the other extreme, ready to support collective action). While the differences over Italy had been acute, by the time the threat from Hitler became real all urged a policy of appeasement.

Japan

The Japanese action was the first challenge to the principles of the Covenant and an obvious threat to the interests of the Western Powers; it is remarkable therefore that it caused such relatively little agitation in the Commonwealth. Failing a clear lead from the USA and under the uncertain guidance of Simon as Foreign Secretary, Britain had no desire to stir things up; the one Commonwealth country which might have been expected to take alarm – Australia – was herself more concerned not to antagonize the powerful militarism arising in what she regarded as her Near North. There was no considerable discussion among Commonwealth Governments and little dissent from the policy (or lack of it) being pursued by the British Government. The idea of League sanctions against Japan had been rejected at the end of 1931 by both the British and US Governments. A year later the D.O. set out its considered views on 'the value of sanctions' which canvassed effectively all the difficulties (need for universality, for unanimity in the League Council, for a more effective instrument than the League). It concluded high-mindedly on the elevated note that the only real sanction would be a moral sanction and that in this the Commonwealth might play a decisive part at some future date.[19]

Italy

The Italian attack on Abyssinia produced a crisis much nearer home for Britain and it revealed substantial divergences in the attitudes of Commonwealth Governments. In the early stages there was a duality in the conduct of British foreign policy, with the Foreign Secretary (Hoare) frankly sceptical of the wisdom of sanctions while the separate Minister of League of Nations Affairs (Eden) was pledged to uphold the principles of the Covenant. Hoare, having at the League meeting in September 1935 appeared to have supported the policy of collective security and sanctions, followed this in December by signing the Hoare–Laval Pact which the British Cabinet at first endorsed and then rejected. The Pact led to strong protests from New Zealand who were 'quite unable to associate themselves with the proposals'[20] and still more from South Africa, whose P.M. expressed 'profound dismay ... [at] the departure of France and Great Britain from the strong stand taken by them' and added the withering comment: 'The Union, and doubtless the lesser Member States of the League, will not be prepared to continue their support of a body which is ready to sacrifice their interests in time of need to the arbitrary dictates of more powerful nations.'[21]

Addis Ababa fell while the consequences of intensifying sanctions (including one on oil) were still being pondered. Its fall produced a division in the British Cabinet between those who favoured continuing sanctions on grounds of principle together with the hope of obtaining some quid pro quo and those who favoured taking a lead to end sanctions. Eden (who had succeeded Hoare as Foreign Secretary) finally proposed the raising of sanctions in July 1936 and the League Members duly followed his lead. The decision was taken in spite of opposition from the Irish, from the South Africans and from the New Zealanders. The South Africans were scathing in public and General Hertzog told his Parliament: 'If the League did its duty it must maintain and continue these measures ... No country will desire to continue to be a member of a League that has proved itself to be a broken reed.'[22] In fact South Africa cast the only dissenting vote at the League Council. New Zealand also felt strongly and persisted in her objections; when in 1938 Britain decided to give full de jure recognition to the Italian conquest, New Zealand declined to follow her lead: indeed she formed a minority of two in the League Council, opposing recognition – her partner being the USSR.

The attitudes of the High Commissioners who were in regular session with the Foreign Secretary and Dominions Secretary in London reflected those of their Government. The Canadian representative was even more inhibited than usual since the Canadian delegate in Geneva, misunderstanding his instructions, had himself proposed an oil embargo only to be repudiated by his Government.[23] Dulanty, the Irish High Commissioner, also took no particular line. Te Water, the South African High Commissioner, had begun by favouring concessions to Italy by the device of establishing some kind of mandate; but he later advocated the strongest action including the severance of diplomatic relations. The most consistent members, but from opposite standpoints, were the Australian and New Zealand High Commissioners. Bruce was a realist and feared that Italy might be provoked into a mad-dog act; he shuddered at the prospect of a naval conflict in the Mediterranean which might prejudice the ability of the Royal Navy to operate in the Far East for Australia's protection. He also felt, and urged on British Ministers, that it would be dangerous to establish a precedent by imposing sanctions on Italy which they would not be able to live up to in the case of

Germany.[24] Parr, on the other hand, expressed his Government's confidence in the League and its determination to stand for good faith in international relations.

Since Te Water was so marked an opponent of later British policy, it is of interest that Malcolm MacDonald specifically asked him (on 16 June 1936) whether he regarded the procedure adopted as adequate consultation, to which the High Commissioner replied that 'So far as he was concerned and he thought so far as his Government was concerned, the consultation had been real and full. He thought the same applied in the case of the other Dominions except that Canada refused to be consulted...'[25]

The Italian defiance inevitably provoked considerable thought about the effectiveness of the League and in the latter part of 1936 there was much discussion by the British Cabinet about a possible reform of the League. MacDonald contributed a memorandum to the Cabinet in which he argued that, while many people under-estimated the strength of imperial sentiment in the Dominions, the fact was that all the Dominions were members of the League and regarded it as the best means of maintaining peace. Therefore taking the long view he felt that the question of League reform was possibly the most important one touching the future of the Commonwealth.[26]

Germany

The threat from Nazi Germany grew from 1933 onwards, but the outside world showed considerable uncertainty. British policy veered between resistance and accommodation. When in 1935 Ribbentrop offered the bait of an Anglo-German Naval Agreement, laying down a relationship between the fleets in the proportion of 100 to 35 (the figure of 100 being for the whole Commonwealth), the British leapt with almost indecent haste to sign. The agreement was a triumph for German diplomacy and gave rise to great bitterness in France where it caused deep distrust of British motives. The Dominion Governments were consulted by telegram. They were first told of the idea in a preliminary way only twelve days before the final signature; they were later given the terms of the Agreement and asked for any observations 'at the earliest possible date'. In spite of this rushed consultation, it is nevertheless remarkable that, over so momentous an event, only the Australian Government replied at all – and they merely said that they had no comments.

The crucial event, which set the pace for the long series of Nazi acts of aggression, was the militarization of the Rhineland in 1936. The French and still more the Poles urged that this open defiance of the Versailles Treaty should be resisted by force and many have argued with hindsight that this was the moment to stop Hitler. There was, however, no disposition in

Britain to go to war and even some sympathy for Germany moving troops into her own territory. Harding for example took the view that it was out of the question to resist a man 'walking into his own back garden'.[27] Nevertheless some of the High Commissioners were anxious lest Britain should follow the French line. Massey confided in his diary (14 March 1936): 'The influence of France is growing stronger every day ... This is the moment when the point of view of the Dominions is of the greatest importance ... We have suffered enough in the past from French vindictiveness against Germany and French pedantry ...'[28] He cabled to his Government pointing to the dangers and asking them to authorize him to state the Canadian attitude to British Ministers 'as an encouragement to moderate opinion in the Cabinet'.[29] His request was not granted. Te Water, however, received firm instructions from his Government and insisted that any military threat on Britain's part would be 'madness'. The Union Government repeated their view of the 'unequal terms' of the Versailles Treaty[30] and asked Te Water to impress on the British Government 'the most serious consequences of any participation in a war ... which ... the Union Government could not but condemn in the strongest manner and from which it would feel compelled to withhold its support'.[31] Interestingly, the Australian Government, commenting on the Union Government's attitude, could 'not agree severe indictment of France's past policy nor implication that U.K. is unduly supporting France',[32] but continued that 'war would find little support in Australia' and concurred 'wholeheartedly in U.K. attitude'. In the event the British decision not to take action earned the unqualified approval of General Smuts (who was 'tremendously proud') and the general, if tacit, support of all the Dominions.

The Imperial Conference 1937

The Imperial Conference of 1937, following on the Coronation of King George VI, was held at a crucial time; it was in fact the last of the old-style Imperial Conferences. Despite the urgency of the times and the desire of the British Government to achieve a closer co-ordination in defence, little progress was made; indeed the main significance of the meeting was that it lit up with almost brutal clarity the limits that were set to any unified and concerted defence policy for the Commonwealth as a whole. Unlike previous Conferences, that of 1937 was virtually confined to the single theme of foreign affairs and defence. Such an agenda was imposed by the threats from the Axis powers and the breakdown of collective security under an impotent League of Nations. In any case, for separate reasons, economic and constitutional questions were not considered. Ever since 1935 when the D.O.

first proposed a Conference, the Board of Trade had sought to avoid any collective discussion of the revision of the Ottawa Agreements. In 1937 Malcolm MacDonald shared this view and warned of the dangers of a multi-lateral discussion at which most if not all the Dominions would be ranged against the UK. Discussion on economic matters at the full Conference was accordingly confined to a general review of Empire trade. As regards constitutional questions South Africa submitted a number of highly controversial proposals, but the Irish did not attend and, in their absence, Hertzog was in a minority of one. The British, who disliked his proposals in any case, succeeded in persuading Hertzog not to insist and, by what was described in the F.O. as 'a happy oversight', the difficult proposals were omitted from the agenda.

The international situation was introduced by a comprehensive exposé by the Foreign Secretary and the discussion on defence was based on a review by the Chiefs of Staff of the political and strategic aspects of imperial defence. This set out in great detail possible forms of Dominion co-operation, even if it left certain vaguenesses about British intentions and capabilities. MacDonald, the Dominions Secretary, worked closely through-out with the Foreign Secretary (Eden) and D.O. officials played their usual part in the Secretariat.

The discussion about the individual areas brought out substantial differences in the attitudes of the Dominions.

Japan and the Far East

This was the area of prime concern to Australia (and New Zealand). Australia was anxious to reach a détente with Japan and pressed her proposal for a Pacific Pact. This would have been a non-aggression pact and could have come about only on the basis of Anglo-American-Japanese agreement. The plan did not receive much support and was not pursued, partly because of the reluctance of the USA to assume any fresh obligations in the Far East. In the presentation of their case about the defence of the Far East, the British representatives painted a sanguine picture of the prospects to avoid discouraging Australia and New Zealand from cooperating in Imperial defence schemes.

Italy

Though Eden still thought the more immediate danger of hostilities came from Italy rather than from Germany, by the time the Conference met most Members accepted that there was no prospect of restoring either Abyssinia or the League of Nations and that an understanding with Mussolini was called for. Even Hertzog was now of this view. It remained for little New Zealand to hold out to the end – Savage and still more his High Commissioner (Jordan) continued to feel that their principles had been betrayed – and to fight for the Covenant and for collective security; but Savage lacked the personality and prestige to make a major impact and had to be content with a curious footnote to the final communiqué which permitted each country to advocate its own policy at Geneva.

Germany

Hertzog could not escape from making the comparison of the Boers after Vereeniging and the Germans after Versailles and drawing the conclusion that if the British showed the same generosity towards German claims as they had shown to the Boers in 1909 they would be similarly rewarded. He took the lead in advocating an understanding with Germany, but he was by no means alone. Casey for Australia urged that Britain should cease to oppose any Anschluss between Germany and Austria and make clear that she was not prepared to go to war in defence of Czechoslovakia. Germany's colonial claims gave rise to conflicting considerations. On these, MacDonald had reported to the Foreign Policy Committee in March 1937 that 'the Dominion position was clear. The Union of South Africa and the Commonwealth of Australia had both indicated in unmistakable language their refusal to entertain any idea of the return to Germany' of the territories under mandate to them.[33] In fact Hertzog favoured a restoration of some Colonies, hoping that in return he would be able to secure German recognition of the South African mandate over South West Africa. His sympathetic attitude received some support from other Dominions (and was not out of line with Chamberlain's own thinking, though he was reluctant to disclose his full hand to the Conference). But South Africa, Australia and New Zealand[34] were not prepared to give up their mandates, though characteristically Savage did offer to give up Western Samoa if, but only if, it was part of a general settlement and if native interests were given prime consideration.

The Conference recognized that collective security had broken down and that there was no prospect of strengthening or replacing the League. The universal hope therefore was that differences between political creeds need not be an obstacle to reaching an accommodation and there was unanimity that the aim should be to seek a détente with the Dictators. At the same time the British concern about the threat in Europe was brought home to Dominion leaders; they were made aware both of the British rearmament plans and of the British Government's view of the need for Commonwealth cooperation. Nevertheless neither Canada nor the Union could be persuaded to adopt the British concept of defence and King secured confirmation from the Conference that it was the sole responsibility of the several Parliaments of the Commonwealth to decide the nature and scope of their defence policy.[35]

Since the concrete results were so meagre it is not surprising that an effort was made to give the impression in public that the Conference had achieved more than in fact was the case. This led to much time-wasting and in the end largely futile discussion about the wording of the communiqué. There was an important shift in emphasis in the attitude of the British delegation during the Conference: Eden and MacDonald had set out with the clear intention of thrashing out a Commonwealth foreign policy; MacDonald had defined the main task of the Conference as being to make the Dominions 'realise their common interest in these European questions'[36] and he had predicted in advance to his Cabinet colleagues that the Dominions 'would be very amenable to persuasion since they were all rather frightened at the present time and fully realised the value of membership of the Empire'.[37] He persistently warned the Conference that international security depended on peace in Europe, that this was threatened by German intransigence and expansionism and that a threat to Britain was a threat to the Commonwealth. This line ran into difficulties and, when Chamberlain succeeded Baldwin as P.M. while the Conference was still on, he did not press it. Chamberlain sought to salvage as much as he could with the aim of recording the highest degree of agreement that was acceptable. In the process he withheld some information from his Commonwealth colleagues. The Admiralty was less than frank in discussing British naval prospects in the Far East and both MacDonald and the F.O. were concerned by Chamberlain's reluctance to reveal to the Dominions the extent of his readiness to consider German colonial claims. The tone of the Conference was set by Mackenzie King, particularly as he was given full support by Hertzog. Chamberlain recognized this; he was willing to meet Canadian susceptibilities and to compromise in order to achieve unanimity, even at a low level. In this, though the outcome did not impress the outside world, he was outstandingly successful and, thanks to his influence, the Delegations left London with public expressions of gratification. Chamberlain therefore felt justified later in the year in claiming that 'never in all the history of Imperial Conferences was a sense of kinship deeper and the fundamental unity ... more clearly demonstrated.'[38]

When the Conference was over, MacDonald in his report to the Cabinet[39] noted a change of emphasis from constitutional relations to cooperation. The Conference had begun on a critical note towards the conduct of foreign policy; each P.M. with different reasons for his criticism. But gradually the attitude had swung round and Britain had won the confidence of Dominion Ministers. MacDonald concluded by repeating the assurances of Australia and New Zealand that if Britain were to be at war they would be at her side, by recounting what Mackenzie King planned to say to Hitler* and by quoting Hertzog as saying that he had never felt so completely within the family circle.

The Conference has since become identified with the word 'appeasement', later so much abused and to carry such sinister meaning. In so far as appeasement called for an attempt to come to an understanding with the Dictators, this was not a policy forced on the Dominions by Chamberlain; most of them expressed this general idea before the Conference started. Nor was the policy dictated to Chamberlain by the Dominions, though in yielding later to Hitler's demands over Czechoslovakia, Chamberlain may well have recalled the refusal of all the Dominions to be involved in British policy vis-à-vis Central and Eastern Europe. The significance of the Conference was that it set certain limits on British policy and in the years that followed, Chamberlain kept within those limits for as long as possible (though not necessarily for Commonwealth reasons); by doing so, Chamberlain ensured that British policy continued to enjoy the broad support of Dominion Governments.

The Approach of War

After 1937, as events took a more serious turn, all the Dominions were anxious to avoid any course that might lead to war; New Zealand alone continued to place faith in the by now discredited League. The Nazi annexation of Austria provided the occasion for a useful statement of the position of the Dominions by the Dominions Secretary. With Dominion susceptibilities in mind, MacDonald sent to the Foreign Secretary (Halifax) in the aftermath of Hitler's invasion of Austria, a memorandum[40] warning him to avoid first saying that there had been 'consultation' between the Dominions and Britain and secondly making any pronouncement as to the views of the Dominions themselves. After explaining that the D.O. communicated very fully with the Dominions on every aspect of international affairs, he made it clear that very little came back in return. Australia and South Africa were getting into the habit of sending back expressions of their own views, but a 'telegram from Mr. Mackenzie King ... is a very rare event. We have not heard a single word from him in recent weeks.' As to the issue of Austria he said that none of the Dominions were in favour of Britain taking on any further commitments. Hertzog and Lyons had stated this categorically. MacDonald did not think that New Zealand would expect Britain to do more than abide by the

---

* When King called on Hitler after the Conference he gave him a warning (with typical verbosity) that if 'Any part of the Empire felt that freedom ... was impaired through any act of aggression ... it would be seen that all would join together to protect the freedom which we were determined should not be imperilled' (James Eayrs, *In Defence of Canada*, Toronto 1964, pp. 226–31).

commitments under the Covenant and he had reason to know that Eire would take the same line. Canadian Governments had always been opposed to fresh commitments.

The threat of war in Europe greatly agitated the Dominions. Moreover because of the ill-defined legal status of the Commonwealth internationally they were inevitably mixed up in British diplomacy. For example after the French Foreign Minister had asked on 10 September 1938 what Britain would do if Hitler attacked Czechoslovakia and France mobilized and marched, the Cabinet authorized a reply which, after refusing to be drawn in hypothetical circumstances, added:

> Moreover, in this matter it is impossible for H.M.G. to have regard only to their own position, inasmuch as in any decision they may reach or action they may take, they would in fact be committing the Dominions. Their Governments would quite certainly be unwilling to have their position in any way decided for them in advance of the actual circumstances, of which they would desire themselves to judge.[41]

The events leading up to Munich inevitably caused a sense of crisis. In the D.O., both Harding and Batterbee were opposed to any British military involvement. MacDonald found it distasteful not to stand up to Hitler's demands, but eventually acquiesced in the Munich Settlement. During the crisis, he kept the Dominion Governments fully informed of every development, sending them an almost non-stop succession of telegrams and receiving from them in return statements of their views. He also maintained close personal contacts with all the High Commissioners – including Dulanty* for Eire – and sometimes two or three times a day. The High Commissioners in London constituted themselves strong advocates of appeasement. Bruce, in particular, brought all his guns to bear† and at critical moments sought an interview with Chamberlain himself. Lyons at one time suggested in a telephone call to Chamberlain that Bruce might act as mediator in Czechoslovakia. Massey was less effective and remained without any instructions from his Government,‡ but he shared Bruce's views and recorded on 24 September[42] (i.e. when there was a risk of a breakdown at Godesberg):

> A meeting with the High Commissioners and Malcolm MacDonald ... All four of the High Commissioners (Jordan of New Zealand is at Geneva) take a view on the basic issue rather different from MacDonald's emphasis. We are all prepared

---

* According to Massey, Dulanty at these meetings felt 'like a whore at a Christening' (Massey, p. 298).
† Bruce's activity did not please Cadogan. He confided in his diary entry for 14 September 1939: 'I think they [the High Commissioners] are the most undependable busybodies. Bruce is bad' (Cadogan, *Diaries*, p. 216).
‡ *See* diary entry by Ritchie for 26 August 1939: 'Still not a word of enquiry or guidance from the Canadian Government. They refuse to take any responsibility in this crisis which endangers the future of Canada. Mackenzie King is condemned in my view as unworthy to hold office as P.M.' (*The Siren Years*, p. 42).

to pay a higher price for peace than he ... Bruce feels very strongly that the German proposals *can't* be allowed to be a casus belli and says so on behalf of his Government. Te Water and Dulanty speak with great vehemence as well.

Of a meeting on 27 September he reported that all the High Commissioners 'made clear there might be dangerous reactions in the Dominions to a decision to plunge Europe into war'.[43]

On 30 September, the day of the meeting in Munich, MacDonald arranged for all the High Commissioners to be standing by. Suddenly he was summoned to take a long distance telephone call. It was from Chamberlain personally to tell him that agreement had been reached. He was able to let the High Commissioners know at once.[44]

All the Dominion Governments urged that Britain should avoid war. The Australian Government was the most forthright, Lyons revealing in a statement in Parliament on 28 September 1938[45] that:

The U.K. Government was informed that the Commonwealth Government urged that the Government of Czechoslovakia should not delay in making a public announcement of the most liberal concessions which it could offer and that representations should be made to the Czechoslovak Government with a view to securing an immediate public statement of such concessions.

MacDonald's view was that, if the Sudetenland issue had resulted in war, all the other Commonwealth Governments would have been placed in a dilemma. His estimate was that only New Zealand would readily join as an ally, Australia would, on balance, fight rather reluctantly, whilst the Canadians would probably feel unable to do so. In South Africa and Eire the prospect was clear; both countries would stay neutral. MacDonald judged that this disarray could well have been fatal for the Commonwealth which would scarcely survive and also for Britain, whose power to win the war might have been crippled beyond repair. That was a principal reason why he supported Chamberlain in his Munich policy.[46] The Settlement, distasteful as it was, was welcomed by the senior staff in the D.O. – as throughout the country as a whole – with all but unanimous relief. The hierarchy, especially Harding, Batterbee, Stephenson, Dixon, were essentially men of peace and were ready, with Chamberlain, to go a very long way to avoid the horror of war. It is perhaps more surprising that the younger members of the staff also welcomed the Settlement. Possibly some independent spirits who were abroad at the time might have taken a different view. As it was, one lone voice (that of Kimber, then a Principal) was raised to condemn what had been done and to warn that war had now become inevitable and had merely been dishonourably delayed.

The Munich Settlement was also greeted with relief throughout the Dominions. The policy of appeasement however crashed with Hitler's rape of Czechoslovakia in March 1939. This time it was Chamberlain's patience that was exhausted and a sudden and dramatic reversal of British policy was revealed in the unilateral Anglo-French guarantee given to Poland on 31 March. Smuts' first reaction was one of shock: 'Chamberlain's Polish guarantee has simply made us gasp – from the Commonwealth point of view. I cannot see the Dominions following Great Britain in this sort of imperial policy the dangers of which to the Commonwealth are obvious ...'[47] Far from having been fully consulted, the Dominions were not even forewarned about this volte-face. Naturally they were not formally bound by its terms – but they were in substance committed, as events were to prove. Remarkably, there was no disposition on the part of any Government to cavil; and Smuts himself qualified his earlier view. The fact is perhaps that Munich had served its purpose: Britain had gone to the limit of concession; there was a general acceptance that she could not go further and must make a stand. The point was tacitly left to her choosing. In 1938, by no means all the Dominions would have gone to war for Czechoslovakia; in 1939 they all (except the IFS) did declare war. This is the measure of the difference wrought by Munich. As Mansergh says,[48] a new Commonwealth consensus on resistance followed close upon the old Commonwealth consensus on appeasement.

CHAPTER 8

Defence and Preparations for War

Though there was plentiful exchange of information and good collaboration at the working level between the armed services of Britain and the Dominions, there was no agreed strategic plan; the British Government were unwilling to share responsibility for the major decisions and Dominion Governments in varying degrees were reluctant to undertake commitments in advance. In any case defence matters are handled in an atmosphere of secrecy where decisions tend to be taken by a small group of senior Ministers, and did not provide an area where the Dominions Secretary could normally exercise substantial influence. The most favourable time was while Ramsay MacDonald was P.M. since J. H. Thomas was always close to him. But in the National Government power was slipping from MacDonald's grasp and control was exercised increasingly by Baldwin and still more by Chamberlain. Thomas in any case had no expertise in defence matters and Malcolm MacDonald but little more, and neither carried weight with the dominant Tory hierarchy. Nevertheless MacDonald consistently sought to encourage cooperation with the Dominions and a greater effort on their part. In this he was strongly supported by senior officials in the D.O. In particular Batterbee was always zealous for opportunities to strengthen defence collaboration and enthusiastically encouraged Hankey in his unceasing but largely unsuccessful efforts at successive Imperial Conferences to associate the Dominions more effectively with the work of the Committee of Imperial Defence. Batterbee also maintained friendly contacts with senior Dominion officials such as Vanier (Canada House), Casey and Stirling (Liaison Officers from Australia), Shedden (Australian Defence Department) and Berendsen (New Zealand P.M.'s Department). In 1934, Stephen Holmes was the first of a long line of members of the administrative staff to be seconded for a year to the Imperial Defence College which widened the contacts of the Office in military circles both in Britain and in the Dominions.

War Preparations

The most important contribution which the D.O. made to the British Government's preparations for war was in a series of exercises beginning in

1937, to consider the possibility of neutrality on the part of any Dominions and to recommend action to mitigate the consequences. Following on correspondence with the F.O. earlier in the year, the D.O. completed during the summer of 1937 a memorandum entitled *Procedure for Declaration of War*. This was the work of Dixon, Stephenson and Batterbee and was sent to the F.O. in October.[1] The memorandum gives an illuminating indication of the thinking in the D.O. at that time. Behind the formulas that were discussed lay far-reaching principles; if these were breached D.O. officials feared that the repercussions could be wide and serious. Officials recognized the sovereign right of each Dominion to decide its own attitude and accepted realistically that some Dominions might insist on remaining neutral. At the same time they were concerned to maintain the indivisibility of the Crown and the concept of Empire unity. In the last resort however these two principles were incompatible. What could best be done to avoid irreparable damage to either?

The memorandum assumed at the outset that the country would not go to war except in self-defence or in pursuance of an international obligation. It also assumed that, though a formal declaration of war as a prelude to hostilities 'seems largely (if not entirely) to have fallen into disuse', nevertheless Britain would not be regarded as justified if she neglected a clear obligation under the Hague Convention. Assuming therefore that a declaration of war was necessary, the memorandum suggested that it was important that the wording should make it clear that the country was acting in self-defence or in pursuance of an international obligation. It then, somewhat quaintly, quoted the Declaration issued on the outbreak of the Crimean War ('Her Majesty feels called upon ... to take up arms ... in defence of the Sultan') as providing a suitable analogy. (The declaration in 1914 made no mention of the King and merely referred to a state of war between the countries concerned.)

The question then was whether the declaration should be in the name of the King or of the Government. If the declaration were made in the name of the King, the ideal would be that there should be a single declaration on the advice of all His Majesty's Governments. But the memorandum pointed out that this would only be practicable if there was no doubt about the participation of all Commonwealth Members (and even so there might be unacceptable delays before approval could be obtained).

There were arguments on both sides as to the form of any declaration. On the one hand, it was important that formal acts should as far as possible be performed in the King's name throughout the Commonwealth. Moreover there might be greater readiness by a Dominion to take part if it could be represented that there had been an affront to the King rather than that they were being asked to help the UK Government. On the other hand, some Dominion Governments might regard the use of the King's name as constitutionally inappropriate unless H.M. had been advised by all His Governments. Moreover in some cases it might be necessary to refer specifically to HMG in the UK. (In the event, the Declaration that a state of war existed with Germany was made in the name of the King; Australia and New Zealand asked the British Government to take the necessary steps to inform the German Government that they associated themselves with the British action; separate Proclamations were issued in Canada and South Africa.) Harding's comment[2] on this memorandum was realistic. He observed that the objective of any Government would certainly be to secure that all parts of the British Commonwealth would take an active part in any war, but he thought that it would be a waste of energy to obscure this general objective, and possibly to impede its attainment, by any avoidable discussion on a question of form. Also he thought it most unlikely that it would be possible to get a single declaration of war by the King on the advice of all His Governments; the probable attitude of the IFS, as well as that of Canada and the Union, would all be against such a result. For these reasons he suggested trying to get agreement with the F.O. that any formal announcement of the existence of a state of war should be between *countries*. 'Each of the Dominions would then be left in a position to make its own announcement ... The doctrine that when the King is at war all his subjects are at war is not, I think, prejudiced by an attitude or by action of this kind.'

The position of the Dominions in the event of war was later further examined by officials in the D.O. Batterbee reflected at length on the problems in December 1937 and explored the prospects, if one or more Dominions decided on neutrality, of extracting the maximum of advantage from the situation and of being ready, as he put it, to 'accept a half-way house'.

He argued: ' "Common belligerency" has hitherto been generally regarded as one of the axioms of the British Commonwealth and it has been assumed that the abandonment of this doctrine would mean the end of the Commonwealth.... This view is of course based on the doctrine that the King is one and indivisible. Clearly we ought to do all in our power to uphold this doctrine, and further we ought to make it the object of our diplomacy to see that no question of Dominion neutrality will in practice arise.

'But if, notwithstanding all our efforts, one or more of the Dominions insisted in the event of war on declaring their neutrality, what attitude are we to take up? Are we quite clear that such a declaration of neutrality should be regarded as severing from the Commonwealth any Dominion making it? Is there possibly a half-way house between the position of a member of the Commonwealth as we have hitherto understood it and that of a foreign country – a half-way position which might be summed up in the formula "not pledged to fight, but pledged to help and not to hinder"?' Batterbee thought that, even if Canada, the Union and the IFS could not be counted upon to accept the doctrine of 'common belligerency' they would be willing to accept a half-way position. It was important that both Canada and the Union should be willing to grant naval facilities in their ports and that Canada with her immense potential capacity should become a source of war material, all the more so since the passage of the US Neutrality Act. Batterbee fully recognized the objections to whittling away any of the duties and responsibilities of the Members of the British Commonwealth, but sensibly faced the fact that it might be impossible to preserve them.[3]

In a later minute of January 1938,[4] Batterbee submitted to MacDonald a memorandum entitled *Position of the Dominions in the event of War*. This underwent intensive study at inter-departmental level and was continually revised. In putting forward the first draft, Batterbee recalled that Floud (the High Commissioner in Ottawa) had warned that, in the event of war, there was a grave possibility of an interval taking place between the declaration of war by the UK and the date on which it would apply to Canada; in addition the Office had been worried for some time past at the possibility that some of the Dominions might not be ready to keep step at the outset, thereby throwing the machinery of the War Book out of gear, or worse still not coming in at all. He concluded 'We all hope that "it will be all right on the night" – if the night ever comes which we trust it won't – but it is impossible to be sure of this and foolish therefore to pursue the policy of the ostrich.' MacDonald agreed and wrote:[5] 'Very important. The proposed examination of the problem should proceed as rapidly as convenient in these rather hectic days. We must at all costs avoid any risk of being "caught napping" on this point.'

The memorandum did not command immediate agreement in Whitehall and the process of inter-departmental consultation took an unusually long time. In fact, the draft of January 1938 did not receive finality until May 1939. While the events of the time made the subject matter one of increasing urgency, it is fair to say that the Czechoslovak crisis, Munich, the Polish guarantee, re-armament all presented even more pressing problems. The main disagreement was with the Admiralty; in essence the Admiralty attached importance to devising machinery for ascertaining very early the attitude of the Dominions and would have preferred to force their hands. The D.O. on the other hand did not think that any good result could be expected from a too abrupt approach to a Dominion Government during a period of uncertainty and wished to leave the High Commissioners to choose the right time and method for action. There were also arguments about procedure – whether matters should be discussed bilaterally between the D.O. and Admiralty, inter-departmentally, at the Overseas Defence Committee (which the D.O. did not favour) or even referred for a decision to the Committee for Imperial Defence (CID).[6] Eventually the D.O. view prevailed and all Departments concerned agreed to the terms of the memorandum. It was sent to the UK High Commissioners in Canada and the Union 'for guidance' and to the High Commissioners in Australia and New Zealand 'for information'.[7] The memorandum was circulated as a Defence Policy (Plans) paper and also sent by the Dominions Secretary to his Cabinet colleagues. Harding minuted that the paper 'should be useful – in theory anyhow!' and it was commended by Inskip (by now S. of S.).[8] By the time the memorandum was completed, the attitude of both Canada and the Union looked more forthcoming than had been the case earlier. Campbell reported on 8 December 1938[9] that, in retrospect of Munich, King 'seemed to be reasonably certain that once Parliament had been called he would have had a large majority in favour of going to war on the side of Great Britain'. Similarly on 20 February 1939,[10] Clark reported that Smuts had told him he had 'almost made up his mind that war was the only solution' and when asked where the Union would stand had replied that 'he had no doubt that the Union Parliament would decide to come in with us,' though he admitted that there might be a period of 'utter confusion'. However he felt that it had now been abundantly demonstrated that Great Britain had done everything in her power to avert war; 'world opinion, especially in the U.S. will be on her side; and the Dominions will be ready to come to her support.'

The memorandum in its final form[11] began by pointing out that the Government War Book was drawn up on the assumption that the Dominion Governments would decide to associate themselves with the action taken by the UK Government, but that, in the case of Canada, the Union of South Africa and Eire, it was doubtful how far the assumption was justified. The memorandum examined the probable attitudes of these three Dominions in turn:

> Canada: It seemed probable that Canada would participate in any likely war, but it would be necessary for Parliament to be consulted; if Parliament were not in session, there would be a week's delay before it could be summoned and any debate might then last two or three days.
>
> Union of South Africa: Force of circumstances would probably compel the Union Government eventually to participate but they were deeply committed to prior consultation with Parliament. The inclination of the Government would be to postpone a decision and they might defer summoning Parliament if it was not already sitting.
>
> Eire: De Valera had indicated that the first desire of the Government would be to maintain 'friendly neutrality' though Eire might well be involved before long for reasons of geography. De Valera himself had recognized the difficulties of maintaining neutrality; but as late as April 1939 he had proclaimed: 'The desire of the Irish people and of the Irish Government is to keep our nation out of war. The aim of Government policy is to maintain and preserve our neutrality in the event of war.'

The memorandum went on to describe the general policy of the British Government. This must be directed to ensuring that no Dominion Government would issue a formal declaration of neutrality and that Dominion Governments would participate to the fullest possible extent in all defence measures. With this in view, it would be undesirable that any impression should be given that neutrality or non-participation was regarded as an attitude likely to be adopted by any Dominion Government; on the other hand any assumption that a Dominion Government was committed to full participation in advance might provoke an embarrassing reaction. If any Dominion were to issue a formal declaration of neutrality, very difficult questions would arise. The memorandum however deliberately did not deal with this question (which was thought unlikely to arise in Canada and the Union), but confined itself to considering what should be the general aims of the UK Government if any Dominion showed reluctance to immediate participation. It suggested that these should be to ensure that:

1. No constitutional issue as to continued membership of the British Commonwealth would be raised.
2. The Dominion in question would take no action and make no statement implying in any way the intention to remain neutral.
3. A decision, involving consultation with the Dominion Parliament, if necessary, would be reached at the earliest possible moment (care being, of course, taken not to press the matter to a point at which the reaction might be unfavourable).
4. In the interval before a decision was reached, the Dominion Government concerned would, even if it did not formally associate itself with the war, adopt an attitude equivalent to non-active participation, i.e. afford to the United Kingdom such facilities and assistance as were immediately desired, while denying corresponding facilities and assistance to the enemy (irrespective of whether such action might be a breach of formal neutrality).
5. If an attitude equivalent to non-active participation were impossible to procure, at least one of sympathetic (or benevolent) aloofness would be adopted.

The memorandum pointed out that both Mackenzie King and de Valera had recognized publicly that, if the UK were involved in war, the enemy country might consider itself entitled to regard itself at war with the Dominions and to attack either the Dominions themselves or Dominion shipping. The Dominions would therefore be well advised in their own interests to take precautionary measures.

The memorandum then went on to examine in detail the forms of Dominion cooperation to be secured, if possible, in the earliest stages of a war. This provided an exhaustive list covering, most importantly, various forms of naval cooperation (intelligence, contraband, naval control, use of ports and facilities), but including censorship, enemy aliens, use of aerodromes and air facilities, supply of munitions and food, training for entry into the UK forces. As regards the use of ports, the memorandum observed that there would be no reason why, in time of emergency, the Canadian Government should not be asked for any facilities required at Canadian ports (with the implication that they would probably be granted), but the D.O. insisted that it would be advisable for the matter to be raised by the UK High Commissioner with the Canadian authorities rather than taken up by the naval authorities direct. Similarly it was thought that the Union Government would probably be willing to allow the Royal Navy the continued use of Simonstown, but if any approach became necessary it should be made informally by the High Commissioner. As to Eire, the memorandum contented itself with the observation that it would be necessary to consider the extent to which the use of Eire ports would be necessary and the best method of approaching the Government.

On minor points the memorandum mentioned the special importance of the internment of enemy civilians in the case of Eire, the desirability of the Canadian Government not putting any obstacles in the way of Canadians who wished to volunteer to join the UK forces though 'there would probably be considerable reluctance on [their] part to send their own forces to fight overseas' and on the importance of retaining any arrangements for training in Dominion territories (especially the training in Canada of pilots for the RAF). Finally the memorandum dealt with severance of diplomatic relations, pointing out that diplomatic relations can be and often are severed in peacetime and putting forward the idea that, if Dominion Governments showed reluctance themselves to make the break, they might be persuaded to place such restrictions on the enemy representatives as would provoke the enemy government to withdraw their representative and require Dominion representatives at the enemy capital to leave.

In conclusion the memorandum commented on various War Book procedures. It pointed out for example that existing instructions to Naval Commanders-in-Chief provided for their approaching Dominion Governments with a view to cooperation in pre-arranged schemes. Commanders-in-Chief were being instructed by the Admiralty that they should not make any formal approach to the Canadian or Union Governments without prior consultation with the UK High Commissioner. In its closing paragraph the memorandum repeated that it would be inadvisable to raise with Dominion Governments, in advance of an emergency, any of the questions discussed in the paper and that 'the preferable course would be to wait until an emergency arises, when the situation could be dealt with on the lines indicated in this memorandum.'

There are several features of the memorandum that are likely to bring a gasp of astonishment at a later date. The memorandum never once exudes the slightest breath of urgency: there is no sense here that Britain might be engaged in a life-and-death struggle and that all-out support from the Dominions would be vital. On the contrary the language is calm and deliberate, the procedure for consideration was leisurely and such conclusions as were reached were expressed tentatively and with caution. The authors of the report seem to have been so obsessed with the dangers of provoking an adverse reaction that they preferred any approach to be deferred until the emergency actually arose. In a serious matter of such overwhelming importance, such pusillanimity looks today like dangerous irresponsibility. Even less justifiable seems the insistence of the D.O. that there should be no direct approach by the Royal Navy to the Canadian or South African naval authorities. It is hardly surprising that there was such strong disagreement for so long between the D.O. and the Admiralty; indeed, when relations between the various Navies were so close it is difficult not to believe that things were said in wardrooms that went far beyond the limitations laid down in the careful memorandum.

The memorandum is virtually confined to Canada and the Union of South Africa. Australia and New Zealand, curiously, are not even mentioned anywhere – but the clear implication is that their whole-hearted support could be counted on. Eire is certainly mentioned, but no attempt is made to face the problems that would arise in the event of Irish neutrality; or to suggest how Britain could make sure of the facilities which she would require, for instance in the ports. It is the essence of the paper that the awkward decisions are left to be dealt with when the emergency arises. Indeed the most questionable feature of the memorandum is the implicit optimism (based on intuitive judgement rather than any evidence submitted) that everything would be for the best which seems in contradiction with the extreme caution recommended.

The memorandum did not foresee the extent or violence of the war into which Britain would in fact be plunged. But nor did the D.O. foresee that a phoney war period would in the event provide the breathing-space required by their own plans so that the delays in declaring war in Canada and South Africa did not in practice matter. The D.O. was however broadly right in its assessment of the attitudes in the different Dominions; all four major Dominions did declare war, Canada and South Africa after a delay of a few days only. It *was* 'all right on the night' and wartime co-operation proceeded smoothly. Whether the D.O. caution was excessive or not is no doubt open to argument; the policy failed in Eire, but the most likely effect of pressure on that country would have been to bring about not a neutrality that became benevolent, but hostility. As events turned out, the confidence in the D.O. that it would be best for the Dominions to reach the decision in their own way, with no nagging from Whitehall, was not misplaced.

CHAPTER 9

Economic Relations

In the years between the wars, the subject of economics played a far smaller part in government business than in a later period. This reflected the intellectual climate of the time when pre-Keynesian views prevailed and the scope for government activity was regarded as limited. Departments made no attempt to recruit professional economists to the staff and the D.O. showed some of the disdain for the subject which had been common in the F.O. A department charged solely with economic matters was not set up until after the Ottawa Conference and it was symptomatic that this was commonly known as the 'Pork and Beans Department'. While economic policy was in the hands of such bastions of the Whitehall establishment as the Treasury and the Board of Trade, the new, small D.O. could not be expected to play a major role.

There was no dearth of novel ideas (there were suggestions for an Empire Bank and an Empire currency) and hopes were high for the World Monetary Conference, held in London in 1933, to which all the Dominions sent delegations and at which Holmes was the observer from the D.O. But the economic crisis paralysed all and no progress was made. Though Warren Fisher assured the Chancellor of the Exchequer that there was 'continuous contact between the Treasury and other Government Departments on all matters arising out of the crisis',[1] there was no prior consultation with the Dominions about the suspension of the Gold Standard in which they were vitally interested, both Australia and New Zealand indeed following Britain's example. In truth the financial relationships between London and Dominion capitals between the wars provided less for consultation at government level than at the banking level, though until the 1930s, there were no central banks in the full sense of the term and the Dominions' oversea reserves were largely managed by the commercial banks. The financial ties of the Dominions were therefore pre-eminently with the City of London and with the Bank of England, which was still largely a law unto itself in this sphere, and expected others to heed its word. Questions were not welcomed and the D.O. did not normally have any direct contact with Threadneedle Street. The general understanding was that, if the Dominions ran surpluses they kept their external reserves in the form of sterling in London; in return the City met the requirements of the Dominions for the development capital they could not find themselves. On the whole these arrangements worked satis-factorily without raising any political problems, but they were not formalized in any way until after the 1939 war.

The D.O. was inevitably caught up in the battle between Free Trade and Protection. The dream of Empire as seen by the Imperialists envisaged a virtuous and ever expanding circle, each action leading to a favourable consequence in another. Thus Britain would export capital and people; overseas these would increase production and, with the increased wealth created, additional British goods would be imported. In the main Britain would export manufactures in return for primary products. These processes would be strengthened if preferential tariffs were adopted throughout the Empire. Preferential tariffs would make Empire development more profit-able, thus increasing the demand for capital and people, adding also to trade with Britain. Such a policy if boldly pursued would help to mitigate the unemployment problem in Britain (an argument with strong appeal during the Depression), lead to growth in the strength of the Dominions (which could be important for defence) and generally add to the influence of the Empire in the world. These ideas which stemmed from Joseph Chamberlain were given contemporary justification by Milner and were preached in and out of season by Amery. The matter became one of party politics and what governed the situation in a Department were the views and beliefs of the Minister and the weight that he carried in Cabinet. At the departmental level officials in the D.O. took a pragmatic rather than doctrinaire view, but welcomed any opportunity for increasing trade with Commonwealth coun-tries. Two early Dominion Secretaries (Amery and Thomas) were both active in all economic matters and left a decisive mark, even if neither achieved his objective. There were two aspects of economic work in which the D.O. possessed the initiative and had some positive achievements to its credit – Empire marketing and migration.

Trade with other Empire countries (nearly half the total) had always been important to Britain and trade with Britain had been important (and for some commodities vital) to the countries of the Empire. Britain's interest in Empire trade was additionally stimulated by the loss of her previously pre-eminent position to her rivals on the Continent of Europe and in the USA, by the haemorrhage of the war and by the problem of unemployment and stagnation caused by the worldwide Depression.

Imperial Preference had appropriately made its début in the year of the Diamond Jubilee when Canada unilaterally had granted a lower preference on British goods. Joseph Chamberlain was fired with the potential for Imperial development offered by Tariff Reform and left the Balfour Cabinet in 1903 in order to campaign in the country. His campaign made little headway with the public and the Liberal avalanche in 1906 swept all before it. Chamberlain could only bequeath his idea to his sons and particularly to Neville. The Dominions saw to it that the item of Imperial Preference was on the agenda for every Conference in the century, but Britain moved cautiously, remaining basically a Free Trade country until 1932. A modest start had been made in 1917 and, at the 1923 Conference, the British Government promised to grant further preferences. Since these required duties on foreign imports including food, Baldwin deemed it necessary to seek a mandate; he called an election in 1923 and lost. When he returned to power the following year the Government, to Amery's fury, refused to extend the preferential system. Since the 1923 pledge had not been honoured, Amery sought new and imaginative ways to stimulate Empire Trade.

The Empire Marketing Board (EMB)

Amery persuaded the Government to spend £1 million a year (calculated to be the approximate value of the preferences withheld) on improving the marketing of Empire products.[2] Such an expenditure was not readily agreed to and the old antagonists – Amery for imperialism, Churchill for economy – were on opposing sides. Amery won and even succeeded in obtaining a direct grant, with no liability to return any sums unexpended in any one year[3] (the Labour Government in 1930 refused to continue this arrangement).[4] The setting up of the Board in 1926 apparently owed much to Harding.[5] The preferences later accorded by Britain after the Ottawa Conference 1932 (*see below*) removed the justification for the existence of the EMB; there were also other reasons against it, especially the feeling that marketing was best left to private enterprise. The Ottawa Conference set up a committee to consider economic consultation and cooperation; the committee made a survey of the many agencies already in operation and, with one exception, recommended their continuance.[6] The exception was the EMB. In spite of a spirited campaign to save the Board, there was no effective pressure for its continuance and Thomas put up no fight. It was brought to an end in 1933, with only Amery left to lament and deplore.

The EMB had a short but remarkable life. Amery succeeded in securing the services of Stephen Tallents whom he described as having 'unlimited fertility of imagination and contrivance'[7] and who ran his show with panache. The Board initiated the 'Buy British' campaign, developed a new style in posters, engaged in market research and pioneered the documentary film. It was served by many remarkable people, outstanding among them being John Grierson whose reputation in films was first made in the EMB. Well can one understand Amery's exclamation in those years that it was 'Heaven to be alive'.[8] The EMB certainly left a remarkable legacy, but was an odd agency for the staid D.O. to be mixed up with.

The Imperial Economic Committee (IEC)

One of the institutions commended by the Ottawa Conference report was the IEC. There had for long been suggestions for an economic secretariat; at first the Dominions Department had been opposed to the idea, Harding describing it as a 'convenient waste basket for schemes of no particular interest'.[9] It was set up in 1925 and continued until its absorption in the Commonwealth Secretariat in 1967. It is remarkable as the first example of a permanent body composed of representatives of all Commonwealth Governments; it steered clear of political controversy, but performed valuable work, mostly by the production of reports on particular commodities.

The Ottawa Economic Conference 1932

At the Imperial Conference of 1930, the question of Imperial Preference was raised yet again, but on this occasion more stridently. The Depression had affected virtually all countries in the world and all were looking for solutions. In Canada, R. B. Bennett, the Conservative Leader, had come to power on a protectionist platform only a few months before the Conference met. Bennett's proposal appeared to be dramatic. In a gesture that seems to foreshadow a statement by Diefenbaker in 1957, he undertook to divert trade by offering a 10 per cent reciprocal preference to all countries of the Commonwealth. The British Cabinet were paralysed throughout the Conference, locked between the rigid Cobdenism of Snowden and the desperate efforts of J. H. Thomas and others to make some positive offer to the Dominions. The Conference failed to reach any decision on trade matters and decided to reconvene in the following year in Ottawa. The Conference did not in fact meet until 1932, by which time the world had changed and the National Government was in power in Britain. J. H. Thomas had made a remarkable impact on the 1930 Conference. On a vote of censure of the Government's handling of the Conference, Thomas, criticizing Bennett's 10 per cent offer, delivered himself of the notorious words 'There never was such 'umbug as this proposal' – on the grounds that the Dominion tariffs would remain prohibitively high, whereas Britain was called upon to tax food and other commodities which were coming in free from foreign countries. The remark caused a furore and was bitterly resented by Bennett. Shortly before this, Thomas had begged his Cabinet colleagues to take some decisions and make some concessions to the Dominions. In his unmistakably blunt and over-emphatic style, he asserted that the 'people of this country, as indeed of the whole Empire, are hoping for ... real and tangible economic results.' On preference he said '... every one of us knows that in fact we have no intention of [removing preferences] within the next three or four years at least. Then why in the name of common sense, should we not say so? Is it not plain folly to risk breaking up this Conference and thereby cutting our own political throats by refusing to say what we and everyone else here knows to be the truth?'[10] Thomas felt strongly on these matters and his frustration with his own colleagues may well account for his public outburst against Bennett.

The preparations for the Ottawa Conference were considerable. In Britain, a Cabinet Committee decided to abandon the old principle of unilateral preferential concessions – which Thomas sought to retain; instead Britain would offer to barter advantages, as Neville Chamberlain (now Chancellor of the Exchequer) wanted. Early in the New Year, the D.O. despatched to the Dominions 'schedules' of items on which they sought concessions and asked the British High Commissioner and Senior Trade Commissioner to discuss the items with the Dominion authorities.[11] In view of all the preparation, it is remarkable that the British Delegation left with no decision on some major matters of principle that were bound to arise. There were, however, acute differences within the coalition Cabinet; moreover Ministers – not for the first or last time – may have relied on being able, when the time came, to get their own way with the Dominions. It has been said that Thomas was originally to have led the British Delegation, but that Chamberlain was determined that he should not.[12] Chamberlain saw the Conference as a glorious opportunity to turn the imperial vision of his father into reality and could not bring himself to serve under a man who had poured scorn on that vision and, for good measure, only recently given grave offence to the host at the Conference. There is no doubt that Thomas would originally have liked to lead the Delegation; but as the time for the Conference drew near he began to see some difficulties looming ahead. Whether making a virtue of necessity or not, he acquiesced in Baldwin assuming the leadership, sending a message to the P.M. that he did not want it since it was clear that the leader would 'return with no bloody halo, but with a crown of thorns'.[13] In the event, Baldwin (then Lord President) headed the Delegation which consisted of no fewer than seven Cabinet Ministers. He played no active part and spent most of the time whiling away the hours playing patience in his hotel bedroom. Chamberlain in effect took charge.

The Ottawa Conference was in many ways an unique event in the history of the Commonwealth – or indeed of international relations. It was the first major Imperial Conference to be held outside London, the only one before the war to be confined to economics and, with the failure of the World Economic Conference, it became the largest multilateral tariff negotiation in the world until the days of the General Agreement on Tariffs and Trade

(GATT). It was a toughly fought Conference at the time and it has since enjoyed a mixed reputation. There is no doubt that it did usher in a brief era of increase in intra-Commonwealth trade, though some of this would probably have occurred in any case. Britain imposed substantial restrictions on foreign imports and guaranteed free entry to most Commonwealth products and a preference elsewhere. In return she obtained an increase in the preferential rate for her exports and acceptance of the principle that British exporters would be entitled to 'domestic competition' in the Canadian and Australian markets (i.e. they would not be excluded by a prohibitive tariff). As might have been foreseen, it proved impossible to turn the fair words of this generalization into equally satisfactory interpretation in practice.

One result of Ottawa which was to have serious long-term effects was that its exclusive nature was seen by some foreigners as offending against the spirit of internationalism and freedom for multilateral trade. This view was held most forcibly by the US Administration, but others including many Canadians, came to share it. From then on the USA lost no opportunity to seek to eliminate preferences – in their trade treaties with Commonwealth countries, in the wartime Lend-Lease arrangements, in the negotiations over the GATT. Nevertheless, in spite of this, in spite too of the unseemly haggling during the negotiations, some unsatisfactory features in the agreements themselves and the disappointment at the results, the Conference was generally seen as giving a fillip to intra-imperial trade and as marking a strengthening of the bonds of Empire.

The Conference has a special interest in any account of the D.O., derived from the accident that it was held out of London. Whiskard, the Under-Secretary in charge of the economic side, accompanied Thomas to Ottawa and sent a series of letters to Harding describing and commenting on the Conference. These convey the flavour of the Conference and throw some light on the relations between Ministers and officials.

Whiskard's letters from Ottawa contain an extraordinary picture of muddle and confusion within Delegations, of acrimony and brow-beating between Ministers on the different sides and of final agreements reached in the early hours of the morning without any detailed consideration and indeed apparently without any certainty as to their full significance. One striking feature in the letters is that, while he mentions a number of Ministers, he scarcely refers at all to Baldwin, nominally the leader of the Delegation, making it clear that Neville Chamberlain was the man who counted, though he implies that Thomas played his part. Although Thomas was not prominent in the negotiations (he was more in evidence on social rather than Committee occasions), he made an important contribution at the end by giving way on a duty on meat. Indeed he may well have played a vital part in ensuring the final agreement. Australia and New Zealand both refused to make an agreement unless there was a duty on meat. But any duty on food was anathema to the free traders in the Liberal and National Labour Parties and risked a damaging split in the Cabinet. At the crucial moment it was Thomas who secured the P.M.'s authority. He was ready to sacrifice his views in order to avoid a breakdown; as Baldwin recalled: 'I told him I saw nothing for it but to put the deadlock before the P.M. and that as an old colleague he had better put it. Then Jim played up splendidly and said "I'll put it and I'll tell Ramsay a lie. I'll tell him I am for the meat duty – which I am not – and that will settle it" ... it was very decent of Jim.'[14]

In his first letter[15] Whiskard said that it was already clear that Bennett intended to run the Conference. In another[16] he thought Harding would be amused to learn that, when he went to see Thomas, he found him playing bridge with two of the South African advisers and Lemass (IFS Delegate)! Whiskard reported the rumour that Thomas hoped by the end of the Conference to have won enough to settle the Annuities question – though 'whether, if so, he would turn it over to the Exchequer is another question!' A letter of 3 August[17] made it clear that Whiskard had to fight to 'keep the D.O. end up' and that he found difficulty in getting on with Horace Wilson (the senior British official) whose 'taciturnity, however, is thawing by degrees as he finds it more and more impossible to run the whole Conference single-handed.' In a later letter[18] he confessed that he felt terribly in a minority of one, adding 'J.H. is not a very strong staff to lean upon ... he's quite interested, but carries no weight with his colleagues.' He had earlier reported that Thomas was 'very tiresome in some respects though quite good in others'. Whiskard explained:[19] 'The trouble is that in the main question – tariff preferences – his colleagues put him somewhat in the shade and he is the more eager to take a leading part in such matters as economic co-operation etc. with the result that he *will* not keep his mouth shut. He agrees beforehand (really and truly agrees) to lie low and say nothing: but as soon as discussion begins, out it all comes!'

In a letter of 13 August,[20] Whiskard described the negotiations with the Canadians in scarcely complimentary terms. 'We have had alternating periods of extreme optimism and violent depression ... I am told that one of his opponents in the House described R.B. [Bennett] as having the manners of a Chicago policeman and the temperament of a Hollywood film star and he has certainly displayed both during the last few days.' A later letter reported a prediction that 'before the end of the Conference, Bennett would either be in a lunatic asylum or would have cut his throat.' The letter continued: 'I find difficulty in understanding the attitude of Ministers. They have offered, and quite properly offered, very substantial concessions to Canada and Australia. In reply Bennett and Bruce have stated quite brutally that, unless we give more, they will give us nothing. It is, however, inconceivable to me that either of them would, in fact, reject the very substantial concessions already offered if our Ministers dug in their toes and said, "No, we cannot agree to such fantastic proposals as these." I fear, however, that there is no strength left in them.' Whiskard added a post-script[21] in m.s. 'Everything is in the melting pot. God knows how it will end. We officials are all in despair. None of our masters has the backbone of a louse.' An earlier reference to Ministers showed an element of glee: 'The extent to which the Dominions are prepared to ask for everything and concede nothing has been an eye-opener for Hailsham, Neville, Cunliffe-Lister and Gilmour.'

In his final letter[22] (dated 19 August but finished on board ship on the 22nd), Whiskard conveys a dramatic picture of the hectic last few days. Recounting a crisis which had been reached on the 13th, he recorded Neville Chamberlain as saying that 'he had put up at Ottawa with insults from Bennett and Bruce such as he would never have imagined it possible that he should have borne. He had borne them, however, for the sake of bringing to fruition the policy which his father had initiated and he asked his colleagues not now to throw away the chance of success when he had already paid so much to earn it.' Thomas and Runciman had resisted this emotional appeal and declared that they had gone as far as it was possible to go. After 'a series of trying moments, it was decided to take a firm stand...' But 'when they saw both Bruce and Bennett the next morning they were far less bold than they had been in the seclusion of the Chateau and by themselves the night before.' It is clear that Bennett and Bruce were the bugbears from the British standpoint. Whiskard thought it 'difficult to know which of the two – Bruce or Bennett – now infuriates Ministers most' and added, 'The trouble is that they are afraid of both of them.'

In the postscript written at sea,[23] Whiskard attempted to sort out the impressions of the last hectic day. 'Both Bruce and Bennett demanded further concessions – brutally and as if they were dictating terms to a beaten enemy, as indeed they were – and all were at once conceded.' And 'Ministers did, as I expected they would, give way to Bruce over meat.' A remarkable revelation in the letter is that, after commenting that the Agreements signed on the 20th 'looked pretty bad to me when I saw them in the early hours' of that day, Whiskard confessed two days later that he had 'not really had time to study them'.

Whiskard concluded that he believed that after all the evil thoughts had been forgotten, the Agreements would not be found 'too bad'. He thought one lesson to be learned from the Conference was that there should never be more than three Ministers going to an oversea conference; seven 'was nearly fatal to us'. Similarly there should not be more than five or six advisers: it was because there were seven Ministers 'and we were legion that we advisers were so little consulted – never, in my experience, have Ministers used their advisers so little, or disregarded so wholly such advice as they did receive.' He added devastatingly: 'Also it would be desirable, if such an occasion ever occurs again, to have something faintly resembling a policy before we start. As it was we had all the materials ... for formulating a policy, but made very little use of them – and in the end Bennett and Bruce made up our minds for us.'

The aftermath of the Ottawa Conference witnessed constant wrangles by Britain with Dominion Governments. The most prolonged and the most serious arguments were over meat imports and concerned primarily Australia and New Zealand, but they covered all food products at one time or another. Some of the trouble arose over interpretation; some over the commitments which Britain felt compelled to enter into to safeguard her own export trade (notably with the Argentine), but most stemmed from increased domestic production. In a significant letter to the P.M. in 1934,[24] Thomas argued that the Dominions would not 'dispute our need to foster our export trade by all means in our power' nor putting 'our existing agricultural economy on a proper economic footing ... What they *are* afraid of,' he insisted, 'and what we did *not* make clear at Ottawa (because at that time our agricultural policy had not advanced nearly so far as it has today) is that our own agricultural output may increase so much as to check our imports of primary produce.' Thomas saw the conflict very acutely and concluded his argument to the P.M.: 'I am bound to say ... that I think that the Cabinet will soon have to make up its mind within what limits we can properly develop our agricultural policy consistently with the necessities of our Imperial and foreign trade.' Until his transfer from the D.O. in 1935, Thomas was in charge of the main negotiations and took the chair at meetings in London with Ministers or High Commissioners. Unfortunately, as his biographer recounts, he 'relied primarily on the impact of his personality, on his jocular bonhomie and his cut-out-the-frills approach'[25] which had served him so well in his trade union negotiations, but which were a mistake in dealing with Dominion visitors. Perhaps his crudeness, indiscriminate use of Christian names and horse-trading tactics would not have mattered so much if he had shown mastery of his subject, but only too often he revealed that he was relying on bluff. Menzies wrote at one point: 'Thomas is shrewd but really has no under-standing of the Dominions or of their point of view, and appears to be obsessed with the idea that Australia has behaved dishonestly over the tariff matters dealt with at Ottawa.'[26]

Discussions on one item or another went on intermittently until the out-break of war. They moved into calmer waters however after the appointment of MacDonald to succeed Thomas at the D.O. and, with a Minister more at home with the ways of Whitehall, it became easier for officials to conduct useful discussions.[27] Whatever may have been the practical results from all the negotiations about Empire trade during the 1930s, it is hard to avoid the conclusion that intervention in these matters by Governments contributed more discord than harmony to the cause of Commonwealth relations.

Migration

Migration was important to the D.O. if only because it provided one of the few subjects where policy was primarily the responsibility of the D.O. itself. Immediately before 1914 there had been very extensive emigration to Canada, Australia and other parts of the Empire. This movement had taken place largely without direct Government support.[28] After the end of the war, the Oversea Settlement Committee was set up, under the chairmanship of the Parly US at the C.O. and staffed by the Oversea Settlement Department. Though the Committee was intended to be ad hoc and temporary, it lasted for two decades.

Amery said unequivocally of his time as Under-Secretary that 'So far as the Dominions' side of the Office was concerned the most important issue was that of Empire migration and settlement.'[29] He was responsible for steering through Parliament the Empire Settlement Act of 1922[30] which for the first time provided substantial British Government aid for settlement overseas. The Act ran for fifteen years and was subsequently twice renewed.

The euphoria of those days is well captured in Amery's speech introducing the bill: 'The transfer of population to the Dominions before the war ... acted like a great fly-wheel steadying the whole industrial process ... I ask the House to give it a new momentum sufficient for the magnitude of the economic task before us.' He spoke of his vision of 'millions of square miles of the richest lands of the world – boundless plains, forests without end, water and coal power without computation'. And, if that were not enough, he commended the bill as a measure of Imperial defence.[31]

Unfortunately the separate D.O. was established just as migration was reaching the watershed. The Depression caused the direction of the flow to be reversed. As the Secretary of the Oversea Settlement Committee sadly expressed it:[32] 'Unexpected difficulties were always cropping up: a political crisis overseas; the vagaries of climates, too much rain in one area, too little in another; a superabundant harvest or a crop failure; a demand for people in Canada when we had trained them for Australia and vice versa; a flood of recruits when openings were few and a scarcity when openings were more numerous.' He ruefully confessed: 'The machinery was not working smoothly ... The combination of the political and economic difficulties with the human factor posed a problem which proved beyond the Committee's powers.'

All this led to much criticism of the Oversea Settlement Committee and the Vice-Chairman, Macnaghten, resigned. In 1936 the Oversea Settlement Department was wound up as a separate organization and its staff and work absorbed by the D.O. At the same time the old Oversea Settlement Committee was replaced by a new Board. This was designed as a high-level body which would be free to devote its attention to questions of general policy, without being hampered by day-to-day questions of executive work. The Parly US at the D.O. continued as chairman and the members included such eminent persons as the Dowager Marchioness of Reading (later head of WVS) and Dr W. G. S. Adams (Warden of All Souls).

Because of the special problems in Australia, there had been a separate British Government Representative for Migration stationed in Melbourne since 1925; in 1931 the Migration Representative (Crutchley) was appointed to open a political Mission in Canberra and thereafter migration work was absorbed by the High Commission.

Communications

Physical communications were vital for the cohesion of the Empire and no less important for the prosperity of the Commonwealth. The D.O. was continuously concerned in securing more effective means of maritime transport and of postal services (including the special rate for Empire press cables); telegraph and telephone communications were becoming ever more important. A conference in 1928 recommended that all Empire cable and wireless interests should be amalgamated. A Merger Company (Cable and Wireless) was accordingly formed and an Imperial Advisory Committee, including representatives of all parts of the Empire, was set up in 1929. After the Second World War, the telecommunications undertakings in the UK and in many Commonwealth countries were nationalized and a Commonwealth Communications Board was established in 1949. This has consistently kept abreast of all modern developments and has proved one of the most successful of joint Commonwealth efforts.

There were dramatic developments in air services. Some in the D.O. possessed the vision to see the impact that rapid air communications would have on the Commonwealth and none worked with more enthusiasm and energy in this new field than Batterbee. He saw to it that the D.O. gave every possible encouragement to the development, on a cooperative basis, of air services to Australia, to South Africa and across the Atlantic from Shannon to Newfoundland. The most significant achievement for the D.O. was the inauguration of the Empire Air Mail Scheme in 1937. A key message in securing Commonwealth agreement was that sent by Baldwin to Lyons (Prime Minister of Australia) in 1936 covering a more detailed memorandum by the Dominions Secretary. The message emphasized that 'We remain firmly convinced that only on the foundations of "all-up" mail policy in which all members of the British Commonwealth of Nations participate can the Empire take its proper place in successful development of air transport at reasonable cost in competition with persistent efforts of other nations.' The message continued that a series of sectional services organized piecemeal could not possibly compete with the unified organization of Pan-American Airways: 'We are thinking in terms of trunk inter-empire services.'[33] These were the essential points for which the D.O. persistently fought. With Australia there was to be much argument about details and at one point Lyons protested: 'The peremptory tone of this [telegram] in negotiations between governments related as we are to each other seems to me unfortunate ... I think that possibly present difficulties of Air Mail Scheme lie partly from [*sic*] the manner of presentation.'[34] Australia insisted on certain conditions and these were accepted in the final scheme. An important consideration in the mind of the British Government, and one strongly shared by Batterbee, was that the development of commercial air services and the consequent establishment of an aircraft industry were of vital significance for defence generally and in particular for providing an industrial base for the expansion, if necessary, of the RAF.

CHAPTER 10

Ireland

The tangled web of relations between Britain and Ireland shows the D.O. in a revealing light, since it appears in three very different moods in three sharply differentiated situations. After the signature of the Treaty of 1921, calm descended on what had so recently been the violent turbulence of Anglo-Irish relations. For the time being the troubles were now confined to Ireland itself and the storm between contestants across the Irish Channel subsided. Irish Ministers often made the running in the constitutional arguments particularly at the 1926 Imperial Conference, but the Fine Gael party accepted the settlement and sought a workable relationship with Britain, though controversy became acute at the time of the 1930 Imperial Conference, particularly over the question of appeals to the Privy Council. This changed abruptly when the Fianna Fail party under the leadership of de Valera gained power in 1932. De Valera had never accepted the Treaty or its provisions and, though the arguments between the two countries in the next few years were apparently to be about lesser matters, what lay at the root of the quarrel was de Valera's passionate nationalism; he had strong feelings about three matters which brought him into collision with Britain. He was a convinced Republican and sought to make Ireland totally free: he objected to the King of England continuing also as King of Ireland; this was offensive to most people in Britain at the time who regarded his attitude as disloyal. Secondly he did not accept the partition of Ireland and objected to Ulster remaining part of the UK; this again brought him into conflict with many in Britain and bitterly with those who wished to stand by Ulster. Thirdly he objected to the British continuing to occupy the naval bases of a supposedly fully independent Ireland; this was bound to be resented in Britain where it was thought that in wartime the facilities would be vital.

There were therefore (as invariably in the relations between the two countries) fundamental differences between them which aroused deep emotions; the quarrel however began with other issues. The immediate cause was de Valera's announced intention, soon after his return to power, to fulfil his election pledges and to abolish the required Oath of Allegiance and to withhold the Land Annuities payable to Britain. The controversy was handled in two distinct stages, which coincide, almost exactly, with the tenure of office in London by two very different Secretaries of State.

The first period may be described as that of enforcement when an unsuccessful attempt was made to ensure by sanctions compliance with Britain's will; the second as that of appeasement when an attempt was made by negotiation to secure a settlement which would serve the wider interests of both countries.

The Minister identified with the first period was J. H. Thomas; with the second Malcolm MacDonald. They formed in themselves a striking contrast and each in a curious way symbolized the policy followed during his period of office. Thomas was nearing the end of his long career and had already lost the resilience he had shown in his prime. A Trade Unionist by origin, he instinctively looked for and saw the other party to any discussion as an opponent to be overcome. He was unsophisticated and did not grasp the complexities of law or economics (both of which were involved in the Irish dispute). He seemed more concerned with preventing his opponent from obtaining his purpose than in seeking a settlement. His weapon was the bludgeon rather than the rapier and he did not disdain crudeness (he referred to de Valera as 'the Spanish onion in the Irish stew'). MacDonald's qualities were quite different and proved of immense value in his dealings with the Irish. A Celt himself, he was sensitive and not unsympathetic to the Irish viewpoint; he had immense patience, but was ready to compromise; he was not averse to a little flattery if he judged that it would help; above all he was determined to spare no effort to reach a fair settlement. As de Valera's biographers put it, 'But in autumn 1935 a crucial event occurred and one of immense benefit to Ireland – the advent of Malcolm MacDonald.'[1]

What was the attitude of officials in the D.O. on being called upon to support, at different times, these seemingly contradictory policies? Even apart from compliance with Ministerial decisions, there were reasons why senior officials were originally in favour of a display of firmness towards de Valera's demands. There was perhaps a natural antagonism between the mystical Celt and the prosaic English bureaucrat; certainly the Irish, at successive Imperial Conferences, had pressed their demands in an extreme fashion; they had given cause for irritation by their failure to play the game according to strict D.O. rules. As a result, there was a degree of animosity against the Irish among the D.O. hierarchy, particularly in the case of Harding. There was a second, more powerful and perhaps more respectable reason. The status of the IFS had, in the Treaty, specifically been equated with that of the Dominions. With what was to prove devastatingly accurate logic, officials saw that the reverse would also apply; that any concessions accorded to Ireland would be claimed by other Dominions (especially the Union of South Africa in the first place) and that Irish extremism could threaten the whole carefully contrived structure of the Commonwealth itself.

Harding's attitude is made clear in a record he made of a conversation with Smuts in 1933.[2] Smuts had been insistent that the situation amounted in fact to war between two parts of the Commonwealth and was a blot on inter-imperial relations which could not be tolerated. (He later played a helpful part in bringing the two sides together.) Harding explained to him that there were three difficulties which had to be kept specially in mind:

1. The King: The Government could not do anything which would even have the appearance of weakening his position in relation to the IFS.
2. The Cosgrave Party: They had done their utmost to carry out the 1921 Treaty. The British Government could not let them down.
3. Northern Ireland: The time was not yet ripe for a united Ireland and any 'weakening' in relation to the IFS would present obvious difficulties from the point of view of Northern Ireland.

Harding also made it clear that he feared a split between de Valera and the IRA if an agreement were reached, in which case we should be back at the same situation as in 1921. Nevertheless the voices in the D.O. were far from unanimous. From the beginning, MacDonald (who was then Parly US) had favoured conciliation or arbitration rather than coercion;[3] so too had Batterbee whom Dixon described as 'a genius for getting over objections to Government policy privately and not by official action'.[4] Dixon himself too was always doubtful of the wisdom of applying economic sanctions to settle political disputes. But for the moment, the view of Thomas prevailed. After nearly four years of somewhat half-hearted warfare, it was clear that the policy was neither popular nor successful. Again there was a deeper reason for the change of view; the international outlook in 1936 was very different from what it had been in 1932. The threat of Nazi aggression was coming nearer; it was vital to be sure of Irish goodwill in the event of war and it was important to maintain friendly relations with the USA (where many were critical of Britain's apparent 'bullying' of Ireland). And so officials found little difficulty in switching to a course which some had already been advocating.

De Valera won the election in February 1932. The D.O. lost no time in preparing to do battle with him. Already before the month was out Thomas had circulated a memorandum to the Cabinet.[5] This analysed the consequences of action being taken in the two matters on which de Valera had given an election pledge. On the abolition of the Oath, Thomas took the simple view that 'the compulsory taking of the Oath is an essential part of the settlement of 1921, and that [its] abolition ... would in consequence be a breach of that settlement.' His firm conclusion was 'We must take our stand on the Treaty' and, even at this early stage, he faced squarely the fact that 'if and when the Bill becomes law, the question of the application of sanctions will arise.' On the Land Annuities, Thomas took the equally straightforward view that they represented the repayment to individuals by Irish tenants of the money lent for the purchase of their holdings, to which the British Government had an entirely valid claim. He recommended that the British Government should examine the desirability of accepting or offering arbitration before a British Commonwealth Tribunal. Again, if de Valera were to persist in withholding the annuities, he asserted that the question of sanctions would arise. Dealing with sanctions, the memorandum said that there were two possible classes – political (restrictions on IFS citizens and denial of diplomatic facilities) and economic (application of the full 10 per cent tariff rate to IFS goods or a special levy on livestock). Thomas recognized the difficulties and recommended an expert study. On tactics, the memorandum emphasized that 'if the I.F.S. is to attempt to break away, it is vitally important that it should be clear that it is entirely the responsibility of the I.F.S.; in other words we must not take action which would enable Mr de Valera to say that we were forcing him out of the British Commonwealth.' Thomas further suggested that 'we must allow the first move to come from Mr de Valera and there should be no provocative action on our part.' But he concluded in ringing tones, after a reference to Irishmen who had given their lives for the Treaty or still risked doing so, 'we should stand absolutely by the sanctity of the Treaty. On this there can be no compromise: our attitude should be clear and definite.'

Unfortunately de Valera's attitude was equally clear and definite; namely that an independent nation had a right to order its own affairs and a democratic government a duty to carry out the popular will. On 5 April 1932 he wrote: 'Whether the oath was or was not an integral part of the Treaty made ten years ago is not now the issue. The real issue is that the oath is an intolerable burden to the people of this state and they have declared in the most formal manner that they desire its instant removal.'[6] A later judgement by the Privy Council[7] implied that de Valera may have been right over the Oath, though he had no strong legal case over the annuities. But what mattered was the emotion aroused on either side, rather than the legal justification. And so the two nations engaged on a collision course, with neither protagonist ready to yield. It is understandable that de Valera, the ascetic revolutionary, achieving power after nearly twenty years of struggle, should have been so embittered; it is more puzzling that Thomas should have shown himself so reactionary. After all his general outlook disposed him to feel for the underdog; his record over Ireland had been consistently sympathetic from his support of the railwaymen, his advocacy of Dominion Status in 1921 and his enforcement of the boundary clauses of the Treaty against a recalcitrant Ulster in 1924. Moreover he was by nature a practical man, not interested in the finer constitutional points. There were various reasons why he was so stubborn; perhaps the very fact that his record over Ireland was one of which he was so proud, in itself gave him a feeling that he had been let down. Secondly and unfortunately, he found de Valera antipathetic; many Irishmen, as he knew from experience over the years, were congenial companions on the turf, at the bridge table, in the bar. Not so de Valera; and meetings between the two only worsened the feud. There was also a deep simplicity about Thomas' feeling of loyalty and he felt offended at de Valera's treatment of the Crown. And there was perhaps a less worthy motive – the National Labour Party was a minute minority in the Government and politically its representatives had to work with the Conservatives, many of whom like Hailsham were all for strong measures. Socially Thomas was enough of a snob to want to stand well with the hunting and racing Tory land-owning class who were invariably anti-Irish. Another factor which caused him to stick to his views with such tenacity was, as his biographer admits,[8] that his mental vitality was on the wane and he had lost his flexibility. Finally he was always conscious of the effect on the rest of the Commonwealth. In a private letter he proudly wrote: 'I am the first Minister that ever stood up to Ireland; and remember, I am doing it quite determined to maintain British rights and interests, having in mind all the time the situation in South Africa, Canada and Australia, which are watching very closely and not unsympathetically the Irish case.'[9] And so the conflict continued. In an early effort to try to avoid a collision, Thomas and Hailsham (at that time Secretary of State for War) visited Dublin and the talks were resumed in London. But no agreement could be reached. When de Valera abolished the Oath and withheld the annuities, the British Government retaliated with a tariff on Irish foodstuffs; the Irish replied with a tariff on British coal. In 1934 there was a glimmer of sense in the economic war with the Coal-Cattle agreement; but the quarrel continued and indeed became extended, with de Valera ending appeals to the Privy Council, making a mockery of the Office of Governor-General, abolishing the Senate and introducing separate citizenship.

The tide turned with the appointment of MacDonald as Dominions Secretary in November 1935. From the first he devoted himself painstakingly, with patience and determination, to the ambitious plan of reaching some general solution of Britain's relationship with Ireland. The effort took nearly three years.

Soon after his appointment, MacDonald was courageous and lucky enough to be able to arrange a secret meeting with de Valera then on his way through London to his oculist in Switzerland. It was a friendly, if inevitably inconclusive, meeting. At least MacDonald had shown de Valera that the British were willing to search for acceptable solutions. Psychologically this first step may have been very important. With Baldwin's acquiescence (it could not be put at more than that for Baldwin remained non-committal, even sceptical), MacDonald then examined with care every issue in Anglo-Irish relations and in May 1936 submitted a comprehensive memorandum to the

Cabinet.[10] This was very strong meat. In form it was unusual for a political matter of this kind; it consisted of twelve closely argued pages with numerous appendices and set out no fewer than twelve separate conclusions. In substance, it was bound to raise the hackles of the right-wing element in the Cabinet. The memorandum began with a statement of the author's belief that the time had come to reconcile differences; he mentioned opinion in both countries and referred to the need, in the threatening international situation, to settle the question of the defences of Southern Ireland in the interests of Britain's own security. He considered whether the aim should be to make progress step by step or by a general agreement and argued strongly in favour of the latter. One matter, however, he suggested should be handled separately, namely the appointment of a British High Commissioner in the IFS. He then went on to examine each aspect of Ango-Irish relations in turn. First he laid down two fundamental principles: i) that the IFS must continue as a member of the British Commonwealth recognizing the constitutional position of the King and ii) that any action towards the establishment of a United Ireland would require the consent of Northern Ireland.

MacDonald recognized that the crux of the negotiations would be the question of the Crown. He accepted that sentimentally the Southern Irish were Republican, but pointed out that de Valera had never gone beyond the point of saying that he would 'recognise the King as head of the British Commonwealth of Nations' (of which a Republican IFS would somehow be a member) 'in its Imperial and Foreign relations' – curiously a formula very like the one accepted for India thirteen years later! But MacDonald did not think the prospect hopeless if Britain, for her part, could make some gesture; de Valera knew that many of his people favoured the imperial connexion and realized that a Republic was incompatible with his other ideal – a United Ireland. MacDonald went on to consider a number of ways in which a helpful gesture might be possible. One would be a carefully worded declaration that the IFS was mistress of her own destiny. As to the Crown, we could not agree to the Crown being recognized by a Dominion for some purposes and not for others. Yet there might be alternative ways in which the Crown's authority could be maintained – and he outlined five such ways including, for example, the appointment by the King of a Commission of Three. He also sought to meet de Valera's objections to the constitutional status of one party being a matter of treaty obligation to the other and, referring to Germany's breaches of the Versailles Treaty, argued that we could scarcely 'without ridicule and damage to ourselves be less realistic and less generous in our treatment of a Dominion Government than in our treatment of a Foreign Government'. He then gave detailed attention to the matters in dispute.

1. Nationality: He recommended that the matter should be left, resting on the

British understanding that allegiance to the King and status as British subjects were not affected by the Irish citizenship legislation.

2. Defence: He circulated a report by the Chiefs of Staff and recommended that it should be considered by the CID.

3. Financial dispute: Having regard to the history of inter-governmental debts since the war, he argued in favour of a lump-sum settlement.

4. Trade arrangements: If a financial settlement were achieved, the Special Duties on IFS goods should be abolished and the Trade Agreement should be re-negotiated.

Finally as to procedure, MacDonald said that his suggestions did not represent hard-and-fast proposals: he thought that formal negotiations would be a mistake and advised that informal discussions should be opened with the High Commissioner in London or between officials.

The memorandum was a monster mouthful for his colleagues to swallow from so young and new a Cabinet member and forms a striking contrast with the opening paper by his predecessor, both in style and in content. It is not surprising that the Cabinet showed such reluctance to come to grips with it. The Cabinet declined to discuss the paper when first submitted and referred it to a Committee of which the P.M. was chairman. There it met with a strong attack from Hailsham (by now Lord Chancellor) and the meeting adjourned. Discussions proceeded for months, MacDonald having gained the important support of the Chancellor of the Exchequer (Neville Chamberlain). Before conclusions had been reached, MacDonald, with Baldwin's approval, contrived a further secret meeting with de Valera.[11] This in a sense proved to be the real break-through, since it was agreed that officials should examine in greater detail some of the outstanding questions and that a further discussion would be held between Ministers. But the path was not easy, the real stumbling-block being de Valera's obsession that the vital need was to create a United Ireland and his refusal, until partition was ended, to make any concessions on other questions. The discussions therefore made slow progress and, in any case, were suddenly jolted into a new context by the Abdication. There was no problem about the substance since the views of Catholic Ireland were at one with the rest of the Commonwealth about the King marrying a twice divorced woman, but about form, for the Abdication required approval of all the Dominions and called for legislation. (Curiously de Valera told Maffey at one of their early meetings that Edward VIII was popular in Ireland. Maffey's account quoting de Valera rather bafflingly reads: 'For some extraordinary reason or other Edward VIII was popular over here. If he had been King at the time of his abdication you would have had trouble in Ireland. Queen Victoria is very much disliked.')[12] The need for legislation precipitated a definition of Ireland's attitude to the Crown. De Valera's Government decided to remove all reference to the Crown in the Constitution and to enact the External Relations Act which specifically defined the functions that might be discharged by the Crown at the discretion of the Executive Council of the IFS. (The Bill caused King George VI to exclaim that he did not so much mind being called an 'organ or instrument' but did object strongly to being described as 'a method of procedure'.)[13] This Act certainly weakened the position of the Crown, almost to vanishing point. Eire (as it now came to be called) had in effect thrown overboard the common allegiance test, held in 1926 to be so vital. She did not attend the 1937 Imperial Conference and there was even doubt whether she remained a Dominion. But de Valera had made some concessions; he had not formally proclaimed a Republic or given up Commonwealth membership. In a mood very different from that in which they had embarked on the quarrel in the days of J. H. Thomas, the D.O. favoured acceptance of the Irish position and took the view that Eire remained sufficient of a monarchy to continue in the Commonwealth. In a sense de Valera had turned the Abdication to his own ends, but at least he had conformed and not made trouble. In any case, clearly nothing was going to deflect him from his purpose. This was MacDonald's view and he did not want to lose sight of the prospect of a general agreement. He was strongly supported by Batterbee and even the meticulous Dixon considered acceptance of the Constitution not a sign of weakness but of strength, showing 'the Commonwealth as a living organisation capable of the greatest flexibility'.[14]

There remained one problem. The Constitution provided (Article 4): 'The name of the State is Eire or, in the English language, Ireland.' HMG in the United Kingdom of Great Britain and Northern Ireland clearly could not recognize any claim by the State to have jurisdiction over all Ireland. A memorandum[15] by Dixon went into the matter exhaustively, examining the precedents of countries like Persia which had changed their name, and exploring the constitutional implications. In substance the position was not open to doubt since the British Government had made clear that they regarded the use of any name as relating only to that area which had hitherto been known as the IFS; they were however still in a quandary as to how to designate the area themselves. Eventually it was ascertained[16] that de Valera would not object to the British using the term 'Eire'. It was therefore decided, while refusing to use the English word, to accept the Erse equivalent and the legislation provided accordingly that the territory 'should be styled and known as Eire'.[17] It was perhaps an appropriately Irish solution!

With the constitutional argument[18] out of the way, the road seemed clear for the general accord. But de Valera still showed himself stubborn, almost fanatical; MacDonald described him at this time as expecting 'us British to do almost all the giving; and to hope for only the gift of Irish goodwill ... in return'.[19] MacDonald steadily persevered; at the end of 1937 it was agreed that formal negotiations would be begun and in January 1938 de Valera came .

to London for the Conference, with Chamberlain, now P.M., leading the British team. Chamberlain had been a consistent supporter of MacDonald's policy; he now embraced it wholeheartedly and, with his authority, pushed it through to a conclusion. There was bound to be opposition from some Tories (of whom Churchill was the most vociferous) and there was continuing hostility from Ulster (though MacDonald himself had taken care to tell Craigavon the Cabinet's plans before the formal negotiations started). Throughout the fluctuating progress of the negotiations, MacDonald, described by the biographer of King George VI as 'indefatigable', kept the King informed in a series of lengthy letters. The King, we are told, read these reports 'with great interest and growing bewilderment'.[20]

The Irish Agreement was concluded in March 1938 and covered all issues. The main provisions were that Ireland was offered possession of the ports and Britain gave up any other rights which, in time of war, she might have demanded. There was no defence agreement. The financial dispute was ended by payment of a single amount of £10 million. The special duties imposed by both sides were to end. There were no special trade concessions to Northern Ireland (as had earlier been hoped). Viewed objectively it was a one-sided agreement, but the British negotiators were hoping for benefits in the longer term. The Agreement came under fire in Britain, the most controversial item being the surrender of the bases. The issue can be looked at from many angles. Inevitably Churchill (who had fought the matter so fiercely at the time) deplored the inability to use them when the U-boat campaign began. On the other hand, it can be argued that if Britain had insisted on maintaining the right, she might have been able to operate the bases only against a hostile population with the likelihood of an enemy landing in Ireland. The D.O. hoped that, if the right were voluntarily given up, it would be possible to win Irish friendship so that in case of war Britain could enjoy the use of the ports with their goodwill.

In this view they had the support of the Chiefs of Staff. (Their attitude was expressed most succinctly in the memoirs of Lord Chatfield[21] who was Chairman of the Chiefs of Staff at the time. He explained that there were three alternatives; that Ireland would be: 1) an active ally, 2) a friendly neutral or 3) hostile. 1) was obviously the best solution and 3) was to be averted at all costs. But consent to use the ports could not be imposed on Ireland against her will; to attempt to use the ports without consent would land Britain 'in a series of Gibraltars'. Therefore, if a defence agreement could not be achieved, friendly neutrality was the best solution.) In the event, the use of the ports was denied to Britain, but conceivably things might have turned out more favourably if the war had not come so soon or followed the course it did.

The Agreement in fact was an act of faith – and a compromise. No party received all it wanted – de Valera achieved neither a formal Republic nor a United Ireland, Britain made many concessions in the constitutional and financial fields and gave up the ports; Northern Ireland was not satisfied. And the D.O. was denied what MacDonald had long cherished – the establishment of a High Commissioner in Dublin. Yet the Agreement did at least enable the neutrality of Eire to be benevolent throughout the war and it set the two nations on a path of greater cordiality which (in spite of some bad moments) has continued. It can fairly be claimed that the main credit for initiating the new policy belongs to MacDonald.

In the longer term, the most significant consequence – certainly for the D.O. – lay beyond the confines of Anglo-Irish relations. The British insistence that the IFS when established should be forced into the Common-wealth pattern and have the status of a Dominion governed the attitude of the D.O. throughout. The whole ethos of the D.O. was based on the validity of the Commonwealth principle of mutual trust and cooperation for the common good; the act of faith in 1938 was rooted in the history of the Commonwealth which suggested that generosity would be rewarded as it had seemed to be in South Africa. Equally the D.O. saw early the danger of the Irish setting the pace for other members of the Commonwealth and had hitherto resisted encroachments on the ties that bound the Dominions to the Crown. The many concessions now made – particularly on common allegiance and in the pretence that 'external association' so long rejected need not affect Dominion status – inevitably weakened the cohesion of the Commonwealth; they led in turn to the whittling away of ties by South Africa and other Dominions, the acceptance of Republican India as a member of the Commonwealth and the progressive loosening of links when the other states in Asia and Africa later achieved independence.

Territorial Responsibilities

𝕒𝕒𝕒

Newfoundland

Although there were ample precedents for withdrawing a Constitution from a Colonial territory, Newfoundland provides the unique instance of doing so in the case of a Dominion; it afforded a novel experience for the Office since, after the loss of responsible government, the island came under the administrative control of the D.O. itself.

Newfoundland with a population of some 300,000 had never sought control of external affairs (she had not therefore separately signed the Versailles Treaty or become a member of the League of Nations) and her Chief Officer was styled a Governor and not Governor-General; nevertheless she had in all other respects been equated with the Dominions; she had regularly attended meetings of the Imperial Conference by right and she had specifically been named as a Dominion in the Statute of Westminster. There was therefore in law no doubt about her sovereign independence.

But in 1932 she was bankrupt and heading for total collapse. There were many causes for this, both local and global. At home, governments had too frequently been corrupt and profligate, business interests had shown short-sightedness and selfishness (with the merchants holding the fishermen in thrall); most of the population were scattered in small outposts along a rugged coastline with little communication except by sea.

The island was dependent on markets abroad and was hit by the economic blizzard as hard as any primary producer in the world. In 1933 the public debt was about to reach the $100 million mark* and interest payments had reached the staggering proportion of 65 per cent of average revenue. The current deficit again threatened to be substantial. Yet with the onset of the Depression, the supply of loans, so freely offered hitherto, dried up overnight. The Government could not carry on unaided and appealed urgently to London for advice. An effort was made to set the financial house in order and some temporary relief was given. Even so, the Government realized that they could

---

* These statistics and much of the information that follows are taken from *Newfoundland: Island into Province* by St John Chadwick. Chadwick was a member of the D. O. who, after Clutterbuck, had most dealings with Newfoundland and was joint author of the report on the financial and economic position of Newfoundland in 1946.

go no further without external help and they themselves proposed a Royal Commission to investigate the whole situation. The Commission · was appointed without delay and was quickly off the mark. The Chairman was Lord Amulree, an eminent lawyer who had been made a peer after being Chairman of an impressive series of commissions of enquiry since as early as 1917. He was assisted by Sir William Stavert, a Canadian retired from banking who had advised the Newfoundland Government and was their nominee, and by C. A. Magrath, a Canadian of wide experience both in politics and business. They constituted a distinguished group; they also formed an agreeable and harmonious team. In particular Amulree was punctilious in always consulting those concerned, though he seldom gave a strong lead. All three Commissioners were, however, over seventy at the time and all of them were faced with unfamiliar problems; most of the detailed work of analysis and of formulation of recommendations fell on the Secretary, P. A. Clutterbuck, then a Principal in the D.O.

Clutterbuck was one of the youngest but also one of the ablest of the war-time generation in the Office, having just been old enough to serve for the last two years of the war in the Coldstream Guards. He had a penetrating and scrupulous mind, vigour and enthusiasm; his manner was easy and friendly and he himself was modest and even-tempered; he was quite incapable of ruthlessness or unfairness. He was thus singularly well qualified to guide his team in strange waters. He had recently been the D.O. representative at League of Nations meetings and other international conferences; his association with Newfoundland endured. He took charge of the Newfoundland department after his return and was responsible for implementing the recommendations of the report and for the administration of the island until the war. Later, as Under Secretary, he continued to supervise the affairs of Newfoundland during the war and he was High Commissioner in Ottawa at the time Newfoundland joined the Confederation. There was some irony in the fact that he, who had been Secretary to the Donoughmore Commission which resulted in the grant of a Constitution to Ceylon, should then have served a Commission which resulted in the withdrawal of a Constitution.

As soon as the Royal Commission had been set up, Amulree had intensive discussions with Harding, Batterbee and others in the D.O. and with senior officials in the Treasury, at all of which Clutterbuck was present. These covered in some depth both constitutional (particularly measures for strengthening the powers of the Executive and ensuring control) and also financial matters (reducing indebtedness and increasing resources). From the start, it was clear that some form of association with Canada would provide the most satisfactory long-term solution and the prospects of confederation with Canada were explored, linked with the possibility of the purchase of Labrador by Canada. At a meeting on 24 February 1933,[1] Archer (then serving in Ottawa) was present and gave his impression that confederation would not be welcomed by the Canadian Government on financial grounds. Harding confirmed this, having mentioned the matter to Skelton (Under-Secretary in the Canadian Department of External Affairs) who had been in London. Skelton felt that Canadian public opinion would not be keen on confederation, particularly at that time in view of the plight of the Maritime Provinces, nor would it be interested in paying a big price for Labrador which was 'a morsel which would drop into their mouth sooner or later'. Archer added that the gossip in Canada was that Newfoundland would prefer to default rather than join the Confederation of Canada.

Before the Commission left, Harding, on behalf of the S. of S., suggested to Amulree that it would be essential for the Commission to make sure that any solution which they might recommend would be acceptable not only to Newfoundland, but also to Canada and the UK; and Amulree maintained close contact with London throughout the course of the Commission's enquiries. His first report[2] from Newfoundland gave a gloomy account of the plight of the people and was discouraging about his initial discussions with Ministers; 'the trouble is that the Prime Minister here and, as far as I have been able to gather, his Cabinet, are against confederation, Crown Colony Government by Commissioner, sale of Labrador (unless on advantageous terms), or any further borrowing. The alternatives to default are thus narrowed down.' Amulree said that Alderdice (the P.M.) was against confederation and was of the opinion that his Cabinet and the House of Assembly would be against it also, but that even if they agreed he could not assent without the approval of the electorate, expressed in a referendum, and it was generally assumed that, on a referendum, confederation would be rejected. Therefore, Amulree reported to the S. of S., it had occurred to him that, if default were to be avoided, the only course now open would be for Newfoundland to join up with the UK – in other words that there should be a Parliamentary Union as between England and Scotland, with Newfoundland sending (say four or five) members to Westminster but with her separate Legislature abolished. He asked Thomas to let him have his reactions privately and in confidence.[3]

Thomas replied, after consulting the Chancellor of the Exchequer, that they both felt his suggestion would not be acceptable. They were disturbed at the pessimistic terms in which Amulree referred to the island's prospects and thought he had not sufficiently distinguished between worldwide, but temporary difficulties and permanent difficulties special to Newfoundland. In their view, Alderdice had not appreciated the very serious objections to default: 'a thing which the Empire has avoided as shameful ... it will have a lasting effect on the credit of Newfoundland and react adversely on the Empire as a whole.' Amulree was asked, if he could not carry Alderdice with him, to put forward his own solution. It would be impossible for Britain to provide a mere dole, and if further assistance were required she would require some control over financial policy and administration. Amulree was urged to use his influence to secure Newfoundland's acceptance of some such scheme rather than default.[4] In separate message,[5] Harding spelled out to Clutterbuck the kind of scheme which might be regarded by the Treasury as acceptable as a measure of temporary control. In essence, the scheme provided for a Controller of Finance, appointed and paid by the British Government, and for certain undertakings by the Newfoundland Government. It was designed to secure effective control in practice, with the minimum of constitutional alteration.

In May the Commission moved to Ottawa but, though they had an initial meeting with Bennett who 'seemed anxious to help', progress was very slow and Amulree never secured the private interview with Bennett which he sought throughout his three weeks' stay.[6] Doubtful of securing Canadian support, Amulree considered possible alternatives and sought[7] instructions on a possible solution under which Newfoundland would offer to exchange existing bonds for new bonds at 2 per cent to run for 30 to 40 years. The bonds were to be guaranteed by Canada in return for the transfer of Labrador. This proposal gravely alarmed London who considered that such a scheme meant wiping out the best part of half the debt. This would therefore be a default and, in their view, it would be disastrous if, for the first time in history, a part of the British Empire defaulted. So alarmed were the Treasury by this spectre that they told Amulree[8] 'if the worst comes to the worst ... we are definitely prepared to put our hands into our pockets and pay whatever is necessary to avoid default, at any rate during say the course of the next 3 years.'

In the meantime the Commission had met with Bennett and his Cabinet. While making it clear that he had no authority to negotiate, Amulree expressed the view that, if some scheme could be devised whereby Canada might acquire Labrador at such a figure as would enable Newfoundland to carry on with a balanced budget, it could be made acceptable to Newfoundland and would be the most satisfactory solution.[9] Bennett seemed to be attracted at first, but later was inclined to hedge. Eventually he sent a written reply,[10] saying that it would be inadvisable for the Canadian Government to offer any suggestions at that stage. Skelton called to explain the Canadian Government's stand. They did not favour either the guarantee suggestion or the purchase of Labrador: in general they did not think it was for the Canadian Government to express an opinion until they knew what the Newfoundland Government were prepared to do. Bennett felt that the guarantee suggestion would cause much heart-burning both in Newfoundland and among bond-holders and, as for Labrador, he now felt that it would be more of a liability than an asset for the Federal Government at any rate. Skelton however ventured his own opinion that confederation, if it could be made acceptable to the Newfoundland people, afforded the only hope.

As to the immediate future he held out hope that Canada would take her part in a further joint advance when the next bond payments were due. A further message from Amulree on the same day reported[11]: 'We have worked out with some care a scheme for a modified form of political union which might possibly have been made acceptable to Newfoundland as it stands' – but he added ruefully, 'However, alterations in the sense indicated by Skelton would probably destroy its chances of success.'

In a further message, Clutterbuck reported[12] that 'Upshot of discussions here is that there is little likelihood of Canadian Government viewing with favour any proposal which would involve them in any substantial financial commitments either direct or contingent though it might, if appealed to by Newfoundland, agree in the last resort to some comprehensive scheme for political union. Difficulty about last resort is that political union would not be acceptable to Newfoundland public opinion unless terms were strikingly generous.'

Bennett went to London for the World Economic Conference; Chamberlain spoke to him there but told Amulree that he had found him 'entirely unwilling to lend any further aid'.[13] When the Commission propounded their scheme, Bennett 'manifested cordial admiration of the scheme as a whole and especially the generosity of H.M.G. in the U.K. in shouldering financial responsibility'.[14] Well he might!

The Commission's Report was published in October 1933.[15] It was generally considered to contain a penetrating analysis of the island's ills and to propose some drastic remedies. It pulled no punches and lay much of the blame on the reckless use of public funds by politicians and on the irresponsible attitude of the local merchants. The Commission considered, only to reject, the possibilities of the sale of Labrador and of union with Canada. There being no further help from Canada and no solution within the island, they perforce had to turn to Britain. The positive recommendation in their Report therefore was that 'an immediate appeal should be made to the sympathy and good offices of the Government of the U.K.'. They recommended that the assistance should take two forms: financial and political.

The practical steps proposed were novel – and regarded by many as undemocratic. These included the suspension of the existing Parliament and Government and the appointment of Commissioners (three from the UK and three from Newfoundland) to be presided over by the Governor. Full legislative and executive power would be vested in the Commission who would be responsible to the British Government. In return, the British Government would assume responsibility for the Island's finances. The Commission felt that only by some such drastic change could Newfoundland hope to recover from the 'malign influences which, developing from a prolonged period of misgovernment, have demoralised the people and warped their outlook'. Amulree was conscious of the difficulties which such a novel solution would arouse. At a meeting with Harding and other officials in September,[16] he made it clear that he did 'not despair of getting the proposed constitutional changes accepted in Newfoundland, provided that the financial proposals were such as to offer the island the prospect of an early return to its former status; but he was anxious that the new Constitution should be as far removed from the ordinary colonial type as possible.'

Indeed it might have been expected that such drastic, and for Newfoundland almost humiliating, proposals would have been resisted on all sides – based as they were on an unremitting attack on Newfoundland's previous leaders, on the withdrawal of independence and the abolition of democratic control; further they contained no long-term plan for development, no measure even of any local government and they held out no prospect of a return to responsible government except 'until the country is again self-supporting'. Moreover from the British standpoint the Treasury was presented with an open-dated cheque. And yet, remarkably, the Report was accepted on both sides of the Atlantic. On each side there was a minority in opposition; in Newfoundland there was a small section virulently opposed to the suspension of responsible government; but in the Assembly, the proposed action was approved by a large majority. In the British Parliament, the small Labour Opposition vehemently opposed the measure on grounds both of principle (demanding suspension of the Constitution rather than revocation, calling for a plebiscite) and of expediency (the British taxpayer should not be called upon to make good bankruptcy brought about by wrong-doing); Attlee even claimed that 'all the best countries default nowadays' and, as for honour, he would like to see more of it directed towards South Wales. The Labour Party bitterly contested every stage and in the process humiliated Thomas. According to his biographer,[17] 'the Opposition ... saw its chance to exploit his weakness on details' and Thomas 'was baited mercilessly ... and was obliged on more than one occasion to hold an undignified consultation with his Under Secretary ... at 3 a.m. he left the Chamber in disgust, an open admission of defeat which drew derision from the Labour benches.' Nevertheless the legislation was passed by an overwhelming majority in the Commons and without a division in the Lords.

Considering the complexity of the issues raised the timetable was a remarkable one:

February 1933	Appointment of Royal Commission
March	Commission at work in Newfoundland
October	Publication of Report
November	British Government accept recommendations in Report
December	Legislation passed at Westminster

| January 1934 | Commissioners appointed |
| February | Commissioners take up duties |

Not only was the operation conducted throughout with a real sense of urgency but, despite the necessary haste, the structure laid down was destined to continue without substantial alteration for fifteen years. Much of the responsibility for all this fell on Clutterbuck.

It has been said that 'the performance of the Commission of Government was one rather of sober and solid administration than of spectacular advance.'[18] This is probably fair. Criticisms were made by Lodge, one of the early British Commissioners, which contain something of an indictment of the D.O.[19] Lodge's main complaints were: that the Royal Commission had been misled in concluding that Newfoundland's ills had stemmed from corrupt and spendthrift administration rather than from external economic causes beyond her own control; the constitution 'suffered from the vice of inflexibility', since any amendment could be made only by Westminster; the D.O. was not equipped to handle administration problems in what was in effect a dependent territory; finally that control by Westminster was bound to have an inhibiting effect on the long-term policies of the Commission. There is some validity in these shafts against the Office. It is also true that, under the Commission, Newfoundland forsook the ways of democracy and economically was in little different shape when war broke out from what she had been when the Commission took over. But the Commission could not control the terms of world trade; they brought order into the state of the finances, introduced many reforms especially in the social services and provided honest and impartial administration. This enabled the island to take advantage first of the boom which war conditions brought and later of the Canadian offer to join the Confederation.

Southern Rhodesia

If Newfoundland was an instance of a territory being accorded the full status of a Dominion without in fact having the attributes necessary to sustain a separate independence, Southern Rhodesia was an even more remarkable example of a territory being treated in a manner out of proportion to its intrinsic importance. Though never formally a Dominion (mainly because of the degree of control over native matters reserved to the Imperial Government), Southern Rhodesia was in practice granted most of the privileges of one. She had a High Commissioner in London (though he did not attend meetings on foreign affairs, he attended all other meetings); she had a Prime Minister (so-called and not 'Premier' which might have been more appropriate); Southern Rhodesia took part in her own right at international and other

Conferences on financial, economic and commercial matters (e.g. the Ottawa Economic Conference) and regularly attended the meetings of the Imperial Conference. All this for a country with a European population of a mere 45,000 (though with a native – and largely unenfranchised – population of one million), described in 1931 in a joint memorandum by Thomas and Passfield as 'primarily a community of farmers' with a Government referred to almost contemptuously as a 'farmers'' Government.[20] But it no doubt seemed natural to accord broad parity of treatment in days before Dominion status had been defined, when the distinction between Empire and Commonwealth was blurred and when no conditions for membership had been prescribed. Amery, for example, had earlier felt doubts whether so small a community could find the men to conduct its affairs successfully, but these were dispelled on his visit in 1927 when he was 'most favourably impressed' by what he saw of the Southern Rhodesia Government.[21]

The main problem of concern to the D.O. was that of the relationship of Southern Rhodesia to Northern Rhodesia (then under C.O. rule). The Europeans in Northern Rhodesia were always looking for amalgamation and in 1930 the Southern Rhodesians supported this and urged that a conference should consider the matter. Whitehall was well aware of the difficulties. In their joint memorandum to the Cabinet, Thomas and Passfield wrote with remarkable candour of the BSA Company: 'On taking over, it was found that hardly anything had been done for the native population, except to tax it.' The two Secretaries of State were clear that there could be no immediate question of amalgamation, but they were anxious not to disappoint Europeans' hopes too sharply. The main motive was laudable – native areas (like Barotseland) were not suitable for handing over to a self-governing white administration, but the need to retain control of the mining area was also in mind. With some percipience, the memorandum considered what it termed 'the fundamental issue', namely 'where in the future the boundary is to lie between a Southern Africa, with one type of civilization, and a central or central and eastern, Africa with another type of civilization'. That line has still not been finally drawn.

Since total amalgamation was ruled out, the Secretaries of State offered to discuss the amalgamation with Southern Rhodesia of the Livingstone area only, but this was not acceptable. The issue was quiescent during the Depression but was revived by Southern Rhodesia in 1936; after considerable discussion the British Government agreed to the appointment of a Royal Commission to enquire into the feasibility of closer cooperation or association between the two Rhodesias and also Nyasaland, 'with due regard to the interests of both races'.

The Bledisloe Commission was appointed in 1938. It consisted of five members in all, including representatives of the three political parties. The Secretary was G. F. Seel (C.O.) with Pritchard (D.O.) as Assistant Secretary.

The Commission spent time in all three territories and produced their report in the following year. The main conclusion (though there were minority reports) was that while amalgamation should be kept in view as the ultimate objective, this policy was not capable of immediate application and that in the meantime various steps should be taken to extend and improve existing facilities for cooperation. In August 1939 a formula[22] setting out the British Government's attitude was agreed between British Ministers and Huggins (P.M. of Southern Rhodesia), but the war intervened before any action could be taken. The formula stated somewhat lamely that the Government 'agree that the eventual amalgamation of the Territories would have considerable advantages from many points of view' but drew attention to the various objections which would first have to be met.

The fact was that Southern Rhodesia did not loom large in the minds of the British Cabinet at this time. In general the D.O. sought to keep things in a low key and to postpone any crucial decisions. It successfully avoided any direct confrontation and, to achieve this, was willing to give a large measure of support to the Europeans. The climate of opinion of the day did not make this so difficult a task as it would have been thirty years later. The events were not so much important in themselves as they were as portents for the future, since they contained rumblings both of the short-lived Federation of the 1950s and of the declaration of independence in the 1960s. Both ideas had been given some plausibility by the attitude of the British Government in the 1930s. But at least the D.O. could claim credit for resisting the demands to extend white minority rule over the African territories in the North.

The High Commission Territories

Basutoland, the Bechuanaland Protectorate and Swaziland had been under British protection since the end of the nineteenth century; Basutoland and Bechuanaland since 1884 and 1885, both at the specific request of the Chiefs who were fearful of the Boer Republic: Swaziland since 1907, after a period of administration shared with the Transvaal. When the South Africa Constitution was drawn up, the Chiefs of the Three Territories objected to any scheme which would bring them under the rule of South Africa. The South Africa Act of 1909 provided for their incorporation in the Union in due course, but the British Government made it clear that they must bear the ultimate responsibility and gave a pledge that transfer would not take place without the consent of Parliament and until the wishes of the inhabitants had been ascertained and considered.

Basutoland is wholly, Swaziland and Bechuanaland (except for her common frontier with Rhodesia) largely, surrounded by South Africa. They had always been dependent on South Africa and, because of the close connexion between the Territories and South Africa, they had been administered by the Dominions Office. They were governed by the High Commissioner for South Africa who had previously also been the Governor of the Transvaal, but who, since 1910, combined the post with that of Governor-General. This arrangement continued until a separate High Commissioner was appointed in 1931. Since they were administered by a High Commissioner, the Territories were frequently referred to as 'The High Commission Territories'.

Following the change in status of the Governor-General, Sir Herbert Stanley was in 1931 appointed to a dual role with the confusing titles of High Commissioner in the Union (i.e. representative in relation to the Union Government) and High Commissioner for South Africa (i.e. administrative in relation to the Territories). He was an officer of considerable experience in the Colonial Service and had been Governor of Northern Rhodesia and of Ceylon; he was succeeded in 1935 by Clark, previously High Commissioner in Canada. High Commissioners of this calibre and distinction were clearly able to devote themselves to questions of administration in a way that had not previously been possible – the Governor-General himself was mainly a ceremonial figure and the Imperial Secretary, though always a competent and relatively senior member of the Colonial Service, was his subordinate. Each Territory had a Resident Commissioner; it increasingly became the practice to recruit both him and senior members of the Administration from the Colonial Service.

Responsibility for administration in London was for many years concentrated in the hands of H. N. Tait. Tait had joined the Colonial Office in 1911, the same year as Dixon with whom he had been at school at Clifton. In spite of their previous acquaintance and the fact that they were to serve in the same small office for nearly forty years, Dixon incredibly could write at the end 'I saw very little of Tait'; he went on to describe him as 'of a very quiet and retiring disposition, partly due ... to shyness'.[23] He added 'although his advice was always sound, he was somewhat excessively bureaucratic' and recalled a comment that his 'minutes and drafts are positively inhuman.' All this was true – Tait was also excessively cautious, always favoured the minimum of action and, when going on leave, once advised 'Try not to send any papers up to higher authority: it always causes so much trouble when one does.' He was therefore the epitome of the negative bureaucrat, pursuing a *laissez-faire* policy. But he had been to Southern Africa in 1919 as Secretary to the Southern Rhodesia Commission and had ever since acquired the reputation of being an expert. He had many of the civil servant's virtues – integrity, orderliness, expertise – and he would never make a mistake; but for years there was little progress in the Territories and, sadly, Tait stands as the symbol of Whitehall's neglect.

The main political problem for the D.O. in relation to the High Commission Territories was that of transfer. There were many reasons why the Union were anxious to be able to incorporate the Territories. They wanted the land (increasingly important with racial segregation in the Union); they wanted recognition of their status (it was galling to be regarded as unfit to administer the Territories) and they did not welcome the idea of a different native policy being applied on their borders. But the British Government had substantial difficulties and were committed by their pledges. On the other hand, there was the commitment in the South Africa Act, there were the undertakings given to Union Ministers in the past and there was the fact that the Union held the three Territories virtually in an economic strangle-hold. The British therefore needed to tread warily and the story during these years is one of the effort of the D.O. to avoid either an immediate acceptance of the demand for transfer or an outright rejection. Nor was this altogether a cynical policy, since all involved on the British side – the D.O. officials, Ministers and the British High Commissioners – accepted that transfer was inevitable in due course; equally all felt that, because of the Union's native policy, it would be wrong to contemplate transfer at any early date. Amery, Thomas, MacDonald all gave substantially the same answer in different ways.

The issue for the D.O. was first raised by Hertzog at the 1926 Conference. The newly formed Office inherited a situation under which it was accepted that incorporation was the ultimate destination, but that the change should be gradual with agreement that Swaziland (with its European settlers) should be the first to be transferred. In his talks with Hertzog in London, Amery succeeded in postponing any substantive discussion until his own visit to South Africa in 1927. Amery then came to the conclusion that any early transfer was out of the question (mainly, in his own mind, because the British first had to make up for past neglect and 'bring forward the peoples till they were more fit to stand up to the impact of transfer'[24]) and he made it clear to Hertzog that at least ten years would have to pass before a beginning could be made. Amery reported to the Cabinet that he was able to secure Hertzog's 'ready acceptance of what was to him no doubt a disappointing decision'.[25] Amery described the Territories as 'human Whipsnades' and explained 'instead of spending money and thought in developing their resources and, still more importantly, raising the general standard of their people, we had been content to protect them from outside interference, leaving them to carry on under a very unprogressive form of tribal rule as museum pieces ... in an Africa that was being transformed at a breathless pace.'[26] Amery was therefore determined to bring to an end the period of stagnation and he envisaged a three-point programme – to revitalize the administration, to inject money for development, and to promote British settlement. The first need was to infuse new blood in place of what had been 'officially little stagnant pools, the same people staying on in the same job for 20 years on end'. He appointed Colonel Rey, a 'live wire', as Resident Commissioner in the Bechuanaland Protectorate 'to put the Bechuana on their feet economically'. Whiskard, who had been with him throughout his tour, became the superintending Under Secretary in Whitehall. (Later, in 1934, Machtig replaced Tait as head of the Department and gave a more energetic lead.) On development, it was Amery's aim to make progress for both Africans and Europeans. He met with stubborn resistance from the Treasury, but eventually secured from Churchill approval for some modest loans to meet immediate needs. Amery had been powerfully impressed by the influence which a progressive and intensely British Southern Rhodesia could exercise upon the Union. The Europeans were opposed to transfer because of Afrikaner control and the treatment meted out to 'poor whites' in the Union. It was for these reasons that he wanted to see 'centres of progress and British sentiment' in appropriate areas in Swaziland and parts of Bechuanaland.[27] In due course a few families were settled in Swaziland, but otherwise little came of Amery's vision. Amery made a forcible impact on the Territories and is entitled to full credit for two major achievements. First he handled the transfer issue with such skill and conviction that Hertzog did not raise it again until 1932. A respite from controversy for five years was welcome in itself and removed a disturbing element in the Territories. Secondly, though his full vision was not realized and progress was destined to be slow, he at last instilled a new spirit into the affairs of the Territories and began a move towards a more progressive administration which steadily gathered momentum.

Overtures for transfer were first renewed at the Ottawa Conference in 1932; discussions were continued until Thomas reached a concordat with Hertzog in 1935. Thomas's own view was clear from the start. As he put it in a memorandum[28] to the Cabinet in 1933, the Union's general attitude to Africans 'to say the least, does not induce to confidence here that we could properly hand over our trusteeship'. He was influenced mainly by the Africans' hatred for the Union; he did not so much share Amery's dislike of Afrikanerdom or enthusiasm for white settlement. Indeed, as he told a deputation in 1934, he had a wider point in mind: 'In this troubled world today, I am more convinced every hour that I am in office, that the British Empire as a whole must play a dominant part in the future and anything that would widen the breach in South Africa, when so much has been done to heal it, would be bad statesmanship.'[29] Therefore, as an outright rejection was impracticable, he played for postponement.

After reaching agreement with Hertzog, Thomas handed him an *aide-mémoire*[30] which recorded that 'the policy of both governments for the next few years should be directed to bringing about a situation in which, if transfer were to become a matter of practical politics, it could be effected with the full acquiescence of the populations concerned.' The sentiment was impeccable, but it was also a hypothetical and conditional one that certainly gave nothing away. The turgidity of the language suggests that the author may have been the Secretary of State himself and that the draftsmanship may not have been so deliberately vague as might appear. In the meantime the *aide-mémoire* looked for 'the closest possible cooperation ... between the Union Government and the Administrations of the Territories...' so that 'the native population should feel that the Union Government are working ... with a real and generous desire to develop and improve conditions in the Territories.'

Unfortunately the nature of the understanding reached and the vagueness of the language used in the *aide-mémoire* contained the seeds of later trouble. Hertzog alleged in a debate in the Union Parliament that a definite time-table had been agreed, beginning with Swaziland in two years' time, but was forced to withdraw his statement that Thomas had mentioned a specific number of years. Later Hertzog accused Britain of failing to carry out their undertaking that local officials would exert their influence in favour of transfer. It seems clear that in each case Hertzog had read too much into the original understanding; he himself was passionate, capable of self-deception and apt to make mistakes. On the other hand he was not a liar; and for his part Thomas, already in something of a decline and accident-prone, may easily with his rather woolly language and his bluff, jocular manner have given an impression which he did not intend.

When Hertzog next came to London for the Imperial Conference of 1937, MacDonald had replaced Thomas as Dominions Secretary. MacDonald's view of the Territories was, in line with tradition, that in the long run transfer was likely to be in the best interests of the inhabitants, but that Britain could not agree to it in the face of strongly expressed African opinion and Parliamentary disapproval. He recognized however that it was necessary to satisfy the Union that Britain was doing all she properly could to obtain African acquiescence. When Hertzog pressed for early transfer, MacDonald made it clear that African opinion was too strongly opposed and that the two Governments must pursue the policy of cooperation laid down in 1935. While MacDonald saw the need to be tough ('I thought it best to rub in ... the realities of the situation',[31] he recorded of a talk with Hertzog and Havenga), he did not want a quarrel. When the South African High Commissioner reported that the General had decided to fight, MacDonald replied that he would 'tell him in return that he would refuse to fight ... The question was the one question between the Union and ourselves which might lead to a break between us.'[32] He therefore sought to lower the temperature and undertook to draft a joint statement of policy. Hertzog was deeply disappointed and, before leaving England, issued a threat of 'unpleasant consequences'.

Agreement on the Statement took time and it was not issued until March

1938. It included two suggestions of MacDonald's which Hertzog had accepted – that a joint committee should be set up to study openings for cooperation and that the Union Government would prepare memoranda clarifying the terms for transfer which they would propose. The main memorandum was not finally ready until August 1939 and was never published owing to the war. With the declaration of war and with Smuts replacing Hertzog as P.M., a new situation arose.

In the meantime, some economic development began. (On his tour in 1934 Hankey found the Territories 'a nasty scandal' and wrote 'Either we shall have to spend more money or hand them over'.)[33] Sir Alan Pim reported on the economic and financial situation of Swaziland in 1932 and followed this up with surveys of Bechuanaland in 1933 and Basutoland in 1935. A programme for development was put in hand; mining in Swaziland, cattle in Bechuanaland, communications and agriculture throughout were encouraged. Moreover the Depression was lifting; the Treasury began to take a less parsimonious view and assistance was forthcoming from the Colonial Development and Welfare Fund which had been set up in 1921. Over the ten-year period before the war, more than £1½ million was made available in grants and loans.

There was a dramatic episode in Bechuanaland in 1933 when Tshekedi Khama, the vigorous, ambitious and highly intelligent Acting Chief of the Bamangwato was suspended. After making ineffective complaints about a European who was notorious for cohabiting with African girls, Tshekedi allowed action to be taken in the Native courts; the man was convicted and ordered to be whipped; the sentence was duly carried out. The reaction of the Administration was swift and severe. Tshekedi had long been at loggerheads with the Resident Commissioner and it so happened that, as the High Commissioner (Stanley) was on leave, the Dormant Commission was held by the C in C South Atlantic, at that time Admiral Evans ('Evans of the Broke' and later Lord Mountevans). Evans had a paternalistic and simplistic view of the African;* moreover he seems to have been satisfied that Tshekedi was getting above himself and needed teaching a lesson.† Since immediate action seemed desirable and this might excite opposition in the tribe and because there was no effective force of police in the Protectorate, he ordered an armed naval escort (100 marines, 100 seamen with naval guns) to proceed at once to Palapye Road (the nearest railway station to Tshekedi's capital). He also arranged, with military precision, that Tshekedi should be suspended, that an

---

* In his autobiography Evans has many revealing comments about the African – 'a great liar', 'naturally lazy', 'really undeveloped children a long, long way from civilization as we know it'. He also wrote 'the nastiest are the Bechuanas' and spoke disparagingly of Tshekedi's 'Bible-thumping'.[34]

† Evans' biographer leaves no doubt that he regarded Tshekedi as obstructive and the punishment of the European as merely 'The latest in a protracted series of provocative actions'.[35] Evans himself recorded unambiguously 'having flouted the administration . . ., he had to be deposed'.[36]

administrative enquiry should be held and that his decision should be announced to a full tribal gathering – all within the compass of a week.[37]

The Committee of Enquiry was composed of the Administration Secretary in the Office of the High Commissioner for South Africa (Captain Neale) and the Acting High Commissioner in the Union (Liesching) and completed its work in a day. The Committee was scathing about the conduct of the European (and another European) but found that he was tried, convicted and flogged in the Chief's Kgotla and that 'This was done deliberately by the Acting Chief Tshekedi, who was fully aware that, as a Native Chief, he had no jurisdiction to deal with a case in which a European was concerned.'[38] A second enquiry under the Resident Commissioner and Liesching was also held the same day into the allegation by Tshekedi that the Resident Magistrate at Serowe had failed to act on Tshekedi's complaints.[39] The Report effectively exonerated the Magistrate (whose powers at the time were limited), but Liesching entered a strong reservation that, while the specific complaints had been disposed of, the Administration had a responsibility for action to remedy the conditions which had given rise to the specific incidents. The Admiral accepted that Tshekedi was actuated by a desire to serve the best interests of his tribe, but regarded the 'principle at issue' as so important that it involved 'a claim to be virtually independent'. He therefore forthwith suspended Tshekedi from the Chieftainship during His Majesty's pleasure and directed the tribe to nominate an acting Chief. He accompanied this with an expulsion order on the Europeans involved.

This high-handed action roused much criticism* in England when the facts became known – and not only in liberal circles. The reaction was all the stronger since it was clear that there was some justice in Tshekedi's claim that he had only taken action because of the inability of the Administration to deal with the matter. Stanley on leave in England was dismayed; the D.O. expressed concern; even Buckingham Palace asked anxious questions. And the business offended Thomas who had a deep-seated belief in the dignity of man and little use for bemedalled Admirals. On 20 September, Thomas secured Cabinet approval[41] for his proposal that, if Tshekedi would express his regret to the Acting High Commissioner, his reinstatement would be sanctioned. This was duly secured and a repentant Tshekedi was reinstated. The incident could be regarded as closed – but it left a scar and was a strange forerunner of the occasion 20 years later when Tshekedi's nephew was also removed from the Chieftainship – for marrying a white woman.

---

* *The Times* in an editorial of 29 September 1933 commented even-handedly: 'As for Admiral Evans and his bodyguard of marines, the whole paraphernalia may seem a little ridiculous in the light of the complete tranquillity in which that gallant seaman, unexpectedly thrust into an unfamiliar and most difficult position, conducted his proceedings to Palapye Road. But there was always the prospect ... of disturbances.' Evans himself certainly did what he believed to be 'the right thing' and did not regret it.[40]

The attitude of the D.O. towards the Territories for much of the time could be summarized as conscious inactivity; this attitude was not heroic and it was responsible for much neglect of the Territories in the early years. But it also resulted in maintaining the political status quo; while avoiding an outright clash with the Union, the D.O. successfully resisted all demands for transfer and their inaction accorded with the wishes of the inhabitants. As a South African historian has put it:[42] 'The continual frustration by the Colonial and Dominions Offices of South African informal overtures in the half-century after the passing of the Act of Union is a notable tribute to twentieth-century imperial trusteeship exercised at the expense of Imperial political advantage.'

CHAPTER 12

The Dominions Office
from Outside

It cannot be claimed that the D.O. ever loomed large on the stage in Britain itself or that it made any dramatic impact on Parliament, the Press or public opinion. Indeed to a wider public it remained largely unknown. This is not surprising since the Office was relatively new, seldom in the limelight and, even with events in which it was directly concerned, the P.M. or another Minister often acted as the Government spokesman or the figurehead whom the public identified as the key performer. Successive Ministers made their mark, but none was particularly identified with the D.O. as such; Amery was known best as Colonial Secretary and was associated with the Empire as a whole; Thomas was regarded as a Trade Unionist and connected in the public mind with labour matters; Malcolm MacDonald was little known, other than as the son of his father. Moreover each successive S. of S. left a very different mark, Amery one of enthusiasm for an exciting adventure, Thomas one of fumbling and bluff, MacDonald one of quiet industry. Even among politicians, opinion towards the D.O. was not noticeably favourable. When the National Government was formed in 1931, Eden relates that he hoped for a post in the F.O. and understood that Malcolm MacDonald would be going to the D.O. as Parly US. Baldwin however warned him that Ramsay MacDonald now wanted his son to go to the F.O.; Eden made it clear to Baldwin that he himself preferred the F.O. 'Of course you would, of course you would,' replied Baldwin with repetitive insistence.[1] In appointing Inskip to the D.O. in 1939 Chamberlain remarked in unambiguous terms: 'It is not a very absorbing department. You will be available for Committees.'[2] In Parliament, the fixed opinion died hard that the D.O. was nothing but a Post Office. In spite of all the explanations given, the Select Committee on Estimates[3] in 1937 could not be weaned from this obsession. When in 1938, the Offices of the D.O. and C.O. were put in charge of a single S. of S. (MacDonald) the *Daily Express* rejoiced at an 'excellent decision' and continued, 'The D.O. is no more than a post office. Its functions could be merged with those of Major Tryon's [the Postmaster-General]. Indeed that is perhaps the best place for it. The Dominions Secretaryship will add to Mr. Malcolm MacDonald's dignity but will add nothing to his responsibilities.'[4]

For its part, the D.O. never sought the limelight and made little attempt to influence opinion. Its Press Officer provided scarcely more than an enquiry desk; though the Office enjoyed amicable relations with the so-called 'patriotic societies' (notably, as it then was, the Royal Empire Society), it never attempted to make use of them for its own purposes. The Anti-Slavery Society and other bodies made representations from time to time, but it kept aloof from them and treated the Empire Crusade with disdain. (The EMB which, in its short life, developed such a flair for publicity was in this respect quite separate from the mainstream of the Office.) There were two occasions when the D.O. was prominent in the news; one such occasion was the Tshekedi affair. Another was the body-line bowling controversy in the Test Matches against Australia in 1932–3 when Thomas went to the MCC in order to help bring the temperature down.[5] But such occasions were rare.

Though the Dominions had for so long pressed for a separate Department in the British Government, there is no evidence that it was an extended warm welcome; they never acquired any feeling of proprietary pride and, though their attitudes varied, their most vocal comments were critical. In Canada, Mackenzie King was primarily concerned to avoid any embarrassing centralization or anything that would involve Canada in commitments; he was therefore fearful of change and did not wish to voice any complaints. Indeed he frequently paid tribute in public to the existing system. Later on, however, Massey as High Commissioner criticized what he called the D.O. bottle-neck and expressed his preference for direct dealings with the F.O. In his *Memoirs* he recalled that, when the D.O. had been created in 1925, he had written to Geoffrey Dawson of *The Times* '... one essential step towards better understanding is to bring the Dominion representatives into direct contact with the F.O. An intermediate department, however able its staff or well-intentioned its head will serve only to cause circumlocution, delays and misunderstandings.'[6] He claims that his experience bore this out, and recorded in his diary for 17 March 1936:[7] 'The machinery of the D.O. instead of keeping us in close touch with foreign crises at present seems somehow to provide an obstacle or rather delay in getting news which we could get and sometimes do receive informally from F.O. What good purpose does the D.O. serve?' With some prescience he then went on to ask: 'Could not its functions be better performed by a Dominions Section of the F.O. with the S. of S. being known as the S. of S. for Foreign and Dominion Affairs?' It is perhaps fair comment that Massey's interests were almost exclusively in foreign affairs and that, as already noted, he himself recognized that some of the irritation he directed at the D.O. should really have been addressed to his own Government. We have seen that South Africa also sought direct dealings with the F.O.[8] New Zealand seems to have expressed few complaints; it was from Australia that came the most formidable and persistent criticisms, and there was good reason for this. Australia took the view that the British Commonwealth should speak with one voice and was in no doubt that it was not possible for Australia to remain neutral in a war involving Britain; until 1940 she had no independent representative in any foreign country and relied wholly on British sources; she was therefore content to leave to Great Britain the actual handling of foreign affairs. But, in her view, this justified her in demanding to be consulted over matters affecting her vital interests in time for her views to be considered and before crucial decisions were taken.[9] W. M. Hughes castigated the D.O. 'Instead of rushing like a swiftly-running cataract, it crawls like a half-baked centipede'.[10] Menzies used to delight in recounting how he imagined that an F.O. draft was emasculated in the D.O., first one, then another paragraph being excised because it might offend one or other of the Dominions until what was served up to Dominion Governments was meaningless. More serious and more important was the accusation made by Casey. Recalling the time when he was Australian Liaison Officer in London (1924–31), he recounted[11] that it had been the traditional policy of the British Government never to give voice, in private or even more particularly in public, to any critical comment on any statement of the Government of any Commonwealth country. Casey thought this policy was first put into practice when the D.O. came into being and he discussed it with Harding. He pointed out 'That the avoidance of plain speaking was a negation of leadership' and asked 'how could there be any basis of mutual understanding without the plainest of plain speaking at least in private?' Harding apparently would have none of this and maintained that the policy stemmed from the doctrine of equality of status: when Casey persisted, Harding firmly, but in uncharacteristic language, closed the argument by saying 'Nice stink you'd like to land us into.' The fact is that, given the Australian feeling of closeness with Britain and of the need for Commonwealth unity, Australia would never be completely satisfied that the information was full enough or received soon enough. But that matters did not work out too badly in practice is suggested by the comment made, with some perhaps pardonable pride, by Bruce: 'From the time Casey went to London as my Liaison Officer until I ceased to be High Commissioner in 1945, Australia was invariably better informed on international affairs and had far more influence on the U.K. Government and its policy than all the rest of the Empire put together.'[12]

Misunderstandings and difficulties also occurred nearer home. The D.O., to be effective, needed to establish itself with other Departments in Whitehall, but the account of its early development has already shown the strong opposition it had to contend with from such established Departments as the Treasury and the F.O. and the new Office seldom met with understanding when it felt called upon to urge wider Commonwealth considerations against a narrower departmental interest.*

* There was a story in Whitehall that Harding had tattooed on his back the words 'If you are a Dominion, kick me.' A variant, according to Menzies current in Australia, was that he was known as 'Kick me, Harding!'

Undoubtedly the closest relations remained with the C.O. This was natural as the staff was interchangeable, shared the same building and common services and there were many personal friendships of long standing. In these early days there was little desire to cut the ties and it was not until the late 30s that any resentment at this continued tutelage began to manifest itself. For its part, the C.O. could afford to be paternal and well-disposed since the D.O. staff was so small. Even so the difference in function of the two Departments showed itself with increasing clarity; each properly took a pride in its own special responsibility, but this could develop into a feeling of superiority on each side, the D.O. considering that it dealt with important matters of international policy contrasted with mere colonial administration, the C.O. feeling it had a real job concerned with improving the lot of whole peoples compared with the ineffective Post Office functions of its neighbour. Nevertheless a common tradition and common interests kept the two Departments together in facing the rest of Whitehall.

The relationship of the D.O. with the F.O. was far more complex. The nature of the work in the D.O. began increasingly to approximate to that of the F.O.; nevertheless relations with that Department never enjoyed real intimacy during this period. There was an ambivalence in the relationship on both sides. They had much in common and each needed the other – the D.O. was totally dependent on the F.O. for one of the most important strands in consultation (though not the only one) in the supply of information about the world situation; the F.O. was equally dependent on the D.O. (though not wholly so) for the support of the Dominions in the pursuit of British policies abroad. But there was much that divided them – the F.O. had great prestige, a long tradition, a foreign service, a large staff. The D.O. was a newcomer, with as yet no reputation, a tiny staff, of which only a handful was beginning to go overseas. The F.O. had always been a distinct service on its own and was conscious and proud of this. Moreover the F.O. was an élitist Department and had traditionally attracted members of the aristocracy to its Service. The D.O. remained part of the Home Civil Service and seemed bourgeois by comparison. One difficulty was that neither Department knew very much from first-hand knowledge about the responsibilities of the other; this was only slowly remedied by the secondment of officers from each Department to the service of the other (and before the war this was confined to a handful of F.O. staff serving in D.O. posts abroad). There was also frequently a genuine difference of standpoint between the two Departments – as instanced by the running fights between Harding and Hurst. There was fundamentally the D.O. conviction that relations inter se between Commonwealth countries were different in kind from relations with foreign countries. The D.O. felt that it was dealing with proved friends on a basis of frankness and partnership and that this called for techniques quite distinct from those for dealing with foreign countries where a greater degree of formality and reserve was required. No doubt the D.O. tended to exaggerate the differences, partly perhaps because the distinction in function was the sole justification for its separate existence. The F.O. for its part did not deny the distinction between relations with foreign and Commonwealth countries, but expected Dominion support for British policies and tended to blame the D.O. for feebleness when this was not forthcoming. Finally a governing factor in the situation was the unresolved conflict between the two Departments in regard to their responsibilities. In spite of the rebuff administered to it through the appointment of a High Commissioner in Canada (and subsequently elsewhere) solely responsible to the D.O., the F.O. still hankered after the right to communicate direct with the Dominions, feeling that only thus could British foreign policy be made fully effective. The D.O. however was extremely sensitive to any encroachments on its own authority and was not prepared to allow the F.O. to handle Commonwealth relations on its own.

There was perhaps something more, amounting almost to a difference in ideological outlook. Symptomatic of the contrast in atmosphere is the fact that a wealth of material exists in the form of biographies or memoirs about a variety of men who served under the F.O. at this period; for the D.O., apart from Amery's memoirs, there is virtually nothing. Any references to contemporary sources are therefore inevitably one-sided and any quotations are bound to be selective. The following quotations at least all point towards a certain disdain on the part of the F.O. towards the Dominion idea. In 1927 Chamberlain commented sourly on a visit from the South African High Commissioner: 'Instead of dealing with great principles, it turned out that Smit wished to discuss some aspect of protocol dealing with the export of ostrich feathers to countries outside the British Empire!'[13] Gladwyn Jebb in his memoirs says that 'the entire Government machine on the foreign side, outside No. 10, was at the beginning of the war dominated by Old Etonians.'[14] No such claim could be advanced for the Commonwealth side. In a minute dealing with the discussion of the Colonial problem at the 1937 Conference, Vansittart recorded that the statement was made 'in strict confidence and for a special purpose to a family gathering and a rather ignorant one at that'[15] (i.e. Dominion P.M.s and their advisers). Vansittart also noted that King George V's Silver Jubilee broadcast was addressed to the Commonwealth as 'my very dear, dear people' and commented: 'On the whole they were. They were also very, very difficult but not to him.'[16]* On any comparison between the F.O. and D.O. perhaps it would be fair to let an

---

* Expression of contempt for the Dominions was not confined to the F.O. Even so scrupulous a commentator as Hankey, in a letter from Australia to Harding wrote about Menzies (of all people): 'He is, according to British standards, rather a rough diamond; very contemptuous of soft and sappy policies, but a good fellow at bottom and quite fearless of responsibility.'[17] The D.O. itself was not above an attitude of condescension: Whiskard, on his tour with Amery in 1927, had written about Canada: 'Of all the Dominions, Canada differed most from my previous conception and differed by being so much better than I had imagined. The standard of civilization is very greatly superior to that of the other Dominions.'[18]

independent outsider give a verdict. L. B. Pearson, who was posted to London in the 1930s and knew both Departments well, described them as follows:

> The Dominions Office, in its people, its attitudes, and atmosphere, was similar to other civil service departments. But the Foreign Office was the Holy of Holies, occupied by an aristocratic, well-endowed élite who formed part of the British diplomatic service, and who saw to it that the imperial interest was protected and enlarged in accord with policies worked out in their high-ceilinged, frescoed Victorian offices, to be accepted, they usually assumed, by their political masters in Cabinet and Parliament.[19]

For all these reasons it is not surprising that the attitude of the F.O. varied from patronizing tolerance to mild derision and that of the D.O. from envy to suspicion. It is a striking fact and one which reflects little credit on the D.O. that, though the D.O. needed to look outside the Office to fill many of the new posts of High Commissioner, no member of the Foreign Service was appointed to be a High Commissioner until the transfer of power in India. Nevertheless at the working level, good understanding and cooperation were much in evidence. Moreover close friendships were often formed and there were many who held their opposite numbers in the other Department in high regard. This applied particularly to D.O. officials associated with their F.O. colleagues in international conferences and also to the F.O. officials seconded to the staff of High Commission posts in the Dominions.

Throughout this period the Treasury remained primarily a Department for the control of Government expenditure rather than for the stimulation of the national economy. Its relations with other Departments could not therefore be expected to be those of open-handed generosity. Most of the projects which the D.O. favoured involved substantial expenditure. The Treasury, particularly under Warren Fisher, certainly kept a wary eye on the D.O., fighting a rearguard action over its establishment, the size of overseas posts, delaying the establishment of a full High Commission in Australia, restricting the size of the home staff. The fact that the salary of the PUS continued until 1940 at the rate of a Deputy in any other Department suggests that the Treasury did not put a high value on the political importance of the Department. In spite of these differences there was in fact a reasonable degree of cooperation between the two Departments, particularly at the working level, and the D.O. accepted, and indeed to a large extent often shared the general Treasury standpoint. There were two spheres in which collaboration between the two Departments was especially close – by the 1930s the Treasury was beginning to accept the need for development assistance and, on the basis of carefully worked out plans, provided grants in aid and development loans for the High Commission Territories; the plight of Newfoundland alarmed the Treasury because of the effect on confidence in sterling if the Island were to default and it worked in close partnership with the D.O. over the functioning of the Commission Government in Newfoundland.

The pattern of the relationship with other Departments in Whitehall was more routine. It was inevitably close and continuous with the Board of Trade and, though there were undoubtedly occasions when the Board would have liked the D.O. to adopt a tougher approach to the Dominions, normally cooperative. Relations were particularly fruitful with the Service Departments (especially the Air Ministry over air transport) and the General Post Office (notably over the Empire Air Mail Scheme). In the light of later developments, it is curious to note that relations with the India Office were slender. There seems to have been surprisingly little interest in the D.O. about constitutional developments in India and little discussion with Dominion Governments on the subject; they were sent for information copies of the Simon Commission Report and of the Command Paper issued after the Round Table Conference, but there was no advance consultation. The main contact between the D.O. and the I.O. was on the awkward question of Indians in South Africa. The D.O.'s association with the Cabinet Office received a stimulus from the fact that the Cabinet Secretary was also Secretary of the CID and acted as Secretary to Imperial Conferences (at which he was always assisted by D.O. staff). Hankey, like nearly all his successors, was well acquainted with the Dominions and had a strong feeling for the Commonwealth. He seems to have had a high regard for Harding and Batterbee both of whom worked closely with him and he could normally be counted upon to be a strong supporter of the D.O. Liaison with the P.M.'s Office was also good and in 1937, in the person of Cecil Syers, the first of a long line of D.O. (later CRO) staff was seconded to serve in the Private Office of No. 10.

With the staff at Buckingham Palace close touch was always maintained: this was especially necessary at a time when the constitutional status of the Dominions was being transformed and the position of the Sovereign in relation to each of his Dominions was assuming greater significance. Batterbee ensured that relations with the Palace were both intimate and discreet; in their different spheres Bromley and Dixon could also be counted on to solve any problems of protocol. The understanding shown by the staff at the Palace was enhanced by the fact that most of them had either served as ADC to one of the Governors-General in a Dominion or accompanied a member of the Royal Family on an Empire Tour.

The role played by the D.O. was inevitably influenced by factors affecting the Government as a whole. There were both handicaps and advantages in Britain's relationship with the Dominions. It was on the whole (though not always) a handicap that the Dominions seldom agreed among themselves. It was certainly a handicap that the one area in which the Dominions agreed was making demands on Britain; the Dominions had specific things (particularly in the economic sphere) which they wanted from Britain, but were able to side-step what Britain wanted from them. The result was that Britain was often in a minority at Commonwealth Conferences (notably at Ottawa). The British suffered another disadvantage since they needed a successful outcome from any Commonwealth occasion and could not afford to be accused of lack of generosity to a Dominion; the reverse was far from true, since in a Dominion it was frequently a political gain to show that its representatives had stood up for the country's rights and not yielded to dictation from London. On the other hand, Britain's position was strengthened because she had the effective power; moreover public sentiment both in Britain and in the Dominions encouraged cohesion.

All these factors limited the role which the D.O. could play. As Bruce Miller has put it: 'The D.O. could hardly have acted as a dynamic force, since the task which it had of conducting relations with the Dominions was one of great delicacy.'[20] And there was a further factor which accentuated the difficulties for the Office and made their position in Whitehall uneasy. This was that the D.O. was in itself a compromise. The Dominions, generally speaking, wanted the best of both worlds – the recognition of equality (and so direct dealings with the F.O.), but also and at the same time special treatment with, in some cases, a voice in the British Cabinet. These were incompatible. The Dominions were given the D.O. which ensured for them special treatment but they were denied direct dealings with the F.O. and an effective voice in the actual formulation of policy. This made them discontented, especially as they took special treatment for granted and showed little gratitude in having a separate Office to ensure it.

As for the British Government, Ministers accepted that responsibility for relations with the Dominions could not just be handed over to the F.O. (who did not want the job in any case). Many would have preferred to leave things alone with the C.O. continuing in charge; but the Cabinet deferred to Amery's insistence. However they saw no need for the new Department to be more than a face-saver and the Treasury's attempt to downgrade the Office reflected the general view. Like all compromises the result was uneasy and the D.O. was discouraged from embarking on a bold course.

Criticisms directed against the D.O. both at the time and since are many and varied. The most frequent complaint was that the D.O. was a 'Post Office'. In a narrow sense the accusation was misplaced since it was precisely the function of the Office to be responsible for communications between the British and Dominion Governments. The criticism was however extended to complaints either that it was a 'mere' Post Office (with the implication that it served no other function and was therefore unnecessary) or that it was an inefficient Post Office (because it acted as a bottle-neck or censor). The first argument was unjustified, but the second lay at the root of complaints both

in the Departments of Whitehall and among Dominion Governments that the
D.O. diluted the material it passed on and did not press with sufficient vigour
the case it had been asked to put. The charge of delay was sometimes
justified, but not always reasonable. The D.O. sought to give a considered
appreciation and never pretended to provide a news service which could
compete with the press. As to dilution there were no doubt occasions when,
for reasons of tact or caution, the D.O. watered down a message. There was
substance in Casey's point that the D.O. paid undue attention to Dominion
susceptibilities and, in going out of its way to avoid causing offence, was at
times lacking in candour. More important were the occasions when, for
reasons beyond the control of the D.O., the British Government decided to
act before there was time to warn Dominion Governments in advance or on
occasion deemed it desirable to withhold some information.

A related cause for complaint was that the D.O. tended to treat all
Dominions alike. The Dominions were equal in status; but they were not
equal in other respects – in function or in power. The D.O. practice of
treating them on the same basis had many consequences. In its simplest form,
it encouraged the D.O. to send identical messages to all Dominion
Governments whatever their degree of interest in the contents. This was the
basis for Menzies' complaint that information was concealed from Australia
because of some irrelevant consideration affecting another Dominion (and led
Churchill in wartime to anathematize the D.O. 'circulars'). Under these
methods the concept of a Dominion became a stereotype to which all were
expected to conform; and the Commonwealth convoy tended to travel at the
pace of the slowest ship. With hindsight it seems that the D.O. made a serious
mistake in treating all the Dominions alike; it was short-sighted to proceed
on a basis which ignored the real and fundamental differences that existed.
Of course the over-riding aim of the D.O. was to secure unity; but the D.O.
did not always display sufficient consciousness of the force of the considerations on the other side. This involved a departure from the normal policy of
basing relations on a hard and realistic assessment of the bilateral facts – this
was in contradistinction to the practice of the F.O. and was one of the reasons
for its dislike of the Commonwealth concept. There were also practical
consequences. Until the suspension of the Constitution, Newfoundland was a
'Dominion' and therefore treated as such; Southern Rhodesia, though not
technically a Dominion, tended to be equated with one in a way that would
not have occurred had she remained the responsibility of the C.O. Some of
the misunderstandings and unhappiness in Rhodesia in later years had their
origins in this period.

There are wider criticisms too. Looking at the matter from the Australian
point of view, Hasluck came to the conclusion that 'one of the most unfortunate results of the attempts made at the 1926 Imperial Conference to
give precision to the imprecise growth of custom and to freeze the fluid course

of political change was that emphasis was placed on constitutional principles rather than on the practice of politics. From that point onwards discussion of British Commonwealth relations tended to stay among the lawyers rather than spread to the politicians.'[21] This is a characteristically pragmatic Australian (or even British) view that would not have been shared in Canada, South Africa and Eire. Nevertheless it has validity and the argument could indeed be carried further. Harding, Batterbee, Stephenson, Dixon were all 'lawyers' in the sense that their first concern was for constitutional principles; they had less relish for mundane forms of practical cooperation. It was not only politics they neglected, but still more economics.

There is a further accusation. Did the D.O., which played a key part in bringing about the changed status of the Dominions, nevertheless seek to rest on its laurels and resist any change? Amery always made clear his view that the Empire was a unity, owing loyalty to the Crown and that no part could be neutral when the King was at war.[22] Did the D.O. stand fast on this kind of view of the Commonwealth and seek to freeze the position as it had been agreed in 1926? To a large extent the answer must be in the affirmative. The D.O. attached importance to the 'common status' of British nationality, with the right of entry into Britain for all British subjects, to the qualification for Commonwealth membership written into the Balfour Declaration 'united in a common allegiance to the Crown', to the concept of a single Monarch with the implication that no Dominion could be neutral in war. All these notions were to lose their validity and would be overturned in due course: Eire did remain neutral in war, India was accepted as a Commonwealth member without owing allegiance, the common status was in practice lost and the doctrine of free entry for all British subjects was reversed with much pain 36 years after the Balfour Declaration.

What was the attitude of the D.O. itself towards these general issues? As a Department of the British Government, its primary duty was to have regard to and to further the interests of Britain. The purpose of its effort and diplomacy was to ensure that Dominion Governments understood as fully as possible the reasons for British policies and to endeavour to secure the cooperation of the Dominions where needed in the carrying out of those policies. The medal of course had its reverse side and, in the endeavour to secure full Dominion cooperation, it was incumbent on the D.O. to make known to policy-makers in the British Government the likely views and attitudes of Dominion Governments and to suggest in what ways British policies would best attract full cooperation. The D.O. could never act as the 'representative' of the Dominions in any formal sense; but it did see itself as the guardian of the British undertakings to recognize the equal status of the Dominions and at the same time to maintain the essential unity of purpose of the Commonwealth. It acted as the 'conscience' of the British Government; it therefore became jealous in upholding the rights of Dominion Governments against any lingering Imperialist tendencies in Britain. It also strove to preserve a sense of unity in situations where there were acute differences – and at times this led it to advocate courses of compromise. Inevitably the task was a delicate one and the D.O. often came to be caught between two fires.

The more serious question is whether the D.O. could or should have done more to press the views of the Dominions on the British Government and, perhaps more importantly, the British case on Dominion Governments.

As to the first point, the fact is that on all major issues Dominion views (which were by no means unanimous) were always taken into account though they were seldom the decisive factor. At the time of Hitler's march on Vienna, MacDonald made clear to the Cabinet[23] that he 'had never favoured our adopting a particular policy merely in order to please the Dominions'; if we came to the conclusion that a particular policy was right, we ought to adopt it irrespective of their views. But he warned of the consequences and argued that if Britain acted over Austria, the Commonwealth might well break in pieces. 'Australia and New Zealand will almost certainly follow our lead. Eire would no doubt toe the same line . . . but South Africa and Canada would see no reason whatever why they should join in a war to prevent certain Germans from rejoining their fatherland.' This factor would have to be taken into account though he recognized that other factors might outweight it.

This indeed was the traditional British attitude. The British Government had no intention of abrogating their responsibilities or of putting the decision-making process into commission, realizing that objections by anyone could then have paralysed action. Nor was Britain's right to act as she saw fit in matters that primarily concerned her ever questioned by the Dominions. (Naturally if there was support from the Dominions, Ministers did not shrink from quoting this to foreign Governments.)

As regards the other side of the coin (as Austen Chamberlain would have put it, seeing that the Dominions 'kept in step') the argument goes to the heart of the question as to the nature of the Commonwealth. There were no doubt occasions where the D.O.* could have sought to bring greater pressure on the Dominions, but there were clear limits to the extent of pressure which would have been prudent or practicable. For the association had long ceased to be one in which Britain could impose her own ideas. Under another system, the Dominions might have been meshed in more closely with the British diplomatic and military machine. This had not happened and if Britain had attempted to force the pace, the Dominions might have been less whole-hearted in support and their military effort less effective than proved to be the case when war came.

---

* In the major decisions, the D.O. could only be effective if the Minister carried weight in the Cabinet and was included in the inner circle of decision-makers. This was seldom the case and, in the crucial last two years before the war, Chamberlain worked with a very small inner group which did not include the Dominions Secretary.

After all what the D.O. was attempting was something quite new. There were many obstacles, but also both in Britain and overseas many favourable factors. Sentiment was always a factor in the Commonwealth association; the adherents of Realpolitik were wrong to think that the Commonwealth need not be taken seriously because it was not a formal alliance. In all this, the work of the D.O. was broadly in tune with popular feeling, and the attempt succeeded. The considerable change in Dominion status was brought about by friendly negotiation, ending in complete agreement and the new techniques for Commonwealth consultation by and large operated smoothly.

Two later events seem to attest to the acceptability of the system of Commonwealth partnership that was developed under the aegis of the D.O. – though other factors were involved in each case. In 1939, when Britain declared war, all the Dominions (with the exception only of Eire) declared war and each made a generous-hearted contribution throughout the years of struggle. Secondly from 1947 onwards whenever Britain has granted independence to former dependent territories, they have all (with only few exceptions) of their own free will asked for Commonwealth membership. It may be doubted whether India (and the long line of successors) would have sought admission to the Commonwealth, had not the Dominions formed with Britain an association that made their sovereign independence evident to all, that rested on friendship and not force and that commanded respect through the whole world.*

* Since this was written, the author's attention has been drawn to a doctoral thesis completed at Oxford in 1977 by Dr R. F. Holland, currently Lecturer in Imperial History at the Institute of Commonwealth Studies in the University of London. This looks broadly at the way in which the Commonwealth relationship was perceived, but is particularly concerned with the workings of the Dominions Office from 1925 to 1937. It concludes that its officials had, by the end of the 1920s and throughout the 1930s, developed an effective understanding of how the Commonwealth relationship was best 'managed'; above all, Batterbee, Harding and their colleagues showed political sensitivity and did not share Leo Amery's 'integrationist' approach to imperial cooperation. D.O. officials at the Ottawa Conference tried to tone down exaggerated notions of Empire protectionism, since they feared that the cleavages to which it might give rise would prejudice those forms of cooperation which were more readily obtainable; at home, whenever the Treasury or one of the Service departments tried to contend that the Dominions were implicitly obligated to cooperate on military matters, they realistically point out that any attempt to insist on an advance commitment would be counter-productive; whilst from the beginning of the dispute with de Valera they recognized the need to maintain a negotiable posture. Generally, Dr Holland finds that the D.O. consistently opposed any other department which seemed to be approaching Commonwealth relations without the finely turned political sense which, after the mid-1920s, he considers was critical.

PART II

The War and Post-War Reconstruction
1939–47

CHAPTER 1

The Dominions and the War

The four overseas Dominions were all actively involved in the struggle against the Axis Powers for the six years of war. Each made prodigious efforts and endured tragic losses. The D.O. was little more than a spectator of many of the purely military operations, but the war provided unremittingly the background to its work and the enmeshing of the war effort of the Dominions with that of Britain remained throughout the prime task of the Office.

Britain's declaration of war did not in form cover the Dominions and the extent of any participation was entirely a matter for each Government to decide. In the event all declared war, though in different ways. Australia and New Zealand considered themselves committed by Britain's declaration.[1] In Canada, Mackenzie King insisted on leaving the decision to Parliament which had to be summoned; a motion to declare war was then accepted without a division. Canada had been neutral for a week, but this had the practical advantage that war supplies could cross the frontier without infringing the US Neutrality Act. In South Africa, the Cabinet was divided but the majority in Parliament voted in favour of war. Hertzog was succeeded by Smuts and war was declared. Only Eire remained neutral. There all sections of public opinion and all parties in the Dail were opposed to war; as has been said 'Ireland at this juncture, with characteristic paradox, would rather fight than go to war.'[2]

War Effort

There was no concerted strategic plan and no agreement in advance as to how or where Dominion forces would be deployed; indeed no Dominion Government had taken serious action to put the country in a position to meet the challenge that now faced it. When war broke out, the British themselves laid emphasis at first on the need for essential supplies of all kinds, including food and munitions. Nevertheless, partly under strong popular pressure, the expansion of the armed services went rapidly ahead. The First Canadian Division arrived in the UK in December 1939 and the Second followed before long. The New Zealand and Australian Governments (in that order chronologically) announced their intention to send a Division overseas and the first convoys sailed early in the New Year. In South Africa, where the two wings of the Nationalist Party combined against participation in the war and represented at least a substantial section of the electorate, Smuts at first had to move warily.

The armed forces of the Dominions served in all areas. While Germany was and remained the main threat to Britain (and in consequence to the Commonwealth as a whole) and remained her prime preoccupation, the entry of Italy into the war in June 1940 and still more of Japan in December 1941 transformed the scene for the Dominions. Italy's declaration brought the war to the soil of Africa and posed a direct threat to the Union. Henceforth, though Hertzog still counted on the defeat of Britain, South Africans saw the threat to their own country and could take pride in helping to expel the enemy from the Continent. Japan's aggression, particularly in the early months when it was so spectacularly successful, was of moment for the whole Commonwealth. It placed a strain on Britain which, with her other commitments, she was unable to withstand. The threat to all British territories in the Far East, to India and Ceylon and also to Australia was close and direct.

Dominion Attitudes

Throughout the English-speaking parts of the Commonwealth, there was virtually unanimous popular demand for the prosecution of the war with the utmost vigour. In Canada there was an acute problem in domestic politics not in opposition to the war itself, but with regard to the way in which it should be conducted: partly because of the history of the First World War, Quebec and the French-speaking people generally were bitterly opposed to conscription. Many English-speaking Canadians on the other hand felt that the whole population should make an all-out effort and the Conservative Party (in opposition throughout the war) accused the Government of feebleness. The conscription issue which had hovered sombrely over the scene for so long flared into a crisis with the heavy Canadian casualties in Europe in the last year of the war. In South Africa, the divisions went deeper and were more clear-cut; the Nationalist party were opposed to the war in principle and for long continued to prophesy a German victory. In Australia and New Zealand there was no doubt about the urgency of fighting and defeating the enemy with the utmost despatch; the problems that arose with Australia were mainly over the higher direction of the war and the settlement of priorities after the entry of Japan into the war.

Personalities were important in wartime cooperation with the Dominions and it is striking that, sometimes after an early change, the P.M.s of Britain and of the Dominions remained in power for most of the war; there were also few changes in the High Commissioners in all capitals. This continuity made all the more significant the personal factor in the conduct of Commonwealth relations.

The dominant personal influence was that of Churchill. He knew many of the peoples and countries of the Commonwealth intimately and had done so throughout his long life (though he did not know Australia or New Zealand at first hand). He had seen service in India, had been to Africa as soldier, correspondent and politician, his frequent visits to North America had made him familiar with Canada. His first political post had been as Parly US at the C.O. in 1906–8 and in 1921–2 he had been S. of S. for the Colonies (or 'S. of S. for the Dominions and Colonies' as, with characteristic disregard for orthodoxy, he described the Office); he had been closely associated with the Irish Settlement in 1922 and in the 1930s had fought a long campaign against the Government's policy towards India. At the same time, despite the length of his experience and the depth of his knowledge, he harboured quaint notions about the Commonwealth. His attitude was a romantic one and his mind harked back to the Empire at its apogee as he knew it in early manhood; he took pride in the continuing Commonwealth, but sometimes treated it with more rhetoric than realism. It was characteristic for example that he sought to popularize the phrase 'Commonwealth and Empire' (for which there was no official support), that he had opposed the Statute of Westminster and resisted the constitutional advances in India and that he kicked against any concessions to Southern Ireland.

So long as events marched according to Churchill's own ideas, all was well. Both by conviction – because in war whoever is set in authority must be in command – and also frankly by temperament, Churchill was determined to have things his own way. While he paid generous and warm-hearted tribute to the Dominions in principle, in practice his response to the accepted canons of the Commonwealth fell short of total observance in such matters as equality of status with the UK, freedom to make decisions in the light of the circumstances affecting the Dominion concerned, the right to receive all the information available and to be able to influence decisions before they were taken in London. Churchill was resolved never to tie his own hands by committing himself to a procedure about consultation which might prejudice a rapid decision. He saw his role as that of the guardian of the Commonwealth as a whole and was determined not to put strategic policy into commission. This was at the root of the trouble with Australia over their demand for representation in the War Cabinet. Churchill's attitude to the Commonwealth was also a highly personal one, based largely on his relationship with the individual P.M.s. Smuts and King he had known all his political life, but the P.M.s from Australia and New Zealand were strangers until he met them during the war. His relations with the Union Government were the least complicated. South Africa was a country that Churchill knew, understood and loved; Smuts had been an opponent in the Boer War, but a friend ever since and a colleague in the British Government during the First World War. Like Churchill, Smuts was a soldier-statesman (and also a philosopher); Churchill admired his energy, courage and the keenness of his mind; he placed a high value on his judgement and confided in him completely. Churchill was positively anxious to exchange his thoughts with Smuts and did so more than with anyone else outside Britain except perhaps Roosevelt. They were in fact comrades-in-arms and no cloud marred their warm-hearted friendship. With New Zealand too, the relationship was a straightforward one, partly because of New Zealand's innate 'loyalty' and readiness to act on the advice of the Mother Country, partly because of the sheer decency of Fraser, whom Churchill admired for his solid support, his forthright honesty and his steadfastness. It was remarkable that after the Japanese aggression, New Zealand showed none of the panic evident in Australia.*

Towards Canada there was some ambivalence, partly perhaps because of the country's position in the world, partly because of Mackenzie King's strange personality. No longer dependent on Britain for defence, Canada nevertheless whole-heartedly took the initiative in waging war, whilst her powerful neighbour remained neutral for more than two years. Mackenzie King's great service was that he led a united nation into war and, in spite of a dangerous moment in 1944, kept it united throughout the war years. This was a remarkable achievement for which he was not always given the credit he deserved. He was also in many ways, the architect of the modern Commonwealth. He was strangely sentimental and had an emotional attachment to the British monarchy and to the traditions of British life. There was another remarkable facet to King's behaviour – he accepted Churchill's great gifts of wartime leadership, he recognized that here was the organizer of victory and, unless a matter of vital concern to Canada arose, he was content to follow Churchill's lead without quibble or complaint. In this his attitude was one of self-effacement, not unlike that of Attlee. Churchill recognized this and, according to King, said to him, 'You have been so fine about letting England lead, not making it difficult for us by insisting on several having direction.'[4] But King had another side – he was pedantic, prosaic, cautious and suspicious. Though he could at times reveal an old-world courtesy, he had little charm and no magnetism. His whole political life had been devoted to fighting 'Imperialism' and he deeply resented any

* In a note on the situation in New Zealand sent on 20 December 1941 Batterbee reported: 'Though there was never any trace of panic, it would, I think, be true to say that the events at Pearl Harbor and off the coast of Malaya caused the man in the street here for the first time to feel the war in the pit of his stomach ... members of the Government and of the War Cabinet ... take a very grave view of the present situation, and indeed one or two have shown symptoms of extreme nervousness as to the dangers ahead ... The Prime Minister himself has adopted the robust sensible attitude which was to be expected of him.'[3]

attempt by the British to continue treating Canada as a Colony. His diaries reveal that he frequently regarded Churchill as a dangerous Imperialist and was often suspicious of his motives. All these factors made the relations between him and Churchill invariably correct but seldom intimate. There was an element of reserve on both sides – King, jealous, timid and anxious not to be committed to anything with possibly dangerous implications; Churchill, despite his admiration for what King had achieved, nevertheless finding him a rather fussy old woman and a bore.*

Australia proved the most difficult partner and caused the greatest strain. Indeed, as Canada (with support from South Africa and the Irish) had set the pace for the Commonwealth convoy in the inter-war years and as first the Asian and then the African Commonwealth members dominated the scene in the decades that followed, so Australia made the running during wartime. Australian anxieties were peculiar to Australia; but they were very real. The annihilation of the US Pacific Fleet overnight and of the British capital ships in the Far East gave Japan supremacy in the Pacific. Singapore – Australia's bastion which had been regarded as impregnable – fell without effective resistance, with the loss of an entire Australian Division. Australia herself appeared to be wide open to attack; the Japanese raided Darwin from the air and threatened other parts with submarines. At this moment, Australia's trained divisions were overseas, her naval forces were divided in several areas, she was denuded of aircraft and had no fighters. Her long coastlines were indefensible. The only British reinforcements had either been lost in Singapore or were about to be chased from Burma.

In the first shock of facing this new peril, there was for a time in Australia a mood of bitterness and anger, fed by fear and a feeling of having been 'let down' by the Mother Country. This would pass, but never again would Australia allow herself to be so dependent on Britain or show as previously, implicit confidence in her judgement.† There were other reasons which lent an edge to the Australian distrust. The very closeness of the relationship itself heightened the emotion; Australia had felt herself to be one with

---

* There was, however, a lighter side. Mackenzie King describes how after dinner at Chequers one evening Churchill turned on the radio and performed a sort of dance. He turned to King and the two of them 'took each other by the arm and performed a dance together. All present were almost in hysterics with laughter.'[5]

This must have taken Mackenzie King by surprise for he was staid and old-fashioned in manner. He was, for example, the only man I have ever heard use the word 'Pshaw' and pronounce it as spelt.

† Sir Alan Watt who was in the Australian Government Service at the time and therefore a close observer of the scene wrote subsequently: [The quick succession of Japanese victories] 'resulted not only in serious conflicts of interest between Great Britain and Australia but also public revelation of acrimonious exchanges of telegrams ... Under the emotional strains of war, honest differences of judgement and of opinion became tinged with doubts as to courage and good faith. It is open to argument that the scars left by these disputes never healed completely, that from this period onwards throughout the war years, and even as late in the post-war period as Britain's application to join the Common Market, British-Australian relations never recovered fully their old degree of intimacy.'[6]

Britain and had relied on her. The constant theme of all Australian Governments since the beginning of the century had been the need for Australia to share in all the information available to the Imperial Government and to have the opportunity of influencing decisions before they were taken. This had been denied to her and she had not always received full information. The conduct of the war seemed to bear out the Australian contention. Apart from the broken assurances over Singapore, the campaigns in Greece and Crete ended in disaster involving heavy casualties among the Australian and New Zealand forces. The Army Commanders of both the forces had serious misgivings (though they did not press them) and there is no reason to question the verdict of the Australian Official History which forthrightly declared that though the question of the employment of troops was referred to Australia, there was no consultation on major questions, the policy towards Greece and the conduct of the war in S.E. Europe being decided wholly in London.[7] Menzies had been P.M. on the outbreak of war. He was not a blind admirer of Churchill in the beginning; but on his visit in 1941 he learned to know and respect Churchill and the latter, in spite of the differences between them, held him in high regard. But when the crisis in Anglo-Australian relations arose, a new Prime Minister was in office. In October 1941 the Labour Party came to power under the leadership of John Curtin. His early encounters with the British were unfortunate and there was much in his situation that did not commend itself to Churchill. He came from an Irish Catholic family; he had been a pacifist in the First World War and, between the wars, had advocated a policy of Australia minding her own business. His political position was weak – his party had been out of power for ten years and he depended on a precarious majority of two. The Labour Party refused to contemplate a coalition government or, at the outset, general conscription. Churchill was irked by these attitudes which he regarded as 'partisan decisions [which] did less than justice to the spirit of the Australian nation'[8] and he did not disguise his views in his personal messages to Curtin. In turn, Curtin did not mince his words. In a newspaper article, he made it clear that 'without any inhibitions of any kind ... Australia looks to America free of any pangs as to our traditional links with the UK'.[9] It does not appear that this was a planned or deliberate announcement of a switch in loyalties, but it caused consternation and a good deal of anger in Britain. Churchill was furious and even 'weighed painfully in [his] mind the idea of making a broadcast direct to the Australian people'.[10] The nadir was reached when in January 1942 Curtin learnt (not by British design) that the Defence Committee in London had been considering the evacuation of Malaya and Singapore. Inevitably the Australian Government were alarmed: Curtin telegraphed at once to Churchill: 'After all the assurances we have been given, the evacuation of Singapore would be regarded here and elsewhere as an inexcusable betrayal.'[11] Churchill commented: 'The expression "inexcusable betrayal" was not in accordance with the truth or with military facts. A frightful disaster was approaching. Could we avoid it?'[12]

Despite the bitter tone of some of the Australian messages, Churchill did understand Curtin's difficulties and himself admitted that 'the Australian Government had little reason to feel confidence at this time in British direction of the war'.[13] He sought to establish a closer relationship with Curtin and devised special code words for personal messages between them, his own beginning WINCH and those of the Australian P.M. JOCU. Later on when things were easier and Curtin came over to England, Churchill felt that he got to know him well and recorded that there was 'general liking for this eminent and striking Australian personality'.[14] In Menzies' phrase, he showed a clear patriotism 'in the crunch' and developed a capacity for inspiring confidence.[15] In the manner of Truman (who had just become President when Curtin died), he rose to unsuspected heights when the occasion demanded.

While the different parts of the Commonwealth had different problems and different anxieties – and some of these at times led to fierce controversy – nevertheless there were many factors encouraging a sense of unity and ease of cooperation. Among the more intangible was loyalty to the Crown, the shared language and the common outlook. Although they fought in all corners of the earth, all felt themselves to be fighting the same war for the same cause. Moreover there was the memory for most of victory together in an earlier war against the forces of aggression. There were also severely practical reasons which facilitated cooperation – a similar system of military organization, co-ordination in training, standardization of weapons and equipment. There was a common system which all understood. This made it easier to work out arrangements for command in the field – the most eloquent example being the Army which fought in North Africa from 1940 to 1943 and comprised Australian, New Zealand, South African and Indian as well as British divisions and operated as a single, effective fighting unit.

There was a special matter in which the Dominions exerted a powerful if incalculable influence. All looked upon the USA as a friend and knew that, if they could survive by their own efforts, they could win victory only with the massive support of America. The Dominions played their own part in ensuring this. It may be doubted whether the President would have been so forthcoming in 1940 if Britain had merely been an off-shore island on her own. But she did not stand alone and Roosevelt by his actions, particularly in defence arrangements with Canada and Australia, showed that he was impressed by the strength of the whole Commonwealth. The Dominions undoubtedly played a part in adding to the credibility of Britain's ability to resist. The Dominions also added to Britain's confidence in herself – and in a very tangible way. After Dunkirk, the British Army had virtually to be re-formed, re-trained and re-equipped. The only effective barrier of fighting formations in readiness were Dominion troops, particularly the Canadian Divisions with their armour. The Dominions brought not only material aid; the moral value of their support was incalculable. The knowledge that Britain could count on unstinted reinforcements of strength from overseas was a potent encouragement to endure.

CHAPTER 2

The Dominions Office in Wartime

The contribution which the Dominions made to the war effort was significant in itself and was well known to the British public. This helped to enhance the reputation of the D.O., though at the same time – since relations with the Dominions were but part of the conduct of the war as a whole – there were limitations on the role which the Office could play.

In wartime there was little scope for the niceties and delays of diplomacy; in a sense policy became less complex (though not less difficult) and could not afford the luxury of prolonged argument; there were fewer options open since everything had to be subordinated to the supreme purpose of winning the war. There took place in the government machine a degree of centralization that would not have been acceptable in normal conditions. Even more strikingly, Churchill by the quality of his leadership established a personal ascendency unequalled before, even in wartime. His direction of the war effort ensured his control in all spheres and his assertion of authority was nowhere more conspicuous than in relation to the Dominions. He was in personal contact with all Dominion P.M.s and other war leaders and reported direct to them on the conduct of the war. He himself handled the question of Dominion representation in the various organs for the higher direction of the war. He constantly sought to take the initiative with Ireland over the bases in Southern Ireland. He appointed former Ministers to be British High Commissioners in the Dominions. The D.O. was intimately concerned in the major issues of the war and was closer to the centre of things than it ever had been in peacetime; all messages to Dominion Governments including all those from the P.M. continued to be sent through the D.O. channels of communication. All this gave a sense of reality and relevance to the work. Nevertheless the scope for initiative on the part of any Secretary of State was limited and the D.O. did not regularly play a major part in taking the vital decisions.

The Secretary of State

This position was reflected in the status accorded to the Dominions Secretary.

Except for the short period that Attlee was at the D.O., the Dominions Secretary was not a member of the inner War Cabinet, though he was normally invited to be present when matters affecting the Dominions were under discussion. The Dominions Secretary, along with other Ministers not in the War Cabinet such as the Leader of the House of Lords, was regarded as a 'constant attender' and summoned to a full Cabinet meeting, normally once a week. Under ordinary conditions this might have operated satis-factorily, but in fact all the Dominions Secretaries chafed under it: Eden because he was used to being a full member of the Cabinet, Cranborne because he felt that he was not kept fully in the picture and, if Caldecote did not himself protest, others did on his behalf. In war conditions, many decisions needed to be taken urgently and were frequently taken in the Defence Committee or in a restricted War Cabinet meeting; they had often already been acted upon before they could be reported to the full Cabinet. Cranborne raised the matter soon after his appointment; he accepted the position with good grace but, in doing so, made the point to the P.M.[1] that he found that 'what the Dominions value most is the sense that they are taken into the full confidence of H.M.G.', inferring that this could not be achieved unless the Dominions Secretary knew what was going on (Caldecote had in fact not known about Dakar).

The matter was neatly put right in February 1942 when Churchill, with one stone involving several Cabinet changes, skilfully contrived to kill more than two birds. After returning from being Ambassador in Moscow, Cripps was brought into the Cabinet to lead the House of Commons. To make way for him, Attlee gave up his post as Lord Privy Seal and became Dominions Secretary and also Deputy P.M. The title 'Deputy Prime Minister' was not known in the British constitution and was an innovation by Churchill. He explained that no constitutional change was involved, that the change was one in form rather than fact and that a special reason for appointing Attlee to the D.O. was that many had pressed that the post should be held by a member of the War Cabinet.[2] Cranborne took over the Colonial Office and also became Leader of the House of Lords. All three were thus simultaneously promoted.

Though the roll of Secretaries of State contained the names of two future P.M.s and both Eden and Attlee exerted a strong influence, this was due to their established reputation and to their qualities rather than to the Office they temporarily held. Eden had become the symbol of resistance to aggression and was closely linked to Churchill; Attlee was the Leader of the Labour Party in the Coalition. Such distinguished men reflected prestige on the Office, but their reputation was made elsewhere.

Throughout the war, only two Secretaries of State held the office for any substantial length of time – Cranborne and Attlee. Eden was brought back into the Government on the outbreak of war, but stayed in the D.O. for only eight months, being moved to the War Office when Churchill formed his new Government. He presided therefore during the unsatisfactory 'phoney war period'. It was particularly frustrating for Eden who found himself serving again for patriotic reasons in a Government from which he had thought it right to resign; he chafed at not being included as a full Member of the War Cabinet and at working in what he regarded, after he had been so long in the Foreign Office, as the lesser Department of the D.O.; above all his restless energy could not be tamed to endure the futile inactivity of this strange period. He gave an impression of superficiality with no profound interest in the problems of the Commonwealth. In his auto-biography he himself wrote:[3] 'While I liked the idea of working with the Dominions I could feel no enthusiasm for the general arrangement of the Government, nor for my own somewhat anomalous position in the Cabinet. If it had not been for the emergency of war, nothing would have induced me to return. The next few months were for me uneasy because, though I was a spectator of most War Cabinet proceedings, I had no real part in them.' Eden excelled in the D.O. on any occasions when he could bring his diplomatic skill and experience to bear. He inaugurated the practice of daily wartime meetings with the Dominion High Commissioners (though of course there had for long been occasional meetings), and the High Commissioners greatly appreciated having in the chair one who kept them in the picture in so informed a way and with such a sense of style.

He was succeeded by Viscount Caldecote, who as Sir Thomas Inskip had been Dominions Secretary for some six months up to the outbreak of war. On this second occasion his term was equally for barely six months. He formed a marked contrast with Eden, being high-minded, conscientious, painstaking, and indifferent to the opinions of others. But he had none of Eden's brilliance, political flair or broad sweep. Caldecote had his limitations. To some he could appear aloof if not pedantic and it was unfortunate that he was never able to gain the confidence of the High Commissioners.* But he was a man of transparent integrity and considerable moral courage. He served the Office well; he knew how to make the best use of the permanent staff and was respected by them. And when satisfied that he was right, he was prepared to take responsibility, refusing to be overborne by the P.M.'s whims.

Cranborne succeeded Caldecote for a short time but returned again for a longer term and Attlee became Dominions Secretary for a year (1942–3) between these two periods. In spite of the future that lay ahead for him, Attlee made less impact on the Office than might have been expected. He

---

* When he informed the High Commissioners of his departure in order to become Lord Chief Justice, Jordan with no pause for reflection retorted: 'I hope there'll be no moaning at the Bar.'

was primarily concerned with the prosecution of the war on all fronts and, in the overall scene, the Dominions played an important but subsidiary role; in any case questions affecting the home front inevitably loomed large in the eyes of the Leader of the Labour Party. Moreover he undertook while he was at the D.O. two major assignments – the first at the P.M.'s request to conduct a one-man enquiry into the problems of tank production; the second as Chairman of a Cabinet Committee on India, which resulted in the despatch of the Cripps Mission to India in 1942. There was a further reason – Attlee recognized, with his simple modesty and loyalty, that Churchill was the indispensable war leader who deserved whole-hearted support from his colleagues unless the reasons to the contrary were over-riding. In any case he did not relish an argument with Churchill and, by temperament, was always disposed to defer to him. Attlee's performance at the D.O. was affected also by certain personal characteristics. He showed an excessive diffidence, as if some inner restraint inhibited him from being forthcoming with other people. It was not merely modesty, for he had complete self-respect and was not lacking in courage. And beneath the shy exterior was a man of simple virtue, of humility and humanity, with a strong social conscience and a dedicated sense of public service. Nevertheless some demon within him prevented him, in spite of himself, from any expansion of his personality, though occasionally when relaxed – and particularly after a glass of sherry – he produced flashes of wit. His manner had an inhibiting effect on his relations with staff in the Office: he never really appeared at ease and was not close with any. Indeed his contacts in the Office – as with his colleagues – were kept to a minimum; he saw only the senior members of the staff with any frequency and, when discussion took place, he preferred it to be brief, business-like and preferably tête-à-tête; seldom did he summon a general meeting. In any case details did not interest him and he showed little inquisitiveness about the normal running of the Office. By contrast, he was far more at home in humbler walks of life and appeared at his best, for example, with loggers from Newfoundland at a lumber camp.

Even allowing for the laconic understatement of Attlee's style, his reference to the D.O. in his autobiography is hardly enthusiastic: 'The D.O. is more akin to the F.O. than to other Departments, and I had plenty of time for my other duties. There was, however, much to be done in keeping in close touch with the other countries of the Commonwealth.'[4] Attlee's main distinction at the D.O. was perhaps that he was, throughout the war, the only Secretary of State to have a seat in the War Cabinet. This gave him a considerable advantage and greatly helped to make his appointment welcome to the High Commissioners. Nevertheless he found time to leave an indelible mark in one sphere within the area of D.O. responsibilities – Newfoundland. He had opposed the establishment of the Commission Government in New-foundland in 1933 and, characteristically, when he became Dominions

Secretary was not prepared to continue it without satisfying himself by personal enquiry on the spot.*

Cranborne's† tenure of office at the D.O. was distinguished on many counts. In the first place he was in charge for nearly five years in all (1940–2 and 1943–5) and therefore for most of the war years (he was also Commonwealth Secretary in 1952). Secondly he was a man of an unusual range of gifts and accomplishments. Although this was his first appointment as Minister of Cabinet rank, he had already gained a high reputation and in particular had made a remarkable impression by the courage and forthrightness of his speech when, on Eden's resignation in 1938, he had also resigned as Parly US at the F.O. Being the heir to the Cecils gave subtlety to his intelligence, quality to his work and robustness to his character. He had nothing of the bluster of a J. H. Thomas, even less the diffidence of an Attlee. But if there was an implicit assumption of superiority and even a strong sense of pride, there was never arrogance. On the contrary, he had a natural courtesy towards all; he was at ease with himself and in society and had a strong sense of humanity. Born to a high position when his grandfather was P.M., he had little obvious ambition for personal advantage, though always a strong sense of public service. Withal he had a lively and amusing mind, with a keen sense of humour. These qualities fitted him admirably for his post in the D.O. and made him successful in his relations with the High Commissioners; he also showed the right touch in discussions with members of his staff – always willing to listen, but equally always ready to assert his view strongly where he differed.

At the D.O., Cranborne was more conscious than his predecessors had been of the restraints imposed by the P.M. on the functioning of the Office and he was less disposed to submit to them. Indeed, more than most Ministers, Cranborne was prepared to stand up to Churchill for what he thought was right. This does not mean that there was a running battle between the P.M. and his Dominions Secretary. On the contrary; each had a high regard for the other (and Churchill's respect for Cranborne was no

---

* Geoffrey Shakespeare, who was Parly US in the D.O. during the war and just before Attlee's term, has recorded his impressions in a way which confirm Attlee's undramatic version. The D.O., he said '... was, in wartime, largely a post office passing on the information of our war effort to the Dominion Governments and receiving from them their views on policy and how the Dominion forces could best cooperate. Although there was little Parliamentary work, it was a fascinating position to hold in wartime, because it brought me in close touch with the conduct of military operations. We held, for example, a daily meeting with the Dominion High Commissioners, and discussed every aspect of the war and kept their Governments in the closest touch. As I was not fully occupied ... I reviewed arrangements in reception areas for the billetting of evacuated mothers and children.'[5]

† As the son of the Marquess of Salisbury, he enjoyed the courtesy title of Viscount Cranborne until he succeeded his father in 1947. He continued to use this title when in 1942 (in order to increase the number of peers in the Government) he was created Baron Cecil (though this title was never used except for formal purposes). 'Cranborne' was therefore used both when he was in the Commons and in 1942–7 when he was in the Lords; thereafter he was known as Salisbury.

doubt increased by the evidence that he was no yes-man). There was here an inherent clash in responsibilities which was well expressed in a minute by Bridges (Secretary to the Cabinet) in 1943:

> I think it would be difficult to segregate any set of questions to be handled by the P.M. to the exclusion of the Dominions Office, without the risk of either i) reducing the D.O. to a post office which can't touch policy matters at all; or ii) having two ministers responsible for policy in the same field. I should expect a solution to be found in recognition of the fact that, in Dominion Affairs as in Foreign Affairs, the degree of supervision exercised by the Prime Minister must, in the nature of the case, be closer than the supervision exercised over other Departments, and that the Secretary of State in charge of each of these two departments, while his responsibilities are not impaired, would be expected to keep in the closest touch with the Prime Minister in the formulation of policy on important issues.[6]

There were from time to time genuine differences between the P.M. and the Dominions Secretary and on such occasions Cranborne did not flinch from expressing and, if necessary, fighting for his view. An attractive example of Cranborne's style with Churchill was shown in minutes about the attitude of the New Zealand Government towards Poland in 1945. Fraser had sent a telegram which had annoyed Churchill who wanted to send a stiff reply. Cranborne minuted to him: 'But is it worth while giving him such a very sharp retort? It will wound him, and he will come to the conclusion that when he offers his comments in perfect good faith, he only gets a slap in the face.'[7]

On the following day, in response to Churchill's demurrer, he added an argument that was likely to appeal: 'we have heard this morning that Mrs. Fraser, to whom he is deeply devoted, is mortally ill. You will therefore, I am sure, wish to deal gently with him.'[8]

Senior Staff

The war marked a distinct change in the character of the Office – not only in the aims and attitudes of those in control, but still more perhaps in the sort of people they were. Some of these changes were due to war exigencies which demanded the speedy conduct of business and encouraged the emergence of men who could adjust to the new pace. But partly the change was fortuitous: it so happened that the beginning of the war coincided with the departure of the 'old guard', the three senior members all going overseas as High Commissioners, Whiskard to Australia (in 1936), Batterbee to New Zealand (in 1939) and Harding to South Africa (in 1940). The Office also began for the first time to derive benefit from those who had returned from service overseas and who took up key positions at home. Machtig was PUS virtually throughout the war period (and remained until 1948). But there was an unhappy period of uncertainty at the start. For reasons that took account more of the C.O. than of the D.O., it had been arranged that Parkinson (PUS, C.O.) should succeed Harding and himself be replaced by Sir George Gater. When war broke out, it was not found possible to release Gater; consequently Parkinson remained at the C.O. and Machtig acted temporarily as PUS. In February 1940 however Gater was released and Parkinson took charge in the D.O., Machtig taking over a new post as DUS. On the formation of Churchill's Government, Herbert Morrison asked for Gater at the Home Office, whereupon Parkinson returned to the C.O.; his term in the D.O. had lasted only from February until May 1940. Parkinson was a man of great erudition, charm and administrative skill. But he was in the D.O. for too short a time ever to come to real grips with its affairs or to make any considerable impact. As he had spent all his official life in the C.O., his appointment was not a very tactful gesture to sensitive Dominion Governments;* it was still more unfortunate in its effect on the staff of the Office generally and notably on Machtig himself. It appeared to imply that the D.O. did not contain a man of sufficient calibre to become permanent head and, though the supersession was short, Machtig was not unnaturally embittered by what he regarded as a signal lack of confidence in himself. The matter was made all the more galling as the salary for the PUS job in the D.O. had been fixed at £2,200 a year, but Parkinson was without question paid at his previous rate of £3,000.

Machtig was a man of many parts and brought to his task some high qualities. He possessed an exceptionally clear mind and expressed himself lucidly: he was a pragmatist and interested in practical results. Above all he was a first-class administrator and knew how to cut his way through to achieve the object desired. All these qualities marked him off very distinctly from the previous tradition; here was no pedant, he was not interested in mere form or in tradition for its own sake; moreover, in the dire demands of war, preconceived theories had of necessity to be jettisoned. He was, too, far more approachable than some of the earlier generation had been; he was essentially human, with no false ideas of his own dignity and was natural in his manner towards junior members of staff. He equally cultivated the knack of making himself agreeable to Ministers. He had many outside interests: his parents had come from Germany, he enjoyed foreign travel and knew the Continent well. He was a keen musician, both in enjoyment and in performance, being a skilled violinist. He was always an enthusiastic and remarkably competent squash player and played well into middle age.

* Pearson in his autobiography (*Mike*, p. 167) refers to a memorandum from the British Government which he amended as it was certain to make the worst possible impression in Ottawa. It had been drafted by a senior official recently transferred from the C.O. to the D.O. 'in a form to which he had no doubt become accustomed in communicating with North Borneo or British Guiana'.

Yet in spite of his many attributes and a manner that could show itself charming to others, he was curiously shy and found it difficult to make contacts of an intimate character.* As a result he failed to establish personal links in those quarters where this was of importance to the Office: first, among his equals in the rest of Whitehall, secondly with Dominion representatives generally and with High Commissioners; thirdly to a large extent with his contemporaries in the Office. The first was perhaps the most serious lack. In peacetime the D.O. had sometimes been an object of mild derision in the rest of Whitehall, but in wartime it had become much more part of the Government machine and had grown in significance. In the D.O.'s own interest it was important to develop an understanding at the top level and establish a close relationship with the permanent heads of the major Departments. Machtig, however, concentrated on his duties inside the Office and seldom left his ivory tower. Even inside the Office he was over eager to assure his own position and showed a streak of jealousy and authoritarianism which prevented him from giving his full confidence or even allowing credit when it was due.

He never visited a Dominion (except Ireland) until after he had retired and it was a handicap to him that he knew nothing of Commonwealth countries at first hand, in contrast to an increasing number of his junior officers. In formulating policy he ran two risks: the first was that his mind was so clear and his whole tone so admirably decisive that there was sometimes a danger of his moving too quickly and of his taking up a fixed position before all the factors had been probed in depth. This danger was all the greater since there was an obstinate streak in Machtig and, once convinced that he was in the right, he was not easily moved. The second risk was that his determination to achieve a practical result could incline him towards the easy solution. His was no striving after the stars and he sought to avoid unnecessary complications; he was not by nature a fighter. This gave him the appearance of being an appeaser, certainly in the many arrangements which had to be made in wartime with neutral 'Eire' and even at times in the conduct of the war with Germany.

In all, Machtig, though no enthusiast for change, reached the top at a time of cataclysmic change; no innovator, his rule yet marked a complete break with the past. In the end he did not prove equal to the transformation of the Office demanded by the new responsibilities for the Asian Commonwealth; but during the war years he steered the Office and successive Secretaries of State sometimes with subtlety, often with wisdom, always with effectiveness. He presided over the Office for nearly ten years during a period of considerable expansion and constant pressure, with all the strains of the war and immediate post-war years. Throughout the war period at least he

---

* It was characteristic of the era perhaps, but also tells something of Machtig, that all his Secretaries of State used his surname in conversation and writing; Addison even addressed him as 'Sir Eric'.

ensured that the machine responded to the challenges made upon it.

Machtig's unfailing support in all matters affecting policy was his Deputy, Stephenson (*see* Chapter 5 of Part I). In many ways he and Machtig complemented each other; each sparked off the other and their joint collaboration invariably produced a better result than would have come from either acting alone. Stephenson was the senior of the generation of men who joined the Office after serving in the First World War and were now reaching the higher ranks. Many of them had now also served their term in posts abroad – Liesching pre-eminently who had served in turn in Canada, South Africa and Australia; Archer and Holmes in Ottawa, Clutterbuck and Price in South Africa, Hankinson in Australia. These in turn were followed by a stream of officers who had done their tour overseas, so that the Office was never again without the ability to call on recent first-hand experience of each Commonwealth country. Perhaps it is not fanciful to suggest that the generation which grew to manhood in the trenches of the First World War was specially qualified to deal with the problems of the Second World War and to cut a straight swathe. They had learned in a hard school and exemplified the virtues of manliness, straightforward dealing and realism. Another generation of those too young to serve in the First War was now gaining experience and the qualities of the two generations blended to give the Office a vigour and an alertness which it had not previously known.

The war also gave new life to one member of the staff – the Ceremonial and Reception Secretary, Rear-Admiral Sir Arthur Bromley. He cannot have been wholly at home dealing with questions of protocol in the stuffy corridors of the Office as he first knew it and the changed atmosphere of the war gave him the feeling of being back on the quarterdeck. He was delighted to be despatched to Greenock to greet the arriving contingents, to conduct the Secretary of State on a visit to a Commonwealth Air Squadron or a Newfoundlanders' logging-camp in Scotland. He was at hand to greet all distinguished visitors and to look after them during their stay. His breezy enthusiasm and his full-blooded manner perhaps gave additional cheer to the many thousands whom he welcomed. From the beginning to the end of the war, his was not the least of the services rendered by the D.O.

Functions and Organization

The main function of the D.O. – to organize cooperation with the Dominions for the prosecution of the war – called for a mass of messages on every variety of topic. At the apex were the messages from the P.M.: if these were personal and reporting the P.M.'s view of a situation, they were frequently drafted by Churchill himself, but many messages despatched in the P.M.'s name were sent on the initiative of the Dominions Secretary and drafted in the D.O. Most messages were sent officially in the name of the Dominions Secretary; these covered important questions of policy requiring the co-operation of Dominion Governments, background reports sent for information and a host of detailed matters calling for reference to Dominion Governments. These detailed matters could include questions as varied as munitions supply, sterling area arrangements, campaign medals or food production. On the international situation the British Government operated an extensive information service for all Dominion Governments; the information was furnished by the F.O. and, in agreement with them, despatched by the D.O. Although by the beginning of the war the Dominions now had their own representatives in Washington, and Canada and Australia had a Minister in Tokyo, they still looked to the British Government for information on foreign affairs generally and were largely dependent on them for appreciations about the enemy countries. One of the innovations at this time was a Daily War telegram (named D.W.) which was sent regularly every day throughout the war; this gave the latest available information on military operations and intelligence.

Contact was also maintained with Dominion Governments in other ways – through the British High Commissioners in the Dominions and Dominion High Commissioners in London. Increasingly, communications of importance from the British Government were sent through the British High Commissioners. The biggest changes in organization took place overseas where the network in the five Dominions (including Eire) was completed by the end of 1939 and all posts shouldered an additional volume of work. At headquarters, there was no major reorganization. Before the war it had been thought likely that air raids might require wholesale dispersal and elaborate plans had been made for key staff to be evacuated to a secret retreat in the country. What would have been the problems – whether all would have arrived safely, whether they would have been able to function effectively and what might have been the social consequences – will fortunately never be known, since in fact no one moved. One effect of the war that was felt immediately was the loss of manpower. Although all Civil Servants were regarded as being in a 'reserved' occupation, some of the younger members were already in the Territorial Reserve and immediately joined the forces; others were called up as in due course the limit was raised to include those of their age. At the same time some members of the staff were seconded for duty in the new wartime Departments. Perhaps it should also be revealed that some promising younger members were – to their own great chagrin – posted overseas and kept abroad so that they were unable to take up military service.

The D.O. became enmeshed in the military machinery of the British war effort and was consequently brought into a close relationship with the Ministry of Defence, the military secretariat of the War Cabinet Offices and the Service Departments. One of the first-fruits of this new relationship was the appointment in May 1940 of a liaison officer with the War Cabinet for the D.O., the I.O. and the C.O. The officer selected for this post was the then Colonel Bishop who had just returned from East Africa with a serious foot injury: no better choice could have been made; he had previously served as Staff Officer to the Inspector-General, African Colonial Forces, Colonial Office; he was already well known to and liked by his colleagues in the D.O. and C.O. He was succeeded in 1942 by (at that time) Major Reid (later Commander of the Ceylon Army and Secretary to the Speaker). In the Dominions, the Service Departments for the first time had their own staffs serving under the direction of the High Commissioner.

In London, on the recommendation of Cranborne, Dominion Governments were in 1942 invited to appoint Service Liaison Officers to keep in touch with the COS organization.[9] Australia, New Zealand and South Africa all took advantage of the offer. Canada did not do so in the first instance; in March 1944, however, when their forces were due to take part in the Normandy landings, to Cranborne's satisfaction they agreed to appoint a Joint Staff Mission in London.[10]

Another change was the creation both at home and overseas of an Information Service. It flowed from the establishment of the Ministry of Information as an important new Department and reflected the current philosophy that effective publicity was an essential weapon of war. There had been propaganda in the First World War, but in the years between the wars most of the bureaucracy in Whitehall would not have thought it practicable or indeed proper for Government Departments to seek to influence public opinion other than through White Papers or Ministerial statements. Before the war the Press Officer in the D.O. was not taken on the permanent establishment, he had no access to confidential papers and was not treated as a regular member of the team. This outlook was brushed away by the war and the D.O. was equipped with a fully staffed new Department to deal with information matters. In the early years, the D.O. itself did not have staff to spare and the senior posts in the new Department were filled from outside the Service with men who had had some previous experience of public relations. The first effective head of the new Department was E. Rawdon Smith whose previous service had been in the public relations branch of London Transport; his businessman's style did not fit easily into a bureaucratic routine and before long he was succeeded by Nicholas Mansergh who proved a capable administrator and also lent distinction to the Office. Throughout the war years R. B. Pugh from the Public Record Office* served as the link-man in the Department and did sterling

* To demonstrate the obtuseness of the D.O., the story was told at the time that Pugh was chosen because the D.O. thought that the initials P.R.O. indicated that he was a Public Relations Officer. It was unfortunately apocryphal.

work in maintaining order throughout what became a growing and sometimes ill-disciplined empire.

From 1941 onwards, UK Information Offices were established under the High Commission in all Dominion capitals, including Dublin, though in the smaller posts a single Officer was appointed as Information Adviser to the High Commissioner. Administrative staff for these new posts were all found from outside the D.O. and indeed came from a wide variety of walks in life; subordinate staff was invariably recruited locally. Some of those who served in the Information posts abroad were men of distinction who made a considerable reputation for themselves in other fields; they included, in Canada, R. M. K. Burge (author of a number of detective stories under the name of Milward Kennedy), and R. H. Marrett (author of *An Eye Witness in Mexico*); in South Africa (after the war), Nicholas Monsarrat (author of *The Cruel Sea* and other books); and in Dublin, John Betjeman (later Poet Laureate).

These developments and other wartime responsibilities led to some increase in the staff at headquarters and the additional post of DUS created for Machtig in 1940 was retained permanently.

CORB

Early in the war, the D.O. became associated with the unexpected activity of sending schoolchildren overseas. The threat of invasion caused many parents to think that their children would be safer overseas and a host of families in the Dominions and in the USA offered hospitality. There was at first little disposition in Government circles to support the idea, but Shakespeare (then Parly US at the D.O.) came to see the need. On the outbreak of war, the Government had already been involved in the evacuation of schoolchildren to the country from London and other cities; and since many children were being sent privately there was pressure for the Government to offer the same chance to those who could not afford to pay. A recommendation by Shakespeare's Committee that the Government should sponsor a scheme was endorsed by the Ministers concerned and approved by the Cabinet.* A Board was set up (with Shakespeare as Chairman) in the

---

* Shakespeare has described the atmosphere at the Cabinet Meeting in June 1940: he had hardly finished his explanation when a message that France had capitulated was delivered to the P.M.; he recorded 'It can readily be imagined how all interest in the evacuation of children was eclipsed by the stark magnitude of the news ... The Cabinet minutes on this occasion recorded the endorsement of the Children's Overseas Reception Scheme. But if I were asked for a frank opinion, I should say that Winston Churchill did not appreciate what had happened ... He was present while I unfolded the plan but only present in the sense that his body was sunk in the P.M.'s chair. His spirit was far away – soaring over the battlefields of France.' (*Let Candles Be Brought In*, p. 245.)

premises of Thomas Cook's with the title of Children's Overseas Reception Board, giving the monosyllabic acronym of CORB.

The Board faced immense difficulties; they were flooded out with applications (nearly a quarter of a million); the war upset all arrangements; there were human problems. Churchill never liked the idea, as he made very clear when invited to send a message: 'I certainly do not propose to send a message by the senior child to Mr. Mackenzie King, or by the junior child either. If I sent any message by anyone, it would be that I entirely deprecate any stampede from this country at the present time.'[11] Above all sinkings in the Atlantic became worse and after some eighty children went down in September the scheme was disbanded.

It is sad that a scheme conceived with such generosity and often calling for heroism in its operation, should have ended in tragedy. It is open to question whether the Government should have sponsored such a scheme; it is in any case clear that it would have been better not to have attempted things in such a hurry and to have operated more modestly. But the overwhelming response took officialdom by surprise. In fact some 3,500 actually went overseas (nearly half to Canada) and in spite of inevitable problems the experiment seems to have been broadly a success as far as the children were concerned, as Shakespeare (by then known as 'Uncle Geoffrey') discovered for himself on a visit to North America in 1941. The scheme also fostered goodwill and, like other wartime manifestations, illustrated the strength of personal links in the English-speaking world.

Office Atmosphere

Though the work was performed with greater expedition, the volume had increased so substantially that there was constant pressure on the staff. In common with the rest of the Civil Service, holidays in the D.O. were cut to two weeks from the munificent pre-war allowance of six. Hours became much longer and work started as early as 9 a.m. instead of the lordly 10 a.m. or even in some cases 11 a.m. of the leisurely pre-war days. The working day also lasted much longer. Indeed in a sense the work never stopped and the Office always had to be ready to deal with an incoming message of urgency or to despatch an important telegram from No. 10 in the early hours of the morning. It was a great convenience on such occasions that the Resident Clerk was able to consult a senior member of the staff, many of whom slept at the Office for Home Guard or ARP duties. Many officers worked extremely long hours and one even made a practice of working through the night on a 24-hour shift; his colleagues working a more normal shift, conscience-stricken at first, soon perceived that their output exceeded his.

The D.O. made one break with tradition in wartime. It employed women on administrative duties for the first time.* Without exception they were all popular with their colleagues (though only one married a member of the staff) and commendably competent, some of them outstandingly so. All appointments in wartime were temporary, but nearly all those women who wished to stay on were successful in being appointed to the permanent establishment after the war. Two wry comments may be offered on the employment of women in the Service. In the years before the war, the Dominions Secretary regularly received women's delegations urging the appointment of women to the staff. Until 1938 he was always advised to take the line, in common with the C.O. and also the F.O., that this was unthinkable since women could not be posted overseas. This argument may have had some validity in the case of certain posts in the other Services but it could not reasonably be claimed that women could not serve in the capitals of the white Dominions. The second comment is that after the citadel was stormed and the doors of the Foreign Service as well as the Commonwealth Service were opened to women the number of applications from women after the first flush never amounted to more than a trickle.

It has become part of the national folklore that the Blitz helped to make the people of Britain more friendly towards each other. Certainly it had this effect on the D.O. which was transformed, after normal working hours, into something resembling a Butlin's Camp. The whole of the basement was turned into living (and sleeping) quarters for those required to stay late either for Office work (Telegraph Section, etc.) or for Home Guard, ARP or other duties. There were dormitories, recreation rooms and a canteen where most of those staying the night ate in common. Facing a common danger, there was a sense of camaraderie, but no hysteria. Differences in rank, class, sex were forgotten and the staff ate, played, gossiped and joked together – Under Secretary and Typist, Messenger and Chief Clerk.† The games included table-tennis, bridge, a sing-song and, most popular of all, poker in the so-called gambling 'Hell'. The bombs may have been falling outside (and some went about their duties on this account) but for the rest, inside and down below, there was an atmosphere of friendliness and warmth.

---

* Before the war there was a bar to the employment of women in the administrative staff of the Foreign Service and also of the C.O. and D.O. because of the requirement to serve abroad. In 1938 however it was decided to remove the restriction in the case of the C.O. and D.O. 'as experimental in order that the matter may be reviewed, after a few years, in the light of experience'.[12] In fact no women were appointed before the war and no appointments to the permanent establishment could be made during the war.

† A very tough Messenger (formerly in the Navy) was on one occasion giving instructions for connecting a hose in fire drill to a senior and somewhat squeamish Under Secretary. To his astonishment, and the amusement of the spectators, he was ordered: 'Grab the male end firmly in your right hand, shove it into the female and ram him home'!!

Relations with Other Departments

The war also changed the pattern of the contacts which the Office had in Whitehall. In particular, the D.O. was more continuously in touch with the Prime Minister's Office than at any previous or indeed subsequent period. This was a consequence of the concentration of power in Churchill's hands. Relations with the staff at No. 10 were invariably close and cooperative and were helped by the fact that a succession of the P.M.'s Private Secretaries had served in the D.O./C.O., John Martin, Leslie Rowan and David Pitblado (all of whom rose to distinction). Nevertheless it was always difficult even with such well-disposed friends to secure any alteration in the *ipsissima verba* of the Master.

Another striking change showed itself in the development of the relationship with the Colonial Office. After being a small part of a greater whole for so long and willingly looking to the stronger partner for support, the D.O. suddenly grew up. It itself developed from a Protected State to one claiming the right of self-government. There were many reasons for this. A new generation was growing up in each Department, unconscious of the shared tradition; the D.O. had slowly developed its own identity and, though in theory the establishment remained a joint one, in practice there was little interchange of staff at any senior level. The war accelerated this change. The exigency of war itself demanded some measure of divorce – for example, the D.O. found it essential to establish its own separate cypher section; the war also altered the relative status of the two Departments, the D.O. becoming more and the C.O. less important than before; above all it demonstrated that their work was different.

The extent to which the two Departments were drifting apart was illustrated by some discussions which took place in 1943. Paul Emrys-Evans (Parly US at the D.O.) was concerned that in the last twenty-five years the Dominions, in putting all the emphasis on independence, had lost touch with the Colonial Empire; he urged that the British Government should take the lead in developing an Imperial policy in which the Dominions could be more closely associated with Colonial administration.[13] His ideas were received with no great enthusiasm by officials either in the D.O. or the C.O. Machtig commented that interest in the Colonies by the Dominions (particularly Australia and South Africa) was already sufficiently embarrassing;[14] Attlee was non-committal.[15] Eventually a meeting was held with a somewhat reluctant C.O., with Oliver Stanley at their head. The C.O. ruled out any possibility of associating Dominion Governments with the administration of a particular territory and the meeting contented itself with considering certain practical steps for increasing contacts,[16] but there was no effective follow-up.

In the same year Smuts, with rather different motives, drew attention to the dual system under which 'in the Commonwealth we follow to the limit the principle of decentralization' but not in the Colonial Empire[17] and he warned that to have two groups developed on different lines raised grave questions for the future. It did indeed; a solution would ultimately be found and the division between the two parts ended by extending the principle of decentralization into what later was termed the transformation of Empire into Commonwealth.

In some ways this growing apart from the C.O. gave the Office a sense of closer affinity with the F.O.; certainly there was a growing acceptance that their functions were similar (and this tended to be truer in war conditions when both Departments put aside some of their particular peacetime activities). Moreover the D.O. began to shed some of its feelings of inferiority towards the F.O. In the first place it was no longer dependent on the F.O. for so large a part of the information relayed to Dominion Governments. Secondly the world of foreign diplomacy had shrunk with most of the nations at war; if the F.O. was responsible for relations with our two major Allies, the D.O. was responsible for relations with the next four.

It is tempting to suggest that a new spirit of harmony prevailed between the F.O. and the D.O. in the years of war deriving from their joint devotion to a single cause. Yet Cadogan, who was PUS at the F.O., wrote of Menzies in February 1941 'What irresponsible rubbish these Antipodeans talk' and described a meeting with Dominion representatives in 1945 in the following terms: 'Dominions meeting at No. 10. Being in the chair, I rushed it through before midnight and left it to others to draft report. This is really impossible. These bloody Dominions take up six hours of my working day.'[18]

For their part D.O. officials were ever vigilant to protect the Office against any encroachment by the F.O. Some missions abroad had argued that the D.O. and the F.O. should be amalgamated. In reply the F.O. proposed to take the somewhat patronizing line that the Dominions had the best of both worlds, enjoying a separate Minister *and* the services of the F.O. and were likely to be satisfied with this state of affairs for some time to come. Machtig did not think this was the position at all and commented: 'The fundamental consideration is that the relations between the Dominions and the UK are (and, it is to be hoped, long will be) very different from those between foreign countries and the UK, and that this is necessarily reflected in business with the Dominions being entrusted to a separate Minister and service with special experience and outlook.'[19] The F.O. reply was amended in this sense. Specially close liaison was established with the Ministry of Defence, the Service Departments and the COS Secretariat. Contacts were also important and were developed with the new Departments that mushroomed in wartime – the Ministries of Economic Warfare, War Transport, Supply, Production, Food and Information. Particularly towards the end of the war when questions of post-war planning were to the fore, co-operation with the Treasury and Board of Trade was close. On the other hand, with Departments concerned with domestic affairs only, contacts were minimal. With the I.O., business on economic matters, for example with the Eastern G)up Supply Council or on commodity agreements, was generally conducted at a junior level; on political matters, in spite of the presence of an Indian representative at the War Cabinet, contacts were not close and there was never any question of an Indian representative at the meetings with High Commissioners. Apart from the involvement of Attlee in his personal capacity, the D.O. took little interest in the future of India.

CHAPTER 3

Representation Overseas

The war threw up new challenges for posts overseas. The volume of work increased, its scope was more varied and the importance of the job itself was enhanced. Shortly after the beginning of the war the D.O. was, for the first time, represented in all the Dominion capitals. By the outbreak of war, the posts in Canada, Australia and South Africa could be regarded as well established (though the High Commissioner himself had been in Canberra for barely two years); Batterbee, the first High Commissioner in New Zealand, arrived six months before the war and the first post in Dublin was set up in October 1939.

Beaverbrook and the High Commissioner in Ottawa

In wartime, with the growing role of the Dominions and the need to keep in touch with all Dominion P.M.s it became even more important for the Government at home to have complete confidence in their representatives overseas. Churchill with his practice of personal contact with Dominion leaders was very alive to this and always took a keen interest in appointments. In October 1940, at the behest of Beaverbrook, he demanded the recall of Sir Gerald Campbell the British High Commissioner in Ottawa. Beaverbrook, who was born in Canada and was at that time Churchill's Minister of Aircraft Production, had never been popular in his own country; he was especially unpopular with the ruling Liberal Party and Mackenzie King mistrusted him profoundly. As Minister for Aircraft Production, he was determined to have the maximum number of aircraft for combat purposes and opposed sending any planes to Canada for training; he constantly denigrated the Air Training Scheme. In October a number of stories circulated in senior RCAF circles about disparaging remarks which Beaverbrook had made about the Canadian war effort, including the operation of the Scheme. These remarks were retailed to Canadian Ministers and formed the subject of bitter discussion at a Cabinet meeting. As a result Mackenzie King told Campbell that he was wondering whether to send a personal telegram to Churchill telling him that 'Canada cannot continue her war effort in a loyal spirit if Beaverbrook is allowed to make such malicious and untruthful charges to all and sundry, Americans included.' Campbell thought it his duty to pass this warning on to London; he did so in a personal and confidential message to Machtig, the PUS.[1] Machtig gave the telegram to Caldecote who in turn passed it to Churchill and left a copy with him. The first reaction was not unduly violent. Churchill himself telegraphed to the High Commissioner: 'Your telegram seems to me extravagant in tone and I cannot believe that the passing of hot words to and fro is in any way helpful.' He went on almost apologetically, 'There is repeated friction between the Air Ministry and the MAP which I endeavour to soften as much as I can, always remembering that nothing but the marvellous expansion of supplies which Lord Beaverbrook has produced would have carried us through this crisis which is by no means ended.'[2] He told the High Commissioner that he was sending a message to Mackenzie King; this too contained a strangely ambivalent comment for after saying, 'While I am sure [that] he [Beaverbrook] never said anything like what is wrongly attributed to him,' he continued nevertheless, 'one must understand his point of view.' He added, 'Do not, on any account, my friend, suppose that we do not value the great Empire Training Scheme or that we are not going to push it with our utmost strength,' but concluded, unexpectedly, 'But there is the inevitable conflict between the short-term and the long-term view.'[3]

By the following day Beaverbrook, who had been told by Churchill what had been going on, wrote officially to Cranborne demanding that Campbell should be dismissed; he denied that he had spoken slightingly of the Air Training Scheme and he quoted witnesses to prove his point. He also telegraphed to Mackenzie King, who sent an ingratiating reply which appeared to deny Campbell's account.* Beaverbrook clearly also went to work on Churchill, for the following day the P.M. addressed a stern minute to Cranborne, accepting in effect the Beaverbrook version and accusing Campbell of identifying himself with a story without in any way satisfying himself as

* The Machtig papers contain much documentation on this affair. Campbell had reported many scathing comments by Canadians on Beaverbrook (*see* letters of 8 October 1940 to Capt. Balfour and Sir Henry Tizard). Shuckburgh (then a Secretary on Campbell's staff who had been present at the interview with King) telegraphed to confirm that King had spoken as reported by Campbell (telegram of 22 October). Campbell felt most bitterly about Mackenzie King's duplicity. On 15 October he telegraphed that the storm had been brewing a long time and was bound to break, but it had broken unfortunately for him: 'Yet it is almost worth it since M.K. is revealed through his talk to Beaverbrook at last in his true colours ... I shall be more wary in future but I realize clearly now why my predecessor was glad to leave.' In a letter to Machtig of 28 October he wrote that he had learnt a lesson and that in future when Mackenzie King said he was going to telegraph he would wait for him to send his telegram. He suspected that King was adopting this method of getting his views known without actually committing himself. 'When challenged this enables him to deny and even kiss the hand which he would have bitten and I am then left holding the bag ...'

to its truth, showing heat and prejudice and being disrespectful to a member of the War Cabinet. He concluded: 'In these circumstances you should call for a precise and full explanation from Mr. [*sic*] Campbell. I ought not to leave you in doubt, however, that unless these explanations throw an entirely new light upon his conduct, he should be recalled and removed from his post.'[4]

Cranborne consulted Campbell before replying and was able to give 'the fullest assurance that he [Campbell] has never been actuated by malice against Lord Beaverbrook nor identified himself with any criticism of Lord Beaverbrook in Canada.' Cranborne asserted that there could be no doubt that marked annoyance was in fact developing among Canadian Ministers in a manner prejudicial to our good relations with Canada. The High Commissioner felt it his duty 'as, indeed, I suggest it was' to report fully on this situation. 'This is surely one of the most important duties – indeed an essential duty – of a High Commissioner.'[5]

Churchill was not to be mollified – but did his petulance perhaps betray irritation with Beaverbrook's importunity? Still making heavy weather he asserted that he could not allow a colleague to be attacked like this on wrong grounds and false evidence without injury to the whole structure of government. He complained that he had been caused a lot of trouble and work unnecessarily and ended 'I trust that I may receive from you some assistance in lightening my burden.'[6]

Cranborne was adamant that, though Campbell's language may have been intemperate, his conduct had been correct and that he did not merit dismissal. Although he had himself only been in office a few days, he felt he had a duty and a responsibility towards the Service and he refused to be a party to any injustice. In all this he had the strong support of his official advisers. He went to the length of making clear that he would rather resign, writing to the P.M. that the censure which Campbell had received and a further reprimand which he proposed should be fully adequate to meet the case. 'To do more would, I feel most strongly be out of all proportion to the offence and would make my position as Secretary of State, holding the views I do, an impossible one.'[7] Again Churchill was not to be appeased. 'I do not see how you can expect me to leave the matter here. You brought me into it ... My confidence in the High Commissioner has been seriously affected' – then, a curious volte-face – 'but I have not at any time contemplated his removal from office on account of this incident.'[8]

In the event, Campbell was required to make a further full apology and Churchill insisted that the D.O. send him a formal rebuke.* Campbell was

* Machtig, having consulted Sir Horace Wilson (Head of the Civil Service) telegraphed: 'I am satisfied that, after consulting those who carry responsibility for our Service, that you will be helping a difficult situation by complying with what is asked of you.' Campbell replied that he was only too happy to comply and was most anxious to find a way to help.

humiliated therefore, but not publicly and he was allowed to remain.* He did not remain long; before many months he was appointed Minister in the Embassy in Washington under Halifax to take charge of public relations. It was a task for which his previous experience well qualified him and could hardly be regarded as a demotion; but it was not a fair reward for his services and he never found fulfilment in the new post.

The episode must have provided a totally disproportionate distraction for the P.M. at a time when the Blitz on London was still raging; it reflects no great credit on anyone except on Cranborne. Considering his junior status (he had only just been appointed a Minister of Cabinet rank for the first time) and his inexperience in the D.O. (he had not even met Campbell), he showed remarkable firmness and strength. The matter marks one of the very few occasions when a Dominions Secretary not only crossed swords with a P.M. but succeeded in gaining his point. That this was achieved in wartime with a dynamic P.M., instigated by Beaverbrook, then at the height of his power, is all the more remarkable. Perhaps only a Cecil could have carried the day in this way with a Churchill.

Appointment of Members of Government as High Commissioners

Campbell was succeeded in May 1941 by Malcolm MacDonald, until that time Minister of Health in Churchill's Government. It was the first time that anyone from political life had been appointed High Commissioner in a Dominion capital (though of course, all Dominion Governments had from time to time – and some invariably – been represented by politicians in London). The appointment, following shortly after that of Halifax to Washington, set the pattern for a new style of wartime diplomacy under which Churchill appointed representatives from political life not only to Embassies in foreign countries but also to posts in the Dominions, in the Far East, Middle East and West Africa.

MacDonald's appointment set a precedent in another way too, as Churchill wished to arrange that Members of Parliament should not have to give up their position when undertaking a post overseas in wartime. To achieve this, the House of Commons Disqualification Bill was introduced; it did not meet with universal approval. Several Members voiced objections on constitutional grounds, but criticism of the individuals involved was not absent. Major

---

* Beaverbrook's biographer mentions this incident (without referring to Campbell by name) and concludes that Beaverbrook 'dropped the affair, perhaps because he had lost interest or maybe because the story was not all that far from the truth.' (A. J. P. Taylor, *Beaverbrook*, p. 433). But Beaverbrook does not appear to have lost interest until after it was clear that his demand for dismissal would not prevail.

amendments were moved and Churchill's intervention was called for to make clear (in the middle of a raid) that he would regard the outcome as a vote of confidence; the Bill was passed, but the Government had to yield to the demand for a Select Committee to go into the general question of places of profit under the Crown (on which the law was full of uncertainties and anomalies).[9] The Act operated for one year only; it was last renewed in 1944 when the Attorney-General perfunctorily moved the Second Reading on the assumption that the renewal would again be little more than a formality.[10] However, there was strong dissent from Aneurin Bevan and other left-wing Members of the Labour Party and also from some Conservatives. The objections were on grounds of the virtual disfranchisement of the constituency concerned and also on the alleged risk of corruption by the Government's powers of patronage; personal attacks were also made on MacDonald, Cross and Hoare (Ambassador in Madrid). The debate was continued on the following day when Eden gave a pledge that the Government would review the matter before asking for a further renewal.[11] Owing to the end of hostilities the Act was not further renewed, but in accordance with its provisions MacDonald and his colleagues retained their status as Members of Parliament while serving abroad until the dissolution in 1945.

It is clear that Churchill had, at the time, no high regard for Malcolm MacDonald:* they had been diametrically opposed on some of the issues on which Churchill felt most passionately – appeasement, Palestine and the Irish ports; moreover Malcolm was the son of the man whom he had once described as 'the boneless wonder of our age'. MacDonald in fact performed outstanding service in Canada. He became an experienced and eloquent public speaker throughout the length and breadth of Canada on Britain's war effort and her peace aims; he was obviously one 'set in authority', yet he also displayed a disarming informality: these qualities enabled him to establish the closest and friendliest relations with Ministers and officials alike. Perhaps MacDonald's greatest success owed something too to good fortune as well as to his merits. It so happened that Mackenzie King, on one of his early visits to England, paid a visit to Ramsay MacDonald's home and there saw Malcolm as a child. King was absurdly sentimental and indeed a believer in omens. With the new High Commissioner therefore, the strangely lonely P.M. was disarmed from the start and MacDonald had all the gifts to take advantage of his good chance. One difficulty developed occasionally from the very closeness of this relationship. King felt so at ease and would often express himself very frankly, in a way

* Cadogan's reference to Churchill regarding MacDonald as 'rat-poison' is sometimes quoted. But the full context of his comment was more favourable: 'The P.M. pressed him [Halifax] on Washington and would appoint Anthony in his place ... H. asks me to think of other candidates. There are very few. Mine would be Malcolm M. but I gather P.M. regards him as rat-poison on account of his connexion with Eire ports' (Cadogan, Entry for 18 December 1940, p. 341).

in which he would not have spoken to British Ministers; this was helpful, but on occasion led MacDonald to report Canadian attitudes which in the event were not maintained.

The other political appointments made in wartime were of Sir Ronald Cross to Australia* and Lord Harlech to South Africa, both in 1941. Cross, at the time of his appointment, was Minister of Shipping. He stayed throughout the war years and returned in 1951 to be Governor of Tasmania. Harlech, as Ormsby-Gore, had been Colonial Secretary until he succeeded to the title in 1938. He was succeeded by Baring (Governor of Southern Rhodesia) in 1944.

Whatever may have been Churchill's reasons for making such appointments, men of this eminence in public life elevated the status of the High Commissioner. No longer could he be treated as a mere postman or glorified sales representative. While appointments from outside were accepted in wartime, prospects in the Service would have been affected if the practice had continued in peacetime. Even so it was not welcomed; Batterbee was sarcastic and Whiskard (before Cross's appointment) doubted whether a Ministerial appointment would be wise in Canberra; he thought that a senior UK civil servant carried 'terrific guns' – quite heavy enough for anything likely to be wanted in Australia.[12] One consequence of the appointment of politicians as High Commissioners was the creation of a new post of Deputy High Commissioner (DHC) held by a senior official. The first such post was that of DHC in Ottawa to which Duff, previously Private Secretary to the P.M. and at the time Permanent Secretary, Ministry of Works, was assigned on MacDonald's appointment. It was then explained that this was an exceptional appointment because of the special nature of MacDonald's appointment. But bureaucracy has a congenital distaste for giving up any post; the title was not only retained in Canada, but was soon extended elsewhere and became so much a part of the establishment that, at the time of merger with the F.O. in 1968, there was no post in a Commonwealth country without a Deputy High Commissioner!

It is remarkable that, even with the very close cooperation that was established during the war, Malcolm MacDonald was the only High Commissioner who developed a warm relationship with the P.M. or gave wholehearted support to the war effort of the Dominion to which he was posted. Campbell in Canada was rightly indignant over the pusillanimity of Mackenzie King and was struck by his unpopularity in the country. But he tended to overlook the sentimental, almost mystical streak in that strange man and to underestimate his political problems; he was more conscious of

---

*How the appointment struck a colleague is revealed in the Diaries of Sir Henry Channon [at that time P.P.S. to R. A. Butler] who recorded 'Poor Ronnie Cross is to go to Australia as High Commissioner! Degommé! I told Rab that he would one day be sent to the Falkland Islands and he was annoyed' (p. 302).

that part in King which was, if not hostile to, at least suspicious of Britain. Moreover in his personal dealings with the P.M., Campbell had cause to complain of duplicity and deviousness as the Beaverbrook episode showed. In Australia, Whiskard was scathing about all Australian Ministers including Menzies. Cross on the other hand had already established a friendly relationship with Menzies – but Menzies survived for only six weeks after Cross's arrival. Cross was therefore called upon to deal with Fadden for whom he had no high regard and subsequently with the Labour Government of Curtin. In the aftermath of the disasters in the Far East and the resulting Australian anger against Britain, relations between Labour Ministers and the Tory High Commissioner were frigid and Cross felt acutely that he was being bypassed. In due course he developed a regard for Curtin, but the relationship was never intimate and he regarded Evatt throughout with suspicion and disdain.

In South Africa, no British High Commissioner either in peace or war developed any deep understanding with politicians in the Nationalist Party; but with Smuts as P.M. during the war the position was easier. Even with him however, neither Harding nor Harlech established a warm relationship. It is difficult to judge Harding's performance since he had served for barely a year when he suffered a heart attack and was required by Churchill to give up his post (though he recovered sufficiently to act for the Office as their correspondent at the Cape until the end of the war). He brought great experience and high qualities to bear, but did not have the ability to get on easily with people and his public performances, particularly as a speaker, were not happy. His successor, Harlech, tended to be autocratic and impetuous. In any case Smuts preferred to do business with Price, the deputy, rather than with the High Commissioner. It is significant that the Office in reporting to the D.O. constantly criticized the wartime apathy in South Africa (only exempting the women's patriotic organizations) and the limitations set by the Government on the country's war effort.

In New Zealand, Batterbee (appointed in 1939) threw himself into the job with vigour and enthusiasm and was fully alive to the needs of public relations. But though his rapport with the Government was close, his excitability did not always appeal to the stolid New Zealand temperament and his over-eagerness at times irritated Ministers and officials. He used a revealing phrase after Pearl Harbor when he asked for the visit of a Minister 'to rouse the people and stir them to greater effort', adding that he was doing his best to 'put courage and confidence in everyone from the P.M. downwards'.[13] But for all his exaggeration (indeed perhaps because of it) he was regarded everywhere with affection and he always radiated goodwill. Duff was appointed to succeed him in 1945. Cranborne secured Churchill's approval with the assurance that Duff had 'made himself very acceptable and popular in all quarters in Canada', no doubt disarming him with the comment that 'one does not need a very big gun there and he seems to have just about the right status'.[14] Duff had considerable charm and was at pains to make himself agreeable. At the same time he developed a passion for public speaking, on which he concentrated almost to the exclusion of anything else. Sir William Clark (carrying out an inspection in 1947) commented that Duff had 'gone all crazy on speechmaking'; he felt that 'it had gone to Duff's head and that, though it did a lot of good, it must have taken up a disproportionate amount of his time.'[15]

For junior staff, a posting in normal times to a Dominion was welcome enough. In wartime it was doubly so; it replaced the discipline of Whitehall with the relative freedom of a small mission and added the prospect of travel; it provided security for the family in contrast to the strain in wartime Britain; at the same time it called for much hard work and gave the feeling that one was carrying out and not escaping the obligations of service to the nation. The feeling of contentment was increased still further in those posts where new members were welcomed and made to feel at once part of the team. The creation of an atmosphere in a mission depends on a number of subtle factors, including the personalities of the High Commissioner and his deputy and, just as important, of their wives.* The author recalls that under various chiefs something of a special family atmosphere prevailed in Ottawa, partly because a tradition had been established, partly because with a larger staff the need was greater and partly because the post was fortunate in its successive heads.

Not all fitted in easily; many had twinges of conscience that they were extremely fortunate compared with others in the war. This applied particularly to men within the call-up limits, one of whom sought unavailingly to be in the front line with his friends. There were others too who had proved admirable officers in Whitehall and worked prodigiously, but were not adapted to life overseas, did not mix readily or make friends and hankered to return to 'the' Office. There were curiously two almost identical cases in different posts where conscientiousness in the office had become a vice and the High Commissioner asked that the officer should return home. There were inevitably other misfits from time to time.†

---

* Though it is invidious to mention individuals where so many played their part, the contribution made by Lady Clutterbuck at that time was by all accounts outstanding.
† In *The Siren Years – Undiplomatic Diaries 1937–1945*, Charles Ritchie records for the 23 June 1942 that he had lunch with 'the new Dominions Office appointee to Canada'. He went on: 'He must be as sick of meeting me at lunch as I am certainly sick of meeting him. Mentally and socially he is a permanent pre-last-war subaltern in a not too good line regiment. What a man to send to Ottawa to cope with that little group of bristling professional Canadian nationalists who would welcome him as a heaven-sent confirmation of all they have ever said about the Old School Tie! The anti-British members of the Canadian intelligentsia will never be happy until they have pulled down the Old England of Tradition and can dance on its grave. He is the sort of Englishman who makes one understand why.' Ritchie's judgement was not belied by events, but the appointee was not a member of the D.O. staff, but a wartime recruit to the Information Service.

The Duties of a High Commissioner

The High Commissioner continued to carry out the normal functions of conducting business with the Dominion Government, reporting regularly on developments and representing Britain in the country as a whole. In wartime he was also called upon to produce each week a report on opinion in the Dominion (termed OPDOM) replacing one for the Ministry of Information on press comments (termed MINIM PRECO which Attlee, on joining the D.O., thought meant a very little prayer). For public occasions, the High Commissioner was more in demand than ever and publicity about Britain's war effort was considered an essential task; High Commissioners made frequent visits to all parts of their territory, addressing audiences of every description.

Ottawa

The increase in work is shown clearly in Canada where the High Commissioner became responsible for: (i) Trade Commission; (ii) Ministry of Pensions Representative; (iii) Treasury Representative; (iv) UK Information Office (UKIO); (v) Air Training Mission; (vi) British Army Staff; (vii) Naval Mission; (viii) Food Mission; (ix) Supply Mission; (x) CORB Representative. Of these only the Trade Commission and Ministry of Pensions had existed before the war. In addition, RAF Transport Command had a station in Montreal where there was also a Ministry of War Transport representative. Representatives of the British Security and Intelligence authorities in Washington paid regular visits to Ottawa, and the scientific staff at the Montreal Laboratory (working on atomic energy, at that time known as 'Tube Alloys') also kept in touch with the High Commissioner. There was too a BBC representative in Toronto.

Of this variety of Missions, only the Treasury Representative and the UKIO came under the direct control of the High Commissioner. The Treasury staff consisted for most of the war years of Gordon Munro, a merchant banker, assisted by a junior official from the Treasury. The senior staff of the Information Office came from all walks of life in Britain, the junior staff being recruited locally. Trade promotion work virtually vanished in wartime, but the regional posts were called upon to perform a variety of new functions, in effect as outposts of the High Commission. After the outbreak of war, the Senior Trade Commissioner moved his headquarters from Montreal to Ottawa and became formally a member of the High Commissioner's staff in 1946 when Senior Trade Commissioners were appointed Economic Advisers to the High Commissioner. But for all practical purposes he had acted in this capacity throughout the war.

Most of the other Missions operated autonomously and communicated direct with their parent Departments. But they were required to conform to any policy directions laid down by the High Commissioner and were normally ready to accept advice (indeed they frequently sought it themselves). Moreover they were dependent on the High Commission for the receipt and despatch of all their communications (both by mail and telegram). Much of their work touched on political matters and called for co-ordination. Though the D.O. never formally adopted the 'Head of Chancery' practice of the Foreign Service, any necessary co-ordination was normally performed by the Senior Secretary (i.e. no. 3 on the political staff). The greatest increase was seen in the mounting mass of messages, particularly those to be despatched in cypher. The sheer volume of telegraphy threatened to become unmanageable. It was saved by two developments – first the enrolment of wives of members of the staff who volunteered to do their stint during the day, but were also liable to be called upon in the middle of the night, to deal with urgent messages; secondly and more permanently by the introduction of cypher machines which improved security and enabled the work to be done in a tenth of the tedious time of operating a book cypher.

The closeness of MacDonald's relations with Mackenzie King was well illustrated by the conscription crisis of 1944 and by the Gouzenko affair. The conscription crisis threatened to split the Liberal party and to divide the country. It was Mackenzie King's most agonizing moment, but it was difficult for him to share his thoughts with other Canadians and he turned to MacDonald in whom he confided throughout. When King was in perplexity, it was MacDonald who to his relief offered to ascertain Churchill's view on whether he thought the general strategy required a resort to conscription[16] (Churchill refused to be drawn) and when later MacDonald flew to England, Mackenzie King rejoiced and wrote in his diary, 'He [MacDonald] is a true friend and understands the situation and will be able to get Churchill to understand it.'[17]

The Gouzenko affair also deserves mention since it involved the only occasion on which anyone in the Commonwealth Service was convicted of espionage. In September 1945 Gouzenko, a cypher clerk in the Soviet Embassy, escaped: Mackenzie King at once told MacDonald and later said that information made available by Gouzenko contained a list of persons in Canada working for Soviet intelligence.* Mackenzie King asked MacDonald to inform the British Prime Minister and meanwhile invited him together with his deputy to serve on a small committee to advise on each stage of the handling of this affair; membership of the committee enabled the High Commissioner to report fully and promptly to his Government. The affair

---

* *See* MacDonald, *People and Places*: 182–3 for an account of an extraordinary conversation with the Soviet Ambassador which must have convinced him that MacDonald knew about his all-night search for Gouzenko before he had heard anything of the matter.

provided an apposite example of the close understanding between Canada and Britain in an unfamiliar situation.

The affair was investigated by a Royal Commission, operating at first in secret. Thirteen persons in all were charged, most (but not all) being convicted. Two of those convicted were in the service of the British Government: one was Dr Nunn May. The other was an employee in the British High Commission itself – Miss Willsher, the Assistant Registrar. Kathleen Willsher was a graduate of the LSE and had been recruited in Britain as the senior stenographer when the Office was first opened in 1927. She went back to England on the expiry of her tour when her post was filled by her assistant; however she returned to Canada, pressed for re-employment as a local recruit and accepted the post of second stenographer. Her life was a sadly lonely one and she became a Communist sympathizer; she was vulnerable to Communist pressure and eventually became an agent of the Soviet spy system. There is no evidence that she passed on any written information nor that she passed information to anyone other than a Canadian on the staff of the Bank of Canada, who she knew was a Communist. It is possible that she had no idea that the information she passed on went to the Kremlin. However, she chose to plead guilty and was one of the first to face trial; she was convicted under the Official Secrets Act and sentenced to three years' imprisonment. It was ironic that some of those tried later were acquitted – including the man to whom she had passed the information. On this count the British High Commission unofficially made representations and she was released a few months early.

Towards the end of his term, MacDonald, after consultation with his staff, forwarded views about the future form of British representation in Canada.[18] He emphasized the importance of Canada as a 'middle-sized' nation and the qualities he required in a High Commissioner rivalled those enjoyed by the Archangel Gabriel.* He thought the High Commissioner should serve for five years, other staff normally three. MacDonald considered the advantages and disadvantages of politicians and civil servants and concluded that only in exceptional circumstances should men from outside be chosen. He made various recommendations to strengthen the staff, including the retention of many wartime posts, and he thought that the Trade Commissioner Service should be incorporated as part of an expanded Dominion Service. He hoped that junior staff would be recruited from all Departments in Whitehall to spread the experience and would be encouraged to travel and engage in public

---

* The High Commissioner would have both diplomatic and public relations duties; he would need to carry conviction not only with the Government but with the 'man-in-the-street', in fact with the public as a whole. As a diplomat he would need 'a presentable character, knowledge of public affairs, experience in government, tact, broad sympathies and skill in negotiation'. For public relations he would need the 'capacity to be a good mixer and to make an effective public speech'. In addition, he should be able to speak French and, since Canada was climatically and otherwise a tough country, he should be young and vigorous. In peacetime he should also have a talent for entertaining and being entertained socially.

speaking. He attached importance to wives whose qualifications should be taken into account when any postings were made. His recommendations involved a large permanent increase in the establishment and he pressed that a new Office should be built to house the whole team in one building.

All his recommendations were in due course acted upon, some with modifications – but it was not until 1963 that a new building was opened.

Australia

Much of the above description would apply to posts other than Ottawa – though on a lesser scale. In Australia there was also the difference that Defence Headquarters and Supply Staff (and consequently the British Service Missions) were in Melbourne and the Senior Trade Commissioner remained in Sydney. But there were other and quite exceptional circumstances in Australia. Though there were many periods of tension between Britain and Australia, the opening months of the Japanese onslaught showed relations at a low point which was not typical. It was essential for Australia to turn towards the USA if she was to secure military support, but her attitude was marked with bitterness towards Britain since she felt that she had been let down and was resentful that Churchill was not prepared to change his 'Europe first' policy. The anti-British campaign which developed was largely incited by Evatt, the brilliant but erratic External Affairs Minister. On the British side, Cross was hardly a sympathetic reporter. As his own messages show, he was not taken into confidence by Australian Ministers; in fact he was generally regarded in Canberra as a British ministerial failure who had been foisted on the Australian Government and he was treated with scant respect.

In a review of his appointment in 1944, Cross explained that,[19] after Pearl Harbor, the Labour Government, a collection of very inexperienced and rather ignorant men, felt at a loss in face both of the enemy and of their own supporters. They could not blame the Opposition for failing to prepare – their own record was weaker. 'Blame Britain' provided a solution and perhaps had the advantage of containing some fraction of truth. He went on: 'The anti-British campaign had swept all Australia and few were the stalwarts who stood by the "old country" in those testing days. My own position had become difficult in the extreme. I had arrived in the country as a friend of the reigning (Conservative) Prime Minister, at a time when the tenacity of Britain at Dunkirk, in the Battle of Britain, and in the blitz, had aroused widespread admiration. The wicket had indeed been favourable. Within a matter of months I found myself associated with a suspicious Labour Prime Minister, a Tory label tied round my neck, and the representative of a country almost universally condemned by the populace. A newcomer, I was without the perspective with which to appreciate the scene, and I lacked established friendships through which to view it. To make matters worse my office lacked functions that would demand frequent official contacts and were at times without information of negotiations that were being carried on by the Australian High Commissioner in London. Thus we were not only strangers in the country, but also conscious of some isolation from the dealings between our own Government and that of the Commonwealth. In a short space of time our circumstances had fallen from the heights of advantage to the depths of disadvantage, and it was obvious that a long uphill task lay ahead.'

This background helps to explain some of the remarkable recommendations made by Cross in 1942. He introduced[20] his case in dramatic terms:

United Kingdom Government relations with the Commonwealth Government have been always conditioned by the assumption that the Commonwealth Government shared the spirit of Imperial Partnership. At present, the Commonwealth Government are ignoring the obligations of that spirit. The propagation of a Nationalist outlook and abuse of United Kingdom authorities, including the Government, persists unabated in certain newspapers possessing a wide circulation ... The time has come to collect all our weapons and to fight for British prestige in Australia. Apart from this immediate situation it is my view, after six months' experience, that a stiffer attitude on the part of the United Kingdom Government is normally necessary to maintain balanced relations between the two countries, and in particular, that the position of the United Kingdom High Commissioner must be strengthened.

The High Commissioner went on to particularize: 'First, it can be of real importance to invest the office of the UKHC with means of acquiring and maintaining a status which will command the wholesome respect of Ministers and officials. This influence appears at present to be subservient, if not entirely lacking. Secondly, to develop means of making the displeasure of the United Kingdom Government felt as from time to time may be desirable.'

His first point was that, as a *quid pro quo* for Australian representation in the War Cabinet in London, the British Government should demand that the British High Commissioner in Canberra should be invited to attend in an Australian Council. (The two were clearly not on all fours and in a minute to the P.M., Cranborne said that this had already been considered in London and the conclusion reached that on balance it would be inadvisable to put this forward.)[21]

Cross then complained that he was not kept fully in the picture by his own Government and in particular was not shown the personal and private telegrams exchanged between the two P.M.s.* This was a thoroughly reasonable and understandable request; the difficulty was that Churchill attached great importance to the strictly personal nature of his messages to

* Presumably Cross was referring to messages sent from Curtin through Bruce, since Churchill's messages would normally have been sent through him.

Curtin and would not have accepted the corollary that they should be shown to Bruce in London. Cross argued that the authority of his position was much weakened by the increasing tendency to conduct all important negotiations without his knowledge and that it was difficult if not impossible to carry on with a Government that 'knows that ... they can and do by-pass me ... and that there is ordinarily no need to reckon with me.' He even claimed that, although he had been chosen as High Commissioner from among Ministers of Cabinet rank as a matter of special importance for the duration of the war, an attempt was made by Australian officials to withhold from him telegrams of special secrecy on the ground that he was 'debarred from the knowledge of the special telegram in question.' He concluded that, if he and his Office knew all that was going on and were in a position to reveal this to Australian Ministers and officials then they would have 'the possibility of making them feel that they have got to take account of the attitude I may adopt, and advice I may give to my Government. It is also desirable that they should have a misgiving that, if they are disobliging in one matter, I may cause the United Kingdom Government to be disobliging in another.'

The High Commissioner's final recommendation was even more unusual in the context of relations between Commonwealth partners and allies in the same war. He urged that 'negotiations of a commercial and financial character should be brought within and related generally to political relations with Australia ... Thus, for example, we should prove unaccommodating on every possible front at the time when the Commonwealth Government was failing adequately to repudiate an anti-U.K. press.' This seemed to hark back more to Cross's time as Minister of Economic Warfare than to reflect the needs of his current diplomatic post. Cranborne himself was quite clear on the matter and recommended firmly:[21] 'I am satisfied that any attempt to use economic or financial pressure against Australia would do no good at all. It would merely exasperate the Australian Government and give further stimulus to their tendency to look to the United States for help. So far from promoting their cooperation with us and strengthening those elements in Australia which genuinely are anxious to strengthen the ties between the two countries, it would have exactly the opposite effect. I do not, therefore, share Sir Ronald Cross's outlook on this, and I would propose to explain my view to him ...'

Post-War Appointments

In 1947 it was thought advisable to have an enquiry into the D.O. posts abroad and the task was allotted to Clark, assisted by Antrobus. Clark had been High Commissioner in Canada and South Africa, Antrobus had served in South Africa, Ireland, Australia and New Zealand so between them they had ample experience of all posts. The report did not raise any major new questions of policy and its general tenor was that the posts had been established on the right lines. Most of its recommendations dealt with matters of establishment and organization. On general matters, they thought that the question of whether politicians or civil servants should be appointed as High Commissioners should generally be decided on the merits of the case, but that in Australia a politician had some advantages and that the title might be changed to Ambassador. They made no new proposals about the Trade Commissioner Service; gave considerable praise to the work of the Information Service but insisted that some limit must be set to the amount of work undertaken; urged that High Commissioners should be instructed to look out for suitable residences or sites to purchase; and recommended that before appointment to the D.O. a candidate's suitability for oversea service should be taken into account. Impressed with the complications of oversea life especially for a family, they also made a number of recommendations to improve amenities and allowances.*

When towards the end of the war, the question of replacing or renewing the terms of High Commissioners overseas came up, Cranborne, with the encouragement of his advisers, recommended some reduction in the number of political appointments. Misunderstanding his motives, Churchill assumed that he was advocating filling all posts from the D.O. In his reply,[22] Cranborne recognized that the time had not yet come to revert entirely to the pre-war practice of appointing civil servants and reassured Churchill that it was never his intention that the posts should always be filled by civil servants from the D.O. itself and that what he had in mind was the whole Civil Service. Although Churchill had various candidates in mind, no further political appointments were in fact made by Churchill's wartime administration. MacDonald and Cross each stayed on till after the end of the war. Clutterbuck succeeded MacDonald in 1946 and was the first official from the D.O. to be appointed High Commissioner in Ottawa. In the same year Cross was succeeded by E. J. Williams (later Sir Ted Williams) then serving in Attlee's Government as Minister of Information – a post about to come to an end. By a curious twist of the political wheel, just as Cross the Conservative had spent his time accredited to a Labour Government, so Williams, for most of his term, saw the replacement of Labour by the Menzies Government.

The conclusion to be drawn from the appointments to High Commissioner posts in the war and post-war years is that what matters is the character and quality of the man selected and not his previous experience, whether as

---

* The author was in two minds about the recommendation that the DHC Ottawa should be an Assistant Secretary of some years' standing and not a junior Assistant Secretary, since he himself held the post at that time and was a very junior Assistant Secretary!

politician or official. MacDonald (as later Clutterbuck) was outstandingly successful in Ottawa; so was Maffey in Dublin. Both Cross and Williams failed to make themselves acceptable in Australia, but so also had Whiskard. In the early years, Canada received High Commissioners who for the most part fitted easily into the North American scene; South Africa and New Zealand also tended to receive representatives who, though effective rather than outstanding, all made themselves welcome. With Australia, Britain's relations in wartime were under exceptional strain and it is fair to add that the Australians themselves did not make things easy for the High Commissioner; moreover it is possible that the restricted and isolated life of Canberra in the early days made it hard to grasp Australia as a whole. Whatever the cause, only in Australia did British representatives take time to become attuned to the atmosphere. In a later period the balance was redressed and a succession of High Commissioners, notably Carrington, came to know the country and in return were liked and respected. It was unfortunate that British representatives, in the country in which they might have been expected to feel so much at home and at a critical time when it mattered most, seemed unable to develop qualities of friendship and understanding which they displayed to such a high degree elsewhere.

CHAPTER 4

Problems in Wartime Cooperation

The recognition that each Dominion was free to make its own decision was obscured in the years leading up to war by the fact that the Dominions broadly supported the changing policies of the British Government: ambivalence towards Japan, support for limited action against Italian aggression but not beyond a certain point, appeasement of the Dictators and finally the decision to resist further Nazi aggression ending in the declaration of war. Constitutionally the Dominions were free to take a different decision. That they did not do so was no derogation from their equality of status. It was in function, not in status, that there was inequality. Britain in 1939 was still the hub of the Empire and indisputably its most important member in numbers, wealth, resources and military power. She controlled the Indian Empire and the Colonial Empire; she was at the centre of the struggle in Europe; she alone had any substantial representation in all foreign countries; she was recognized as a Great Power and dealt as an equal with the USA and the USSR.

The central problem throughout the war years was how to reconcile unity with diversity; the war inevitably sharpened this problem because its effective prosecution demanded a synchronization of military action; yet because the issues were those of life and death, it was all the more essential for Dominion Governments to be satisfied that any action undertaken would be sustained by their own people. The difficulties in achieving this were increased by considerations of security that did not apply in peacetime: much information could not be used publicly and some of operational secrecy was not conveyed to all Dominion Governments. Mansergh posed the problem 'could the partner nations of the Commonwealth hope to wage war . . . [especially against Hitler] . . . without some radical modification of their individualistic, decentralised peace-time relationship involving separate control of defence and foreign policies?'[1]

There was a variety of ways in which the war effort of the whole Commonwealth could be organized. The first question was where was the decision-making power to lie? Was it to be confined to Britain or shared in some way with other Commonwealth Governments? The 'Imperial' solution was contrary to the whole trend of Commonwealth development, but it offered some attractions. In the First World War there had been meetings of what was called the 'Imperial War Cabinet', and some hankered after such a solution. But the importance of the Imperial War Cabinet can easily be exaggerated; though marking a significant development, it never sat continuously and therefore exercised no regular control; it merely met for some days in the summer of 1917 and in the spring and autumn of 1918; its weakness was that it was not, strictly speaking, a Cabinet at all, since the members were neither collectively responsible to, nor members of, a single Parliament.* When early in 1940 the possibility of reviving the Imperial War Cabinet was mentioned by Lothian (then Ambassador in Washington), officials in the D.O. expressed their opposition on constitutional grounds. Machtig commented that 'the whole trend of Dominion feeling during the last years has been to indicate that anything in the nature of a super-Cabinet which would take decisions for the UK and the Dominions as a whole would be unacceptable and would indeed meet with strong opposition.'[2] He thought the only practicable way of approaching the matter was to arrange for a Meeting of Dominion Prime Ministers though he recognized the difficulties; P.M.s would not find it easy to get away themselves, but on the other hand would not agree to send deputies entrusted 'with sufficient discretionary authority to make their presence here of real value'. The D.O. reaction was a mixture of genuine conviction, of pride in existing arrangements and a belief that they would serve equally well in war.

Short of an Imperial War Cabinet, there were various ways in which the Dominions could be brought into closer consultation:

1. A meeting of the Imperial Conference (The British Government did in fact call regularly for this, but Dominion P.M.s were not able to meet together until 1944.)
2. Visits by individual P.M.s (These occurred regularly and the visitor was always invited to attend meetings of the War Cabinet.)
3. Dominion Governments could appoint special representatives (This was the arrangement sought by Australia.)

In the event no single solution emerged and there was a characteristically British attempt to deal with matters empirically. No departure from existing forms was made and no significant new Commonwealth machinery was set up, though after the Japanese onslaught, the belligerency of the US added a new dimension to the Alliance† and called for special arrangements among all the Allies.

The war transformed the normal methods of consultation; the revolutionary development in travel (when crossing the Atlantic and Pacific by air

* There were two distinct arrangements in the First World War which have sometimes been confused. The Imperial War Conference and Cabinet are described above. The second was the quite separate arrangement under which General Smuts, at that time a member of the Union Parliament but not of the Union Government, was appointed to membership of the (British) War Cabinet.
† There was of course no formal Alliance among Commonwealth countries; but they formed a de facto Alliance – a concept which they had rejected in peacetime and would not contemplate once the war was over.

became regular for the first time) greatly facilitated Ministerial visits in both directions, the despatch of special missions and teams and speeded up mail communication. Churchill's touch made a unique addition to the exchange of messages; there was a sense of urgency in the need to arrange collective Ministerial discussions and greater frequency in the meetings with High Commissioners in London.

Churchill's Messages

From the moment of his becoming P.M., Churchill's messages played a key part in the whole business of consultation with the Dominions. In his own words, they became 'in fact the channel of much vital business and played a part in my conduct of the war not less, and sometimes even more, important than my duties as Minister of Defence.'[3]

These messages now have their place in history; they were in the main composed by Churchill himself and were intensely personal. They were also idiosyncratic and bear some of the traces of Churchill's individualism. Often they argued a case, rather than containing an objective appreciation; they tended to be selective both in the material purveyed and in the destinations to which they were sent. Churchill's account at the time of Dakar, 'I kept General Smuts fully informed',[4] and his surprising comment on the imminent collapse of France, 'It was decided to tell the Dominions the whole facts',[5] both imply that the Dominions were not all kept fully in the picture.

Churchill's phrase that he regarded the messages as 'intimate and informal correspondence with friends'[6] is exactly right; but this approach, whilst having inestimable advantages, had some drawbacks; it meant that the information was tailored to the personality of the recipient and his relationship with Churchill rather than to the needs of the country in question; it also meant that the Dominions did not receive the information in the same form nor, sometimes, even the same information. Churchill revealed his attitude to the D.O. in his frank confession that he circulated his messages 'in some cases after they had been sent, to the principal members of the War Cabinet and, where he was concerned, to the Dominions Secretary'.[7] Nevertheless in the early days of his Premiership, Churchill's messages to the Dominions filled the need as nothing else could have done.

However, Churchill held strong views about communicating information to Dominion Governments and the D.O. encountered frequent opposition from him. After a number of occasions when Churchill sought to restrict the amount of information sent to the Dominions, Cranborne was provoked into minuting to the P.M. that he had the impression that the P.M. had serious doubts as to the whole policy of communicating secret military information to

Dominion Prime Ministers.[8] He reminded the P.M. of complaints, particularly from Australia and New Zealand, that they had not been kept as fully
informed as they would have wished and made it clear that his telegrams on
these matters were not for general circulation, but were sent through most
secret channels for personal communication to the four P.M.s and that there
had never been a leakage. He pleaded for a 'steady and continuous supply
of suitable information' as the best method of checking unhelpful tendencies.

The P.M.'s reply[9] was dated Christmas Day and he clearly relished
composing it. It read: 'No departure in principle is contemplated from
the practice of keeping the Dominions fully informed of the progress
of the war. Specially full information must necessarily be given in
respect of theatres where Dominion troops are serving, but it is not
necessary to circulate this to the other Dominions not affected. However,
on the whole an effort should be made not to scatter so much deadly and
secret information over this very large circle. The Prime Ministers of every
Dominion are bound to inform their colleagues, who no doubt inform their
wives and private secretaries. There is a danger that the Dominions Office
staff get into the habit of running a kind of newspaper, full of deadly secrets,
which are circularised to the four principal Governments with which they
deal. The idea is that the more they circulate, the better they are serving the
State ... While, therefore, there is no change in principle, there should be
considerable soft-pedalling in practice.'

In March 1941, Cranborne sought approval to send to Dominion
Governments an appreciation by the military authorities about the likelihood
of an invasion. He received the following reply: 'What is the point of worrying
the Dominions with all this questionable stuff? Have they asked for such an
appreciation? Surely the other side should be stated too ... Frankly however
I do not see the object of spouting all this stuff out – some of it injurious
if it leaked – unless it is thought that the Dominions require to be frightened
into doing their duty'.[10] Towards the end of 1941, Cranborne sent a strongly
worded letter[11] to the P.M. He complained that lately he had been unable to
do his liaison job with Dominion Governments. He himself did not know
what was going on, many of the most important decisions being taken at
meetings at which he was not present. Moreover most of the important
telegrams were exchanged by the P.M.s personally and these he was not
empowered to show or even to mention to the High Commissioners. He
continued 'I cannot feel that this is right from any point of view and from my
own it is disastrous ... In such circumstances, the position of the Dominions
Secretary becomes a farce ... I do feel very strongly that I should be given full
discretion to tell and show to the High Commissioners anything I think right,
with the well understood exception of operational matters. But I do want a
free hand, without which it is quite impossible to carry on the only part of the
work of Dominions Secretary which is of the first importance ...'

The P.M., however, never relaxed his vigilance; in March 1942 after Attlee had succeeded Cranborne, Churchill told him in relation to an appreciation of the situation in the Far East: 'I do not see much use in pumping all this pessimism throughout the Empire. It is the fashion here: but it will do great harm wherever it goes ... Altogether there is too much talk.'[12]

An exchange of telegrams which took place shortly after Cranborne's return to the D.O. in 1943 while Churchill was at the first Quebec Conference, throws a clear light on Churchill's attitude to Commonwealth consultation. The D.O. had informed Dominion Governments about proposals for the future of Austria. In expressing appreciation of this, the Australian Government asked for a further opportunity of expressing their views before the proposed talks took place with the USA and USSR. Churchill read this and flashed back to Cranborne: 'The demands now put forward by the Curtin Government would have the effect of strangling our foreign policy and preventing us from taking any action without the endless process of consulting all four Dominions. Living as we do within twenty miles of Europe, bearing as we are nine-tenths of the whole British Commonwealth and Empire war burden we must be accorded reasonable latitude.'[13]

Cranborne replied at once: 'This is a question of the future of Austria after the war consequently of the European settlement rather than of immediate military purposes ... Even if Dominion contributions to the war are small in comparison with ours, they are very great in proportion to Dominion resources. In my view the whole future of cooperation within the Commonwealth and Empire depends on the Dominions being given opportunity to put their full weight with us in considering the post-war settlement ... On first-class issues like this I am sure that we ought to consult the Dominions before the Major Allies and even before we reach final conclusions ourselves. To present the Dominions at the Peace Conference with cut and dried decisions, whether of our own or taken jointly with the United States (or Russia) would lead us into far more difficulties than we should avoid ...'[14]

Churchill had a number of separate objections to the circulation of information to Dominion Governments on the grounds of:

1. Secrecy of military operations. This was of course fully accepted; the question was where to draw the line.
2. Risk of leakage. Churchill had a far stronger case here than Cranborne was prepared to accept. Even the 'most secret channel' involved a minimum of some twenty members in the British Government service alone seeing a message when all the typists, cypher staff, filing clerks, private secretaries in No. 10, the D.O. and the High Commissioners' Offices are added up; and the total was probably nearer fifty.
3. Dislike of circulars. Churchill accepted the need to inform the Governments about a theatre where their troops were serving, but not otherwise. This showed a misunderstanding of Commonwealth consultation and of the needs of Dominion

Governments. They were all alike concerned in any theatres that affected the general course of the war and might at any stage become involved in them.

4. The need to know. Churchill put a strict limitation on this whereas the D.O. felt that the Dominions had a right to know the facts at the disposal of the British Government.

5. The nature of consultation. In a sense this was the crux of the matter. In a minute to General Ismay about strategy against Japan in January 1944, Churchill wrote: 'We must await the arrival of the Officers whom Admiral Mountbatten is sending, to go into the matter fully with them, and we cannot send any telegrams to the Dominions until we have at least formed our own view.'[15] He may have been right on this occasion, but the doctrine he was propounding (and by which he was guided) was not in accord with the principle of Commonwealth consultation and was in direct contradiction with the Australian insistence on their voice being heard *before* the British Government had formed their own view.

6. The P.M.'s personal authority. Churchill insisted that all messages of import-ance should be submitted to him for approval. This should not normally have been necessary; even where it did not lead to a veto, it frequently involved some delay.

The problem remained throughout the war, but grew appreciably less awkward with the improving war situation, when Dominion Governments had less reason to press for further information and the P.M. less reason to withhold it.

Ministerial Meetings

Shortly after the outbreak of war, in reply to a Parliamentary Question asking for some form of Imperial War Council, Chamberlain said that there was already close contact with the Dominion Governments and that the constitution of an Empire Council with a representative in the War Cabinet was not immediately practicable.[16] Nevertheless the British Government wished to make personal contact with Dominion leaders. Eden, as Dominions Secretary, attached particular importance to arranging a gathering, both for the value that such an exchange of views would have in itself and for the effect that a demonstration of solidarity would have on public opinion at home and perhaps also on the enemy. A Ministerial Committee consisting of Hankey (Chancellor, Duchy of Lancaster), Chatfield (Minister for Co-ordina-tion of Defence) and Eden was appointed to consider relations with the Dominions and decided to invite Dominion Governments to send representa-tives to London in October and November. The Ministers (none of whom curiously was directly responsible for the war effort) discussed matters of practical cooperation and paid a visit to France. The Conference did not make any proposals for a change in existing arrangements. The most noteworthy result of the gathering was the discussion with Fraser (NZ) about the Far East which satisfied him that the situation was sufficiently clear to justify the New Zealand forces being sent to Egypt. Reitz (Union of South Africa) attended a meeting of the Defence Committee which he regarded as an outstanding event. He was less impressed with the Western Front and told Churchill bluntly that 'the Germans will go through there [the Western Front] like a knife through cheese.'[17] His doubts were to some extent shared by Casey (Australia) who accused some of the British of 'self-satisfaction'[18] and also claimed that his report 'was a factor in the resignation' of Hore-Belisha.

In April 1940 before the German attack on Scandinavia and the Low Countries, the British Government proposed the holding of an Imperial Conference, but this was not found acceptable: Mackenzie King disliked an Imperial Conference in wartime in principle and in any case neither he nor Smuts felt free to leave his own country. Moreover all the Dominions were then satisfied with existing arrangements. Churchill pressed the proposal in 1941 and again in 1943; Mackenzie King was reluctant on each occasion; the idea was dropped in 1941 because Smuts could not come and in 1943 because it was overtaken by the Quebec Conference that year. In fact therefore no Meeting of Prime Ministers was held until 1944.

High Commissioners' Meetings in London

Cooperation with Dominion Governments was also facilitated by meetings with High Commissioners. At the outbreak of the war, it was decided to hold such meetings daily (except at weekends): and the practice continued throughout. For special occasions other Ministers or representatives of the Chiefs of Staff were present, but it was always a small and intimate gathering, and it was understood that the invitation was for the High Commissioner personally who could not be represented by a deputy.

This series of meetings was typical of Commonwealth consultation – informal, secret, intimate, frank. High Commissioners were given much information that would not normally have found its way into the official messages and they were able to assess the atmosphere behind the facts; they were free to ask any questions they liked and in general the meetings provided an opportunity for them to warn of any storms brewing either in their own minds or in the minds of their Governments. They were encouraged to offer any criticisms or suggestions and on many occasions they produced ideas which were passed on and eventually acted upon. They were after all in a unique position – they were vitally interested in the British war effort, yet completely detached from its conduct; they, unlike Parliament or the Press, had access to most of the official sources of information; they were men of experience and mature judgement; and, however carping some of their criticisms might seem to be, their motive was to be helpful.

The usefulness of such a continuous conference depended on the ability of those taking part and on the rapport which the High Commissioners were able to build up with the Minister. On the whole, London was favoured by the High Commissioners at the time – of whom two at least (Bruce and Massey) were outstanding. Bruce towered among them – he had himself been Prime Minister of Australia twenty years previously, but was still vigorous and in the prime of life; he possessed shrewd judgement, was remarkably well-informed on a great many subjects – particularly on practical matters – and was persistent in making his points. Massey was set in a very different mould: he was the aristocrat, the intellectual of the party; he enjoyed wide social contacts but sometimes contrived to bring his elevated mind to bear on the mundane problems of the war. By contrast, Jordan (the ex-London policeman who was High Commissioner for New Zealand) stood for the common people and despised what he regarded as Massey's snobbery; he had broad human sympathies, but little comprehension of the more profound aspects of affairs.* Waterson, the South African, was a light-weight; he was succeeded by Reitz (the Boer Commander and author of *Commando*) and later Leif Egeland, both of whom were agreeable but made no great impact.

The character of the meeting changed under successive Secretaries of State. Led by Bruce, the High Commissioners showed scant respect for Caldecote. They stamped outside the door if kept waiting and the meetings seldom achieved a temperature above tepid. Cranborne's advent changed the atmosphere – here was a man they all knew and admired. He was familiar with the ways of the Foreign Office, was close with Eden and was always ready to discuss wartime diplomacy. He was forthcoming, but equally ready to listen. The meetings were therefore at once lifted on to a different plane. Any change from this happy arrangement would normally have been resented, but his successor was Attlee who was also Deputy Prime Minister and, unlike his predecessors, had a seat in the War Cabinet. However it was the nature of the man to be laconic; he seldom volunteered information and, when questioned, was scarcely forthcoming. But he had authority and the High Commissioners treated him with respect. Moreover by this time, Bruce himself attended War Cabinet meetings and was able to draw Attlee out or, if necessary, could offer some gloss himself.

These meetings were not in themselves an adequate means of consultation between Britain and the Dominions. They were never intended to be that either by Britain or by the Dominions. Australia wanted something more formal and looked for machinery which would enable her to participate in the

---

* Cranborne's Freudian slip at a farewell dinner is eloquent: 'When Bill Jordan got up to speak in the League of Nations, it was like a breath of hot air!'

decision-making process itself. At the other end of the scale, Mackenzie King shrank from anything that might commit Canada in any way; he therefore refused to regard the meetings as an occasion for the expression of Canadian policy and Massey had difficulty in extracting any information from his Government which would indicate their views. There was no question therefore of High Commissioners at these meetings being authorized or equipped to represent their Governments' views, still less of their having any authority to take decisions or act as a body.

Nor should it be imagined that an idyllic harmony always prevailed. Indeed the High Commissioners never ceased to make protests about the lack of information and frequently found much to criticize in what was imparted to them. The memoirs of both Bruce and Massey contain copious references to these meetings. Bruce for example was scathing about the plan in 1940 to land at Narvik and stop the flow of iron ore to Germany: he dubbed it 'nearly madness'; in the event it was not proceeded with. He also posed the obvious but devastating questions about the ill-thought-out ideas of helping Finland and later about the disastrous Norwegian campaign. Before the fall of France, he flatly asserted that it was 'criminal' that the War Cabinet had not yet examined what should be done if France did collapse and later, to Churchill's irritation, he never ceased his press for a definition of peace aims.[19] After Japan had entered the war, Bruce had many memorable passages of arms with the British but the story belongs in a wider context.

Massey and Bruce were both imbued with the British tradition, Bruce having lived as long in Britain as in the country of his birth: Massey succumbed more easily to the charms of English life. Though on his arrival Massey had spoken disparagingly of the machinery of the D.O., he later came to regard the wartime meetings with the Dominions Secretary with affection and almost veneration. In his autobiography he records:[20] 'These meetings at the D.O. were an admirable demonstration of the family relationship that existed between the countries of the Commonwealth. No other association of States could, through their representatives, have met regularly in such an informal, intimate, unrecorded, almost cosy atmosphere.' Perhaps he enjoyed the meetings all the more since they had at one time been for him forbidden fruit.

Massey perceived that the value of the meetings depended on the performance of the incumbent. Anthony Eden 'could not have performed his duties more admirably' but Caldecote 'hasn't the qualities for the D.O. at this of all times' and 'was not sufficiently close to the centre of the stage'. Cranborne was an 'admirable choice' but even his 'very great ability could not compensate for his exclusion from the inner circle [of the War Cabinet].' Attlee, though Deputy Prime Minister and a full member of the War Cabinet, was soon found to be 'unduly reluctant in passing information on to us'. Massey even commented with a hyperbole that was revealing 'It is very irksome to hear from shopkeepers and taxi-drivers information you should have received officially.' But while the position of the High Commissioners was affected and sometimes adversely affected by the personalities of the various Dominions Secretaries, Massey recognized that the real cause of the British failure to supply full information lay elsewhere – namely with Churchill.[21] Massey remonstrated with Churchill when he learnt that first Caldecote and then Cranborne were to attend only two meetings of the War Cabinet each week, but confessed that he met with only partial success.

There were no doubt faults on both sides. Sometimes for good reasons, but more often for reasons that were less than compelling, the British withheld information which High Commissioners thought they should have. Sometimes the High Commissioners in turn were unreasonable in pressing a Government under great strain. Nevertheless the ultimate objective remained a common one, and five 'good men and true' working in daily contact over the years inevitably built up a certain tradition of their own. At the least, the daily meetings provided a useful subsidiary means of keeping the Dominions in touch at the centre of the united war effort; they also acted as a safety valve for High Commissioners and they served as a minor but salutary check (at a time when with censorship and security there were so few others) for the testing of British policies by a well-disposed but objective group.

Particular Issues

A number of difficulties arose, especially in the early stages of the war; some of these affected all Dominion Governments, some were peculiar to one country.

The dramatic but desperate offer of 'indissoluble union' to France on 16 June 1940 was made without any consultation with Dominion Governments – though, if it had come into force, they would have been affected by its terms in many ways. In fact the implications of this magnanimous offer had not been subjected to any inter-departmental study in Whitehall and were never fully examined. The D.O. had very grave reservations about the proposal because of the effect on the common status of British subjects and Caldecote, the Dominions Secretary at the time, in his rectitude threatened resignation.[22] The D.O. was however given no chance to express its views – in fact in a matter of such moment and urgency its intervention could not have achieved anything.

Curiously the decision to continue the war after the collapse of France was never the subject of formal consultation, any more than it was discussed within the British Cabinet itself. After the Nazi attack on the Soviet Union, Dominion Governments were not consulted about Churchill's broadcast of

22 June 1941, welcoming the Soviet Union as an ally on the day of the invasion – Churchill deemed it essential to make an immediate announcement. It was greeted with varying degrees of warmth by the Dominions: they were however consulted about the terms of the Anglo–Russian Agreement, published on 15 July, to which they were formally parties.

There were other occasions when full advance information was not accorded to all Dominion Governments: the agonizing decision to attack the French Fleet at Oran (with implications for all the Dominions, but especially for Canada on account of the bitter Francophile reaction) and the luckless attempt to take Dakar (again of concern to Canada, and also to Australia as an Australian cruiser was actually engaged in the operations). The failure of the Dakar expedition led to an unusually sharp exchange between Menzies and Churchill, though the correspondence ended on a softer note. Menzies complained that it was 'absolutely wrong' that the Australian Government should not be told details of the engagement and should know nothing of the decision to abandon it until after newspaper publication. After a stern lecture in reply from Churchill he repeated his point, but concluded: 'Australia knows courage when it sees it and will follow you to a finish.'[23] There were other serious differences between the British and Australian Governments; in 1941 when Rommel first drove back the Imperial forces in the Western Desert they bypassed Tobruk where a considerable force was invested. In September the Australian Government demanded the withdrawal of the Australian Division. Its replacement was a risky operation, it was opposed by Auchinleck and strongly resisted by Churchill, then eagerly counting on an early counter-offensive. The Australians insisted and the incident caused bad blood.[24] There was a further 'painful episode' when, after the Japanese had entered the war and Australian troops were being withdrawn from the Middle East, Churchill sought to have the leading Australian Division sent to Burma and, although the Australian Government had not agreed, gave orders for the convoy to be diverted. Curtin greatly resented Australia's approval being treated as merely a matter of form and insisted on the troops being sent to Australia.[25]

The appointment of Casey (then Australian Minister in Washington) to be Minister of State in the Middle East, which was intended to put the seal on the Anglo-Australian partnership, also unfortunately caused controversy and wrangling. Curtin did not relish releasing Casey at such a time but Evatt did not object, perhaps because this would get him out of the way in Washington.[26] The decision was left to Casey who accepted. The appointment led to what Casey described as 'an acid and embarrassing exchange of telegrams'; he felt that he had 'come between the hammer of Mr. Curtin and the anvil of Mr. Churchill'.[27] Roosevelt telegraphed that 'the publicity from the Casey business disturbs me greatly ... I sense in this country a growing feeling of impatience at what publicly appears to be a rather strained relationship between the UK and Australia.'[28] The fact was that Australia did not relish the implication that British interests in the Middle East were more important than Australia's relations with the US and Churchill had not improved matters by his lack of tact and sensitivity.

With New Zealand, any differences were minimal (indeed less than the differences in foreign policy had been in the years before the war). In South Africa too the personal ties between the two leaders were so strong that there was no thought of contention. The assault on Madagascar provided a good example; Churchill was interested only in securing the port and vital installations, but Smuts seized the bit between his teeth and began to nourish plans to occupy the whole island. Similarly in June 1942 when Rommel pushed the Eighth Army back a second time, he surrounded Tobruk (which on the previous occasion had held out for a year) and the force of some 33,000 under the command of a South African, General Klopper, surrendered; it was the worst single disaster in the war after Singapore. Yet both leaders showed magnanimity and neither made any attempt to blame the other.

With Canada there was a number of difficult situations. These gave rise to no overt friction; but there were some serious strains behind the scenes. Canada was deeply disturbed by the loss of two Canadian battalions in Hong Kong and by the heavy Canadian losses at Dieppe, and they were opposed to the shackling of German prisoners after Dieppe in retaliation for German action.[29]

The most serious political problem arose over a UK-US decision, on grounds of military security, to make no reference in the public announcement to the participation of Canadian forces in the invasion of Sicily. Mackenzie King protested vigorously and, when he got nowhere in London, telephoned direct to Roosevelt; he reported all this to the Canadian Parliament (and commented bitterly in his diary).[30] Churchill did not like it. 'It will not I fear be physically possible to guarantee that any statement agreed upon between the President and myself shall be submitted to and concurred in by the four Dominions. This would indeed amount to paralysis of action.' He went on, 'The form of your remarks in the Canadian House of Commons seemed rather to suggest that Canada got better treatment from the United States authorities than from us. This was painful reading.'[31] It was partly MacDonald's skill that averted a quarrel between the two. King reacted acidly to an enquiry from Churchill as to what he should say in reply to a question in Parliament and even talked of going to the country on the issue; but MacDonald drafted a reply and coaxed King into letting it go in his own name. Churchill's eventual statement was courteous to King and moderate in tone. Nevertheless King did not think it a fair statement but concluded his diary entry philosophically 'however, with war on, it is perhaps as well to let the matter lie where it is.'

By a happy chance, Churchill was able to mention the Quebec Conference at this time and, though the meeting would present problems of its own, lesser difficulties paled before this glittering occasion.

In a letter to the D.O., MacDonald explained the importance of the incident and analysed the grievances which the Canadian Government felt: 'It was an expression of accumulated resentment over a succession of other incidents. This resentment has been more or less bottled up in the interests of maintaining apparent complete harmony between Britain and Canada fighting as comrades side by side ... United Kingdom ministers who visit Canada get an incomplete impression of Canada's sentiments towards Britain ... When you have left Ottawa, believing that all is for the best in the best of all possible Canadas they [Canadian ministers] turn round and tell me exactly what they feel about Britain.* Their sentiments are a mixture of affection, admiration, gratitude and annoyance ...' MacDonald went on to list half a dozen matters ranging from composition of the Combined Boards to consultation over the peace settlement where the Canadians thought the British Government were not paying them proper heed.[33]

All these incidents denoted inevitable differences in points of view rather than controversies over policy or basic objectives. In the Canadian view, they arose from mistaken judgements, but did not reveal any flaws in the machinery for consultation. Indeed King never ceased paying fulsome, even excessive tribute to the existing arrangements, declaring on his visit to London in August 1941[34] that there was 'in existence today in actual practice the most perfect continuous conference of Cabinets that any group of nations could possibly have ... He could not conceive of more effective means of communication than those which existed at present ... So far as the relations between the two Governments are concerned, there never has been a time when they were closer. No single point of difference has arisen since the beginning of war between us in matters which are essential. The reason ... is that before any important step is taken we have been consulted.' This was a valuable view to have on record; but it strayed at times somewhat beyond the facts and it was not a picture that King's colleagues in Australia at that time would readily have recognized.†

---

* MacDonald's view is confirmed in a comment made in another context by Pearson; King, he said, might 'smoulder privately', but when he met Heads of Government 'would be smiling, friendly and mild in his reactions'.[32]

† Towards the end of the war, different viewpoints were expressed by other Dominions. Smuts was unhappy about diverting attention from the underbelly of Germany by opening up a new front in Northern France. The New Zealand Government disliked the recognition of the Lublin Committee in Poland. Smuts as well as King had anxieties about the British acceptance of the invitation to intervene in Greece in 1944.

Quebec Conferences

Canada's relaxed attitude to the question of higher direction of the war was convincingly demonstrated in her behaviour at the two Conferences between Roosevelt and Churchill and their Chiefs of Staff held in Quebec in 1943 and 1944.

The Dominion Governments played no part in the many Summit Conferences between the major Allies during the war, though they were informed of the results in general terms. Two in the series of Anglo-American conferences took place on Canadian soil. Canada however was not a party to the Conference; Roosevelt and Churchill were quite clear about that; this could have caused embarrassment but fortunately all was happily arranged.

On 19 July 1943, Churchill told Mackenzie King that he and Roosevelt wanted to have a meeting in the near future and would like to have it in Quebec. King's first reaction was one of elation, but Norman Robertson and Malcolm MacDonald, who were with him, both pointed out that it would be necessary to protect his own position and that it would be a mistake to have a meeting unless King were more than in the position merely of host; MacDonald felt it would be embarrassing for King to raise the question himself and undertook to do so on his behalf. Churchill's reply contemplated the Canadians attending all plenary sessions of what King understood Churchill saw as an 'Anglo-American-Canadian Conference'. But Roosevelt felt that this would create grave difficulties with other Allies and Churchill accepted this, realizing that there would also be complications with Australia. It was arranged therefore that the British and Canadians should confer together, but that Britain alone was present at the meetings with the US. Churchill and some of his colleagues also had meetings with the War Committee of the Canadian Government and there were plentiful occasions for private talks and social gatherings. In the event Mackenzie King was delighted that the Conference was held in Canada and gratified at the attentions paid to himself. But Churchill paid him due credit for the 'broad-minded outlook' in letting the two major Allies have the Conference to themselves.

No staff from the D.O. in London were included in the British Delegation, but MacDonald was asked to be on hand and stayed in Quebec throughout; he was also instructed to make available a member of his staff.* The most important contribution which the D.O. made to the Conference was to provide an Information Officer from the UKIO in Ottawa (M. K. R. Burge). He and the Head of USIS in Ottawa served with the Head of the Canadian

* The author can confirm that the only duties required of him were to deal with the extensive fan-mail sent to the P.M.

Wartime Information Board to form a very effective trio who, on unfamiliar territory, nevertheless successfully handled all publicity questions for this major Conference and did so on a basis of completely equal partnership.

Most of the problems in wartime cooperation with Dominion Governments arose from military decisions in which the D.O. itself frequently did not participate. But the Office was always involved in the handling of the problems and the effort to reach an accommodation, either by virtue of its responsibility for the transmission of the messages or because of the part which could be played by the British High Commissions or by the D.O. itself with Dominion High Commissioners in interpreting the British standpoint. Before 1942 few of these problems caused political confrontation at the top level or called for any major adjustment in the general arrangements for consultation. The success of Japanese arms in the Pacific however created a new situation in which Australia insisted on representation in the War Cabinet and, with the advent of the US as an ally, called in question the whole matter of the higher direction of the war.

CHAPTER 5

Higher Direction of the War

Australian Anxieties

The supply of information to Dominion Governments and consultation with them on specific issues represented a continuation of the normal peacetime functions of the D.O., but enhanced by the crucial nature of what was at stake and made more difficult by considerations of security and operational secrecy to which Churchill attached such importance. The traditional procedures were, as we have seen, strengthened by Ministerial meetings with High Commissioners and, above all, by Churchill's own personal messages to Dominion leaders.

All this left Canada, South Africa and New Zealand reasonably content. Not so Australia. What Australia sought was participation in the higher direction of the war – a problem quite different in kind from any peacetime questions of information or consultation. There was much that was traditional in the Australian attitude; Australia had for a generation pressed for the right to be consulted on major external issues at the formative stage and before the UK Government had taken a decision. Australia's wartime situation, different from that of the other Dominions, added a special significance and urgency. For decisions on grand strategy could affect the safety of the Australian homeland itself, and no Australian Government could accept that such decisions should be wholly out of Australian hands.

By the middle of 1941, Australia was seriously concerned over the conduct of the war, both in the handling of operations in Greece and the Middle East and in the lack of preparedness to meet the growing threat from Japan. The former have already been touched on; the latter had a long background. Basically the degree of interest of Britain and Australia in the Far East was of a different order: the Far East was important to Britain; to Australia the Near North was vital. The conflicting interests of the metropolitan power and the overseas territory highlighted the fact that the Commonwealth was in a transitional stage; the Imperial power was still looked upon as having the duty to protect all its domains. When it came to the point in 1942, Australia and Britain each saw itself as fighting for survival – but Britain's whole life was not at stake in the Far East; Australia's was. No such situation arose in relation to any other Dominion – New Zealand considered her fate more dependent on Britain than on Singapore.

There had for long been rumblings of the different ways in which Britain and Australia saw matters. In the inter-war years when economy was the watchword, Britain tended to economize on Singapore first; moreover she had at times been lacking in frankness about naval plans and the inadequacies of defence. Equally Australia had shown a reluctance to send her own forces to Singapore.

Reviewing naval policy at the beginning of the war, Churchill was confident that 'as long as the British Navy was undefeated and as long as we held Singapore, no invasion of Australia or New Zealand by Japan was deemed possible.' But he added significantly: 'We could give Australia a good guarantee to protect them from this danger, but we must do it in our own way, in the proper sequence of operations.'[1] Even before the invasion threat to Britain herself could be regarded as over, Churchill addressed himself to the reinforcement of the Middle East. In a message to the Prime Ministers of Australia and New Zealand,[2] he faced the prospect of war with Japan, but asserted that, in the event, Singapore would of course be defended and 'if attacked – which is unlikely – ought to stand a long siege'. Moreover the naval forces available would act as a very powerful deterrent. However if the worst happened and Japan set about invading Australia or New Zealand, he had the explicit authority of the Cabinet to give the assurance that 'we should then cut our losses in the Mediterranean ... and would proceed in good time to your aid.'[3]

In Churchill's eyes the Middle East always loomed larger than the Far East and his feeling was that, if Japan attacked, the US would come in. He accepted that if Japan invaded Australia or New Zealand the Middle East 'should be sacrificed to the defence of our own kith and kin'; but he did not believe that this would be necessary and, in spite of Australian alarm at an awkward moment, proved in the event to be right.

All this led Australia to press her case for a greater voice in the conduct of the war. The case was first put by Menzies in 1941. On his visit to London Menzies' first impression had been that 'If the P.M. were a better listener and less disposed to dispense with all expert opinion, I might feel a little easier about it. But there's no doubt about it; he's a holy terror.'[4] However he was immensely impressed with the war spirit in Britain and fell under Churchill's spell. In turn, he created a favourable impression and despite their differences Churchill regarded his visit as 'most valuable'. Menzies' mind had to some extent been prejudiced in advance by the views of Bruce, his High Commissioner in London, who over the years had many brushes with Churchill. When Menzies arrived in London, he was warned by Bruce that major policy was increasingly concentrated in the P.M.'s hands, and that he was little influenced by other members of the War Cabinet who were, frankly, not prepared to stand up to him. Bruce forecast that the P.M. would offer the utmost courtesy but that when 'you tried to pin him down ... you would find him discursive and elusive' which led either to a show-down or frustration.[5] During his visit, Menzies modified his first unfavourable opinion of Churchill, but he still feared that 'his real tyrant is the glittering phrase.'[6]

Churchill, for his part, was well aware that Menzies was not satisfied 'either with the organization of the Cabinet or with my exercise of such wide powers in the conduct of the war'.[7] They discussed the matter on several occasions and Churchill gave his reasons for disagreeing with Menzies. In effect the Australian P.M. wanted a radical change in the higher direction of the war and, in particular, an Imperial War Cabinet, containing representatives from each of the Dominions. Menzies formally submitted his proposals to the Prime Ministers of the other Dominions and took the opportunity of discussing them with Mackenzie King in Ottawa on the way home. Mackenzie King was the decisive figure – his opposition to any organization with an Imperial flavour might have been predicted. Not for the first or last time, King brought to bear a host of objections – the difficulties of P.M.s leaving their countries for any length of time; a meeting of any length would be 'unthinkable'; equally an occasional meeting could see the situation change as soon as the meeting was over and 'you would have incurred responsibility without power'; the need for any P.M., if strategic matters were to be discussed, to be accompanied by expert advisers whose presence was most needed in their own country.[8]

This, as Churchill recorded, 'deployed formidable constitutional arguments' and neither Smuts nor Fraser favoured the change. As if to clinch matters, Churchill, in sending Menzies a message[9] on 19 August to say how welcome a return visit would be, took the opportunity to emphasize that it would not be possible for a Dominion Minister other than the P.M. to sit in the War Cabinet, as representation of all four Dominions would then be involved, resulting in too large an addition to the permanent members; and he rubbed in that his enquiries suggested that there would be no chance of the other Dominions agreeing to a Minister from a single Dominion representing them in the War Cabinet. But the sands for Menzies in control of the Australian war effort were running out – within ten days of the receipt of the message he was defeated.

Even if anything like an Imperial Council had to be ruled out, it seems a pity that, at this stage of the war, it was not found possible to provide for the Dominions in some way a greater sense of what later, in a different context, would be called power-sharing. For Menzies had a legitimate grievance. Mackenzie King recorded brutally that what Menzies' complaint really amounted to was that 'there was no British Cabinet, no War Cabinet – that Churchill was the whole show, and that those who were around him were "yes-men" and nothing else ... He did all the talking and no one dared to say anything.'[10] And Menzies confided to his Cabinet on his return to Australia that Churchill had no conception of the Dominions as 'separate entities' and that the more distant the problem from the heart of the Empire, the less he thought of it. Churchill was 'a great European', but on questions in which Dominion interests were involved, his attitude was 'unsatisfactory'.[11] Even Mackenzie King was moved to complain at that time that Canada was 'ignored altogether' and 'left completely to one side' by the meeting of Churchill and Roosevelt in the Atlantic and was not consulted about the terms of the Atlantic Charter with which Canada, as all parts of the Empire, was very immediately concerned.[12] Frequently there were strong reasons why consultation could not be as full as Dominion Governments could have wished – because of operational secrecy or genuine urgency (as with the Atlantic Charter); sometimes the reasons stemming from the P.M.'s pre-occupations were equally formidable if not so valid.

Not long after Menzies' return to Canberra, the Australian War Cabinet in August 1941 decided that Menzies should go back to London to represent Australian interests in the British War Cabinet. But Menzies' majority was slender and his popularity at home diminished; there was opposition in all quarters to the proposal and he resigned. Churchill heard of his fall with regret – 'although my disagreements with him were serious, our relations had been most friendly,'[13] but lost no time in sending his good wishes to his successor Fadden. In this he took the opportunity of giving the new Prime Minister a full exposition 'of the Imperial and constitutional aspects' of the issues raised by Menzies.[14] This lecture contained a clear and succinct description of Churchill's view. He began by restating that all Dominion Governments were equal in status to that [sic] of the Mother Country. The British Cabinet 'is responsible to our own Parliament ... it would not be possible therefore without organic changes, about which all the Dominions would have to be consulted, to make an Australian Minister who is responsible to the Commonwealth legislature, a member of our body. In practice however whenever a Dominion Prime Minister visits this country ... he is always invited to sit with us and take a full part ... This is because he is the head of the Government, engaged with us in a common struggle, and has presumably the power to speak with authority and not only upon instructions ... The position of a Dominion Minister, other than the Prime Minister, would be very different, as he would not be a principal, but only an envoy. The suggestion that each Dominion should have a Minister other than the Prime Minister sitting in the Cabinet' presented many difficulties – the other Dominions did not desire such an arrangement and the numbers would be unmanageable for effective business. Nevertheless Churchill offered that 'if you desire to send anyone from Australia as a special envoy to discuss any particular aspect of our common war effort, we should of course welcome him with the utmost consideration and honour, but he would not be, and could not be, a responsible partner in the daily work of our Government.' Churchill warned that if an envoy remained as a regular institution, the existing functions of the High Commissioner would to some extent be duplicated and the relations of the Dominions Secretary with the High Commissioners might be affected. Such difficulties would not be insuperable, but 'the whole system of the work of the High Commissioners in daily contact with the Dominions Secretary has worked well and I am assured that the three other Dominions would be opposed to any change.' The message concluded 'we should of course welcome a Meeting of Dominion Prime Ministers if this could be arranged' and – rather unexpectedly – 'we are also quite ready to consider the question of an Imperial War Cabinet – though so far-reaching a change could be brought about only by the general wish of all Governments now serving His Majesty.'

Although the message was cast in official form and carried the concurrence of the D.O., the inspiration for it came from Churchill himself and many of the arguments were his own. Some of them may be somewhat specious; nevertheless the message made an imposing case. Australia however did want at least an accredited representative and in a contemporary debate the Labour leader insisted that Australia had the right to be represented in the British War Cabinet, not by the Prime Minister who was needed in Australia, not by the representative whom Britain would choose, but by the representative of Australia whom the Australian Government would choose.

The Australian Government decided to appoint an 'Envoy Extraordinary to the British Cabinet' and their choice fell on Sir Earle Page (the decision was taken by the Fadden Government and maintained by the Curtin Government). It was in some ways an unfortunate choice. Earle Page was an elder statesman with considerable political experience and the fortuitous advantage of having been Prime Minister for two weeks in 1939, but he had little knowledge of defence or foreign affairs, no experience in diplomacy (he was a doctor by profession; he owned a cattle station and was Minister of Commerce when appointed to London), and lacked the strength of character required to stand up to Churchill. He was genial, but fussy and rather stupid and it was no recommendation in high quarters in London that he did not get on with Menzies or any help to him that Bruce so clearly resented his presence and despised him. He suffered from two further handicaps. By the time he arrived in London, the Fadden Government had fallen and he was therefore a member of the Opposition; within little more than a month Japan struck and Page found himself in unfamiliar waters that were too deep for him.* Immediately after the Japanese attacks, Page asked Curtin to have

* Bruce recorded that in October 1941 an early meeting with the War Cabinet was arranged to enable Page to make a statement, in which Page planned to 'introduce innumerable irrelevant matters' and not to make the main point, namely the reinforcement of Singapore. Perhaps it is not surprising that the name Earle Page scarcely finds a mention in Churchill's history!

Bruce and himself appointed fully accredited representatives of the Australian Government so that they could be fully informed and consulted and would be able to express views before decisions were taken. He pointed out that the Dominions Secretary was far from fully informed and that he often received information too late for proper consultation (the message was no doubt inspired by Bruce). The British Government agreed that communication and distribution of appreciations should be better organized, but the Australians were not satisfied. Page then recommended that a fully accredited representative of Australia should be appointed to inaugurate a new system and that this should be Bruce. On 1 January 1942 accordingly Curtin asked for the agreement of the British Government to the appointment of a representative with the 'right to be heard in the War Cabinet and in the formulation and direction of policy'. Cross (the British High Commissioner) telegraphed[15] that Curtin's request was at variance with the personal view he had expressed to Cross the previous week and he attributed this change to the 'strong influence wielded by the Government left-wing in the person of Evatt and to a lesser extent of Beasley', though he thought too that these 'would have secured support from some Opposition members of the War Council, including Spender and very possibly Menzies. The High Commissioner attributed the request to the wave of nationalism instigated by some Ministers and fanned by the press; he particularly emphasized the strength of the influence of Evatt who 'is exceedingly ambitious ... has anti-Whitehall prejudice and would not hesitate to use highly intensified national feeling to gain his own ends'. But Cross recognized the need to have regard to Australia's tender susceptibilities about her nationhood and warned that 'if Australia suffers acutely in this struggle she will blame Britain the more and a permanent weakening of Australia's ties with the UK may well result.'

The High Commissioner refrained from giving advice but concluded magisterially: 'The question whether some extraordinary step should be taken to meet Curtin's request for representation should be viewed against the above background' and added that 'the demand is interwoven with Australian national dignity and feeling that the movement of the centre of gravity of the war towards the East has given Australia an urgent and increasing claim to a direct voice in the higher strategy of the war.'

In additional messages, as recorded in Chapter 3, Cross also made a number of suggestions for ensuring a more effective British voice in Australia.

On 21st January, Cranborne submitted two powerfully argued memoranda to the War Cabinet on cooperation with the Dominions. The second memorandum[16] made detailed recommendations, after discussion with the other departments concerned, for closer liaison with Dominion Governments on military, supply and foreign affairs matters. In the first memorandum[17] he wrote: '... the question of further Dominion representation in the conduct of the war has, as a result of the extension of the conflict to the Far East, again come very much to the fore ... It would, I believe, be a great and possibly disastrous mistake for us to underestimate the strength of the feeling which is arising in the Commonwealth [of Australia] on this question. Evidence of this is coming in from all quarters ... If this tendency is not to gain in velocity and become uncontrollable, it must, I suggest, be tackled now and by radical methods. And it must be tackled by a generous gesture to Australia, the main centre of trouble. Already, His Majesty's Government are studying proposals for affording to her a closer liaison ... These developments are all to the good. But I suggest that even more is needed. If Australia wants, as a right, to attend the War Cabinet in London on all occasions when questions affecting the war, as a whole, are being discussed, this right should be granted to her. It is a gesture that would pay us a hundredfold.'

Cranborne suggested that it should be made an absolute condition (though in the event this was not pressed) that the representative must be given authority to take decisions on behalf of the Australian Government in urgent matters; if this condition were refused, Australia would put herself in the wrong. She 'would have repulsed us. How much better than the present situation under which we are regarded by wide sections of opinion here and abroad as refusing a legitimate claim by one of our partners in the Empire.' Cranborne added that to concede such a right to Australia would mean doing the same for all the other Dominions: it was doubtful whether they would take advantage of it. 'But in my view any risk of unfortunate consequences of putting these proposals to the Dominion Governments is smaller than the risk of a gradual disintegration of the Empire.'

Cranborne concluded with the following peroration:

> It is an issue not merely of machinery, but even more of status. On this question of representation have boiled up nearly all the great crises of our history, the long struggles of the Middle Ages which led to the creation of Parliament, the disputes between the King and Parliament which culminated in the Civil War, and most analogous of all, the conflict with the American Colonies which led to their separation from the Empire. Such another crisis may be approaching with regard to Imperial relations. There are today in the British Empire centrifugal tendencies which no-one can ignore. The situation cannot and will not remain as it is. It rests with us to see whether the crisis comes to a head, with all the incalculable consequences involved, or is by wise statesmanship averted. The issue is immediate. It cannot be delayed.

The King read the two Cabinet papers and his Private Secretary wrote[18] to the P.M. to express the King's anxiety and indeed alarm and to hope that some satisfactory procedure could be devised.

Churchill was prevailed upon to accede to the Australian request. He telegraphed to Curtin accordingly and the Dominions Secretary told the other Dominions that the Australian Government were being informed that 'we are prepared to agree to this request and that Earle Page who is at present in

London as the special representative of the Australian Cabinet will attend meetings of the War Cabinet here for the purposes indicated [namely the 'right to be heard in the War Cabinet in the formulation and direction of policy'].' The message to the other Dominions stated somewhat flatly: 'We feel that Canada/New Zealand/the Union should know this in case they feel disposed to avail themselves of the new offer.' None of them did (though India, who was later invited to appoint a representative to attend the Pacific Council and also the War Cabinet, accepted the offer.[19]*). The P.M.s of Canada, the Union of South Africa and New Zealand rejected the offer for somewhat different reasons. Canada did not feel herself to be remote from the centres of power or to be faced by any direct threat to her own land, as did Australia; in any case Mackenzie King was not prepared to contemplate any changes that might lead in the direction of Imperial centralization. Smuts for his part also was satisfied. He knew that he was in Churchill's confidence and that he could transmit his views to Churchill confident that they would receive full attention. He would have been less than the human person he was, had he sought to substitute an intermediary in London for this personal contact. New Zealand's reaction was perhaps more surprising; she could complain, with even more justice than Australia, of the conduct of the campaigns in Greece and Crete and of the whittling down of the successive British assurances about reinforcing the Far East; she was as vulnerable to Japanese invasion as Australia and even more defenceless. Yet Fraser throughout remained imperturbably content and uninterested in constitutional innovations.

In explaining to Parliament[21] the offer to Australia, Churchill made clear that 'the presence at the Cabinet table of Dominion representatives who have no power to take decisions and can only report to their Governments evidently raises some serious problems.' He added it must not be supposed 'that in any circumstances the presence of Dominion representatives for certain purposes would in any way affect the collective responsibility of H.M.'s servants in Great Britain to the Crown and Parliament.' The Australian Advisory War Council met on 30 January and considered the gloss which Churchill's statement had put on the matter. The Council, which included Menzies and W. M. Hughes as well as members of the Government, disagreed with Churchill's interpretation. They considered that the constitutional position depended upon the convention existing at any particular time and was necessarily subject to change. As Australian representation in the War Cabinet, with the right to be heard in the formulation and direction of policy, had been agreed to, they considered it inadvisable to continue any argument about the academic aspects of the question and concluded that the effectiveness of the results would largely depend on the individual selected.[22]

* Amery recorded that the offer to India was not made without certain flourishes from Winston as to the necessity for hiring the Albert Hall for Cabinet meetings, etc...[20]

A further statement in Parliament by Churchill on 5 February[23] rubbed in how he saw matters when he blandly suggested that Earle Page 'for a good many months has been exercising these rights'. The Australian Government forbore to argue further and Earle Page carried on 'on the present footing'.

In the spring Earle Page was indisposed and for a time Evatt, the Australian Minister of External Affairs, sat in his place at Cabinet Meetings. Finally Bruce was appointed to succeed him in June 1942, remaining also High Commissioner. In accepting the appointment, he reminded Curtin that the British Government had not honoured their undertakings to provide[24] Australia with full information before decisions were taken. Bruce attributed this not to any deliberate intention, but to the personality of the P.M. and the defects of his qualities. He added that 'my task as I understand it is, quietly and if possible without friction, to ensure that we will be fully informed ... before decisions are taken. I believe I should be able to ensure this, but I have no illusions that the task will be an easy one.' Bruce's biographer comments[25] that the task was more than difficult; it was impossible. No doubt there were faults on both sides; Bruce had a running battle to ensure that he was not left out of meetings, that he received full documentation and that his own memoranda were circulated promptly. He did not always succeed and then made representations to the Cabinet Secretary, senior Ministers (especially Attlee and Cripps) and where necessary the P.M. himself. He was not invited to the War Cabinet meetings which decided on many matters which, in Bruce's view, were of clear concern to Australia. On such occasions Bridges consulted Machtig who, with Attlee's agreement, pressed that Bruce should be invited to discuss war production negotiations with the USA:[26] in the event he was not – and protested again. In July 1942,[27] Bridges minuted to the P.M. that, since Bruce had been the accredited representative, he had attended ten meetings in all, but had not been invited to twelve. In a tactful understatement, Bridges represented that, unless Bruce were invited to more meetings, he was likely to ask whether the procedure adopted accorded with the invitation extended to Dominion Governments. Churchill's reply was revealing:[28] 'This is the best we can do. The British Cabinet must sometimes be allowed to sit together. We do not sit in the Australian Cabinet.' Late in 1942 Bruce sent Churchill a memorandum arguing unbelievably that there was 'a serious defect in the higher direction of the war', that the 'emotional' period of Dunkirk had passed and what was required was not inspiration for the people but organization and planning and finally 'it is true as many people would contend that this is due to the P.M.'s temperament.'[29] It is hardly surprising that Bruce received no reply (though apparently an 'acid' letter was drafted) or that the P.M. addressed his letters 'Dear Mr Bruce'.

Something of Bruce's equivocal behaviour at this time is revealed by his contacts with other Ministers. He talked with Cripps about Cripps's opposition which might even bring down Churchill; at the same time he told Eden: 'If Winston does not do something [about a small War Cabinet], it is better that he should go,' and said the same to Attlee. Significantly he 'did not tell either one I had seen Cripps'.[30] Some months later, Hankey concluded his diary entry about a talk with Bruce with the surprising verdict 'I believe he might make a possible P.M.'.[31] Perhaps Churchill had cause for his dislike of Bruce! The fact was that Bruce's manner was often abrasive; he involved himself in British politics, seeing himself as a member of the War Cabinet in his own right (as Smuts had been in the First World War) rather than as the representative of Australia. He was astonishingly insensitive towards Churchill and increasingly appeared to act from motives of personal ambition instead of on instructions from his Government.

After the last Australian Division had been withdrawn from the Middle East, Churchill saw an opportunity to get rid of Bruce: he minuted to Attlee:[32] 'The position of Mr. Bruce is highly anomalous. The Australians have now moved their last troops away from the general war zone to their own affairs. Why then should Australia be represented in the Cabinet when Canada, which has five divisions, and New Zealand and South Africa, which each have one, are not similarly represented? I hear that Mr. Bruce is writing a lot of hostile stuff to his government and some time ago he made serious demands to become a full working member of the War Cabinet of the U.K. I think he should be brought up with a round turn.' Attlee defended the arrangement,[33] pointing out that the position, accorded at Curtin's insistent demand, was not based on the presence of Australian troops in the Middle East, that similar representation had been offered to all the Dominions and that it would be extremely difficult to rescind the offer to Australia without by implication 'disinteresting ourselves in the Pacific theatre ... and without grave dangers of friction with the Australian Government, who are still obsessed with the idea that they are not sufficiently taken into counsel as regards their strategic interests.' With his invariable common sense, Attlee concluded: 'It has always been difficult to delimit the functions of Bruce as a member of the War Cabinet in view of the very wide terms of our offer and the position has been complicated by the fact that he is permanently here as Australian High Commissioner. It has, however, not worked too badly in practice considering all the difficulties and given goodwill I do not regard it as unworkable. We might easily go further and fare worse.' On both sides the war of attrition seemed to be wearing itself out. On 5 October 1943 Cranborne, after a talk with Bruce, reported that 'it was a somewhat frosty conversation; but he appeared to accept the position rather reluctantly'.[34] Finally the arrangement came to an end in 1944 after Churchill had accepted Curtin's suggestion at the meeting of Dominion Prime Ministers that there should be monthly meetings at which the P.M. with the Dominion Secretary would meet the High Commissioners. He wrote to Curtin recognizing that 'this arrangement would make it unnecessary for Mr. Bruce ... to attend meetings of the War Cabinet regularly' and associated himself with the remarks made 'as to the distinguished services which Mr. Bruce has rendered'.[35] Bruce continued to receive selected Cabinet papers and military reports. Bridges concluded in a letter to Machtig: 'I am bound to say that I never thought that this particular trouble would end so easily and I for my part, feel very grateful to Bruce for the attitude which he has adopted about this business.'[36]

In spite of the mutual irritations and expostulations and although the Australian Government could on occasion claim that they did not always receive all the information at the earliest moment, the arrangement worked for the critical period of the war. No doubt it was helped to function to some extent by the fact that Bruce not only had his contacts with the War Cabinet, but also as High Commissioner enjoyed all the normal services provided by the D.O. The increasing involvement of the USA also removed many of Australia's worst anxieties and there was less obvious cause for complaint as the series of disasters began to be replaced by successes.

Alliance with the USA

Australia succeeded, therefore, in securing special arrangements with the British Government even if her needs were not always fully met. But, with the entry of Japan into the war, the higher direction of the war no longer rested solely or even largely with the British Government; the USA had become the senior partner. This set a new dimension to the Australian problem. The President and P.M. and also all their main advisers were at one in favouring an Anglo-American combination as the means of directing the war in matters both of strategy and of supply. Both parties disliked the possible trend towards a multinational superior authority for the conduct of operations in wartime, though they accepted that a place had to be found for Allies, as the United Nations Declaration and the establishment of the Pacific Councils showed later. The Anglo-American predominance was devised to be on a basis of equal partnership between the two. This recognized Britain's monopoly of battle experience and at that time her greater war production and deployment of forces. Nevertheless it was a sign of things to come that the Combined Chiefs of Staff and all the Combined Boards were set up in Washington. The basis of the Anglo-American understanding was that unity would be achieved stemming from agreement reached at the top level between the President and the P.M. The two leaders set up Combined Chiefs of Staff who were responsible for all recommendations on strategy and in effect became an Executive Committee for the prosecution of a global war. The decisions of the Combined Chiefs of Staff and Combined Boards were of crucial importance to all the Allies, not least to the Dominions.

Ways found for associating the Dominions with the Combined Boards are discussed in a later chapter. Australia, not surprisingly, was not content with a situation in which higher strategic and policy direction was, through the Combined Chiefs of Staff, effectively retained exclusively in US/UK hands. Some means of regular and direct access to both the senior partners seemed to her essential, at any rate to cover the area in which she was directly involved. Accordingly from the outbreak of hostilities with Japan, the alliance with the USA raised in a new form the question of the higher direction of what had now become a global war. The Australian Government (with the solid support of New Zealand) demanded the constitution of a supreme authority for the higher direction and control of Allied strategy in the Pacific area. The demand was made with all the more stridency and insistence as Evatt had become Minister for External Affairs and quickly impressed his brilliant but harsh and egocentric character on the scene. Evatt sought the limelight and was avid for power. He also felt that he had a mission and believed that the survival of Australia depended on his success. This made him over-bearing, but also deeply distrustful of others and quick to resent any slight. As an Australian diplomat put it, 'The status which he succeeded in winning for Australia during his overseas visits was diminished by his aggressive and thrusting manner, which took small account of the susceptibilities of other countries, including the U.K.'[37]

Early in his Washington visit, Churchill had agreed to the President's proposal that unity of command should be established in the South West Pacific and that Wavell should be appointed Supreme Commander of all US, British, British Empire, and Dutch forces in the theatre. He had given his approval without any advance consultation with the Dominions; they readily accepted, but insisted on an adequate voice in control. Churchill did not welcome the Australian and New Zealand view that the supreme body should be set up in Washington, but was eventually persuaded to recommend a Pacific Council in London under his chairmanship with representatives from Australia, New Zealand and the Netherlands, but strangely not the USA or Canada or China (though China did attend later sessions). The President was content with this, since the US services had no enthusiasm for setting up a body in Washington. The Australians however were not; they wanted a share in the higher direction of the war in the Pacific. Churchill argued that the London Council would not be merely advisory and would give Australia an equal voice with the UK. But Cranborne in his memorandum to the Cabinet,[38] recognizing that the Council went a long way to meet the Australian demands, pointed out that it failed to meet those demands in two ways – Australia regarded consultation as inadequate unless it enabled her to influence decisions; secondly the Council was limited to the Far East and did not cover the whole aspect of war strategy.

The Americans became increasingly impressed with the Australian case and eventually the President, largely on advice from Harry Hopkins, decided to set up a counterpart Council in Washington. The Council in London had its first meeting on 10 February 1942. The Council in Washington met for the first time on 1 April, under the President's chairmanship, with Evatt representing Australia and Nash (the Deputy Prime Minister) New Zealand. Other countries were represented at a high level and Mackenzie King and Churchill attended meetings on visits to Washington. Churchill and Roosevelt both had phrases about the two Councils being co-equal and keeping in close touch; but the London Council never really came to life; inevitably the Washington Council assumed greater importance. Neither was a decision-making body.

Meanwhile Evatt had been bombarding Churchill in Washington with gloomy, but not inaccurate appreciations of the situation in Singapore and with frantic appeals for help; he followed these up in London. Though he was unsuccessful in securing an aircraft-carrier (the one intended for Australia was sunk), Churchill was able to offer three squadrons of Spitfires for the defence of Darwin. Part of the reason for Evatt's success in London may well have been that, after the traumatic experience of the first months of the Japanese war, both sides sought to avoid further controversy. Despite Bruce's urgings (or perhaps because of them!), Evatt did not press the case for clarification of Australian representation in the War Cabinet. On the contrary, according to Bruce's notes, he took the view that Churchill had 'an amazing grip upon the people' and felt that 'it would be a bad thing for us to have a quarrel with Winston as it might hurt Australia's interests in obtaining reinforcements and supplies we need if we antagonize him.'[39] Evatt told Bruce that 'it was not for us to upset what the members of the War Cabinet were prepared to accept.' Bruce commented with some justice that this was a very changed atmosphere from the somewhat blood-and-thunder one that Evatt had adopted on arrival and he concluded that 'It is clear Winston has exercised his charm and unquestionable astuteness upon Evatt. I see some difficulties in Evatt's really facing Winston up with the position...'[40]

For his part, Churchill was anxious to be conciliatory and he was conscious of his own responsibilities towards Australia. While recognizing that an aircraft-carrier could not be spared at that stage, he minuted[41] to the First Sea Lord: 'We have to consider our permanent relationship with Australia, and it seems very detrimental to the future of the Empire for us not to be represented in any way in her defence.'

Cross, reviewing his time in Australia in 1944, commented[42] that the tide of anti-British feeling turned from the moment of Evatt's visit to London in mid-1942 and attributed it to the immense impression which Churchill made on him. 'Evatt, the erst-while doubter and critic, was publicly bending the knee to the biggest figure in oft-condemned Whitehall ... That influence has endured to this day.'

By the end of 1942 the tide began to turn against Hitler and Japanese naval supremacy had come to an end. The worst was over and, with it, the worst of Australia's anxieties. Her concern had been understandable enough; even before the war Australia had been worried about the place of the Far East in British strategic thinking and, while a direct threat to Australia remained, she would not be reconciled to the decision (reached without her) by Churchill and Roosevelt in favour of 'Europe first'. It was her anxiety on this score that lay behind the complaints of Churchill's conduct of affairs and the constant efforts to get closer to Roosevelt and involved in the decision-making process. (Whether the representations were made in the way best calculated to achieve the purpose is another matter.) Effectively Australia did not achieve her aim of participating in decisions on over-all policy though nominally she was accorded what she requested – a voice in the War Cabinet and a seat on the Pacific Council. There was a good deal of window-dressing about both – the plain fact being that Churchill and Roosevelt were equally determined to retain control of strategy in their own hands and not to share this with others to any extent greater than they themselves considered necessary. Nevertheless in practical ways Australian requirements were largely met: both Bruce in London and Casey and his successors in Washington established close personal relations outside the formal bodies and managed to secure most of the essential information in informal ways. Moreover as time passed, supplies to the Australian theatre were increased and her security was assured when MacArthur established his base on Australian territory. There was almost a note of irony in the sequel after the end of the war against Hitler; Churchill was determined that there should be an adequate British contribution to the defeat of Japan, but met with implacable opposition by Admiral King to the inclusion of British forces in the assault on Japan itself. The risk of a serious and open rift between Britain and the US, which would have concerned all the Allies and dismayed Australia and New Zealand, was fortunately removed by the sudden capitulation of Japan after the dropping of the atomic bomb. A final gesture to Australia was paid by the decision to hold in Canberra in 1947 a Commonwealth Conference to consider the proposed peace treaty with Japan; the meeting achieved little of practical importance, but it symbolized the recognition accorded to Australia's place in the Pacific. The wheel had come full circle.

CHAPTER 6

Economic Relations

In wartime economic relations covered a far wider field than hitherto and extended to such matters as exchange control, supply and procurement of munitions, raw materials and foodstuffs, and the resultant need to arrange financing for purchases on so vast a scale; they were affected by new arrangements made to meet wartime needs such as the British Commonwealth Air Training Plan and the Combined Boards set up in Washington to organize allocation after the US became a belligerent. They also embraced matters of economic warfare and proposals for post-war financial, economic and commercial policy. The war inevitably set the content of economic relations in a new context and greatly increased the role of Government since so much in this sphere, previously left to private enterprise, became subject to control.

In trade matters, the war brought about a reversal in the normal pattern. After 1939 it became clear that the survival of Britain depended on growing as much as possible of her own food (instead of encouraging cheap imports from overseas); it also depended on the Dominions manufacturing as much as they could of the hardware that Britain needed (instead of keeping industrial development down to encourage British exports). Nevertheless, with the Continent cut off, Britain looked to the Dominions for many vital food supplies; she also sought to maintain as much of her export trade as possible. In war conditions Imperial Preference lost most of its practical importance, but there was constant concern at the efforts of the Americans to get rid of it. In the Atlantic Charter, Churchill with strong support from the War Cabinet (in which Attlee played his part as Acting Prime Minister and Dominions Secretary) secured reservations to protect the Ottawa Agreements. In the Lease-Lend Agreement the British were compelled to promise the reduction of trade barriers and the elimination of discrimination after the war. The American attitude caused alarm both in Britain and in the Southern Dominions and formed a major topic at conferences of Commonwealth officials. The D.O. was closely involved but did not play a lone hand as the principle of preference was supported in Whitehall and at this stage particularly by the Board of Trade. The fear was that Churchill, for wider reasons, would give in to US pressure. In truth here, as over India, there was no meeting of minds between him and Roosevelt.

The war also forced the conduct of financial relations within the Common-wealth into a new pattern and brought about a clearer definition of the Sterling Area. The Bank of England and the Treasury found it necessary to formalize the financial arrangements which had hitherto operated without any formal agreement. Previously nothing had been written down; now it became necessary to define limits and give them the force of law. The Sterling Area thus came officially into being. A single ring fence of exchange control was placed round the UK, the Dominions (excluding Canada) and all the other members of the Sterling Area (including all Colonies and other dependencies). Within the area, funds continued in theory to move freely; but each member of the Sterling Area controlled with comparable strictness, as laid down in London, exports of capital outside the Area. These measures called for the active cooperation of Commonwealth authorities and there was of necessity a much closer degree of consultation than had been found desirable in the years before 1939, though characteristically there was no formal inter-governmental agreement. The understanding was also continued that members of the Area put any surplus they earned into the reserves of the Sterling Area held in London; this became increasingly important in providing a means of payment for Britain's purchases in Sterling Area countries.

The Dominions were vitally affected by all these changes and assumed a new importance in world trade particularly by the series of bilateral trade discussions which each in turn had with the USA during the war years. Matters affecting international trade and finance were discussed at a series of meetings of Commonwealth officials in London and at the CPM Meeting in 1944 there was a discussion of post-war plans, including such matters as the International Monetary Fund and bulk purchasing. All this gave the D.O. a new and important role to play. Liesching, Clutterbuck and, in the later stages of post-war planning, Snelling all worked closely with the Treasury, the Bank of England, the Board of Trade and the new wartime Departments concerned. Snelling was also a regular member of the team which accom-panied Keynes on his missions to North America and to the Conference at Bretton Woods.

Munitions Supply

Since war production in Canada and, to a lesser extent in Australia, rose so dramatically, it is remarkable how exiguous was the productive capacity of the Dominions at the beginning of the war. Britain missed a chance to stimulate production overseas when the rearmament programme first got under way: there was consultation, there were enquiries but, apart from some minor projects, nothing substantial was started. It was not until war was imminent that the advance party of what became the British Purchasing Mission left for Canada. As soon as war was declared, the Mission was set up; it was considerably strengthened and cooperated closely with the Canadian War Supply Board. The Mission initially was responsible for purchases in the USA (then still neutral) as well as Canada (Canada being given precedence over the US as the main supplementary arsenal). After the fall of France, a separate organization was set up in New York and, since the Canadian authorities preferred themselves to handle all orders in Canada, the Board as such was then wound up in Canada, its functions being taken over either by the Canadian authorities or by separate British missions operating under the British High Commissioner.

Munitions supply from the Southern Dominions was co-ordinated by the Eastern Group Supply Council set up in Delhi in 1942; although it could not match either in sophistication or quantity the mass production of North America, it was significant because of the importance of production near to the theatre of operations and the consequent saving in shipping.

Britain's wartime purchases were paid for in a variety of ways; sale of external assets, dollar loans, grants or free gifts and also by an increase in the sterling balances held in London by other members of the Sterling Area. By the end of the war Britain had incurred an immense indebtedness by this last method; much the largest holding belonged to India, arising from the cost to Britain of supplies and services to the Indian and British armed forces in the Middle East and Far East; the balances held by Australia and some Colonies were also substantial (though lower than those of Egypt). After the First World War, Britain's war debts were mainly to the United States; in the Second, most goods from North America that were not paid for were supplied on lend-lease (or comparable terms) and there was no substantial dollar indebtedness until after the end of the war. Britain's main debts were to her Commonwealth and Colonial partners holding balances in sterling and repayment created formidable problems in the post-war period.

Payment for purchases in Canada created a special problem as Canada was not a member of the Sterling Area and did not contribute to the reserves of the Sterling Area in London. Even in peacetime, Britain had an adverse balance of payments with Canada and it was clear that in wartime Britain's requirements of munitions, raw materials and food would far exceed Canada's likely purchases in Britain. From the earliest days of the war therefore the authorities in both countries sought for ways to overcome the exchange barrier: these included British payments in gold, sale of British securities, an interest-free loan of $700 million (January 1942), the billion dollar gift (January 1942), the sale of British capital assets in Canada (1943) and Mutual Aid (which amounted to $1,800 million, 1943 and 1944). After the war, following on the US Loan, a 'final settlement of all outstanding accounts' with Canada was reached in 1946 and a loan of $1,250 million was made for 50 years. Under the wartime arrangements, the deficit was met by Canada until the end of the war. Canadian assistance was therefore considerable; in the last two years of the war however Britain was still able to pay for twice as much as she received in aid (largely from increasing receipts for services to Canadian troops in Britain).

British Commonwealth Air Training Plan (BCATP)

The BCATP was an outstanding example of wartime cooperation between the participating Commonwealth countries; it relied on a smooth-running organization and it produced a steady flow of pilots of high quality in the numbers required for the air forces of the Commonwealth. The scheme was launched in a message from Chamberlain to Mackenzie King in September 1939,[1] which suggested the training of Australians and New Zealanders as well as Canadians and British and, after acceptance in principle, the British sent a mission to work out the Plan and there were also missions from Australia and New Zealand. With these there were no problems, but between the British and Canadian negotiators there was trouble from the start and friction continued for the full two months of the negotiation. Both sides were to blame for this and each from time to time acted stupidly. The British side were in too much of a hurry and took Canadians too much for granted; the Canadians were unduly suspicious of British motives and insisted on unnecessary assurances. In all the argumentation that went on, the British High Commissioner (Campbell) had the invidious responsibility of advising the British team and of trying to help each side see the other's point of view.

The negotiations were described by Campbell in a remarkable despatch.[2] He began by stating bluntly that the UK delegation (and to a lesser extent the Australian and New Zealand delegations) approached the problem from an entirely different angle from the Canadian Government. The three delegations never forgot that their purpose was to forge a weapon for use against the common enemy; the Canadian Government on the contrary saw everything in terms of the advantage which they might gain for themselves. They saw from the first that they could employ the scheme for the greater honour and glory of Canada and that the plan promised a far better return in the way of political capital than the despatch of a mere division or two to the Western Front. Campbell then demonstrated how cleverly the Canadians had played their hand to secure concessions for themselves, particularly the British admission that Canada's part in the scheme should be regarded as having preference over all her other forms of war effort and, most valuable of all, that Canadian pupils should be organized in RCAF

Squadrons. Campbell charged that in their efforts to secure this, the Canadians were guilty of 'a deliberate distortion of the truth' in pretending that the Canadian public would not stand for any other arrangement. He drew the sharpest distinction between the attitude of the Canadian Government and the Canadian public and he saw King as the villain of the piece. 'The P.M. is the Government and he is a very complex character. On the one hand he goes far beyond the average Canadian in his mystical and idealist talk of a crusade or a holy war against the enemies of civilization and democracy. On the other hand he is the narrowest of narrow Canadian nationalists.' Campbell concluded that the agreement would prolong the life of the Canadian Government and he was clearly doubtful whether this would be to Britain's advantage. He ended with a vision of the UK driving a team of the three Dominions – he had little doubt that the somewhat unwieldy equipage would reach its destination, but 'the driver must not now be surprised ... if one of the team from time to time turns round to argue on the subject of the road to take, the speed to be used, or even the advisability or possibility of proceeding further at all.' This was a singularly bitter and even ungenerous report; it was perhaps written too close to the event and reflects the irritations at Mackenzie King's tactics and the tension of the two months' negotiation.

Official minuting in the D.O. contained little critical comment and accepted Campbell's judgement, but the Duke of Devonshire suggested that the P.M. and other Ministers should see the despatch since some Ministers 'are apt to think that we have only to make our wishes known to get them carried out at once' and should therefore 'know what kind of difficulties we have to contend with'.[3]

Once agreement had been reached, the organization of the Plan went ahead rapidly under capable and enthusiastic Canadian administration.[4] There were inevitably clashes of personality from time to time and there continued to be argument about the implementation of the employment of Canadians in the RCAF, but there were no major political problems and the D.O. as such ceased to be closely involved. The responsibility was now clearly on Canada's shoulders. The British High Commissioner (or his Deputy) and his RAF Adviser attended the regular meetings of the Board set up in Ottawa to administer the Plan, and most issues were settled on the spot.

Combined Boards

One of the most far-reaching Allied decisions after Japanese entry into the war was the setting up of Combined Boards to deal with matters of production and supply, covering munitions, raw materials and foodstuffs. Both the US and British Governments sought to keep matters in their own hands and to avoid the dangers and delays that might result from spreading responsibility among too many Allies. As far as the Dominions were concerned, the British Government preferred to handle matters in London where already a network of Committees had been established. Much of the business could best be done there and, except for Canada, London remained the effective clearing-house. Nevertheless Washington was where the decisions were taken and inevitably attracted Dominion attention. Stephen Holmes, a member of the D.O. staff, was appointed at this time to the Embassy in Washington with the rank of Minister to coordinate liaison with the Dominions on all supply questions.

In principle, and if only for reasons of prestige, the Dominions could not feel satisfaction with their lack of formal association, though they welcomed the enormous effort being made by the USA and were glad to see an effective partnership with Britain. All the Dominions had complaints. In the case of Canada these were not pressed mainly because Canada already had a close liaison with the USA under existing bilateral arrangements. Australia was more vociferous and had more cause. Evatt complained bitterly that while Australia could of course submit her point of view to London or Washington, 'nonetheless any claims made by Australia in relation to aircraft, shipping, army or naval strength are dealt with by such bodies in a way that places us in the role of a petitioner.' Yet there was some flexibility: the Canadian Minister of Munitions and Supply was invited to become a member of the British Supply Council in North America; a Consultative Committee was also set up consisting of representatives of all the Dominions, India and the Colonial Empire. Moreover while the membership of the Combined Boards was limited to British and Americans, the term 'British' could in practice be used to cover the British Commonwealth. The interpretation of this dying doctrine led to every variety of confusion, misunderstanding and contradiction. The Americans took the view that the Commonwealth countries should first co-ordinate their needs with the British Government and use a common channel for their approach to the US Government. Somewhat inconsistently they later suggested that Canada, Australia and New Zealand should all become members of the Food Board in their own right. The British for their part did not wish anything to upset the 'dual control' they had established with the USA. They preferred that Australia and New Zealand should be represented only on the London Food Council, but agreed to Canadian membership of the Combined Food Board (CFB) in Washington.*

* Adolf Berle recorded that Churchill redrafted the President's message of invitation to Canada in a form which 'cuts down recognition of Canada's right to be consulted. We do not agree; but it is not worth a fuss.' This was not quite the case. The President's message had referred to Canada's existing membership of the CPRB and to the desirability that Canada should 'participate fully with the U.K.

On another occasion, Evatt in the Pacific War Council proposed that Canada should be appointed a member of the Combined Production and Resources Board (CPRB) and should act as a representative of all the Dominions. King would not have this and took the view that if Canada were to become a member, she should represent herself and nobody else. In the event Canada, alone of the Dominions, became a full member of any of the Boards, joining the CPRB in November 1942 and the CFB in October 1943. But representatives of other Commonwealth countries were invited to sit on combined committees, and, as time passed, it became increasingly the practice for representatives of other countries to be present when matters of concern to them were discussed: these arrangements worked all the more effectively because they were operated on an informal basis.

While Britain continued to be by far the largest supplier of all British Commonwealth military requirements, the contribution made by the Dominions in supplies of all kinds was impressive. Canada by the massive increase in all heavy production and Australia by the striking adaptation of her industry to produce tanks and aircraft both far outstripped any prospects thought likely before the war. And munitions formed only a part of the supplies imported from the Dominions to sustain Britain's war effort – raw materials and foodstuffs were equally vital elements in the import programme; for the first two years of the war, they amounted to far more in value than munitions and over the whole period of war to nearly as much. A new phase in trading was marked by the extensive bulk purchase agreements entered into by the Ministry of Food, of which outstanding examples were the Commonwealth Sugar Agreement and the Wheat Agreement with Canada.

With the exception of the period when Australia felt herself to be under threat from Japan and complained that her appeals for aircraft and guns did not receive a fair response, all these non-political matters were handled with a remarkable absence of public friction. And the Australian complaint – significantly voiced mainly by Evatt – was largely political in origin and formed part of the Australian demand for a greater voice in the conduct of affairs generally. Otherwise there was no conflict. This was perhaps not surprising in the case of South Africa and New Zealand where any problems were manageable; but it was more remarkable in the case of Canada. Both Britain and Canada were under strain; Britain was denuding herself of her assets but the deficit steadily mounted; Canada was facing unprecedented

---

and the U.S. in the consultations and decisions which are made in this vital field as well'. The D.O. diplomatically watered down these phrases in an effort to 'avoid any form of words which might be embarrassing to other Dominion Governments' (and no doubt which might be quoted against them by Australia), but these were verbal changes which had no effect on the substance of Canadian membership.[5]

expenditure; the problems were complex and urgent and involved vast new schemes. Fierce pressures too were exerted by the commercial interests both in agriculture and industry on each side. Yet, though there were from time to time acute differences of viewpoint and not infrequently misunderstandings, there was no open conflict. Many factors help to explain this. Apart from the subordination of everything to the task of winning the war, the issues were not easily understood by public opinion as a whole and did not arouse political controversy (on the contrary in Mackenzie King's view the pressures were positively in favour of showing that sacrifices were being made – since generous aid for Britain might lessen the demand for conscription). Above all a good understanding was reached by those at the working level on each side; these included many first-class minds not only among officials and serving officers, but bankers, scientists, businessmen and others whom the war brought into Government service and who were determined to achieve practical results. The number of British visitors to Canada during the war years was legion and covered every field from atomic energy to exchange control, aircraft design to food production. Outstanding in the later years was Keynes, but there was a host of others who made their mark in a variety of ways. Much also was due to the effective diplomacy of Malcolm MacDonald, to the expert advice given by the various missions under his wing and to the sympathetic understanding of Gordon Munro, a peacetime banker, who was Financial Adviser to the High Commissioner from 1941 until the end of the war and enjoyed the friendliest relations with his Canadian colleagues.

A contemporary minute in the British Treasury contained the verdict that British requirements in Canada were covered throughout the war 'without any undue legacy of debt or any undue strain on our depleted resources'. Both countries come well out of the story; Britain paid Canada all it could across the exchanges; Canada provided most of the rest virtually free, only asking that her own deficit with the US be met from her much larger surplus with Britain.

Towards the end of the war, a number of international conferences was held, mainly in agreeable resorts in the USA, to plan the future world for the United Nations. Many of these were concerned with economic matters and all were attended by Dominion Governments. The D.O. followed closely the proceedings and a member of the D.O. was invariably included in the British Delegation. The reports forwarded by Snelling from Bretton Woods and Shannon from Chicago convey the flavour of relations with the Dominions at two contrasting Conferences.

Bretton Woods: International Monetary Conference

Snelling summed up[6] that the Conference had done much to demonstrate that the countries of the Commonwealth by no means always speak with one voice and that the Dominions certainly could not be relied upon to dance to the tune which London called. Informal meetings, of course, frequently took place with all Commonwealth delegations, but the exigencies of the timetable prevented full meetings from being held after the initial one. Nevertheless there were remarkably few public clashes between the various Commonwealth members and, where differences were ventilated, they arose normally from fundamental divergence of interest which no amount of discussion could have reconciled.

Snelling then commented on the individual delegations: Canada showed at the Conference that she was fully alive to the responsibilities of her new-found status as an almost-great Power and possessed officials with breadth of vision and intellectual equipment equal to the role. The Australian delegation was under rigid instructions from their Government who intended to make use of the Fund quota to the maximum possible extent and therefore pressed for an increase in the Australian quota to a point beyond what was practicable. Snelling himself found the Australian delegation extremely co-operative, but records the embarrassing fact that Keynes and Melville (the Australian Leader) did not get on. Relations with the New Zealand delegation could also have been better. The team was weak and the vanity of its leader (Nash) whose powers seemed to have deteriorated, presented an obstacle to close personal relations. The South Africans were among the enthusiasts, they sent a good team and had no axes to grind. Relations with them were excellent. The Indian delegation was composed both of British members of the Government and of Indian politicians. There was potential embarrassment since the Indian members were determined to use the mechanism of the Fund for clearing off a large part of their sterling balances. They were especially anxious to avoid giving the Congress Party a handle to agitate against India joining the Fund. These considerations made them acutely sensitive to questions of national prestige. Snelling made four general observations: i) the essentials for a conference of this kind are that the leader should be physically robust and should have sufficient time at his disposal. Neither condition was satisfied. The result was that some things were left undone – among the omissions were daily delegation meetings and regular meetings with Dominion delegations; ii) the closeness of the cooperation with individual Dominion delegations and their satisfaction at the attitude of the UK representatives towards them tend to vary directly with the quality of the Dominion personnel concerned; iii) liaison work with Dominion delegations should not have to be combined with secretarial duties; iv) close co-operation with Dominion delegations at international conferences cannot be effected when the time-table is grossly overloaded. Reasonable time to complete the job in hand should secure adequate consultation, because the willingness is almost always there. Fortunately the frequency of conferences of this kind meant that a number of UK and Dominion officials were getting to know and respect each other and Snelling hoped that this would help to make friendly consultation natural and easy in future.

Chicago: Civil Aviation Conference

The International Civil Aviation Conference, held during the war, marked the first occasion when the Allies scrambled for their own post-war advantage; equally, though Britain and the Dominions had by no means always expressed identical views at the League of Nations, this was the first international conference to reveal the Empire in serious disarray.

It was agreed to hold an international conference in Chicago in November 1944 and this was preceded by a Commonwealth meeting held in Montreal. The leader of the British delegation was Swinton, then Minister of Civil Aviation; Boyd-Shannon (Assistant Secretary in the D.O.) was included in the delegation and sent a detailed report to the Office. On Churchill's insistence, Eire was excluded from the Commonwealth meeting allegedly on the grounds that war matters would be discussed, but in spite of Churchill's protest she was invited to and attended the Chicago Conference.

Some of the detailed argument at the Conference was complicated and highly technical; broadly the facts were that the USA had been able to steal a march on all other countries during the war years and pressed for the maximum opportunities for US airlines on a basis of private enterprise to operate with the greatest freedom. Most other countries sought a degree of international regulation and control. Britain was in the middle of the argument since, as she held bases all round the world, she counted on being able to develop services in spite of the powerful American competition. The trouble at Chicago arose largely because the British delegation changed its position; after initially opposing the Americans and being ready for a break, it then sought a compromise.

Shannon[7] felt that seldom could the British delegation to an international conference have held so many meetings with other Commonwealth delegations; they were held almost every day and sometimes, towards the end, twice a day. On the other hand, fewer than half the meetings were attended by the Canadian representative; Swinton reported on the separate UK-USA-Canadian talks at those meetings which the Canadians preferred not to attend since they did not agree with the British line of opposition to the USA. Despite the frequency of the meetings, Shannon reported that UK policy at the Conference changed so often and so quickly, and at times seemed so inconsistent, that the Dominion delegations found difficulty in adjusting themselves and, in the latter part of the Conference, gave up trying, especially as it was made clear to them that the British Government, having set their course, intended to pursue it, whatever other Commonwealth delegations might say.

Shannon commented that the initial UK decision to be ready for a break with the USA did not win the inner conviction of the Dominions and that the UK appeared to be isolated not only from her foreign friends but even from other Commonwealth members. Swinton retorted alike to the impassioned appeal of the Canadians and to the more moderate arguments of the Australians that he had the most explicit instructions from the War Cabinet not to budge an inch and that the political implications had been considered and decided by Churchill 'with fuller knowledge and greater wisdom than anybody at Chicago'. When eventually the decision was taken in London to make concessions, the volte-face caused a shock in Chicago and Commonwealth delegations were dumbfounded; their resentment being all the greater because they had not been told before the public announcement was made. It was clearly an unhappy conference and Shannon concluded his report: 'This was the first of the political conferences which may be expected to mark the transition period. The outstanding feature on the British Commonwealth side was the strong desire of all the Dominions and India for mutual agreement and co-operation between the countries of the British Commonwealth and the U.S.'

In London, Machtig commented with almost negligent understatement: 'One cannot escape the conclusion that the result of the Conference has *not* been to improve our relations with the Dominions, especially with Canada. Could this have been avoided? I should not like to say.' Cranborne took matters more seriously. He was concerned that he personally had had no idea of the extent of the divergence within the Commonwealth and it was news to him that the UK was primarily responsible for the absence of the Canadians from Commonwealth meetings. He regarded this as most unfortunate and felt that it was a pity that Swinton was not given a freer hand. While Swinton felt tied by his instructions, London were unaware of the constantly changing position and Cranborne urged that the lesson ought to be learnt for future conferences held outside Britain.[8]

Nevertheless something was salvaged for Commonwealth cooperation.[9] At the invitation of the Canadian delegation, Commonwealth delegations all met again in Montreal for a few days after the Chicago Conference was over. Here and at a later meeting in London, arrangements for Commonwealth cooperation were discussed and set in hand. A Commonwealth Air Transport

Council was set up in 1945 (and one in the South Pacific in the following year). The British did not achieve all their aims – they had only modified success with the sale of British aircraft and they failed to develop an all-red route under the British Pacific Airlines scheme in a deliberate attempt to undercut the USA. But business arrangements between airlines proved fruitful. BOAC (under its various names) helped to set up national airlines in the Commonwealth countries and cooperated with them when established. Effective partnership arrangements were made with airlines in all the Dominions for the sharing of technical services and pooling of receipts. This pattern was extended to include the airlines in virtually all Commonwealth countries as they were established; it proved a commercial success and endured with a notable absence of friction.

CHAPTER 7

Ireland: Neutral Dominion

The events of the Second World War gave many surprising twists to the Irish question. It was strange that a people so turbulent, partisan and pugnacious as the Irish should smother its emotions and display throughout a phlegmatic restraint. With so much bitterness from the past and so much tension from the war, it is remarkable too that the situation between the two countries was nevertheless contained and that no confrontation occurred. Churchill never ceased to fret over the unnecessary burden resulting from the loss of the Irish ports or to devise plans for their use; he and de Valera had long been antagonists and during the war Churchill had many harsh things to say – yet though his tempestuous demands secured no response from the ice-cold steel of de Valera's rigidity, there was no resort to force.

The phrase 'Neutral Dominion' has an element of artificiality; Eire was hardly a normal Dominion and was never referred to as such on either side of the St George's Channel. De Valera, for understandable reasons, evaded precision, but claimed that Eire was a Republic, in external association only with the Commonwealth. The British and other Commonwealth Governments chose to regard the 1937 Constitution as not effecting a fundamental alteration in the position of the IFS as a member of the British Commonwealth and, until the war, the D.O. treated Eire for all practical purposes as a Dominion. Eire was also not wholly neutral; geography alone forbade any total insulation and there were many ways in which Britain secured advantages not available to Germany.

Although Churchill took an idiosyncratic line, refusing to regard Eire as a sovereign independent State or to recognize her right to neutrality, there was in fact no fundamental disagreement as to what the position between the two countries was. Each side had signed the Agreements in 1938 in good faith, knowing that neither was committed beyond the terms of the Agreement; Chamberlain was not committed to ending partition, nor de Valera to providing any facilities in the event of war. Each side looked forward genuinely to an improvement in Anglo-Irish relations and hoped that in the easier atmosphere its aim would be realized. But the war came too soon, before there was time to begin the process of bringing the two sides together either on defence cooperation or partition.

From the day of Britain's declaration of war, the neutrality of Eire threw up a host of extremely difficult practical problems. Largest of all loomed the question of the use of the facilities at Berehaven and other ports. Hardly less serious was the possibility of a German invasion (even more practicable after the fall of France) and the problem of devising in advance measures of military cooperation. There were complications over belligerent rights at sea. There was the question of the Axis Missions in Dublin (and their right freely to communicate information to their Governments). There was finally a number of complex wartime matters – economic warfare, censorship, espionage, landing of armed personnel (for example, by baling out from an aircraft) and all the problems involved in supplies for a neutral country.

The Bases

The British hoped, but without conviction, that Eire would fight on the Allied side (the hope was revived for a moment when the US entered the war). This hope was never fulfilled and the D.O. accepted with painful realism the fact of Irish neutrality and the consequence that the use of the naval bases was ruled out, unless Britain's very survival necessitated taking them by force. Churchill never reconciled himself to what he described as the 'numbing loss of the Southern Irish ports' and turned his attention to them from the moment of his appointment to the Admiralty at the beginning of the war. On 5 September 1939 he called for a special report on the 'questions arising from the so-called neutrality of the so-called Eire'. He was sufficiently circumspect to warn that the matter raised political issues 'which the First Lord is not certain he can solve'; but he asked that the full case be made for consideration.[1] On 24 September he returned to the charge with the claim that 'Three-quarters of the people of Southern Ireland are with us, but the implacable, malignant minority can make so much trouble that de Valera dare not do anything to offend them.' He thought there was evidence to suggest that U-boats were being succoured from the West of Ireland. He concluded that if the U-boat campaign became more dangerous 'we should coerce Southern Ireland', but if it slackened off that the Cabinet would not be inclined to face the serious issues which forcible measures would entail. While he feared that 'the present bad situation will continue for the present', he was insistent that 'on no account must we appear to acquiesce in, still less be contented with, the odious treatment we are receiving.'[2] It was a theme to which he would recur over the next five years.

Churchill recognized that there were wider considerations than the purely naval ones. In response to a request from the War Cabinet, Eden presented on 20 November a memorandum on 'the financial, economic and political considerations involved in the termination of Eire's membership of the

British Commonwealth' which had been drawn up as a result of an inter-departmental meeting of all Departments concerned. The paper[3] drew the conclusion that 'while there are several measures by which pressure could be exerted on the Government of Eire, these measures are likely to affect detrimentally the interests of this country either directly or indirectly.' After drawing attention to the losses in trade and elsewhere which would result from any serious deterioration in relations, the report emphasized that to bring pressure to bear upon Eire might provoke serious reactions in some at any rate of the Dominions on purely constitutional grounds and would alienate the sympathies of the large Irish population abroad, especially in the United States of America. Moreover a breach with Eire would add seriously to the military commitments in Northern Ireland. The authors of the report, with tongue almost visible in cheek, understood 'that the object of bringing pressure to bear upon Eire to an extent which might result in Eire leaving the British Commonwealth would be to obtain for ourselves the full facilities we require in defence matters, including a base for the operation of our anti-submarine forces both ships and aircraft. The question whether the need for these facilities and the advantages to be derived from them are so great as to outweigh all the disadvantages which might result from a breach with Eire is a general matter of policy with which it is not within the scope of the present report to deal.' They concluded with as great a degree of decisiveness as bureaucratic caution would allow: 'It should, however, be added that it seems very doubtful whether any pressure which we could bring to bear upon Eire in the various directions to which reference has been made would, in fact, induce the Government of Eire to accord us the facilities desired, while a breach with Eire would result in the loss of such cooperation, whatever it may be worth, as the Government of Eire are at present disposed to accord.'

This remained throughout the attitude of officials in the D.O.

'UK Representative to Eire'

The first need in wartime relations between the two countries was to set up a British mission in Dublin (hitherto there had been a Trade Commissioner only). There had been a High Commissioner in London since the establishment of the Free State and the post had since 1930 been held by J. W. Dulanty. He had many outstanding qualifications for the job; he had lived most of his life in England (at the University of Manchester and as a British Civil Servant); he understood the British and was in return liked by them; he was a convivial character and readily made friends. At the same time he was a loyal servant of his own Government and was in the confidence of de Valera though the difference in their temperaments prevented any great intimacy. He was small in stature and mild in manner; he was not a powerful figure in any sense of the term and de Valera frankly admitted his deficiencies to Maffey. Churchill (under whom curiously enough Dulanty served in the Ministry of Munitions in the First World War) said of him not unfairly that he was 'thoroughly friendly to England' but that he had no control or authority in Eire and acted 'as a general smoother, representing everything Irish in the most favourable light'.[4] In any case Dulanty – or anyone else for that matter – in London was no substitute for a British political representative in Dublin. For some time both Governments had felt the desirability of a British representative in Dublin and Harding had investigated the possibility of establishing a post in 1936 when he got as far as discussing a draft scale of emoluments with the Treasury. There were, however, inevitably in the Irish context, complexities over the title. The British could not agree to Ambassador or Minister since such titles would be appropriate only in an appointment to a foreign country; an Ambassador moreover was the representative of the Sovereign and it was argued that the King could not appoint an Ambassador to himself. (This was specifically a D.O. doctrine; the Office was always at pains to maintain a distinction between Commonwealth relations and foreign affairs and for long resisted the application to Commonwealth posts of the nomenclature of diplomacy.) For their part, the Irish found the title 'High Commissioner' unacceptable in view of its imperial history, though they themselves had used this title for their representative in London for nearly twenty years and would shortly receive in Dublin High Commissioners from Canada and Australia. Early in September 1939, the Eire Government sent to London J. P. Walshe, Secretary to the DEA, to explain to the British authorities the general position of the Eire Government. While insisting on maintaining the essentials of neutrality, Walshe gave assurances that de Valera wished to be as helpful as he could. In the course of his talks, he indicated that de Valera would be willing to accept a British mission in Dublin. As a follow-up, Sir John Maffey was sent to Dublin to arrange for the establishment of the post. Maffey had retired in 1937 from the post of PUS Colonial Office on reaching the age limit, after a distinguished career in the ICS (Political Department) culminating in his appointment as Governor-General of the Sudan. He was therefore a public servant of the highest reputation; he was also a man of commanding stature with a personality that combined both strength and charm. His imperial past might have made him unwelcome to de Valera; fortunately he made a most favourable impression at these first meetings and he earned and retained the goodwill of the Irish Government throughout the ten years that he stayed in Dublin. He was also immensely popular with a wider public, being gregarious by nature, a keen sportsman and ardent race-goer. De Valera's biographers record of him: 'Sir John

Maffey was to prove an admirable choice, tactful, discreet and discerning. He won de Valera's confidence, the respect of all who met him and the friendship of many of the people of Ireland, while remaining a thorough Englishman throughout. He was a key figure in the testing years of neutrality.'[5]

It proved no easy task to get agreement for the new post. On his first visit in September 1939, Maffey was surprised to find that the President emphasized the difficulties in the way of creating an appointment of a new and special character. On thinking the matter over, de Valera said he had come to see more closely the dangers – particularly from the forces working against him. Dramatically pointing to a map, he asserted that the trouble was all due to Partition. Maffey turned to discuss the interpretation of the rules of neutrality and felt he made some impression when he stated that the action which the Irish contemplated would be adding to Chamberlain's difficulties. They discussed the problems of a ward and watch system for submarines and of RAF planes landing in Eire.* In the talk, de Valera admitted that two-thirds of his people were pro-British, but he always came back to Partition (the 'tyranny' and 'oppression' in Northern Ireland must lead to 'disaster'). At the end of the talk, de Valera reverted to the question of representation; he repeated that the creation of a post of special status would be dangerous, but that the appointment of a Minister would involve no such risks and asked Maffey to tell Chamberlain that he would agree to receive a Minister.

Summing up his talk,[6] Maffey concluded that 'Mr. de Valera evidently at present does not wish any consideration to obscure his vision of neutrality. The only possible line at present is to retain his goodwill and to render his neutrality as benevolent as possible.' Maffey felt that his visit might have done some good in opening de Valera's eyes to the difficulties and embarrassments he caused by issuing formal orders under his policy of neutrality without previously feeling his way with Britain. But he had to leave without any decision on the question of representation. Within a week, Maffey was back in Dublin, bearing a letter† from Chamberlain; this explained that the title 'Minister' would raise most contentious issues which it would not be possible for him to accept and pressed for the acceptance of 'Representative' as a compromise between the two points of view, appropriate for an emergency arrangement.[7] Maffey had nearly two hours alone with de Valera (his previous talk had lasted even longer) who 'had a good run on the old scent' and raised a cloud of difficulties. Maffey waited for his opportunity

---

* By a coincidence, while they were talking, the telephone rang and the President said; 'There you are! One of your planes is down in Ventry Bay. What am I to do?' Fortunately the telephone rang later to report that the plane had 'managed' to get away.

† Maffey had to apologize that the letter was addressed 'Dear Prime Minister' which was not regarded as a correct translation of the Erse term.

to intervene when, after pointing to the obvious dangers from an enemy like Germany, he begged de Valera to see that, unless a closer relationship was established, unless the Admiralty felt that they had established a real liaison, any happenings off the Irish coast would start a justifiable outcry and the two Governments would meet in head-long collision simply because they had not established reasonable contacts. De Valera was not to be moved from his stand that the solution proposed was not acceptable. Maffey then turned to the problem of liaison with the Admiralty and the need to tackle promptly any German vessels reported. De Valera was more cooperative here though clearly he preferred not to know about RN destroyers attacking a U-boat in territorial waters. There was also talk about arms for the Eire forces and de Valera gave an assurance that no obstacles were placed in the way of recruiting for the British forces (though he asked that the men should not return to Eire in uniform).

The next day at dinner Walshe warned Maffey that de Valera had gone back to his apprehensions and that the draft reply to Chamberlain was getting more and more controversial. On the following day, Walshe reported that the difficulty now was the name '*UK* Representative' since the UK included Northern Ireland. Later that evening, however, after a Cabinet meeting, de Valera asked Maffey to call when he gave him a reply to Chamberlain accepting in principle his request. De Valera only made the points that he did not wish the term to be regarded as other than temporary and that, while he accepted that in Britain the incumbent would be referred to as UK Representative, in Eire they would use 'British' Representative in common parlance.* He also asked that the Representative should not employ secret service funds or methods. De Valera went on to raise a number of miscellaneous points (including the price paid for Irish cattle in London), before bidding Maffey 'a most friendly goodbye' and expressing 'his high hopes of future association'. In his reply to Chamberlain's letter, de Valera said that he had explained the difficulties to Maffey who would no doubt make clear how much would depend on the character of the person chosen. He added that he believed Maffey had the experience and understanding necessary to make a success of the post. Maffey was duly appointed and took up his duties early in October.

A delicate task was imposed on Maffey almost before he had settled in. Churchill strenuously and repeatedly took up the question of naval facilities; under his stimulus the Naval Staff showed forcibly the benefit derived by German U-boats from the inability of escorts and aircraft to cover adequately from English bases the Western Approaches and pressed for the use of one

---

* The prolonged discussions hardly bear out the account in de Valera's biography that, after studying for a few minutes Chamberlain's letter suggesting 'UK Representative in Eire', de Valera crossed out 'in' and substituted 'to' – the problem was solved! This is based on an article 'Lord Rugby Remembers'. No doubt Rugby's memory was as diplomatic as Maffey's mission had always been.

or more of the Irish ports. On the instructions of the War Cabinet and after an interview with Chamberlain, Maffey took the matter up with de Valera in October, but he did not present it in the form of a demand. De Valera's answer to every line of approach was a categorical 'non possumus'. In his report, Maffey made it clear that the policy of neutrality commanded wide-spread approval among all classes and interests in Eire, including even pro-British groups, and he showed how de Valera had sought to be helpful within the limits of neutrality in a variety of ways. He instanced the reporting and signalling arrangements in regard to German submarines, the acceptance of a naval attaché, the holding up at Maffey's request of a series of emergency orders, acquiescence in British surface craft attacking in territorial waters and in British aircraft overflying Eire territory.

In circulating this report to the War Cabinet on 28 October, Eden commented[8] that it showed the 'rigid and unsatisfactory attitude' of de Valera and set out three possible courses: i) to seek further discussion with de Valera: he did not think this would serve any useful purpose; ii) to acquiesce in de Valera's attitude and endeavour to secure what was possible, bit by bit: he feared, however, that this would produce only minor concessions of comparatively little value; iii) to make forcible use of the harbours. If this were done, he did not think that de Valera would oppose with military force, but he would indict Britain before the world and rally his people against her. There would be serious repercussions in the US and in the Dominions, and the passive support which Britain received from great numbers of Irish people would be alienated. In addition, Eire might grant facilities to the enemy.

Churchill urged that the constitutional basis of Eire's neutrality should be challenged, but recognized that it would be advisable to wait until the US Neutrality Act had been repealed; he suggested that 'we should take stock of the weapons of coercion'. The Cabinet decided that force should be used only if the matter became one of life or death. The view of Chamberlain which was also that of the D.O. prevailed and a show-down was averted. By the end of November, the Cabinet felt that the U-boat menace was sufficiently under control to regard the danger as passed for the time being.

There were three further critical points in Anglo-Irish relations during the war. The first was in the early summer after the collapse of France. The second occurred when, after Pearl Harbor, the USA became an ally which Churchill vainly hoped would provide the occasion for Irish participation. The third was before the Normandy landings when the British and the Americans were equally concerned about the possibility of a security leak through Dublin.

MacDonald's Mission (June 1940)

In June 1940 the authors of the 1938 Agreement surprisingly were given a chance to play a last hand. Chamberlain remained Lord President of the Council in Churchill's government and, in reply to a letter from de Valera on his resignation as P.M., warned him of the dangers of enemy landings from troop-carrying planes. On 12 June he followed this with a further letter saying that the danger of an invasion of Ireland was so real that a personal consultation was essential and that Craigavon (Premier of Northern Ireland) should attend any meeting. Chamberlain therefore suggested a meeting between himself, de Valera, the Dominions Secretary and Craigavon. De Valera was not to be caught in a trap of this kind in London, but welcomed the possibility of talks, particularly as at this time he was anxious for urgent military supplies which the British were not willing to release. Malcolm MacDonald, who had won de Valera's confidence in 1938 and was now Minister of Health, was accordingly instructed by Churchill to fly to Dublin for a secret talk with de Valera to try to persuade him to join the war. He operated throughout in the closest contact with, and the strong support of, officials in the D.O.

MacDonald had a series of prolonged talks with de Valera in the latter half of June, interrupted by visits to London for discussion with the Cabinet. The first talks were largely exploratory and often repetitive. MacDonald forcibly made the point that, in the British view, there was serious danger of a German invasion of Ireland, that the risk of a quick success for a comparatively small invading force was so real that Britain could not afford to release valuable equipment and therefore that the only hope of safety lay in inviting the cooperation of British forces. De Valera for his part maintained that an invitation to British forces would be a fatal mistake and would almost certainly lead to IRA sniping at them; he argued that it was in the general interest including the British that any equipment available should be given to Irish forces. Inevitably he referred to Partition and suggested that, without it, there might already have been an alliance between the two countries. MacDonald retorted that the best chance of Ireland becoming united would be if Eire and Ulster were fighting side by side. MacDonald and de Valera then examined three possibilities. i) Declaration of a United Ireland in principle; Ulster to remain belligerent, Eire neutral at least for the time being, but to allow British forces (land, sea and air) at agreed points and to receive additional military equipment. De Valera rejected this on the grounds that it would be a violation of neutrality and would stir up trouble with the extremists. ii) Eire and Ulster to be merged in a United Ireland, its neutrality to be guaranteed by both Britain and the USA.

MacDonald rejected any idea of Ulster becoming neutral in a war in which it was already engaged. iii) Declaration of United Ireland in principle, to become at once a belligerent on the Allied side.

The last was a suggestion thrown out by MacDonald which de Valera did not reject out of hand: he even said that if there was not only agreement in principle but also agreement on the constitution of the new Union then the Government of Eire might agree to enter the war at once. He made it clear that he envisaged the Eire constitution being applied to the whole country and that its relation to the Commonwealth would be that of external association only. MacDonald pointed out that a German invasion would not wait for all the difficult constitutional matters to be negotiated and settled. However, de Valera refused to go further than to say that Eire 'might' enter the war; MacDonald thought that this was mainly because he was concerned that the Eire armed forces and the people were completely unprepared for war.[9]

The talks had occupied three long meetings and, after a visit to London, MacDonald handed de Valera on 26 June a document containing a considered statement from the War Cabinet.[10] This set out a plan which, if acceptable to the Government of Eire, would be put to the Government of Northern Ireland for their assent. The proposals in the plan were:

1. A declaration to be issued by the United Kingdom Government forthwith accepting the principle of a United Ireland.
2. A joint body including representatives of the Governments of Eire and of Northern Ireland to be set up at once to work out the constitutional and other practical details of the Union of Ireland.
3. A joint Defence Council representative of Eire and Northern Ireland to be set up immediately.
4. Eire to enter the war on the side of the United Kingdom and her Allies forthwith, and Eire and British forces to cooperate in the defence of Eire.
5. The Government of Eire to intern all German and Italian aliens in the country and to suppress Fifth Column activities.
6. The United Kingdom Government to provide military equipment at once.

De Valera's first reaction to the plan was unfavourable, mainly because there was no assurance that a United Ireland would actually materialize. The argument continued, with MacDonald emphasizing the urgent risk of a German attack in the near future and the fact that British support would make invasion less rather than more likely. De Valera would not have this, but was drawn into discussing the possibility of a joint Defence Council and even speculated on the idea of joining the two Parliaments of Ireland in one body. In the end he came back to his conviction that the best course would be for the United Ireland to be neutral, at least to begin with. MacDonald had the impression that one of the decisive influences on de Valera's mind was his view that Britain was now likely to lose the war.[11]

De Valera put the plan to his Cabinet and the following day MacDonald had a meeting with him, Lemass and Aiken;[12] he discovered that Aiken was even more persistent than de Valera in urging neutrality for a United Ireland. MacDonald formed the definite opinion that the Cabinet would reject the plan, mainly because they thought Britain was going to lose the war and that it would be a mistake for them to throw in their lot with her. Nevertheless he recommended certain amendments to the plan to which the British Government agreed. These were incorporated in a letter[13] from Chamberlain to de Valera and included the following important additions: The British Government to give a 'solemn undertaking that the Union is to become ... an accomplished fact from which there shall be no turning back'; the joint body to establish at as early a date as possible the whole machinery of government of the Union; the British Government to consider a proposal that the two Parliaments should meet together with sovereign powers to legislate for the whole of Ireland; the British Government not to press for Eire's entry into the war provided British forces were stationed in Eire.

But de Valera was not to be moved; he finally replied to Chamberlain on 4 July that 'the plan would commit us definitely to an immediate abandonment of our neutrality. On the other hand it gives us no guarantee that in the end we would have a United Ireland unless indeed concessions were made to Lord Craigavon opposed to the sentiments and aspirations of the great majority of the Irish people.'[14]

MacDonald himself has confessed that from the beginning he felt sceptical about the chances of success.[15] There were good reasons for this; there was no real equivalence between immediate belligerency (which Eire never regarded as being in itself in her own interests) and the coming about of a United Ireland in the future under conditions which remained to be settled. The greatest difficulty was the likely reponse of Ulster; here de Valera who otherwise was often blind to the facts of Northern Ireland seems to have shown a shrewder judgement than the British. Although the whole arrangement depended on the agreement of Ulster, there was no prior understanding with them. The British Government's view as expressed by Chamberlain was that Craigavon 'would have to be told that the interests of Northern Ireland could not be allowed to stand against the vital interests of the British Empire' and though Churchill made it clear that he would not urge those who had worked loyally within the Empire to join with those who wished to stay outside it, he went along with what was proposed; the general assumption was that, if agreement could be reached with de Valera, Churchill's authority at a moment of crisis would be able to persuade Craigavon. What would have been the response had de Valera accepted was never put to the test. As it was, Craigavon reacted angrily to the talks maintaining, when Chamberlain explained that MacDonald had been sent over because of the danger of the Germans invading, that de Valera would welcome them!

Superficially the offer seemed to bear some resemblance to the offer of Union made to France a few weeks earlier; it was equally dramatic and equally doomed to rejection. But it was more practicable than the offer to France and had greater historical and geographical justification. The prize was immensely worthwhile; had a United Ireland stood together in the war, subsequent history would not have been the same and could have been far happier. Emotions on both sides however were too deep and, in retrospect, it is remarkable how lightly the British Government seemed to regard the strength of feeling in Ulster.

When MacDonald reported on the failure of the talks in London, Churchill was, according to MacDonald, 'deeply disappointed, and bitterly critical of de Valera'.[16] This was understandable, yet he was not one to get things out of proportion. His wrath may have been tempered by his confidence that 'nothing that can happen in Ireland can be immediately decisive.'[17] In any case the bases themselves became less important after the German occupation of the West Coast of France ruled out the South West approaches for convoys and, though there were German plans for landings in Eire, nothing serious was in fact ever attempted. In January 1941, Churchill himself admitted to Cranborne that the most one could say was that the lack of the bases was a grievous injury and impediment, though naturally in the event of a German descent 'with or without an invitation we should have to go to turn out the invaders'.[18] By March 1943 Attlee,[19] commenting on a suggestion that Roosevelt might ask for the bases on behalf of the United Nations, observed that he thought the strategic facilities would probably be very dearly bought as he doubted whether Britain could afford to pay the price of the military and civilian supplies which would be necessary to provide for Eire's protection.

Economic Pressure

In the first months of the war, Eire was treated as an export market and the despatch of goods was positively encouraged. On coming to power, Churchill at once put a stop to this and sought to bring pressure to bear by a policy of 'squeeze'. In November 1940, he minuted to Cranborne: 'I think it would be better to let de Valera stew in his own juice ... Sir John Maffey should be made aware of the rising anger in England and Scotland ... and should not be encouraged to think that his only task is to mollify de Valera and make everything, including our ruin, pass off lightly.'[20] In the following month he addressed the Chancellor of the Exchequer: 'The

straits to which we are being reduced by Irish action compel a recon-
sideration of the subsidies [paid on agricultural produce]. It can hardly be
argued that we can go on paying them till our last gasp.'[21] He referred to
the 'de Valera-aided German blockade' and in a message to Roosevelt at this
time talked of having 'to carry Irish supplies through air and U-boat attacks
and subsidise them handsomely when de Valera is quite content to sit happy
and see us strangled.'[22]

In response to Churchill's pressure, Kingsley Wood presented in December 1940[23] two plans, the first designed to make the population 'feel uncomfortable in a few weeks' while the second would be the equivalent of economic
war. Cranborne told the Cabinet that he favoured the first plan, with the
omission of action on coal and dollars. Accordingly it was decided to require
export licences for a variety of commodities including foodstuffs, materials
and machinery and that these would then be withheld at the instance of the
Department concerned; the Ministry of Shipping would also find itself
unable to arrange ships for Eire. In each case action would be taken
administratively and no announcement was made of any policy decision. An
informal committee was set up under Cranborne to keep up the pressure
and in March 1941 he claimed that the new economic policy had opened
the eyes of the Irish to their true situation and that they were very uncomfortable.[24] There were many shortages and the sudden curtailment of
raw materials was a severe blow. Nevertheless Britain was never severely
taken to task and de Valera spoke at the end of the war of the 'fair way'
Britain had treated Ireland over supplies.[25]

Machtig and senior officials in the D.O., with Maffey in strong support,
were never happy about the policy of squeeze and sought in any way
possible to lessen its severity. It could be argued that officials showed undue
complaisance towards de Valera and sought to continue the policy of
Chamberlain under the rule of Churchill. Their aim was to keep relations
between the two countries as normal as possible and to avoid any exacer-
bation which might affect Irish cooperation in other ways – in particular
the supply of vital foodstuffs and the various breaches of neutrality in which
the Eire Government acquiesced, many of which were of great importance.
Remarkably, resistance to Churchill's policy continued over a period of years
without causing an explosion, indeed without any open confrontation. This
was possibly because the policy was never publicly announced and was
carried out by administrative action. It was also partly due to the charm and
skill of Maffey's diplomacy and to the dexterity with which Machtig gained
the ear of successive Secretaries of State and avoided exposing his full hand.
But it must also have been due to Churchill. Any policy smacking of appeasement was anathema to him – above all when it involved the Irish. Wheedling
the Irish certainly never gained his approval; but he could have stamped
on any sign of this at once had he really wanted to. That he did not do

so may have been due to an inner recognition that it was not worth pushing his ideas to extremes – the more so as he knew he could not count on American support; he therefore did not interfere beyond giving an occasional growl to indicate his displeasure. The difference between the views of the D.O. and those of the P.M. and the exasperation they sometimes felt at Churchill's fulminations was revealingly if diplomatically expressed by Maffey when he was asked to comment, at the end of the war, on Churchill's gibe in a broadcast about de Valera's Government frolicking 'with the German and later with the Japanese representatives to their hearts' content'. Maffey explained that he himself had been pursuing towards Eire the policy approved by the D.O. and described as the 'absent treatment'.[26] This policy had yielded good results, but the P.M. 'handling world problems on a vast stage, finds it expedient from time to time to come into collision with that policy, thereby producing local reactions to those on the spot but which no doubt serve a useful purpose in another and higher dimension. If milk happens to be spilt here it would be presumptuous on my part to suggest any criticism of the hand which spilt it.'

An item of supply that raised peculiar difficulties was that of arms. De Valera frequently made a grievance of this and made a strong plea for more arms. Commenting on one of these requests in January 1941, Maffey recommended that the situation could be left to develop unless the British Government felt that there was urgent need to give Ireland the strength to defend her soil and prevent another Denmark.[27] Cranborne commented to the P.M. that as regards supply of arms clearly there were arguments on both sides. The answer depended on whether a German invasion or a deterioration in the shipping position was the more likely. If the former, it might be wise to supply arms to encourage the Irish to resist. But if the latter, it would be foolish to present de Valera with the means to prevent Britain from taking over the ports.[28] Churchill's reply was unambiguous: 'If we were assured that it was Southern Ireland's intention to enter the war, we would of course if possible beforehand share our anti-aircraft weapons with them, and make secretly with them all possible necessary arrangements for their defence. Until we are so satisfied, we do not wish them to have further arms, and certainly will not give them ourselves.' He went on to speak of the 'depth and intensity of feeling against the policy of Irish neutrality' and ended prophetically: 'Should the present situation last till the end of the war, which is unlikely, a gulf will have opened between Northern and Southern Ireland, which it will be impossible to bridge in this generation.'[29]

Maffey's task was indeed an unenviable one. While he did his best to understand the Irish attitude, he found de Valera on one occasion in 1941 in an exceedingly 'nagging' mood and was driven to an outburst that de Valera seemed uneasy because in the past he could use Irish fanaticism to achieve international prestige: 'He could stir worldwide interest in the soul of

Ireland. But it is the soul of England which stirs the world today and Eire is a bog with a petty leader raking over old muck heaps.'[30]

Nevertheless there were some lighter moments. When in 1940, Maffey's office told the D.O. that the Irish Government would provide a military guard for the Office, the D.O. deprecated this in case there might be IRA infiltrators and gave the splendid advice that the practice of the F.O. was to ensure that a post abroad should be capable of being closed and defended against infiltrators 'by one or two sturdy messengers equipped with truncheons'.[31] Another report in those bleak days is worth recalling if only because it sheds a less harsh light on relations between the two countries. There had been a proposal to extend conscription to Northern Ireland which had greatly alarmed de Valera since the repercussions of Nationalist resentment might have been very serious. The War Cabinet decided in the end not to go ahead. Maffey lunched with three Ministers shortly after receiving the news and reported to Machtig: 'their joy was equally divided over the sinking of conscription and the sinking of the Bismarck.'[32]

Cranborne's Mission (December 1941)

In January 1941, Churchill told Cranborne firmly that he saw no policy towards Eire other than to see how the economic and shipping pressures worked. In spite of Churchill's attitude, Cranborne felt that there were a number of matters calling for personal discussion and in February 1941 he suggested to the P.M. that there might be advantages in a visit by him to Dublin; Churchill rejected this however, asking 'would you not find difficulties in repelling the charge that our action was a deliberate attempt to squeeze Ireland? I have a great dislike of dealing in humbug especially with a nation like the Irish. – You might easily have to make some inconvenient admissions or else say what is not true.'[33] Churchill felt that we 'should follow through the hard policy it is our duty to pursue'. The idea of a visit was not pursued at the time, but Cranborne's chance came before long.

The entry of the USA into the war changed the whole situation overnight and came as a tonic to Churchill. He lost no time in telegraphing to de Valera: 'Now is your chance. Now or never! A nation once again! I will meet you wherever you wish.'[34]* The exuberance in the terms was matched by the dramatic nature of its delivery shortly after 2 a.m. following a telephone call from Maffey to say that he had been instructed to deliver the message at once. De Valera did not respond in kind. After deliberating for two days he sent a message simply suggesting that 'Perhaps a visit from Lord Cranborne

* According to the biography of de Valera, the last sentence of the message as delivered read 'Am very ready to meet you at any time' which de Valera took as a summons to London.[35]

would be the best way towards a fuller understanding of our position here.' Cranborne arrived in Dublin on 16 December and on the following day received what was becoming the standard treatment in a two hours' lecture. He reported to the Cabinet:[36] 'I had a long, friendly, but fruitless talk ... He began immediately on Partition.' A large section of the country felt that 'so long as a part of their country was actually occupied by an alien power which had always been their enemy in the past, they could not align themselves with that Power.' Cranborne urged de Valera to use his great personal prestige, remonstrated that neutrality was bound to postpone indefinitely a solution of the Partition problem and underlined Eire's vulnerability through a shortage of supplies or invasion by Germany. He emphasized the help which the USA and the UK could give to an ally. De Valera seemed to accept the validity of all this, but insisted that his difficulty in rallying to the Allied cause came not from a lack of sympathy but because, with the Partition problem an open sore, any attempt to bring a United Ireland into the war would be doomed to failure. Cranborne concluded his melancholy report: 'From this position I could not budge him.'

Axis Missions in Dublin

The only major question to arise in the later war years was that of security before the Normandy landings. Before the outbreak of the war, the D.O. had considered the position of the Axis Missions in Dublin in the event of Eire (or the Union of South Africa) opting for neutrality and pointed out that a nation could still remain neutral while breaking off diplomatic relations. The Cabinet considered the matter on 1 September 1939, but took no action.[37] The D.O. kept in close touch with Dulanty who assured Harding on 4 September that he feared de Valera would not break off diplomatic relations with Germany, but that 'we could be sure that there would be no practical danger,' implying that the German Minister would be kept under surveillance.[38] In the main, this assurance was honourably carried out. German agents were landed from time to time, but their numbers were not large and they never constituted a serious threat* (there were equally from time to time British agents who were an embarrassment to Maffey and about whom the Eire Government complained). The situation was helped by the German Minister who seems to have behaved correctly and with circumspection.†

---

* De Valera's biographers mention a figure of 'the half dozen or so' all of whom were interned.[39]
† At the outbreak of war, the Eire Government wanted to appoint a Minister to their Legation in Berlin. Eden explained to de Valera: 'You will appreciate the difficulties arising over the formal procedure such as asking the King to sign credentials addressed to Herr Hitler.' De Valera did not press the matter and the Mission remained in the hands of the Chargé d'affaires.

With the approach of the Normandy landings, there was a danger that vital information might be passed through Dublin. By this time there was in Dublin an extremely active US Minister in the person of David Gray who was determined to ensure the dismissal of the Axis Missions. He did not succeed in his purpose, but in the process diverted some of the Irish animosity to his own head and away from Britain. Short of dismissing the Axis Missions, the Eire Government were as helpful as they felt they could be if they were to remain neutral. Early in 1944 at British instigation they compelled the German Minister to surrender his wireless transmitter and he was limited to ordinary cable communications which the British controlled and which were sent in a cypher which the British could in any case read.[40]

Britain's attitude towards Eire during the war was thus shown at two levels – the carrot and the stick were offered simultaneously. On the one hand was the effort at reasonableness, of seeking to meet the legitimate needs of a neutral with the aim of securing maximum cooperation; this was the stand consistently taken by Maffey and by Machtig and Stephenson. On the other hand was the exasperation of Churchill which led him to favour a course of recrimination and harsh treatment. Yet, recognizing that to justify the risks of seizing the ports the need would have to be one of survival, Churchill refrained. His moderation, in face of what from his idiosyncratic assessment he regarded as insupportable provocation, deserves some acclaim.

In one sense, the inconsistency in British attitudes tended to get the worst of both worlds. Churchill's bitterness hardened the Irish resolve to withhold the ports and made it more difficult for them to accord some of the benefits which the line taken by British officials was designed to secure. In the long run however the result was perhaps beneficial to Anglo-Irish relations. Churchill's vehemence brought home how sorely the British had been tried in their hour of danger; Maffey's diplomacy satisfied the Irish that nonetheless Britain was able to understand and was anxious to help when possible. After the strains and vicissitudes of war the fact is that relations between the two countries began to show greater mutual respect and even cordiality than at almost any previous time in their history. For this no small share of the credit is due to Maffey who, with the consistent support and encouragement of officials in the D.O., discharged his difficult mission in so acceptable a manner.

Territorial Responsibilities

Newfoundland

When war broke out, Newfoundland had been under Commission Government for a little more than five years. During that time, order had been brought into the finances, corruption had been checked, some development work had been undertaken and social services had been improved. But the regime, however benevolent, was not democratic and no progress had been made politically; economically too the island was in little different shape. The war brought about a total transformation. As in the First World War, Newfoundlanders rallied to the colours and this alone helped to relieve unemployment. They served in all the Armed Services, in the Merchant Marine, in the Pioneer Corps and in forestry work. The fall of France created a new situation; the extension of the U-boat campaign and later the advent of the long-range bomber involved Newfoundland in playing a key role in the Atlantic convoy system; this placed her suddenly in an undefended and exposed position. Overnight her strategic value to Britain was greater than it had ever been before – and it was even greater to Canada and the USA. Symbolic of the island's new significance was the first meeting of Roosevelt and Churchill at Argentia in August 1941 when the Atlantic Charter was signed. In due course the Canadians and the US (but not the British) established military, naval and air bases in the island. The resulting employment (at far higher wages than Newfoundland had been accustomed to) transformed the economy; from bankruptcy Newfoundland became prosperous and by the end of the war had a substantial surplus. Her horizons were widened and her main outside contacts became North American rather than European.

The major problem which first preoccupied the D.O. was the matter which later became known as the Bases Destroyers Agreement. By September 1940 the British and US Governments were negotiating to provide fifty old US destroyers to Britain and simultaneously for the lease to the US of bases in Newfoundland and the Caribbean for a period of 99 years 'freely and without consideration'.[1] The Newfoundland Members of the Commission were seriously alarmed by the British Government's intentions. They were in a dilemma; naturally they wanted to do everything possible to assist the war effort and indeed had a clear duty to take all possible steps to assure the security of the island. On the other hand, they had no representative institutions to support them and did not wish to put themselves in the position of selling the island's birthright. Two of the Commissioners, Penson and Emerson, visited London for the final negotiations with the US. Emerson was a St John's lawyer and was dogged in sticking to a point; Penson (a Treasury official) was one of the British Commissioners but showed himself more royalist than the King. Both felt strongly about what they regarded as unjustified claims by the US encroaching on the sovereignty of Newfoundland. Dixon was the Under Secretary in charge at the D.O.; he has related[2] that he felt a good deal of sympathy for the Newfoundland case and that he represented their point of view to the Secretary of State with all his power. The need for US cooperation at this critical stage of the war, both generally and over the particular related transaction of the fifty destroyers, was however of over-riding importance. The Government therefore felt it necessary to meet US demands over the bases (those in the Carribbean were included in the same agreement) to a greater extent than might otherwise have been considered right. Churchill had already committed himself to the principle of the leased bases in his speech in Parliament on 20 August 1940 in which he referred to the 'British Empire and the United States [being] somewhat mixed up together in some of their affairs.' The urgency of the situation permitted no moment for niggling departmental points. Nevertheless Churchill was persuaded that Newfoundlanders might be disturbed by what they might regard as a 'surrender' and agreed to send a personal letter to the Newfoundland Delegates which could be published. Dixon drafted such a message; this recognized the great sacrifices which Newfoundland was asked to accept, but pointed out that these were a direct and most valuable contribution to the winning of the war. To Dixon's surprise, the P.M. did not alter a single word and the letter was despatched as it stood. Dixon records that it gave great pleasure to the two Delegates and helped greatly to stifle criticism. In fact the Newfoundland people were not disposed to cavil and could well understand the importance of the fifty destroyers in the dangerous days of 1941. Moreover the construction of the bases soon began to bring prospects of employment and prosperity.

September 1941 saw the first visit to Newfoundland by members of the D.O., apart from a visit by Clutterbuck in 1938, since the time of the Royal Commission. In fact the visit to Newfoundland was incidental – Geoffrey Shakespeare, Parly US, was responsible for the evacuation of children overseas and visited various centres in North America including St John's, Newfoundland. Though the purpose of the visit was to see the British children, a Ministerial stay in Newfoundland was bound to attract attention; it was unfortunate therefore that, owing to the vagaries of early wartime Transatlantic flying, his programme had to be severely curtailed, giving little time for serious political discussion. This disappointed public opinion which had been looking – without any justification – for something more substantial. The following summarizes Shakespeare's main impressions:[3] *

> Apart from interested parties, there is no demand for responsible government at the present time. It is therefore clear that, for the duration of the war at least, no change in the *form* of government need be contemplated. The question is whether it is being operated to the best advantage. The Commissioners are not popular and, though some of the abuse levelled at them is unfair, there is a consistent view that they lack contact with the public. There is no Commissioner with the gift of putting a case across (the Governor sees his role primarily as the King's representative) and there would be much to be said for appointing at least one British member with political experience. In any case some machinery should be established to enable each Commissioner to meet representatives of the public, hear their complaints and expound the Commission's policies. The bases have revolutionised the economy of the whole island and brought a period of extraordinary prosperity; the U.S. and Canadian forces appear to have established excellent relations with each other and with the people of Newfoundland; but there is grave concern as to the future, Newfoundlanders seeing British control of defence matters slowly being withdrawn and wondering if they would one day wake to find themselves an American State or a Canadian Province (each of which would be equally unpopular). In general the island gives the impression of being in a neglected and dilapidated state and calls for large-scale improvements in all community services. Development and reconstruction would be of vital importance as soon as the war was over and planning should start at once.

The Ministerial changes at the D.O. in 1942 were important for Newfoundland. Cranborne was replaced by Attlee and Shakespeare, who left Ministerial office and was awarded a baronetcy for his services, was succeeded by Emrys-Evans, a Conservative M.P. (previously P.P.S. to Cranborne). Emrys-Evans was not a man of action and gained a poor reputation as a Parliamentary performer, but he was a keen student of Imperial problems and thought seriously about them. In June 1942 he submitted a thoughtful memorandum on Newfoundland.[4] In this he pondered over the 'only failure in the history of the British Empire of our own people to govern themselves' and pointed out that the solution adopted involved reversing a policy which had become established and universally accepted in Britain and in the Dominions. Because of this it was felt that local susceptibilities should be treated very tenderly and the Commission form of government was a compromise; while the island was nominally brought under British rule, the Commission was left to manage its own affairs as far as possible and was given

---

* Shakespeare's Private Secretary was a lady and could not at that time be carried by RAF across the Atlantic. The author (who was P.S. to the Secretary of State at the time) was selected to accompany Shakespeare, partly because his family was in the US and the Office gave him the opportunity to see them.

little guidance from the D.O. For their part the Commission acted cautiously and took a short-term view. Emrys-Evans pointed out that the recent record in Newfoundland showed no dramatic or impressive achievements and that this was noted both in Canada and the US. He thought that after the war it was likely that small nationalities, while retaining their sovereignty, would wish to form part of blocks for defence and economic purposes. He therefore urged, both on general as well as particular grounds, a new and vigorous policy with regard to Newfoundland. The immediate aim should be the improvement of the condition of the people and the development of natural resources so that the country would be able to manage its own affairs again as soon as possible. The ultimate aim should be to bring Newfoundland into the Confederation of Canada. The question was how to put this policy into operation. The Commission itself was not an effective body for carrying out a dynamic policy and the Governor (Admiral Sir Humphrey Walwyn) saw his role as that of Chairman only. The need was for a Governor who could provide leadership. Emrys-Evans called for a man of outstanding character and ability, with the gift of inspiring people – someone of the stamp of Milner in South Africa – and concluded with a plea for decision on a policy and on the man to carry it out.

Machtig, in what he described as a 'somewhat hurried minute'[5] agreed with the broad conclusion (though for different reasons), but denied that the D.O. had given little guidance to the Commission or that the Commissioners had failed to make much impression. However he agreed that the Commission had never been a very happy instrument and felt that the Newfoundland members of it had not fulfilled their function of testing public opinion. He also agreed that, after the war, there would be an irresistible move in favour of the restoration of self-government and that it would not be feasible to wait for the report of a further Royal Commission. He found himself also in 'very great agreement' that the aim of our policy should be to bring Newfoundland into the Canadian Federation, arguing that it would be politically impossible to retain control from Britain, but that a small country lacking in essential resources was likely to be unable to govern itself effectively. He did not share Emrys-Evans' view about the Governor and pointed out that the arrangement by which the Governor acted on the advice of his Commission and was therefore a titular head rather than a P.M. was one of the conditions on which the Newfoundland Parliament agreed to its own extinction. However the question of a Governor was really only a piece of machinery; what was needed was to decide what future was looked for for Newfoundland. His conclusion was that the only hope for a future within the British Empire was some union with Canada 'and the sooner this can be brought about the better'. Public opinion in Newfoundland had always been intensely against Union, but this was largely due to the fact that the Canadians had regarded them as poor relations and done little to help. If Canada could be induced to offer more liberal terms (perhaps backed by some help from Britain) then Newfoundland opinion might change. This would be a constructive policy worth trying. If we could aim at a big development, it would be better to keep the present system of Governorship, rather than embark on a Colonial type of Governor which would be inconsistent with the objective.

The matter was discussed with Attlee who decided to investigate the situation on the spot. As he recorded in his biography:[6] 'I had visited Newfoundlanders serving in the Forces and on lumber work and was much concerned at what would happen after the war. No Secretary of State had ever visited the island, so I decided to make a new start.' On the face of it, it may seem strange that the Leader of the Labour Party and the Deputy P.M. in the War Cabinet should have paid a special visit in the middle of the war to this relatively unimportant island. But Attlee had a passionate belief in justice and in democracy and had a natural sympathy for the underdog; he had never accepted that Commission government was the right answer and he had not forgotten his fierce campaign against the 1934 Act. Moreover in the D.O., Newfoundland offered the one area where he could exercise his full responsibility and where he felt he could make some personal contribution. The need for a visit was established after an initial exchange of messages between the Secretary of State and the Governor which revealed little meeting of minds between the two. Attlee regarded the Governor as reactionary with no political sense; in return the Governor felt that Attlee was a left-wing radical with an itch to interfere when he had no knowledge of conditions on the spot. On the face of it there was little in common between the waspish Socialist politician and the breezy, autocratic Admiral and it seemed inevitable that the Governor would be replaced.

Attlee set out in September 1942.* The visit showed the value of personal discussion and was a tribute to the quality of the two protagonists; from the moment of meeting Attlee and Walwyn established a remarkable rapport. Attlee was big enough to recognize that Commission Government would have to remain for the duration of the war and that Walwyn was the right man for the job. Equally important were the views formed by Attlee and the steps he set in train which led by successive stages to the final dénouement.

Attlee recorded some impressions in his autobiography.[7] He described St John's as 'a depressing place' and the vaunted picturesque villages as 'very slummy'. He found them a great contrast with the plushness of the American bases and the high standards in the company paper-making towns. He summed up: 'I came to the conclusion that the ills from which the island suffered were partly due to the fact that its economic resources were not

---

* Attlee was accompanied by his P.P.S., Clutterbuck and his P.S. His P.P.S. was Arthur Jenkins the M.P. for Pontypool (and father of Roy Jenkins). Clutterbuck, after a posting to South Africa, was again concerned with Newfoundland affairs when he became an Under Secretary in the D.O. in 1942. The author was P.S. at that time.

253

sufficient to allow it to stand on its own feet and partly to the lack of public spirit which had in the past resulted in a good deal of corruption. Besides this, the island was dominated by a group of capitalists who monopolised trade.'

After his return to London, Attlee battered out on his typewriter in characteristically pungent vein his impressions of his visit.[8] He had found that in Newfoundland 'a population rather less than that of Cornwall inhabits an island rather larger than Ireland.' There was practically no leisured class and in the absence of organized labour the work of government had fallen upon lawyers and merchants. He was not unduly impressed by reports of corruption, taking the view that the overseas standard of probity was not so high as in the UK (Newfoundland politicians merely had a narrower margin to work on than those of Canada or Australia). The Commission Government had raised hopes, but those went unfulfilled particularly as they were set up under Treasury influence at a time when 'retrenchment was all the rage'. Nevertheless hardly anyone thought it was possible during the war to return to full responsible government; many desired to find some half-way house. Attlee summed up their attitude as being that of a man who having had a spell of drunkenness has taken the pledge, is tired of it and would like to be a moderate drinker but does not quite trust himself. He found that the chief failure of the Commissioners was that they were aloof from the people and in particular that they had not prepared them for the resumption of self-government. He scathingly commented on Emerson (who thought the Commission should continue for twenty years): 'he would keep his football team all the season in the dressing room without even a punt about and expect them to be fit to win a match at the end.' Attlee recorded bluntly his long-held view that the whole conception of the Commission was wrong and devised by persons who, however skilled in administration, were inexpert in the practice of democracy. He concluded, 'We can with general assent continue the Commission till the end of the war. There will then be an irresistible demand ... for a return to self-government.' He proceeded to list various ways of facing the problem:

1. Accede to the demand with the probability of a Government spending the available balance and a return to bankruptcy;
2. Refuse the demand with the result that Britain would have to meet all the odium of the post-war slump;
3. Formulate some compromise, but this would promote irresponsibility and probably ensure that Britain got the blame for everything that went wrong;
4. Try to devise some different form of Government which, while democratic, did not conform to the Westminster model;
5. Put off the evil day by appointing a Commission of Enquiry.

The note ended without reaching any conclusion and curiously made no specific mention of two matters which were throughout in Attlee's mind – in the short term the need to foster democratic education (first at the local government level) and in the long term the possibility of union with Canada. But while a clear policy for the distant future eluded him, his practical mind fastened on the immediate steps which could be taken and these centred on making the people of Newfoundland more familiar with the ways of democracy. He therefore hit on the expedient of sending a small mission of Members of Parliament. Announcing this in the House of Commons,[9] Attlee said that, while concentrating on the winning of the war, the Government must think and plan ahead for the future of Newfoundland as far as this could be done. It would be premature to attempt to reach conclusions at present, but it would be valuable if fuller knowledge could be made available to Parliament. The mission he suggested would not be a formal body, it would have no terms of reference and would not present a written report; it would be of an informal goodwill character. To some extent, the device of a mission of this kind was a delaying tactic; it also served to go some way to meet demands in Newfoundland for a Royal Commission. But in any event it achieved the objective of stimulating political discussion in the island and of acquainting Parliament more fully with the affairs of a people for whom they had assumed a special responsibility.

The Members of Parliament selected for this task were C. G. Ammon, later Lord Ammon (Labour), Sir Derrick Gunston (Conservative) and A. P. Herbert, later Sir Alan Herbert (Independent). They were accompanied by a Secretary from the D.O. – G. W. St John Chadwick. The Mission formed a curiously assorted trio and held widely diverging views. Ammon was an unbending disciplinarian, Gunston a compulsive fisherman and Herbert a bon viveur and writer in addition to his other qualities. The Secretary later recorded[10] that the more the Mission saw of Newfoundlanders the more they came to like and respect them; but the more they talked with them, the more bewildered they became. They were unable to produce a unanimous report. A. P. Herbert described[11] how each of the three merchants of goodwill wrote his own independent report. 'When I saw Derrick Gunston again I found that, in odd corners and moments he had nearly finished tapping out his version ... And John Chadwick, at the more stately speed of the Civil Service, was drafting a most able report for our leader.' The three reports were submitted to the Government, but never published and, before any move could be made, Attlee had left the D.O. and been succeeded by Cranborne.

In November, Cranborne reported[12] to the Cabinet on the results of the Mission; he summarized their different viewpoints, but concluded that all three had found the islanders agreed on three main points: 1) no change during the war, 2) any change should *not* take the form of return to full responsible government and 3) confederation with Canada was wholly out of the question. Cranborne commented that 1) was very satisfactory since we should clearly wish to avoid any distraction from the war effort; that 2) resulted from Newfoundlanders' distrust of their politicians and lack of confidence in themselves and that while 3) would in many ways be the best long-term solution and the Canadian Government were certainly not disinterested in Newfoundland's future, nevertheless the British Government could not directly intervene and must take account of the traditional dislike of Canada. He himself recommended that there should be no change while the war lasted and that after the war the Newfoundland people should express their views by means of a National Convention. He asked for authority to made an early announcement on these lines and this was done by Emrys-Evans in December 1943.[13] The subsequent debate gave an opportunity for all members of the Mission to express their views, but was chiefly remarkable for Herbert's assertion that Newfoundland seemed to him 'about the most testing and complicated problem in the whole Imperial scene', having 'some of the religious, political and indeed industrial problems of Ireland and of India, the size of Ireland, the title of a Dominion, the population of Bradford, the history and habits of Dominion Government and the social services of a neglected Crown Colony.'[14]

Towards the end of the war, a scheme was drawn up to ensure that any new Government taking over would be able to do so with good prospects of financial stability. Shortly after becoming Prime Minister, Attlee characteristically wrote to Addison: 'You will recall that when I held your office I took a great deal of interest in the future of Newfoundland. I shall hope to receive your proposals before long.'[15] Addison had to report that progress on the scheme had been held up by the difficulties of the dollar situation; but he added that in the meantime the Canadians had indicated informally that they were much interested and wished to exchange ideas with the British Government before decisions on future policy were taken. Addison accordingly proposed to send Clutterbuck to Ottawa to compare notes informally and non-committedly.[16] Attlee replied that he was interested to know of Canadian forthcomingness and commented, 'They will have to make a very good offer to overcome the particularity and local prejudice of the Newfoundlanders to say nothing of the vested interests of the Water Street merchants.'[17] Clutterbuck flew to Ottawa in September 1945; his mission was not very encouraging: he reported[18] that he had had some useful talks but that the initial reactions was 'disappointing in that it appeared that, so far from Canadians having any positive ideas to put to us, there was little or no interest even in official circles and no serious consideration has been given to the problem.' However 'we have jollied them along and they have not been unreceptive.'

Three members of the Commission Government had visited London in August 1944 for discussions about the future and shortly afterwards a senior district magistrate was made available to prepare a scheme for elections to a Convention; the prolongation of the war in Europe however delayed matters and it was not until 11 December 1945[19] that Attlee announced the decision to set up an elected National Convention early in 1946. This would have the task of making recommendations as to possible forms of future Government which would be put before the people in a national referendum. To help the Convention, the British Government made available the services of Professor Wheare as an expert adviser in constitutional matters. The P.M. also promised that a factual statement of the island's financial and economic situation would be provided. Two officials, Edgar Jones of the Treasury and Chadwick of the D.O., were accordingly despatched to prepare the survey.

The survey was to be the last substantial contribution which the D.O. helped to make to Newfoundland. It was presented to the Convention and published as a White Paper.[20] The report was a self-contained commentary on the Commission of Government's stewardship and on the state of the island as it had emerged at the end of the war. It analysed a mass of statistics and did not hesitate to draw conclusions. The part-author later summed up: 'although the Report's immediate message was (to coin a phrase) "You've never had it so good," the lesson it sought (rather too polysyllabically) to drive home was "It may be too good to last".'[21]

The Convention met in September 1946 and decided early in 1947 to send delegations both to Britain and to Canada. Addison, by now the Dominions Secretary, received the Delegation in London and made it clear that it would always be Britain's desire to help within her means. If the people of Newfoundland decided in favour of the continuation of the Commission, HMG would continue to be responsible for Newfoundland's financial stability: if however they decided in favour of responsible government, this would mean that full responsibility for finance would rest with the Newfoundland Government and he could hold out no hope that HMG would take over liability for the public debt. This provided a chilly reception, but 1947 was a most difficult moment for Britain to afford generosity; the moral was perhaps therefore driven home with all the more force, that full independence meant standing in a cold world alone and facing the risk of another collapse. The Delegation to Ottawa met with a different reception; they received an offer, in the event of Newfoundland joining the Confederation, that on any interpretation was a generous one.

The report of the Convention in January 1948 showed that many favoured responsible government, few a continuation of the Commission while a number gave Confederation as a second choice. Although the Convention had not in their formal resolution recommended Confederation as one of the choices, the British Government decided that the referendum should put the three alternatives: i) Commission of Government for a further period of five years; ii) Responsible Government as it existed in 1934; iii) Confederation with Canada.

The first ballot in June was indecisive, but showed fewest votes for responsible government. This was therefore omitted in the second ballot held a month later when the voting was 71,000 for continuance of the Commission and 78,000 for Confederation. The campaign had been bitter and the margin was narrow. But it was enough – and enabled the three Governments of Britain, Newfoundland and Canada to announce, following consultations, that the Canadian Government were ready to proceed with arrangements for the entry of Newfoundland into Confederation and that the next step would be for Newfoundland representatives to agree on the terms of union. In the negotiations, the Canadians improved still further on their earlier proposals and full agreement was reached.

A bitter campaign against the Union was fought in all three countries: persistently and brilliantly in Britain by A. P. Herbert both in and out of Parliament; in Canada by Drew, Leader of the Conservative Opposition whose case was that such a step required consultation with the other Provinces in Canada; and in Newfoundland where the business and professional classes saw a threat to their monopoly. But none was of any avail and the Union came about on 1 April 1949.[22]

After so many years of uncertainty, the end came with almost dramatic suddenness. Moreover, though union with Canada seemed natural and had been talked of since the beginning of Confederation, the upshot was a surprise since before the referendum all observers were agreed that a majority were opposed to joining with Canada. The D.O. itself had consistently taken the view, at least since the 1931 collapse, that Confederation offered the best solution – and certainly the one that was in the interests of the UK; Britain's post-war weakness powerfully reinforced the case. There had of course always been close and friendly contact between the Canadian and British Governments. In the later stages Clutterbuck, since 1946 High Commissioner in Canada, was in constant and frank touch. But though the British Government wished for this result, they did little to will it. There was the minimum of collusion with the Canadians. The reason is clear; until a late stage (at least until the Canadians formulated their terms) there was no real prospect of a vote in favour of Confederation; moreover nothing would have destroyed the chances more effectively than the knowledge that the British were plotting for a 'sell-out'. Nevertheless when a decision was called for, the D.O. did not hesitate. It took the decision to place Confederation on the list of choices (and thus run the risk of obscuring the issue by adding a third alternative) and strongly supported the view that, despite the narrow majority, the second vote was sufficient to settle the future of the island. The history of the subsequent quarter of a century has hardly proved it wrong.

The High Commission Territories

In spite of the war, steady progress continued to be made in the introduction of Indirect Rule. In accordance with Lord Hailey's advice and in line with the general practice in other African colonial territories, the reform of African administration was gradually completed with the systemization of the powers of native authorities, courts and treasuries. In addition the Territories shared in the assistance made available under the Colonial Development and Welfare Act of 1929, the amounts for which had been substantially increased in 1940 and again in 1944.

With Smuts replacing Hertzog as the P.M. and with South Africa as an ally in the war, it might have been expected that the question of the transfer of the Territories would lie dormant. Such evidently was Eden's assumption when he came to the D.O. for he minuted, 'It is clear that here is a "sleeping dog" which we are fortunate to be able to let lie.'[23] Unfortunately the dog soon barked.

Colonel Reitz (Minister for Native Affairs) had after the outbreak of war agreed with the British High Commissioner that the question of transfer should be left in abeyance and that the Memorandum (on which both Governments had been working in fulfilment of the Thomas-Hertzog agreement) should not be published. But Smuts felt differently and in October indicated that he wished the matter raised in London. The British Government were not pleased by Smuts' behaviour and Eden sent a stiff reply saying 'It has come as an unpleasant surprise to me that General Smuts wishes to raise question of transfer again at this moment;' while being ready to discuss the matter with Reitz as requested, he made it clear that 'it would certainly be wrong to assume that Parliament would be indifferent . . . if there should be strong opposition from the native inhabitants.'[24] Reitz, who went to London for the meeting of Dominion Ministers in October 1939, was instructed to take up the matter of transfer and did so in talks with Eden and also separately with Devonshire (Parly US).

In the talks Eden firmly said that it would be a grave mistake to underrate the public interest; nothing could make a worse impression than if the British were to appear to hand over these Territories during a war fought for the interests of small nations; he refused to give any kind of assurance. Devonshire, who had himself visited South Africa in 1939 and been impressed with the strength and unanimity of the Chiefs' views, was host to Reitz at Chatsworth. He was gentler in manner and pursued various suggestions in discussion, but was nevertheless equally clear that 'while I thought transfer should be our ultimate policy, I did not regard it as a practical possibility and that our policy should be rather to produce conditions which made transfer possible.'[25] Reitz appears to have taken all this calmly; at one point he told Devonshire that, if some sort of move could be made in the next ten years, he thought his Government would be satisfied and Devonshire got the impression that Reitz had been instructed to 'fly a kite but not to press matters'. In any case no more was heard of the matter for another three years; in 1943 Smuts agreed that it should be suspended, partly perhaps because the agitation inside South Africa was dying down and partly because Smuts, pursuing Rhodes' dream, had other more grandiose ideas in mind. His raising the matter in this way provided an uncharacteristic incident in the relations between the two Governments and suggests Smuts more in the role of the 'slim' politician than the Imperial statesman.

Some light on D.O. policy can be glimpsed in the contrasting views expressed by successive High Commissioners. In his final summing up, Clark who retired as High Commissioner early in 1940 posed the dilemma that faced Britain: on the one hand the necessity for South African goodwill if Britain was to achieve anything and the undertakings on transfer to the Union Government. And on the other hand the interests of the Africans and the pledges to consult them. He was not sure that there was a way out, unless it were for Swaziland to accept a spectacular offer from Smuts. He suggested that Swaziland might be a test case, contributing to a final solution either, if successful, making possible a confident transfer of the other Territories or, if not, persuading the Union not to press its claim further.[26] Machtig expressed the D.O. view that, if faced with the political necessity of appeasing the Union, action confined to Swaziland would be 'a convenient solution', but only provided transfer could be effected with the goodwill of the Swazi.[27]

Harlech who became High Commissioner in 1941 favoured an early all-round settlement and a 'long-range' deal while Smuts was still in power. He envisaged the outright transfer of Swaziland, 'rectification' of the boundaries of Bechuanaland and no change in Basutoland. He was prepared to see Swaziland go because British rule was unpopular there, the territory was too small to make an efficient unit of administration and he feared it would always be a liability. The Nationalists, when they came to power, would certainly demand it and he would prefer to deal with Smuts. He concluded that to be tied for ever to the legal wording of the Act of Union without making any adjustment after the passage of more than thirty years was the 'negation of humanity, justice and commonsense'.[28] Tait did not accept this view and felt that Harlech did not realize how delicate the British position was on account of the pledges. There could be no question of seeking to upset the status quo until negotiations were forced upon Britain by the Union. He recognized that in theory the 1935 policy of cooperation held the field, but unashamedly regarded this as a paper formula: 'Lip-service could be paid to it, but it could never reconcile divergent attitudes.'[29]

Baring, who moved from Southern Rhodesia to become High Commissioner in 1944, had decided by April 1945 that, despite the increasing Imperial importance of South Africa, 'we should never sacrifice the true interests of Africans to a desire to remain friendly with a United Party Government at Pretoria.' But he added that, if the Territories were to be retained, the position would be impossible to defend unless there was proper development in agricultural, health and education services. If the High Commission Territories fell below the new modern standards of good administration, this could exacerbate feeling in South Africa.[30] Here spoke again the authentic voice of British liberalism and Baring's words expressed the aim that the British Government sought to follow.

Hailey later charged that the attitude of the British Government over transfer 'revealed a measure of hesitation, and at times even of evasion, which must have appeared unworthy of a great nation'.[31] But the dilemma in which Britain found herself imposed the necessity for compromise. Even if wider considerations of British interests were left aside, Britain needed the cooperation of South Africa for the sake of the inhabitants of the Territories themselves. And even if moral considerations were absent (and they were not) the British Government could not have agreed to transfer because Parliament would not have approved; all parties – radical and imperialist alike – were agreed on this. It would not have been practicable for the answer to be either a blunt No or a complaisant Yes. The equivocation of the D.O. was required by the situation and was not dictated by narrow self-interest (the Territories themselves were liabilities and not assets). Indeed the policy was conceived as being in the interests of the inhabitants and in fact it enabled each of the Territories in turn later to achieve full independence.

CHAPTER 9

The Post-War Settlement

In the closing years of the war, the D.O. devoted attention to two main issues – the form which the Commonwealth association should take in the post-war years and secondly the nature of the peace settlement and the international machinery required to enforce it.

The future of the Commonwealth was discussed in a number of public speeches during 1943 and 1944, and its machinery was considered at the Dominion Prime Ministers' Meeting in May 1944. The idea of a United Nations was proclaimed in the Declaration at Washington in January 1942 and finally settled at the Conference of all the Allies in San Francisco in April 1945; in addition a number of international agencies dealing with specific subjects was established; all of these were of importance to the Dominions.

The Future of the Commonwealth

The question of the future of the Commonwealth raised a number of distinct issues; about its nature, its extent, its role in the United Nations and its own organization.

As to its future, two extreme courses were ruled out in advance. It would have been possible to dissolve the bonds of Empire altogether on the grounds that an exclusive association such as the Commonwealth had no place in a world of international cooperation under the United Nations. Though the Empire had detractors and some opponents in all Commonwealth countries, this argument found no serious support anywhere in the Commonwealth. The almost universal verdict at the time of the ending of the war was that the degree of unity achieved during the war had proved its value and that the association should continue; the D.O. for its part did all it could to encourage this attitude. At the other extreme, it could have been argued that the war had shown how dangerously ill-prepared all Commonwealth countries had been and that the course of prudence was to band together in advance and for each to guarantee to defend other Members against aggression. It is remarkable, after a war in which there had in effect been a successful alliance between all Commonwealth members and just before many of them undertook defence commitments against communism under a variety of Regional Pacts, that the possibility of the Commonwealth itself developing on NATO lines was never considered; the D.O. for its part considered such an idea impracticable and gave it no support.

Among the many contributions to public debate about the future of the Commonwealth, three made a special impact. The first was a series of speeches by Curtin in which he advocated an Imperial Council and Secretariat.[1] The second was a talk by Smuts to the Empire Parliamentary Association in London in November 1943.[2] He saw after the war a Britain 'with glory, honour and prestige' but from a material point of view poor. Power would be concentrated in the USA and USSR. Rather than a closer union with the USA, Smuts advocated Britain working with the smaller countries of Western Europe, for whom the Commonwealth would provide an easy association. It was in this speech that, as we have seen in Chapter 2, he also urged a strengthening of the Commonwealth with emphasis on decentralization.

The third was a speech by Halifax, at that time British Ambassador in Washington, given in Toronto in January 1944.[3] On the face of it, most of what he said seemed innocuous enough, if not platitudinous; but given the circumstances it caused an explosion. The Ambassador's theme was the need for closer Commonwealth unity after the war. He fully recognized the independence of the Dominions and had no idea of retracing steps. But it had, he thought, been a weakness that the weight of decision on many problems of defence was not more widely shared. He urged therefore that nothing should be left 'undone to bring our people into closer unity of thought and action'. Halifax did not regard the speech as a major pronouncement and he had not thought it necessary to clear it in advance with the British High Commissioner in Ottawa, still less with the Government in London. Unwisely however he concluded with what appeared to be a pronouncement of British Government policy:

> If, in the future, Britain is to play her part without assuming burdens greater than she can support, she must have with her in peace the same strength that has sustained her in this war. Not Great Britain only, but the British Commonwealth and Empire must be the fourth power in that group upon which, under Providence, the peace of the world will henceforth depend.

According to Massey, Mackenzie King's reaction was one of 'paranoic fury'.[4] In his diary King himself recorded that he was 'simply dumbfounded' and immediately began to suspect that 'Halifax's work was all part of a plan which had been worked out with Churchill ... As Englishmen, of course, they seek to recover for Britain and the United Kingdom and the Empire the prestige which they are losing as a nation.'[5] The British High Commission telegraphed to the D.O. an account of the critical Press reactions throughout

Canada and commented that nationalist opinion was in one of its touchy moods and regarded appeals for unity with quite unwarranted suspicion.[6] On 26 January after a talk with King, MacDonald reported:[7] 'he gave two reasons for his resentment ... First, it looked to him like part of a deliberate design by the United Kingdom Government and some Dominion statesmen to revive an imperialism which left the Dominions something less than national sovereignty ... [secondly] ... Lord Halifax's speech had amounted to an attack on his personal position. Lord Halifax must have known that he [Mackenzie King] would not agree with some of the principal views he expressed and that those views would be used against him by his political opponents ...'

Churchill took the stern view that Halifax ought not to have made the speech without reference home beforehand, since it was in effect an interference in Canadian politics, 'turning markedly against Mackenzie King'.[8]

When the dust had settled, Cranborne wrote in April 1944 that he was quite sure that nothing was further from Halifax's mind than to suggest any wish on the part of the British to assume control of Canadian foreign policy. 'All he intended to indicate was that consultation between the various Empire countries was essential and that consultation should be as constant and as close as possible. It only shows how very sensitive Canadian opinion is at the present time. We are fully aware of this in the D.O., but I am afraid it is not sufficiently recognized outside ...'[9]

Meeting of the Dominion Prime Ministers 1944

Ever since the early days of 1940, the British Government had sought to bring all the Dominion leaders together in conference but, though individual Prime Ministers came from time to time, a collective meeting had not been found practicable. By 1943 however there was a general wish that a meeting should be held before long. Cranborne had a special reason for wanting a meeting since he felt that there must be adequate prior consultation with Dominion Governments before decisions were taken at the Summit of the Big Three about the post-war settlement in Europe. A meeting could not be arranged in 1943 however and finally took place in May 1944. Cranborne suggested to the War Cabinet that it should be made clear that the meeting was intended to be a meeting of Prime Ministers and not a full Imperial Conference. He recommended that the discussion should cover general matters concerning the military situation, the probable two-stage ending of the war, the post-war settlement and cooperation within the British Commonwealth.[10] The Cabinet rejected Cranborne's recommendation that, as this would not be an Imperial Conference, no invitation should be sent to the Prime Minister of

Southern Rhodesia; Huggins (like the Indian representative to the War Cabinet) was invited to be available when matters of special concern to his country were discussed.[11] The 1944 Meeting had a special value since it provided a unique demonstration of Commonwealth solidarity to the world as a whole and enabled Dominion Prime Ministers to learn in secrecy of the war plans. It was not an occasion for taking decisions; the vital decisions would be made elsewhere on the fields of battle.

There was no dearth of ideas at the Meeting; though Churchill's mind was preoccupied by the war, in a moment of enthusiasm he spoke to Mackenzie King of an Annual Conference of Prime Ministers, meeting from time to time in the Dominions and also of regular meetings of the Committee of Defence (which King took to mean meetings of the Chiefs of Staff).[12] Churchill also had notions about regional organization. Smuts was fertile in ideas favouring at this time some association with the countries of North West Europe; Mackenzie King was elaborating his thoughts for the address he had been invited to give to both Houses of Parliament. But it was Curtin's ideas for changes in organization which created the most dramatic impact.

The Curtin proposals were in line with the consistent Australian stand throughout the war and had been formulated in his speeches at the end of 1943. They involved a) recognition of the Dominion High Commissioners in London and the Dominions Secretary as a standing sub-Committee of the Imperial Conference and b) establishment of a joint permanent Secretariat of the Imperial Conference.

In a memorandum to the War Cabinet before the Meeting,[13] Cranborne analysed the proposals and suggested that they were designed to ensure that the Australian voice was listened to and accepted rather than to emphasize the need for a common policy. He summed up the attitude of other Dominion Governments as follows:

> Canada had the same objective as Australia, namely control of Canadian policy by the people of Canada, but would not consider that this would best be achieved by a close linking of Canada's policy with that of other Commonwealth Members.
> New Zealand: Fraser might reasonably be expected to support the Australian point of view.
> South Africa: Smuts supported the idea for a cooperative body of states to counter-balance the Great Powers of Russia and the USA.

Cranborne pointed out that hitherto the British Government had been careful to refrain from committing themselves to either side, but as King and Curtin would not agree, it would be well to be prepared with some compromise suggestions. He therefore explored the possibilities of regular annual meetings of Foreign Ministers and some kind of formalization of the system of London meetings with High Commissioners. Cranborne thought it likely that Mackenzie King would still regard as unacceptable any proposal for a

Secretariat, but possibly he might be reconciled to the idea if the Secretariat were not to be concerned with policy and would be no more than an office for the exchange and collection of information: in any case 'there is, of course, no reason why we ourselves should oppose any scheme which would make for closer machinery.'

In the event, the Curtin proposals never got off the ground. The item seems to have been handled in a perfunctory fashion. It was taken at the last meeting but one after the draft of the communiqué had been disposed of; Mackenzie King seems to have been taken aback by Curtin's 'lengthy statement which we were supposed to discuss ... after we had come to an agreement on the whole proceedings.'[14] Churchill was not present (being detained by operational matters) and Attlee took the chair. Curtin was deeply hurt by this treatment, though it does not appear that any slight was intended.[15]

Not only was the opposition stronger than Cranborne had predicted; there was no strong support at all. The attitude of King and Smuts was predictably hostile to any idea of centralization; and, though Fraser asserted that there was little in the Australian proposals with which he disagreed, he gave no active support. The Meeting dismissed the proposals under the polite formula of remitting them for further study. It is a wry comment on the 1944 Meeting that one of the few changes in a matter of Commonwealth cooperation on which all agreed was that the British Prime Minister should meet the Dominion High Commissioners once a month – in fact, after a first Meeting in June and another in December even that idea was not acted upon.

As to the results in the longer term, it is possible to take more than one view. Mansergh argues that the discussions about the functioning of the Commonwealth took place within a context of agreement upon the essential nature and purposes of the Commonwealth, that the flexible system of cooperation (as opposed to institutionalization by setting up a rigid Secretariat) showed in fact a continuing capacity for development and that the rejection of proposals for more formal machinery may be regarded as evidence of a degree of unity in aims and outlook which made additional machinery superfluous at that time.[16] It is equally possible to maintain that the retention of the easy, informal, flexible Commonwealth system contained within it the seeds of its own ultimate dissolution. The nature of the Commonwealth as re-affirmed at the 1944 Meeting showed it to be the sort of association to which, on the transfer of power in Asia and Africa, the newly independent countries need have no inhibitions in seeking membership; equally the new Members were able to take advantage of the freedom and independence accorded to all Members in a way that led to such disarray when acute differences of policy arose with Britain in the sixties. What emerges clearly is that the Meeting marked the apotheosis of Mackenzie King and all that he stood for: ever since the Chanak incident in 1922 and at each succeeding Imperial Conference he had fought against centralization and Imperialism. This was for him virtually the last round – and he won completely. As if to emphasize his achievement, he was invited to address both Houses of Parliament when he took the opportunity to assert the view of the Commonwealth that he had held for a lifetime. He referred again in phrases that were hardly original to the 'continuing Conference of the Cabinets of the Commonwealth' and he expressed his complete satisfaction with the existing arrangements for Commonwealth consultation.[17] Even if not all his colleagues would have agreed with such hyperbolic language, his tribute can not unfairly be regarded as an endorsement of all that the D.O. had striven for since its establishment; its importance lay in recording the agreement that there should be no change in the way that the D.O. had sought to carry out its responsibilities for Commonwealth consultation.

The attitude of the D.O. itself to these matters showed that it was more concerned with finding a solution that would be acceptable to all Dominion Governments than with crusading for any changes that it thought would serve British interests best. The response was therefore cautious rather than imaginative, pragmatic rather than idealistic. The balanced if complacent position which the D.O. took up is well illustrated in a minute Cranborne addressed to Churchill about a debate on Dominion affairs in which he suggested the following points.

1. Closer cooperation. It would be deplorable to give the impression that the United Kingdom was trying to dictate to the Dominions how their joint affairs should be managed.
2. Defence cooperation. The answer to any criticism that this was inadequate before the war might be that we did in fact rely on the whole-hearted participation of the Dominions in any war and were fully justified by the event.
3. To the criticism that there was no proper machinery before the war for providing a joint foreign policy, the answer might be that there was full and constant discussion of foreign policy and general agreement as to the policy that should be pursued. Machinery can, of course, be improved, but no matter of machinery can of itself secure more than this.

International Affairs

The first steps towards the organization of a new world order were taken by the Great Powers of their own motion. The intention to found a United Nations Organization was made clear at the 1943 Quebec Conference and an announcement in the name of the Four Powers* was contained in the Moscow Declaration of October 1943. Subsequently the Four Powers alone met in

* The 'Big Three' were the USA, USSR and UK. The 'Big Four' added France and the 'Big Five' China.

August 1944 at Dumbarton Oaks to draw up a draft Charter. The Dominions were neither parties to these discussions nor were they consulted in advance by the British Government. Churchill was very firm about this: he expressed his views in a paper[18] written before the meeting of Foreign Ministers in Moscow: 'It will not, I am sure, be physically possible to consult the Dominions before the main meeting in November, upon the whole future of the world. This meeting ... can only lead to broad understandings between the three Governments, and it will of course be necessary to impart the Russian view and our reactions to it, to the Dominions after the meeting has taken place. I am afraid it will not be practicable either here or in the future to have meetings between Britain, the United States and Soviet Russia at which Britain is represented by five principals of equal status and Russia and the United States by only one. It will not be possible to tell the Dominions in advance what our views are because we are trying to go with open minds to hear for the first time the formidable demands which will be made by Monsieur Stalin after the great victories which the Russian armies have won and are winning. On the other hand, it would seem a great pity to abandon the meeting altogether in view of the immense demand there is that it should take place. We must be careful that the Dominion claims to representation at discussions do not make all discussions impossible.'

This failure to consult the Dominions extended to the Cairo Conference where major decisions were made about the future of Manchuria, Korea and the Japanese Islands in the Pacific, which took Australia and New Zealand completely by surprise. Cranborne constantly sought, but in vain, to communicate more information to Dominion Governments or to summon an early meeting of Prime Ministers at which any difficulties could be discussed. The Australian and New Zealand Governments, who had special interests in the Pacific, were alarmed that a pattern was being set for post-war settlements to be determined exclusively by the Great Powers. Their anxiety led, on Evatt's initiative, to the Australian–New Zealand Agreement of 1944. This was a formidable document, in the form of a formal treaty, consisting of no less than 42 Articles covering a declaration of principles governing cooperation between the two Governments, setting out their views on all outstanding problems and establishing permanent machinery. One of the main purposes of the Agreement undoubtedly was to serve notice on the Great Powers of the Australian and New Zealand claims. This was achieved, but owing to the assertiveness of the language at some cost to friendly relationships with the USA. Evatt claimed that the Agreement had had a warm and encouraging welcome on all sides, especially in the UK and also among the other United Nations. This was not true of the USA and was excessive in relation to other countries. Cranborne disliked it, but the British Government refrained from any public rebuke. Their reaction is exemplified in the following somewhat sour reflexion by Shannon, the head of the department concerned in the

D.O.: 'But when all allowances have been made it remains a deplorable monument of egregious amateurism in international affairs. It will not, I think, prove helpful to the Commonwealth Government or to Dr. Evatt personally in international affairs.'[19]

The predominance of the Great Powers was of concern to all the Dominions. Though there were variations in their attitudes, all were agreed on certain major points and especially: i) they were all strong supporters of an effective World Organization; ii) they all wished to be Members in their own right, not by virtue of membership of the British Commonwealth, and wished to play their own independent role; Canada in particular resisted any idea that Britain (or any other Commonwealth country) could act in any sense on behalf of the Commonwealth as a whole; iii) they hoped to influence decisions in an effective way and looked forward to an organization which would not be dominated by the Great Powers. Both Canada and Australia were insistent on their rights to direct representation in the subordinate bodies.

The second point was of close concern to the Dominions Office and raised a major problem. The British Empire was frequently accused by its critics of seeking six votes. Partly on the strength of this, the USSR had originally claimed 17. Eventually at Yalta, the UK and USA agreed to the admission of White Russia and the Ukraine, Roosevelt reserving the right to ask for additional votes for the USA to secure parity. (In the event though the Soviet claim was accepted, the USA refrained from pressing for three seats herself.) Dominion views about membership of the UN in their own right ran counter to some of the notions which attracted Churchill. He wanted the world instrument to be founded on a regional basis; in his view most of the principal regions suggested themselves and he thought it right that issues of local controversy should be thrashed out in the Regional Council which would then report to the Supreme Body. Churchill's further idea was that the appropriate Commonwealth Member should represent the whole Commonwealth on the Regional Councils. He set out his ideas in a memorandum, 'Regional Leagues under the World Council', which was discussed by the Cabinet in April 1944. At the Cabinet meeting, Churchill explained that, in the world structure he had in view, ultimate authority for keeping the peace would be concentrated in the hands of the three Great Powers, but that the Dominions and other important and historic countries would be associated with the Great Powers through the working of the Regional Councils.[20] His scheme found little favour with his colleagues and was not liked by Eden. Cranborne addressed him a strong minute of dissent, confessing that he could not help feeling that the scheme 'contains within it the possible seeds of Imperial disruption'. He feared that the Dominions would tend to concentrate their attention more and more on their own areas and less on the Empire as a whole and, in particular, that Canada would be tempted to attach herself to the USA.[21]

During the Cabinet discussion, Attlee drew attention to the importance of ensuring that the British Commonwealth should speak as a single unit (it was as if Halifax had never uttered!). If that could be secured, Attlee thought that the Empire would be in as strong a position, in dealing with the problems of the post-war world, as the USA and the USSR. But if the Dominions insisted on taking their own line as separate nations, the Empire as a whole would be in a much less satisfactory position.[22]

In an informal talk with Churchill before the 1944 Meeting, Mackenzie King made it clear that he did not welcome his ideas. In particular he took exception to the idea of Canada representing Britain on the American Regional Council. With characteristic ingenuity, Churchill at once suggested that the UK could sit on the Council in her own right by virtue of her possession of the West Indies.[23] When the matter came up in the 1944 Meeting, Churchill spoke eloquently but found little support. King described the occasion as the 'hardest battle of the Conference thus far'[24] but found an ally in Smuts. However Fraser of New Zealand proved himself to be its strongest opponent; in a letter to Eden he set out with crisp cogency the objections of the New Zealand Government towards any division into regions:

> a) It will encourage the reluctance of states to take part in sanctions against an offending state which is not located in their regions. To be effective, sanctions, which are the core of effective action for the preservation of peace, must be universally applied, e.g. would European States cooperate in Pacific sanctions and vice versa? b) It is not a suitable foundation for the eligibility of States to membership of a World Council. As a small power, New Zealand would wish to have the right to make its voice heard on the World Council and not lose its identity in a regional organization. c) In particular, New Zealand feels that a Pacific or Asiatic region, regarded as a permanent unit, is an unreal conception.[25]

After the discussion, Churchill agreed to withdraw his paper, while adhering to his own personal viewpoint: he sent a minute to Cranborne accepting that the idea of Regional Leagues was full of dangers, but added: 'I hope however to rescue the "United States of Europe" from the midst of them.'[26]

With the ending of the war, problems arose with the defeat of the enemy both in Europe and in the Far East. The Paris Peace Conference was held in the shadow of growing dissension between the Western Allies and Soviet Russia; it equally revealed differences between Britain and the Dominions. As regards Japan, an innovation in Commonwealth techniques was marked by the decision to hold in Canberra early in 1947 a Commonwealth Conference at a level below that of Prime Minister to consider the specific subject of the proposed Peace Treaty with Japan. The Chairman was Evatt. The British Delegation was led by the Dominions Secretary, Addison (curiously the only occasion when the Dominions Secretary, or for that matter the Commonwealth Secretary, led the British delegation at a significant multilateral

Conference). The Conference was largely window-dressing for Evatt's benefit and achieved few results. All Commonwealth Governments (except Eire) attended; they included for the first time India and Pakistan (who achieved independence during the Meeting) and, for the first and only time, Burma (who later chose independence outside the Commonwealth).

In Europe, Canadian forces operated with the British as part of the occupying forces in the British zone of Germany and Australian and New Zealand forces took part in the occupation of Japan. An Australian represented not only Australia but the UK, India and New Zealand as well on the Allied Council for Japan in Tokyo and an Australian General commanded all British Commonwealth Occupation Forces in Japan. All these matters were considered at the first meeting of Dominion Prime Ministers after the ending of the war, held in 1946. The Conference continued the informal pattern set in 1944 and, under Attlee's quiet but effective guidance, did useful if unspectacular work. The Meeting considered the draft Peace Treaties, the future of Germany and other matters connected with the peace settlements. The representatives also placed on record (it was virtually King's last appearance) their appreciation of the value of 'the existing methods of consultation among Commonwealth countries which were peculiarly appropriate to the character of the British Commonwealth and preferable to rigid centralised machinery'.[27]

The United Nations

Though Dominion Governments were not parties to the Moscow Declaration, foreshadowing the new World Organization, the Dominions Office did its best to keep them informed of all developments and considered that they were in fact fully consulted. They were not present at the Dumbarton Oaks Conference, but the British Government were at pains to keep them in the picture and Lester Pearson later recorded that, in contrast to the USA, the British 'as a matter of policy kept Canada and the other Dominions well informed about these preliminary negotiations'.[28] The British Government further arranged a Conference in London with all Dominion delegates immediately before the Conference in San Francisco. It was a distinguished gathering including Smuts, Evatt, Fraser and indeed the heads of all Commonwealth Delegations except Canada. Churchill presided at one of the meetings, but otherwise Cranborne led the British team. The Conference was useful, but was played in a low key and disagreements were not emphasized. Cranborne evidently handled matters with tact and skill. Before the Conference, Cockram from the D.O. sent to Gladwyn Jebb in the F.O. a note[29] on the probable attitude of Dominion Governments which made the following points.

Canada. The Canadian Government have been pressuring the US Administration with the idea that the Dumbarton Oaks proposals must be modified if they are not to be put in a very difficult position politically, the major difficulty for them being that Canada would be committed to participating in coercive action against an aggressor without herself having any say in the matter. Canada seeks better representation for secondary powers throughout the UN structure.

Australia. The delegation is likely to be unwieldly and under-staffed, will probably be disunited and split by personal ambitions and dislikes, mainly because of Evatt. Australia therefore is unpredictable and may be unreliable.

New Zealand. Fraser is both reliable and cooperative. New Zealand is unworried by ambitions to be recognized as a secondary power; she is strongly attached to the notion of international trusteeship for dependent peoples, but otherwise can be relied upon to support Britain.

South Africa. Smuts will to all intents and purposes be the delegation. The Union wants to incorporate South West Africa in some form or other and Smuts may feel obliged to refuse commitment to military sanctions without the Union's consent; but he is not anxious to be considered a secondary power. The South African delegation ought therefore to be an effective and relatively disinterested one with whom it will be easier to co-operate than with any other Commonwealth delegation and from whom more effective support can be obtained.

The main point which concerned the Dominions in the draft Charter was the authority to be accorded to the Great Powers: their control of the Security Council, their use of the veto which could lead to the dominance of those Powers, contrasted with the lack of provision for the smaller powers to make their views felt before decisions were taken. There were a dazzling variety of amendments on a number of differing items which the fertile brain of Evatt devised and which his ambition and determination often successfully pushed through to adoption, and the New Zealanders were insistent with him on pressing for provision of trusteeship. But the central question for both Canada and Australia was that of great-power control and the right of veto. Canada in particular at this time pressed the doctrine of 'functionalism'; this was based on the view that representation on international bodies should neither be confined exclusively to the largest powers, nor divided equally among all states: it should be extended on a functional basis so that states, whatever their size, which had the greatest contribution to make should be admitted as members. Another argument in favour of greater representation of secondary powers lay in the development of the regional principle. In a sense, the Australian–New Zealand agreement represented an ambitious example in regional planning, but the concept of concentrating on regional bodies was not a solution to the problem as a whole.*

The British delegation to the Conference at San Francisco comprised a formidable team, including Attlee, Eden (both of whom had held the office of Dominions Secretary), and an array of junior Ministers in all parties. The D.O. members throughout were Cranborne with his P.S. (Clark) and Cockram, then serving in the Washington Embassy. The British General Election was announced while the Conference was in session; Halifax was left in charge of the British Delegation with Cranborne as the only senior Minister.

The arrangements at the Conference for Commonwealth consultation as described by Cockram were very thorough. His first letter reported that there seemed every sign that as a result of the talks in London all Dominion Delegations were doing their best to be as helpful and cooperative as possible. Two weeks later he reported that 'last week was unconscionably grim and earnest'.[30] The main cause was Evatt who 'is probably the most generally disliked man at the Conference' and 'considers that Australia is being let down if he does not obtain immediate and unquestioning support for every suggestion which he makes, whether it be dictated by the genuine interests of Australia, the platform of the Australian Labour Party or the prestige of one of its representatives at San Francisco...'[31] A later letter drew an alarming picture of Evatt, having seen one after another of his amendments voted down, taking the bit between his teeth and trying to drag the entire Conference into 'a bolt'. He offended in one day each of the Big Five, Holland and Belgium, the Arabs *and* the Jews, and the Latin-American countries! In a final explosion he vented his spleen on Cockram who in his letter to the D.O. 'apologised humbly for breaking the rules and answering back'.[32] A letter sent in the final days of the Conference revealed Cockram's gloom and doubt whether it would prove possible to solve the problem of the veto and conditions for the amendment of the Charter (the Soviet Delegation were in the event authorized to make a sufficient concession which Evatt accepted). The letter mentioned differences between Britain and Australia on the provisions about domestic jurisdiction and for trusteeship. On the latter item which 'possessed too strong an emotional appeal', Evatt had 'harped ceaselessly to Fraser on the necessity of protecting dependent people from exploitation'.[33]

---

* In a curious way, however, the principle of regionalism did survive in the UN. The Dominions all signed the UN Charter separately according to their alphabetical order and not, as they had signed the League of Nations Covenant, grouped together under the general heading 'British Empire'. They were recognized as fully independent sovereign States; yet when it came to elections to the Security Council they were in effect grouped together as if members of a region and, until the Council was enlarged in 1965 and different arrangements were in any case called for to provide for the increase in Commonwealth members, there was traditionally a 'Commonwealth' seat, filled in turn by Commonwealth members other than the UK.

There was an important discussion at one of the last meetings of the British Commonwealth delegations in which Halifax explained the general UK standpoint. He said that the UK had a dual role at the Conference, as a Member of the British Commonwealth and as one of the four sponsoring powers. In the latter role they had to bear in mind the major objects at the Conference, first that the USA should be brought into the new world organization and secondly that there should be no breach with Russia. He thought it valuable that the expression, sometimes forcible, of the different points of view in the Commonwealth had dispelled the illusion of six votes; nevertheless if the UK were to maintain its position among the Big Three and to exert the greatest possible influence, it would be important to foster the idea that the British Commonwealth was a group, the members of which generally thought alike on major issues and that, while the UK could only speak for itself, nevertheless it could generally be assumed that its views represented the ultimate interest of the group.[34]

Fraser immediately responded to express his general agreement and his appreciation of the ceaseless efforts at conciliation of Halifax and Cranborne who had been 'models of tact and diplomacy' but went on to complain bitterly of junior members of the British delegation who had treated remarks of Dominion representatives with 'lofty superiority' (he made it clear that his criticism did not apply to D.O. officials who had been unfailingly helpful). Evatt supported this criticism; he thought that any difficulty had been due to the British Government's failure to carry out the conclusions of the London meeting and he claimed that 'the F.O. officials too often appeared to think that the Dominion delegations should be seen but not heard.' The Canadians placed on record that, as between officials, co-operation between the British and Canadian delegations had been perfect, though they thought that the necessity to clear every question with the Big Five placed a hopeless load on the British and hampered complete Commonwealth agreement. Smuts concluded that a great public service had been performed by the Conference in dispelling the illusion that the Commonwealth was a close-knit bloc which took its orders from London. Yet there had throughout been effective Commonwealth consultation and, if the Conference proved to be a success, it would be due to the British Commonwealth group and to the fact that the UK had been able to explain the point of view of the other Members and to act as middleman between the Big Five and the smaller powers.

The official report[35] sent at the conclusion of the Conference confirmed Cockram's general impressions about the Dominion delegations. It summarized the position:

Field Marshal Smuts has in countless ways both in public and private been consistently helpful. The Canadians have been one of the strongest and ablest teams at the Conference. They have displayed a real solicitude for the welfare of the organisation and have worked closely with us. The New Zealand delegation has been friendly, although Mr. Fraser has, occasionally, been carried away by his feelings and his interventions in debate have not (repeat not) always been judicious. The Australian delegation has been divided within itself. Mr. Forde, all the unofficial delegates, and almost all the officials have been anxious to co-operate fully with the other Commonwealth delegations. Dr. Evatt and one or two of his personal staff on the other hand, have been hasty and suspicious: constantly pressing for full support for his various purposes, sometimes contra-dictory, and outspokenly critical if it was not instantly forthcoming. He has felt under little obligation to reciprocate. His attitude to other Commonwealth dele-gations has been similar and it has been particularly resented by the Canadians ... the Conference, in consequence of Dr. Evatt's conduct and Mr. Fraser's occasional effervescences has certainly dispelled the illusion that Dominion representation means six votes for the United Kingdom. It has also demonstrated that the Commonwealth countries breed independent and vigorous personalities, and the Commonwealth contribution, both individual and collective, has been outstanding.

The British delegation was able to support the Dominions in several matters to which they attached cardinal importance and particularly domestic juris-diction for Australia, the future of South West Africa for General Smuts and, for Canada, the provision that when decisions regarding the use of a State's own armed forces for UN purposes were taken, that State could become a co-opted member of the Security Council.

By the end of the war, the D.O. had come of age, both in years and metaphorically speaking. The Dominions had made an outstanding contri-bution throughout the war and had successfully claimed their right to speak for themselves in any international forum. In the early post-war years, with the Axis powers no longer of account, with much of Europe prostrate and before the nations of Asia and Africa achieved their independence and made their voice heard, the Dominions played a more considerable role than at any other time.

With the ending of the war a new stage was reached. Men's minds turned to the problems of peace and to the place of the Commonwealth in the new world order. While there was general accord that the Commonwealth had proved itself during the war, there was no disposition to strengthen it by any centralized control, closer economic union or military alliance. On the contrary, none of the Dominions wished to be as dependent on Britain as they had been in the past and all recognized (though in differing degrees) that their interests in the post-war world might differ sharply from those of Britain and other Commonwealth members. All counted on the effective-ness of a new and strengthened World Organization and did not want to prejudice its success in any way. Many found it easier to accept obligations to the UN rather than to the British Commonwealth and were anxious to avoid any appearance of 'ganging up'. The problems of the Office in the post-war world would be different, but not obviously easier.

The Office too had been changed by the war years. There had been a revolution in pace and style. Gone were the days of cautious argument and finely balanced memoranda; the bemonocled figure of Eddie Marsh had departed for ever. The telephone and discussion played a larger part, informal correspondence replaced the pompous official letter and abroad the telegram superseded the despatch by mail. The Office became not only modernized; its work ceased to be generalized and increased in scope and variety. The staff acquired new expertise and became professionally more competent. More of its members were developing first-hand knowledge of the Dominions and the posts overseas had established themselves as important links.

In general the atmosphere in the Office was easier and more informal and personal relations at all levels were less stiff. The approach was more down-to-earth and direct. The Office adapted itself and its thinking to a Commonwealth which, more than ever before, would depend on consent and could not count on unity. But it had done little to prepare itself for the greater diversity that would come into the Commonwealth with the admission of the Asian members in 1947.

PART III

The Asian Dimension 1947–57

CHAPTER 1

The Scene

Abroad and at Home

The years following 1947 have often been hailed in extravagant terms as marking the triumph of the Commonwealth idea. While Britain herself showed a growing weakening of her economy and to some extent of her will, and her relative status declined, the full extent of this was not at first perceived and in any case seemed compensated for by the growing strength of the other Commonwealth countries. Canada had become a considerable industrial power and both she and Australia seemed assured of a rapid development that would one day lead them to outstrip the Mother Country. Each was already playing a role on the world scene. Post-war Canada, under St Laurent and Pearson, reversed the Mackenzie King doctrine of 'no commitments'; she took an energetic part in the UN and all its activities, was a member of NATO, the Colombo Plan and the Supervisory Commission in Indo-China, thus involving herself in Europe, South Asia and the Far East; she regarded herself – and was widely accepted – as the leader of the Middle Powers. The Australian contribution may have been less solid and less restrained, for under the leadership of Evatt during the peace-making, it had been aggressive, indeed strident; certainly Australia made her voice heard in the world. With the defeat of Labour in 1949, Menzies came to dominate the Australian scene; eloquent in his loyalty to the Crown Commonwealth, strong in his broad support of Britain, but increasingly critical of the 'new' Commonwealth and its Republican Members. In South Africa on Smuts' defeat in 1948, the country began its long rule under the Nationalist Party. The Afrikaners were dedicated to Apartheid, but first they wished to settle the other racial score – that between Britain and Boer and so to reverse the verdict of the Boer War. Meanwhile fate smiled on this favoured land and prosperity for the ruling minority leapt ahead. New Zealand too, applying new techniques to agriculture, continued an important and efficient supplier of Britain's food supplies and developed a stable and comfortable society. The Dominions were therefore not only important to Britain for all the traditional reasons; they were of value no longer as appendages, but in themselves.

The power-base in the post-war world lay at first with the USA and later also with the USSR; but a new dynamic in world affairs came from the continent with the oldest civilization of all – Asia. In the years immediately after the war, some of the most original new impulses stemmed from the India of Jawaharlal Nehru. India championed the cause of nationalism and encouraged first the emancipation of Indonesia and Indo-China and later the ending of all overseas Colonial rule. She led the fight for equal rights for all races and first preached the doctrine of non-alignment which led to the independent stand adopted throughout what became known as the Third World.

India's influence on the development of the Commonwealth and the organization of the CRO was no less far-reaching. In spite of the talk for so long about Dominion status, the general assumption before the transfer of power was that India, on independence, would wish to break her links with the Commonwealth and be treated as a foreign power. But two remarkable things happened: first the settlement by Mountbatten in 1947 provided for accelerated independence on the basis of partition, with the formation of two Dominions who would be welcomed as Commonwealth Members. Secondly, and contrary to the previously accepted doctrine, it was agreed in 1949 that India, on becoming a Republic, could remain a Commonwealth Member. If it was a matter of some surprise that India became and remained a Member of the Commonwealth, it was thought to be a matter of gratification also and the change took place among the utmost goodwill. Nehru's leadership promised to be stable, progressive, democratic and much of the British legacy remained. There were grave blemishes in the picture – worst of all the tragic massacres of Moslems and Hindus at the time of the transfer of power. Nehru never found it in his heart to show generosity to the smaller country, Pakistan, and he remained obdurate over Kashmir. Later the seizure of Goa by force of arms seemed out of character and shocked many; his reputation was in shreds after his humiliation at the hands of the Chinese. Against this background many in Britain found it hard to stomach his lecturing on the wickedness of the use of force, of military alliances, of colonialism. Nevertheless the early years of Indian independence seemed full of promise. It was perhaps in the Commonwealth setting that Nehru performed at his best. He valued membership of the Commonwealth because he felt that it could bring a healing influence to bear on international problems; he welcomed the opportunity of uninhibited discussion with major statesmen of the day, his nature was aristocratic not revolutionary, naturally courteous not strident; he preferred to work for a constructive solution rather than to plan for confrontation. Unlike his African successors of a decade later, he avoided the open attack and sought to work within the agreed conventions.

The decision to admit India to full Commonwealth membership marked a clear turning point. The changed power structure in the sub-Continent upset the strategic balance with effects throughout the Middle East and South East Asia. Moreover there were important changes in the operation and indeed the nature of the Commonwealth itself. It ceased to be a loose, informal grouping of friendly like-minded States. It consisted of nations who recognized that they did not all think alike; inevitably the association became more formalized. Above all it ceased to be the preserve of one race and one colour; it became multi-racial based on the principle of racial equality. It implied that all other former dependencies could be admitted in course of time, if they desired. All this had many consequences for the future – some of which would be disagreeable. Thus what was called the 'new' Commonwealth came about and was for the time being given a welcome.

The Labour Government after the war faced immense difficulties at home and abroad, many of greater dimensions than was grasped at the time. The record is one of no mean achievement and effected a permanent change in the life of the country. Perhaps Attlee's greatest claim to fame will remain the settlement in India – Mountbatten's was a dazzling performance, but the responsibility lay with Attlee. Attlee is commonly credited with being an effective chairman and it was under his quiet leadership that a social revolution was accomplished – not without troubles and grumbles but with general support. The Attlee administration was equally remarkable for its commitment to defence and robust resistance to Communist designs. Later under the Conservatives, with the ending of the war in Korea and recovery in Western Europe, the world returned to something resembling normality and things at home became easier. It was a time for stabilization rather than innovation and, until the shock of Suez, the bitterness of party conflict was abated.

It is noteworthy that the three P.M.s (as also Home at a later date) were well acquainted not only with Commonwealth matters generally, but also with the Commonwealth Office itself. Attlee had been Dominions Secretary in wartime and had been a member of the Simon Commission on India; Churchill had been connected with the C.O. since 1906; he had been Colonial Secretary in 1921 and had enjoyed close dealings with Commonwealth leaders over a period of fifty years; Eden had also always had substantial contacts with Commonwealth Governments during his many years as Foreign Secretary and had been Dominions Secretary during the war.

Secretaries of State

Addison had been appointed Dominions Secretary in Attlee's Government, but he retired in 1947 shortly after the establishment of the CRO. He was succeeded by Philip Noel-Baker, who came to the Office after long experience in political and diplomatic life. At Cambridge he had distinguished himself equally as a speaker (he was President of the Union), a scholar and an athlete (he was an Olympic runner). A Quaker by origin, he had served with distinction in the Friends Ambulance Unit during the First World War. The son of an MP, he had contested a seat for Labour in 1924 and been elected in 1929. He had served as Parliamentary Secretary to the Ministry of War Transport in Churchill's Government and, in Attlee's administration, became Secretary of State for Air. But his over-riding interest was in the maintenance of peace. He had worked in the League of Nations Secretariat, had been P.P.S. to Arthur Henderson as Foreign Secretary and had written much on disarmament. He had limitless compassion, unquenchable faith and courage and inexhaustible energy. Above all he had a great heart. He was an idealist with all the virtues of the pure in heart – but also some of the drawbacks. He reached for the stars, but was not one to calculate nicely and under-rated the art of the possible. Often he appeared to direct his energies over too wide a field of interest. The very sweetness of his nature prevented him from showing the ruthlessness that politics sometimes demanded. He was unfortunate too that his passion was for international pacification but that in this field he was overshadowed by the burly figure of Bevin, of whom he was a great admirer. Noel-Baker did not always show a firm grip on administration or the capacity to give a decisive lead; he pursued his own individualistic line too enthusiastically to be able to make the best use of his staff and, though the blame sometimes lay with others, he did not enjoy the full confidence of his senior advisers. But whatever frustrations his methods may have caused, he was recognized by all as one of the kindest of men and one always inspired by the highest motives.

It was a tribute to the mark which Patrick Gordon Walker had made in three years as Parly US that, in looking for a successor to Noel-Baker, Attlee took the unusual step of promoting the junior Minister from the same Department. Though he was S. of S. for a bare two years, Gordon Walker stands out as one of the most effective Commonwealth Secretaries and also one of the most popular with the staff generally. He was in a different generation from his predecessors, being nearly 20 years younger than Noel-Baker. Like his colleagues Harold Wilson and Hugh Gaitskell, he had been a tutor at Oxford before the war, did war service (with the BBC) in London and entered Parliament in 1945. His academic training in history gave him a good intellectual background and he applied his mind to the philosophical problems of the Commonwealth. Indeed it is remarkable that, in an academic sense, both Noel-Baker and Gordon Walker were as experienced professionals about the Commonwealth as any of their official advisers; Noel-Baker was the author of the authoritative *The Juridical Status of the British Dominions in International Law* (1929) and Gordon Walker had been History Tutor at Christ Church, Oxford for nine years before the war. But Gordon

Walker had also had much practical experience and grasped problems with a confident touch; invariably he found a commonsense solution. When Parly US he had learned to know both senior and not so senior officials and got on well with them; he took great pains with staff relations and a keen interest in postings.

Above all he was knowledgeable about and cared greatly for the Commonwealth. Later he gave eloquent expression to his thoughts in his book on the Commonwealth.[1] He was the first S. of S. since Amery to be able to visit Commonwealth countries generally and he made by air a number of tours, all of which were highly successful. In particular he held strongly to the view that the Commonwealth is an association of peoples rather than an alliance of governments and he attached the highest importance to the fullest development of all links – in the professions, in commerce, in sports, in the arts. He wanted to see Government help given for these purposes under what, on Liesching's suggestion, he called the Commonwealth 'umbrella'. In this way he anticipated much of the later work of the Commonwealth Foundation – and to some extent also that of the Commonwealth Secretariat and other organizations concerned with Commonwealth links.

Gordon Walker's subsequent career has led commentators to suggest that in spite of his many gifts, he lacked one essential in political life – namely luck. However that may be in general, it was true of his days as Commonwealth Secretary. He presided at an unhappy time in his party's fortunes when the giants – Bevin and Cripps – had worn themselves out, when there was dissension in the Cabinet and foreign policy was in the inadequate hands of Herbert Morrison. He inherited from his predecessor the unsolved problem of Seretse Khama and, though he was carrying out Cabinet policy and his handling of the matter was honest, nevertheless the incident cruelly damaged his reputation in the Labour Party.

Of the three Conservative Secretaries of State, the first, Ismay, stayed for barely six months. Throughout the war he had been Chief of Staff to Churchill as Minister of Defence and, when Mountbatten went to India as Viceroy, Ismay was his Chief of Staff. Ismay had never been in political life and was astonished at being offered the post; recording modestly 'Officials do not usually make good Cabinet Ministers and there was no reason why I should be an exception to the rule. But I was overjoyed at the prospect of serving under Churchill again.'[2] In a chapter called 'A Medley of Assignments', his autobiography says merely that the Office 'proved to be heavier, and the hours longer, than I had anticipated',[3] and makes it clear that, pending Alexander's return from Canada to be Minister of Defence, much of his time was spent in being consulted on defence matters by Churchill. His appointment to be Secretary General of NATO was certainly more in accordance with his bent and provided a post where he felt more at home.

Ismay's successor, Swinton, achieved the unusual distinction of being almost equally known under three different names – Philip Lloyd-Greame at the Board of Trade under Lloyd George and Bonar Law, Philip Cunliffe-Lister as President of the Board of Trade and Colonial Secretary in the National Government of MacDonald, and Viscount (later Earl of) Swinton as Air Minister under Baldwin and in a variety of wartime jobs under Churchill. He had been continuously involved in political life since the end of the First World War.

He was essentially conservative; immensely proud of his tradition and his country; a countryman at heart, he delighted in his Yorkshire origin and connexions; a product of the Edwardian era he shared the values of that age – the English country house, the public school system (he was at Winchester), Oxbridge (though he had nothing but contempt for written examinations), the Empire, the bar (to which he had been called), a 'good' marriage, the chase, high living. Racily extrovert, fun-loving, with a pungent sense of wit, relishing politics as an 'endless adventure', he was something of a buccaneer or could have fitted into the life of an eighteenth-century squire.

He prided himself on being a realist, a man of commonsense whose guide was experience not dogma. He had a shrewd eye for business and could be ruthless in achieving what he wanted. His tone was emphatic, he used sweeping gestures and deliberately created an impression of forcefulness* (to the extent of imitating some of Churchill's characteristics) and despised any manifestation of weakness.† Yet (provided things were going his way) he could display considerable tolerance and even kindliness. This showed itself particularly in the Office. He was always determined to do the best job of which he was capable; as he himself said, the attraction lay in getting things done. But he also developed a strong feeling towards any Department in which he served and took a keen personal interest in members of the staff. When at the C.O., he had warned: 'I should send for people, young or old, and get the facts from them and their ideas in conversation,' adding 'If he is the office boy and knows about sugar, I want to see him.'[4] He still carried this out in the CRO twenty years later and his habit of calling in quite junior officials and encouraging them to speak their minds gave a welcome fillip to staff morale. He enjoyed a stimulating relationship with Liesching, each admiring the other's toughness and, if necessary, yielding to it. An elder statesman, with a range of experience rivalled only by Churchill, he had great prestige with the public and carried weight in the Cabinet. His was an uncomplicated way of life and there were no great depths in his mind. He broke little new ground in diplomacy or constitutional

* A senior official advised a colleague returning from overseas: 'If you want Swinton to change something, suggest what you want but introduce it by saying "Would it not be much stronger to say...?" He will invariably fall for it.'
† Yet he was no Colonel Blimp. When an official reported that some of the BBC staff had been Communists at the University he exploded 'Good God; if a man can't be a Communist when he is at Oxford or Cambridge when the Hell can he be?'

affairs, but was effective in such practical matters as trade and defence (in both of which he had a wealth of experience). He was also interested in questions of organization and made frequent interventions in management matters – in greater detail than would concern most Ministers and not always with happy results. As Commonwealth Secretary he revealed unashamedly his affection for the old Dominions and Rhodesia (all of which he visited during his term) making the most of high-level contacts made over the previous 30 years. Nehru he found antipathetic and he had little feeling for India. It cannot be claimed therefore that he saw the Commonwealth 'whole' or advanced the development of the 'new' Commonwealth. But he fought a doughty battle for British interests as he construed them and can fairly be said to have lived up to his watchwords of sincerity and courage. His bark was always far worse than his bite and his bluff geniality caused him to be regarded almost with affection. He was certainly the most colourful S. of S. in the history of the Office.

When Eden succeeded Churchill as P.M., he made a change at the CRO bringing in Alec Home to succeed Swinton. The appointment provided a striking contrast with one at the end, the other at the beginning of his Ministerial career. Previously Home's best known activity had been his part in 1938 in handing to Chamberlain, in the course of his speech in Parliament, the message announcing the meeting in Munich. In Churchill's Cabinet after the war he had been Minister of State at the Scottish Office. To a wider public he was unknown and, after an (interrupted) spell of 25 years altogether in Parliament, he had no reason to expect any dramatic change in fortune. In one sense this was a fair judgement; at the same time there was a quiet determination about the diffident new Minister which became increasingly impressive. On his very first day, on the advice of his officials, he reversed the intransigent line which Swinton had consistently taken over textile imports from the Indian sub-Continent.

Home's subsequent career brought him so prominently into the limelight that his character and achievements are well-known. He is, not without reason, regarded as being devoid of rancour or strong personal ambition. He himself made no claim to intellectuality or to any deep comprehension of economic matters. But he was highly intelligent as a Minister and was incidentally a very good draftsman with a gift for simplification. The outstanding qualities he displayed at the CRO were integrity and fairmindedness. He was totally without meanness in his thoughts or actions; he was concerned solely to be of service without any ulterior motive or thought of personal reward. Moreover if he did not probe every problem in great depth (which, properly, he would have regarded as the job of his officials), he always understood it in the round; he invariably got to the essential and saw things in perspective. But more than that he revealed positive qualities of his own; he enjoyed that indefinable quality – charm;

he always had a fresh outlook on things; he had spontaneous wit and could on occasion be extremely entertaining; he was a good public speaker and found it easy to get on with all sorts and conditions of different people. All these qualities stood him in excellent stead in the two major tasks to which he turned his attention – administration and diplomacy. In diplomacy, his main object was to develop the closest cooperation with all Commonwealth Governments on a basis of complete equality and to build up personal links with all Commonwealth leaders. He paid many visits to all Commonwealth countries and played a prominent part in all major Commonwealth Conferences. It was his misfortune that the Suez crisis occurred when he had been in the Cabinet for little more than a year, but he was admirably qualified to play a leading part in the healing process after Macmillan's assumption of power. Within the Office, it was a time for consolidation rather than innovation and his even-tempered and sympathetic leadership helped the process of settling down and of preparing for the challenges which would come in the next decade. Alike with Commonwealth leaders and with members of his staff he ensured respect for his integrity and inspired confidence.

CHAPTER 2

The Office

In 1947 three things marked a break with the past for the D.O.: first in time, in the spring, was the separation from the C.O.; last, in August, was the absorption of the I.O.; to symbolize both, in July came the change in title to that of Commonwealth Relations Office.

Office accommodation had always been a problem and became worse during the war, when hardships had to be tolerated. But in the post-war period, with the expansion envisaged both for the C.O. and the D.O., sharing the same building (even with the additional I.O. rooms) could no longer be managed. There were arguments both ways as to which should move. The C.O. was the older and had a historic claim to the site; on the other hand it looked forward to a grand new building opposite Westminster Abbey. The D.O., though the junior Department, had greater need to stay close to No. 10 Downing Street and to the F.O. So the C.O. moved to temporary accommodation in Church House (where they remained for nearly 20 years; the Westminster Hospital site alas! still remains an unlovely car park) and the D.O. inherited the whole office space, including the splendid room traditionally occupied by the Colonial Secretary. For the first time the Dominions Secretary possessed an imposing office – and a few months only before he assumed the wider responsibilities under his new style. The D.O. broke the final links with its parent Department and, on coming of age, acquired a dignified estate.

Although the change in title was accelerated by the prospect of responsibility for relations with India and Pakistan, it would no doubt have come about in any case since 'Dominion' was becoming an outmoded term, particularly with its implication of British rule over distant territories. It seemed right and inevitable that the term 'Commonwealth' should be included and the alternative of 'Commonwealth Affairs' and 'Commonwealth Relations' were canvassed and put to Dominion Governments. None expressed any strong view, but Smuts preferred 'relations' since this did not imply any responsibility for the affairs of any Commonwealth country. This was accordingly adopted and the Office became known as the Commonwealth Relations Office (CRO).

India and Pakistan achieved their independence on 15 August 1947; the CRO absorbed the I.O. and assumed responsibility for relations with the two new countries as from that date. The uncertainty in advance whether, on independence, India and Pakistan would become Members of the Commonwealth and, still more, whether they would remain so was reflected in the way the Office went about its new tasks. This was shown both in the organization of the Office at home and in the establishment of diplomatic posts in the new Member countries.

In Whitehall the reform brought few visible changes. Admittedly the historic title of the S. of S. for India and with it the name of the India Office disappeared. The I.O. Ministers (Listowel and Henderson) withdrew from the scene and their duties were taken over by the CRO (formerly D.O.) Ministers, Addison and Bottomley, who themselves were replaced within two months by Noel-Baker and Gordon Walker in the Cabinet re-shuffle in October. With the exception of this shuffling-up of Ministerial functions, the Departments remained distinct; they were named Division A (former D.O.) and Division B (former India Office); they continued for the most part to occupy their previous accommodation; each operated under a separate PUS and retained its own services. There was no attempt at integration, very little at co-ordination and any differences between the two sides could in principle be resolved only at the Ministerial level, where alone the problems of the two sides were viewed as a whole. The former members of the I.O. underwent a greater sea-change than their colleagues in the former D.O. whose accommodation, organization and functions scarcely changed at all. The I.O. on the other hand shed overnight responsibilities it had so long exercised; its duty was no longer to govern or to give directions, but to be responsible for relations with independent countries. The staff felt uncertainties about the security of service in the new Department: moreover they became liable for service abroad which had not existed in the I.O. In any case the greatly changed responsibilities called for reductions in staff. For all these reasons, a number of I.O. staff sought transfer to other Departments in Whitehall rather than absorption in the CRO.

In February 1948, not many months after the acceptance of India and Pakistan as independent Commonwealth members, Ceylon was also granted independence and accepted as a full Commonwealth Member. The administrative arrangements formed a contrast with those made for India and Pakistan. Ceylon had hitherto been administered by the C.O.; there were therefore those in the D.O. who were familiar with the island to an extent that very few were with India and Pakistan and close liaison had been maintained with the C.O. throughout the whole of the preparatory period. When responsibility for relations with Ceylon was transferred to the CRO, a Ceylon department was set up to which the C.O. loaned for six months the services of their Ceylon expert. The new department was included not, as would have seemed more logical in Division B along with India and Pakistan, but in Division A.

The atmosphere in the Office in these early days was not a happy one. Though the responsibilities of the D.O. and C.O. had been diverging markedly and though in each Department a new generation was growing up without close contact with the other, nevertheless something of the old tradition of camaraderie remained; at least the staffs knew each other and understood the other's problems. Between the I.O. and the D.O. there had however been no such tradition. The Departments had never been close and now their juxtaposition without integration merely added to the strains and nourished mutual suspicions. Perhaps the worst effect of the dyarchy was that it did not allow any sentiment of common loyalty to grow. On the contrary, officers in the two Divisions were responsible to their own PUS and Establishment Officer and each went his own way according to the hallowed traditions of the previous Department. At meetings with other Departments, two officers would speak separately for the two Divisions in the Office – and frequently with discordant voices. The bad feeling between the two Divisions was symbolized by the distant relationship existing between the two PUSs; inevitably any feeling of lack of cooperation at the top quickly communicated itself to all lower levels and there was no incentive to work things out together.

The organization into two Divisions may have been justified in the un-certain circumstances of the time and could serve as a temporary arrange-ment. It could not be tolerated if, as seemed increasingly likely, India and Pakistan (as well as Ceylon) continued as Commonwealth Members. It was inefficient and cumbersome; it was bad for morale among the staff and for the reputation of the Office in the rest of Whitehall and in the public mind; and it ran counter to the prevailing philosophy that Commonwealth Members were on a footing of complete equality and that there must be no two-tier system or differential treatment. In the admirably expressive words of Nye to the Select Committee, 'It was a proper dog's breakfast.'[1]

The question of principle was further complicated by a clash in person-alities. The two PUSs were Machtig (Division A) and Carter (Division B). Each had a considerable record of service and each was nearing retiring age. Indeed Carter had already been offered and accepted the post of Chairman of the Monopolies Commission. Noel-Baker was by now Commonwealth Secretary; for his part he did not object to the double arrangement. Indeed he would have liked Carter to continue, but felt that it would not be right or fair to press him to stay on. Machtig on the other hand disinterested himself in the Asian side of the work; he was not suitable to be the single head of both Divisions, nor was it likely that he would cooperate with any successor better than he had with Carter himself. Noel-Baker reached the conclusion that here too there would have to be a change.

There were deeper reasons for this. Machtig had been PUS for nearly ten years and had grown increasingly autocratic and obstinate. With his long experience he thought he knew best and was determined to get his own way. There were personal factors too. After being a bachelor for over 50 years he made an extremely happy marriage in 1941, but his wife died tragically within two years. This left him morose and lonely and he led the life of a recluse with his aged mother. A second important factor was the death of Stephenson in 1948; Machtig was distressed by the loss of his closest colleague and it was a misfortune that his sage counsel was missing at the crisis in Machtig's official life. Machtig had always made a point of being agreeable to Ministers, but he failed with Noel-Baker to whom he was completely unhelpful. His natural shyness and his aloofness kept him from mixing freely in the top Whitehall circles and he was not on close terms with any of his opposite numbers in other Departments.

The removal of a PUS is a rare event and is hedged about with the requirement that the P.M.'s approval (on the advice of the Head of the Civil Service) must first be obtained. Noel-Baker discussed the matter with Bridges and Attlee; agreement was reached that Machtig should leave the CRO on assignment for special duties. (A number of possibilities was in mind, but Machtig resisted the decision as long as possible and refused to consider any alternative Government employment.) Machtig retired at the end of 1948.

There was general agreement that in future there should be a single PUS; only in this way could the Office operate as an integrated unit. The essential thing was to find the right man for the new post. Undoubtedly the most able officer of his generation in the D.O. and a man with unrivalled experience of Commonwealth relations was Percivale Liesching. He had been sent in turn to open up the new High Commission posts in Canada, South Africa and Australia, serving in each for a period of some three years. He returned to the D.O. in 1939 for three years but he was not in sympathy with Machtig, chafed at the control in London after enjoying for so long the opportunity of doing his own job abroad and longed in the crisis of war to be fully stretched. He was seconded to the Board of Trade in 1942 as Second Secretary until 1946 when he was promoted to be Permanent Secretary to the Ministry of Food.

So it happened that at this critical moment for the Office, not only was Liesching the most highly qualified candidate for the job in terms of experience of Commonwealth relations, but his prestige and impartiality also guaranteed an equal welcome from both Divisions. He had experience of two domestic Departments of the front rank, had been Permanent Secretary of one of the most politically sensitive and had a formidable reputation throughout Whitehall. In one sense he was coming home to his former Department, but equally he had been away from it for six years and was totally aloof from the jealousies of Divisions A and B. Incidentally Liesching was the first PUS ever to have served abroad (all his successors on appointment had served in at least two posts). Liesching's name was originally put forward by Bridges; it was supported by Norman Brook and others in Whitehall (notably J. H. Woods and Frank Lee); it was also welcome in the CRO – to Gordon Walker, Syers (then Deputy) and to all who knew the situation from the inside. Liesching took up his duties on 1 January 1949.

Liesching played a considerable part in the history of the Office and he left his stamp on it in more ways than most. He was educated at Bedford School and Oxford, but his education was interrupted by the First World War in which he served throughout. He had a gruelling war, serving both on the Western Front and in the East African Campaign and it left its mark on him, leading him to make a cool assessment of any situation, not to flinch from any task however unpleasant and at all times to be ready to take decisive action. These lessons from the battle-field Liesching applied alike in his relations with people and in his administration of the Office. He was far removed from the traditional caricature of the bureaucrat as indecisive, shuffling responsibility and a clock-watcher; he also differed in temperament and methods from the hierarchy who had controlled the Office hitherto. Where their watchword had been conciliation, if not at times appeasement, Liesching was aggressive and ever ready to fight for the principles he considered right. Moreover he never forgot that his prime duty was to defend British interests and he was ever on the alert for ways in which the Dominions might damage these. Here therefore was no starry-eyed idealist, but a coldly calculating realist. He was firm, not gentle, suspicious more than enthusiastic, tough rather than tolerant. On occasion he could be ruthless; and always gave the impression of 'the smack of firm government'.

Superimposed on this background were many qualities which he developed and which stood him in good stead. Although he made no claim to intellectual eminence or academic distinction, he was a master of crisp lucid English prose; because he thought clearly he expressed his thoughts with the utmost clarity and with no possibility of words darkening counsel. He also had good judgement – more perhaps in material things and in people than in abstract concepts. He chose his men with the utmost care and skill and, having done so, was wise enough to devolve full responsibility to them. This confident use of the power of delegation was no small part of his success as an administrator. He came nearer than most officials to the ideal of being 'the whole man'; he could be charming in society; he was an excellent if sometimes combative conversationalist; he was civilized enough to enjoy the delights of the table and did not deny the claims of Bacchus. All this contrived to make him at ease in company; he was equally successful in expounding a case vigorously to an attentive Minister, in comparing notes with a Commonwealth colleague, making a dominant impression at an official dinner party or entertaining with kindness some juniors who had done a job for him.

He had therefore decisiveness, determination and dignity; but his decisions were pragmatic and based on a shrewd calculation of the facts – they were not intuitive; his determination did not mean that he was unwilling to listen to advice and his dignity had only that quality which he himself frequently described – 'a man does not stand on his dignity, he carries it around with him.'

Unfortunately – and perhaps because of his very strengths – Liesching ran into a head-on clash with Noel-Baker. Basically they were not interested in the same things and each thought that the other did not give him the help that was his due – Noel-Baker was obsessed with the search for a solution in Kashmir which Liesching regarded as futile; Liesching was concerned with the practical jobs of producing an efficient machine in the Office and resisting F.O. claims; such matters held little interest for Noel-Baker. More seriously they disagreed on the question of colour; Noel-Baker abhorred colour prejudice to an extent which Liesching regarded as unrealistic. Their differences came to a head over the plan for a Federation in Central Africa which Liesching supported and Noel-Baker resisted. Temperamentally they were poles apart – Noel-Baker regarded Liesching as a racialist and thought he was disloyal. Liesching considered Noel-Baker an ineffective busybody and relished repeating a comment that he was an 'intellectual mosquito'. The partnership did not last more than a year. Noel-Baker always suspected that Liesching influenced his removal. If so it would be ironic if he removed one PUS, only to appoint another who succeeded in removing him!

The plans for the re-organization of the Office took three months to draw up and were introduced in a talk which Liesching gave to the administrative staff. He made no attempt to make light of the new heavy loads that would be put on the staff and addressed them in the style of a commander to his troops on the eve of battle.

Liesching brought with him into the Office W. A. B. Hamilton who served throughout as his Director of Establishments. He was a young Scot of great promise, having passed first in the Civil Service examination, and had had a brilliant career in the Board of Education and Ministry of Food, reaching the rank of Under Secretary at the early age of 37. Before his appointment to the CRO, he had for the previous three years been Director of Establishments in the Ministry of Education. He had therefore ideal qualifications for the operation in hand – he had a first-class aptitude for administration, considerable general experience, but was aloof from any squabbles between the two Divisions and therefore in a position to view the problem with complete objectivity. Later this aloofness and almost clinical objectivity came to appear as lack of imaginativeness and insensitiveness and, allied with the fact that he never served in a post in a Commonwealth country (though he was later Director of Personnel at the UN), proved a handicap when his responsibilities were so largely concerned with representation overseas. But for the immediate situation he was incomparable. The circumstances called for someone who could be relied upon to wield the axe without emotion, with even-handed justice and to make a clean job of it.

The re-organization was basically simple. There was a single PUS – so much had already been decided. But just as there was a single Parly US supporting the S. of S. at the political level, so now there was to be a single deputy below the PUS. Laithwaite had been DUS in Division B, but his appointment as Ambassador in Dublin left Syers as the single deputy in the Office. The allocation of work is shown in Appendix A, Table 3; it was on a functional basis (political, foreign affairs, economics, establishments, etc.), the only exception being the departments responsible for the High Commission Territories and Southern Rhodesia. The one drawback of this functional distribution was that there was no single focus for the affairs of any individual country – there was no equivalent of the 'desk officer' to whom one could refer on all matters affecting that country.

If the scheme appeared an exercise in simplicity it involved nonetheless a major surgical operation. It required the abolition of the two separate Divisions, and the creation of a single integrated and unified Office. This could not be achieved without a degree of pain and anguish. In the first place it involved inevitably some reduction in total numbers of staff – this was achieved in a variety of ways; by retirements, transfers to other Departments and postings. Secondly, many officers were called upon to carry a heavy load, being required to carry out functions previously performed by two full-time officers. (This was deliberate policy on Liesching's part in order to ensure concentration on essentials and to force work downwards.) Thirdly, it involved moving those who had, as a result of a lifetime's experience, acquired a vested interest in a particular area in which they took a proprietary interest. (This again was deliberate and the Administration sought as much cross-posting as possible.)

There were therefore inevitable strains, hardships and grumbles. Nevertheless the staff adjusted itself to the new organization with commendable speed; its immediate impact on staff morale was stimulating and in the long run its effect was wholly salutary. Indeed it was remarkable how rapidly the old suspicions, jealousies, prejudices between A and B vanished and the staff saw themselves as members of a single service. It was an eloquent example of what staff attitudes can be achieved by leadership at the top.

The re-organization undoubtedly simplified and improved the Office machinery; in administration it avoided duplication; in policy it ensured a single chain of command and a single flow of advice to Ministers; it made the Office more effective in giving support to posts overseas and increased its credibility in Whitehall. One proof of its quality is that the basic structure remained broadly unaltered until the merger with the F.O. nearly 20 years later.

Liesching attached special importance to what a later generation would call the problem of communication – to ensure that all staff knew what was going on in the Office as a whole; this was all the more necessary with a functional distribution of work. In addition to normal staff meetings (sometimes with the S. of S., sometimes with the PUS and more regularly at a lower level), special talks by knowledgeable people both from the Office and from outside were arranged; copies of all telegrams (except those restricted for reasons of secrecy) were circulated daily; all important despatches from the CRO, many of which reached a high standard in political reporting, were printed and given a wide circulation in the Office, in Whitehall generally and in all posts abroad. All this was invaluable in giving background not only to members of the Office, but to Ministers* and others concerned.

When Liesching was appointed High Commissioner in South Africa in 1955, Laithwaite was selected to succeed him. Laithwaite's previous official service had been under the I.O. – he had been P.S. to the Viceroy during the war, had returned to become an Under-Secretary in the Cabinet Office at the end of the war and later DUS in the Burma Office. He became a member of the CRO when the Burma Office was dissolved in 1948 and served as Ambassador in Dublin and later as High Commissioner in Pakistan. He had therefore acquired wide experience both in Whitehall and abroad when he became PUS. Some eyebrows had been raised in Ulster at the appointment of a Catholic who had been at school at Clongowes, but any fears on this score proved groundless as Laithwaite from the start made a special effort to get on with the Anglo-Irish Protestant establishment – and completely succeeded. He was called upon to become the first Ambassador following Eire's decision to become a Republic and leave the Commonwealth. This set numerous constitutional problems, but Laithwaite surmounted these with skill; after the break there were few major political problems and Laithwaite was able to devote himself to fostering Anglo-Irish relations – a task to which he turned with relish. He conducted his mission with dignity, even with panache; although he had no wife, he entertained sumptuously and widely and was at pains to show himself an excellent host. He was a connoisseur of food and wine; in conversation he was quick of mind and had a ready fund of amusing gossip. He had the good sense as a host not to push himself forward, but by careful manipulation stimulated others into a lively confrontation. He was elegant and cultivated and brought a quality of brightness and old-world charm into social life.

Laithwaite continued the same tradition on his appointment to Karachi, where he established cordial relations with the Moslem leaders and felt thoroughly at home when on tour, staying with the great. (He also won respect by his unremitting habit of wearing impeccable English clothes,

* The author recalls for example receiving an appreciative letter from R. A. Butler (then Home Secretary) after he had read a report on the political situation in Canada.

including a stiff collar and a waistcoat even in the most oppressive days of the hot weather.) In the politics of the sub-Continent he was on familiar territory; by his sympathetic but unemotional approach to Pakistan's problems and by the soundness of his advice, he carried much influence with Government leaders and helped to put Anglo-Pakistan relations on a more even keel. On one point in particular Laithwaite showed his good sense; his predecessor, Grafftey-Smith, had kept up a running battle with his colleague in Delhi and neither had visited the other. Laithwaite at once put a stop to this; he himself became a regular visitor to Delhi and encouraged visits to Karachi by members of the Delhi staff. Inevitably the two High Commissioners tended to see problems in different ways and did not always agree; but from that time on they had a continuous dialogue and always sought to reconcile any conflicts.

An experience which was crucial in moulding Laithwaite was his service for seven years (1936–43) as P.S. to the Viceroy (Linlithgow). This developed his talents and established his reputation. The post necessitated dealing with big problems, seeing them in the round and in their setting, reconciling the many conflicting interests, but nevertheless moving to a clear decision and taking firm action without sensitivity to criticism. All this gave him a taste for la haute politique, encouraged the development of an already brilliant mind and compelled it to reach quick decisions. He absorbed the art of statecraft. At the same time he learned to admire the ways of the viceregal Court in which he himself shone; he acquired the art of the courtier, making himself agreeable to all; he developed a strong interest in people as human beings and acquired an uncanny faculty for remembering names – a gift which never deserted him.

The new Head of the Office was clearly a man of parts who would lend it an air of distinction. From the first he threw himself into all aspects of the job with enthusiasm: he attached primary importance to the advice to be given to the S. of S. and on most important matters would himself compose the necessary briefing; he was equally concerned in matters of administration and took keen personal interest in postings of even quite junior officers; he was at pains to develop good relations with the heads of all the major departments in Whitehall and with all the Commonwealth High Commissioners in London; he also led an extremely active social life, entertaining frequently and never missing any Commonwealth occasion of importance. In addition to all this, he sought to keep in close personal touch with developments throughout the Commonwealth and made regular and lengthy visits to all the independent Commonwealth countries, paying particular attention to the 'old' members with which he had previously not been familiar.

His was an exuberant personality, the ideas overflowed; words, both in speech and in writing, tumbled over in a cascade; his zest and his tireless energy never failed. Few other men could have given so much personal attention to so wide a variety of tasks, but he had fortunately cultivated the habit of making a quick judgement. In general he tended to be content with things as they were; here was no radical reformer. Nevertheless he was ready to accept change when inevitable and, brought up in the viceregal tradition, rapidly adapted his ways to those of the new Commonwealth. Indeed he prided himself on 'flexibility' especially in matters of office organization (though he found difficulty in convincing the Select Committee that the organization was as perfect as he claimed). Perhaps his ceaseless activity did not allow time to probe deeply into all matters and perhaps he was at times disposed to take too generous a view of the Office's performance. But these were very human traits; he was devoted to his duty as he conceived it and served to the best of his remarkable ability the cause of Britain and the Commonwealth and the Office which linked the two together. Tribute is due to one so tireless and so affable. Even if some problems remained unsolved, he always took pride in the skill with which he manipulated the pieces on the increasingly complicated chequerboard and unravelled the skeins in the intricate web of diplomacy.

CPM Meetings

In many respects there was a change of style and of tempo in the ways in which the CRO carried out its liaison with other Commonwealth Governments. This was shown in the pattern for CPM Meetings. The last meeting of the Imperial Conference had been held in 1937; thereafter following the model set in wartime in 1944 (and again in 1946), Heads of Government met informally at Commonwealth Prime Ministers Meetings (CPM Meetings). These were held in the Cabinet Room of No. 10, with the British P.M. in the chair. Normally each P.M. came in person and was accompanied by a Minister or his High Commissioner at the table, with not more than two officials sitting behind. Although the British Government invariably had larger numbers, the rules meant that there were seldom more than 30 people in the room (indeed there was not space for many more) and the atmosphere was genuinely informal. The convention was that no fixed agenda was agreed in advance; in fact each delegation had a reasonably clear idea of the matters that were likely to come up and broad heads for the discussion were invariably provided in advance by the Cabinet Office in consultation with the CRO and circulated by the British Government. Frequently a British Minister led off the discussion, but an effort was always made to give Commonwealth P.M.s an opportunity to introduce a subject. The introductory speech was carefully prepared, but was seldom read in extenso and was always liable to be interrupted for a comment or a question. The Chairman called on anyone who indicated that he wished to speak, but there was no bar on interruption and in fact across-the-table discussion was frequent and often uninhibited. The atmosphere cannot have been very dissimilar from that of a Cabinet meeting and contrasted with the much larger and publicized meetings held at Marlborough House in the following decade.

Nehru fitted naturally into a P.M.'s Meeting. So did his Asian colleagues: Liaquat Ali Khan from Pakistan and Senanayake from Ceylon, both of whom proved very acceptable members of the Club. There were however two complications which arose from India's membership. The first was the conflict between India and Pakistan over Kashmir. This caused continuous embarrassment at Commonwealth gatherings; in particular at the Meeting in 1951 after Nehru refused to allow the issue to be discussed at the Conference, Liaquat Ali Khan refused to come unless it were discussed. A compromise was eventually reached under which it was agreed that informal discussions should be held outside the Conference itself (in fact they were held in Menzies' suite at the Savoy Hotel). Many strong differences of view were inevitably aired at P.M.'s Meetings, but this was the only issue, before the storms of the next decade, which gave rise to public controversy and caused bitterness at the Conference itself. There was a potential difficulty in any discussion on defence since in this delicate area there were clearly matters which could not be imparted on an equal basis to all Commonwealth Governments. This arose from India's policy of non-alignment (and there were sometimes also security difficulties). The CRO sought, perhaps to excess, to avoid discrimination or anything in the nature of a two-tier Commonwealth. In the early years therefore various subterfuges were resorted to in order to arrange meetings to which not all were invited. In practice there was no problem* and it soon became accepted that meetings could be restricted to those directly concerned.

The CRO played its part in the organization of P.M.'s Meetings. The Commonwealth Secretary attended throughout, acted as the P.M.'s chief adviser and was invariably made responsible on behalf of the Conference as a whole for publicity matters. The PUS was regarded as the leader of the official team; a senior CRO member was normally seconded to act as the Cabinet Secretary's deputy; the CRO in concert with the Cabinet Office was responsible for all the preparations for the Meeting and for any follow-up work.

---

* On one occasion Bevin (in the middle of a speech) was handed a note warning him not to mention a certain topic 'as we have not passed any information to India, Pakistan or Ceylon' which he proceeded to read out! When he blandly said, 'Oh! I suppose I was not meant to read that out – but that seems to be the position' it was received good-humouredly.

Other Ministerial Meetings

An important post-war development was the greater frequency and variety of meetings at Ministerial level; previously Ministers (other than P.M.s) had normally met together only under the aegis of an Imperial Conference. In view of the importance of maintaining cooperation in the Sterling Area, it became the regular practice for Commonwealth Finance Ministers to meet annually before the meetings of the World Bank and International Monetary Fund. There were also yearly meetings of the Colombo Plan countries at Ministerial level. An innovation was made in holding in 1950 a Meeting of Foreign Ministers in Colombo. The meeting provided a much needed opportunity to review the question of the recognition of Communist China and the discussion on economic cooperation resulted eventually in the formulation of the Colombo Plan, but the experiment was never repeated. The main reason no doubt was that CPM Meetings themselves were largely concerned with foreign affairs and Foreign Ministers frequently accompanied the P.M. to them.

The scope of Ministerial meetings was greatly extended and later included meetings of Ministers concerned with supply questions, trade, education, youth matters, law and justice, medicine.

The lead at such Meetings was normally taken by the Whitehall Department primarily concerned; but the CRO played its part and its officials attended the meetings. Until the establishment of the Ministry of Overseas Development, the CRO took the lead at Colombo Plan meetings; it had been prominent in the delegation to the Colombo Conference which was led by Bevin but included Noel-Baker, Liesching, Hankinson (the High Commissioner) and other CRO officials. The Conference gave an opportunity for Noel-Baker and Liesching to make visits to India and Pakistan soon after their independence.

United Nations

There were frequent meetings of Commonwealth delegations throughout the Sessions of the Assembly; though, under Krishna Menon's baleful influence, goodwill was lacking and the meetings became less useful, nevertheless they were regularly held until in the 60s the ill-will engendered over Rhodesia caused them to be dropped for a time. Apart from Noel-Baker's attendances for the Kashmir issue, the Commonwealth Secretary did not normally attend UN meetings; if a CRO Minister was not included in the Assembly delegation, arrangements were made for a member of the delegation to be specially responsible for liaison with other Commonwealth delegations; for some years after his retirement Hankinson carried out this duty – and on later occasions it was entrusted to Parliamentarians in the delegation like John Tweedsmuir and Peter Lothian. To advise him an officer was invariably sent from the CRO for the duration of the Assembly. In addition a member from the CRO was always seconded to the permanent delegation in New York where his special expertise in Commonwealth matters was invaluable. A number of CRO officers developed a flair for UN diplomacy, among them Cockram (who was by now an old hand at the game), Curson, Cole and Fowler (who earned a particularly warm commendation from Gladwyn Jebb).

High Commissioners in London

The CRO regarded it as part of its responsibility to keep Commonwealth High Commissioners in London in the picture. Meetings were held from time to time both on foreign affairs and on economic questions at which the Commonwealth Secretary took the chair, accompanied when necessary by the Foreign Secretary, Chancellor or other Minister concerned. Unfortunately these meetings changed their character and lost much of their usefulness owing to the behaviour of some of the High Commissioners at that time. Beasley for Australia struck a new note of aggressiveness, but even he was exceeded by the strange, contorted figure of Krishna Menon who indulged in bitter tirades of personal abuse. At one time his unprovoked attacks on Gordon Walker led the CRO to ask the High Commissioner in New Delhi to make a protest informally to Nehru. These unfortunate displays vitiated the atmosphere at these meetings which lost much of their value and tended to be held less frequently. The most effective liaison with High Commissioners was maintained in bilateral contacts. Many High Commissioners (such as Mrs Pandit from India who succeeded Krishna Menon, Norman Robertson from Canada, Ikramullah from Pakistan) were outstanding and enjoyed a close relationship at all levels with the British Government. Others were appointed for some personal or party reason and did not fit easily into a diplomatic posting. In such cases it often happened that the Deputy filled in any gaps. Contacts between officials were invariably effective; Canadian and Australian diplomats in the two High Commissions developed particularly close liaison with the F.O.

Throughout this period it remained the practice to circulate to Commonwealth Governments and to High Commissioners in London a selection of the more important despatches and telegrams from F.O. posts. It was hoped that in course of time Commonwealth Governments would reciprocate by circulating despatches from their posts. Certainly a few excellent despatches were received from Canada and one or two from Australia, but from the rest there were none and the practice never became general.

No doubt many Commonwealth Governments were reluctant to commit themselves to a regular practice since they wished to be free to say things which they might not always want the British to see and to be able if necessary to comment adversely on British policy. It may also be that there was an element of timidity in appearing in competition with the polished phrases in the tradition of despatches from Her Britannic Majesty's Ambassadors.* In any case the fact that all Commonwealth Governments were establishing their own posts in all the foreign countries of concern to them and the restrictions placed on circulating sensitive material equally to the growing number of Commonwealth members caused the practice in Britain too to be less complete and eventually fall into desuetude.

Relations with the F.O.

The differences between the F.O. and the D.O. in functions and outlook during the war and pre-war period have already been described. The differences after 1947 took on a new dimension. The two Departments were more closely involved in the same problems and the functions of the CRO began to come nearer to the diplomatic tasks of the F.O. On the other hand the very closeness of the association led to strains and controversy. The F.O. saw the world as a whole, did not accept that international relations could be carved up into categories and, particularly with the significant arrival of India on the scene, resented the fact that communications with Commonwealth Governments on foreign affairs were the responsibility of another Department. This marked a change from the earlier attitude of the F.O. which, though never convinced that there was a special mystique about Commonwealth relations, was content that the D.O. should look after the Dominions which it regarded as tiresome. The D.O. view, on the other hand, which the CRO inherited, was that the Commonwealth was a unique association, that Commonwealth relations were different in kind from relations with foreign countries and that, to preserve the cohesion of the Commonwealth, it was essential to have a separate Minister in the Cabinet responsible for relations with them. This was regarded as all the more important if new Members were admitted since there was a risk that the F.O., given its attitude towards the Commonwealth, would dilute the sense of partnership.

* *See* Charles Ritchie's reference to the prose of any British Ambassador – 'the casual style, the careful avoidance of purple patches and fine phrases, and every now and then the rather wry, tired, little joke' (*The Siren Years*, p. 35).

Bevin's general attitude is perhaps best described in Gordon Walker's accounts of discussions at the time when India's membership of the Commonwealth was being considered. Bevin is reported by Gordon Walker as 'saying in effect that the Commonwealth ought to be dissolved'.[2] Gordon Walker added his own comment: 'His officials had been at him; they are sore at Indian and Australian resentment over our attitude towards the Dutch aggression in Indonesia and over Evatt's escapades. At the bottom of their hearts they think they could run foreign policy better than we can run Commonwealth relations: they want Ambassadors under direct instructions.' Of a later discussion Gordon Walker recorded[3] that 'Bevin argued the F.O. line – that it was not worth keeping India in the Commonwealth: it was not going to be morally committed to us, but we to it. To keep India in would lead to the breakdown of the old Commonwealth.'

The differences between the two Departments came to a head in a written request from the F.O. at the end of 1948 for the right to communicate direct with Commonwealth Governments in matters of foreign affairs.* Looking back with the benefit of hindsight and in the knowledge of the eventual merger, it may seem strange that the request aroused such violent passions at the time; but the argument concerned the very existence of the CRO. The arrival of the new Commonwealth Members sharpened the argument since India played a far greater role in foreign affairs than the Dominions had done before the war (and Canada and Australia were also more significant than they had formerly been); the new status of India and Pakistan fundamentally affected the basic elements of British policy throughout the Gulf and South East Asia – areas of prime F.O. responsibility; the F.O. had expected to take over responsibility for India and Pakistan on independence. Since they did not in the event gain control, they sought to achieve the substance in another way.

From the F.O. point of view, the request was not unreasonable. The CRO after all took pride in the fact that all Commonwealth representatives, unlike foreign representatives, were free to make a direct approach to any Government Department (and particularly to the F.O.); the Foreign Secretary dealt directly with his opposite numbers in Commonwealth countries at international conferences and knew them personally; indeed there was nothing to prevent the Foreign Secretary from sending, through the CRO channel, a personal message to Commonwealth Foreign Ministers as other Ministers from time to time did to their opposite numbers. From its own standpoint therefore, the F.O. did not seem to be asking very much.

From the CRO point of view, the F.O. was asking for the right to send official messages on foreign affairs in the Foreign Secretary's name without their being seen in advance, still less subject to possible amendment in the

* In fact the letter was sent at PUS level towards the end of 1948. It was addressed to Liesching and sent to him before he took over on 1 January; this tactic did not please him.

CRO. The CRO regarded this as a challenge to the principle that relations with each Commonwealth Government required to be considered as a whole; if so important a sector of relations as foreign affairs were to be handled in isolation, where was the justification for its continued separate existence? This became the real nub of the controversy since the CRO feared that the request was merely the prelude to an eventual take-over and, as the CRO was so much smaller at that time, that any merger would lead to its being swallowed up. Moreover the CRO was aware that the F.O. was not always happy at the way the CRO carried out consultation; the F.O. felt that the consultation was one-sided, that Britain consulted and informed Commonwealth countries, but that they seldom reciprocated. The CRO for its part did not welcome the idea of another Department carrying out Commonwealth consultation on different principles from its own.

The battle raged fiercely for several weeks, with the CRO building up a formidable case. It was fought mainly at official level; indeed Ministers seemed to keep aloof from the controversy. But the matter clearly concerned Ministers and could be settled only by them. It was eventually referred to the P.M. Attlee, keeping a characteristically low profile, ruled that matters should remain as they were – and so they did. Possibly he remembered his own days at the D.O. and was quick to see how the proposal might undermine the Commonwealth Secretary's position with Commonwealth Governments. In the event, after the storm had broken, a period of calm set in and relations between the two Departments developed on a more realistic and cooperative basis. The F.O. learned to respect a Department which had put up so vigorous and successful a fight. For its part the CRO, having gained the day, was at pains to avoid provocation and achieve a more effective cooperation. This was assisted by various arrangements agreed between the two Departments. These included: increased secondment of staff between the two services, F.S. officers to hold the posts of DHC in Delhi and Karachi alternately with CRO staff; corresponding departments in the two Offices to be accommodated in rooms as close to each other as possible, better communication being made by openings in the walls; a single Under-Secretary* in the CRO to be responsible for foreign affairs and directed to pay special attention to relations with the F.O.

Inevitably there were occasions when the interests of the two Offices were in conflict and many differences remained. But in the main with the growing international importance of Commonwealth countries the areas of common interests grew and habits of cooperation began to take root.

* The author.

Relations with other Government Departments

While with the F.O. the relationship grew continuously closer, from the Colonial Office the CRO grew farther apart. There was the physical separation; the hole in the wall symbolized the closeness with the F.O., but the C.O. had moved from Whitehall to Great Smith Street. The common establishment was forgotten and there were no more tea clubs to bring the two staffs together. Secondly the difference in the nature of their responsibilities was more sharply seen – particularly with the advent of the new Commonwealth countries; the CRO with its own overseas service was a diplomatic and external affairs department, far more closely resembling the F.O. than the home-based administrative department of the C.O. There were other factors too. The concept of the new Commonwealth was a popular one and met with general public approval; Colonialism on the other hand was going out of fashion – moreover it was during these years that the C.O. attracted criticism for the violence which arose in many areas under its control – Malaya, Kenya, Cyprus, British Guiana – and which called for the use of British troops. The CRO, somewhat unctuously perhaps, sought to avoid being too closely identified with a Department increasingly regarded as a relic of the past. In particular in dealing with the new Asian countries, the CRO did not wish to be tarred with the Colonial brush.

The strongest single influence in Whitehall on the CRO throughout this period was perhaps the Cabinet Office. There continued to be frequent contact with the staff at No. 10 Downing Street; but no P.M. in peacetime could hope to maintain the grip on the whole machine as Churchill had done in war and no peacetime P.M. engaged in such continuous consultation with Commonwealth Heads of Government: relations with No. 10 therefore reverted to a normal, routine pattern. For the two decades after the war, the role of the Cabinet Office – and more particularly of the Cabinet Secretary – proved crucial. One important reason for this was the almost accidental arrangement that the British Cabinet Secretary served as Secretary to CPM Meetings. This gave the Cabinet Secretary a special responsibility; it also ensured that he became involved in Commonwealth problems. There were additional reasons in the case of Norman Brook; for much of his time he combined his Cabinet post with that of Head of the Civil Service with control over appointments at the top level in other departments. He had been associated with the arrangements for bringing Liesching to the CRO and was brought into the conflict between the F.O. and the CRO. He played a key part in the arrangements for the recognition of India as a Republic and was chosen as one of the three special emissaries. He gained a quite special knowledge of Commonwealth affairs and came to regard his opposite numbers in Commonwealth Governments as personal friends: his knowledge ripened into a very genuine affection for Commonwealth interests. All this meant that here was a powerful ally ready to give support to the Office itself and to use his influence in the furtherance of Commonwealth interests. Nevertheless it is not always easy to draw the line between a friendly hint and the appearance of interfering in matters that are the concern of someone else. Undoubtedly there were occasions when he was thought by the PUS of the day to have transgressed that line. This sometimes produced a momentary cloud, but there can be no doubt that his intention was well-meant, his judgement usually sound and, in the long run, his influence on the development of Commonwealth affairs beneficial.

In the sphere of defence the relations of the CRO with the Service Departments were closer and more developed than those of the D.O. had ever been. There were various reasons for this. The Second World War had shown Commonwealth military cooperation at its best in all three Services: close liaison had been maintained and many genuine personal friendships formed. Secondly the Army had an intimate knowledge of the Indian sub-Continent and could not disinterest itself overnight in an area of such long traditional association (indeed for some years British officers continued to hold the top posts in the Navy and Air Force and high posts in all three Services in both India and Pakistan). Thirdly the war had proved the strategic importance and military strength of Commonwealth countries and these were likely to grow. The continued cooperation of Commonwealth countries was thus eagerly sought and for the first time Britain, instead of being the bastion of Imperial defence to whom all turned for succour, was now herself in the role of suppliant. The importance of defence matters in the CRO was underlined by the appointment of a senior Army Officer as Principal Staff Officer to the Secretary of State. This was a legacy of the India Office tradition, but the incumbent's responsibilities covered the whole of the Commonwealth. An officer of his prestige eased cooperation with the Service Departments and encouraged full participation by the CRO (both at military and at civilian level) in the network of Committees set up under the Chiefs of Staff, including the COS Committee itself. The first three Staff Officers had all held senior active appointments and all served later as High Commissioners. They were: Sir Geoffrey Scoones (NZ), Sir Alec Bishop (Cyprus) and Sir William Oliver (Australia).

With other Departments in Whitehall and particularly with those concerned with the economy, there had been a similar transformation since the pre-war days; Commonwealth countries were now playing a more important role and Britain, with her own economy in such critical shape, needed their cooperation. The Treasury was concerned to conserve sterling and reduce dollar expenditure. The Ministry of Food sought the bulk of our food imports in the three old Dominions. The Board of Trade were under compulsion to expand our exports and were especially anxious for access to Commonwealth markets. In many ways therefore in the economic sphere too, the British were in the position of suppliants.

There were many factors which helped to bring Commonwealth officials into closer contact with their colleagues. The airplane had made a great difference to the frequency of visits for conferences or *ad hoc* discussions; key officials met each other regularly at CPM Meetings, the UN and Finance Ministers' meetings and a genuine spirit of camaraderie grew up. In the CRO by this time senior staff had had personal experience of life in a Commonwealth country and in London enjoyed easy contact with the increasingly more highly trained staff in Commonwealth High Commissions. In all countries, including Britain, there had been a process of growing up; each had gained experience in working the Commonwealth experiment; the fear of British domination had disappeared and each now treated his fellows without emotion, prejudice or suspicion. The effect of all this was that many firm friendships were formed and relationships between individuals were based on mutual trust. This was of immense importance to the working of the Commonwealth system and helped to overcome difficulties (such as the crisis over Suez) far more easily than might otherwise have been the case.

In general after the re-organization in the early 1950s, the Office exuded a confident atmosphere for the future which marks off this period from both the preceding and the succeeding periods. This arose from a combination of favourable circumstances: the general view that the Commonwealth was of value, that Commonwealth countries were no longer minor players on the world stage but had key roles to play, the realization in Government that their views had to be listened to and that the handling of relations with them was important, the consequent appointment as High Commissioners from outside the Service of men who in some cases were of obvious stature, put there because of the job and not for party reasons. Members of the Office (including, increasingly, the executive grade) were for the first time moving back and forth to overseas posts where young men were allowed, and even encouraged, to take initiatives; they saw the prospects of new horizons with the creation of new Commonwealth members becoming imminent. At home, Liesching's leadership and re-organization provided an ambience of purpose and progress; the active interest of the economic and defence departments in the Commonwealth brought the Office into the centre of Whitehall activity; the circulation of telegrams and despatches to the Cabinet encouraged the feeling that the work was of more than ordinary importance, and there developed a sense of belonging to a distinct and significant service – regarded by its members as the Commonwealth Service – in which pride could be taken.

CHAPTER 3

The Service Overseas

With the resumption of normal contacts after the war, High Commissioners in Commonwealth countries played a more varied and prominent part than before; they became more significant to the Government at home as agents for furthering the aims of British policy and they gained increasingly in public recognition and esteem. This was enhanced by the establishment of the new posts in Asia, particularly that in New Delhi where the High Commissioner was expected to carry on something of the tradition of the Viceroy; he watched over the biggest British community outside the British Isles and was responsible for a larger post than any other British Head of Mission outside the Embassy in Washington.

There had for long been Trade Commissioners in India and also, more surprisingly, since 1920 an Indian High Commissioner in London. But as the Viceroy also represented the British Government, no need was felt for a political representative in India. The intention to appoint one was first announced in 1945 by Amery (then S. of S. for India in the caretaker Government), the reason given being 'for the better representation of the particular interest of the UK'.[1] It was a year before the post was established partly because of the constitutional discussions, partly for a procedural reason. The Government of India from the first was insistent that the High Commissioner should be regarded as the agent of the Government as a whole and not simply of the India Office.[2] Pethick-Lawrence (S. of S. for India in the Labour Government) however at first disagreed, arguing that the 'pretence' of placing him under the D.O. 'would be very clearly and, on occasion, embarrassingly exposed'.[3] When he put this to the Cabinet,[4] however, Attlee would not have it.[5] There was much Ministerial discussion and Cripps suggested as a provisional solution that instructions should be passed to the High Commissioner through the Cabinet Office.[6] Addison jibbed at this[7,8] but was persuaded by his officials to accept since their only concern was to avoid anything being done to prejudice the responsibility to the D.O. of High Commissioners in the Dominions. Eventually Attlee approved a submission that the conduct of relations with the High Commissioner should be put in the hands of a standing committee of officials to be served by the Cabinet Office; the High Commissioner was thus not responsible to one

Minister rather than another and Parliamentary questions about him were answered by the P.M.[9]

The matter hung fire during the Cabinet Mission's discussions in India and at one point the Viceroy was provoked to enquire whether the High Commission had been 'sunk without trace'.[10] Finally the post was established in the summer of 1946, with Alec Symon (from the India Office) setting it up and being joined in October by Terence Shone (a member of the Foreign Service, previously Minister in Beirut) as the first High Commissioner. The Mission was small in the first instance, its total strength in July 1947 being 54, consisting of 9 administrative staff, 25 subordinate staff from the UK and 20 locally recruited.[11] With the advance in the programme for the transfer of power, the special arrangements for the Delhi post lasted for less than a year; on independence in August 1947 the post in Delhi and the new one set up in Karachi became the responsibility of the CRO. Grafftey-Smith (a former member of the Levant Service who had spent most of his career in Moslem countries and was, at the time of his appointment, Minister to Saudi Arabia) was appointed the first High Commissioner to Pakistan.* A surprising feature of the posts in the sub-Continent was that the D.O. was not involved in the staffing arrangements and did not initially provide any of its members for the new posts (and the India Office provided only Symon at a senior level). Many posts were filled in the first instance by retiring members of the ICS and only after 1950 did it become the normal practice to appoint CRO staff to all posts in the sub-Continent. There were many reasons for this; the D.O. had no responsibility when the High Commission in Delhi was set up; later there was doubt, until this was resolved in 1949, whether India and Pakistan would remain Commonwealth members; finally it was difficult, so long as the separate Divisions continued in the Office, to view matters as a whole – the I.O. had never been an overseas service and there was a reluctance on Machtig's part to be involved in the problems of the sub-Continent. Ceylon marked a sharp contrast; Hankinson (formerly D.O.) was appointed the first High Commissioner on independence in February 1948 and all senior staff came from the CRO. In India with the imminence of his own return, Mountbatten pressed for a high-level appointment to be made; he recommended Nye (then serving successfully as Governor of Madras) and Attlee, who had formed a high regard for him as VCIGS in wartime, readily agreed. Nye took up his post at the end of 1948.

In the years after the war something of a new style was developed in the conduct of diplomacy in Commonwealth relations. The change perhaps was one of degree and emphasis and was not necessarily adopted by all High

---

* The reader is referred to the section 'Dominion Status' in Sir L. Grafftey-Smith's book *Hands to Play* for a moving account of the agonizing birthpangs of Pakistan and a mordant description of the trials of the first British High Commissioner.

Commissioners, at least to the same extent. The essence of the change was that the style was more direct and more personal; it called for less time in the capital, but more in touring; it took a man out of the Office to factories, festivals, mines and colleges; it involved less diplomatic entertaining, more mixing with all sorts of people, less political reporting, more public relations, less emphasis on the policies of the government of the day, more on presenting a picture of Britain as a whole. In general the tempo was faster (communication was by telephone or telegram rather than by mail), the physical area far more extensive (the airplane facilitated frequent visits and made possible tours to the Far North in Canada, the remote outback in Australia or the vast expanse of the sub-Continent) and the coverage more varied (the traditional topics of pre-war diplomacy were extended to cover questions affecting the domestic economy, the arts, industrial relations, scientific developments). The new style also involved the wife who made her contribution as a full-time partner in the job. In brief, the Commonwealth Service was developing its own style of diplomacy which depended on a close knowledge of the country and placed less stress on the professional skills of diplomacy.

Many could be taken as representing the new style. Malcolm MacDonald in wartime had already shown the way; Clutterbuck, Liesching and Laithwaite, who are described elsewhere, in their different ways all exemplified the new attitude; Carrington, somewhat later in Australia, was not only an outstanding personal success but set the Canberra post in a new dimension; Baring (later Lord Howick) between service as Governor of Southern Rhodesia during wartime and as Governor of Kenya during the Mau-Mau troubles had qualities of head and heart which made him equally effective as Britain's diplomatic representative in South Africa and Governor of the High Commission Territories. But it was another newcomer to the Service – Archie Nye – who perhaps gave the sharpest definition to the new style.

Archie Nye had just left school when the First World War broke out. He enlisted in the ranks, received a commission the following year, remained in the Army and never looked back. He achieved the unusual distinction of reading for the bar while at the War Office and being admitted to the Inner Temple. He was appointed VCIGS in 1941, served throughout the War as deputy to Alanbrooke and carried a major responsibility for the planning of the invasion of Normandy. After the War he was appointed Governor of Madras, where he was immensely popular and was one of the two Governors invited to stay on after independence. He was High Commissioner in India and then in Canada, each for nearly four years. He had therefore already established a considerable reputation when he embraced a diplomatic career. Tall, good-looking, well-groomed, with a military bearing, he gave the impression of a man of action and one having complete confidence in himself. His mind was not profound but few others combined a clearer intelligence, a more retentive memory, a keener eye for the essentials, a greater gift for lucid exposition or a more compelling power of decision. His strength of character, courage and skill added up to a formidable combination and he made a unique contribution to the Service which he had joined late in life.

Nye's training as a soldier inclined him to military rather than diplomatic methods. This could sometimes be a weakness; he tended to see the country as a 'Command', to place people into clearly defined categories and to consider that any action was better than doing nothing (by no means always true in diplomacy). He was an autocrat with the habit of command, he had an eye for detail and a passion for precision.* He was apt to vent his wrath in no uncertain manner at any member of his staff who he thought was not pulling his weight and on anyone in Whitehall who failed to grasp the local situation. Outside the Office too his prejudices could sometimes prove a handicap. For a non-smoker and teetotaller he was remarkably tolerant as a host; but he did not enjoy the diplomatic round, the cocktail circuit or being one of a crowd. Moreover he was by nature dogmatic and, though he mellowed in his later years, he could on occasion be abrasive. Some of these characteristics caused resentment among his staff, but they were the warts inevitable on the face of a strong character.

In India, Nye's main achievement was that he was called upon, at the Delhi end, to be in charge of relations between India and Britain at a crucial time when those relations were being completely transformed. By his example and his own efforts, he established them on a basis which – with some deviations through the years – endured. The essential point to his mind was to achieve understanding and friendship and he made every effort to hold out a helping hand to the new India. From the start it was a great advantage that he, with his wife, had established a reputation while Governor of Madras as a friend of India. His determination to develop a good understanding did not by any means blind him to Indian faults or mean that he did not represent British interests with vigour. On the contrary, the fact that he was known to be sympathetic to the new India allowed him to speak with all the greater frankness and to be listened to with all the more respect (but on Kashmir he failed, like so many others, to move Nehru at all). His concentration on his job with the Government and people of India made him sometimes less sympathetic to the British community and certainly to their old style of life. Nevertheless the senior ones respected him and realized that he was working to establish a climate in India in which they could hope

---

* Nye carried his degree of personal supervision to surprising extremes – in Delhi checking the time of arrival of members of the staff at the front door of the Office (and sending a chaprassi daily to every room with an alarm clock so that all could check their watches); in Ottawa personally regulating the Office thermostatic control – to give central heating at some 10 degrees less than most local staff found comfortable.

to continue to operate and be assured of a hearing by the Government of India for any reasonable representations they wished to make.

Always strong in administration, Nye devoted himself both in India and Canada to building up British organization both at the capital and in the Provinces. His first principle was that the object of any mission abroad was the pursuit of British interests. This called for the closest relationship at all levels between the mission and the Government to which it was accredited. It also required British representatives to show themselves over as wide an area as possible and to gain an understanding of the country as a whole. Under both headings he himself was highly successful. He (with his wife) achieved a friendship with Nehru which was equalled by no other diplomatic representative at any time; and he had a remorseless touring programme (as later in Canada) which took him to all parts of India in a special RAF plane provided by the Government. He insisted on all members of the staff making their contacts in Delhi and doing their share of touring the country. For these broad reasons he placed in the top priority relations with the people of the country, second relations with the British community and other Commonwealth representatives; foreign diplomats came at the end. He made his point too by insisting that no one knew India until he had made his journey in a bullock-cart.

Nye also had clear views about the role of a High Commissioner in relation both to the Government at home and to his own staff. On the substance of any matter he would argue a case with all the strength at his command, but once a decision was taken he accepted it completely and would defend it loyally. But he was emphatic that the way a High Commissioner carried out his instructions must be left to his discretion to act as he thought best. With his staff, he insisted that the High Commissioner must be accepted as in control of all British interests in the country. Nye was in charge not only of the political work, but of the work of the Trade Commissioners, Defence Advisers and Information staff (to a degree which was not always welcomed); at the same time he sought to ensure that everyone felt himself to be a member of a single team. He excelled in delegation and made it clear that he regarded his Deputy as an alter ego, supporting him unreservedly in public (though reserving the right to blow him up in private if necessary).

Nye's first question was always 'What is the object of the exercise?' He was impatient alike of verbiage, unnecessary reporting (he took the view that all information should be at the post and made available as occasion required, but that only essential information should regularly be sent home); he saw no point in arguing a matter unless it led to definite action; he was unmoved by precedents and judged each issue on its merits. He believed in face to face discussion rather than lengthy memoranda. He was irritated with any red tape and particularly with the nonsense of 'Buggins' turn' in the Civil Service; he was always keen to give younger men their chance and to secure promotion for any who deserved it. To those with whom he worked closely he gave his complete confidence; he stimulated their loyalty and gave them a sense of purpose. In a word he had the gift of leadership.

On the transfer of power, a number of British members of the ICS transferred to the Foreign Service and others went to other Departments in the British Government (notably the Board of Trade). Not many came to the CRO partly because, with the absorption of the India Office, there was no immediate shortage of staff; partly perhaps because there was no certainty that responsibility for India and Pakistan would remain with the CRO. Later Nye forcibly expressed the view that anyone with a pre-1947 outlook was not suitable to serve in the modern India. This has given rise to a belief that the CRO was opposed to using the experience of the former members of the ICS. This was not altogether so; Nye himself, in evidence before the Select Committee on Estimates, said that the CRO 'missed a wonderful opportunity', that other Departments got 'first class chaps' from the ICS, but the CRO got very few.[12] In fact in 1947 the posts of DHC in the outposts in the sub-Continent were all filled on contract by former ICS members; in addition eight former ICS members were taken on to the permanent establishment, all of whom served in senior posts in the sub-Continent in the next few years. (At a later date, the CRO expressed more strongly its objections to employing former Colonial Service members in the former Colonies.)

The extension of diplomatic responsibilities to India and Pakistan led to a new development in organization abroad; hitherto the British Government had for many years appointed commercial representatives with the title of Trade Commissioner in major towns throughout the Dominions, but political representation had been confined exclusively to the Capital. India and Pakistan however presented new problems. Areas were vast and heavily populated; in many centres there remained a sizeable British population (some 20,000 for example in Calcutta). In any case there had been the tradition of a British presence and it was thought unfitting that the symbols of British power should vanish overnight. It was decided therefore to establish political posts in the key provincial centres, with the title of Deputy High Commissioner. (Similar posts with the same title were later set up in Malaysia and Nigeria; curiously it was only after the creation of the Diplomatic Service in 1965 that the posts in the provincial centres of Canada, Australia and New Zealand ceased to be controlled by the Board of Trade and came under the control of the CRO with the appointment of Diplomatic Service Officers.)

The presence of large British communities in the sub-Continent added a new function. Consular duties as such had never been performed by British High Commissions and no Consular officers had been appointed in Commonwealth countries. The reason for this was that Commonwealth countries were not regarded as foreign to each other and that the citizens of all Commonwealth countries shared the common status of British subjects; therefore if any citizen needed assistance he addressed himself to the local government rather than to the representative of the country to which he might belong. In fact, in the old Dominions, the settler from Britain normally faded into the landscape and ceased to be identified or to identify himself with the Mother Country. These conventions no longer applied in the Indian sub-Continent; the Britisher was clearly distinguishable from the rest of the population and only rarely became a permanent resident. He might be at risk in the event of civil disturbance or riot, he might be harassed by the local government: British-owned companies, business houses, plantations continued to operate as before and were accustomed to look to the British Government to protect their interests. UK Citizens Associations were formed and all UK citizens were encouraged to register with the High Commission. The High Commissions in India and Pakistan accepted a responsibility for maintaining contact with UK citizens, giving advice and guidance, making representations where necessary and visiting those in remote areas. These duties added a function that had never been performed in the old Dominions and gave a new dimension of consular responsibility to the Commonwealth Service overseas. 'Consular' duties covered also a number of matters which had never arisen in the Dominions such as the supervision of cemeteries, protection of ancient monuments, the status of Anglo-Indians and responsibility for large numbers of previous employees and pensioners.

While these consular responsibilities were special to the sub-Continent, British missions in all Commonwealth countries found themselves with added functions in the more complex post-war world and resulting increased staff. One of the main causes for the increase in work was that the British Government used the British High Commissioners for passing virtually all information to Commonwealth Governments. The use of the High Commission channel had several advantages. It enabled the High Commissioner to comment before irrevocable action was taken; more frequently it enabled him to deliver the message with a suitable explanation. Moreover, though the message was normally sent to all posts in identical terms, this method allowed for a differentiation in practice which would not have been possible in the case of a circular despatched to all Governments simultaneously. This became increasingly important with the objections seen to communicating full information on certain matters to all Governments alike. On such occasions the full text was sent to all High Commissioners for their information and it was open to any High Commissioner to recommend that the information should not be withheld from the Government to which he was accredited; more frequently he was able to use the information as background and could in this way satisfy any enquiries received.

There were also three new areas of work which affected all posts.

1. *Trade*

Until the creation of the Diplomatic Service, the Trade Commissioner Service remained a distinct service responsible to the Board of Trade (though the Senior Trade Commissioner and members of his staff were appointed Economic Advisers and as such were members of the High Commission staff). The war had shown the need for cooperation between the political and commercial arms and the Senior Trade Commissioner was by this time in all countries based in the capital city. In the old Dominions, Trade Commissioners in provincial centres normally reported direct to the Board of Trade; in the outposts in India and Pakistan the position was complicated by the appointment of DHCs. In view of the importance of the export drive (which sometimes required support at the political level) and of the frequent need of the High Commission for political advice about the Provinces, there was a call for mutual cooperation and this was not at all times forthcoming. In the absence of a single service and of a clear unified chain of command, too much was left to the personal factor. Normally the High Commissioner's own authority was accepted without question by all members of the Trade Commission Service; but, owing to clashes between individuals, there were sometimes damaging conflicts between Trade Commissioners and the Deputy High Commissioner, both in the outposts (where they were thrown closely together, frequently sharing the same accommodation) and even at the centre.

2. *Information*

The second new function which war exigencies had already added to posts abroad was Information. Publicity continued in peacetime to be regarded as an important function of Government; abroad it became increasingly the duty of High Commissioners to sustain British interests and help project the British way of life. Missions in all Commonwealth countries both at Headquarters and in Provincial capitals deployed a substantial staff on information work, a high proportion of which was locally recruited. This was efficient, appropriate and economical since the work was seldom of a confidential character and often called for local knowledge for effective presentation. Although the information staff in practice formed a separate cadre they were not a distinct service and, in spite of the use of the term 'British Information Service', operated as part of the CRO. There were therefore few problems of jurisdiction such as occurred with the Trade Commissioner Service.

3. *Defence*

In diplomatic missions in foreign countries, the service attaché had been a traditional figure for centuries. Strangely no similar appointments had been made in relation to Commonwealth countries before the 1939 war. The military cooperation in wartime spawned a variety of missions of all three Services and the need for some continuing machinery to ensure cooperation in defence matters in peacetime was accepted without question. In India and Pakistan there was special need to establish a military liaison in countries where Britain had been so intimately involved (and continued to have responsibilities); and in the old Dominions the Service Departments in Whitehall attached no less importance to maintaining and strengthening the wartime habits of cooperation. Sizeable British Joint Service Liaison Staffs were established in Canada and Australia and Service representatives were appointed in all Commonwealth countries; for convenience and to make a distinction from attachés serving in foreign countries they were regarded as members of the High Commissioner's staff and were designated Advisers – but the degree of the High Commissioner's control varied and in some cases was nominal.

In addition to these three areas there were special functions in particular countries. Thus there was a Financial Adviser in Ottawa, in Delhi and for a time also in Canberra and Karachi: there was an Agricultural Adviser in Ottawa, Canberra and Wellington. There continued for a short time after the war to be resident representatives of the Ministry of Food and Ministry of Supply. In addition when circumstances called for special liaison on security matters a representative of the Security Service was appointed to the High Commission staff.

In view of all these increased responsibilities it is not surprising that the size of the High Commissions expanded substantially. In Canada the number of diplomatic staff (i.e. excluding local staff) grew from 3 in 1925 to 14 in 1950. In India the comparable figure for 1950 was a total of 45 (made up of 28 in Delhi and 17 in the outposts). The staffing of the posts in the sub-Continent made a complete change in the balance of the service; there were nearly four times as many appointments in India as in Canada and nearly as many as in all the four old Dominions put together; well over half the CRO staff posted abroad were serving in Asia. The figures in the sub-Continent for total staff reached a formidable figure, resulting to some extent perhaps from carrying on the lavish traditions of the Raj in the employment of subordinate staff. Successive missions were despatched from London and sought to achieve economies; over the first few years substantial cuts were made.

In contrast to the spate of political appointments by Churchill during the war and also of those that followed later under Macmillan, the Attlee Government made only one political appointment (Williams to Australia) as did also the Conservative Government of Churchill and Eden (Carrington, also to Australia). The period is remarkable for the fact that for the first time the

314

posts of High Commissioner (including the major ones) were filled by members of the CRO.

Two footnotes call for mention. The Government of Eire had objected to receiving in Dublin an agent of the British Government with the title of High Commissioner. He was therefore appointed with the neutral designation of 'Representative'. This title could well have continued when the Republic was proclaimed, since the Republic was to be neither a foreign country nor a member of the Commonwealth. But the title of the High Commissioner in London would have to be changed in any case and it was agreed that both should be called Ambassadors. The change was not effected immediately and did not come about until July 1950. Thus a further anomaly was added in that the CRO for the first time was officially in direct relation with an Ambassador of a country not in the Commonwealth and indeed included an Ambassador in its own Service.

In 1951 another unusual appointment was made, namely the appointment of a High Commissioner in Southern Rhodesia. Southern Rhodesia had been since 1923 a self-governing Colony under a Governor appointed by the Secretary of State. There were however plans to form a Federation of the three Territories of Southern Rhodesia, Northern Rhodesia and Nyasaland and it was of obvious convenience for the British Government to have on the spot its own political representative who would not, like the Governor, be concerned with responsibility for one particular territory only. The Federation came about in 1953 and the High Commissioner was then accredited to the Federation as a whole. Thus the CRO included in its Service not only an Ambassador to a country that was not foreign, but also a High Commissioner to a country that was not a full independent Member of the Commonwealth.

In recognition of the increased significance of High Commissioners changes came about in their status and the formal degree of precedence accorded to them. Hitherto they had been oddities in the international world of diplomacy; they were not appointed by or accredited to a Head of State, they were not conducting relations between foreign nations and they were not members of the Diplomatic Corps (the D.O. indeed had always been at pains to distinguish between the diplomatic relationship between foreign countries and the more informal relationship between Commonwealth countries). As High Commissioners' functions began to draw nearer to those of Ambassadors this formal differentiation seemed artificial and it tended to create unnecessary jealousies between High Commissioners and the representatives of foreign countries.* The changes came about by degrees. In 1946 it was decided for the first time that the title 'Excellency' should be

* It remained a source of complaint among foreigners that, at meetings with the Diplomatic Corps in Commonwealth capitals, the Queen received Commonwealth High Commissioners first and invited them to stand with Her when She received the Ambassadors.

accorded to all High Commissioners (as already to Ambassadors). In 1948 international agreement was secured to the acceptance of High Commissioners as members of the Diplomatic Corps, and to the grant to them of precedence on the same basis as Ambassadors. Two modifications of this general rule were observed in London – for purposes of precedence Ambassadors and High Commissioners were regarded as 'interleaved', and it was conceded that, even if he had seniority, a High Commissioner would not become Dean of the Corps.*

In view of these changes the suggestion was frequently made that the title High Commissioner should be changed to Ambassador. The case in favour was straightforward and simple and has always found some supporters, but they have never been more than a minority. The matter first came up at the CPM Meeting in 1948 and has been raised from time to time since, always with the same result. The main argument against has been that the distinctness of the Commonwealth association still makes it appropriate to retain a title different from that in ordinary international usage. There was also the negative argument that a change might be misinterpreted as indicating some weakening of the association. By coincidence the matter first came up when, after the war, the prevailing practice of reserving the title 'Ambassador' for the great powers (leaving the smaller powers to be content with 'Minister') was going out of fashion. Ambassadors 'cropped up like hay' and, by contrast, there seemed to be something select about 'High Commissioner'.†

---

* The rule did not apply in other Commonwealth countries where the British High Commissioner frequently became Dean and in many cases was the first to do so. The rule in London was changed when Lindo, the Jamaican High Commissioner, became Dean in 1973.

† The title High Commissioner has since become relatively less select in London than that of Ambassador – 1 in 4, compared to 1 in 8 thirty years ago.

CHAPTER 4

The Issues

The cordiality and fruitfulness of the consultation carried on with Common-weath Governments varied with different Governments, at different periods and on different issues. In general there was active and close cooperation with Canada over all issues affecting the defence of the free world, foreign affairs and the development of the 'new' Commonwealth; on trade and economic matters however there were often acute differences and occasionally bitter arguments. The reverse was the case with India – here there was in the main effective collaboration in economic matters and in planning aid for Indian development; but though views were shared in some international problems there was a fundamental disagreement over the strategy called for in containing the threat of Communism. Moreover the British reluctance to take sides in the quarrels between India and Pakistan inevitably led both countries to complain of lack of support. South Africa presented a special case. On the one hand there was broad identity of view on world problems (though reluctance on South Africa's part to undertake defence commit-ments) and there was close collaboration in all matters of finance, trade and commerce; moreover the CRO was always conscious of the need to retain South African goodwill towards the High Commission Territories. On the other hand the more rigid adherence to Apartheid antagonized opinion in Britain and, in contrast with the admiration shown for Smuts, no sympathy was felt in the CRO for the high priests of Afrikanerdom. Australia too presented both light and shade; there was substantial British investment both in men and money and there was basic agreement on world issues. But trade matters often provided scope for recrimination and on political issues there were differences alike on account of Evatt's abrasive insistence on Australia's place in, and of Menzies' growing disenchantment with, the development of the Commonwealth.

Suez was unique in arousing such intense opposition to British policies from so many Commonwealth partners; but there were minor irritations affecting one member or another from time to time which made the task of the CRO all the more challenging. Some of them are considered below.

Constitutional

The Indian Republic

The most important constitutional issue was the agreement that India, on becoming a Republic, would be welcome to remain a Member of the Commonwealth – a decision which altered the basis for Commonwealth membership and foreshadowed other changes in the future. The doctrine that had hitherto prevailed was that the association was based on being 'united by a common allegiance to the Crown'; this view was held with tenacity and sometimes with emotion. As far back as 1938, Malcolm Mac-Donald had envisaged the possibility of a Republic within the Commonwealth which might have accorded with de Valera's ideas at that time. But he found no readiness among his colleagues to entertain the notion and it was dropped. At the time of the transfer of power, Dixon expressed the Office view when he rejected the suggestion that, since India could not be expected to accept the common allegiance to the Crown, the Commonwealth should in future consist of two categories – Members accepting the 1926 formula and Associates who would have all the benefits of membership, without the acceptance of allegiance. Dixon pointed out that this distinction would undoubtedly be interpreted as implying that the status of Associates was in some way inferior; if therefore India could not accept membership on the 1926 condition, the only course seemed to him to be that, like Burma earlier, she should leave the Commonwealth and become a foreign country, but have a Treaty relationship with the UK on the lines of the Brussels Treaty of 1947.[1]

In 1949 Eire had ceased to be a Member of the Commonwealth on becoming a Republic and this had been generally accepted. Having regard to the background therefore, it is remarkable that a few months later Republican India was accepted as a continuing Member with such speed, goodwill and unanimity. One reason for this lay in the thoroughness of the preparations for the 1949 CPM Meeting. The British Government resorted for the first time to a device (which was later followed when an application to join the EEC was being considered) of despatching emissaries to Commonwealth Governments; Gordon Walker visiting India, Pakistan and Ceylon, Norman Brook Canada, Listowel Australia and New Zealand and Liesching South Africa. These careful and thorough consultations enabled the Prime Ministers when they met to reach a unanimous conclusion in less than a week. The key to the settlement lay in India's acceptance of the King 'as the symbol of the free association of its [the Commonwealth's] independent member nations and as such the Head of the Commonwealth'.[2] As Mansergh has pointed out[3] the settlement seemed almost metaphysical in its refinement, but had the merit of reconciling constitutional forms with political realities. The King's Headship of the Commonwealth was the symbol only of the free association of its members (as the words 'as such' make clear): as Head of the Commonwealth, the King was owed no allegiance and had no authority.

On the British side, the CRO can take a large share of the credit for the successful outcome; Gordon Walker in particular, strongly supported by Liesching, played a leading part. (In his books he states his belief that he was responsible for the first suggestion of the common allegiance to the King as Head of the Commonwealth).[4] On the Indian side Krishna Menon was anxious to retain the Commonwealth link and to show no disrespect to the King; in this matter at least he was most helpful in urging Nehru to accept a compromise.

Coronation

The decision called for an alteration in the Royal Style and Titles and an Act was eventually passed in 1953 which described the Queen as Queen of 'Her other Realms and Territories' and as 'Head of the Commonwealth'.*

The formalities for the Accession and Coronation in the changed circumstances were worked out carefully in advance and the CRO ensured that the interests of Commonwealth Governments were taken into account. In the event everything went smoothly.† This was the first time that a Sovereign was crowned as Head of the Commonwealth and full emphasis was given to the Commonwealth character of the occasion; Commonwealth leaders attended in person and Commonwealth contingents took a full part in the procession. All this was a happy example of Commonwealth collaboration. The CRO officials concerned included two members of the staff who had already retired but were happy to find themselves on the familiar ground they had already covered together for the previous Coronation in 1937 – Dixon for constitutional and Bromley for ceremonial matters.

---

* The change had not been made when King George VI died. When the King had to undergo an operation, Dixon was deputed to explain to Krishna Menon the procedure on a Demise of the Crown, including the arrangement whereby High Commissioners attended the meeting of the Accession Council and signed the Proclamation of the new Sovereign. He pointed out that the Proclamation had been in use without alteration for three or four centuries and contained expressions which were not appropriate for a Republic; Menon said that he would be sorry if he could not show his respect for the new Sovereign by signing the Proclamation and asked if it would be possible for the expression 'Head of the Commonwealth' (for which he claimed authorship) to be included. Dixon was extremely doubtful, but a Committee under Brook's chairmanship agreed to the change. When the time came, Menon therefore had no difficulty in signing.[5]

† The only discordant note was struck by Malta (in status still a Colony) where Dr Borg Olivier demanded as P.M. to be provided with a separate carriage with such persistence that Churchill yielded.

Ireland

It is a curious coincidence that only a few months before the decision on India was taken, Eire became a Republic and left the Commonwealth. Naturally the question poses itself whether, if the Indian decision had been taken first, the Irish might have decided otherwise. It is an intriguing question, if of no great significance. The Indian solution came near to de Valera's own earlier idea of 'external association' and it is conceivable that he himself might have accepted such an arrangement. But curiously it was his opponents (the party which had originally supported the Treaty) who took action; Costello when Prime Minister made no attempt to bargain and announced the decision to become a Republic and to leave the Commonwealth in the same breath.* The decision made little difference in practice; for ten years Eire had ceased to take part in Commonwealth meetings or in the normal Commonwealth cooperation. On leaving the Commonwealth, she nevertheless retained by agreement two of the most important benefits of membership – continued enjoyment of Imperial Preference and free entry into the UK for Irish citizens.†

One obvious change was that the titles of the representatives exchanged between Ireland and Commonwealth countries were changed to Ambassadors. Even here there was delay in accrediting the British Ambassador since the Irish insisted on the letters referring to Republic of Ireland and not Irish Republic (which did not necessarily imply the whole island). As if to underline the undramatic nature of the change, the CRO continued to be responsible for relations with the Republic.‡ It was all a very Irish solution!

* Costello's announcement was made suddenly and without warning at a press conference in Ottawa where he was on a visit. He had been entertained the previous evening at a dinner at Government House. Alexander told the author that Costello had taken offence at the centrepiece on the dining-table (somehow symbolic of Ulster) and alleged that it was intended as a deliberate insult to him. This of course was not the case in any way, but Alexander wondered whether this imagined slight might have proved the last straw. It was certainly odd that Costello's announcement should have been made in Canada apparently on the spur of the moment.

† Dixon had proposed that Eire citizens should be treated on the analogy of British protected persons, i.e. they would not be subject to the disabilities specifically imposed on aliens e.g. as regards entry and residence, but they would not be entitled to benefits specifically conferred by legislation on British subjects. Gordon Walker was impressed with the idea, but it was rejected by the Home Office who felt that it would create insuperable administrative difficulties (e.g. sorting out among Irish residents in the UK who were and who were not British subjects). The 1949 Act therefore provided that Eire citizens should be treated for the purposes of UK legislation as though they in fact possessed the status of British subjects.

‡ The formulation that the Republic, though outside the Commonwealth, was to be treated as if she were a Commonwealth member was agreed between Dominion Governments at a hastily convened informal meeting between the Commonwealth Secretary (Noel-Baker) and the Lord Chancellor (Jowitt) with Commonwealth Ministers who happened to be attending the 1948 UN Assembly in Paris. The main discussion took place at a small dinner at the Ritz whose gastronomic excellence contributed to the resolution of differences and of which the astronomic cost could not be questioned in the light of the political results.

Nationality

Far-reaching consequences developed from what might have appeared to be a technical change in the nationality law. The effect was to turn upside-down the basis on which British nationality throughout the Empire had hitherto been founded. The matter was brought to a head in 1946 by the passing of a Canadian Citizenship Act;[6] instead of defining the various classes of persons who were British subjects, this defined who were Canadian citizens, but went on to provide that they would be British subjects. As someone put it at the time, instead of beginning with a whole cake and cutting it into a number of slices, it began with a number of slices and built them into one cake. The Canadian action caused alarm in Whitehall at first since it upset the traditional basis, but it was readily recognized that nothing but confusion would result from two separate systems existing side by side. The British Government called a conference of experts from all parts of the Commonwealth. This met at the beginning of 1947; the Chairman was Sir Alexander Maxwell, PUS at the Home Office, and the UK Delegation included, from the CRO, Stephenson, Dixon and Dale (then Assistant Legal Adviser). The Conference recommended the general adoption of a scheme whereby each Member of the Commonwealth would define its own citizens, while providing that citizens of all Members would possess a 'common status' as Commonwealth citizens or British subjects. This led to the enactment in Britain of the British Nationality Act of 1948[7] which provided for the first time for the status of 'citizenship of the U.K. and the Colonies'. This apparent breach in the principle of the common allegiance to the Crown and the common status as British subjects was strongly attacked by many Conservatives – it did violence to the life-long views held by L. S. Amery and was mercilessly criticized in Parliament by Enoch Powell. In the light of hindsight it is remarkable that what the CRO fought so hard to retain in the interests of maintaining Commonwealth unity was the continuing validity of the principle of the common status; they (like others at the time) did not foresee that a time would come when Britain would need to restrict the entry of those belonging to other Commonwealth countries.

There was another feature of the Act which had repercussions later. It provided that existing British subjects who did not acquire the citizenship of another Commonwealth country under its law would automatically become citizens of the UK and Colonies. This was based on the assumption that, on independence, a Commonwealth country would confer its citizenship on all British subjects in its borders and all 'belonging' to it outside. This did not always happen in India and Pakistan owing to their dispute over refugees, but this gave rise to no serious difficulties. Later however a number of Asians in East Africa failed to acquire the citizenship of their country of adoption and qualified for entry to Britain as UK passport-holders. This led to much controversy in the 1960s when African Governments sought to expel them. Looking back one can hardly fault Dixon's wry comment[8] that 'This is only another instance of a policy, embarked on as an act of good faith, which has profoundly disappointed our hopes.'

Foreign Affairs

Kashmir

Of all the issues in international affairs, Kashmir – which served as a symbol for the acute differences dividing India and Pakistan – was the most continuous and prolonged preoccupation for the CRO. It was for them a particularly unhappy problem since the underlying assumption in the Commonwealth relationship was that war between any of its members was unthinkable; hostilities in fact took place on Independence in 1947, there was sporadic fighting over a long period with the constant threat of war which erupted in military confrontation in 1965 and again in 1971; yet until that latter year both countries remained members of the Commonwealth. The dispute between them was serious because it remained a continuous threat to the peace and was consequently frequently before the UN, it was a grave embarrassment to the Commonwealth, it prevented the sub-Continent from playing any effective role in international security and, above all, as a result of the armaments race in which both indulged and of their failure to achieve reasonable economic cooperation, it applied a severe brake to development and progress in each country.

The conflict was of deep concern to the British Government and strenuous though unsuccessful efforts were made to compose it. A number of different motives impelled the British. First was their genuine concern to end so damaging a quarrel. In any case they bore a measure of responsibility for its existence. But the whole tradition of the Commonwealth was to avoid intervention in the affairs of other Members and the CRO sought throughout to maintain impartiality. Nevertheless there were factors influencing attitudes in favour of one side or the other. From the point of view of self-interest, India was far more significant than Pakistan for reasons both of trade and diplomatic influence; it was important to retain her goodwill and to avoid arousing her antagonism or causing her to rely too dangerously on the USSR. On the other hand, while India remained non-aligned and at times unhelpful to Western policies, Pakistan was well disposed and later became an ally firmly linked with the West. The merits of the case were confused by the complicated legal argumentation. But in general it is perhaps fair to say that many impartial observers felt a measure of sympathy with

Pakistan in spite of her initial 'aggression' on the grounds that Kashmir was in the main Moslem and the general expectation had been that it would opt for Pakistan, that a last-minute decision by a discredited Maharajah was hardly the fair way to settle the fate of a people, that India accepted the principle of a plebiscite and then refused to allow one to be held except on conditions which Pakistan would not accept as fair and that India, as the party in possession and at the same time the more powerful one, could afford to show more understanding of the other side.

These different standpoints were to some extent reflected in the minds of British leaders at the time. Mountbatten and Cripps were strong supporters of India. Attlee and Nye were sympathetic to India, but not without reservations. Bevin, Gordon Walker, Ismay, Cadogan did not favour either side. Noel-Baker, whose ceaseless efforts were made futile by Indian stonewalling, tended in practice to sympathize with Pakistan and her case was strongly presented by Grafftey-Smith, the British High Commissioner. In the CRO itself, the majority, in the face of so baffling and novel an issue, sought to adhere to Talleyrand's maxim and avoid over-zealousness. But it had been traditional in the sub-Continent that many, particularly in the Army, had found the Moslems more loyal than the Hindu and had developed considerable affection for them; moreover many in the ICS and in the Services in India had spent much of their life in opposition to Congress and had little liking for the ways of its politicians. The most vocal and pungent exponent of this viewpoint in the CRO was General Scoones, who had seen most of his service in India and was Principal Staff Officer to the Secretary of State until his appointment as High Commissioner to New Zealand in 1953, but his advice was confined to military matters and he had little influence on policy decisions.

Kashmir involved the CRO in a considerable effort at many points. In London it was engaged in working out policies and formulating instructions to the two High Commissioners and the UK Delegation in New York. This required continuous liaison with the F.O. with whom there were frequently acute differences of opinion; these were not always easy to resolve since while the CRO was responsible for relations with the two countries, the F.O. was responsible for instructing the UK delegation to the UN. The main difference between the two Departments was that the CRO had a wealth of detailed knowledge about the background in the sub-Continent, was more optimistic of the possibility of achievement and sought to be active; the F.O. saw Kashmir as only one of the many international issues which concerned Britain, took a more cynical or realistic view of what could be accomplished and did not wish to take an initiative that might well prove unrewarding and prejudice other interests.

The issue involved the CRO heavily in the discussions in the UN. In 1948 Noel-Baker spent several months in New York in negotiations; a member of the CRO staff was always attached to the UK Delegation, in addition it was the practice to send a senior official from the CRO for all important discussions at the Security Council. The differences between the F.O. and CRO came to a head in New York where Noel-Baker was constantly pressing for action in the Security Council which Cadogan sought to postpone or avoid altogether. In the list of those who laboured in search of a solution, special tribute must be paid to Noel-Baker who devoted his energies with passion to the problem and on more than one occasion felt, thanks to his close collaboration with Bajpai,* that he was on the point of reaching a settlement. It is arguable however that his intense and successful efforts to associate the UN with the principles of a possible settlement by plebiscite eliminated any slender chance of reaching an agreement by negotiation. Officials in the CRO and in the two High Commissions gave all the help they could to the many who tried at various times and in various ways to bring the two countries together – MacNaughton at the Security Council, Menzies at the 1950 CPM Meeting, Chester Bowles the US Ambassador in India, and the succession of UN representatives – Nimitz, Owen Dixon and Jarring; later they worked closely and more fruitfully with the World Bank in the plans for the settlement of the Canal Waters dispute.

In the capitals of the two countries, the two High Commissions constantly used their influence to counsel moderation and sought ways to bring the two sides together. In particular the High Commission in New Delhi missed no opportunity of trying to bring home to the Indians the dangers of their failing to reach a settlement – Nye was perhaps the most emphatic and because of his known affection for India carried the most weight;† but there were also others; all urgings however fell on deaf ears. Unfortunately in the early years the two High Commissioners not only tended to share the standpoint of the Government to which they were accredited, but quarrelled among themselves and were unable to submit agreed advice. This was especially the case when Grafftey-Smith was the High Commissioner in Karachi; he and Nye made no attempt to meet and a recommendation from one was invariably followed by a note of dissent from the other, in crisp and pithy language.‡ Later when officers from the Commonwealth Service were appointed, they were at pains to keep in close touch. Laithwaite in Pakistan was the first High Commissioner to pay regular visits to the capital of the other country; this later became standard practice. The closeness of the contact was symbolized in the unique record of Morrice James who

---

* Cadogan was head of the UK delegation to the UN. Bajpai was head of D.E.A. in the Indian Government.

† In his farewell meeting with Nehru before leaving India for good, Nye made a powerful appeal to Nehru to show magnanimity and so increase his stature in the world – but it was to no avail.

‡ In *Hands to Play* (p. 136) Grafftey-Smith wrote: 'In our personal discovery of India, vast areas of interest and attraction were denied to us by my official Pakistani label. We were officially unwelcome in the considerable parish of my colleague in Delhi, Sir Archibald Nye.'

between 1952 and 1971 served as DHC Lahore and then in turn as Deputy in Karachi and Delhi and High Commissioner in each capital.

After the early heady days at the UN, it became clear, with India militarily and economically the stronger, physically in possession and strengthening her hold on Kashmir all the time, that Pakistan aspirations would not be met short of some dramatic change in the situation. Some time after he became PUS, Liesching came to the conclusion that there was no prospect of being able to impose a solution from outside and that nothing but the threatened bloodbath would force the parties to come together. He gave instructions to his deputy that he was to waste no more time in the futile task of searching for a solution. But the problem would not go away and the CRO was never rid of it.

Defence Pacts

The various Defence Pacts gave rise to conflicting considerations. Over NATO there was no problem apart from India's general hostility to military alliances. There was close cooperation with Canada and full support from Australia and New Zealand. The arrangements for a Treaty with the USA made by Australia and New Zealand (ANZUS) seemed to the CRO natural and sensible and they were approved by the Attlee Government. Churchill and Eden however regretted this turning towards the USA and, when the Conservatives came to power, they made their protest. This had no effect and it seemed in the CRO a pity to question the right of a Commonwealth country to make whatever arrangements it thought best for its own security.

The military alliances in South East Asia (SEATO) and the Middle East (CENTO) presented the CRO with something of a dilemma. SEATO was a USA concept and, in Dulles' view, provided a means of rescuing something from what he regarded as the disastrous Geneva settlement. The British went along with it because it provided the best means of ensuring continued USA cooperation in South East Asia and it met to some extent the needs of Australia and New Zealand. Nehru however doubly disliked a military alliance on his doorstep and one which included Pakistan (who was not without an ulterior motive). Nye warned his Government that, if the idea of the Pact were pursued, serious damage would be done to Indo-British relations and any settlement with Pakistan would be impeded. The CRO had misgivings, but did not seek to resist the formation of SEATO (or later of CENTO). It is arguable that both helped to bring a degree of stability but at some cost to the closeness of India's relationship with the West, though the deterioration was more marked with the USA than with Britain because of the American supply of armaments to Pakistan.

In the military sphere, Korea provided a remarkable occasion for forces from various Commonwealth countries (including an ambulance unit from

India) to form the Commonwealth Brigade which served with great distinction and considerable harmony.

Suez

Until the full story is told, any account of this strange business runs a risk of misleading. But its importance for the CRO was profound and, to this day, not wholly calculable. Suez presented the biggest challenge to Britain's leadership of the Commonwealth since the American War of Independence and saw the Commonwealth in greater disarray than ever before. The hostility of the USA and the USSR was so extreme that the opposition in Commonwealth countries became overlooked and apologists for Suez have tended to play down the weight of Commonwealth objections.* It is true that Australia (under Menzies) gave full support and New Zealand (under Holland) somewhat more muted support and that South Africa kept aloof;† Pakistan was torn and, under strong pressure from Symon (the British High Commissioner) Suhrawardy, after a struggle, at least did not oppose his ally in CENTO and SEATO. But there is no doubt that the Anglo-French action came as a great shock to public opinion throughout the Commonwealth or that the unfavourable Commonwealth reactions were a major factor in the eventual decision to withdraw. It must also be said that there was nothing whatever surprising in those reactions; the CRO had for several weeks known what they were likely to be if resort were had to unilateral military action and had been scrupulous in ensuring that regular reports of the likely attitudes of Commonwealth Governments were submitted to Ministers.

The eventual solution was largely the work of a Commonwealth Government. Canada and India were in the lead in bringing the matter before the UN and Pearson was the author and promoter of the resolution which brought about the cease-fire. Building on a reference by Eden to the possibility of the UN 'being willing to take over the physical task of maintaining peace in the area',[9] Pearson with extraordinary skill and speed secured the approval of the Assembly for a resolution setting up the UN Emergency Force; in doing so he showed great determination in resisting the demands of the US who, in a strange frenzy, sought the humiliation of the British. Pearson's plan met

---

* Macmillan (*Riding the Storm*) does not mention Commonwealth objections and Eden (*Full Circle*) makes light of them. Home's autobiography (*The Way the Wind Blows* pp. 138–41) mentions the sensitivity of any revival of colonialism on the part of India (and also the difficulty of Pakistan) but does not refer to any influence that Commonwealth attitudes may have had. His conclusion is that had it not been for a sad lapse on the part of American diplomacy peaceful persuasion had a good chance of gaining the day. Butler (*The Art of the Possible* p. 193) however says 'Censure by the United Nations in which most of the Commonwealth was arrayed against us, certainly had its effect upon many members of the Government.'

† Strydom said at the time 'it is best to keep our heads out of the bee-hive'.

the requirements of the Assembly by ensuring the withdrawal of the Anglo-French forces; but replaced them with the new and imaginative concept of a UN force; in this way he provided Britain with an acceptable and honourable means of retreat. It is this action which brought Pearson the tributes paid to him by British Ministers – but he would never have been able to win the support of the Assembly if it had not been clear that he was opposed to the Anglo-French unilateral action in the first instance.

In spite of the deep emotions that had been aroused on all sides, the British Government succeeded in restoring a relationship of trust and friendliness with other Commonwealth countries in a remarkably short time. The main credit may fairly be given to Pearson since Canadian policy deliberately took account of the need to avoid conflict within the Commonwealth and he himself claimed that Canadian action had been designed to help to heal the differences. Something was also due to the good sense and the dignity with which the British Government behaved and to the success of the UN operation itself. No doubt also the strength of the relationship between Britain and her Commonwealth partners could survive a temporary aberration, especially as it was clear that many in Britain had opposed the initial policy and, after Eden's departure, Macmillan implicitly (but with such skill that this was scarcely recognizable) reversed the policy. Nevertheless the whole business left deep scars and had serious consequences. Perhaps the most important effect was the growing recognition in Britain of her changed status in the world. By the initial decision, Britain threw away the moral position on which her world status largely depended; she revealed her weakness by stopping the action.

In the CRO itself, Home was at that stage a newcomer to diplomacy and had been in the Cabinet for little more than a year. He lacked the experience or authority to question the P.M.'s lead and he always expressed confidence that Eden knew what he was doing and must be loyally supported. The PUS at the time was Laithwaite; he alone in the Office was taken into the Government's confidence and was made privy to their plans; his hands were therefore tied. To the rest of the Office, however, the affair came as a shock and, in many cases, caused deep distress. It seemed to many to be a turning back on all that the CRO had been established for and had sought to achieve – not least (though equally this was not the vital consideration in the importance attached to Commonwealth consultation. (The attitude of officials in the CRO was not markedly different from their colleagues in the F.O. and other Departments in the Government.)* Some High Commissioners also felt embarrassment and found themselves in an exposed position since none had any prior warning. Malcolm MacDonald who was High

---

* *See* for example Pierson Dixon, 'I remember feeling very strongly that we had by our action reduced ourselves from a 1st class to a 3rd class power.' (*A Double Diploma*, London, 1968, p. 278); and also Gore-Booth (*With Great Truth and Respect* pp. 227–34); Trevelyan (*Diplomatic Channels* p. 65).

Commissioner in India actually drafted a telegram submitting his resignation, but slept on the matter and awoke in the morning to learn of the British Government's agreement to a cease-fire; the message was not sent. Garner who was about to take up his appointment as High Commissioner in Canada and who had always made clear his opposition to the unilateral use of force offered to stand down since he could not conscientiously defend the policy; but the offer was brushed aside by Home who insisted that Ministers were counting on his help and he proceeded to his post.

Economic

Britain's efforts in the early post-war years to bring about reform at home and to maintain her position abroad imposed a heavy strain on her resources. In spite of modernization in industry and the skill and firmness of the Treasury under the guidance of Stafford Cripps, the economic outlook remained bleak. There was continual difficulty over the unfavourable balance of payments and the shortage of dollars and in 1949 sterling was devalued. Britain's economic situation had important effects on all Commonwealth countries, leading in some cases to closer cooperation within the Sterling Area (though the restrictions enforced caused difficulties); there remained a continuous problem with Canada.

The difficulties with countries in the Sterling Area arose from different causes. Contributors to the dollar pool (Australia and also Hong Kong and Malaya) complained that they were unduly restricted in expenditure necessary for their own development. But the main problem resulted from the sterling balances which had accumulated during the war years and, in the case of India and Pakistan, represented considerable sums. For a decade or more after the war there were a series of negotiations between the British Government and the Commonwealth creditor Governments in an attempt to limit the rate at which the latter could draw down their balances and so exercise a call upon Britain's current production of goods and services (referred to as 'unrequited exports'). Annual negotiations, in which the CRO was involved, were held; sometimes these were acrimonious with Commonwealth Governments showing resentment at what they regarded as the unwillingness of their banker to allow them to have back their own money.

Britain's unwillingness (or, as she would have claimed, inability) to discharge her sterling obligations as quickly as her Commonwealth creditors wished had the result of making them anxious to avoid in future a situation in which the rate at which they could draw upon their own external resources was dependent upon securing the agreement of the British Government. This led Commonwealth Governments to diversify their reserves – to hold part of them in gold or dollars or other acceptable international tokens and to cease to keep them wholly in sterling. Any indication of sterling weakness and successive devaluations increased that urge. The Bank of England, with the CRO as an ally, spent a large part of the 1960s trying to slow down the rate of this diversification. Finally in 1968 its inevitability was recognized and arrangements were negotiated with most of the countries of the Sterling Area to afford them dollar guarantees against further depreciations of sterling to the extent that they continued to hold part of their external resources in London. Though the Sterling Area continued for some time, it was losing its cohesion. The beginning of the end was signalled by the British devaluation in 1967, following on the restraints on investment in old Commonwealth countries. The Sterling Area came to an end not by plan, or by mutual agreement of its members or even, apparently by intention. But its demise in the next decade, together with British membership of the EEC, which foreshadowed the ending of the Imperial Preference system, removed a traditional part of the economic content of the Commonwealth.

To all this facet of the story, South Africa and Canada are partial exceptions. South Africa was within the ring fence of the Sterling Area, and benefited greatly from the flow of British capital to finance her industrial and mining development; but she held most of her reserves in the form of the gold she mined rather than in sterling in London. Canada, though part of the system of tariff preferences, stayed outside the Sterling Area because of the over-riding importance to her of her economic and financial relations with the United States. Consequently, during the war, Canada's unwillingness, like that of the United States, to acquire and hold inconvertible sterling, coupled with Britain's lack of dollars and inability to guarantee convertibility of sterling, caused Canada, as we have seen, to make generous financial provisions. From the point of view of relations between Britain and the Commonwealth in the post-war decades, the Canadian story is the exception to the general rule on two counts. First because Britain emerged in 1945 with massive war debts to the other Dominions, to the Colonies and above all to India. Secondly because in spite of Canadian help during the war and a substantial loan in 1946, Britain was quite unable to continue to pay for imports from Canada on the normal scale. In 1947 a Mission led by Liesching as Permanent Secretary at the Ministry of Food arrived to inform the Canadian Government that Britain proposed to purchase virtually no more foodstuffs except wheat. This came as a blow to Canadian farmers who had built up production for the British market and had been strongly encouraged by Britain to do so during the war years. Even on wheat there was controversy since Britain, basing herself on a technicality in the Wheat Agreement, refused to pay the price demanded. The situation could have created an ugly atmosphere. This did not happen, partly because Britain was still held generally in high regard after the war by Canadians who recognized that her plight was serious and commanded sympathy; partly because both sides were prepared to do what they could to remedy the situation: the British modified the severity of their intended cuts; for their part, the Canadians were anxious to encourage British exports to Canada and Western farmers staged valuable 'Buy British' campaigns; partly because this was thought to be a temporary phenomenon and indeed the clouds began to lift before long. When things were at their worst, imaginativeness among officials led them to set up what came to be known as the UK-Canadian Continuing Committee. At the outset it consisted only of the official heads in each country of the three Departments mainly concerned – Treasury, Trade and Agriculture. The Committee met every six months or so, in each capital by turns, for an intensive, but informal discussion. A curiosity was that the chair was not taken by the host country but by the High Commissioner accredited to that country. Though the CRO and DEA were not formally members of the Committee, they took part in the preparations, were present at meetings in their own capital and provided the first two Chairmen (Clutterbuck and Robertson). The main credit for the idea must go to John Henry Woods (Permanent Secretary at the Board of Trade) who felt strongly that an atmosphere of rancour and mutual recrimination was no way for rational people to live together. The meetings were seen primarily as an opportunity for 'letting down hair'; each side could voice its grievances or take the opportunity to give advance warning of any unpleasantness to come. The discussion was tough, but the participants all showed bigness of mind; they were also highly congenial and there was much conviviality, sometimes far into the night and at weekends. It is not too much to claim that the Committee transformed the atmosphere and restored Anglo-Canadian relations to a basis of mutual confidence. If there were differences (and there were many), there was at least no misunderstanding. In later years the personalities changed, the need was less urgent and the meetings became more formal and less frequent; but the Committee still continued to do useful work and, because of the understanding between top officials, ensured that neither side was taken unawares by any action of the other.

In other ways too, the CRO helped to promote machinery for consultation with Commonwealth Governments on economic matters. Before the war there had been virtually none. Under the shadow of economic difficulties after the war, it became the novel, but accepted pattern, in addition to the regular meetings of Finance Ministers, for officials from all Commonwealth countries to meet in formally constituted Committees. A pattern was begun which developed still further later, in a way characteristic of the flexible Commonwealth system. Apart from the Continuing Committee with Canada, the most important bodies were the European Liaison Committee (originally under the chairmanship of Roger Makins, F.O., with a CRO deputy) to discuss developments of policy in Europe, and the Sterling Area Statistical

Committee. In 1949 the functions of the Liaison Committee were extended to include the discussion of Sterling Area policies in general; it was renamed Commonwealth Liaison Committee and placed under CRO Chairmanship (later still it absorbed the Statistical Committee and was given still further terms of reference). These Committees did valuable work and gave British officials an opportunity to explain the background to British policies; discussion was informal and free from the acrimony which characterized meetings of High Commissioners at this time on political matters.

In Whitehall itself the inter-departmental machinery had been closely co-ordinated during the war; the tradition continued and, in the early years after the war, economic matters were handled by a network of Committees at various levels, serviced by the Cabinet Office. Ministerial Committees settled the general lines of policy; Committees at senior official level were responsible for their application. There were two such Committees comprising all the interested Departments to deal with Overseas Negotiations and Dollar Exports; there was also a smaller group under the chairmanship of Bridges (then head of the Treasury) to consider problems of the Sterling Area. The CRO sent a representative at Under Secretary level to all these Committees. These were grim days when tough decisions had to be taken promptly, without undue sympathy for the susceptibilities of outsiders. The essential decisions necessarily had to be taken by the Departments responsible for economic policy and the CRO could not be expected to exert any major influence on policy (especially as none of the Ministers in the CRO at the time was strong on the economic side). In many quarters the CRO was still regarded as primarily the advocate for its own clients and in some the Commonwealth was regarded as a hindrance rather than a help and Commonwealth countries were thought to have done better out of Imperial Preference than Britain. Nevertheless the Office played its part in the decision-making process. It was able to make a more solid contribution with a staff that had now become larger, was better equipped to specialize and whose members were gaining first-hand experience of Commonwealth countries. The task of the CRO was also greatly eased by the fact that the calibre and outlook of officials in charge of economic policy differed from the narrow pre-war mentality of the Treasury. Bridges, Wilson-Smith, Rowan at the Treasury, Woods, Helmore, Lee at the Board of Trade were all broadminded with a wide experience, knew their Commonwealth colleagues and had an understanding of Commonwealth interests. Another helpful factor in mutual education was the secondment of CRO officers to economic Departments (Syers to the Treasury, Liesching and Holmes to the Board of Trade). Above all Liesching as PUS commanded respect in Whitehall and could be counted on to ensure that any important CRO case did not go by default.

Throughout this period the CRO was becoming increasingly involved in the new post-war attitude to economic relationships between the richer and the poorer countries and was playing its part in the schemes advanced both bilaterally and internationally after the war – and increasingly so in the 1960s – for the provision of technical assistance and of capital aid for development purposes. It was the scale and scope of the new programme rather than the idea itself that marked such a departure from the past. An early example of the new pattern in multilateral aid was the Colombo Plan. Paternity has been claimed in various quarters, by Spender of Australia and by Jayawardene of Ceylon. The fact is that the idea was in the air before the Foreign Ministers' Meeting in Ceylon in 1950. It was certainly in the mind of the CRO; the possibility of economic cooperation was mentioned by Noel-Baker at his first press conference in Colombo and Bevin was groping for something to put flesh on the bones. In any event, in 1950 the Foreign Ministers approved the general idea and remitted it for further study to the Commonwealth Economic Consultative Committee which met in Sydney and again in London later that year. The plan provided for multilateral official aid to South East Asia on the basis of development plans drawn up nationally but submitted to a Committee of the scheme; the main Commonwealth aid came from its more developed members, but the Plan also provided for mutual aid between the countries in the area. Originally conceived as a Commonwealth project, it was later extended to cover foreign countries both as donors and recipients. The Plan had many virtues: it was not exclusive to the Commonwealth and became international; it was aid entirely without strings and based on mutual cooperation; it was essentially practical.

The Plan maintained a permanent Secretariat in Colombo and progress was reviewed at annual Ministerial meetings. Until the creation of the Ministry of Overseas Development (ODM) in 1964, the CRO was primarily responsible in the British Government and Alec Symon deserves the most credit on the British side for the success of the Plan. Symon had been in the Indian Supply Mission in Washington during the war and when a mission was opened in Delhi was the first DHC (he returned later as High Commissioner in Pakistan). Not popular in the Office generally because of his obvious ambition, still less with his subordinates on account of his autocratic ways and lack of sensitivity, he nevertheless had a strong practical bent, was clear-headed and could be relied on to achieve results. He lacked the depth or subtlety to achieve the highest posts, but he was admirably suited for organizing a Scheme like the Colombo Plan about which he acquired a wealth of knowledge and in which he took a keen personal interest. There were two practical tasks in which he also distinguished himself. It had long been the practice to contribute to the relief of natural disasters in Asia or Africa. In 1950 there were serious floods in Winnipeg and, with memories of Canadian generosity during the war, there was an immediate emotional

332

response and Government assistance was demanded. Symon took on the task single-handed, making all the arrangements with great urgency and flying to Winnipeg to supervise the distribution of blankets and medicines. It was a job which a more fastidious diplomat might have disdained; Symon embraced it with enthusiasm and discharged it energetically. He was also given an unusual assignment in 1954 when he undertook a special mission to review the financial and economic position of the High Commission Territories. With no previous experience in the area he looked at problems with a fresh eye and produced a report that was both down-to-earth and stimulating.

The dimension of international aid was changed during the 1950s when the USA and the USSR both became involved in giving assistance to other countries in what was becoming known as the Third World, sometimes for defence, sometimes for ideological and sometimes for altruistic reasons. Simultaneously the economic organs of the UN began organizing multilateral assistance in a great variety of ways, amounting in all to a substantial effort.

The CRO was involved in all this from the beginning, partly because of its sponsorship of the Colombo Plan, partly because the new spirit of economic cooperation seemed in tune with the new patterns that were sought in the multiracial Commonwealth, and partly because by far the biggest single applicant – India – was the direct concern of the CRO.

The attitude in the CRO was seldom one of uncritical advocacy of the demands of the newly independent countries; on the contrary it did not hesitate to resist plans that it regarded as extravagant or impracticable (such as the grandiose Indian plans for rapid industrialization or the later proposal for a railway through Tanzania connecting Zambia with the sea). Indeed there were occasions, particularly with Frank Lee as head of the Treasury, when his enthusiastic but hard-headed advocacy of Indian plans over-rode the more cautious attitude of CRO officials. But when CRO officials were satisfied that a scheme was well founded and should yield valuable results, they gave unstinting support, as throughout the long negotiations by the World Bank to secure an agreement between India and Pakistan for the division of the Indus Waters; this resulted in a massive project financed by a consortium of countries under the aegis of the Bank.

Territorial

In the High Commission Territories a new impetus was given to the development of local institutions and to the training of Africans for the administration; thanks to assistance from the Colonial Development and Welfare Fund and to the activities of the Colonial Development Corporation considerable progress was also made in the development of the economy. The matter which caused the greatest stir however was the banishment of Seretse Khama, the heir to the Chieftainship of the Bamangwato tribe.

The banishment of Seretse Khama affords a striking example of an apparently minor matter on the periphery of the main interests of the CRO which nevertheless distracted the Office over a long period and affected its reputation and that of successive Ministers. It attracted more sustained criticism of the Office than any other single matter and, curiously, it was the second time that the Chieftainship of the same small tribe had caused such a stir.

Seretse Khama, the son of the Chief of the Bamangwato, married an Englishwoman in 1948 while he was completing his studies in England and his uncle (Tshekedi Khama) was acting as Regent. Tshekedi himself opposed the marriage and the tribe at first refused to accept the wife as the future Chief's consort. European opinion in South Africa and also in Southern Rhodesia condemned the marriage and many African Chiefs also expressed their opposition. The situation was however confused by a second tribal meeting (Kgotla) in March 1949 which produced an overwhelming majority in favour of Seretse as Chief with his wife and made it clear that a continuation of Tshekedi's rule would be unacceptable. Throughout 1949 the British Government prevaricated, hoping that the situation would sort itself out, but early in 1950 Noel-Baker invited Seretse to London hoping to induce him to renounce the Chieftainship. This he refused to do and it fell to Noel-Baker's successor, Gordon Walker, to bring the matter to a conclusion. In March 1950[10] within a week of assuming Office he announced that, in view of the danger which recognition of Seretse as Chief would 'cause to the unity and well-being of the tribe' this would be withheld for five years during which time he and his wife would be required to live outside the Territory 'with a suitable allowance'; at the same time, while the Chieftainship was in suspense, Tshekedi would be exiled outside the Reserve.*

This decision led to a storm of abuse in Parliament† and was hotly criticized in the Press. It also ushered in an era of unrest and non-cooperation in the tribe. Criticism in Britain fastened especially on the terms of Tshekedi's banishment and some of the restrictions on him were successively eased by Conservative Ministers – Ismay, Swinton and Home.

---

* The Bamangwato therefore became in a literal sense 'The Tribe that Lost Its Head' (the title of a novel by Nicholas Monsarrat based partly on this incident and also on incidents in the Mau Mau trouble).
† Gordon Walker's statement led to a spate of questions including Churchill's denunciation that 'It is a very discreditable transaction.' On 26 January 1951[11] the Liberal leader (Clement Davies) moved that the order of banishment on Seretse should be rescinded. This was treated as a vote of confidence and the winding-up speeches were made by Churchill and Attlee; the Government secured a majority but many members in the Labour Party were far from happy. On 31 July 1951 there was a further debate on the adjournment.[12] Meanwhile on 27 June a full-scale debate took place in the House of Lords.[13] It was notable for the strong criticism of three previous Colonial Secretaries – Salisbury, Swinton, Harlech – and resulted in a 2 : 1 defeat for the Government.

Finally in 1956 Seretse and Tshekedi reached an agreement under which both renounced any claim to the Chieftainship; this was welcomed by the Government and Home announced in October 1956[14] that both would be allowed to return as private citizens (Seretse with his family) and play their part in the affairs of the tribe.* Peace thereafter returned to the Protectorate – but the unrest had lasted for six years. Few on the British side emerge with great credit. The local administration was limited; Baring who was High Commissioner for most of the time was clearly unhappy in being cast in an unwelcome role. The greatest damage was suffered by Gordon Walker whose reputation and position in the Labour Party were both affected. One person who emerged with credit was W. A. W. Clark.† He was Administration Secretary in the High Commissioner's Office at the beginning; he came to know both Seretse and Tshekedi well personally and was regarded by both as a friend. Later he was head of the department in the CRO dealing with the affairs of the Territories. He was invariably on hand to lend a sympathetic hearing, to explain the Government's difficulties and above all to keep the lines open with a view to an eventual settlement.

The controversy inevitably raised the question of whether the CRO was the right Department to be responsible for the administration of the High Commission Territories and two former High Commissioners entered the fray on different sides. Clark (Sir William) resisted the suggestion that responsibility should be transferred to the Colonial Office, maintaining that in his experience it was essential that the High Commissioner in his dealings with Union Ministers 'should be able to speak with an intimate personal knowledge of the Territories and their peoples'.[15] Harlech however took the contrary view, asserting that the time had come when the Territories 'must be dealt with by the same Office, the same people and treated with the same policy as Central Africa, East Africa and West Africa'.[16] He went on to complain 'Our staff is entirely a C.R.O. staff. The C.R.O. people have had nothing to do with the Territories ... and the result has been that two completely water-tight compartments have existed.' In the event no change was made until after South Africa left the Commonwealth in 1961 when responsibility for the High Commission Territories was transferred to the C.O. Curiously the views of the two former High Commissioners not only cancelled each other out; each contained an illogicality. Clark's point would equally have been met if, in his administration of the Territories, he had been responsible to the Colonial Secretary: on the other hand Harlech's proposal for transfer to the C.O. would have made the compartments even

---

* It was in accordance with this undertaking that Seretse contested the first elections and went on to become the first President of Botswana.

† In her life of Tshekedi Khama (London 1960) Mary Benson quotes Buchanan as saying of Clark in 1950 'he is the only live wire at this end. With him away, I just don't know what will happen here' and Tshekedi as recording in 1951 'he was the one official of any help to me whilst I was in London.'

more water-tight since at least both sides of his Office took their orders from a single S. of S.

Such were the main issues which preoccupied the CRO during the fifties. Before the war the D.O. had been concerned to secure the equality of status of the independent members of the Commonwealth, but nevertheless to seek the fullest cooperation between them in all matters, especially – if need be – in the event of war. After the war, in the decade between the acceptance of the Indian Republic and Ghana's admission, there were few problems of status and no major constitutional changes. The task was to preserve the vitality of the Commonwealth partnership when it had ceased to be composed of like-minded nations with a common background and contained members who voiced strong ideological differences with their partners; these differences ruled out a common approach to the dangers which threatened them and led to strong argument and frank speaking. Nevertheless discussion was conducted with courtesy and a degree of harmony prevailed. In the sixties to which we now turn, racial issues involving Britain's colonial rule came to the fore and, with the explosion of African nationalism, a very different atmosphere prevailed when other Commonwealth Governments gave forcible expression to their dissatisfaction with British policies.

PART IV

The African Dimension 1957–68

CHAPTER 1

The Wind of Change

The General Scene

The events of 1956 surrounding Suez caused a shift in the attitude of other Commonwealth countries towards Britain as well as a change in Britain's position in the world. Yet, as time passed, the scars healed. The process of reconciliation began as soon as Britain accepted the cease-fire. It derived impetus from the personality and policy of Britain's new leader, Harold Macmillan, who sought to attune himself to world opinion, to prove himself a good internationalist and set out to make friends. His rapprochement with the USA was symbolized by his meeting with his old wartime comrade, President Eisenhower, in Bermuda in the spring of 1957; he was careful to invite St Laurent and his colleagues to meet him there also and so set the seal on renewed cordiality between the British and Canadian Governments. Macmillan was tireless in his efforts to repair Britain's friendships and restore her position. In no area was his personal diplomacy more active – or indeed more successful – than in relations with other Commonwealth countries. Macmillan made a series of substantial tours to Commonwealth countries almost in the tradition of the Monarch, being the first P.M. in office to 'embark on such an adventure'.[1] These tours had a number of visible effects; they unmistakably added to Macmillan's self-confidence and prestige; they gave him a new understanding and stirred his imagination about the role which the Commonwealth could play in the world; they were also a visible reminder to the Commonwealth peoples of Britain's continuing interest in them.

These early years of the Macmillan regime perhaps mark the apogee of the Commonwealth idea. The CPM Meeting in the summer of 1957 was held in circumstances of easy familiarity and some enthusiasm, engendered by the apocalyptic appearance of Diefenbaker, breathless from his surprise election triumph in Canada. Eager to exploit the full potentiality of Commonwealth collaboration, Diefenbaker invited a special Conference to meet in Montreal in 1958 which registered a high point in post-war co-operation. Not only Ghana (now a full member) but also many Colonial Territories attended and the Conference looked forward hopefully to a steady expansion in Commonwealth membership; Britain's economic situation had improved and she was able to announce a new programme for investment in developing countries; the base also was laid for one of the most imaginative joint Commonwealth enterprises – the Commonwealth Scholarship Scheme.

Later the atmosphere changed, for a new portent came on the world scene. The place of Asia as the continent of dynamic change in the fifties was seized in the sixties by the stridency of Africa. After the independence explosion of the 1960s, the African nations provided a striking example of a pressure group exploiting to the full the techniques of propaganda available to international diplomacy. These efforts perhaps drew additional strength and bitterness from the domestic campaign being carried on at the same time by the Blacks within the USA. If one tries to form a picture of the history of the Office as a whole, the last decade may be compared to a film that has been speeded up at a ridiculous rate where everything happens at once and the characters seem to be rushing in all directions. The pace in the Commonwealth had shifted indeed from the slow deliberation of the interwar years, when it took five years for the Statute of Westminster to follow the Imperial Conference of 1926 – and then another fifteen years before its final adoption in New Zealand. Crisis succeeded crisis unpredictably and problems arose in every part of the Commonwealth. At the same time the British Government were constantly preoccupied with the problems of British entry into the European Community, of sterling and the balance of payments, of major adjustments in defence policy and of immigration into Britain; all of which had important consequences for Commonwealth countries.

Since the war a change had taken place in the attitudes of the political parties towards the Commonwealth. Before the war, the Conservative Party had prided itself on being the party of Empire, while the Labour Party had taken its stand against any form of imperialism. But after the war, Attlee had been responsible for the transfer of power in the sub-Continent and the Labour Party gave whole-hearted support to the new concept of the Commonwealth. The change in the Conservative Party was even more striking. Under Macmillan, the Conservative Government proceeded apace with decolonization and disturbed a sizeable section of the Conservative Party on that account. While Macmillan, in the early years of his rule, had the good fortune to preside when Commonwealth cooperation was at its height (though later there were squalls), Wilson had the ill-luck to be in power when everything seemed to go wrong and the Commonwealth endured its greatest strains. In the short interregnum, Alec Douglas-Home sought to carry on the Macmillan tradition but also, in the bitter wrangling over Rhodesia at the CPM Meeting in 1964, received a foretaste of what was to follow.

There was something peculiarly unfair to Wilson in the way events turned out, since he believed in the Commonwealth cause and constantly sought for closer cooperation between Britain and other Commonwealth countries. At the first CPM Meeting over which he presided in 1965, Wilson made an eloquent plea for a Commonwealth initiative on Vietnam and succeeded in gaining approval for a Commonwealth peace mission of Heads of Government (including remarkably Nkrumah). Though the conference agreed on an important 'Statement of Guidance'[2] which set out basic objectives (in itself a remarkable achievement in the heated atmosphere), the Mission never got off the ground.* Wilson had always advocated increased Commonwealth trade and at the 1965 Meeting he also put forward a 'Plan for Commonwealth Trade', which he had originally suggested while still Leader of the Opposition. As he himself recorded, he was 'acutely disappointed at the outcome' and he came to the view that 'there was virtually no willingness to improve intra-Commonwealth trading arrangements'.[4] This for a time somewhat soured his attitude to the rest of the Commonwealth and he was necessarily on the defensive as Britain was put in the dock over Rhodesia. The bitterness to which the controversy over Rhodesia gave rise destroyed much of the usefulness of CPM Meetings and led many to question the continuing value of the Commonwealth. Yet the changes in attitude that took place were by no means solely due to the clash over Rhodesia or to the African element. The changes were profound, far-reaching and due to a variety of underlying causes. They led to a slow, but nonetheless marked process of diminishing interest on the part of public opinion generally in all Commonwealth countries, to strains and stresses between individual countries and to the generation of friction between Commonwealth Governments, often publicly displayed. Though for very different and even sometimes opposite reasons, this attitude made itself felt in virtually all Commonwealth countries.

British opinion in particular was affected by many factors. In the first place the very word 'disillusionment' implies that there previously was illusion and that to some extent the process was one of coming alive to reality. The concept of Empire into Commonwealth was a valuable one and continued to remain valid in general terms and emotionally, but the argument clearly could not be pushed to its logical extremity. The new Commonwealth was *not* the old Empire; Britain could look forward to fruitful relations with a number of friendly nations, but they were and intended to be fully independent; they were proud, sometimes arrogant and always – and inevitably – had

---

* Some scepticism was shown at the time about Wilson's motives in insisting that his 'Peace Plan' for Vietnam should take precedence over all other business at the CPM Meeting. The Diaries of Richard Crossman make it clear that he regarded it as a 'stunt' both to rally support in the left wing of the Parliamentary Labour Party and to avoid a break-up of the Commonwealth Conference on the issue of Rhodesia; Crossman's view was that in each case the initiative had the desired effect.[3]

prime regard for their own interests. The underlying implications of the independence of Commonwealth countries were becoming more consciously accepted. They had been brought forcibly to notice by the bombshell of Suez, but there were other counts on which the British complained of being 'let down' by their Commonwealth partners. All the old Commonwealth countries were accused of paying too much court to the USA, at the expense of Britain. In addition, there were bitter feelings towards the Canada of the Diefenbaker regime which, in spite of all its fair words, failed to take action to secure any increase in British imports and to match with deeds the highly publicized promise of a '15% diversion' of trade. Australia in different ways was also arraigned for failing to show sufficient readiness to help Britain by encouraging trade or undertaking firm defence commitments. South Africa became an increasing embarrassment with her policies towards Apartheid and South West Africa – and the embarrassment did not cease when, on becoming a Republic, South Africa withdrew from Commonwealth membership. British criticisms of their Asian and African Commonwealth partners were more diverse and more profound; they ran the gamut from the feeling that the new members were not living up to the rules of the Club, to accusations of the adoption of double standards in the UN and of lack of support for and even positive hostility towards British interests. For the general public in Britain there was a new factor which overshadowed all others – the mass immigration of coloured citizens from Commonwealth countries. This gave rise to deep-seated if illogical fears and, because of official emphasis on the term 'Commonwealth immigrant', tended to give an ill reputation to the Commonwealth as a whole.

The complaints were by no means one-sided and Britain herself was the cause of strong criticism. This arose on account of what was regarded as a departure by Britain from her policies. The first was in her attitude towards Europe. Britain's early steps in favour of a Free Trade Area were tentative enough and, even when she sought full membership of the Community, she pledged herself to safeguard Commonwealth interests. Nevertheless the move represented a distinct change, even if it did not involve a turning away from the Commonwealth; it was rightly seen as a clear intention on Britain's part to put her own interests first and was inevitably interpreted as spelling the end to preferential treatment for Commonwealth interests as such. In every Commonwealth country some section saw a threat to its trading interests and there were many which felt that Britain's move to Europe would irreversibly weaken the Commonwealth fabric. The second area was in defence. It was accepted that Britain could no longer police the world as she had done in the days of Pax Britannica and indeed was no longer able to guarantee the defence of other Commonwealth members. Nevertheless successive reductions in the British defence programme and, in particular, the sudden decision at the end of 1967 to withdraw from East of Suez contrary to recent previous assurances came as an unexpected and most unwelcome shock to Australia and New Zealand as well as to Malaysia and Singapore. The third sphere was immigration control, where Britain contrived to obtain the worst of both worlds. The Commonwealth Immigrants Act of 1962 was clearly designed to restrict and control the immigration of coloured people and it operated with increasing efficiency against continued large-scale immigration from the West Indies and the sub-Continent. Inevitably there was resentment at the withdrawal of what had come to be regarded as a 'natural right' and there were understandable objections that the law was being operated racially. But in form the law was non-discriminatory and applied equally to white as to coloured citizens of the Commonwealth, even if there was some latitude in practice. This led to heated protests particularly from Australia who complained with bitter logic that Britain's understandable desire to restrict coloured immigrants was no reason for barring her own kin. Throughout the whole of this period, Australia felt and expressed her sense of aggrievement far more strongly than any other Commonwealth country; she felt that Britain was ready to forsake her old friends (the former Dominions of the Crown Commonwealth), was no longer true to her own greatness and was turning her back on her principles; Britain was seen as seeking to come to terms with the new and irresponsible nations in Asia and Africa and treading the dangerous path of appeasement. Australia wanted a tougher response to the double-standard diplomacy of the new Commonwealth members; a rejection of their insistence on interfering in matters within Britain's responsibility and a more vigorous, self-assertive, less hypocritical attitude on Britain's part.

From a complex of genuine and deep-seated differences of this character, from a host of petty complaints and perhaps also from the inevitable fact of growing up and therefore to some extent growing apart, there came upon all Commonwealth countries a mood of disenchantment. The dissatisfaction was most keenly expressed in Britain by a series of contributions in the more responsible organs of the press and notably in a mocking but mordant article entitled 'Cwthmanship' in *The Economist*[5] and in an uncompromising condemnation in *The Times* by an anonymous 'Conservative' (generally assumed to be Enoch Powell) which described the Commonwealth as 'a gigantic farce'.[6] Yet, despite the discontent and the controversy, the Commonwealth not only survived but in some areas flourished.

Decolonization

The story of British Colonial rule would take us outside the scope of this book; its most significant feature for our purposes was the speed with which it was brought to an end. Before the end of the war, neither Colonial administrators nor the people in the dependent territories – nor indeed observers and critics at home and abroad – had any notion that transference of power would come at so early a date (apart from Ceylon which followed in the wake of India). As late as 1950 most informed opinion, including that of African leaders, would have expected many years to pass before any African territory was ready for full independence; even as late as 1960 few would have believed that, less than five years after the ending of the Mau Mau Emergency, Kenyatta would be President of an independent Kenya or that full independence would ever come to Grenada or Tonga. In Britain, the C.O. was alerted by the report on the riots in the Gold Coast in 1948; steps for providing that Africans should play a larger part in Government were taken and from then on a shortened time-scale was accepted as a political necessity; indeed in the later years the tempo changed from adagio to prestissimo. Decolonization in Africa began with the rather special case of the Sudan in 1956. Ghana followed in 1957 and became a full Member of the Commonwealth. The C.O. virtually completed the process of decolonization in Africa within a decade; it was ironic that the one remaining problem was in the territory that had been the responsibility of the D.O. and CRO – Rhodesia. There had never been any question about the direction in which British policy was moving: self-government by the people in overseas territories had long been accepted as the ultimate goal. The time-table however was less clear. After 1947 the apparent success of the transfer of power in the Indian sub-Continent encouraged the hope that in time it could take place similarly in the territories of Africa; and, outside Africa, a greater degree of self-government was already envisaged for Malaya, Singapore and the Caribbean territories. Contrary to all previous expectations and planning, the pace was hastened for two quite different sets of reasons. In the first place an early move was forced by external events; more compelling even than the pressure in the territories themselves was the influence of foreign opinion. Overseas possessions had been wrested from Germany and Italy; Belgium and France were already planning to give up power; only Portugal (and Spain) sought to defy history. Britain, who would have preferred a more gradual pace, had no wish to stand against the tide, particularly when she was under pressure alike from the enmity of Communist propaganda and the naiveté of American liberalism. There were also domestic reasons favouring an early decision. After two World Wars, British public opinion had moved full circle from the imperialism of the Kipling era, its mood was no longer aggressive or acquisitive; it had lost any desire to dominate other peoples against their will; still less had it any stomach to fight to maintain its power. Finally the Conservative Government were quick to sense the mood and were in a strong position to execute a drastic policy, since they could count on support from the Opposition (which might well not have been forthcoming had the roles been reversed). The Conservative leaders at the time were realists, with the courage and determination to act. Duncan Sandys and Macleod were not trammelled by doctrine or troubled by doubts. They believed that the best way to learn responsibility is to exercise it. Once having set course they did not hesitate; they soon learned that when the idea of 'freedom' is in the air and independence has been promised, the pace is ineluctably accelerated, and that, if one is to leave with dignity and in friendliness, it is best to go with good grace and without prevarication.

It is often asserted that, after the 1959 Election, some dramatic decision was taken to speed up the process of granting independence in Africa.* This is not the case and would not have been in accord with the British tradition. There was no overall plan. The British followed a pragmatic approach, proceeding step by step and seeking agreement with the main political groupings in the way they considered best suited to local needs; certainly by 1960 they understood that they must come to terms with African nationalism. This was recognized in the 'Wind of Change' speech in 1960. It can also be claimed that the British handling ensured that independence was achieved by agreement between ruler and ruled. The struggle was political and not violent;† the settlement was friendly and, in most cases, the new State started with a fund of goodwill and gratefully accepted continuing help from Britain (notably in aid and in the large number of British who offered their services in a variety of ways). The smaller the territory, the more it continued to rely on Britain for support and particularly for diplomatic and consular help.

Until it was formally defined in the Statute of Westminster, Dominion status had not been a matter of any precision; it was one of natural growth and depended on informal understandings, as the examples of Newfoundland and Rhodesia show. The grant of independence to the former Colonial territories required legislation at Westminster; if the territory desired to be accepted as a full Member of the Commonwealth, formal application was made and was accorded, originally by decision at a CPM Meeting, later more frequently in correspondence. In no case was an application refused.‡ Nevertheless something of the old informal tradition persisted and no rules governing membership were ever laid down and no prior conditions needed to be satisfied.

It was however tacitly assumed that any new State would be 'viable' and

* In an article in 1965, Iain Macleod commented on this assumption: 'This is not true. What did happen was that the tempo accelerated as a result of a score of different deliberate decisions'. (*Weekend Telegraph*, 12 March 1965).
  The fact that the CPM Meeting in 1960 paid special attention to the future of the smaller dependent territories and agreed that a detailed study should be made implies that, at least up to that time, no general decision had been taken.
† Where there was fighting (as in Cyprus or British Guiana) it was between rival claimants for power rather than against British rule as such.
‡ The South African application met with considerable opposition, but it was withdrawn and the Union left the Commonwealth of her own accord.

able to maintain its integrity and the British Government sought to ensure that any territory, qualifying for independence, should contain an area of sufficient size and importance to maintain its position. It was for this reason that they advocated amalgamation in suitable cases and encouraged the formation of Federations. The notion was well intentioned, but in no case did the experiment wholly succeed. The Federation of Rhodesia and Nyasaland failed in its object of bringing the two races into 'partnership' and broke up in 1963; the Federation of the West Indies collapsed in 1962 having lasted only four years in spite of some thirteen years of painstaking preparation and the fact that it undoubtedly represented the wishes of all delegates at the time; Singapore withdrew from the Malaysian Federation in 1965 leaving Sabah and Sarawak on their own in union with Malaya; the Federal idea in East and West Africa failed to advance beyond the conflict-prone East African Common Services Organization and residual arrangements for co-ordination of certain services in West Africa.

If it did not prove practicable to establish larger areas able to manage on their own after independence, was there any limit to the minimum size and stature of a country hoping to achieve the status of an independent Commonwealth country? In course of time, many of the underlying assumptions about viability and integrity became undermined. Cyprus in 1960 marked a water-shed. Cyprus had a population of little more than half-a-million people of European origin with its own distinct culture, it is an island in the Mediterranean smaller than either Sardinia or Sicily, its constitution rested on a precarious *modus vivendi* between its Greek and Turkish inhabitants between whom there had been bitter enmity, and its independence required to be guaranteed by Greece, Turkey and Britain (who retained a Sovereign Base Area on the island). Though it was economically viable these circumstances did not provide ideal conditions either for independence or for Commonwealth membership (as later events would show) and many in the British Government initially had doubts whether Cyprus should qualify for Commonwealth membership. After all it was not many years since a British Minister, with reference to Cyprus, had declared that 'there are certain territories in the Commonwealth which, owing to their particular circumstances, can never expect to be fully independent'[7] (the remark proved the unwisdom of using the word 'never' in politics). Nevertheless, as Macmillan himself relates, 'to deal with the rather special case of Cyprus in view of her relationship with Greece and Turkey, I had agreed to canvass the various Prime Ministers as to their attitude.'[8] This was an unusual step, but the result showed that there was no disposition to deny Commonwealth membership to Cyprus. Though this was perhaps not fully realized at the time, the decision set an important precedent. Henceforward no attempt was made to set conditions for Commonwealth membership. In 1964, political considerations pointed to the need to accord independence to Nyasaland in spite of a substantial deficit on her budget.* The later grant of independence to Botswana, Lesotho and Swaziland (who had come under British rule because their people wanted protection from South Africa) finally destroyed the argument that to be independent a territory must be able to secure its defence. Any territory however small, impoverished or defenceless received independence and later the mini-State, with recognition as a member of the United Nations, gained acceptance on the world stage and could scarcely be denied Commonwealth status.

Nevertheless there clearly was a point, particularly in a small island, beyond which the inhabitants would not be able or even wish to form an independent State. Much thought was given to the future of the smaller territories with the object of removing any taint of Colonialism. This included proposals for a more appropriate title, for integration with the UK and for administration (on the analogy of the Channel Islands) under the Home Office. Nothing came of these plans, but a special arrangement was made in the case of the islands in the West Indies which did not wish to become fully independent. They were given the new title of 'Associated States'; they enjoyed full internal autonomy, but continued within the British ambit for defence and foreign affairs; more importantly perhaps they were given the right unilaterally to terminate the Association and become independent.

The question has pertinently been asked why, in view of the difficulties inevitably inherent in a political revolution of the kind that was taking place, African politicians were not content to hasten more slowly and why the British Government did not delay the process until the foundations for independence had stood the test of time.† So far as the British Government is concerned, the answer has already been given; for the rest the Monckton Commission on the Central African Federation in 1960 put the point succinctly in referring to the 20 countries in Africa which by then were independent by recording that it was 'natural and inevitable that the prospect of independence, seven years ago unthinkably remote, should now appear to many Africans a right from which they should no longer be debarred.'[9] The causes need not detain us further, but the result threw an increased burden on the CRO for which it was not well prepared. It is arguable, in the light of hindsight, that the CRO after the success in Asia was unduly complacent about the ease with which the African territories would develop as Commonwealth members on the Westminster model. In any case the CRO had many other matters on its hands and may not have given the priority to new and small territories which their problems demanded. For reasons

---

* Zanzibar was the first British territory to become independent without a balanced budget, but the deficit was small and likely to be temporary.

† *See* the article 'The Process of Decolonisation' by Sir Leslie Monson (p. 274) in *The Modernisation of British Government* (Pitman Publishing, 1975).

described later, relations between the CRO and the C.O. were not always as close as they should have been and there was perhaps not sufficient liaison between the two Departments in advance;* the CRO not wishing to get involved with the Colonial aspects of the problem, the C.O. assuming too readily that all would be well on the night.†

The CRO took a number of steps with the aim of equipping the new country to play its part on the world stage. The first involved what came to be called the despatch of a 'St John the Baptist'. The first such appointment was that to the Gold Coast of Francis Cumming-Bruce (who had by then already served in New Zealand, Canada and India). He was appointed in 1955, some two years before the date of independence, to the post of Adviser on External Affairs to the Governor. His duties were two-fold: first to advise on all matters which would affect Ghana on becoming an independent Commonwealth Member and secondly to assist in forming the nucleus of an External Affairs Department and in training selected officers for this purpose. Similar appointments were made in the case of many, but not all other Territories; the arrangement elsewhere was less formal and of a shorter duration, the normal practice being to despatch an officer of middle rank some months before independence, with the primary task of setting up the British mission, who would also be available to the Government for any help and advice. In most cases the officer stayed on as DHC after independence.

Another step initiated by the CRO was an offer to train candidates for the External Affairs services which were about to be established: arrangements were made for officers to be attached to British missions abroad both in Commonwealth countries and in some significant foreign posts. This was taken advantage of by many countries and proved of great value not only as an introduction to the job of diplomacy, but perhaps still more in forming lasting friendships between those who worked together in this way.

In advance of independence the CRO set up in the Office for each new territory a geographical unit (where this did not already exist) and, in the early days, it was the practice for an officer from the C.O. familiar with the Territory to be seconded for a short time. Increasingly too the organization

---

* The current jibe in the C.O. was that the CRO was 'clueless in Ghana'.
† Zanzibar, though by no means a typical case, showed how slender the foundation and how brief the independence could be. The timetable speaks for itself:

1963
24 June Internal self-government introduced
July General Election. Coalition Government formed by parties which held a majority of seats but not of votes
Sept. Independence Conference in London
10 Dec. Full sovereign independence and Commonwealth membership
1964
12 Jan. Government overthrown. Proclamation of People's Republic
25 Apr. Union with Tanganyika.

of the CRO was put on a geographical rather than functional basis, thus enabling more attention to be paid to the affairs of a particular territory.

CPM Meetings

Though there was no agreed pattern, CPM Meetings tended to be held every two years or so. It is an indication of the change in tempo (and also of the work-load on the CRO) that in the first six years of the 1960s the average was one a year. But the quality of the Meetings also changed for it was here that the African made his most violent impact on the Commonwealth. With the rapid expansion in membership, it was inevitable that these gatherings would become larger and would lose something of their earlier intimacy. The comfortable Cabinet Room at No. 10 soon ceased to be adequate and, by a happy coincidence, the Queen made Marlborough House available to the British Government for Commonwealth purposes; its splendid halls and salons with a separate room for each P.M. were first used as a venue for the Meeting in 1962. Alas! even with restrictions on the size of delegations Marlborough House itself was later thought not to be large enough. It was foreseeable that with bigger numbers the meetings would need to be conducted with more formality, with a greater prospect of set speeches and less of general discussion. After all one does not talk to a man across the table in the same way as through a microphone to someone out of sight at the end of a long conference table. What was not predictable was that the substance of the discussion and the whole character of the Meetings would be altered. The conflict over Rhodesia showed African pressure at its extreme, but an earlier Meeting in 1961 was a clear pointer to the way things were likely to go. In that year South Africa (as other Commonwealth members before) applied for continued membership after she became a Republic. While the British Government, like other Commonwealth Members, deplored Apartheid, they made no secret of the fact that they wished South Africa to continue as a Member. Macmillan pleaded with his colleagues both in advance and with great eloquence at the Meeting itself. He failed. The Africans and Asians were adamant and Verwoerd sensed that he had no alternative but to withdraw his request and leave the Commonwealth. Many factors influenced the decision; one important one was that Canada under Diefenbaker, with the characteristic fervour of an Old Testament prophet, supported the Africans (which at least meant that the division was not based on colour). Another was the brutal honesty of Verwoerd who, when asked, admitted that he would refuse to meet any of his coloured colleagues socially in his own country. Nevertheless it was a clear victory for African pressure. Duncan Sandys sought to put a brave face on the matter and issued a statement[10] taking pride in the fact that the Commonwealth now stood united on the principle of racial equality. There is no doubt that so long as South Africa kept rigidly to the dogma of Apartheid, her membership of the Commonwealth was incompatible with its principles; her departure preserved the Commonwealth. But Menzies was disgusted and Macmillan felt 'weighed down by a sense of grief and foreboding';[11] he asked prophetically: 'Was every problem in the world to be handled by men who altogether failed to understand, still less to compromise with, any other view than their own?'

The Conference in 1962 was largely taken up with the question of the British application for membership of the European Community. The discussion showed little sympathy for Macmillan's appeal and was sometimes rough; the lead was taken by Canada,* Australia and India, with the Africans playing no outstanding part.

The Meeting in 1964 first saw the new pattern emerging in all its starkness. Ironically Douglas-Home set great store in summoning a CPM Meeting before the General Election and he had generous ideas of a number of practical ways in which Commonwealth cooperation could be made more effective. But from the start he found himself up against a solid wall of attack from the Africans who insisted on discussing Rhodesia almost to the exclusion of anything else. There had been a big propaganda build-up in advance, there were lengthy set speeches bitterly criticizing Britain, made available verbatim to the press often before delivery. Every device of propaganda and pressure was brought to bear; the Africans sought to change the character of the Meeting from that of a discussion group to a public forum for pressurizing Britain as they had previously pressurized South Africa. The Meeting began to resemble an acrimonious session of the UN Assembly rather than the quiet of a Cabinet meeting. The older members of the Commonwealth were taken aback by these tactics, so alien to all earlier tradition, but they found no effective way of containing them. A similar tone of hostility was displayed at meetings of officials where the British representatives were the object of accusations of partiality and even of personal abuse. The 1966 Conference reached the high-water mark of African pressure – on this occasion they carried to extremes their practice of forming a caucus to determine their line in advance and operate as a single bloc.† But they over-reached themselves and antagonized moderate opinion; such rough tactics were never tried in quite the same way again.

---

* Macmillan records a 'broadside attack upon us led by Diefenbaker' and describes Canada as 'just playing a sort of political game based on Diefenbaker's strange mystique'.[12]

† Wilson described it as 'a nightmare conference, by common consent the worst ever held up to that time'.[13]

The Commonwealth Secretariat

By 1964, British officials were being placed in an intolerable position at these meetings. By tradition the Secretary to the British Cabinet acted as Secretary-General of the Conference, but it was becoming impossible for him to operate in the gentlemanly tradition of the British Civil Service and at the same time withstand the attacks made on him, his handling of the Conference and the policies of his Government. The idea of a multinational Secretariat was no doubt regarded as in the interests of some of the new members; it was no less emphatically in British interests.* The credit for proposing the Secretariat at the Conference table belongs to Nkrumah. In fact the idea was already in the air and, on a visit to Ottawa earlier that year, Duncan Sandys and Garner had elicited from Pearson that the Canadian Government would no longer oppose the idea if it were thought to be of general value; this marked a break with the stand which Mackenzie King had adopted for so long; but circumstances had changed. Curiously the idea was not discussed by P.M.s themselves in any depth but there was no dissent and it was remitted for study by officials.

The interests of the British Government, as formulated and expressed by the CRO, were to ensure that the British were relieved of an invidious task and that a competent organization took over the servicing of Commonwealth meetings; for political reasons it was also desirable for the British to make clear that they were handing over not only with good grace but willingly. Accordingly at the first meeting of Commonwealth officials, the leader of the British delegation stated at the outset that his Government welcomed the proposal to establish a Secretariat and would give it all possible support.† Commonwealth officials recommended in favour of the idea and the P.M.s' Meeting approved it in principle and instructed officials to consider the best basis for establishing a Secretariat.

A meeting of senior officials was held in London in January 1965, under the chairmanship of Trend, Secretary to the Cabinet, with Garner leading the British delegation. The first objective of the British team was a positive one – namely to set up a body that would do its job as effectively as possible. The crucial question was what sort of job should it be called upon to perform.

* The idea of a Commonwealth Secretariat had been raised in the past, notably by Australia in 1907 and 1944 (*See* Chapter 1 of Part I and Chapter 9 of Part II). It had previously always been resisted by Canada and had never found general favour.
† From time to time outside commentators have castigated the CRO for resisting the formation of the Commonwealth Secretariat and wishing to frustrate it thereafter. The author was the leader of the team of British officials to the meeting in 1965 and also the official responsible for the British Government's relations with the Secretariat until his retirement in 1968. He can only say that from his personal knowledge the facts are as stated above.

Here there was scope for a variety of views. The British took a cautious and pragmatic line, arguing that the first task of the Secretariat was to set up its own organization as a working concern and that it should not undertake any wider responsibilities at least until the Secretariat itself was firmly established. In any case they saw risks of embarrassment if the Secretariat sought too interventionist a role and they wished to avoid its becoming a large and expensive organization which might merely duplicate functions already being adequately performed. This cautionary attitude was strongly supported by all the other British Government Departments who were likely to be affected by the Secretariat – particularly the C.O., the F.O., the Board of Trade and the Treasury. There was also a point of principle on which the British took a firm stand – namely that no information about a country should be circulated by the Secretariat without the approval of the Government of that country.

At the meeting there was a clear-cut division between those who wanted to circumscribe the activities of the Secretariat and those who were in favour of its playing an active role. The Africans were generally in favour of the second course, but unexpectedly the most emphatic statement of the case came from the Canadian delegation (led by Arnold Smith). The British and, even more so the Australians, favoured caution – but again, somewhat un-expectedly, the Indian delegation took the lead in objecting to anything bordering on interference. How ironic that the traditional roles of Mackenzie King and Krishna Menon should have been reversed by their successors! The result was a compromise in the best tradition of British adaptability and led to the first of those splendidly antiphonal documents which became such a feature of Commonwealth communiqués. Paragraphs 6 and 7 of the Memorandum[14] as eventually agreed combine admirably in two sentences the opposing points of view:

6. The Secretariat should not arrogate to itself executive functions. At the same time it should have, and develop, a relationship with other intra-Commonwealth bodies.
7. The Secretariat should have a constructive role to play. At the same time it should operate initially on a modest footing; and its staff and functions should be left to expand pragmatically in the light of experience, subject always to the approval of Governments.

The Memorandum drawn up by officials was approved without substantial amendment at the CPM Meeting in 1965 and the Secretariat was set up. British officials were clear that the first Secretary-General should come from outside Britain and no British candidate was put forward (except that belatedly a name was suggested by Nigeria): some half-dozen candidates were suggested by various governments but there were only two candidates of substance and, after Alister MacIntosh (Head of DEA in New Zealand) withdrew on grounds of health, the field was left open for Arnold Smith of the Canadian Department of External Affairs who, after the other candidates had been eliminated, was unanimously recommended by officials.

The Secretariat was set up in 1965 and rapidly got into its stride. Apart from its routine functions of servicing all Commonwealth Conferences and Committees and acting as a clearing house, the Secretariat carried out a number of new functions all of which, on balance, acted as a powerful stimulus to Commonwealth understanding and cooperation.

Much was due to the character of the man chosen to be the first Secretary-General. Arnold Smith was experienced in diplomacy and possessed of a brilliant, fertile and subtle mind; he had a political flair far above that of a conventional bureaucrat; he had courage, a powerful will, nurtured by ambition and perhaps above all a strong sense of mission. (It was precisely these qualities which at first caused some of the more cautious Australians and Britishers to be doubtful about his candidature.) Arnold Smith never hesitated to grapple personally with any problem, however delicate or complex, which threatened the Commonwealth – including such intractable ones as Rhodesia, Kashmir, Biafra. His efforts did not always succeed, but remarkably they did not occasion any ill-will and certainly put the Secretariat on the map as a significant seat of influence. More importantly perhaps, Smith built up a position for himself from which his advice was listened to. From his vantage point he could put arguments (for example to African Governments about Rhodesia) in a way that no Britisher could have done. Undoubtedly he was often successful in counselling moderation and restraint and in preserving something of the Commonwealth spirit at times when it might otherwise have been threatened.

In the course of a few years the Secretariat embarked on a number of practical schemes of Commonwealth collaboration covering technical assistance, development projects, youth programmes, education. (Again it was the ambitious nature of some of these projects, with their high cost and risk of overlapping with existing schemes, that attracted criticism from officials in some national Governments.)

The Secretariat also launched a Commonwealth Information Programme which, though modest in scope, helped to put matters in perspective and to improve the 'image' of the Commonwealth at a time of difficulty and some misunderstanding.

In thus inheriting the functions of the CRO for general co-ordination, the Secretariat was able to take initiatives which were not open to a Department in the Government of one Member nation. These new functions were a gain for the Commonwealth – and no loss to the CRO. Moreover it was a gain for Britain that the Secretariat in taking over responsibility for servicing meetings acted as a shock-absorber and removed from British officials the impossible task, when there was a conflict, of serving at the same time British interests and those of the Commonwealth as a whole. Henceforward British officials could, as those in every other Delegation, concentrate on the single task of representing the interests of their own nation; within the British Government, the responsibilities of the CRO were not affected.

Commonwealth Links

In 1963 a Conference was organized at Ditchley for the purpose of discussing Britain's role and influence in the modern Commonwealth. There was nothing remarkable in such a gathering, nor in itself did it record any spectacular achievement. The Conference was however interesting as a symptom; it was arranged by the CRO and this in itself was an indication of the more open attitude being adopted by Government Departments towards outside interests. The members came from business, finance, journalism, politics, trade unions and the Universities, as well as from the Civil Service. Such a mixture to discuss matters of official concern would have been unthinkable to the pre-war generation. Moreover the Conference was held, not as a prestige gathering to mark progress when things were going well, but when things were beginning to go badly (though not as badly as they would in the following year) and there was much public questioning about the Commonwealth. The discussion did not gloss over the strains and frictions inherent in the different attitudes of various Commonwealth countries and recognized that the stresses particularly over racial issues could lead the Commonwealth almost to breaking point. In the published Conclusion to the Report,[15] the Conference left political changes aside and concentrated on the scope for practical progress in a variety of ways such as technical aid, training, education, teaching of English, voluntary service.

There had since the nineteenth century been associations in the Empire dealing with trade and commerce, loyal societies and many other groups. As a follow-up to the Ditchley Conference, the CRO organized a conference of all the professional societies with Commonwealth interests to consider in what way the many efforts could be co-ordinated and the links strengthened. This led them to recommend the establishment of a Commonwealth Foundation for the purpose of increasing interchanges between Commonwealth organizations in professional fields. This idea had been favoured in the CRO since Gordon Walker's day; it had been carried further at earlier conferences and the moment now seemed propitious for putting it forward to other Commonwealth Governments. Officials from all Commonwealth countries considered the proposal, at the same meeting as that which dealt with the Secretariat; their report was approved by P.M.s at the Meeting in 1965.

The Foundation was set up in the same year with John Chadwick, an Under-Secretary in the CRO, serving as the first Director. The work of the Foundation is, by its nature, not so spectacular as that of the Secretariat and it has never been so well known. But it performs a valuable function and marks, in a sense, even more clearly than the Secretariat, the change in the content of Commonwealth cooperation; in the past the relationship between Britain and the Dominions had been characterized by consultation on matters of policy concerning foreign affairs, defence, economic cooperation or constitutional issues; in the new multiracial Commonwealth the emphasis changed to cooperation in economic and other matters and the development of professional and other links which became the pattern (and, some claimed, its most significant achievement).

Many other organizations shared in this cooperative task. First of all was the Secretariat which increasingly encouraged schemes of technical assistance, cooperation in education and youth matters. In the British Government itself the Ministry of Overseas Development (ODM) was set up as a separate Department in 1964. The British Council operated fruitfully in many Commonwealth countries, particularly in the teaching of English. The Commonwealth Institute in London took on a new lease of life when its exciting new building was opened in Holland Park in 1962 and, under a Board consisting of representatives of all Commonwealth Governments, rapidly became an educational and art centre where all Commonwealth countries were represented in exhibitions of their way of life. Another manifestation was the Commonwealth Scholarship Scheme inaugurated in 1959 with the aim of providing 1,000 scholars throughout the Commonwealth, which soon achieved its target and gathered a reputation for encouraging students of the highest quality and promise. Beyond was the network of societies, bringing together men and women from every walk of life – Parliament, the Press, the Law, Universities and a host of others from architects to helminthologists.

There never had been a time when personal contacts between people in the many Commonwealth countries had been so easy, so widespread and so fruitful. They covered every calling and included businessmen, tourists, students, exchange teachers; they extended to participation in the popular Commonwealth Games and to many new and adventurous forms such as Voluntary Service Overseas, sponsored expeditions, development of Commonwealth literature and cultural exchanges. Whatever may have been happening to political cooperation in the Commonwealth association, a powerful means had been fashioned to promote communication and encourage understanding between very different peoples scattered round the world.

Perhaps the most significant Commonwealth link of all – if also the most subtle – is provided by the Head of the Commonwealth. The days when the common allegiance to the Crown was an essential condition of Commonwealth membership have long passed; when the title 'Head of the Common-weath' was recognized in 1949 it was accepted that in this capacity the King had no sovereignty and was the source of no authority. Nevertheless the Commonwealth experience has been that, without any formal powers, the Head of the Commonwealth can exercise widespread and helpful influence and provide the role with meaning and value. In a Commonwealth that knows no flag or anthem of its own, the Queen has become the one visible symbol of the free association of its members. It has been an immense asset that the Head of the Commonwealth inherits and has been strengthened by all the tradition and prestige of the British Crown. The Queen has made herself known to millions by her broadcasts to the Commonwealth and her frequent tours to all parts (not only the monarchical countries) and has demonstrated her knowledge of the Commonwealth and her interest in its peoples. Readily adapting to change herself, she has made the changes in the Commonwealth more acceptable and credible and, at a deeper level, she has stood for the simple virtues of family life, friendship and tolerance to all in a way that has found a response in the hearts of countless men and women. Without an acknowledged Head, such as it has enjoyed in recent years, the Commonwealth would undoubtedly be something different and less comprehensible; under the Queen it has had cause to be grateful to her for fostering throughout the world greater understanding of the Common-wealth idea, encouraging any activities designed to further its objects and giving a sense of purpose to all who care for the Commonwealth and what it stands for.

CHAPTER 2

The Office

Though few can have guessed it at the beginning, this period was to see the end of the Office as a separate Department. For the first five years the idea of a merger either with the F.O. or the C.O. was viewed with distaste, but then, in rapid stages, came closer association, a single Service and finally merger.

Though the prime tasks of the Office did not differ in kind from what they had always been, there was a great difference in degree. The magnitude of the task had increased by sheer numbers; the five Dominions of 1947 and the seven overseas Commonwealth members of 1957 had become no fewer than 28 by the end of 1968. Nor was it only a question of numbers: the 'Dominions' had been homogeneous and reflected a pattern in the familiar British tradition; the three new Asian members represented an ancient civilization and enjoyed a degree of stability. The twenty additional members who joined the Commonwealth after 1957 represented every variety of nationhood and stage of development, some with no prolonged contact with British ways. All this called for new qualities of sensitivity and skill both at home and in posts abroad.

Secretaries of State

Under successive Prime Ministers the various Secretaries of State set the tone for the CRO. Home remained as Minister in charge until 1960 when he was succeeded by Duncan Sandys. Sandys remained until the fall of the Conservative Government in October 1964; between them they covered a span of nearly ten years – an unusual record of continuity. Sandys left an impact on the Office because of his personality, because of his attitude and because of his methods. He was a man of immense courage, both moral and physical, of vigour, determination and extraordinary single-mindedness of purpose. He was both forceful and, where necessary, brutal; but, contrary to the legend which surrounded him in Whitehall he was neither bad-tempered, nor impatient nor even intolerant.

He had few preconceived views and regarded himself as a realist, judging

357

every proposition on its merits and reaching the solution which he was satisfied would best meet British interests. Here was no idealist or one to be bound by principles or by precedent. On the contrary here was a radical who could accept nothing on trust. Everything – even the seemingly most obvious or trivial – required to be questioned and probed into.* Recommendation of a particular course on the ground that it was in accordance with some Treaty, followed the line laid down by Cabinet or conformed with Office practice merely incited him to discover reasons for a different way of doing things. All this was salutary for the staff; it kept them alert and forced them to re-examine their assumptions. Sandys' methods created problems because the steps he took to reach a conclusion were laborious and regarded by the staff as frustrating. The fact was that Sandys, though a man of strong determination who held to his course inexorably once his mind was made up, nevertheless made the process of reaching a decision a complicated one. This was partly because he was a perfectionist; he needed to be satisfied not only that his decision was the right one, but also that it had been expressed in the clearest possible terms.† It was also part of a deliberate tactic during a negotiation in order to wear down opposition and grind out the solution he wanted.‡ Groups of advisers (sometimes in considerable numbers) were summoned to the Secretary of State's room for a discussion which might continue literally for hours without a break. Sandys held the stage for most of the time and gave little opportunity to those in attendance to offer advice. This led to resentment by some senior members of the staff, especially when in their view the decisions reached in this painful fashion were not necessarily the best. For a time there was a rather sultry atmosphere. But the correct doctrine in the Civil Service is that it is the duty of permanent officials to give the best advice to Ministers at their disposal, to argue the case to the limit of their ability but, having done so, to accept the decision when taken without sourness and to execute the policy without reservations. Gradually the Minister and his permanent staff came to terms; the staff ceased to oppose every new idea automatically and sought instead to turn it into something acceptable and constructive. Moreover the staff could not fail to reach the conclusion that, however sorely he might drive them, Sandys invariably drove himself even harder.

But if Sandys plodded through the composition of a State document or engaged in time-consuming cross-examination in any negotiation, he could

* Sandys, then a young member of the Foreign Service, was loaned to Hankey at the time of the Lausanne Conference in 1932. Hankey commented: [He] 'is very argumentative and lays down the law on every subect'.[1]

† This ambition led to what often seemed like interminable drafting sessions and caused one of his junior Ministers to exclaim 'Duncan is unique in being able to accomplish in twenty-four hours what would take any other man at least two.'

‡ On one occasion (and it was not unique) Sandys interrupted at 8 a.m. a meeting with two Commonwealth P.M.s which had begun at 9 p.m. the previous evening with the words 'Perhaps we should take an hour off for breakfast.' They pleaded for, and grudgingly received, two hours.

equally act with the surprise of a lightning flash and take an initiative which revealed alike his courage and his reasonableness. Many examples could be given – his decision in the small hours of the morning at Christmastime to fly at once to Cyprus when reports of serious rioting were received; his determination to visit the stricken areas in British Guiana at the height of the communal disturbances; his insistence on President Nkrumah driving with him through the streets of Accra to test if the route would be safe for the Queen on her proposed visit.*

In characteristic fashion, Sandys concentrated on apparently small things as much as on big issues. He was equally thorough and inexorable in trying to settle a war or drafting a new Constitution as in settling questions of form and of style. He insisted that the holder of his office should normally be called 'Commonwealth Secretary' instead of the more formal 'Secretary of State for Commonwealth Relations' and he changed the practice of 'HMG' in the United Kingdom of Great Britain and Northern Ireland by securing agreement that (except for formal purposes) they should in future be known, rather more simply, as the British Government.

The advent of Sandys was a unique experience for the Office; nothing quite like it had happened before or would happen again. But though Sandys may have been unjust to one or two members, in general he left the Office a better Department than when he had arrived. While he ruled, there was no room for slackness, weakness or superficiality. He presented a challenge and the staff were forced to respond. They were compelled to think afresh and to think big. The character of the staff was strengthened and the Department emerged from the ordeal with a new self-confidence, toughness and determination.

That alone would have given Sandys a worthy niche among the Commonwealth statuary, but he was also the minister of 'decolonization' who from 1962 to 1964 combined the offices of Commonwealth Secretary and Colonial Secretary. During his term he added some ten new members to the Commonwealth association and was himself responsible in most cases for the various independence agreements, invariably worked out in prolonged sessions. Never before or since would the pace be so accelerated; in addition Sandys personally engaged in the negotiations for the return of stability to British Guiana as a prelude to independence, for the negotiations between Malaya, Singapore and the Borneo Territories for the establishment of a Greater Malaysia and for a more democratic constitution in Southern Rhodesia. It may be that Sandys' concentration on successive critical situa-

---

* Macmillan expressed in his autobiography his sense of indebtedness for Sandys' persistence and courage, commenting 'with his iron determination he cajoled or forced the reluctant President to drive with him in an open car.' Macmillan also made clear his view that it would be wrong to expect the High Commissioner to make the final recommendation in dealing with the life of the Queen and that this should be made by a Cabinet Minister.[2]

tions prevented his devoting himself in depth to Commonwealth affairs as a whole; but he carried a gigantic load and, on his own insistence, carried it on his own back. Once committed to a matter he gave it his all; nothing was ever done by halves.

After the Labour Government came to power in October 1964 only four more years of separate existence remained for the CRO. In that time there were three Secretaries of State. Each of them was cast in a very different mould from Sandys, but as none of them was in the Department for much more than a year, there was little scope to make the lasting impact which Sandys' dominance had achieved. Moreover the course of events forced Wilson as P.M. to involve himself closely in Commonwealth relations even if that had not already been his inclination. The Rhodesian question became the longest and most difficult problem in external relations and forced no less than three Meetings of Commonwealth P.M.s in the first three years of Labour rule: with the P.M. compelled to take personal charge, there was less opportunity for the Minister to take the lead.

Nevertheless each S. of S. made his own contribution. The first, Arthur Bottomley, bore the brunt of the Rhodesian crisis. He had a wide experience of Commonwealth affairs extending alike to the Dominions, to India (where his credit was high for his settlement of the Burma problem after the war) and to Africa (where he had many personal friends among the leaders of the newly independent countries): he also radiated honesty and goodwill and his patently genuine personality did much to disarm criticism and secure understanding when British policies came under attack. Bottomley was modest and never laid claim to any intellectual eminence; but he was a shrewd judge of men and he also possessed a quite unusual sense of loyalty. Once having given his confidence he gave it whole-heartedly and was almost disarmingly ready to be guided by those whom he trusted; his word was indeed his bond. His distinct contribution can perhaps best be summed up in the one word – friendliness.

Bottomley was succeeded by Herbert Bowden who had none of his predecessor's easy familiarity with Commonwealth personalities and indeed little acquaintance with Commonwealth matters. He made no pretence of being an originator; but he was a Parliamentarian of experience, a man of total probity and clarity of expression and an administrator of business-like efficiency. He was clear-cut and handled matters without fuss or ostentation and was guided by a firm instinct of what was politically feasible.

The third Labour Minister and, as it happened, the last Commonwealth Secretary was George Thomson. Given the opportunity of a longer term and the chance to influence policies, he might have proved an outstanding Commonwealth Secretary. As events turned out, his short term coincided with a time that offered little comfort. He had made clear that he was devoted to the idea of securing British adhesion to the EEC; he could have played a major part in securing Commonwealth understanding, but during his term all was frustrated by the French veto. He engaged in a search for some settlement of the Rhodesian tangle but, in the face of the NIBMAR (No Independence Before Majority African Rule) commitment, no solution was acceptable to both sides. He was called upon to defend to the Governments of Malaysia, Singapore, Australia and New Zealand the British withdrawal from East of Suez – an inevitably disheartening experience. Finally his Department lost its separate existence and for his last six months he was a 'lame duck' Minister, with no promise of any continuing responsibility for Commonwealth relations. Yet he brought many qualities to bear – youthful zest, freshness and originality of thought, a spirit of tolerance and liberalism, a sense of humour, a flair for human relations and a quality of caring – all of which endeared him to his Commonwealth colleagues and made him a leader in the Office who commanded in equal measure both respect and affection.

Staff

Throughout the period there were in all four PUSs – Laithwaite (who has already been considered), Clutterbuck, Garner* and James† (who, in effect, had the cup dashed from his lips since the merger of the CRO and F.O. was announced a bare 10 days after his appointment and he served as PUS for 6 months only). When Laithwaite retired at the end of 1959 it had been the Office plan that Garner should succeed as PUS, but Home (then S. of S.) conceived another idea. This was that Garner should stay for a full five-year term in Ottawa (instead of returning after only three) and that Clutterbuck should be PUS for a two-year period. The idea appealed immediately to Garner himself not only on his personal account but also because he thought that the appointment would be in the interests of the Service and provide a fitting climax to Clutterbuck's career. It did not immediately appeal either to Laithwaite or to Clutterbuck himself. But Laithwaite soon fell in with the S. of S.'s plan and Clutterbuck whose reluctance was interpreted as due to modesty was persuaded that his duty lay in accepting. The objections which Clutterbuck made at the time were two-fold. His most serious doubt was on grounds of age; when the offer was made he had for some time been

---

* Garner was PUS from 1962 to 1968. Owing to Caccia's retirement some three months only after the formation of the Diplomatic Service, Garner who succeeded him was Head of the Diplomatic Service for most of the time that the CRO remained a separate Department.

† James was appointed a member of the Privy Council when he left the post in London – the only member of the Commonwealth Service ever to receive this honour. He went on under the FCO to become High Commissioner in India and Australia and received a life peerage in 1977, taking the title of Lord St Brides.

looking forward to retirement and he would be 62 by the time he took up the appointment; a further anxiety on this score was whether there might not be some disappointment in the Service at his taking over at that age. His second concern was on the question of readjustment of tempo and technique considering he had been out of Whitehall continuously for 12 years; he wondered too whether the interests of the Office would suffer when everybody would know that he was only keeping the seat warm for a couple of years and whether there would be any danger of the Office losing in authority on this account. Laithwaite reassured him on all these points; Clutterbuck had a profound sense of duty and, against his own inclination, allowed himself to be persuaded.

Clutterbuck's previous career has been sketched in earlier chapters – his attendance at international conferences between the wars, his secretaryship of the Newfoundland Royal Commission and subsequent responsibility for the administration of the island, his important work on economic matters during the war; abroad he had been called upon to act as High Commissioner in the Union of South Africa at the beginning of the war, he had been an outstanding success as High Commissioner in Canada in the difficult years after the war, his term in India was dogged by ill-health and eventually cut short, but he had fully recovered in Dublin where he was a most popular British representative.

Clutterbuck came to the Office therefore with a wealth of experience and a high record of achievement. His name commanded respect in Whitehall; he enjoyed social life and made an admirable representative of the Office in all Commonwealth functions. More important still, he was a man of the utmost integrity and loyalty and was held in high regard by all members of the Service. Nevertheless he rightly foresaw that the appointment would not be an easy one. There had been many changes in the Commonwealth, including the advent of the African nations, which altered the character of the Office from the D.O. he had left in 1946; he was not familiar with the pace of the post-war inter-departmental system in Whitehall; moreover he had never found it easy to delegate – which became more important than ever before with the immensely increased number of problems – and, curiously, he normally wrote in a beautiful but laborious manuscript and seldom dictated to a stenographer. In matters of administration there was a further factor; Clutterbuck was essentially a kindly person and this quality greatly endeared him to all his staff; but there was the reverse of the medal and Clutterbuck increasingly found it distasteful to take ruthless action with individuals. He had gentility to a high degree, but in times of difficulty sometimes lacked forcefulness. All these factors made it difficult to ensure smooth running especially when so many critical issues arose simultaneously.

None of this might have mattered seriously if things had gone well at the top. Clutterbuck was appointed by Home; the two men understood and respected each other and no doubt would have worked well together. Un-fortunately Home was moved to the F.O. and, for most of Clutterbuck's time, Duncan Sandys was the Secretary of State. The two were not compatible, each saw only the weaknesses in the other and not the strengths. No Government Department can prosper unless there is complete confidence and collaboration between the Minister and his chief adviser; this did not exist between Sandys and Clutterbuck. Nevertheless Clutterbuck gave a new quality of leadership in the Office, he provided stability and inspired universally among the staff feelings of affection and respect.

One of the first tasks of Office management throughout this period was to secure and train the increasing number of staff required to deal with the growing responsibilities and especially the increasing number of posts abroad. As these became available over a period of some ten years, there was no call for a sudden and once-for-all injection of new blood; each situation was dealt with as seemed best when the need arose. This led to accusations that the solution was one of living from hand to mouth. In fact the needs were met in a variety of different ways.

One obvious course was to increase the rate of inflow of recruits to the Service. Since the Service was growing, this was desirable in any case, but it could not provide any immediate solution towards filling senior posts; moreover from the point of view of the structure of the Service and of the need to ensure a steady flow of promotion in the future, it was important to avoid excessive recruitment over a short period. A second step was to fill new vacancies by appointing existing staff on promotion. In justifiable cases this was resorted to and the resulting improvement of prospects had a good effect on staff morale; as a result the expanding opportunities in the Commonwealth Service tended to give CRO staff an advantage in promotion prospects over their contemporaries in the Foreign Service.* There was however a limit beyond which this could not be encouraged without impairing efficiency. A third step that could readily be taken was to increase the numbers of Foreign Service officers seconded to posts abroad, without paying undue regard to exact numerical reciprocity.

The most important source of additional recruitment was by appointment from outside the CRO, whether on permanent transfer from elsewhere in the Government Service, by late recruitment or by engagement on contract. An obvious field was presented by the Colonial Office and the Colonial Service, both now running down in numbers for the very reason that the CRO in turn was increasing. But the CRO took the view at this time that those who had served in a Territory (and most Colonial Service officers

---

* A fortuitous advantage accruing to the CRO from the number of senior posts overseas was the disproportionally high number of knighthoods awarded. At the peak, the CRO could count on some 20 awards in all, compared with three or four in a major home Department like the Home Office or Board of Trade. This discrepancy was reduced by the cut in awards to Civil Servants in 1967.

wished to continue in the land they knew) would not be acceptable in a new role as members of the Commonwealth Service. The chance therefore was missed of recruiting any considerable body of men with experience in depth of life in the new Commonwealth countries; but, though virtually none came from the Colonial Service at this early stage, a handful of highly qualified men was accepted on transfer from the C.O. itself. A special source of recruitment from outside was the appointment of men in political life as High Commissioners.

A basic problem concerning organization was whether the work should be distributed on a geographical or functional basis. The tendency through-out, first in the D.O., later in the CRO, and specifically reaffirmed in the 1949 reorganization, was to organize the work on a functional basis. By the sixties however there were a number of cogent practical reasons pointing to some shift in the emphasis. Commonwealth members were no longer a small compact group, susceptible of similar treatment; they were not only numerous but were becoming far more individualistic, each calling for more specialized knowledge for an understanding of its problems. The more the Office grew, the bigger these difficulties became since the butter of know-ledge was inevitably spread more thinly throughout the whole Office. There were also strong reasons for greater geographical emphasis from the point of view of relations with the rest of Whitehall. The case for a fresh look was powerfully supported by the Third Report of the Select Committee on Estimates published in 1959. The Committee considered that the CRO had been organized in a way that seemed to them 'anomalous'.[3] The Committee were told that the CRO had been organized on a functional basis, but in the words of the PUS (Laithwaite) that 'it has not worked 100% well and we continue to experiment. It may be that with further experience we shall extend geographically rather than on that basis.' As we have seen, Nye, who had earlier described the 1947 organization as 'a complete dog's breakfast'[4], strongly favoured a functional organization, 'particularly [for] a Commonwealth which is changing and will be changing more'. The Committee were not attracted by Laithwaite's advocacy of a 'completely flexible' system and said with some tartness that they did not regard it as conducive to efficiency; they feared moreover that, as the number of countries with which the CRO had to deal increased, the organization of the Department would become more and more complicated. But they failed to give any lead and in the end were unable to pronounce in favour of either of the two methods 'whatever the rival merits' might be.

There was at no point a sudden master-plan which revolutionized the departmental organization; the changes took place gradually over the years. Some concentration of interest in India, Pakistan and Ceylon developed *ad hoc* in the relevant departments and geographical departments had been formed to handle relations with Ghana and Malaya when they achieved independence in 1957 and 1958. Later further changes were made, the general effect of which was to put more weight on the division of work by region (*see* Appendix A, Table 5). The object was to identify a single focus for each individual country and so ensure that in the formulation of policy all aspects affecting that particular country could be taken into account at an early stage.

On the organization of the Service, the Select Committee made the important recommendation that the Government should investigate the possibility of creating an integrated Commonwealth Service. By this they envisaged a breaking down of the barriers between political, trade promotion and information work. Only the first was performed by regular Commonwealth Service officers; the second was carried out by officers in the Trade Commission Service responsible to the Board of Trade and the third by CRO Information Officers who were specialists and did not normally share in the political work of the Department. The Select Committee wanted the Commonwealth Service to be staffed by officers capable of dealing with all aspects of the Department's work and thus to achieve a position where the highest posts could be filled by men with first-hand experience of all kinds of work performed by their subordinates. They recognized that there would be room for a number of specialists, but they believed that specialization should be the exception rather than the rule.

The Committee were much influenced by Nye who had always been in favour of the generalist, the competent all-rounder and discounted the view that information, trade promotion or any other matter called for some special mystique. In this the Committee were undoubtedly right; but it was a counsel of perfection at the time. The Board of Trade refused to give up their direct control and there were practical problems about the Information Service. Only a radical transformation could provide a solution and this had to wait for the Plowden Report.

In the past staff morale had been consistently good – in the early days of the D.O. there had been the excitement of a new Department creating a unique form of international cooperation. A new fillip had been given after the 1949 reforms with the development of the new Commonwealth and the prospect of further expansion; this seemed to be fulfilled with the admission of further new members after 1957. But by the 1960s troubles abounded and a mood of disillusionment set in. It was not easy for the Office to see clearly the way ahead. There was anxiety among the staff about their prospects – what would be the effect of any merger with the C.O., still more of a take-over by the much larger F.O.? There was concern at the large number of senior posts abroad that were being filled by candidates from outside the Service. Something of the previous sense of intimacy was lost by the very size of the organization. It was no longer so easy to give full attention to the needs of all High Commissioners abroad and some (particularly those who had served continuously abroad) felt left out.

In the last resort what sustained morale was the evidence of continuing and important responsibilities which the Service showed itself competent to discharge, the pride that could be taken in the response which its members had made to challenges of danger and difficulty in some of the posts overseas and the achievement of the Diplomatic Service which gave a sense of purpose and offered a clear prospect for the future.

In the meantime a number of steps could be taken to give a sense of confidence and to satisfy staff that they were performing a worthwhile job. Increased emphasis on continuity and on expertise in relation to particular countries helped to give a feeling that the individual was master of his subject and could make an effective contribution. Insistence on delegation encouraged junior staff to take the initiative and assume responsibility. Many procedures were adopted to ensure that, however narrow might be the field in which an officer worked, he kept in touch with the broader scene all the time and was apprised of general office policies. One innovation was made in relation to High Commissioners. This was the institution in 1962 of a practice by the PUS of sending regularly once a month a personal and confidential letter commenting on the events of the month and giving as frank an account as possible of how the CRO viewed the situation and what policies it was seeking to pursue. In order to ensure that the letter was not inhibited in any way, it was prepared by the PUS himself and deliberately not shown either to Departments or to Ministers.

Minor housekeeping ways to improve efficiency which claimed perennial attention were the need for brevity in language and for economy, particularly in the use of telegrams. Circumlocution is the besetting sin of bureaucracy; obscurity and verbosity are often a cloak for indecision and the CRO was no exception. Clear thinking and clear writing should go together.* Regular exhortations were also made to reduce both the number and the length of

---

*On one occasion in 1963 the PUS circulated a number of choice pieces which had reached his desk, chosen at random, and of which he attempted a shortened version: the following are examples.

1. It is useful to bear these simple facts in mind in any analysis of Commonwealth relations and in any attempt to try to assess the role that the Commonwealth can play in the modern world because it is far too frequently postulated that the Commonwealth does not exist except as a vague concept.	We should remember this because it is often thought that the Commonwealth is only a vague idea.
2. The above illustrations of difficulty of identifying the economic aspects of the Commonwealth reflect the basic considerations which constitute the nature of the problem of Commonwealth economic relations.	This shows that Commonwealth economic relations are difficult.

telegrams. Sheer quantity was defeating itself – the lines tended to get choked and there were sometimes long delays. Everyone suffered from too much documentation to digest and the burden on the mechanics of telegraphy in all its stages became formidable. The growing complexity and urgency in Commonwealth relations ruled out any severe reduction in the number of telegrams; their length was another matter, but rare was the officer who could resist the temptation to embellish his report with more words than were necessary.

The Office did not operate in a vacuum and could not ignore the currents of contemporary opinion. Not only was there increasing disillusionment with the concept of the Commonwealth, there was a constant undercurrent of criticism of the CRO itself by public opinion. This was shown especially in the series of critical reports by Committees of the House of Commons and by numerous attacks in the press, most persistently in *The Times* which questioned the need for a separate CRO. The main thrust of the argument was stilled by the creation of the Diplomatic Service and the merger with the F.O., but in the meantime an attempt was made to keep matters in perspective.

An early requirement was to re-invigorate the Information Service. Although the D.O. had established an Information Department at the beginning of the war and though in each Commonwealth country an efficient Information Service had been set up, somehow the Information Department remained the Cinderella of the Office. Since the Information staff had for the most part spent their whole career on information work, it would take time before they could be genuinely integrated and before there would be complete interchangeability. The first step was to break down a psychological barrier and convince the Information staff that they had their full part to play in carrying out the policies of the Office. In order to create a new spirit, Major-General Bishop who was looking forward to retirement on completing his term as DHC Calcutta, agreed in 1962 to take charge of the Information Service as an Under-Secretary and he held the post until, in 1964, he again responded to the call of duty to serve at a most difficult time as High Commissioner in Cyprus. In a bureaucracy, miracles do not happen overnight; nevertheless over a period a significant change took place. The staff were given new heart and, while no public relations work could hope to reverse the trend of public opinion, at least more was made known of the positive achievements of the CRO, and the original contribution which it had to make. Hitherto the Information Service had concentrated on the projection of Britain overseas; this remained their primary responsibility, but approval was obtained for a modest budget for the projection of the Commonwealth in Britain which enabled several useful activities to be supported. A conscious effort was also made by senior members of the staff to cultivate 'opinion-formers' in all walks of life, by encouraging correspondents to call for individual briefing, by developing contacts with editorial staff in the Press and broadcasting, and by seizing any opportunities for meeting leaders in the business, banking, trade union and University worlds. It was in this spirit that in 1963 the CRO organized the Conference on the Commonwealth at Ditchley which incidentally helped to show that the CRO was not an ivory tower, but was anxious to share with and learn from others.*

Women in the Service

Women had been recruited to the Administrative Grade on a temporary basis during the war years and were admitted permanently in 1946. Though statistically their numbers remained small, they provided a handful of qualified officers who undramatically made progress in the Service; though none was appointed in charge of a post abroad before the merger, Leonore Storar was posted as Consul in Boston in 1969; the first woman to take charge† of a diplomatic post was Eleanor Emery who was appointed High Commissioner in Botswana in 1973; both Storar and Emery had begun their service in the D.O. In grades other than the administrative, women in the CRO distinguished themselves quantitatively as well as qualitatively. From the earliest days of the D.O., women had supplied a large proportion of the clerical grade and, apart from one or two male rarities, had monopolized the typing pool and shorthand staff. In the years after the war they began to occupy prominent posts in the executive grade and particularly distinguished themselves in all those jobs where personal relations were important. Dolores Monreal for years bore the real burden in the Ceremonial and Reception work, Peggy Dalgleish and Nancy Fisher ministered in London to all the needs of British High Commissioners on appointment or on leave, Eleanor Booker, as Press Officer, gained the confidence of the Fourth Estate to a remarkable extent, Margaret Archer as Welfare Officer – all these and many others, in their individual jobs developed the special qualities required and performed with grace as well as efficiency. One other category deserves special mention: personal assistants to senior officials. Stenographers were ill-paid in Government service and they were invariably in short supply. As a result, shorthand writers were frequently overworked and were expected to put in long and sometimes highly irregular hours. Nevertheless a group of them were prepared over a period of years to tolerate all these unsatisfactory conditions, to suffer the vagaries of a series of idiosyncratic chiefs,

---

* Most of the matters referred to in this section arose while the author was PUS and the account is derived from personal knowledge. For a more personal description of how things were seen at the time, the reader is referred to the farewell talk to the Staff given by the author on his retirement which is quoted in Appendix B.

† Barbara Salt was designated as Ambassador to Israel in 1962 but owing to ill-health was unable to take up her appointment.

yet so long as there was a job of work to be done they performed uncomplainingly and always showed a sense of dedication to the Service and perhaps still more of personal devotion to their 'boss'; in a thousand ways they lightened his task and made the daily grind more agreeable. It would be invidious to select individual names and they would no doubt prefer to remain unsung; but they should not be forgotten.

Relations with the rest of Whitehall

Other Departments in Whitehall had consistently taken a realistic and unemotional stance about the Commonwealth; in the 1960s they tended to become even more cynical about its value, regarding it as liable to get in the way of British interests. The Commonwealth was seen as posing an obstacle to Britain's aim of joining the EEC; as imposing a variety of defence obligations, calling for the commitment of British troops; and as swallowing up most of Britain's aid which might otherwise have gone in larger amounts to the Colonial Empire or to foreign countries or been available for a more direct stimulus to the British economy. The CRO was regarded as resisting the policies of other Departments and at times was thought to be little more than a mouthpiece for Commonwealth interests. On the other hand, as the CRO gained more expertise, this came to be recognized and its advice was more eagerly sought, especially when things grew more difficult. It was increasingly seen that, far from being uncritical, the CRO stood up firmly to unreasonable behaviour by Commonwealth countries.

There was also a change in the climate of opinion in Whitehall in the 1950s and 1960s which eased cooperation with other Departments. Before the war a Department could be virtually a law unto itself, under the autocratic control of its official head. Such a state of affairs had vanished. The war had wrought many changes in Whitehall; it broke down the rigidities of the old hierarchy within Departments, replaced the old formal communication between Departments with a new informal style and vastly improved the whole business of interdepartmental consultation. The Committee system which had been devoted largely to co-ordinating action on the economic front, was extended to cover fields of policy. In the 1960s a Committee at PUS level was established to review all questions of foreign affairs and defence. In addition there were *ad hoc* Committees on any matters of importance – including the application to join EEC, the problem of Rhodesia, the withdrawal from East of Suez. This involved the PUS and most of his senior advisers regularly rubbing shoulders with their opposite numbers. In 1960 there was a further development. The practice was instituted of having an annual Conference for Heads of all Departments over a weekend in the country where they could discuss in an uninhibited manner any questions affecting administration and policy. Another factor which was of some significance was that over the years there had been a considerable exodus to other Departments and during the 1960s at one time or another the Heads of the Treasury, the Board of Trade, the Ministries of Food, Supply, Fuel and Power, the Department of Defence (Air) as well as senior officers in a number of these and other Departments were all former colleagues of those in the CRO.

The growing authority exercised from the P.M.'s Office and the increasing importance of the interdepartmental Committee system enhanced the importance of the Cabinet Office, with which the CRO had a close relationship, both under Norman Brook and his successor Burke Trend. The two Offices were brought into particularly close cooperation before the establishment of the Commonwealth Secretariat by their responsibilities in connexion with CPM Meetings. It is probable that the CRO had fewer differences with the Cabinet Office than with any other Department with which it did regular business; but the Cabinet Office was somewhat special and, because of its nature, seldom had its own axe to grind.

The most significant relations in Whitehall were those with the F.O. and the C.O. In each case there were considerable tensions in the early years; yet in each case as related in Chapter 5 the relationship ended in merger to the general satisfaction of all concerned.

In economic matters, the dominating influence in the Office was that of Rumbold, though in later years Lintott (especially over relations with EEC) and Snelling also exercised responsibility at the Deputy level. Rumbold had joined the I.O. in 1929 and had been P.S. to R. A. Butler. He transferred to the CRO in 1947 and served as DHC in the Union of South Africa. He succeeded Symon as the Under-Secretary in charge of the Economic Division in 1954 and was appointed DUS in 1958; for the next eight years he provided a powerful element of continuity at headquarters, on both economic and Asian matters. He was a man of high principle and a civil servant of wide experience and intellectual honesty. His manner was authoritarian and he exerted an unusual degree of personal control over all the work he supervised; he was always firm in his own views and uncompromising in his defence of them. He was a devoted and single-minded protagonist of the interests of the Office and none could question his command of his subject or his total integrity.

Throughout this period there was continuous collaboration with the Treasury over the nexus of problems concerned with the British economy and the need to strengthen sterling. In all this work and also the whole range of problems concerned with aid (Colombo Plan, Scholarship Scheme, aid consortia) the CRO could count on a sympathetic hearing and there were few serious difficulties. There were however inevitable differences over defence expenditure and particularly over reductions in Britain's commitment in the Far East. There was also a gap between the Treasury and the CRO over British entry into the European Community particularly at the time of the first application; fortunately at this stage the crunch was never reached. The Board of Trade was even less sympathetic than the Treasury to the CRO case over the European Community and was strongly critical of other Commonwealth countries – and particularly the old Dominions – for whittling down the British preferential position. By contrast, the European question helped to make allies of the CRO and Ministry of Agriculture, both of whom had their different anxieties. Rhodesia provided another cause for differences between the Board of Trade and the CRO since the Board of Trade could hardly be expected to welcome the restrictions on British trade which would be imposed by the sanctions so strongly advocated by the CRO.

Successive defence reviews, continuous consultation especially with Australia and New Zealand, the East African mutinies, 'confrontation', Cyprus, Malta, the Sino-Indian war – all involved the CRO with the Ministry of Defence to a quite unusual extent and relations with them were not only close but normally most cordial. The repeated demands of the Treasury for severe reductions in defence expenditure placed each Department in a position of acute embarrassment and the successive economy cuts found them, together with the F.O., as bedfellows resisting the threat to the effectiveness of British military power. Nevertheless there were clear differences in the attitudes of the three Departments; the CRO attached importance to Britain's relationship with Australia, New Zealand, Malaysia and Singapore and did not wish to see any diminution in the British contribution to stability in South East Asia; the F.O. was more concerned with relations with the Persian Gulf States and the security of British oil supplies. There was a still greater difference of principle between the Ministry of Defence and the political departments. The CRO sought to avoid damage to relations with Commonwealth countries resulting from any whittling down of British undertakings. This was common ground with the Ministry of Defence at the first stage; but when it became clear that it was Government policy to secure force reductions, then the Ministry of Defence resisted being asked to perform beyond their capability and insisted therefore that if resources were to be cut, commitments must also be reduced.

In 1961, the Government established a new Department with the title of Department of Technical Cooperation (*see* Chapter 5 below). It functioned under a junior Minister and was responsible for technical assistance work previously performed by the F.O., the CRO and the C.O. The new Department received little more than a tepid welcome from the CRO, but no serious problem arose since it acted rather as an agency and was subordinate to the political Departments in all matters of policy. In 1964 however the Labour Government established an independent Ministry of Overseas

Development under a Minister with a seat in the Cabinet, with wide authority over all aid to developing countries. This gave rise to a very different situation. From the CRO point of view, the new Department was resented for being given responsibility over matters which had a vital bearing on the work of the CRO; at the least it was feared that unnecessary duplication and a degree of blurred responsibility would inevitably result. There was therefore some mutual jealousy and constant argument about jurisdiction. There was also a real difference in principle. The CRO regarded aid as part of the total relationship with a Commonwealth country and considered that it should be decided in the context of overall policy. The ODM, on the other hand, felt that aid should be considered objectively, even idealistically; that it should be related solely to the needs of the recipient country and not to the selfish interests of Britain; in other words, in the fashionable jargon of the day, that aid should be 'pure'. There were furthermore differences between individuals in the two Departments. The difficulties felt in the CRO were expressed with emphasis and determination by Rumbold, from his long experience of problems of aid-giving, and he was reluctant to yield the authority that he thought properly belonged to the CRO. But he met more than his match in Andrew Cohen, the first official head of ODM, who was one of the most powerful as well as dynamic Permanent Secretaries in Whitehall.* The ODM also suffered in the eyes of some officials of the CRO from the fact that the bulk of its staff came from the C.O. and were considered to be imbued with Colonial ideas and therefore disposed to adopt an unduly paternalistic line in relation to the newly independent Commonwealth countries. However the ODM representatives in the field gradually built up a corpus of expert knowledge and established excellent relations with their clients. Though there were occasional differences between aid officials and the political staff in the various High Commissions, relations were normally good and the work of the development officers was held in increasingly high regard; with further experience of working together and with greater interchange of staff, the earlier antagonisms between the two Departments in Whitehall also began to subside.

Any differences between the CRO and other Departments were normally related to specific issues for particular reasons and sometimes applied only between individual members of the two Departments. At times but rarely there were genuine differences of viewpoint, which could only be settled at Cabinet level. In general the working relationship was good and it may not be unfair to conclude with the judgement of Burke Trend, the Cabinet Secretary, who had much to do with the CRO and yet was sufficiently detached to be able to look at the Office in relation both to other Departments in Whitehall and, to some extent, to the outside world. In 1968 shortly before the final merger, he authorized the PUS to quote his views as follows:

* It was not without cause that Cohen and his first Minister were dubbed 'The Elephant and Castle'.

He had been increasingly impressed by the way in which, in recent years, the Commonwealth Office had maintained and enhanced both its efficiency and its prestige. It had had to face a number of handicaps – a kind of creeping disillusionment with the concept of the Commonwealth itself, both among the general public and in Whitehall; the psychological shock – if that is the right word – of ceasing to command a separate Service and being merged, to some extent, with a larger and more powerful sister Department; and the wearing frustration of having to go on grappling with three or four obstinate problems – Rhodesia, Cyprus, Kashmir and so forth – which one sometimes despairs of ever solving. The Secretary of the Cabinet said that, in his view, few, if any, other Departments had been expected, since the end of the war, to cope in so short a space of time with such an accumulation of difficulties, both material and psychological; and he felt that far too little credit had been given to the Commonwealth Office for the way in which it surmounted them and had continued to speak up for the Commonwealth concept, while fully recognising that that concept had changed already and would have to change still further.

CHAPTER 3

The Service Overseas

While in essence the job of a High Commissioner had not changed, the scenario was altered beyond recognition. Apart from the increase in the number of posts, the world in the 1960s had become a more complex one, a world of strains and of violence. High Commissioners were subjected to dangers which their predecessors had seldom if ever known. New qualities of strength of character, of sheer nerve and courage were called for in Heads of posts and they needed to be supported by staff with a knowledge in depth of the country. The importance of High Commissioners was well recognized at the political level,* more particularly since Ministers themselves travelled far more frequently than in the past to other Commonwealth countries. Macmillan after his tour of Commonwealth countries commented that 'it was clear that, more than ever before, the future of the nations linked together through the Commonwealth tie must depend upon personal as well as formal relations' and, since it was likely that in the future fewer Governors-General would be appointed from Britain 'it was therefore upon the High Commissioners that we must depend'.†

In much of the Commonwealth the first requirement was to unwind the accursed chain of racial superiority which had blighted the British Empire and to gain acceptance of the fact that tolerance was not an effort in condescension and that behaviour stemmed from a genuine belief in the equal rights of all. The phrases sounded easy but the practice was not always perfect. A minority of individuals in all societies suffer from attitudes of racial prejudice, which cannot be disguised from those against whom they are directed. Qualities of the heart and of understanding are called for if

---

* *See* for example Alport's comment on his appointment to Salisbury: 'The High Commissioner in Salisbury would have more power than a Minister of State in London. The telegram, which is popularly supposed to have destroyed the influence of diplomatic representatives ... had really placed a formidable weapon in their hands. Most telegrams on foreign and Commonwealth affairs receive a pretty wide circulation among Ministers and departments. Skilfully used they could present my views far more effectively than an office minute or an argument at a Cabinet committee.'[1]

† Macmillan added 'In their choice, as in the Foreign Service, the principle must be re-asserted that the man should be chosen most likely to do the Queen's business. Above all there must be no appointment without careful consideration of the personal characteristics, foibles and even susceptibilities of the Government to which our High Commissioner or Ambassador was to be accredited. Above all no question of seniority should be allowed to interfere with the object in view. There must be no "Buggins' turn".'[2]

true friendship is to be gained between those of differently coloured skins.

Nor could the challenge of a High Commissioner's job in the 1960s always be solved by the display of qualities in his own character. Outside events took charge and a High Commissioner was often faced with a dangerous situation – riots and violence in a dozen Commonwealth countries; even in countries not directly affected there were mass demonstrations. All this was obvious at different times in Cyprus and Nigeria, in Dublin or Pakistan; but in no country of the Commonwealth were a High Commissioner and members of his staff wholly exempt from risk, as the kidnapping of James Cross, the British Trade Commissioner in Montreal, demonstrated in 1970.

There was yet another area, hitherto little known to the general public, where a High Commissioner in a Commonwealth country became for the first time vulnerable. Handing his passport to an Ambassador was normally the prelude to a declaration of war and such action had been utterly unknown in diplomatic relations with Dominion Governments. But in the tensions of the 1960s requests were made by various Commonwealth Governments on no fewer than a dozen occasions for the removal of a British High Commissioner from his post. Some of these resulted from the decision of the Government to break off relations because of opposition to British Government policies, some as a mark of displeasure at the High Commissioner's expression of those policies, some on account of some dislike that was entertained towards the High Commissioner on personal grounds; in these latter cases the request was seldom made publicly and sometimes took the form of an informal hint rather than a formal demand; but the indication that effective business would no longer be conducted with the incumbent was sufficiently clear to ensure that, even if he was not withdrawn forthwith (as was frequently the case) he was replaced in due course. The proprieties were therefore observed. Most of the complaints, though not all, came from Commonwealth countries in Africa and could be attributed to an assertion of new-found nationalism. The consequences were not serious or unmanageable; nevertheless changes which involved an average of two Heads of Missions a year and affected more than a third of all Heads of Mission posts in Commonwealth countries constituted an unwelcome hazard and created a new problem for the administration of the Service.

The early 1960s were remarkable for the high number of men from political life appointed as High Commissioners. There was nothing new in this, but the scale was greater than ever before or since; no fewer than ten posts were within a short period filled by former Ministers.* The Select Committee

---

* Between 1956 and 1966, former Ministers were appointed as follows: Lord Amory (Canada), Lord Carrington (Australia), MacDonald (India, Kenya), John Freeman (India), Lord Head (Nigeria, Malaysia), Sir Geoffrey de Freitas (Ghana, Kenya) and Lord Alport (Federation of Rhodesia).

on Estimates devoted the Session of 1958–9 to the CRO and expressed themselves strongly on what they regarded as the excessive number of senior posts that were awarded to persons outside the Service. They observed with some pompsity:[3] 'there is clearly something wrong with a Service when so many of its top posts are offered to men who have made their careers elsewhere. Appointments of this kind are bound to have a bad effect on morale within the Service and, in the long run, may harm recruitment.' They went on to quote the PUS (Laithwaite) as agreeing that the figures for outside appointments 'looked very bad' and they disagreed with his optimism that time would improve the situation. They might have expressed themselves even more strongly had they known that the numbers appointed from outside would increase sharply in the immediately following years.

There was clearly some merit in the point; but equally it was easy to get the matter out of perspective. The normal time lag between recruitment and appointment as a High Commissioner was approximately twenty-five years; it was scarcely surprising therefore that the small staff recruited in the 1930s when there were only two or three posts overseas did not throw up the large numbers required in the 1960s when there were twenty or thirty. Secondly attention tended to focus on posts occupied by outsiders; throughout some of the top posts abroad were always held by men in the Commonwealth Service. Thirdly recruitment from outside on this scale proved to be a temporary phenomenon, due to the rapid evolution of the Commonwealth. If it had continued for long, it might have had a serious effect on morale; as it was, it occurred at a time of rapid expansion when prospects for individuals in the Service were extremely good. Moreover Laithwaite was proved correct; by 1965 when the Diplomatic Service was created, only one post (High Commissioner in Malaysia held by Head) was filled by someone from the political field; by the end of 1968 when merger took place every single Head of Mission in a Commonwealth country was a member of the Diplomatic Service. Above all it was accepted that the aim must be to have in a post overseas the best man available whatever his origin. The CRO at that time demonstrably did not contain sufficient high-flyers to fill all the senior posts abroad and there was no resentment when men from outside were brought in on temporary assignment. In fact, though necessarily their qualities were very different, all the newcomers were of high calibre. It would however be a bold claim to assert that, as a group, they were more successful than the best CRO officers serving in the top posts abroad. It is nevertheless true that, at a lower level, there was a high proportion of CRO High Commissioners of no more than average ability. It is not easy to give a general verdict, but perhaps the judgement of an eminent and impartial observer at one post may be mentioned. Writing in 1970 about representation in Ottawa during the war, Arnold Heeney said:[4] 'At that period and since, I have the impression that in choosing their representatives in Ottawa, Britain has taken more than normal care in their selection. Certainly no country, in my experience, has had such consistently effective spokesmen. Representation of the United States has been uneven, as has that of France.'

Though it is invidious to single out individuals, the record of Malcolm MacDonald is nevertheless unique. His length of service was noticeable: he first visited Commonwealth countries on a University debating tour in 1924–5; in 1976 he was President of the Royal Commonwealth Society and of VSO after nearly forty years in continuous Government service. His career has been remarkable for variety and breadth: he served in four Continents having been Dominions Secretary, Colonial Secretary and Minister of Health in London; High Commissioner in Canada and India; Governor-General and Commissioner-General in South East Asia and holding a series of posts in Africa. In Canada he had greatly facilitated wartime cooperation by the personal relationship he had built up with Mackenzie King. In Malaya and Singapore he, more than anyone else, transformed the pre-war planters' atmosphere depicted by Somerset Maugham into a rejection of racial prejudice and intolerance. In India, he showed a sensitive understanding of Indian feelings (her need to grapple with poverty and her bewilderment over British action at Suez). In Kenya his arrival instantaneously brought a breath of fresh air to the sultry scene and his courage and foresight in recognizing Kenyatta's qualities of leadership were rewarded by the stability and progress which have marked Kenya since independence. It was a double tribute to MacDonald that, after serving as Colonial Governor he was invited to remain as Governor-General on independence and later was accepted as High Commissioner. When his retirement from the High Commissioner post was due, in 1966, Britain was at the height of her difficulties with the African countries over Rhodesia; in view of the understanding which MacDonald had shown first for Asian, later for African peoples and of the remarkable personal position he had built up, he was appointed to a post unique in the British Government service, that of roving Ambassador throughout Africa with the title of Special Representative. For two years he travelled indefatigably throughout all the African countries and his quiet diplomacy did much to take the heat out of dangerous situations, to develop closer understanding and to pave the way for mutually acceptable solutions. He continued even after formal retirement to devote his remarkable skills in understanding and in diplomacy to any problem where his counsel could be of help – over Rhodesia, South Africa, civil war in Nigeria, the difficulties that beset Malaysia and Singapore.

One feature that distinguishes this period from earlier years is that, whereas previously members of the D.O. and the older members of the CRO published virtually no account of their service, a considerable literature is now building up. Up to 1957 only Grafftey-Smith's memoirs[5] (which themselves did not appear until 1971) gave any substantive account of life in a

377

Commonwealth post abroad.* Since then, George Mallaby[7] has described his time in New Zealand, Alport[8] his service in Rhodesia, Gore-Booth's memoirs[9] include a chapter on his period as High Commissioner in India, David Hunt[10] has written about Uganda, Cyprus and Nigeria and there are glimpses of life in Ottawa, Singapore, Delhi and Nairobi in MacDonald's various writings.[11] In their different ways these books emphasize that a High Commissioner's life is not exclusively a solid diet of work. Fortunately a diplomat performs a better job if he is also enjoying his life in the new country and certainly Commonwealth countries offer unrivalled opportunities for every kind of sport and relaxation.

Because of the shared language and culture a High Commissioner in a Commonwealth country normally lives as an integrated member of the local community to a greater extent than the diplomat in a foreign country; his contacts are both wider and deeper. He therefore finds himself involved in a range of activities more reminiscent of minor royalty than of diplomacy.† The dramatic and musical talent of the High Commissioner's staff was frequently employed in performing plays and concerts. Perhaps because of its size the High Commission staff in New Delhi was the most highly organized and staged two or three plays every year as well as Carol Concerts at Christmas and Easter. Nearly every High Commission staff had its own informal style of celebrating the annual Staff Christmas Party; amateur dramatics were often essayed and even pantomimes based on a caricature of the then serving High Commissioner and making fun at the expense of senior members of the staff.

Individually staff members were free to enjoy the delights of the country of their posting: many, particularly in the old Dominions, took advantage of the splendid opportunities for local leave. Every sport was on offer – skiing, surfing, fishing, hunting, mountaineering, rock-climbing, bird-watching, riding, gliding, trekking, sailing. High Commissioners in one country or another took part in such a variety of activities as finishing second in a Marathon race, holding the record for gliding, owning successful racehorses, engaging in serious mountaineering; and many had wives who made accomplished records of the local scene on canvas. Colleen Nye (wife of the High Commissioner in Delhi and Ottawa) painted portraits of many well-known people in India and Canada; the life-sized portrait of Sir Abubakar Tafawa Balewa, commissioned after his assassination to hang in the Nigeria Institute of International Affairs, was painted by Yvonne Cumming-Bruce, wife of the High Commissioner in Lagos.

More than is the case in most other walks of life, the success of a High

* *Of True Experience*[6] by Gerald Campbell (High Commissioner in Canada 1938–41) contained a brief chapter on Ottawa with some light-hearted reminiscences but did not purport to be a serious study.
† The author appeared in 1959 in an extravaganza *The Wizard of Ozzawa* (Finance Minister in the title role) as Fairy Queen mounted on roller skates (which he had never previously used).

Commissioner depended on his wife; she as much as her husband could make or mar his assignment. There are many posts today where the charms of one and the gaffes of another are remembered – though the memory of the latter is often more vivid and long-lasting. In view of the important role a wife can play it is surprising that the Office took so long either to take the wife into account when postings were made or to organize any special training. In the early days of the D.O. it would have been thought indelicate to consider the wife and there are obvious difficulties in withholding appointment from a man otherwise qualified on account of his wife. (There was a similar reluctance to refuse approval for marriage which was required in the case of marriage to a foreigner; the number of those marrying foreigners was in fact high; surprisingly few married citizens of other Commonwealth countries.) As regards training, the assumption was that, just as the officer would 'learn on the job', so his wife would receive any necessary guidance by senior wives at the post. Often this happened, but clearly this was a casual way of doing things and depended on chance. The first written instruction (called Notes for Newcomers) for wives in the Commonwealth Service was prepared by Office wives themselves in Delhi in 1952. This paper was revised and extended and was eventually circulated to all posts officially from the Office in 1956. It also formed the basis of the Memorandum circulated by the Diplomatic Service in 1966. It was in Delhi too at the same time that Office wives, finding the need for some means of putting particularly junior wives in touch with Indian women, founded the Delhi Commonwealth Women's Association. This started modestly enough in 1952 but is still flourishing with increasing numbers more than twenty-five years later.

In 1954, the Commonwealth Relations Office Wives Society* was formed in London. The motive was that while, in a post overseas, there was easy and regular social contact between all members of the Mission and their wives, on return to London that contact was maintained by the men, but was almost completely broken as far as the wives were concerned. The objects of the Society were first to provide a continuing link between wives of members of the Service; secondly to provide any services that would be useful to wives, such as giving information about posts, arranging for children on journeys alone to be met, providing courses on practical matters or organizing visits to places of interest, usually in London, thus enabling the wives to become better acquainted with the country they were helping their husbands to represent overseas; finally to emphasize the Commonwealth idea. For this last purpose the Society organized a Christmas Tea to which they invited the wives of all Commonwealth High Commissions in London. The idea caught on rapidly; the Society proved to be extremely popular with the

---

* Just as the Association in Delhi had soon become popularly known as the 'Common Women', so the body in London was rapidly styled the 'Crows'. No similar society existed for men; there was nothing in the CRO comparable to the Corona Club for members of the C.O. and the Colonial Service.

wives and its efforts were welcomed by the Office. The Society served as a model for many similar societies which were formed later, notably the Foreign Service Wives Association, the British Council Wives Association and the Wives' Societies in the Canadian and Australian External Affairs Service. The Society flourished until, with the coming about of the Diplomatic Service in 1965, it happily merged with the FSWA to form the Diplomatic Service Wives Association.*

Accommodation

When posts were first set up in the Dominions, there was until after the war no thought of the British Government building for their own account and very little of their acquiring their own property by a capital investment. The normal pattern was to rent office accommodation in suitable commercial premises, to rent a house for the High Commissioner and to pay a rent allowance to other members of the staff. The first and for some time only exception to this was the purchase in 1930 of a residence for the British High Commissioner in Ottawa. This was Earnscliffe, the home of Canada's first P.M. (Sir John A. Macdonald) and apart from its excellent site and historic associations had the added advantage for the Treasury that the stables could be converted for use as an office.† Not until 1964 was a new building to house all staff constructed in the centre of the city. The first residence to be built for a High Commissioner was in Canberra in 1956 where the house enjoys a commanding position, is functionally efficient but lacks distinction. In New Zealand, the first High Commissioners lived in a house now occupied by the DHC and described at the end of the war as 'apart from bad drawbacks is comfortable and, with its democratic simplicity, suits the country'. An ample if somewhat old-fashioned house with spacious gardens was acquired in 1958.

The opening of posts in Asia created a variety of problems. There was the tradition of British splendour; there were the difficulties of life in the tropics; hitherto staff in the Dominions had been indistinguishable from their neighbours, now they were living in an alien culture; finally staff were far more numerous (especially in junior grades since local recruitment was not so easy). In Delhi and Karachi, suitable houses were rented for the High Commissioner; but housing for other staff and office accommodation were not solved in Delhi until the British Government accepted an offer by the

*The union was fortunate for the CROWS since otherwise they might have had to become COWS in the following year when the name of the CRO was changed.

†An illustrated account of Earnscliffe was written by Norman Reddaway who served on the staff of the High Commission from 1952–5. It was published in 1955 and revised and reprinted in 1961.[12]

Indian Government to acquire a considerable area of land in the Diplomatic Compound, where they built a new office, half-a-dozen houses for senior staff and blocks of flats, together with a number of amenities including a social centre and swimming pool; and in Pakistan until the capital was moved to Islamabad where the British Government built suitable residences and offices. In other Asian capitals, the climate was less trying and the difficulties on housing staff were far fewer. In Colombo a residence was built which the Ministry of Works sought to make something of a show-piece; in Kuala Lumpur the British Government were happy to be presented by the Government of Malaya with a residence which is more splendid than that enjoyed by any other High Commissioner.

In Africa, different factors again came into play. In general there was little suitable office or residential accommodation available; moreover by the sixties the Treasury philosophy had changed and favoured owning rather than leasing. Residences were accordingly constructed in most countries: in Lagos an imaginative new house on the open plan system was built on a fine site on the lagoon, generously presented by the Nigerian Government; elsewhere and notably in Freetown the style was sometimes inappropriately imposing; later designs followed a more modest pattern but were agreeable and comfortable, as in Botswana. In the Caribbean and other islands suitable accommodation could normally be found either for purchase or renting. The policy of owning property extended to accommodation for junior staff and to residences outside the capital. In some, for example accommodation for junior staff in West Africa and the purchase of a residence for the DHC in Sydney, Australia, the scale was later criticized as unduly extravagant. But in general the real shortcomings experienced in the early days were remedied and increasing attention was rightly paid to a better standard of furnishing and the provision of amenities. The Ministry of Works were inevitably a perennial target for complaints, but over the years they developed a growing awareness of the demands of different climates and conditions of living and when they put their hearts into a job, the quality of their work was of a high standard and was often much admired locally.

In London it was remarkable that, despite the frequent changes in Whitehall, the Office occupied the same accommodation throughout all its years of separate existence. The only significant change in the main building was the refurbishing of the Entrance Hall under Gordon Walker's inspiration, with the arms of all Commonwealth countries displayed on the walls. The India Office Library in 1965 moved from its cramped quarters to spacious modern accommodation at Orbit House in Blackfriars Bridge Road where it was able to provide a far more efficient service than before.

A word of gratitude should also be expressed for the gift by Lord Courtauld-Thompson of Dorneywood, a charming Elizabethan mansion in Buckinghamshire. When not required by the Foreign Secretary, this was made available to and was frequently used by the Commonwealth Secretary for entertaining. After the conversion of Admiralty House, the Commonwealth Secretary was also normally allocated a suite, which because of its central position was a great convenience.

CHAPTER 4

The Issues

Rhodesia

During the 1960s Rhodesia occupied more of the time and energies of the CRO than any other single subject. As Kashmir in the previous decade had marked the concern with Asia, so Rhodesia symbolizes the later preoccupation with Africa. Except for a short period in the 1960s (during the existence of the Central African Office), Southern Rhodesia was throughout the responsibility of the Office (originally the Dominions Department, later the D.O. and then the CRO). The problem facing the Office in the 1960s was not new; rather it derived from and was accentuated by factors from the past.

In the first place, the territory was unique both in status and in its history. It had been acquired by Cecil Rhodes by methods which, to say the least, were dubious; it had thereafter been administered by the BSA Company until in 1922 it was formally annexed to the Crown as a self-governing colony (with some powers reserved to the Crown). Never had it been administered by the British Government; never (apart from the Governor who was nominally Commander-in-Chief) had the British Government maintained any of their own servants whether in administration, the armed services or police; a High Commissioner was first appointed in 1951 but he had solely diplomatic functions. This historical fact with all its psychological implications became important when the British Government were urged to use force to impose their will. Any force could only come from outside – and would have been resisted.

The second factor was that Southern Rhodesia had in practice been accorded virtual Dominion status by the British Government and been encouraged in feeling a sense of independence. In 1922 when Rhodesia's future was settled by a referendum, the British Government accepted the verdict of the electorate though it was virtually confined to the European minority. No question here of consulting the inhabitants as they were pledged to do before transferring the High Commission Territories to the white minority Government of South Africa. Subsequently the D.O. in all practical matters, if not formally, equated Southern Rhodesia with the Dominions; a High Commissioner was appointed in London; the P.M. regularly attended meetings of the Imperial Conference and the D.O. appeared to take a passive line in not withholding assent from reserved legislation. The special status of Southern Rhodesia was emphasized by the fact that its affairs were handled by the D.O. whereas Northern Rhodesia and Nyasaland were the responsibility of the C.O. One could well speculate whether things might have turned out differently if Southern Rhodesia had been dealt with by a Department imbued with a sense of trusteeship for African interests rather than one concerned with developing a partnership with the Dominions of settlement.

The third legacy from the past was that of the Federation. The idea of amalgamation, at least between Southern and Northern Rhodesia, had been in the air since 1930 and had a strong appeal for the Europeans. The idea was revived after the war and at first found favour with the Labour Government, though later some had doubts owing to the growing opposition of African opinion. Owing to the change in Government, it was left to the Conservative Government to bring the Federation into being in 1953. Federation was in many ways an inspiring concept; it began under favourable auspices and soon proved its success in the economic sphere, enabling the construction of the Kariba dam with important results for industrial development in both Rhodesias and sharing the wealth of the whole with Nyasaland. Federation with its association of different races was seen as a means of preventing Apartheid spreading across the Limpopo and there was brave talk of partnership between European and African. But it came too late – with the rapidly rising tide of African nationalism and little sense of urgency in making up for lost time. The plan was perhaps doomed in any case. The fundamental difficulty was that there was no reconciliation between the rival doctrines of 'paramountcy of the African' and 'rights of civilized men'. The Federation was an institutional nonsense joining a self-governing territory with two dependent territories governed by a Metropolitan power.* Federal Ministers were in fact always suspicious of C.O. plans for advance in the North and always sought to apply the brake. The Africans sensed this and this was a main element in their 'almost pathological' hostility to Federation mentioned in the Monckton Report.† This dilemma posed a problem for the British Government which they never succeeded in overcoming. There was no unity either in their policy at home or in its execution overseas. There was no agreement on the key question of whether the Federation was to develop a genuine unity between the three territories or whether it was to be Southern Rhodesia writ large: and events were allowed to take charge with no decisive lead. Symptomatic of the British ambivalence was the con-

---

* The Bledisloe Commission had concluded as long ago as 1938 that 'any attempt at federation between Governments enjoying such different measures of responsibility and in such different stages of social and political development would not in our opinion achieve success. The wide disparity between them constitutes a fundamental objection to any scheme of Federation'.[1]

† The Macmillan Government appointed a special commission under the chairmanship of Lord Monckton to consider the constitutional position of the Federation.[2] Its report was published in 1960: this expressed qualified optimism about the future of the Federation, but faced the facts of African hostility and recommended that the possibility of secession should be accepted.

tinuing authority of two separate Departments, the CRO being responsible for the Federation as a whole and also for Southern Rhodesia, with the C.O. remaining responsible for Northern Rhodesia and Nyasaland. On the crucial question of policy, the two Departments, with their different history, tradition and outlook, were divided. They were divided not only in Whitehall where their differences could always in the last resort be resolved by the P.M. or at Cabinet level; they were also dangerously divided in the field. Had the British influence been thrown whole-heartedly into the effort of making the new system work, things might have been otherwise. But this was not so; many officers in the Colonial Service in Northern Rhodesia and Nyasaland felt that the Federation was not in the best interests of the Africans and encouraged an atmosphere that was hostile to cooperation. On the other hand, the establishment of the capital in Salisbury and the attitude of some European leaders lent colour to the accusation that the Federation was a take-over by the European minority. Yet in this developing conflict, on the spot the British High Commission had no authority either over the Federal Government or over the Territorial Governments.

In the early years, it was still possible to hope that the Federation would fulfil its promise. Economically, the larger unit with a common market prospered; development proceeded apace and the prosperity of Africans (as well as Europeans) increased rapidly. The generous concept of a multiracial University came to fruition. Qualified Africans had the vote for and were elected to the Federal Parliament, two being appointed junior Ministers. The prospects for advancement for Africans were improved and some of the harsher aspects of the colour bar were banished. But the reforms did not go far enough and were not fast enough. Africans in the two Northern Territories remained suspicious. Instead of the two sides becoming reconciled in the wider association, they were farther apart than ever, with the Africans becoming more articulate and active. It was a time of crisis; the fire lit in the Congo could not easily be contained, there was unrest in Northern Rhodesia and rioting in Nyasaland; relations between the British Government and the Federation Government became strained to the point where there was a complete breakdown of confidence. It was not clear whether the Federal idea could be sustained at all and if so, in what way. In this atmosphere, the continuance of the dual control in London acted as a serious brake on policy. The friction* between the two Departments

* The disagreements between the two Departments were fundamental and did not depend on individual Ministers. In 1958 Macmillan wrote in his diary[3] ... 'the C.O. and the Commonwealth Office are at daggers drawn'. The Ministers were then Home and Lennox Boyd. Two years later, over the issue of Banda's release, he wrote:[4] 'For a few days it looked as if I should be faced with the resignation of one or other' – Home and Macleod. The difficulties became still more acute later when Sandys and Macleod were both negotiating in the area of their different responsibilities at the same time. They also existed between Sandys and Maudling; Macmillan commented wryly that Macleod 'is not an easy colleague' but added on Maudling's appointment 'had I thought that there would be some relief in the pressure from the Colonial Office, I was doomed to disappointment...'[5]

not only imposed a heavy strain on relations between them, but involved the P.M. personally and the Cabinet as a whole in far too frequent efforts to bring about a reconciliation. In these circumstances Macmillan decided that the time had come to end duality;* he appointed R. A. Butler (then Home Secretary) to be in charge of a newly created Office and to be responsible for Central Africa as a whole, with the title of 'First Secretary of State'. The Central African Office, set up in March 1962, took over all the responsibilities previously exercised by the two separate Departments in relation to the Federation and its constituent Territories. It was a small unit composed of Mark Tennant (from the Ministry of Labour who had been Secretary of the Monckton Commission) assisted by officials mainly from the CRO and C.O., notably Metcalf (CRO and previously High Commissioner) and Duncan Watson (C.O.).†

In spite of the many achievements of the Federation and, as if to mock the professed objective of fostering partnership between the races, the Federation left a legacy of ill-will, suspicion and hostility. It is one of the tragedies of this unhappy story that Welensky who inherited the mantle of Huggins and was P.M. of the Federation for most of its history lost confidence in British Ministers. There was plenty of bigness of heart about Welensky, he was no extremist and no racialist; he had his own rough feeling for the African and he was genuinely attached to the Commonwealth idea. But he continued to fight his old battles against the C.O. to the detriment of giving a lead in opening up the new opportunities which Federation presented. A series of incidents embittered him and he regarded the Monckton Report with its recommendation that the British Government should announce its willingness to consider a request for secession as a betrayal of assurances which he had received from Macmillan. The fact was that both the Northern Territories were by now straining at the leash to achieve independence on their own on the basis of African majority rule. After tense negotiation with frantic objections from Welensky, agreement was reached with both. At the same time Southern Rhodesia realizing that the Federation could not go on was reconciled to its dissolution, counting on securing her own independence. In the event, with Butler employing all his skill and resourcefulness, the Conference at Victoria Falls in June 1963 which had threatened to be so difficult and acrimonious, reached complete agreement and the Federation was dissolved on the last day of 1963. Butler had left the Central African Office shortly before and it came under Duncan Sandys;

* Macmillan described the situation in his autobiography: 'The last two years had shown me that with all the loyalty that Conservative Cabinets can generally command, the system [of dual control] made the conduct of affairs almost impossible. Moreover, quite naturally, all the local notabilities took advantage of this now obsolete division of power, and it became impossible to conduct negotiations without accusations of lack of good faith or conflict of policies'.[6]
† Butler paid tribute to the 'remarkable capacities for work of Tennant and Watson'; 'in all my long experience of government office I never benefited from better briefs.'[7]

in the spring of 1964 it was wound up and absorbed in the CRO.

There was one other important effect of Federation. The whole effort for advance (inadequate as it may have been) was concentrated on the Federation. When the Federation collapsed, Southern Rhodesians woke up like Rip van Winkle to find that the world around them had moved on irrevocably while for them nothing had changed. In fact the earlier regimes in Southern Rhodesia under Todd and Whitehead gained a reputation for liberalism, but the pace ignored what was happening in the rest of Africa and, so long as the main concern was focused on the Federation, little pressure was brought to bear on Southern Rhodesia itself. In 1961 however Duncan Sandys forced the adoption of a new constitution; this did not go very far but it was a marked advance and for the first time gave significant representation (15 seats out of 65) to Africans. It was originally accepted by the African nationalist parties and it was overwhelmingly endorsed at a referendum. There seemed some hope of success. But there were ominous signs; the African nationalist parties withdrew their support; Africans failed to register and only a small minority took advantage of the right to vote. The Constitution was also opposed by what appeared at the time to be an insignificant break-away group of Europeans under Ian Smith.

The real dilemma arose in 1964 with the dissolution of the Federation and the promise of independence to Zambia and Malawi. The Europeans in control in Southern Rhodesia held tenaciously to certain propositions, not all of which were unreasonable in themselves: they argued that Southern Rhodesia should at least inherit the status of the dissolved Federation and they claimed with more emotion than logic that the adoption of the 1961 Constitution at British request and their acquiescence in the break-up of the Federation entitled them to expect formal recognition of their independence;* in any case it was unthinkable to them that full independence would be granted to the former dependent Territories in the Federation and yet denied to them who had enjoyed self-government for over 40 years. They added a further more dubious, but even more deeply felt argument – that the Europeans had been responsible for developing the country, that the Europeans alone had the skills to administer it, that government must remain in 'civilized' hands or chaos would ensue, as they were persuaded had already happened in African countries to the North.

The African case on the other hand was quite simple – and morally unassailable. Their view was that they were in the overwhelming majority and had the same rights as other Africans to be able to manage their own affairs, that it would be unjust to grant full independence to a minority and

---

* Field (S. Rhodesia P.M.) claimed that Butler offered independence to Southern Rhodesia before the Victoria Falls Conference. The story is not accurate and is strongly denied by Butler;[8] but Butler was a master of the oracular statement which was capable of different interpretations and it is possible that the misunderstanding was genuine.

that the British Government had a duty to prevent this from happening.

This, in essence, was the clash which confronted the British Government in 1964 – and was to remain unsolved for so long. It is a clash between two sides, each of which at the outset had a strong case in principle; with the years, the gap between the two widened and each side pressed its case in more extreme terms.

For their part, the British Government sought throughout to promote a settlement which would meet the reasonable needs of both sides. They insisted that advance for the Africans must be guaranteed, but equally that there could realistically be no question of an immediate transfer of power. They shared the African viewpoint that there could be no grant of independence without the acceptance of prior conditions. The world had changed since 1922 when the constitution of Southern Rhodesia had been settled without consulting the views of the African inhabitants and in that time the CRO had learnt to treat independent Black Governments on the same footing as the White Dominions. They looked for progress by stages as had been the case in former Colonial dependencies, including of course the East and Central African territories all of which had a sizeable number of European residents. But they were prepared for the process to be gradual. (It is significant that whereas, before the break-up of the Federation, there was a continued and successful effort in Northern Rhodesia and Nyasaland to search for solutions to constitutional advancement which both the African leaders and Federal Ministers would accept, no comparable effort was made with the Africans in Southern Rhodesia after they withdrew acceptance of the 1961 Constitution.) They were equally insistent that the grant of independence was the responsibility of the Parliament at Westminster and that they had a duty to pay heed to African interests; they were clear that any unilateral act would have to be resisted.

The essential, prime conditions for independence were first expressed in Butler's time at the Central African Office; they were spelled out by Duncan Sandys, with Douglas-Home's approval, in 1964; they were taken over by the Labour Government and Wilson subsequently added a Sixth Principle.* In general there was broad agreement between the political parties

---

* Macmillan recorded in 1963[9] that Field and his colleagues seemed to think that they could maintain Commonwealth preferences, British investment and all other advantages of the British connexion even if they moved to independence on their own. He 'made it quite clear that they must be told that they could not "have their cake and eat it". If they became rebels they would be treated as rebels.'
The five principles called for
  i) unimpeded progress to majority rule
 ii) guarantees against retrogressive amendment of the Constitution
iii) immediate improvement in the political status of the Africans
iv) progress towards ending racial discrimination
 v) independence to be acceptable to the people of Rhodesia as a whole.
Wilson added
vi) guarantees to the minority after majority rule against exploitation by the majority.

in Britain. The last act of the Conservative Government on the very day of the General Election in 1964 was to refuse to send observers to an indaba which Ian Smith (by then Prime Minister of Southern Rhodesia) proposed as a means of testing African opinion. It was characteristic of Duncan Sandys that he insisted on sending the reply at once instead of leaving it over for whoever might be in charge on the following day. On their defeat, Conservative Ministers agreed, on the advice of officials in the Cabinet Office and the CRO, that all correspondence about Rhodesia could be shown to their successors. This was a very exceptional arrangement and emphasized the bipartisan approach to the problem. The Labour Government, inevitably committed by the undertakings of their predecessors, willingly carried them out and, on the occurrence of UDI, put in force the policy of economic sanctions. Later, when there was general dissatisfaction at their apparent ineffectiveness and Wilson sought to tighten them, differences came to the surface and some, but not all, Conservatives opposed their extension. Yet despite occasional bitter skirmishes in Parliament (stirred up by extremists on both sides) a remarkable degree of bipartisanship was maintained throughout.

Within the British Government policy was decided at the Ministerial level centring on No. 10 and executed at the official level based on the CRO. After UDI, while decisions were taken by the Cabinet when necessary and when important questions of policy were concerned, the effective work was performed by a small, ad hoc group of varying membership under the P.M.'s chairmanship; this met irregularly whenever summoned by the P.M. The Committee consisted of the senior Ministers chiefly concerned and other Ministers as required. The Cabinet Secretary acted as Secretary and, as an exceptional arrangement, the PUS, CRO, regularly and other officials sometimes were invited to attend.

The official machinery was comprehensive, highly streamlined and ensured that action by all Departments in Whitehall was closely co-ordinated. At the top was a small, high-powered Steering Committee, nominally under the Chairmanship of the Commonwealth Secretary though in practice the PUS invariably took the chair. The members were the Cabinet Secretary, the PUSs in the Treasury, Board of Trade and other Departments concerned, including when necessary a representative of the Chiefs of Staff and of the Intelligence Services. It was the function of this Committee to make recommendations to Ministers on all matters of policy, including the formulation of general strategy and the supervision of existing policies.

Secondly there was a much larger Committee of officials from all Departments concerned with sanctions against Rhodesia, under the Chairmanship of the Minister of State at the CRO. It was the function of this Committee to supervise sanctions, both in matters of policy and in the day-to-day operational details. At the time of the imposition of sanctions, a special

Committee was set up to co-ordinate all action in relation to the imposition of sanctions; this was under Treasury Chairmanship specifically at CRO request, since the Office while wishing to be represented felt that a Chairman from an economic Department would be more effective in securing action from other Government Departments. There was also a number of sub-committees to deal with various particular matters, such as publicity (the BBC erected a station in Botswana), aid to Zambia, evasion of sanctions.

There was thus a close link between Ministers and officials. Moreover Wilson was punctilious in bringing CRO officials into consultation, in encouraging them to produce ideas and in giving them his full confidence when they were called upon to conduct what were sometimes extremely delicate negotiations. It is probable that officials from the CRO were more closely and effectively involved with Wilson over Rhodesia than with any other P.M. or over any other subject. The degree of cooperation between Ministers and officials was unusual in Whitehall, though it occurred in other forms in the early days of Wilson's premiership. Nevertheless the two elements did not at all times think in the same dimension; the official Committee sought to formulate a long-term strategy, but was sometimes taken by surprise by the immediate tactical moves initiated without advance notice in the Ministerial Committee* and wondered occasionally whether more attention was not paid to publicity rather than policy and to scoring off the opposition more than Smith. But the Rhodesian problem was an exceptionally difficult one – Wilson himself believed that no British Government had ever had to face a 'problem so complicated or so apparently insoluble'.[10] As he frequently made clear, he had 'four constituencies' to consider – Rhodesian opinion, opinion in Britain, the view of Commonwealth colleagues and world opinion, as expressed particularly in the UN. He himself denied that domestic political considerations swayed his judgement, but they were inevitably one of his constituencies, particularly as the Labour Government had a bare majority in Parliament until the election in 1966.

There is a depressing similarity about the various negotiations that took place over the years, with their juggling over the techniques of constitution-mongering: electoral rolls, 'blocking' percentages, constitutional safeguards, voting qualifications. In any case the events are now a matter of history and have been amply recorded in public statements at the time, official documents and, more recently, memoirs by some of the main participants.[11] What

---

* It was not altogether surprising perhaps that at a meeting of the Steering Committee the following was passed to the Chairman:

> In dealing with Southern Rhodesia
> The machine is in danger of seizure
> Instead of just 'steering'
> We're constantly veering –
> Which doesn't make Garner's task easier.

follows is an attempt to describe how the various facets of this business were seen at the time by officials in the CRO.

In general, officials in the CRO sought for a solution that would be acceptable broadly both to Europeans and Africans. This meant pursuing a middle course, refusing alike to countenance either indefinite continuance of minority rule or immediate application of majority rule. When therefore UDI was declared, though inevitably there were varying shades of opinion among the staff of the CRO, none sided with the Smith regime or was in favour of recognizing independence without any conditions. Most went along readily with what became official policy, though some were sceptical of the likely effectiveness of sanctions.

Before UDI

Before UDI the main objective of policy in the CRO was, by persuasion and threats of the serious consequences, to prevent UDI from taking place; if nevertheless it was proclaimed, the second objective was to act with such effect that there would be a revulsion of feeling in the territory leading to the overthrow of the regime and its replacement by a government of moderates. Both the Governor and other well-placed observers were convinced that, if only the British showed that they meant business, loyalist opinion would rally and that there would be a popular demand for a change. In particular they urged that leaders in the judiciary, in the armed services, in the churches would be reluctant to support an illegal regime and would exert a strong influence. Many of those most experienced in politics – Malvern, Welensky, Tredgold and others – were emphatic that Smith was a man of straw and did not have the support to lead the country into rebellion.

In the light of subsequent events as they turned out, the prospect of bringing about a change seems to have been based on a complete miscalculation at least in any short term. Whether another result might have been achieved if things had been handled differently cannot now be proved. The fact remains that, on the occurrence of UDI, thinking in the CRO, relying on what it considered to be the most experienced local information, was based on the possibility of replacing the illegal regime.

It fell mainly to the CRO to prepare contingency planning in the event of UDI and detailed steps were worked out under a committee in the Cabinet Office which met under Snelling's chairmanship. It was the CRO which pushed through this Committee the idea of sanctions without illusion about their effectiveness by themselves and sometimes against strong opposition from the Board of Trade.

UDI

Immediately on the declaration of independence,* the series of steps which had been planned in advance were put into effect. The Foreign Secretary flew to New York and introduced a resolution in the Security Council. Sanctions were imposed. The Governor received instructions from the Queen to dismiss his Ministers. Legislation was passed through Parliament declaring that Southern Rhodesia continued to be part of HM's dominions and the British Government and Parliament had jurisdiction and responsibility; the Act suspended the Ministerial and legislative system in Southern Rhodesia; it enabled H.M. by Order-in-Council to make provision for Southern Rhodesia and empowered a Secretary of State as well as the Governor to exercise executive authority. These provisions in the event remained a dead letter; they were strongly criticized at the time and caused much offence in the Colony. But it was necessary to mark the 'rebellion' in terms of international law and to provide for all eventualities – for example an appeal from the Governor to preserve law and order. It was also hoped that steps of this kind would bring home to Rhodesian opinion the seriousness of the action taken.

The British High Commissioner (Jack Johnston) was at once withdrawn, but a residual Mission was left behind in charge of the DHC who was first Stanley Fingland, later replaced by John Hennings. Since the British Government did not recognize the illegal regime and the Mission was therefore precluded from any direct dealings with the Government, the position was not only anomalous but also disagreeable for the incumbent. It was however important to have someone at hand to keep in touch with and advise the Governor and, at a later stage when officials came to Salisbury for 'talks about talks' it was valuable to have a post which was able to handle all arrangements and conduct communications. A residual mission for Rhodesia was also for some time retained in London.

Use of armed force

Officials in the CRO would have been prepared to recommend the use of armed force in response to an appeal from the Governor to assist in the preservation of law and order; but such a situation never arose. Nearly all members of the Office were opposed to the unilateral use of armed force, though one or two individuals would have favoured a display of force, if only to the extent of sending a ceremonial guard to support the Governor. Bottomley on a tour of West Africa made it clear in reply to questions before UDI that Britain would not resort to force. He was much criticized for this

* 11 November 1965.

but it would have been dishonest to prevaricate and in any case an implied threat would have rebounded when the Africans realized that it had never been intended.

Sanctions

Since armed force was ruled out and surrender to the regime was politically unthinkable the CRO favoured the use of economic sanctions; it regarded them as the only credible means of bringing pressure to bear on the European minority. It was not possible to make any thorough assessment in advance of the likely effectiveness of sanctions, not least because the Board of Trade and other Departments refused to commit themselves beforehand to effective sanctions (particularly on tobacco). The CRO relied more on the threat of sanctions and the anxiety that would be caused by their effect in the long term and hoped that the totality of the steps taken would succeed in bringing about a change of heart in Rhodesia. The CRO therefore from the beginning favoured the imposition of sanctions, not with the objective of ruining the Rhodesian economy but in the hope of provoking a situation in which the regime would be compelled to yield to a moderate government. In the event sanctions were brought in piecemeal; this tended to cushion the shock and did not constitute the hard-hitting blow which many Rhodesians had advocated. It is also now clear that the firm line against the regime taken in British Government statements was often counter-productive; instead of rallying opinion, they alienated it. By the time mandatory sanctions were imposed at the end of 1966, European opinion had already hardened and resentment was only increased.

Sanctions having failed in their immediate objective, the issue then was what action should be taken. Since the two extremes of the use of military force and of capitulation continued to be ruled out, there seemed no alternative to continuing sanctions for, in effect, a different purpose – by a long haul to bring sufficient pressure on the regime to induce it to make concessions. The effect was likely to be mitigated by assistance in sanctions-breaking from South Africa and Portugal, but this policy inevitably involved an attempt to bring real hardship to Rhodesia; the CRO engaged on this task with no joy; as time went on, it was clear that even if sanctions were not likely to achieve their objective in a short time, they were undeniably slowing down the Rhodesian economy and preventing further development. The effect of sanctions was undoubtedly a major factor inducing the regime to seek a settlement; the closing of the oil pipe line from Beira in early 1966 for example had a part in bringing Smith to agree to what were called the 'talks about talks'. In general it is perhaps fair to claim that Ministers, above all the P.M., were consistently inclined to be more optimistic about how

393

effectively sanctions could be made to work than officials, particularly over the oil sanction* and over mandatory sanctions.

United Nations

The CRO had always regarded Rhodesia as a British problem and resisted attempts at interference from outside (though in recent years the British Government had been willing to make a statement to the CPM Meeting about dependent territories and had allowed discussion to take place about Rhodesia). Nevertheless with UDI, the matter became an international one and, if sanctions were to be applied, then the only way of securing compliance by all countries was through the UN. The CRO agreed that it was right for the British Government to refer the matter at once to the Security Council† and to propose a resolution providing for sanctions. They were distressed to discover that the British initiative met with nothing but abuse from virtually all members of the Afro-Asian group (including nearly all Commonwealth members in the group) and the Communist bloc. Nevertheless the British draft was eventually accepted and the resolution became the basis for international action.

Different considerations arose when the British Government proposed mandatory sanctions in December 1966. Since this arose from an undertaking given at the CPM Meeting, there was no alternative to carrying out the action, when the 'Tiger' talks failed and the time limit expired. The CRO however were concerned at the position which might arise later if after an acceptable settlement the British Government wished to remove sanctions, since there was a risk that, unless the Council agreed, they would be unable to do so without infringing a Security Council resolution initiated by themselves and which they had specifically required to be mandatory.

---

* The oil sanction was decided upon by the British Government in December 1965 while Wilson was in the US. The P.M. secured President Johnson's approval (for without the cooperation of the USA it would have been futile) and subsequently supervised its adoption by the Security Council. It was in a sense his brain-child and he deserves full credit for pushing it through against the more cautionary attitude in Whitehall. At the same time, because he took an almost proprietary interest in it, he was tempted to exaggerate its effects.

This was most noticeable at the Lagos Conference. In his book[12] Wilson explained that this phrase 'weeks not months' was based on advice that the oil sanctions and the closing of the Beira pipe-line would bring the Rhodesia economy to a halt and that there was reason to believe that Portugal would not challenge the determination of the UN. It was also based on the understanding that South Africa would allow only 'normal' supplies (i.e. limited to the previous rate) to be sent to Southern Rhodesia. These certainly were the hopes at the time, but they were not based on any firm evidence available to the CRO, though some officials in the Treasury were optimistic in their forecasts. CRO officials were completely taken by surprise when the statement was made. It proved of course a turning point at the Conference.

† The decision to refer to the UN was acted upon with such speed that the author went to bed on the night of 10 November 1965 with his bag packed to fly to Salisbury with the Commonwealth Secretary and awoke to receive instructions to fly to New York with the Foreign Secretary.

NIBMAR

The most important occasion when action taken at the Ministerial level bore no relation to advice that had been submitted from the official level was the decision of the P.M. (who had received authority from the Cabinet to act at his own discretion) to concede the principle of NIBMAR at the CPM Meeting in 1966. This was something that had been sought by African leaders since 1964 and it had always been resisted by the British Government. It was resisted initially with no less firmness by Wilson at the Meeting in 1966; indeed his refusal to accept it had been the main reason for Nyerere refusing to come to the Meeting. After an exceptionally acrimonious discussion extending over days, the point was finally conceded. This gesture saved the Conference – and may indeed have saved the Commonwealth. This is the sort of political decision that only Ministers can take. And it is important to see the decision in the context in which it was viewed by Ministers at the time. Wilson only conceded NIBMAR and mandatory sanctions conditionally.* In his own mind what he had secured was a three-month delay during which he hoped, with the threat of this action impending, that he would be able to reach a settlement with Smith. In fact he very nearly succeeded; it was a gamble – but a gamble that did not come off, when Smith was unable to secure his Cabinet's approval of the 'Tiger' proposals. CRO officials, who disliked mandatory sanctions for the reason already given, were still more unhappy about NIBMAR. In their view, it could lead to only one of two results, each of which was undesirable: either independence was granted at once with majority rule, in which case chaos was likely; or Rhodesia would return to dependent status for a period which would not be acceptable either to Europeans or Africans in Rhodesia and would have placed the British Government in a most invidious position. The NIBMAR commitment was contrary to all statements of British Government policy in the past – and even after the 'Tiger' talks, it was kept off stage in the subsequent discussions with Ian Smith, on 'Fearless' and in Douglas-Home's proposals in 1972. Moreover it served only to harden the resolution of the Europeans to stick it out till the end, since for them it was the equivalent of a demand for unconditional surrender.

Negotiations with Ian Smith

CRO Ministers and officials were constantly involved in the series of discussions that took place over the years – in 1965 before UDI there were

---

* That Wilson considered he had only conceded NIBMAR and mandatory sanctions conditionally is clear from his own account. In reply to George Brown's question: 'You conceded NIBMAR, I take it,' Wilson replied that he 'had not and told him of the three months' plan'.[13]

visits by Bottomley and the Lord Chancellor, and by Cledwyn Hughes (Minister of State), the discussions with Smith in London and the subsequent visit to Salisbury of the P.M. (accompanied by the Commonwealth Secretary and Attorney General and a large team from the CRO). After UDI, a visit by Bottomley after the Lagos Conference to Rhodesia was planned but called off because of the conditions imposed by the regime:* Duncan Watson and other CRO officials engaged in the prolonged 'talks about talks'; there were two visits by the Commonwealth Secretary (Bowden) and a series by Morrice James leading up to the talks on 'Tiger' in 1966. The third Commonwealth Secretary, George Thomson, went to Salisbury in the following year and again in 1968 after the inconclusive results of the talks that year on 'Fearless'. None succeeded in breaking the deadlock.

No man could have done more to avert the clash than Wilson did in October 1965 in Salisbury. He did not spare himself, but devoted himself for a full week, working hard every day until after midnight, to dreary repetitive discussions with Smith and his colleagues, yet always patient, tolerant, making his points with skill and clarity and taking care to inform himself in detail of all the matters that came up. He contrived to find time for a series of interviews with all sorts of people, representatives from the Church, University, judiciary, all political parties, business, editors, servicemen and civil servants, the Asian communities, Nkomo and Sithole (whom he brought together from internment for the first time in years) and Native Chiefs. At the end of an exhausting week, before departure he delivered a moving and eloquent broadcast, which obviously had an appeal to many in Rhodesia. All this made immense demands on his stamina, yet throughout he showed freshness of mind, resourcefulness, imagination.

Smith is an exceptionally stubborn and suspicious person, afraid to concede anything and living in a strangely blinkered world. All this makes him difficult to negotiate with and no British Minister or official succeeded in reaching a lasting understanding with him. Yet, at the start, there was a degree of mutual respect between Smith and Wilson. Smith was emphatic that he appreciated Wilson's directness, since he claimed that he knew where he stood; and in Smith himself there was evident a rugged if narrow patriotism and even some feeling for the England he had known during the war. Events as they unfurled lessened the respect each had originally felt

---

* Bottomley proposed two visits which did not take place. Immediately after taking office in October 1964 he attended the Zambia Independence Celebrations; he offered to visit Salisbury but made it a condition that he should be allowed to see the African leaders than in detention; Smith would not agree. Subsequently after the Lagos Conference he planned to visit Salisbury. In his book, Wilson states that Smith had reacted to the proposal by saying that Bottomley 'could go to Salisbury – but only as a private citizen. Above all he would have no security protection.'[14] This was only part of the response: Smith's answer was that the visit would be welcome but that Bottomley must either come officially in which case he would be met by the appropriate Minister or privately in which case no facilities would be provided. The first was unacceptable to the British because of their stance on recognition.

for the other and distrust between them grew. One possible reason for this is that Wilson may have underestimated the effect of his own personality on Smith's conduct. He was after all supreme as a tactician in the House of Commons, he was a Minister of long and wide experience on the world stage and he had ready gifts of wit and repartee. Ian Smith was no possible match for him and was painfully aware of this. He was therefore determined not to be trapped and for this reason, it may be suspected, refused to enter into an immediate commitment and sought to withdraw even when he had been pressed into doing so. This gave rise to an impression of dishonest dealing on his part which may have been due primarily to his sense of inferiority.*

Throughout the time of his Premiership, Wilson took personal charge of the whole subject of Rhodesia.† He played the hand in his own way and from time to time took officials by surprise with sudden tactical switches and on occasion appeared to over-dramatize his reaction. But, though there were some erratic moments, throughout he stoutly upheld and carried through the main lines of his policy, namely resistance to illegality and injustice, together with readiness to reach, if humanly possible, an honourable settlement acceptable to all Rhodesians.

The European Community

When after the defeat of Hitler and the reconstruction of Europe the question of Britain's role on the Continent was looked at afresh, the CRO fully supported the plans for economic cooperation in Western Europe after the recovery made possible by the Marshall Plan; equally it favoured the defence arrangements facilitated by the Brussels Treaty and NATO; indeed Canada played a key part in encouraging both economic and military cooperation and thus ensuring that the framework was Atlantic rather than Continental. But the CRO, with its sights set on the new Commonwealth, while supporting any move intended to strengthen Britain and enable her to continue to play a leading part in Commonwealth development, was opposed to any closer integration with Western Europe, particularly if the goal were to be political or economic union. The Office was not called upon to fight on this issue in the early stages since, under both Attlee's and Churchill's leadership, British policy looked askance at too close a British involvement. As the

---

* Even so there was no excuse for Smith's assurance to Morrice James in Salisbury that he had 'full and unequivocal powers to settle' from his Cabinet (an essential condition of the invitation for discussions) and his subsequent denial of this on board 'Tiger'.[15]
† George-Brown later commented 'I always had a feeling that had one then had stronger political heads at the C.O., Rhodesian developments might well have been less personalised than the P.M. made them and would have developed differently.'[16]

collaboration of the Six gathered momentum and promised to be successful, the question of British association arose again, but the solution first
advanced by the Macmillan Government – that of association in an industrial
Free Trade Area – by the exclusion of agriculture kept at bay serious
opposition in Commonwealth countries and did not provoke any anxiety
about political unity. After prolonged, if somewhat desultory probings, it
became clear by 1959 that such an arrangement was not acceptable to France
and would not be practicable. Meanwhile the Common Market prospered
and the issue became whether or not Britain should apply for full membership. So vital a matter gave rise to a host of difficult problems – political,
constitutional, economic, financial – and there were many imponderables.
Eventually the Macmillan Government took the decision that, on balance,
full membership would be in British interests; they accordingly made an
application and entered into negotiations to see what derogations from the
Treaty of Rome could be agreed to satisfy the circumstances of Britain, with
her Commonwealth and other interests.

This decision raised crucial problems for Commonwealth countries for,
however successful any negotiation might be in securing concessions, it was
clear that the traditional pattern of intra-Commonwealth trade based on a
preferential system could not be maintained for long and it was feared in
many Commonwealth countries that Britain's accession to a European
community would inevitably lessen in the long run the strength of her links
with the Commonwealth.*

This situation faced the CRO with what was potentially one of the most
explosive and embarrassing issues with which it was called upon to deal, since
there was the possibility of a direct clash between British interests and the
interests of other Commonwealth countries. While initial reactions by
Commonwealth Governments were often hostile and sometimes expressed
with a vehemence that took little account of British interests or susceptibilities,
the situation fortunately never reached the acute point where it became one
of a straight choice between the two. In the first place, the British took
unusual pains to consult with other Commonwealth Governments; they kept
throughout in the closest possible touch and showed themselves in the
negotiations with the Six ready to press legitimate Commonwealth interests
strongly. In particular before the formal decision to submit an application
was taken by the British Cabinet in 1961, special Ministerial missions were
despatched to Commonwealth countries (the most significant being that of
Duncan Sandys as Commonwealth Secretary to Canada, Australia and New
Zealand). In 1962 the CPM Meeting was largely devoted to the single issue
of the British application. When negotiations were undertaken, they were
conducted on the British side by Heath (Lord Privy Seal) who gave an

* In his autobiography Macmillan wrote about Europe: 'Certainly the Commonwealth aspects of the
problem overshadowed all other – politically, economically and above all emotionally.'[17]

account of all Ministerial meetings not only to Commonwealth represent-atives in Brussels but also to Commonwealth High Commissioners in London; in these he made it clear that he was fully alive to Commonwealth interests and indeed was having some success in seeing that their points were met. Moreover after meetings of officials, Commonwealth representatives in Brussels and the Commonwealth High Commissioners in London were kept fully informed each week (normally by Lintott or Bottomley).

In the event, matters did not come to a head at that time since de Gaulle put a stop to further negotiations in 1963. The veto gave rise to renewed talk of the Commonwealth as an alternative. Macmillan lost little time in scotching this, making clear that the Commonwealth could not be a single economic unit in the sense of any other trading community. For this reason he saw no value in an immediate CPM Meeting, though he agreed that trade between Britain and Commonwealth countries must be extended and he proposed a conference of Commonwealth Trade Ministers. In the main however, the Government looked for a growth in trade to the so-called 'Kennedy Round' of tariff negotiations under the GATT and to the development of EFTA. When the Labour Government in their turn made a second application in 1967, they equally made it clear that agreement depended on satisfying essential Commonwealth interests, but the general situation had already changed and, in the intervening years, many Common-wealth countries (and notably Australia and Canada) had diversified their trade and made themselves less dependent on the British market.* It was left to the Heath Government to carry these negotiations to a successful conclusion in 1972. The end of the matter is therefore outside the compass of this book, but the dénouement confirmed that, in the event, Common-wealth interests were broadly satisfied; by then the passage of years had taken much of the heat out of the problem; trade patterns had changed and Commonwealth opinion had had time to adjust.

Inside the CRO itself there were changing attitudes towards the question of British participation, reflecting the change in circumstances surrounding the problems of British entry. By instinct and tradition, the CRO was dis-posed to be distrustful of European commitments and opposed to any steps which might adversely affect Commonwealth relations or even be thought by other Commonwealth Governments to be likely to have that result. By the end of the 1950s, the view in the F.O. had changed and officials there

* British membership of the European Economic Community was always likely to affect the three old Dominions far more seriously than other Commonwealth countries since they stood to forfeit their advantages in the British market not only over manufactures, but over agricultural products and in some cases to be subject to a reverse preference. There was never any prospect of obtaining substantial con-cessions for temperate foodstuffs and New Zealand faced ruin if the British market was lost; in the event New Zealand was recognized as a special case. The developing Commonwealth countries on balance stood to gain from British membership; indeed Nigeria and other African countries lost no time in negotiating preferences in the Community under the arrangements for association.

were by that time ready to contemplate full membership by Britain. This readiness was not shared in the CRO at so early a date. At this time too, voices in the Board of Trade and in the Treasury were being raised to deplore the failure of Commonwealth countries to take a larger share of British trade and to complain over the erosion of Imperial Preference by Commonwealth Governments; the CRO, while painfully conscious that Canada and Australia notably could have done more to help British trade, nevertheless took the view that much of the talk was exaggerated and that a large part of the blame for the sluggishness of Commonwealth trade lay with Britain herself and the performance of British industry. The CRO however often found itself in close alliance with the Ministry of Agriculture which had its own reasons for objecting to full membership, because of the provisions of the Common Agricultural Policy of the Common Market. Until the early 1960s, officials in general in the CRO were not convinced of the advantages to Britain of joining the Common Market and their attitude at that time could at most be described as negative; but the situation changed. The most important factor in bringing this about was the arrival of Duncan Sandys as Secretary of State. Sandys had from the end of the war been a convinced European and saw it as one of his main tasks to carry Common-wealth opinion if (or, as he would have hoped, when) Britain joined the Common Market.* Officials did not take easily to this new shift. With one exception, none of the senior officials in the CRO was enthusiastic about British entry and some were strongly opposed. The most convinced opponent was Algie Rumbold, DUS on the economic side. On the issue of the Common Market, he was by no means alone in the attitude he took, but he felt more strongly than others; it soon became clear that the differences between two such determined characters as Rumbold and Sandys could not be reconciled and that Sandys would not agree to leave the questions of Britain's entry into the Community in the hands of someone so opposed to his own ideas. The arrangement was therefore made in 1961 that, while Rumbold remained in charge of all other matters on the economic side, Lintott (the other DUS) was made responsible for questions affecting British entry. Lintott had joined the CRO in 1956 with the rank of DUS; he went on in 1963 to become High Commissioner in Canada. He had spent most of his official life in the Board of Trade, but significantly had been seconded to serve with OEEC in Paris where he had been Deputy Secretary-General for eight years before coming to the CRO. Lintott had already had five year in the CRO by the time the British application was made and had

* Macmillan sent Sandys a note after his appointment as Commonwealth Secretary. In addition to calling attention to the growing dangers in Africa – his first major task – this pointed out that the second great question was the problem of the Commonwealth relation to Europe. Macmillan concluded: 'I am not satisfied that there is not a way to be found [of] getting over the Commonwealth difficulty. If you could put your acute and active mind to the study of this you would be doing a great service. It is perhaps the most urgent problem in the Free World today.'[18]

developed great sensitivity for Commonwealth susceptibilities. But his previous experience had also involved him closely in European collaboration of which he was a convinced but never a blind supporter; while he never pushed matters to extremes, his air of detached elegance hid the application of an acute and agile mind; moreover his sympathetic handling of staff had won him a strong position in the Office.* All this helped him to bring balance into the approach of the Office to the problem of Europe and the Commonwealth. Under his guidance, officials in the CRO adapted themselves to the requirements of Government policy and devoted their energies to endeavouring to secure in the negotiations at Brussels whatever modifications were possible to meet legitimate Commonwealth requests. Lintott accompanied Sandys on his tour to Canada, Australia and New Zealand in 1961 and was the CRO representative in the powerful team of officials which handled, under Heath's directions, the negotiations in Brussels. Throughout the negotiations resulting from the application in 1961, the Treasury took the lead in Whitehall (in the later application of 1967 the F.O. tended to take the lead). Co-ordination in London was effected by a Steering Committee of officials, chaired by Frank Lee, Permanent Secretary at the Treasury. He was a determined and indeed aggressive advocate of entry into Europe; but he had worked much with Commonwealth officials in his various capacities in the past and was sympathetic to their problems. It may also have helped the process of Whitehall cooperation that Garner who attended the Committee as the CRO representative happened to be a close personal friend of Lee.

When the negotiations were resumed under the Labour Government in 1967, Jim Bottomley (who had been with Lintott on the previous round) represented the CRO in Brussels; the discussions made slow progress and did not present any new difficulties for Commonwealth interests; the negotiations were not completed until after the CRO's separate existence came to an end. When Britain finally acceded to the Treaty in 1973 there continued to be some controversy about the terms, including the effect on Commonwealth countries. The terms were 're-negotiated' by the Labour Government; there was general agreement that the essential interests of Commonwealth countries had been safeguarded and, at the time of the referendum in 1974, all Commonwealth Governments expressed themselves in favour of British membership.

---

* In his autobiography,[19] Chandos said of Lintott: 'He was rapid and clever, knew my prejudices and methods of working, and had a happy sense of humour allied to a certain disenchantment with his fellow-men.' He added: 'Harry Lintott in earlier life had been described by a gushing Chelsea lady in these terms: "My dear, I've got a wonderful new friend: he looks like the drowned Shelley and is something in the Customs".'

Indo-Pakistan relations

India and Pakistan continued sorely at odds; the Kashmir issue remained unsolved; with the passage of years India became only more determined to retain what had cost her so much effort and Pakistan only more embittered and frustrated. A dangerous feature was that, as India turned to the USSR for support, so Pakistan began to look to China. In general British diplomacy exercised a moderating and benign influence in India and Pakistan for twenty years after independence, nevertheless the strength of that influence inevitably began to wane with a new generation taking control that was no longer familiar with British ways. Britain herself partly limited the extent of her influence also by her attitude of impartiality which prevented a whole-hearted commitment to either side. There was moreover a series of problems which acted as irritants in the relationship. On the Pakistan side there was the constant accusation that Britain did not give the support to Pakistan which the moral justice of her case demanded and that Pakistan's membership of SEATO and CENTO did not ensure the loyalty of her allies on which she had counted. On the Indian side, matters were more complicated. There had been resentment in Britain over the strong Indian reaction to Suez (not accompanied by parallel denunciation of the Soviet invasion of Hungary) and the talk of leaving the Commonwealth. The accusation of the adoption by India of double standards became stronger and drew all the more force from some of India's own actions, above all in December 1961 her seizure by force of Goa. A further cause for concern in Britain was the increasing reliance of India on arms and equipment from the USSR. But then in 1962 occurred an event which made a dent in India's policy of non-alignment and for a time brought about a transformation in the relations between Britain and India. After the early honeymoon period, relations between China and India had deteriorated; the Chinese had built a road to Ladakh and made extravagant territorial claims; there were consequent fears in India of a threat to Kashmir and of Chinese ability to furnish support to Pakistan. There had been constant border disputes; suddenly in 1962, owing to a combination of Chinese toughness and Indian bungling, the Chinese attacked, overwhelmed the ill-prepared Indian forces and seemed poised to descend on the plains below. After a display of force, the Chinese, having taught India a lesson, in fact withdrew. But India had received a traumatic shock; in her first panic she had appealed for aid and the Western Powers – including Britain, the USA, Australia, New Zealand and Canada – had readily responded. Britain in particular provided substantial quantities of arms and was ready to give undertakings about the provision of air cover. Sandys seized the opportunity of this assistance to exert pressure on India to settle her problems with Pakistan. In a concentrated negotiation conducted by the Commonwealth Secretary in Delhi and Rawalpindi, Sandys brought all his influence to bear; the discussions often became tense, but in the end Indian intransigence could not be overcome.

One of the diplomatic problems at this time was the need to concert action with the Americans, who were specially important as the main suppliers of economic aid. The Americans remained alarmed at the threat of Chinese expansionist policies and sought to strengthen India; at the same time they resented, even more than the British, India's reliance on the USSR (particularly for MIG fighters) and they (and also Menzies) were disturbed about the position of Pakistan, an ally in SEATO. They were more inclined than the sceptical British to the view that progress on Kashmir might be possible if India could be made to feel secure against China. For all these reasons the Americans showed more agitation than the British and would have favoured stronger intervention than the British in their caution felt to be necessary. The ultimate aims of British and American policy were in complete harmony but there were often strong differences as to how these could best be achieved; these differences came to a head particularly when Sandys was in India at the same time as George Ball, the very determined US Under-Secretary of State. Eventually Britain and the US agreed to send fighter squadrons to India for training and liaison purposes. The British did not make their supply of military equipment or promise of air cover conditional on the settlement of outstanding differences with Pakistan but they left no doubt of their concern or of the difficulties which help on the scale provided created in their relations with Pakistan.* Eventually with US support, the British succeeded in arranging direct talks between Nehru and Ayub. These took place in 1964, but led to nothing.

In 1965 there was a further dispute between the two countries to which the British Government, largely on the initiative of the CRO, was instrumental in finding a solution. A clash arose over the Rannof Kutch, a desolate area to which both sides could lay plausible claim, and hostilities broke out. The legal complexities, as in the case of all matters in dispute between the two countries, were formidable; but with perseverance and imagination CRO officials, led by Rumbold and Pickard, worked out formulae in consultation with the British High Commissioners (Freeman and James) who kept in close touch with both Governments. Eventually Wilson was able to propose a solution (providing for an international tribunal in default of agreement) that was accepted by Nehru and Ayub. Unfortunately this success was short-lived. Within two months, there was renewed fighting in Kashmir and in September 1965 India, determined to deter the Pakistan forces from crossing the cease-fire line, herself crossed the international frontier in the

---

* *See* for example Macmillan's message to Nehru of 23 December 1962.[20]

Punjab with heavy armour. This caused intense international excitement since the thrust appeared to be aimed at Lahore. The British Government felt that in this serious situation they should make a strong appeal to both parties and, on the advice of the CRO, Wilson despatched personal messages in very similar terms to Shastri and Ayub. He also released a public statement about the messages which he had sent. This was taken in India as a condemnation of them and caused great offence;* as a result relations between Britain and India were strained so long as Wilson remained P.M. In fact, having achieved their objective of posing a threat to the Pakistani forces, the Indians did not advance further. The UN Security Council succeeded in obtaining a cease-fire and eventually the two parties came together under Soviet auspices at Tashkent and agreed on a withdrawal of forces and restoration of relations. It is arguable, in spite of the bad blood caused between Britain and India, that Wilson's forthright action achieved its purpose of bringing home to both parties the seriousness of the situation they were heading for and was one of the factors which helped in the negotiation of the armistice; it certainly made it easier for Pakistan who would have otherwise smarted under a sense of defeat.

Other Issues

It is not possible to cover all the problems with which the Office had to grapple, but some which showed it in an unusual light deserve perhaps a glance. There was the strange confrontation with the Maldive Islands in 1964 when Duncan Sandys, concerned that Britain's defence rights had not been fully secured, declined to confirm an agreement which had already been negotiated; the islanders, suspicious, adopted a hostile attitude, though they were not able to upset the operation of the RAF base at Gan. Lengthy negotiations conducted separately by the Duke of Devonshire and by Snelling led to nothing and though a frigate was despatched Britain seemed powerless to impose her will. A new agreement was eventually negotiated by the Labour Government in the following year. There was Sandys'

---

* This was the statement[21] to which Wilson referred in *The Labour Government*. The actual wording in the statement was: 'I am deeply concerned ... at the news that Indian forces have today attacked Pakistan territory across the international frontier in the Punjab. This is a distressing response to the resolution ... by the Security Council.'[22] Wilson's book stated that 'C.R.O. officials ... inveigled me into issuing ... a statement ... condemning India for an act of aggression. I was wrong in all this ... I had been taken for a ride by a pro-Pakistani faction in C.R.O.; it did not remain there for long.' In a subsequent TV interview[23] Wilson while maintaining that it was a mistake on his part to accept the advice recognized that he must take the responsibility which he did; he also accepted that in his references to officials he had 'been unfair' and that in mentioning the 'faction' not remaining for long he had in mind one official 'who was due to retire with honour' (*see also* letter from Sir Algernon Rumbold to *The Times* of 5 August 1971).

personal involvement in the establishment of Malaysia (comprising Malaya, Singapore and the Borneo Territories); when in 1963 Indonesia and the Philippines sought to prevent the Federation coming about, Sandys flew out to ensure that it did;* he succeeded, but Sukarno found the excuse for the foreign diversion he wanted; in the so-called 'confrontation', Indonesia carried on a guerilla struggle which required a major effort by British forces and was not finally overcome until 1965. There was the disturbing business of the mutinies which occurred in 1964 in Tanganyika, Uganda and Kenya; each Government in turn made a request for British troops which, on Sandys' insistence, were promptly despatched; they rapidly overcame the mutiny in each country with no British casualties. The Office was in instant and direct radio-telephone communication with the three High Commission posts† and much of the credit for the speed and smooth working of the operation was due to Walsh Atkins who was in charge. The success of the British action received much acclaim, but in the East African territories it was not long before the feelings of relief and of gratitude were replaced, for understandable reasons, by those of humiliation and resentment. Later, in the bitter atmosphere of hostility between Greek and Turk in Cyprus, one of the most exacting tasks for any High Commissioner was the unending search, often in circumstances of considerable danger, for a means of bringing the two sides together.

---

* Macmillan, in an apt choice of words, records that 'Sandys, with unrelenting persistence, went himself to Malaya to give encouragement to the Tunku.'[24]
† Sir David Hunt (High Commissioner at the time) has described the incident in detail in his book.[25]

CHAPTER 5

The Merger with the Colonial Office and Foreign Office

We have already seen some of the difficulties which the CRO experienced in the early years of this period with the C.O. on one side and the F.O. on the other. The situation was made more uncomfortable for the CRO because in each case it was the primary target for criticism. In Parliament, in Whitehall and in the Press, it was alleged that the CRO was ineffective; in particular that it failed to make use of the expertise of the Colonial Service and that it did not work closely with the F.O. Critics fastened on the fact that so many of the top posts overseas went to outsiders and some deduced from this that the CRO staff must be inferior.[1] The most vocal critic on this (as well as on other scores) was Humphry Berkeley (then a Conservative MP).* Another persistent critic was *The Times* which made much of the lack of communication between the CRO and F.O. in matters affecting Africa. *The Times* implied that a single authority would be preferable and became a strong advocate of merger. But the most widespread criticism was directed against the CRO's objection to taking on to its staff former members of the Colonial Service.

As early as 1957 Callaghan, recently appointed spokesman for the Labour Party on Colonial matters, expressed in Parliament his lack of confidence in the CRO and compared it unfavourably to the C.O.; he was to revert

---

*Humphry Berkeley conducted a campaign in Parliament in 1961 designed to show the failure of the CRO to seize the opportunity to employ former members of the Colonial Service in the new High Commission posts in Africa. In the course of a debate in November 1961,[2] he asserted that he had found a very real difference in quality between F.O. representatives in Africa and the CRO representatives: the latter he regarded as 'markedly inferior' and he found it 'quite staggering ... that we should have diplomatic representatives in our C.R.O. missions who are inferior as undoubtedly and demonstrably they are.' This unsubstantiated opinion drew a stinging rebuke from Duncan Sandys (then Commonwealth Secretary) who, replying to a subsequent Parliamentary question, stated that the remarks 'cast the gravest asperions on the experience and quality of the staff of the C.R.O. ... [and] have been deeply resented by the Service' and he concluded that he had 'the highest confidence in the capabilities of those serving at home and overseas in the service of my Department'.[3]

to the charge.* In 1960 the Conservative Political Centre issued a report[6] recommending amalgamation between the CRO and the C.O. on the grounds that the existing division was out of date. On this issue too, *The Times* repeatedly urged† the need to continue, under the changed circumstances, the help previously provided by the C.O. Commenting on Humphry Berkeley's campaign in 1961, *The Times* concluded magisterially 'The fact that such a fast-expanding department can see so little merit in the Colonial Service, is so touchy and yet gets quite a lot of its talent from outside is odd. There seems to be a case for enquiry.'[10]

On the main issue of providing for former members of the Colonial Service, the CRO had a perfectly good case. The total number of those serving in HMOCS‡ in 1961 was over 4,000; the total diplomatic staff in the Commonwealth Service was 160. There never was any possibility that the CRO could take on more than a handful and in fact in that year some 32 former members of the Colonial Service were employed under the CRO.[3] There was also substance in the CRO case that former members of the Colonial Service were not necessarily the most suitable candidates for a diplomatic posting in a newly independent Commonwealth country; particularly as, not unnaturally, they frequently wished to continue serving in the territory which they had previously administered. Unfortunately the CRO was sometimes inept in putting the case across and gave the impression that it regarded with hostility the idea of colonialism and the men who had been responsible for operating the system. The rule in the Home Civil Service (of which the CRO was still a part) was that candidates for appointment to the permanent staff were required to sit the appropriate Civil Service examination; this was applied even to senior members of the Colonial Service; it gave great offence. More damaging still was the justification given in public by CRO spokesmen. In 1960 speaking to the Royal Commonwealth Society, Alport[11] said that independence must be and must be seen to be real and urged that it was right to make the moment of independence 'a clean break

---

* In a debate on 6 May 1957[4] Callaghan said: 'The C.R.O. is not one of my favourites. It never seems to me to be much more than a post office and ... to have a purely negative conception of its relationship to the Commonwealth as a whole.' He thought that there should be a fresh look at the relationship between the C.O. and the CRO and their staffing; he would like to see the CRO injected with a little of the 'vigour, energy and positive conception that undoubtedly inspires the C.O.' He reverted to this theme over the years, referring in 1960 to the 'absence of any bold, adventurous and challenging lead from the C.R.O.'[5]

† As early as 1957 a *Times* leader entitled 'New Methods Needed'[7] urged that it was essential to devise machinery by which the help traditionally afforded to Colonial territories through the C.O. could continue to be provided and called for readjustments in Whitehall. Two years later they asked 'What can be done to keep the C.R.O. abreast of this rapid constitutional movement'[8] and insisted that drastic reorganization was called for. Later that same year they published an article by Professor Carrington on familiar lines 'How to improve the C.R.O.'[9]

‡ The Colonial Service had been in existence for over a century. With the progress towards independence and the need to make provision for officers continuing to serve the government of the new State, 'Her Majesty's Overseas Civil Service' (HMOCS) was set up in 1954. It was largely a change of name.

with the Colonial past'. Answering Humphry Berkeley in Parliament a year later, Bernard Braine[12] made the point that, within the Commonwealth Service, too great a degree of geographical specialization in the affairs of either Asia or Africa would not only create undesirable rigidity but eventually throw up at the top senior officers whose experience based only on one part of the Commonwealth would not contribute to the effective discharge of the Commonwealth Service's wider responsibilities. It might perhaps have been foreseen that expressions of this kind would raise the blood pressure of Colonial Governors and senior officials in the C.O.

Colonial Office

At the crucial stage of the dismemberment of the British Empire there were thus factors causing sensitivity both in the CRO and in the C.O. and tension between them. The CRO, assuming heavy new responsibilities, was keen to respond to the challenge in a tolerant and enlightened way and laid stress on the changed atmosphere in the new Commonwealth. It felt itself to be a progressive Department with an exciting future and regarded the C.O. as in decline, prone perhaps to dwell on past glories. There was some element of disdain in the CRO attitude – not dissimilar from the earlier attitude of the F.O. towards the D.O. As George Thomson, speaking from the Opposition benches in 1960,[13] put it: 'When the CRO referred to what it called the C.O. people, it was using the tone of an anthropologist discussing a backward tribe with somewhat backward rituals.' The staff of the C.O. were equally sensitive. They felt that they had honoured their trust to the dependent peoples; moreover they looked with pride on what they considered they had achieved; under pressure for decolonization at a pace faster than anyone had contemplated, they had succeeded in steering countries through periods of tensions and sometimes violence towards an orderly transfer of power; despite all the strains, they had also maintained not merely good relations, but often relations of close friendship with those they helped to independence. They could not therefore understand the desire of the CRO for a 'clean break'; they regarded this as divorced from reality and involving an absence of continuity in developing fruitful relations. In any case the fact that the C.O. was working itself out of a job had an inevitable effect on staff since they saw their responsibilities contracting without any assured future in their careers. Events in the early sixties brought about changes in attitude on both sides. In the early stages at least, most of the wooing came from the C.O. side; the advantages of a marriage were less apparent to the CRO, embarrassed rather than attracted by the dowry.

The relationship between the CRO and the C.O. was examined by the

Select Committee on Estimates in two successive years. The Committee's Fourth Report[14] published in 1960 was devoted to the C.O. It tackled the relationship between the two Departments and came out strongly in favour of merger. It recognized that there would be opposition and primly reported that 'broadly speaking, the witnesses from the C.O. and the independent witnesses favoured the proposal, whereas witnesses from the CRO were less sympathetic.' It tabulated the main arguments, not unfairly, as follows:

Arguments against a merger
  1. The functions of the Offices are different.
  2. In some fields a merger between the C.O. and F.O. would be more appropriate.
  3. The burden of work would be too great for one S. of S.
  4. A merger would be unacceptable to other Commonwealth countries.

Arguments for a merger
  1. There would be a net economy.
  2. It would assure the future of the staff of the C.O.
  3. The CRO would gain correspondingly.
  4. The functions of the two Departments have close affinities.
  5. There are disadvantages in the use of the term 'Colonial Office'.
  6. The transition of dependent territories to independence would be facilitated.
  7. It would ease many economic and technical problems during the transition to independence and afterwards.
  8. It would provide for unified representation of independent countries and dependent territories in the international economic field.

The Committee rightly found little substance in the first three objections and regarded the fourth argument as the strongest one against merger – namely that independent Commonwealth countries would regard it as a reactionary step because it would associate them with a Department exercising direct responsibilities for the Colonies. The Committee attached 'great importance' to this argument, but their considered conclusion in the light of evidence given to them was – curiously enough – that the difficulty was almost wholly one of presentation; they were convinced that, given sufficient thought and care, it should be possible to secure the concurrence of the other independent members of the Commonwealth. They accordingly recommended in favour of a merger, that the step should be taken at once if the full advantages were to be obtained, and that the new Department should be known as the Commonwealth Office and should be administered by a single S. of S.

The Government reacted cautiously to the recommendation in favour of merger. Macmillan, while promising to consider the Select Committee

Report, did not 'underrate the difficulty of combining independent and dependent territories in a single Office'[15] and, in a debate on the Report, the Colonial Secretary (Macleod)[16] announced that in the Government's view the time had not yet come for a merger. Six years elapsed before the Select Committee's recommendation was adopted. In the meantime a number of developments took place which helped to take the heat out of the problem of C.O. staff transferring to the CRO and encouraged closer organic links between the two Departments. The most significant was the Government's decision to act on a proposal (originally put by Poynton to the Select Committee and endorsed by them) that technical aid should be handled on a functional basis, applying to all territories both independent and dependent, Commonwealth and foreign. The Department of Technical Cooperation (DTC) set up in 1961 took over the technical assistance work previously performed by the F.O., CRO and C.O. The staff was seconded from these three Departments, the majority coming from the C.O. Answering questions in March 1962,[17] Macmillan claimed that the removal of appropriate parts of the CRO and of the C.O. and other Departments to form a functional task in the DTC represented a stage 'on the way to what will ultimately come – a single Department – as the dependent territories become very small and almost of minor importance'; but he still insisted that 'although the day will come when the two Departments will be amalgamated ... at the present state of development of the Commonwealth' such a move would be 'misunderstood ' by the independent Commonwealth countries.

The DTC had a substantial impact on the developing relations between the CRO and C.O. For the first time since 1925 there was now an organizational link and some of the affairs of independent and dependent territories were handled in the same unit. More important was the effect on the staff, particularly in the C.O., since many who were reluctant to undertake to serve abroad could now transfer to a Department which seemed to offer an assured future in Whitehall. In 1964 the Ministry of Overseas Development (ODM) took over the functions of the DTC and was made responsible for aid generally. The new Department offered greatly improved prospects of employment for C.O. staff in an office with more prestige than its predecessor and it reduced still further the scope of the work in the C.O. itself. Another departmental reorganization bringing the CRO and C.O. together was the establishment in March 1962 of the Central African Office. The two Departments were also brought closer by the appointment in July 1962 of Duncan Sandys (then Commonwealth Secretary) to the portfolio also of Colonial Secretary; he held the two posts until the fall of the Conservative Government in October 1964. When the Labour Government came in, separate Ministers were again appointed and continued up to and indeed beyond the date of the final merger. All these developments helped to encourage the idea of closer association between the two Departments. The C.O. was shedding its responsibilities at a rapid rate and it was clear that in a few years its business would be confined to dealing with a miscellany of small islands and special territories. The responsibilities of the CRO continued to grow. In this atmosphere, the C.O. lost many of its fears about the CRO, which in turn lost much of its disdain. A general feeling grew up among the staff that merger was inevitable and that it would be wise to prepare for it.

Nevertheless the final step was long in coming. The Conservative Government prepared for merger and in fact carried it through at the Ministerial level in October 1963, when all Ministers in the two Departments were assigned to both Departments, their duties being divided on a functional basis. In February 1964 they announced that they intended the merger to take place in July 1965. However in October 1964 they were replaced by a Labour Government and, to the general surprise, Wilson again appointed a separate S. of S. for the Colonies, Greenwood: at the time of this appointment, the P.M. confirmed that it remained the Government's intention to arrange a merger in due course – though he expressed the view that July 1965 would be too soon. To the taunt by Nigel Fisher that the appointment arose solely from the fact that he thought it expedient to appoint two S.s of S. to do the work of one in the previous Administration, Wilson retorted that 'the Colonial Secretary was told on appointment that his job was to work himself out of a job and that is what he is in process of doing.'[18] But it was not to be; when Greenwood left the C.O. in December 1965, he was replaced as S. of S. by Longford and, on the latter's resignation in April 1966, he in turn was replaced by Fred Lee. Indeed the C.O. took an unconscionable time in dying – or, perhaps more accurately, Ministers took their time in killing it off. The C.O. staff were becoming impatient and desperately anxious for some clear decision about their future. There was a particular urgency in that Poynton, the PUS, was due to retire and clearly would not be replaced. He agreed to stay on and finally retired in August 1966, the date eventually chosen for the merger. The enlarged Department took the name of Commonwealth Office, thus neatly incorporating the name of the CRO and the initials of the C.O. The former C.O. was incorporated in the new Commonwealth Office as the Dependent Territories Division; though the geographical departments remained in essence unchanged, the Division was fully integrated in the Office as a whole and only those willing to serve abroad were taken on the permanent establishment of the Diplomatic Service. Nevertheless Lee still remained until the end of 1966 as a separate Colonial Secretary.

The future of the C.O. was not included in the terms of reference of the Plowden Committee and the Diplomatic Service came about in 1965 with no provision made for the C.O. It was helpful however that the C.O. should merge with the CRO, rather than with the larger FCO; the D.O. had grown out of the C.O. and there was something fitting in completing the circle. In the event the smaller merger with the C.O. preceded the larger one with the F.O. by only just over two years.

Foreign Office

The claim of the F.O. to take over some at least of the responsibilities of the CRO had not been settled by the controversy of 1949. Most members of the F.O., officials as well as Ministers, were intellectually persuaded that it was wrong for responsibility for Britain's external policies to be divided and for the F.O. to have no direct influence on relations with Commonwealth countries which were becoming an important factor in world affairs. On the other hand, most members of the CRO, both Ministers and officials, still felt – perhaps emotionally rather than intellectually – that Britain's relations with her Commonwealth partners were quite distinct, deriving from a shared experience and a continued intimacy, and that Britain's interests would suffer if the Commonwealth relationship were no longer treated as something special.

The F.O. however did not press the issue and as late as 1962, Harold Caccia (then PUS at the F.O.) told his newly arrived counterpart at the CRO that, while there had been much talk of a take-over in the past, his own view was that the burden on the F.O. was already heavy enough and that he had no wish to add to it the growing and complex problems of the CRO. Yet within three years a single Service was created and within six years a single Department; what over the years had been stoutly resisted by the CRO was accepted willingly.

Many factors account for the reconciliation between the opposing views which came about in so short a period. First, no doubt, the logic of events asserted itself and adaptation to changed circumstances was seen to be necessary. But a major factor in bringing the two together so readily lay also in the way matters were handled by the Plowden Committee and the fact that their recommendations were seen as bringing benefits to all.

The division of Britain's external relations into separate departmental categories had always suffered from disadvantages; but while the arrangement had been tolerable when the Dominions were few, were content in the main to follow a British lead and did not play a major role in world affairs, the scene manifestly changed when Commonwealth countries comprised almost a quarter of the total membership of the UN, were prominent in international activities, sometimes in opposition to British policies, and were themselves frequently involved in and indeed the cause of major international conflicts. It was a wasteful arrangement that (apart from the relatively small number of staff exchanged) the Foreign Service knew little at first hand of Commonwealth countries and the Commonwealth Service little of foreign countries. The arguments in particular areas were even stronger; if one moved along the coast of West Africa, one was transferred from the jurisdiction of the F.O. to that of the C.O. and then the CRO and back again; this pattern was repeated elsewhere. In the nexus of problems in Southern Africa, the F.O. dealt with South Africa and Portugal, the CRO with Rhodesia, Zambia and Malawi and the C.O. with the High Commission Territories. And many of the major international disputes – Turkish-Greek rivalry in Cyprus, Indonesian 'confrontation' of Malaysia, the Argentine and Spanish claims to the Falkland Islands and Gibraltar, to say nothing of Hong Kong – found the F.O. and the Commonwealth Office responsible for relations with the opposing sides. Nor were the difficulties in this divided control solely theoretical; some were of severely practical importance. At the height of the Congo crisis, it transpired that there was no common cypher between the British High Commission in Salisbury (Rhodesia) and the British Embassy in Leopoldville (Congo) and, until special arrangements were devised, all messages between the two had to be sent to London and there re-encyphered. All these factors assumed greater importance during the early 1960s.

The fact was that the two Departments were increasingly performing the same sort of job; the world was no longer divisible and in many areas it was not possible to disentangle the 'foreign' and 'Commonwealth' aspects; events forced the two Departments into working together. Experience in the job convinced many of the need for a change. A connected factor was that the staff in the two Departments had grown much more alike – the F.O., after the Eden reforms, had lost the image of being 'stripe-panted diplomats' and the CRO, having cut the tie with the C.O., was establishing its own tradition: the younger generation in each Department were indistinguishable from their colleagues next door in a way that had not been true before.

The factor of gradualness was also important; the point was emphasized by the way in which the Plowden enquiry was set up without any precise idea of what would emerge. No one was required to commit himself at the outset; indeed no one was committed in advance to the recommendations in the Report itself. The Report,[19] while recommending the creation of a unified Service, firmly stated that separate Foreign and Commonwealth Relations Offices 'would be retained' and merely expressed the Committee's view that amalgamation of the two Offices 'must be the ultimate aim'. This recommendation was criticized at the time for showing a departure from logic and indeed some lack of courage. But this solution can also be seen as a typical example of British compromise and it was certainly helpful from both a practical and a psychological standpoint. An immediate merger without any intervening period of preparation could have proved a severe shock.

It was easier to accept the concept of a single Service while the Departments remained separate; this interim period gave time for a sense of unity to grow up among the staff and for the idea of merger to develop naturally from within. There were also considerable administrative advantages in working out the techniques of a single Service before facing the major surgical operation involved in a full merger; this was also helpful since, at the time of the establishment of the Diplomatic Service, the C.O. was still a separate Department.

The concept of the Diplomatic Service was finally all the more acceptable since it brought material advantages in the conditions of service. The background was that the Treasury had consistently treated the CRO as part of the Home Civil Service and had refused to concede to them many of the benefits accorded to members of the Foreign Service. There had originally been some justification for this when postings were confined to the temperate white Dominions but, in an increasing number of posts, Commonwealth Service officers were facing similar conditions to their colleagues in the Foreign Service, yet with lower allowances. Some progress (e.g. in educational allowances) had been made, but the CRO was far from having achieved equivalence. Now at a stroke it was offered the full advantages of the improved Foreign Service conditions simply by joining it. The substantial improvement in conditions of service undoubtedly helped to place the whole concept of the new service in a favourable light.

The origin of the Plowden Committee lay in a request by the F.O., in their perennial battle with the Treasury about conditions of service, that the matter should be referred to an impartial, outside body. Big changes often come from little causes and two quite different considerations conspired to enhance the scope of the resulting enquiry and thus to change the history of Whitehall.

The first was that it came to the notice of the CRO that the F.O. were negotiating to set up an enquiry. If overseas allowances were to be reviewed, then it seemed right that the Commonwealth Service should be included; indeed if they were not, then the CRO staff would not be able to count on benefiting from any improvements that might be secured. Though the F.O. had originally treated the matter as a domestic concern of their own, they raised no objection to a wider enquiry and readily agreed that the CRO should be included.

The second consideration concerned Ministerial views in the CRO. When the Plowden Committee was set up, the CRO was under the charge of Duncan Sandys; he himself had spent the early years of his career as an official in the Foreign Office and, as Minister for Defence, had already been responsible for the closer integration of the Service Departments. He was disposed to favour the idea of amalgamation with the F.O., though at the time CRO officials did not. If the matter were to be pressed there would be advantage in a reference to an impartial outside body; the CRO could ensure that their case would receive a full hearing. The CRO officials therefore came to favour broadening the scope of the enquiry. The F.O. and the Treasury, though possibly for different reasons, both welcomed this extension and it received the warm support of Norman Brook. The following were the terms of reference eventually agreed upon:

> to review the purpose, structure and operation of the services responsible for representing the interests of the United Kingdom Government overseas, both in Commonwealth and in foreign countries; and to make recommendations, having regard to changes in political, social and economic circumstances in this country and overseas.

The terms were extremely broad and did not tie the Committee's hands in any way. Plowden was appointed Chairman; he had considerable Government experience in the Treasury, as Chief Planning Adviser and Head of the UK Atomic Energy Authority; he had had dealings with both Commonwealth and foreign governments; at the time of the enquiry he was Chairman of Tube Investments and therefore removed from any battles in Whitehall. Previous PUSs were included on the Committee – Inchyra (F.O.) and Liesching (CRO). The CRO were entirely satisfied that they could rely on Liesching to ensure that no points of interest to the CRO would go by default.

The Committee was not merely eminent in composition, it also set about its tasks in an unusually businesslike fashion. A helpful feature of the Committee's work was that, as explained in the Introduction to the Report, 'throughout we were almost in daily touch with members of the departments most directly concerned.' The special technique of the Plowden Committee was that the detailed work was processed by sub-Committees on which there was full representation from the Departments concerned; in the sub-Committees the various recommendations were hammered out and not formulated until they had been agreed by all concerned; the result was that, when the Committee's full Report was submitted in February 1964, the Government were able to accept it *in toto* and put its main recommendations into effect without delay.

The following were the most significant recommendations.

1. There should be a unified Service to be known as Her Majesty's Diplomatic Service.

2. Separate Foreign and Commonwealth Relations Offices should be retained.

3. Conditions of service should be improved.

4. Various administrative changes should be made.

Diplomatic Service

The Report recommended that the new Service, in addition to the Foreign and Commonwealth Services, should also take in the Trade Commissioner Service. The Department of Overseas Trade had at one time provided staff for both foreign and Commonwealth countries, but commercial work had been absorbed in the Foreign Service when a unified service was established in 1943. Since that date, Trade Commissioners who were members of and responsible to the Board of Trade had served only in Commonwealth countries. The Board of Trade had always refused to contemplate handing over to the CRO its responsibilities and staff in Commonwealth countries; it no longer raised such an objection when the single Service was set up. The change greatly increased the scope and variety of work within the responsibility of the CRO.

The Report also recommended that members of the Commonwealth and Trade Commissioner Services should be given the option either to join the Diplomatic Service as full members or to remain Home Civil Servants. A generous time interval was allowed and the arrangement was of considerable psychological value (though in practice a mere handful in the Commonwealth Service availed themselves of the offer to opt out).

Separate Departments

The Committee's recommendation that separate Departments of State should remain was perhaps their most controversial one. But the arguments were skilfully balanced. The Committee said forthrightly that the division of responsibility was becoming an anachronism and at times of crisis could prove disastrous. They stated that the logic of events pointed to amalgamation and that unified control 'must, in our view, be the ultimate aim'. However they considered that 'such a step could be misinterpreted as implying a loss of interest in the Commonwealth partnership' and concluded 'We therefore hesitate to recommend the establishment of a single Ministry ... at the present time.' Such a verdict bore all the hallmarks of a compromise, but of a typically British variety. In this case instant amalgamation would have been psychologically disruptive to the staff of the CRO; after three years working of the Diplomatic Service they discovered a new identity. Unlike many compromises the Plowden solution enjoyed the best, rather than the worst of both worlds. Those in favour of amalgamation received authoritative endorsement in principle of their case and a virtual assurance that it would come about in due course; those concerned for Commonwealth relations who were opposed to immediate merger equally received endorsement of the importance to be attached to the Commonwealth and an assurance that merger would not be forced immediately. There was no doubt validity in the argument that immediate merger could have been 'misinterpreted' at the time – but when merger took place five years later there was little disposition to cavil. This was because the ground had by then been prepared and circumstances had changed. The short delay proved itself to be undeniably worth while.

Conditions of Service

The improved conditions of service included a variety of matters covering allowances of all kinds and amenities. The terms for staff in the Commonwealth Service would automatically be improved by being equated to those already existing in the Foreign Service; these further benefits were extra and constituted a powerful inducement to join the new Service.

Administrative Changes

The administrative changes concentrated on efficiency and recommended that the authorized manpower should include a reserve of 10 per cent (virtually the only recommendation that was not fully implemented); they also recommended greater attention to training, unification in certain specialist branches and a grade structure which, by abolishing the former overt division into separate classes, was to some extent a forerunner of the later Fulton reforms in the Home Civil Service.

When the Report was presented in February 1964, officials in both the F.O. and CRO advised their Ministers to support the recommendations in the Report and they were accepted without difficulty by the Conservative Government, curiously under the only P.M. of Britain who had been both Commonwealth Secretary and Foreign Secretary – Alec Douglas-Home. The Labour Government who came to power in October 1964 made no change and the Diplomatic Service accordingly came into being on 1 January 1965.

There were inevitably some disadvantages to compensate for the benefits of a unified Service. The major difficulties stemmed from the problems inherent in any large organization. In the CRO, the sense of intimacy and of personal acquaintance were lost, the organization became aloof and more impersonal. Many officers abroad now found that they had never met their correspondents in Whitehall. Old hands in Whitehall, for the first time, were working with people who were total strangers to them. Business was conducted in a more formal manner; this was shown most dramatically in the system of staff appointments. The CRO with its small numbers could afford to operate by informal methods. The normal procedure was for the Establishment Officer to make suggestions to the PUS who might take some private soundings of others knowledgeable, but eventually made a recommendation to the S. of S. solely on his own authority. The Diplomatic Service, by contrast, found it necessary to set up an elaborate system of Boards, consisting of up to a dozen or even more members, staffed appropriately to make recommendations for different grades. The PUS in the CRO had normally known any officer (even if relatively junior) and also his wife; in the early days of the enlarged Diplomatic Service it frequently happened that some members of the Board had no personal knowledge at all of some of the candidates whose names were before them.

The disadvantages were felt far more keenly in the CRO than in the F.O. for two reasons. The size of the new Service made merely a marginal difference to the F.O.; it involved a complete transformation for the CRO. Moreover (though there were some exceptions to this) the F.O. practice was normally followed when the staff were required to conform to a common pattern – in staff organization (i.e. the 'Head of Chancery' system in posts abroad), in matters affecting security, in the adoption of common systems for communications, registration and filing, in arrangements for premature compulsory retirement.

In face of increasing formality, stricter discipline, an obligation to conform to new procedures, there were some early teething troubles and some complaints on the part of CRO staff. But, except in a very few special cases, these difficulties were never serious. They were counterbalanced by the improved conditions – not merely the Plowden benefits, but the better prospects in a larger Service, the opportunity to serve in new and exciting posts and the sense of being a member of a Service with enhanced prestige.

Another important factor was the atmosphere that prevailed in the early days of the Service. Both the F.O. and the CRO felt that what they stood for had been justified. Each was satisfied and there was no sense either of victory or defeat. The F.O. made no attempt to dominate the junior partner and the CRO showed no distrust. This was in itself a good start when each side sought only the success of the Service as a whole and this soon began to be reflected in the staffs of both Offices. It was the deliberate policy of the Administration to arrange as many cross-postings as practicable and this was psychologically important in encouraging a sense of unity to grow up from within.

There were also some fortuitous circumstances which encouraged a favourable atmosphere. Caccia, PUS at the F.O., was appointed the first Head of the Diplomatic Service; but he was already near to retirement and served for barely two months. Garner, PUS at the CRO, was chosen his successor and served for nearly three years. It was perhaps some reassurance to the staff of the CRO (always the more sensitive party) to know that, in these crucial formative years, they were being treated as equals and that their interests would receive full attention at the highest level. By another stroke of chance, Gore-Booth who succeeded Caccia as PUS, F.O., and later became Head of the Diplomatic Service, had served in the Commonwealth as British High Commissioner in India for four years.

Something may also have been due to the example set by those at the top. At times in the past there had been personality clashes between the F.O. and the CRO, both at Ministerial and official level. In the early days of the Diplomatic Service there were none. In particular those with the chief responsibility for the functioning of the Service, namely the two PUSs and the Chief of Administration (who for the crucial early years was Colin Crowe) were, as it happened, all cooperative rather than combative by nature and all made it their business to work together and to reach agreement. Once the Diplomatic Service had settled down and got into its stride, the two separate Departments found that cooperation came more naturally and that a sense of unity between them developed almost imperceptibly. A key factor in this no doubt was the existence of a single – and strong – administrative control which was able to impose its will and command the loyalty of the staff for the good and sufficient reason that it exercised the power and controlled the postings of all. Symptomatic of the new spirit was the amalgamation of the staff associations; the Diplomatic Service Association became extremely active and effective and was a major factor in bringing all staff in the two Departments together. There was no doubt that the Diplomatic Service was flourishing. It was broadly acceptable to Parliament and public opinion, it was welcome in Whitehall and it was widely popular among the members of the Service. Moreover nearly all those working in the Service came to recognize that a Diplomatic Service serving two separate Departments could not be expected to remain permanently and that it would be right to move towards still closer association. Everything pointed in this direction – the logic of the argument, the habit of cooperation that had grown up, the benefits that had already flowed from unification (e.g. in communications) and finally external events, including the attitudes of Commonwealth Governments. There was little sign that, if unification were now to come, it would give rise to the anxieties which the Plowden Committee had foreseen in 1963.*

In 1967 a submission was made to Ministers with the agreement of senior officials in both Departments. This made a firm recommendation that a decision should be taken to plan positively for a single Department and went on to suggest that the important question was When and not Whether. The submission set out the arguments regarding timing, but did not recom-

---

* The views expressed about the Diplomatic Service are those of the author. He is conscious that some former members of the CRO regard them as unduly glossing over the difficulties. He can only state that the description given is as matters appeared to him at the time and he believes his view to be shared by the majority.

mend merger in the immediate future. Accordingly on Garner's retirement in February 1968, Morrice James was appointed to succeed him as PUS in the CRO. In the event, following the resignation of George Brown as Foreign Secretary in March 1968, it was announced that Michael Stewart had been appointed in his place and that the two Departments would be merged in October 1968 when Stewart would be in charge of the single Department as Foreign and Commonwealth Secretary.* This came as a complete surprise.

The precise timing was thus governed by an extraneous matter and was not related to the planning that was proceeding. This had some minor consequences – the time-table for merger was more rushed than had been contemplated and came about at a time when there were changes in the posts held by all the senior officials concerned. Nevertheless though the suddenness of the final move may have caused some untidiness, perhaps it was no bad thing that a clear-cut decision was taken without delay and that the new combined Department started its life with a completely changed leadership at the top.

The need to announce the new incumbent at once meant that the decision to end the separate existence of the Commonwealth Office was taken without any previous consultation with Commonwealth Governments; in fact there was no reaction from them. As we have seen there had from the earliest days been criticism by Dominion Governments of the D.O. and the way it operated; and many had pressed the need for direct contact with the F.O. which had always readily been granted. Over the years any general criticism diminished (though there might always be causes for specific complaint); Commonwealth Governments in general appreciated the services provided by the CRO and welcomed the fact that there was a separate Minister charged with responsibility for relations with Commonwealth countries. The Plowden Committee were undoubtedly right in thinking that the disappearance of the CRO in the early 1960s could have been 'misinterpreted' in some Commonwealth countries as well as in Britain itself – though Commonwealth Governments would not have been in a strong position to protest since by that time virtually all of them combined responsibility for foreign and Commonwealth affairs in a single Department. By 1968 however there had been many developments – the Rhodesian tangle, the establishment of the Commonwealth Secretariat, the growing acceptance of the fact that Britain was likely to join the EEC, above all perhaps the changed ethos of the Commonwealth idea itself; Commonwealth opinion had in the intervening years been prepared and when merger came about, while individual

---

* In *The Governance of Britain*,[20] Wilson explained almost brutally 'For a long time I had it in mind to merge the enlarged C.O. with the F.O. and as soon as G.B. resigned from the F.O. in March 1968 this was announced.'

officials in Commonwealth Governments voiced their concern informally, no Government made any official representations; indeed there was virtually no public protest either in Commonwealth countries or in Britain itself.*

---

*One of those to regret it publicly was Gordon Walker who expressed the view that 'Britain's relations with other Commonwealth countries depend upon treating them as non-foreign and upon conducting her business with them through officials whose speciality this is.'[21]

CHAPTER 6

Retrospect

The separate existence of the Office had a clear beginning and a clear ending. The period lasted just over forty years and during that time the Office performed a function that was unique in history – namely the responsibility for relations with important territories which had ceased to be possessions of the Metropolitan power but were not foreign countries. This was a reflection of the unique character of the British Empire and Commonwealth itself. From earliest days two factors distinguished that Empire from all others, both those of past ages and of the contemporary world. The first was that the Empire had always been one of settlement as well as one of subjugation – and settlement not merely in a few outposts but in vast lands overseas, where the new arrivals did not mix with indigenous peoples but continued a British way of life. The second distinguishing feature, stemming to some extent from the first, was that from earliest days a measure of autonomy was accorded in the lands of settlement; the powers of local assemblies and the development of parliamentary traditions marked a sharp contrast with the centralizing tendency of most forms of imperialism. The American Revolution confirmed rather than contradicted this; it had indeed the effect of reinforcing the move to devolution.

There were always two facets to the work done by the Office. The prime task was to advance the interests of Britain but there was always the parallel responsibility of preserving the cohesion of the Commonwealth (or unity of the Empire as it would have been expressed in earlier days). A frequent criticism directed at the Office was that, in its efforts for the Commonwealth as a whole, it failed to pay adequate attention to the interests of Britain. As has been said, 'one of the major concerns of the CRO, as of its predecessors, was to avoid giving offence to Britain's Commonwealth partners and this meant that its activities were more emollient than dynamic.'[1] The Office was always accused of seeking to defend Commonwealth interests even when these conflicted with British interests. In its last years the CRO was alleged to be dragging its feet over European integration in deference to representations from Commonwealth countries who themselves showed little concern for Britain; of opposing controls on Commonwealth immigration when the numbers were clearly building up problems for the future; of insisting on maintaining a defence burden East of Suez beyond Britain's capacity to maintain. To these were added criticism of misjudgement in assuming that India and Pakistan could be treated like the white Dominions and that the Westminster model could be transplanted to Africa; dominating all was the long unhappy story of Rhodesia, important not so much in itself but for the way in which it poisoned relations between Britain and the African Commonwealth and put immense strains on the association as a whole. (Without those strains, the Commonwealth, the British Government's attitude towards the Commonwealth and even the position of the CRO itself might have been very different in the 1960s.) But as an eminent Australian historian has put it, 'If the CRO comes forward with a cautionary word each time a Commonwealth Government is likely to feel hurt, it is likely to be doing so all the time. But it is not a case for blaming the CRO; it is rather a case for blaming the Commonwealth as such.'[2] The fact is that the existence of the CRO and the way it operated reflected the reality of things as they were seen at the time. Even in the sixties, though perhaps to a declining extent, British Governments of all complexions continued to give special treatment to all Commonwealth Governments and to adopt a special relationship with them; Britain remained the kingpin of the Commonwealth association and was vital to its existence. The British Government's attitude to the Commonwealth needed to be made manifest in its administrative structure; the future of the Commonwealth did not depend on the existence of a separate Department in Whitehall; but it undoubtedly drew strength from it. In so far as the Commonwealth required an administrative organization of its affairs, this was provided – until the establishment of the Commonwealth Secretariat in 1965 – by the CRO, as earlier it had been by the D.O. This general view of things was supported by all political parties and by public opinion. The deference to Commonwealth interests in the 1961–3 negotiations with EEC owed much to the fact that this was a condition of the assent of a large part of the Conservative Members of Parliament. The introduction of immigration control was strenuously opposed by Gaitskell and the Labour Party because it broke faith with the Commonwealth ethos; later defence commitments were justified by Wilson on Commonwealth grounds and the Commonwealth was a major constitutent in his consideration of Rhodesia.

The effect on the Dominions of the establishment of a separate D.O. also needs to be considered. Though as early as the first decade in the century there were embryo sections dealing with external affairs in the P.M.'s Department in both Canada and Australia, there was no diplomatic representation in foreign countries at all until the 1920s (the pace being set by the Irish); separate External Affairs Departments were not firmly established until the late 1930s and diplomatic representation developed on a substantial scale only after the Second World War. The fact is that the Dominions, though they had their own special interests, were not in the earlier stages deeply concerned about foreign affairs as a whole; only belatedly did they acquire the apparatus to formulate or execute separate policies and develop foreign policies of their own (and only occasionally did they express differences from Britain). It was here that the D.O., in carrying out its role of consultation, played an important part in providing a full information service and ensuring that the requirements of Dominion Governments were met. The establishment of the D.O. had two contrary influences on the development of the Dominions: in the first place the D.O. saw itself as the author and guardian of the doctrine of 'equality of status' and encouraged both the sense and the practice of independence (in a way that probably neither the F.O. nor the C.O. would have done); at the same time by providing the services it did, it tended to delay the need for the Dominions to set up their own machinery which might have encouraged earlier the formulation of separate foreign policies. It is possible therefore that the separate establishment of the D.O., while reinforcing the independent status of the Dominions, prolonged the tendency in the Dominions to continue to rely on the Mother Country in the conduct of relations with the outside world.

If it was right to create a separate Department with responsibility for handling relations with independent Commonwealth countries, what were the appropriate moments in time for setting the arrangement up and for bringing it to an end?

The answer about the origin of the separate Department is lost in the historical process. From the very origins of the Empire in the reign of the first Elizabeth in the sixteenth century, the administration of the Plantations was regarded as distinct from the business of diplomacy with the European Powers, though the impact of each gravely affected the other, notably in the rivalry with the Spanish, French and Dutch overseas. Moreover there was no single clear and precise moment when Britain was able to declare that the status of the Dominions had changed from that of Colonies to independent nationhood; rather there were several such moments and an arbitrary date could have been selected at any time during a period of over half a century, from 1867 to 1931 or even as late as 1947. Within this time-span, was there a moment when the affairs of the Dominions should have been recognized as calling for differential treatment from that accorded to dependent territories and what form should that difference have taken?

A case can be made for arguing that the change came about 20 years too late and that, if the British Government of the day had had the foresight to establish the Department in say 1907 the disadvantages would have been few, if any, and the advantages considerable. There is no doubt that such a move would have been welcome at the time in the Dominions; indeed they had asked for it, but were fobbed off with a Dominions Department within the Colonial Office and with an Imperial Conference Secretariat under the control of that Department.

Establishment at an earlier date might have had a strong impact on the

D.O. itself and could have fostered its development. Had a separate D.O. been established in 1907 it would have experienced its formative period while the whole concept of the Commonwealth partnership was being worked out, it would have endured the challenge of the war years and thereby had the opportunity to enhance its reputation and it would have been in a stronger position than the Dominions Department ever was to take the lead in the constitutional discussions at the Imperial Conferences in the years immediately following the First World War. It seems unlikely moreover that, had the separate Office been set up 20 years earlier, Britain would have waited until as late as 1927 before appointing the first political representative in a Dominion. Had there been over a period some representation in the Dominions, the Office in London would have been better equipped to be more effective. The result might well have been that by 1925, the Office would have overcome its teething troubles; it would have amassed a body of experience, it would have been composed of men knowledgeable about the Dominions; it could therefore have established its reputation and spoken with self-confidence. If all this were so, the D.O. might in 1925 have reached the point which in fact it did not achieve until 1949 under Liesching's leadership. In retrospect it can now be seen that the D.O. was largely concerned with fighting for its position in its early years and secured general recognition only after a period.

Had the separate Office been set up earlier therefore, two consequences might have ensued. The first is that it could have achieved recognition in Whitehall earlier and might not have been forced to dissipate so much of its energies in conflict with such old-established Departments as the Treasury and the F.O. and its voice in questions of policy might have carried more authority. The second consequence is that the Office might have adopted a more resolute stance in relation to Dominion Governments; it would have understood their interests better, and could have afforded to be franker and less timorous in dealing with Dominion susceptibilities. The establishment of the Department at an earlier date by 20 years or so might therefore have affected the character of the Office itself and provided qualities of realism, robustness and resolution which were not always manifest in the early years. The consequences are incalculable but they lie wholly within the realm of speculation.

Leaving aside the question of the timing of any change, there can be little doubt that, in principle, a break from the Colonial Office had to come at some point and would have been demanded by the Dominions themselves. As early as 1897 there had been murmurings against the C.O.; in a later period during the process of decolonization in the 1950s it would have been a grave embarrassment if the Department responsible for developing the Commonwealth concept had been identical with the one responsible for maintaining colonial rule. There was on the other hand a case against further fragmentation of responsibility for Britain's overseas interests which might lead to divided counsels, if not dissipation of effort. (Indeed there were later two areas in which complete separation from the C.O. could be seen as a handicap – in Central Africa where both Departments had responsibilities but did not always see eye to eye and in the transfer of power when it would have been an advantage for the Department responsible after independence to have been more directly associated in the run-up to independence.)

If Dominion affairs were to be divorced from the C.O. and not made the responsibility of a separate Department, the only practicable alternative would have been to place the responsibility with the F.O. (There were suggestions from time to time that the P.M. himself should undertake direct responsibility, sometimes in the context of the Privy Council – but in practice this would merely have involved setting up the separate Department in a different form and under different and probably less effective Ministerial control.) But the case against transferring responsibility to the F.O. was, at least until the Hitler war, overwhelming. The Dominions felt themselves to be British and not foreign; they would have resented their affairs being handled by a Department at that time largely absorbed by the affairs of the European continent and would have feared that their interests would receive less attention by the British Government. More positively, relations between the Dominions and Britain covered a number of matters which were special to members of the Commonwealth – the whole issue of Dominion status involving their sovereignty and independence but covering also such links as the common allegiance to the Crown, the common status of British subjects, the jurisdiction of the Privy Council. Even with other items there was a special element of Commonwealth content – defence, trade, finance, migration, communications. These were matters in which the F.O. had no experience and little interest. Such matters loomed large and were of greater interest to the Dominions than foreign affairs. Transfer to the F.O. offered the prospect that the Dominions might be able to exert a greater influence on British foreign policy – but this became a factor of significance in their eyes only in the years of muddle and uncertainty before the Second World War.

The acceptance of India, Pakistan and Ceylon as full Commonwealth Members – with all that was thereby involved both in Commonwealth concepts and in repercussions on international affairs – provided an occasion when the possibility of transfer to the F.O. might have been considered afresh. It is teasing to speculate what might have been the consequences, if this had come about. A merger in 1949 might have benefited the F.O. and possibly British interests as a whole. Because of the divided responsibilities, the F.O. as a rule had no intimate knowledge of Commonwealth countries and no deep appreciation of the Commonwealth. If the F.O. had assumed responsibility for Commonwealth relations in 1949, its own experience of the Commonwealth would have been enlarged and conceivably Commonwealth interests might have played more of a part in the formulation of British external policy as a whole.

The prospect for the Commonwealth itself if the change had come in 1949 is debatable. On the one hand, there would have been some diminution in the expertise and special attention devoted to its affairs; there might have been a lessening in the degree of sympathy shown and perhaps even in the special links. On the other hand it can be argued that the CRO created a mystique out of Commonwealth relations and that, had the more worldly-wise F.O. been responsible, both the euphoria about the Commonwealth in the 1950s and the subsequent disillusionment that set in might have been avoided.

Such speculation is however fruitless, since a merger did not take place until 20 years later and even the F.O. did not ask for it in terms in 1949. In any case the abolition of the D.O. at that time would have run contrary to the spirit of the age. It was because the F.O. demands were seen as inevitably leading to merger that Attlee so effectively quashed them.

Looking at the period as a whole, there can be little doubt that the Office was able to make its contribution more effectively as a separate Department. At the outset it developed its own organization and set up from scratch an overseas arm; it concentrated on defining the new concept of Dominion status and on working out the techniques for consultation and cooperation between partners who were equal and independent. It maintained ceaseless touch with Dominion Governments over the threatening world situation, but avoided pressing them too hard. In the result all (except only Eire) themselves took the decision to join in the war and made an outstanding contribution. Though inevitably the D.O. played a subsidiary role during the war, it had completed its network of representation abroad and was responsible for the machinery, to which many tributes were paid at the time, for ensuring close collaboration in the war effort by all Commonwealth countries. After the war, the CRO developed still further the concept of the Commonwealth with all members being treated on a footing of equality. It seems likely that the solid foundation laid by the craftsmen of Commonwealth cooperation in the previous twenty years eased the entry of the new Commonwealth members; if responsibility had been transferred to a Department without experience of the Commonwealth or belief in the value of the association, the chances of India leaving the Commonwealth would have increased and, without the sense of purpose given by the 'new' Commonwealth, the old Commonwealth might well have atrophied.

Similarly when the time came for independence to be accorded to the former Colonies, the transition from Colonial to independent status in the Commonwealth was facilitated by the accumulation in the CRO of a wealth of experience about the working of the Commonwealth association and its concentration on the task as its single main concern. This was particularly important in the case of the smaller Territories.

In the 1960s many things went wrong. Nevertheless few of them were peculiarly the responsibility of the CRO and things might not have been handled very differently or better by some agency other than a separate Department for Commonwealth affairs. The one decisive change that could have been made would have been for Britain to wind up the Commonwealth after the war or at least to refuse to allow former dependent territories to join as new members. But such a policy was never a practicable alternative; it would have involved a total turning back on the whole of the British tradition, on the aspirations for a new relationship with her partners and on the promises held out for a century; it would have been regarded as incomprehensible in the Dominions, as a betrayal in the dependent territories and would have been unacceptable to all shades of opinion in Britain itself.

One further question should be faced. We have spoken throughout of the CRO as if it were an entity; of course it was never that, though it inherited a tradition and developed its own distinctive ways. It was an amalgam of many different individuals of varying abilities and of varying views – and the personalities in charge and the representatives overseas changed at times with bewildering frequency. Above all there was the subtle interplay of the relationship between Ministers and officials – the transitory politicians alongside the permanent staff. In general, as is no doubt the case in most Departments, Ministers were responsible for initiating policy decisions and officials for providing the machinery to execute them. There were however two features of the Office that were distinctive; the first was that throughout its history there was little difference between the political parties in their approach to most Commonwealth matters. We have seen that there was occasional opposition to a number of matters over the years, nevertheless there was broad harmony between the parties on all major issues – the doctrine of 'equal status' and its implementation, the conduct of the war, the transfer of power in the sub-Continent, the process of decolonization, the special nature of the association and the development of Commonwealth links. Over all these issues there was a broad degree of bi-partisanship and the Office seldom if ever had to make a rapid adjustment to accommodate an incoming political party. The differences between Ministers were in fact far more those of their personalities than of their party affiliations. The second distinguishing feature was that the Office regarded itself as the guardian of a particular system. No doubt all Ministers are to some extent circumscribed by what has gone before, but this was peculiarly the case in the D.O. (and CRO), especially when officials regarded themselves as the high priests of a somewhat esoteric cult. The Dominions Secretary could develop and extend, but he could not rebuild the structure. Nevertheless in the first days Ministers were responsible for providing the impulse and stimulating new ideas. Above all Amery, with the support of his officials, drove through the new concept of Dominion status and all that was entailed in legal and organizational changes. Malcolm MacDonald and Cranborne, in their different ways, breathed new life into the whole manner of Commonwealth consultation. Throughout this period officials, under Harding and Machtig, ensured that the machine operated smoothly but adopted a cautionary line, being more concerned to placate the Dominions than to stir them into action against their will. Nevertheless Machtig's performance was remarkable for the manner in which, with Maffey's assistance, he contrived to keep relations with Eire during the war on a reasonable footing despite Churchill's exasperation.

The ready acceptance of India and Pakistan into Commonwealth membership owed much to Gordon Walker who sought imaginative ways to give meaning to the concept of the new Commonwealth. By this time however the Office, under Liesching's leadership, was becoming a firmer instrument with a larger and more experienced staff with service overseas as well as at home. Later there was the idiosyncratic rule of two Conservative Ministers – Swinton and Sandys – interspersed with the quiet diplomacy of Home. Sandys pursued with his customary doggedness the policy of decolonization but, as has been shown, his methods of work caused friction in some quarters in the Office. Under the succeeding Labour Government, the three Ministers returned to a more normal pattern and in all the troubles that clouded the scene there was an easy relationship between Ministers and advisers; indeed the last Secretary of State (George Thomson) had he been given the chance might well have been in the highest tradition of the past. The work of the CRO can therefore be taken to be the joint product of Ministers and officials together, normally in close harmony, with the officials providing the expertise but the Minister always enjoying the last word when he chose to use it. In major matters of course the Cabinet laid down the policy; but inside the Office the effective decision was taken by the S. of S. and the PUS working together (with the growing complexity of business, the Minister of State and other senior officials increasingly playing their parts). Inevitably, the S. of S. could always prevail on matters of policy, especially when he was confident that he was expressing the views of the Cabinet; but equally the PUS often had powerful arguments, from his knowledge of past occasions, of the load which the administration could bear, of what was likely to be acceptable where other Departments in Whitehall were concerned. Beyond that who, in any discussions between Minister and officials, carried the greater weight and whether it was a harmonious encounter or a contest of wills depended entirely on the character and strength of the individuals concerned; in this the party affiliations and outside reputation of the Minister made little, if any, difference.

Perhaps nothing befitted the CRO better than the manner of its departure.

There was a refreshing readiness to adapt and an absence of any attempt to cling to power or to remain on the stage longer than was necessary. When the proposal for a Commonwealth Secretariat was first mooted, the CRO did not resist it as an organ that would inevitably in some respects usurp functions hitherto carried on within the British Government machine, but viewed such a development not only as inevitable but desirable and foresaw that it had a constructive role to play in the further working out of concepts of Commonwealth cooperation. The CRO welcomed the proposal from the start and cooperated with it closely to enable it to function as effectively as possible.

Similarly the CRO achieved in the 1960s a degree of very close cooperation with the F.O., never previously entertained. The CRO itself took the initiative in asking for its affairs to be included within the Plowden enquiry; it cooperated with the Plowden Committee and accepted all its recommendations. The CRO and the F.O. worked hard together to make a success of the Diplomatic Service and created an atmosphere in which the merger of the two Departments but three years later took place with grace and dignity and in a manner that reflected credit on both parties. If the CRO acted with good sense, the F.O. also showed magnanimity.

To the final question of whether the end of the separate Office came at the right moment, the response can be briefly stated. Though the actual date of the merger into the FCO resulted from a fortuitous change in the Cabinet, and its precipitate announcement caused some administrative inconvenience, there can be no doubt that, within a year or two, the timing was as near right as one can hope to achieve. The Diplomatic Service had been in existence for nearly four years; it had proved a success and itself provided the atmosphere for merger. The problem of the future of the Colonial Office had been belatedly resolved, with its absorption into the Commonwealth Office a year earlier. The Commonwealth Secretariat had been established as a going concern for over three years and had got into its stride. More generally the merger took place at a time when the Commonwealth had survived the worst period of disillusionment and disarray and there was an atmosphere of growing realism. Though there was still scope for Commonwealth collaboration in a variety of other ways, the content of political cooperation among Commonwealth Governments had diminished and the limitations on the Commonwealth were recognized. Just as the separate existence of the CRO reflected the reality of things as they were seen at the time, so its merger with the F.O. matched the change in circumstances and attitudes towards the end of the 1960s. Nevertheless there were still possibilities for Commonwealth collaboration in a variety of ways; the retention of the name Commonwealth in the title of the new Office proclaimed the British Government's continuing commitment to the Commonwealth and their intention to carry forward the work which this book has attempted to describe.

APPENDICES

Appendix A

Organization and Distribution of Work

Table 1 1928

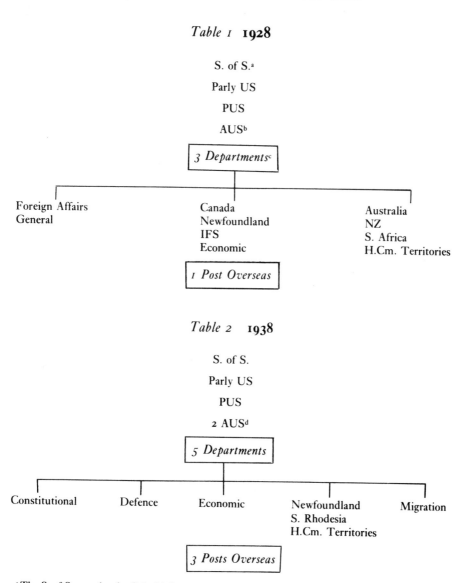

S. of S.[a]

Parly US

PUS

AUS[b]

| 3 Departments[c] |

Foreign Affairs
General

Canada
Newfoundland
IFS
Economic

Australia
NZ
S. Africa
H.Cm. Territories

| 1 Post Overseas |

Table 2 1938

S. of S.

Parly US

PUS

2 AUS[d]

| 5 Departments |

Constitutional   Defence   Economic   Newfoundland   Migration
                                         S. Rhodesia
                                         H.Cm. Territories

| 3 Posts Overseas |

[a] The S. of S. was also the Colonial Secretary until 1930.
[b] The Vice-Chairman of the Oversea Settlement Office was also shown as an AUS on the D.O. staff.
[c] Establishment work was performed by the C.O. until 1946.
[d] A second AUS was added temporarily in 1937 to cover the Silver Jubilee and Imperial Conference.

433

Table 3 **1950**[e]

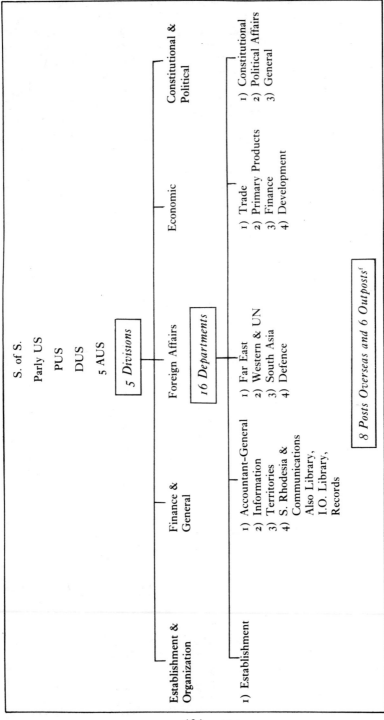

S. of S.

Parly US

PUS

DUS

5 AUS

5 Divisions

Establishment & Organization	Finance & General	Foreign Affairs	Economic	Constitutional & Political

16 Departments

Establishment & Organization	Finance & General	Foreign Affairs	Economic	Constitutional & Political
1) Establishment	1) Accountant-General 2) Information 3) Territories 4) S. Rhodesia & Communications Also Library, I.O. Library, Records	1) Far East 2) Western & UN 3) South Asia 4) Defence	1) Trade 2) Primary Products 3) Finance 4) Development	1) Constitutional 2) Political Affairs 3) General

8 Posts Overseas and 6 Outposts[f]

[e] In 1948 the Office, after the absorption of the I.O., was divided into Divisions A and B. The later date has been selected to show the effect of the Liesching reorganization.

[f] DHC posts were opened in India and Pakistan in 1947 and, on independence, in Malaya and Nigeria. While Information posts were established during and after the war in provincial centres in Canada, Australia, South Africa and New Zealand, the Trade Commissioner posts remained under the control of the Board of Trade until the coming about of the Diplomatic Service in 1965. After that date, the posts in provincial centres came under the CRO.

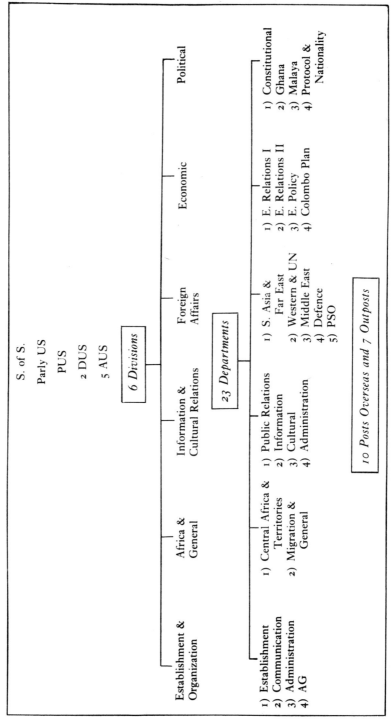

Table 4 **1958**

S. of S.
Parly US
PUS
2 DUS
5 AUS

6 Divisions

Establishment & Organization	Africa & General	Information & Cultural Relations	Foreign Affairs	Economic	Political

23 Departments

1) Establishment	1) Central Africa & Territories	1) Public Relations	1) S. Asia & Far East	1) E. Relations I	1) Constitutional
2) Communication	2) Migration & General	2) Information	2) Western & UN	2) E. Relations II	2) Ghana
3) Administration		3) Cultural	3) Middle East	3) E. Policy	3) Malaya
4) AG		4) Administration	4) Defence	4) Colombo Plan	4) Protocol & Nationality
			5) PSO		

10 Posts Overseas and 7 Outposts

435

Table 5 **1968**

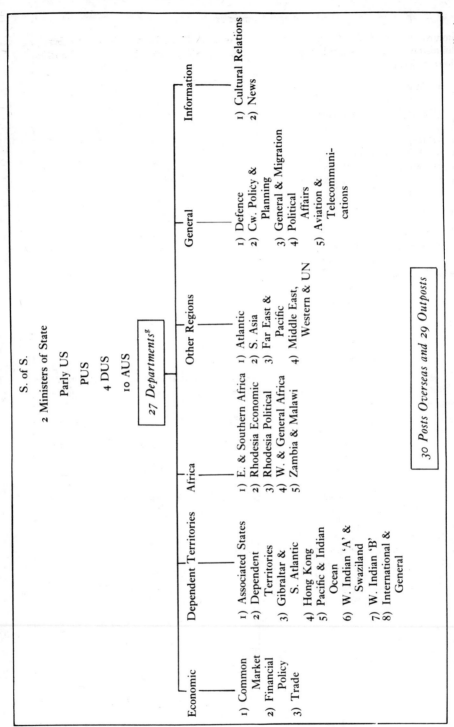

S. of S.

2 Ministers of State

Parly US

PUS

4 DUS

10 AUS

27 *Departments*[g]

Economic	Dependent Territories	Africa	Other Regions	General	Information
1) Common Market	1) Associated States	1) E. & Southern Africa	1) Atlantic	1) Defence	1) Cultural Relations
2) Financial Policy	2) Dependent Territories	2) Rhodesia Economic	2) S. Asia	2) Cw. Policy & Planning	2) News
3) Trade	3) Gibraltar & S. Atlantic	3) Rhodesia Political	3) Far East & Pacific	3) General & Migration	
	4) Hong Kong	4) W. & General Africa	4) Middle East, Western & UN	4) Political Affairs	
	5) Pacific & Indian Ocean	5) Zambia & Malawi		5) Aviation & Telecommuni-cations	
	6) W. Indian 'A' & Swaziland				
	7) W. Indian 'B'				
	8) International & General				

30 Posts Overseas and 29 Outposts

[g]There were no Divisions as such. Supervision of departments was exercised by the 4 DUSs and by 10 AUSs on a basis designed to ensure co-ordination. The departments are grouped above for convenience only.

Administration of H.M. Diplomatic Service was carried out by the Diplomatic Service Administration Office, staffed from both Offices. It consisted of 1 DUS, 1 AUS and the following departments:

1) Accommodation
2) Communications
3) Establishment & Organization
4) Finance
5) Inspectorate
6) Offices Services & Supply
7) Personnel (Operations)
8) Personnel (Training & General)
9) Security

The following were joint Commonwealth Office/F.O. departments:

1) Consular
2) Information Research
3) Information Administration
4) Information Policy and Guidance
5) Information Services
6) Nationality and Treaty
7) Protocol and Conference
8) Research

Advisers and non-departmental staff

From its inception, the D.O. shared with the C.O. a Legal Adviser, a Ceremonial and Reception Secretary and a Librarian, each with appropriate staff. From 1947 after the separation from the C.O., the D.O. had its own advisory staff.

After the absorption of the I.O., the CRO employed a Principal Staff Officer (normally a Major-General (retired)).

In 1964 an Economic Adviser was appointed; his staff was increased and later formed an Economists' Department.

After the absorption of the C.O. in 1966, Advisers were appointed for Overseas Labour and Overseas Police.

By 1968 therefore the non-departmental staff consisted of the following.

1) Ceremonial and Protocol Secretary
2) Legal Adviser and Staff
3) Economic Adviser and Staff
4) Overseas Labour Adviser
5) Overseas Police Adviser
6) Library
7) India Office Library and Records

Appendix B

Talk by the author to CRO Staff on Wednesday, 28 February 1968

I have served in this Office now for nearly thirty-eight years and think I can say without exaggeration or any false pride that the last six years have seen greater activity, more crises and more far-reaching changes in the Office than any other period in its history. It has been, without a break, a frantically busy time. In our aims and policies we have had many disappointments. Yet I like to think that the machine has stood up to every test and – what is infinitely more important – the people manning the machine have had a sense of purpose and of a worthwhile job to do.

But, my goodness, we have been through a lot together in these last six years!

We have had three Prime Ministers and both major political parties in power. We have had four separate Secretaries of State (or nine if you count the Colonial Office and double figures if you throw in the Central African Office!), goodness knows how many Ministers of State and more Parliamentary Under Secretaries than anyone can now remember.

In the Commonwealth we have had:

1. Mutinies in Tanzania, Uganda and Kenya.
2. Civil war in Cyprus.
3. War between India and Pakistan.
4. War between Malaysia and Indonesia.
5. Civil war in Nigeria.
6. Singapore's breakaway from the Federation.
7. Coup d'état in Ghana.
8. Coup d'état in Sierra Leone (the one in Uganda does not count as it was carried out by the Head of Government).
9. A row with Malta over the rundown.
10. Break of relations with us by Tanzania and Ghana.
11. Spanish hostility to Gibraltar.
12. Chinese hostility to Hong Kong.

But that round dozen scarcely begins the catalogue, because overall there has been:

1. The insoluble problem of Rhodesia.
2. The perennial balance of payments crisis with the inevitable cuts and restrictions which affect both the Service and Commonwealth interests.
3. Britain's application for entry into EEC which has profound implications for Commonwealth countries.
4. The successive defence reviews which have imposed a great strain on our relations with all our allies in the Commonwealth.
5. The Commonwealth Immigration Act which has inevitably caused trouble with many of our clients.
6. Five Commonwealth Prime Ministers' Meetings, all of which, for different reasons, have imposed great strains on the relationship.
7. The opening of no fewer than thirteen new posts in the capitals of new Commonwealth countries.

But even this catalogue only touches on half the picture. In addition to the daily work of the Office, we have had major organizational changes inside it. In particular:

1. The creation of the Diplomatic Service.
2. The absorption of the Colonial Office and CRO into a single Commonwealth Office.

Having got through a list of such proportions, I feel that it is enough to claim with Abbé Siéyès (as he did when they asked him what he did during the Terror), 'I survived!'

I do not propose to comment on our many political problems but I would like to say something on the housekeeping side.

Some of the points I suggested in my first talk to the staff were:

1. Some increase in staff at all levels. This has been achieved at the working level in spite of the reduction in total numbers in the combined Commonwealth Service and Foreign Service.

2. Streamlining of the work.

3. Greater emphasis on geographical specialization.

I did not feel that our organization was right and wanted it to be better. One can never get it absolutely right because there is no ideal solution to the problem of geographical versus functional and the emphasis of the work is constantly shifting. But I think that the changes we made were sensible.

4. Increased continuity. Our practice is not perfect with overseas service and the present staff shortages, but I think it is better and DSAO are certainly conscious of the problem.

5. *Whitehall*. Six years ago I was worried about the doubts in Whitehall about the reputation of this Office. Today, broadly, I think we play our full part and our views are respected, if not always accepted; in general I think that we have got our balance just about right – that is, that our prime function is to serve British interests, but to ensure that British interests are not narrowly interpreted, but take into account the interests of the Commonwealth as well.

6. *Public image*. Similarly I was worried about our public image and said that a job of public relations required to be done to bring about a better understanding. Again, I think we have done this, particularly under the leadership of successive Under Secretaries in charge of Information, even if much still remains to be done.

As to the Diplomatic Service, my conclusions are:

1. The creation of the Diplomatic Service has been a success.

2. We should aim at the merger of the F.O. and C.O. into a single Department.

3. Meanwhile we should press on with measures of integration.

4. I have been conscious of a high honour in being Head of the Diplomatic Service but have immensely enjoyed the job.

Finally in regard to the Commonwealth let me say that we have had our difficulties as all of us here know better than anyone else. Nevertheless I believe that some of the simple truths about the Commonwealth remain valid:

1. It is an association of real value and genuine links, in which history, sentiment, self-interest, personal contacts all play their part.

2. It is an association of people in which individuals count and personal friendships matter. All Governments do silly things sometimes and it is wrong to consider the Commonwealth in a political sense only.

3. Britain enjoys a number of built-in advantages in all Commonwealth countries and will continue to be able to bring her influence to bear. There will continue to be a 'British presence' long after any British military presence has been withdrawn.

4. The Commonwealth could be a powerful vehicle for solving the big problems of the last half of the twentieth century: world power rivalry (Communism versus the West), the division between rich and poor countries (the North–South problem), and above all the racial conflict (the relationship between black, brown, yellow and white).

439

Appendix C

List of Territories

Dominions Office 1925

The Dominions Office was responsible for relations with:
Canada
Commonwealth of Australia
New Zealand
Union of South Africa
Irish Free State (Eire) – became Republic and withdrew from Commonwealth 1949
Newfoundland – became Province of Canada 1949

In addition the Dominions Office was responsible for the administration of Southern Rhodesia and of the High Commission Territories of Basutoland, the Bechuanaland Protectorate and Swaziland and it had certain direct responsibilities for the Australian States.

Commonwealth Relations Office 1947

In addition the CRO became responsible for relations with:
1947	India
	Pakistan – left the Commonwealth in 1972
1948	Ceylon – later Sri Lanka
1957	Ghana – formerly Gold Coast
	Malaya – later Malaysia
1960	Cyprus
	Nigeria
1961	Sierra Leone
	Tanganyika – later Tanzania
1962	Jamaica
	Trinidad and Tobago
	Uganda
1963	Zanzibar – later incorporated with Tanganyika as Tanzania
	Kenya
	Singapore – with Sabah and Sarawak joined Malaya to form Federation of Malaysia: seceded 1965
1964	Malawi – formerly Nyasaland
	Malta
	Zambia – formerly Northern Rhodesia
1965	Gambia

Commonwealth Office 1966

1966   Guyana – formerly British Guiana
        Botswana – formerly Bechuanaland Protectorate
        Lesotho – formerly Basutoland
        Barbados
1968   Mauritius
        Swaziland
        Nauru

The Commonwealth Office which incorporated the Colonial Office took over responsibility for the Associated States, dependent territories and Protectorates. Of these the following became independent under the FCO:

1970   Fiji
        Tonga
1973   Bahamas
        Seychelles
        Antigua

In 1972 Pakistan left the Commonwealth and Bangladesh which seceded from Pakistan became a member of the Commonwealth.

References

Part I

Chapter 1 (pp. 3–14)

1. Cmd. 3568, *Report of the Indian Statutory Commission,* 1930
2. 26 Geo. V, c. 2, *Government of India Act,* 1935
3. 20 Geo. V, c. 40, *Colonial Development Act,* 1929
4. CO 323/534, 29255A, C.O. to Treas, Aug. 1907
5. Cd. 3795, Elgin's *Despatch on C.O. reorganization,* Sept. 1907
6. *See* G. Fiddes, *The Dominions and Colonial Offices*:264
7. ibid.:264
8. ibid.:245
9. ibid.:250
10. L. S. Amery, *My Political Life,* vol. I:196
11. ibid.:302
12. ibid.:151
13. DO 121/1, Report of the Committee on the Higher Establishment of the Colonial Office, 20 Feb. 1925
14. PREM 5/32, Fisher to P.M., 27 Feb. 1925
15. DO 121/1, Churchill to Amery 'Private', 7 Dec. 1924
16. T 122/1480, CP 148/25, Memo by Colonial Secretary, 9 Mar. 1925
17. PREM 5/32, Amery to Baldwin, 23 May 1925
18. Amery, vol. II:336
19. HC Deb., vol. 184, 11 June 1925
20. ibid., vol. 187, 27 July 1925

Chapter 2 (pp. 15–24)

1. CAB 24/210, CP 80 (30), Memo by S. of S. for D.A. and for the Cols., 7 Mar. 1930
2. H. B. Wheatley, *London: Past and Present,* London, 1891:132
3. Lavinia Handley-Read, 'Whitehall Sculpture', *The Architectural Review,* Nov. 1970, vol. CXLVIII, no. 885
4. *See* Cosmo Parkinson, *The Colonial Office from Within 1909–1945*
5. Charles Jeffries, *The Colonial Office*
6. K. Middlemas and J. Barnes, *Baldwin: A Biography*:126
7. R. Vansittart, *The Mist Procession*:376
8. R. Skidelsky, *Politicians and the Slump*:70
9. E. S. R. Wertheimer, *Portrait of the Labour Party*: 178–9
10. Harold Nicolson, *King George V: His Life and Reign*:432
11. Amery, vol. II:336
12. C. W. Dixon, *Memoirs*:16
13. ibid.:38

14. Amery, vol. II:381
15. S. Roskill, *Hankey: Man of Secrets*, vol. II:574
16. CAB 24/192, CP 46 (28), Memo on Amery's Tour in Canada. *See also* DO 117/93 containing *short notes on points discussed with Prime Minister at Ottawa*
17. Lord Casey, *The Future of the Commonwealth*:54–5

Chapter 3 (pp. 25–32)

1. DO 35/5488/E, 4/6, Report of Inter-Departmental Committee, 27 Sept. 1937.
2. HC Parly Papers, reports and committees, vii (1937), Select Committee on Estimates 1937, Second Report. *See* 154–69, evidence by Sir E. Harding and Mr Machtig, 3 May 1937
3. Lord Strang, *The Foreign Office*

Chapter 4 (pp. 33–47)

1. *See* H. Llewellyn Smith, *The Board of Trade*: 75–82
2. D. Creighton, *John A. Macdonald, the Old Chieftain*: 275–80
3. FO 372/2444/T 12916, Minute by Chamberlain, 7 Dec. 1928
4. DO 117/44/D 12381, S. of S. to G.G.s of Canada, Australia, N.Z., Union of South Africa, tel., 5 Nov. 1926
5. ibid., G.G. of Canada to S. of S., tel., 8 Nov. 1926
6. ibid., G.G. of Australia to S. of S., tel., 8 Nov. 1926
7. ibid., G.G. of N.Z. to S. of S., tel., 8 Nov. 1926
8. ibid., G.G. of S.A. to S. of S., tels., 8 and 16 Nov. 1926
9. CAB 23/53, Cabinet 57 (26), Minutes of Meeting, 10 Nov. 1926
10. Amery Papers, Diary, 10 Nov. 1926
11. FO 800/259/864–5, Amery to Chamberlain, 12 Nov. 1926
12. FO 800/259/858–60, Chamberlain to Amery, 12 Nov. 1926
13. FO 800/260, f 349–50, Chamberlain to Amery, 29 Mar. 1927
14. CAB 241/192, CP 37 (28), Notes on Amery's Tour in Australia and N.Z., 8 Feb. 1928
15. CAB 24/186, CP 140 (27), May 1927
16. CAB 23/55, Cabinet 31 (27), conclusion 3, 11 May 1927
17. CAB 27/347, *Report, Proceedings and Memoranda of Cabinet Committee on Representation in the Dominions*, BRD (27) Series. Committee paper 3, 4 July 1927
18. ibid., BRD minutes, mtg 1, 22 June 1927
19. DO 35/29/D 8975, Amery to Chamberlain, 15 Aug. 1927
20. FO 372/2322/T 9181, Minutes of 23 June 1927
21. FO 372/2322/T 9182, Minutes of 6 July 1927. *See also* T 9183, Memo of 12 July 1927
22. CAB 27/347, BRD minutes, mtg 13 July 1927. *See also* CP 202/27, BRD committee report, 18 July and Cabinet 42 (27), Minutes of mtg of 20 July
23. FO 372/2442/T 3588, *Memorandum on the Representation in Canada of HMG in Gt. Britain*, 24 Oct. 1927
24. DO 117/106/D 4539, Memo of Dixon and Harding, 7 Mar. 1928
25. CAB 24/192, CP 46 (28)
26. FO 627/2, U 141/4/750, T. Shone (Embassy, Washington) to R. Craigie (F.O.), 8 Mar. 1929
27. FO 627/2, U 205/4/750, Minute by A. Chamberlain, 11 Apr. 1929
28. CAB 24/189, CP 296 (27), *The Position in South Africa*. Memo by Doms. Sec., 24 Nov. 1927
29. DO 117/84, *Diary of a Tour* by G. Whiskard
30. DO 35/4541/3, Clark to Harding, 4 Sept. 1934
31. PREM 1/65, Baldwin to Stamfordham, 22 Mar. 1928
32. DO 35/4541/3, *Notes on Procedure in the High Commissioner's Office and on Matters connected with the discharge of the High Commissioner's Functions*, 4 Sept. 1934
33. DO 35/4541/5, *Organization of the Representative's Office*, Dec. 1934
34. DO 35/4541/3, Clark to Harding, 4 Sept. 1934

35. DO 35/548, C/E 31/5, Floud to Machtig, 30 Sept. 1937
36. DO 35/4541/C97/46, Campbell to Harding, 25 Aug. 1939
37. Gerald Campbell, *Of True Experience*: 93–7
38. Machtig Papers, Whiskard to Machtig, 3 Jan. 1938
39. ibid., Whiskard to Machtig, 6 Apr. 1941
40. ibid., Whiskard to Eden, 22 Feb. 1940

Chapter 5 (pp. 48–61)

1. CAB 24/295, Memo from Hankey to Balfour, 1 Nov. 1926
2. CAB 24/192, CP 37 (28), *Notes on Mr. Amery's Tour in Australia and New Zealand*, 8 Feb. 1928
3. Cmd. 3479, *Conference on the Operation of Dominion Legislation*
4. 22 Geo. V, c. 4, *Statute of Westminster*
5. Dixon: 29
6. Amery, vol. II: 391
7. Roskill, vol. II: 430
8. DO 117/33/2618, *The Constitution of the British Commonwealth* communicated by Gen. Smuts to Mr Amery in 1921
9. DO 117/32/2618, CP 341 (26), Annex A, Hertzog to Amery, 26 July 1926
10. Amery, vol. II: 381
11. CAB 21/295, Memo for P.M. by Hankey, 29 Oct. 1926
12. DO 117/32/2618, CP 341 (26), Memo by Amery, 4 Oct. 1926
13. FO 800/259, f 808–11, Chamberlain to Amery, 16 Oct. 1926
14. *See* Roskill, vol. II: 430
15. Cmd. 2768, Imperial Conference 1926: Summary of Proceedings which contain the Report of the Inter-Imperial Relations Committee. *See also* CAB 32/56, E 129, for drafts of the Report
16. Balfour Papers, B.M. Add. Mss 49697, Balfour to Sir George Foster, 4 May 1927
17. *See* Roskill, vol. II: 433, Hankey to Smuts, 25 Nov. 1927
18. Amery, vol. II: 400
19. CAB 24/189, CP 296 (27), Memo by Amery, *The Position in South Africa*, 24 Nov. 1927
20. Amery, vol. II: 454
21. ibid., vol. II: 387
22. CAB 32/56, E 129, Report of Committee
23. D. W. Harkness, *The Restless Dominion*. Text quoted in full: 101–4
24. Cmd. 3479
25. HC Deb., vol. 259, 20 Nov. 1931
26. DO 35, R3 4020/255, Memo by Dixon, Dec. 1931
27. CAB 21/336, Hankey to CIGS, 14 Nov. 1930
28. Cmd. 3717, Imperial Conference 1930: Summary of Proceedings
29. Dixon: 41
30. ibid.: 42
31. Mansergh, *The Commonwealth Experience*: 239
32. Nicolson: 486
33. DO 35/541/C, 97/3, Clark to Batterbee, 6 Jan. 1937
34. ibid., 97/6, Clark to Batterbee, 3 Feb. 1937
35. ibid., Harding to Hartington and S. of S., 1 Mar. 1937
36. CAB 32/127, E (B) 37, 4 Apr. 1937

Chapter 6 (pp. 62–72)

1. R.A. P 633, 78, Byng to H.M., letter of 29 June 1926. Quoted in Nicolson: 476–7
2. DO 117/4, Minute by Davis, 2 Jan. 1926
3. DO 117/20, CP 263 (26), Memo by Amery, 6 July 1926
4. DO 121/60, Amery to Byng, undated

5. Amery, vol. II:378–9
6. ibid.:378
7. CAB 24/192, CP 37 (28), Memo covering *Notes on Mr. Amery's Tour of Australia and New Zealand*, 8 Feb. 1928
8. DO 11156/47, Note of meeting covering *Notes by Solicitor-General*, 14 July 1931
9. DO 11156/48, Gov. N.S.W. to D.O., 16 July 1931
10. DO 9374/15, Gov. N.S.W. to D.O., 23 Apr. 1932
11. ibid., Bushe to Attorney-General (Inskip), 10 May 1932
12. DO 11622/16, Gov. N.S.W. to D.O., 14 May 1932
13. Dixon:33
14. R.A. K 2077, 2, quoted in Nicolson:483
15. R.A. L 2266, 90, quoted in Nicolson:485
16. CAB 24/213, I.E.C. (30), 6th and 8th mtgs, 7 and 14 July 1930
17. R.A. L 2293, 276, quoted in Nicolson:429
18. R.A. L 2293, 338, quoted in Nicolson:480
19. Nicolson:482
20. Malcolm MacDonald, *People and Places*:123
21. Middlemas and Barnes:991
22. H.R.H. The Duke of Windsor, *A King's Story*:346
23. Mansergh, *The Commonwealth Experience*:241
24. Windsor:344
25. Vincent Massey, *What's Past is Prologue*:250
26. Malcolm MacDonald, *Titans and Others*:68
27. Mansergh, *The Commonwealth Experience*:241
28. MacDonald, *Titans and Others*:66–7

Chapter 7 (pp. 73–90)

1. H. Blair Neatby, *William Lyon Mackenzie King 1924–1932*:40
2. FO 371/19465/W/11200/4972/50, Memo by Chamberlain, 20 Dec. 1924
3. ibid., 20 Dec. 1924
4. CP 5 (30), 27 Dec. 1929
5. FO 800/259, f 984–5, Chamberlain to Amery, 21 Dec. 1926
6. ibid., f 999–1003, Chamberlain to Amery, 26 Dec. 1926
7. DO 35/183, 6776/1A, Dixon to Dunbar, 5 June 1935
8. Amery, vol. II:377
9. Neatby:41
10. ibid.:42–3
11. Massey:238
12. DO 114/68/6109, A/3/54, MacDonald to King, 22 May 1936
13. Massey:241
14. ibid.:258
15. DO 114/94, FS 2/295, Record of Meeting, 30 Sept. 1939
16. Massey:236
17. ibid.:232
18. ibid.:236
19. DO 114/40 MO 263, Memo, 23 Nov. 1932
20. DO 114/67 N.Z., tel. no. 126, 13 Dec. 1935
21. ibid., Te Water to MacDonald, 16 Dec. 1935
22. ibid., extract from *Cape Times*, 7 May 1936
23. ibid., Ottawa to D.O., tel. no. 62, 4 Sept. 1935
24. Cecil Edwards, *Bruce of Melbourne: Man of Two Worlds*:233
25. DO 114/68, Record of Meeting with Te Water, 16 June 1936
26. DO 35/165/6216A/40, FP (36) 12, Memo by MacDonald, 21 Aug, 1936
27. Dixon, *Memoirs* (first version):35
28. Massey:230

29. ibid.:231
30. PREM 1/194, Cape Town, tel. no. 321, 12 Mar. 1936
31. ibid., Cape Town, tel. no. 323, 14 Mar. 1936
32. ibid., Bruce to MacDonald, 17 Mar. 1936
33. CAB 27/622
34. DO 35/551/F, 25/130, Memo by Cockram, 9 Dec. 1937
35. CAB 23/88, Report by MacDonald, 16 June 1937
36. CAB 32/127, UK Delegation 3rd Meeting, 29 Apr. 1937
37. CAB 32/127, E (B) 127
38. FO 371/21216, W 22248, 9 Dec. 1937
39. CAB 23/88, 16 June 1937
40. DO 35/576/F, 706/48, MacDonald to Halifax, 23 Mar. 1938
41. *See* Churchill, vol. I:233
42. Massey:260
43. ibid.:266
44. Information from Mr Malcolm MacDonald
45. Cw. of Aus. Parl. Deb., vol. 157, 28 Sept. 1938
46. MacDonald, *Titans and Others*:80–1
47. Churchill, vol. 1:271
48. Mansergh, *The Commonwealth Experience*:283

Chapter 8 (pp. 91–8)

1. DO 35/543/D, 28/2, Memo: *Procedure for Declaration of War*, Bushe to Malkin, 7 Oct. 1937
2. ibid., D, 28/2, Minute by Sir E. Harding, 18 Sept. 1937
3. ibid., D, 28/5, Minute by Batterbee, Dec. 1937
4. ibid., D, 28/5, Minute by Batterbee, 7 Jan. 1938
5. ibid., D, 28/5, Minute by MacDonald, 21 Jan. 1938
6. ibid., D, 28/21, Bridges to Harding, 13 Feb. 1939
7. ibid., D, 28/32, Minute by Dixon, 24 May 1939
8. ibid., D, 28/32, Minutes of 25 May 1939
9. ibid., C, 87/31, Campbell to Harding, 8 Dec. 1938
10. ibid., D, 28/23, Clark to Harding, 20 Feb. 1939
11. ibid., D, 28/32, Memo: *Position of the Dominions in the Event of War*, May 1939

Chapter 9 (pp. 99–110)

1. T 172/1775, Memo from Warren Fisher to Snowden, 30 Sept. 1931
2. CAB 231/52, Memo by Amery, 11 Feb. 1926
3. Cmd. 3637, EMB Report, July 1930
4. T 172/1668, Grigg to Whiskard, 4 Nov. 1930
5. Dixon:10
6. Cmd. 4335, Imperial Committee on Economic Consultation and Cooperation, 1933
7. Amery, vol. II:347
8. ibid.:354
9. CO 352/262, Harding to Llewellyn Smith, 17 July 1923
10. CAB 24/216, CP 366 (30), Memo by Thomas, 27 Oct. 1930
11. DO 35/236/8831/69, Harding to Clark
12. G. Blaxland, *J. H. Thomas: A Life for Unity*:260
13. Information from Mr Malcolm MacDonald
14. Middlemas and Barnes:683
15. DO 121/61, Whiskard to Harding, 22 June 1932
16. ibid., 25 June 1932
17. ibid., 3 Aug. 1932
18. ibid., 5 Aug. 1932

19. ibid., 3 Aug. 1932
20. ibid., 13 Aug. 1932
21. ibid., P.S., 16 Aug. 1932
22. ibid., 19 Aug. 1932
23. ibid., P.S., 22 Aug. 1932
24. DO 35/37/9513, Thomas to MacDonald, 24 Apr. 1934
25. Blaxland:263
26. National Library of Australia, Sir George Pearce papers, Ms 213
27. DO 35/259/9105/3/172, Machtig to Whiskard, 30 June 1936
28. Cmd. 8462
29. Amery, vol. II:182
30. 12 and 13 Geo. V, CL 13, *Empire Settlement Act*, 1922
31. HC Deb., vol. 153, 26 Apr. 1922
32. G. F. Plant, *Oversea Settlement*, London, 1951:155
33. DO 8345A/62, tel. 253, D.O. to Canberra, 13 Feb. 1936
34. ibid., tel. 267, Lyons to Baldwin, 27 Feb. 1936

Chapter 10 (pp. 111–20)

1. Earl of Longford and T. P. O'Neill, *Eamon de Valera*:303
2. DO 35/398/11111/540, Minute by Harding, 28 June 1933
3. Dixon:47
4. ibid.:45
5. DO 35/397/11111/26, CP 86/32, Memo by Thomas, Feb. 1932
6. Cmd. 4056
7. Mansergh (ed.), *Documents*, vol. I, *Moore and Others versus the Attorney-General for the IFS.*: 305–14
8. Blaxland:262
9. ibid.:262
10. CAB 24/262, CP 124 (36), Memo by MacDonald, May 1936
11. MacDonald, *Titans and Others*:61
12. DO 35/1107/W, XI/5, Memo by Maffey, 17 Sept. 1939
13. Dixon:50
14. ibid.:49
15. DO 35/891/X, 1/98, Memo by Dixon, 21 June 1937
16. DO 35/892/X, 11/21, Minute by Harding, 10 Jan. 1938
17. ibid., Minute by MacDonald, 13 Jan. 1938
18. 1 and 2 Geo. VI, CL 25, *Eire (Confirmation of Agreements) Act*, 1938, s. 1
19. MacDonald, *Titans and Others*:74
20. J. W. Wheeler-Bennett, *King George VI His Life and Reign*:327
21. Lord Chatfield, *The Navy and Defence*, vol. II: 126

Chapter 11 (pp. 121–36)

1. DO 114/58 11754/163, Note of Meeting, 24 Feb. 1933
2. ibid., /180, Amulree to Harding, 3 Apr. 1933
3. ibid., /180, Amulree to Thomas, 3 Apr. 1933
4. ibid., /183, D.O. to Ottawa, tel. 64, 1 May 1933
5. ibid., /183, D.O. to Ottawa, tel. 68, 3 May 1933
6. ibid., /184, Ottawa to D.O., tel. 108, 5 May 1933
7. ibid., /185, Ottawa to D.O., tel. unnumbered, 11 May 1933
8. ibid., /186, D.O. to Ottawa, tel. 72, 16 May 1933
9. ibid., /185, Ottawa to D.O., tel. 120, 14 May 1933
10. ibid., /190, Ottawa to D.O., tel. 134, 22 May 1933
11. ibid., /191, Ottawa to D.O., tel. 135, 22 May 1933
12. ibid., /191, Ottawa to D.O., tel. 137, 22 May 1933

13. ibid., /228, Chamberlain to Amulree, 31 Aug. 1933
14. ibid., /268, Ottawa to D.O., 21 Nov. 1933
15. Cmd. 4479, Royal Commission on Newfoundland, Oct. 1933
16. DO 114/58, 11754/230, Meeting at D.O., 1 Sept. 1933
17. Blaxland:265
18. St John Chadwick, *Newfoundland: Island into Province*: 176
19. T. Lodge, *Dictatorship in Newfoundland*:9–14 and 249–55
20. DO 35/424/11969/15, CP 84 (31), Apr. 1931
21. CAB 24/189, CP 296 (27), *The Position in South Africa*, Memo by Amery, 24 Nov. 1927
22. DO 35/825/ R 8 221, Agreed Formula, 10 Aug. 1939
23. Dixon:78
24. Amery, vol. II:415
25. CAB 24/189, CP 296 (27), *The Position in South Africa*, Memo by Amery, 24 Nov. 1927
26. Amery, vol. II:415
27. DO 117/70, Memo by Amery
28. DO 35/392/75, Memo by Thomas, 10 Nov. 1933
29. R. Hyam, *The Failure of South African Expansion 1908–1948*:130
30. DO 35/393/10991/233, *Aide-mémoire*, 15 May 1935
31. DO 35/900/Y, 6/19, Memo by MacDonald, 16 June 1937
32. ibid., Memo by MacDonald, 7 July 1937
33. DO 35/334/10087/414, Hankey to Batterbee, 14 Sept. 1934
34. Lord Mountevans, *Adventurous Life*:194
35. Reginald Pound, *Evans of the Broke*:228
36. ibid.:221
37. DO 116/5 20283/92, Desp. no. 682, 26 Sept. 1933
38. ibid., Enclosure no. 1, 13 Sept. 1933
39. ibid., Enclosure no. 3, 13 Sept. 1933
40. Rear-Admiral Searle, letter to Pound, 11 Oct. 1962
41. CAB 23/77, Conclusion 1 of Meeting no. 51 (33), 20 Sept. 1933
42. Hyam:183

Chapter 12 (pp. 137–48)

1. A. Eden, *Facing the Dictators*:19
2. T. Inskip, *Diary*, 17 Jan. 1939:230
3. HC Select Committee on Estimates, Second Report, 1937
4. *Daily Express*, 28 Oct. 1938
5. *The Times*, 19 and 24 Jan. 1933
6. Massey:236
7. ibid.
8. CAB 32/27, Paper E (B) (37):4
9. See A. Watt, *The Evolution of Australian Foreign Policy 1938–1965*:22
10. Mansergh, *Survey, 1931–39*:436–7
11. Casey, *The Future of the Commonwealth*:54–5
12. Edwards:87
13. FO 800/260, f 507, Chamberlain to Amery, 28 Apr. 1927
14. Lord Gladwyn, *Memoirs*:106
15. FO 37/21139, R 4048
16. Vansittart:535
17. DO 35/410/11648/84, Hankey to Harding, 28 Nov. 1934
18. DO 117/93, Whiskard, *Diary of a Tour in Canada*
19. L. B. Pearson, *Memoirs*, vol. I:108
20. J. D. B. Miller, 'The C.R.O. and Commonwealth Relations', *International Studies* (New Delhi), vol. II, no. 1, Bombay, July 1960:44
21. P. Hasluck, *The Government and the People 1939–1941*:49
22. DO 117/50/D 12913, Amery to Low, 29 Nov. 1926
23. CAB 27/623, 18 Mar. 1938

Part II

Chapter 1 (pp. 151–3)

1. Sir Robert Menzies, *Afternoon Light*: 15–16
2. Wheeler-Bennett: 412
3. CAB 66/21, W.P. (42) 67, Batterbee to Machtig, 20 Dec. 1941
4. J. W. Pickersgill, *The Mackenzie King Record*, vol. II: 91
5. ibid., vol. I: 245
6. Sir Alan Watt, *The Evolution of Australian Foreign Policy 1938–1965*: 50
7. Hasluck: 335
8. Winston S. Churchill, *The Second World War*, vol. IV: 4
9. *Melbourne Herald*, article by Curtin, 27 Dec. 1941
10. Churchill, vol. IV: 8
11. CAB 66/21, W.P. (42) 34, Curtin to Churchill (JOHCU 21), 23 Jan. 1942
12. Churchill, vol. IV: 51
13. ibid., vol. IV: 138
14. ibid., vol. IV: 5
15. Menzies: 125

Chapter 2 (pp. 154–75)

1. DO 121/10A, Cranborne to P.M., 4 Jan. 1941
2. Churchill, vol. IV: 78
3. Eden, *Memoirs*, vol. 2: 63
4. Attlee, *As It Happened*: 125
5. G. Shakespeare, *Let Candles be Brought In*: 278
6. PREM 4/43A/14, Memo by Bridges, 22 Oct. 1943
7. DO 121/10A, Cranborne to P.M., 22 Feb. 1945
8. ibid., 23 Feb. 1945
9. CAB 66/21, W.P. (42) 30, Memo by Cranborne, 21 Jan. 1942
10. DO 121/10A/46, Cranborne to P.M., 6 Apr. 1944
11. Churchill, vol. II, Appendix A, 18 July 1940
12. HC Deb., vol. 342, Statement by Col. Sec., 14 Dec. 1938
13. DO 35/1896/WR, 213/3, Memo by Emrys-Evans, 13 Jan. 1943
14. ibid., Minute by Machtig, 19 Feb. 1943
15. ibid., Minute by Attlee, 19 Feb. 1943
16. ibid., Minutes of Meeting, 2 Apr. 1943
17. J. C. Smuts, Speech to E.P.A., 25 Nov. 1943 (extracts in Mansergh (ed.), *Documents*, vol. 1: 568–75)
18. A. Cadogan, *The Diaries of Sir Alexander Cadogan 1938–1945*: 359
19. DO 35/1204/WC, 75/39, Proposed F.O. circular on Proposals for Consultation with Commonwealth Governments, Minute by Machtig, 24 July 1944

Chapter 3 (pp. 176–91)

1. PREM 3/82, tel. no. 2105 from Ottawa, 9 Oct. 1940
2. ibid., P.M. Personal tel. to H.C., 11 Oct. 1940
3. ibid., P.M. to P.M. of Canada, 11 Oct. 1940
4. ibid., P.M.'s Minute, 13 Oct. 1940
5. ibid., Doms. Sec. to P.M., 16 Oct. 1940

6. ibid., P.M. to Doms. Sec., 20 Oct. 1940
7. ibid., Doms. Sec. to P.M., 24 Oct. 1940
8. ibid., P.M. to Doms. Sec., 25 Oct. 1940
9. HC Deb., vol. 369, 27 Feb. 1941
10. ibid., vol. 396, 10 Feb. 1944
11. ibid., vol. 396, 11 Feb. 1944
12. Machtig Papers, Whiskard to Machtig, 6 Apr. 1941
13. ibid., Batterbee to Machtig, 16 Aug. 1940
14. DO 121/10A/93, Cranborne to P.M., 17 Nov. 1944
15. Machtig Papers, Clark to Machtig, 16 Mar. 1947
16. Pickersgill, vol. II:140
17. ibid.:205
18. Ottawa desp. no. 512, 6 Nov. 1945
19. Machtig Papers, Cross to Cranborne, 13 Jan. 1944
20. CAB 66/21, W.P. (42) 33, Memo by Cranborne, *Relations with Australia* covering tel. from Cross no. 53, 22 Jan. 1942
21. ibid., Memo by Cranborne, 22 Jan. 1942
22. DO 121/10A/68, Cranborne to P.M., 24 May 1944

Chapter 4 (pp. 192–206)

1. Mansergh, *Survey*:24
2. DO 35/998/WC, 7/1, Minute by Machtig on letter from Lothian to Halifax, 19 Mar. 1940
3. Churchill, vol. II:21
4. ibid., vol. II:431
5. ibid., vol. II:157
6. ibid., vol. II:21
7. ibid., vol. II:21
8. PREM 4/43B/1, Minute from Cranborne to P.M., 23 Dec. 1940
9. ibid., Minute from P.M. to Cranborne, 25 Dec. 1940
10. Churchill, vol. III, Appendix C:667, Minute P.M. to Cranborne, 25 Mar. 1941
11. DO 121/10A/2, letter from Cranborne to P.M., 18 Nov. 1941
12. Churchill, vol. IV, Appendix C:755, P.M. to Doms. Sec., 4 Mar. 1942
13. DO 35/1843/WR 208/22, P.M. to Cranborne, 12 Aug. 1943
14. ibid., Cranborne to P.M., tel. Concrete no. 201, 14 Aug. 1943
15. Churchill, vol. V:506, P.M. to Gen. Ismay, 24 Jan. 1944
16. HC Deb., vol. 351, 21 Sept. 1939
17. Reitz, *No Outspan*, London, 1942:248 and 255
18. Lord Casey, *Personal Experience*:5
19. Edwards, *Bruce of Melbourne*:286–99
20. Massey:297
21. ibid.:298–301
22. Dixon (first version):41
23. Churchill, vol. II, Appendix D, Correspondence relating to Dakar:645
24. Churchill, vol, III:367–9
25. ibid., vol. IV:139–45
26. Watt, *Evolution of Australian Foreign Policy*:59
27. Casey, *Personal Experience*:97
28. R. Sherwood, *Roosevelt and Hopkins*, New York, 1948:508–9
29. Pickersgill, vol. I:417 and 421–2
30. ibid.:521–6
31. PREM 3/83/2, P.M. to P.M. of Canada, T 1048/3, 17 July 1943
32. Pearson:215
33. PREM 3/83/2, MacDonald to D.O., 6 Aug. 1943
34. Pickersgill, vol. I:240

Chapter 5 (pp. 207–20)

1. Churchill, vol. I:326
2. Churchill, vol. II:385, P.M. to P.M.s of Australia & New Zealand, 11 Aug. 1940
3. ibid.
4. Menzies:65
5. Edwards:314
6. Menzies:66
7. Churchill, vol. III:365
8. Pickersgill, vol. I:214
9. Churchill, vol. III:365, P.M. to P.M. of Australia, 19 Aug. 1941
10. Pickersgill, vol. I:214
11. Hasluck:347
12. Pickersgill, vol. I:234
13. Churchill, vol. III:366
14. ibid.:758, P.M. to P.M. of Australia, 29 Aug. 1941
15. CAB 66/21, W.P. (42) 29, covering tel. no. 37 from Cross to D.O., 14 Jan. 1942
16. ibid., W.P. (42) 30, Memo by Cranborne, 21 Jan. 1942
17. ibid., W.P. (42) 29, Memo by Cranborne, 21 Jan. 1942
18. PREM 3/167/1, Harding to P.M., 22 Feb. 1942
19. Amery to Linlithgow, 8 Feb. 1942, covering text of tel. sent to Canada, N.Z., S. Africa on 27 Jan. (*See* no. 86 in HMSO, *The Transfer of Power 1942–7*, vol. I)
20. Amery to Linlithgow, 9 Feb. 1942 (no. 89 in *The Transfer of Power*, vol. I)
21. HC Deb., vol. 377, 27 Jan. 1942
22. Hasluck, *The Government and the People 1942–1945*:54
23. HC Deb., vol. 377, 5 Feb. 1942
24. Edwards:348
25. ibid.
26. DO 35/999/WC7/96, Bridges to Machtig, 27 Oct. 1942
27. ibid., Bridges to P.M., 16 July 1942
28. ibid., P.M. to Bridges, 19 July 1942
29. Edwards:368
30. ibid.:333
31. Roskill, *Hankey*, vol. III:563
32. PREM 4/50/11, P.M. to Attlee, 12 Feb. 1943
33. ibid., Attlee to P.M., 15 Feb. 1943
34. DO 121/10A, Cranborne to P.M., 5 Oct. 1943
35. DO 35/1490/WC 75/37, P.M. to Curtin, 20 May 1944
36. ibid., Bridges to Machtig, 2 June 1944
37. Watt, *Evolution of Australian Foreign Policy*:46
38. CAB 66/21, W.P. (42) 30, Memo by Cranborne, 21 Jan. 1942
39. Edwards:344
40. ibid.:345
41. Churchill, vol. IV, Appendix C, Minute to First Lord and First Sea Lord, 17 May 1942
42. PREM 3/83/2, Cross to D.O., 6 Aug. 1943

Chapter 6 (pp. 221–32)

1. Webster and Frankland, *The Strategic Air Offensive against Germany 1939–1945*, HMSO, London, 1961, vol. I:110
2. DO 35/1072/W.T. 276/115, Desp. from Campbell to D.O., 19 Dec. 1939
3. ibid., Minutes by Holmes, Liesching, Stephenson and Devonshire, 10 and 12 Jan. 1940
4. The King's Printer, *The British Commonwealth Air Training Plan 1939–1945*, Ottawa, 1949
5. DO 121/10A, Cranborne to P.M., 8 Oct. 1943
6. DO 35/1216/W.R./254/1/40, *Notes on the U.N. Monetary & Financial Conference*, 31 July 1944

7. DO 35/1236/A, 341/5/65, Report and Note by Shannon, 15 Dec. 1944
8. ibid., Minutes by Machtig and Cranborne, 9 and 14 Jan. 1945
9. Swinton, *I Remember*: 255

Chapter 7 (pp. 233–48)

1. Churchill, vol. I: 335
2. ibid.: 582–3
3. CAB 67/2 W.P. (G) (39) 102, Memo by Doms. Sec., 20 Feb. 1939
4. Churchill, vol. I: 583
5. Longford and O'Neill, *Eamon de Valera*: 351
6. DO 35/1107/W.X.1/5, Memo by Maffey, Sept. 1939
7. ibid., Notes by Maffey, 24 Sept. 1939
8. CAB 67 2, Memo by Eden, 28 Oct. 1939
9. PREM 3 131/3, Note of talk between MacDonald and de Valera, 23 June 1940
10. ibid., /2, Memo to de Valera, 26 June 1940
11. ibid., /1, Note of talk, 26 June 1940
12. ibid., /2, tel. from Dublin no. 65, 28 June 1940
13. ibid., /2, D.O. tel. to Dublin no. 85, 28 June 1940
14. Longford and O'Neill: 367
15. MacDonald, *Titans and Others*: 84
16. ibid.: 85
17. Churchill, vol. II: 153, Minute to Ismay of 30 June 1940
18. Churchill, vol. III, Appendix C, Minute to Doms. Sec., 17 Jan. 1941
19. FO 371 36002, Attlee to Eden, 5 Mar. 1943
20. Churchill, vol. II, Appendix A, Minute to Doms. Sec., 22 Nov. 1940
21. Churchill, vol. II: 534, Minute to Chancellor, 1 Dec. 1940
22. Churchill, vol. II: 23, P.M. to President, 13 Dec. 1940
23. CAB 66 14, Memo by Chancellor, 6 Dec. 1940
24. CAB 66 15, Memo by Doms. Sec., 19 Mar. 1941
25. DO 35, 1228
26. DO 35, 1229, Maffey to Machtig, May 1945
27. PREM 3 131/3, Memo by Maffey, 20 Jan. 1941
28. ibid., Doms. Sec. to P.M., 30 Jan. 1941
29. ibid., P.M. to Doms. Sec., M 104/1, 31 Jan. 1941
30. ibid. Memo by Maffey, 20 Jan. 1941
31. DO 35/1109
32. DO 35/1109/W.X. 37/4, Maffey to Machtig, 28 May 1941
33. PREM 3 131/4, P.M. to Doms. Sec., M 204/1, 19 Feb. 1941
34. Churchill, vol. III: 539, P.M. to de Valera, 8 Feb. 1941
35. Longford and O'Neill: 393
36. CAB 67/9 W.P. (G) 4/158, Memo by Doms. Sec., 19 Dec. 1941
37. DO 35/543/D 28/46A, CAB Minutes 47 (39) Concl. 3, 1 Sept. 1939
38. ibid., D.O. memo, 1 Sept. 1939
39. Longford and O'Neill: 397
40. DO 121, Doms. Sec. to P.M., 2 Feb. 1944

Chapter 8 (pp. 249–61)

1. Cmd. 6259
2. Dixon: 55–6
3. DO 121/92X/J.464, Notes on Newfoundland by Garner, Oct. 1941
4. DO 35/723/N.2/73, Memo by Emrys-Evans, 10 June 1942
5. ibid., Minute by Machtig, 13 June 1942
6. Attlee, *As It Happened*: 125
7. ibid.: 127

8. DO 35/723/N.2/73, Undated note by Attlee
9. HC Deb., vol. 389, 5 May 1943
10. Chadwick, *Newfoundland: Island into Province*:185
11. A. P. Herbert, *Independent Member*, London, 1950:286–7
12. PREM 4/44/3/W.P. (43) 507, Memo by Doms. Sec., 8 Nov. 1943
13. HC Deb., vol. 395, 2 Dec. 1943
14. ibid., vol. 395, 16 Dec. 1943
15. DO 35/1344/N. 402/39, P.M.'s Minute, 1 Sept. 1945
16. ibid., Dom. Sec.'s Minute, 5 Sept. 1945
17. ibid., P.M.'s Minute, 7 Sept. 1945
18. ibid., Ottawa tel. 1949, 22 Sept. 1945
19. HC Deb., vol. 417, 11 Dec. 1945
20. Cmd. 6849, *Report on the Financial & Economic Position of Newfoundland*
21. Chadwick:195
22. 12 & 13 Geo VI Ch 22 (the Terms of Union are set out in the Schedule to the Act)
23. DO 35/903/Y.6/349, Minute by Eden, 2 Oct. 1939
24. DO 116/7/94, D.O. to H.Cr., 18 Oct. 1939
25. DO 35/904/Y.6/356, Minute by Devonshire, 24 Oct. 1939
26. DO 35/904/Y.6/361, Clark to D.O., Jan. 1940
27. DO 35/904/Y.8/69, Minute by Machtig, 27 Nov. 1942
28. DO 35/1172/Y.706, Harlech to D.O., 1 Nov. 1943 and 17 Jan. 1944
29. ibid., Minutes by Tait, 29 Nov. 1943 and 28 Sept. 1944. (*See also* DO 35/905/Y.8/64, Minute by Tait, 23 June 1942)
30. DO 35/1172/Y.706/7, Baring to D.O., 2 Apr. 1945
31. Lord Hailey, *The Republic of South Africa and the High Commission Territories*, London, 1963

Chapter 9 (pp. 262–76)

1. Mansergh (ed.), *Documents 1931–1952*, vol. I (Extracts from statements by Curtin on 14 Aug. and 6 Sept. 1943 and from speech of 14 Dec. 1943):562–5
2. ibid. (Extracts from speech to EPA, 25 Nov. 1943):568–75
3. ibid. (Extract from speech of 24 Jan. 1944):575–9
4. Massey:393
5. Pickersgill, vol. I:637
6. DO 35/1204/W.C. 75/9, Ottawa tel. no. 261, 26 Jan. 1944
7. ibid., Ottawa tel. no. 263, 27 Jan. 1944
8. ibid., P.M.'s Minute, M 53/4, 31 Jan. 1944
9. Cranborne, Letter to author, 20 Apr. 1944
10. DO 121/10A, Memo by Cranborne, Jan. 1944
11. ibid., Minute to P.M. from Cranborne, 24 Jan. 1944
12. Pickersgill, vol I.:664
13. CAB 66/49 DPM (44) 14, Memo by Doms. Sec., 7 Apr. 1944
14. Pickersgill, vol. I:687
15. DO 35/1490/W.C. 75/37, P.M. to Curtin, 20 May 1944
16. Mansergh, *Survey*:188
17. Mansergh (ed.), *Documents 1931–1952*, vol. I:587–9
18. PREM 4/43A/14, Draft Memo by P.M., 2 Oct. 1943
19. DO 35/1214/W.R./227/11, Minute by Shannon, 25 Jan. 1944
20. F.O. 371/40691/U, 4098 W.M. (44) 58, Minutes, 27 Apr. 1944
21. DO 121/10A, 62, Minute by Cranborne, 11 May 1944
22. *vide* 20
23. Pickersgill, vol. I:675
24. ibid., vol. I:679
25. F.O. 371/40693/U, 4562, Fraser to Eden, 18 May 1944
26. ibid., /U, 4635, P.M. to Cranborne, 22 May 1944
27. CPM Meeting 1946, Final Communiqué, 23 May 1946 (Text in Mansergh (ed.), *Documents*, vol. I:595)

28. Pearson, vol. I:269
29. F.O. 371/50698/U, 2179, Minute by Cockram, 20 Mar. 1945
30. DO 35/1884/W.R. 208/261, Cockram to Machtig, 28 Apr. 1945
31. ibid., Cockram to Stephenson, 15 May 1945
32. ibid., Cockram to Stephenson, 2 June 1945
33. ibid., Cockram to Stephenson, 16 June 1945
34. ibid., Note of Br. Cw. meeting, 18 June 1945
35. ibid., Delegation to F.O., tel. no. 812, 23 June 1945

Part III

Chapter 1 (pp. 279–86)

1. P. Gordon Walker, *The Commonwealth*
2. Ismay, *The Memoirs of General the Lord Ismay*: 453
3. ibid.: 453–4
4. Lord Swinton, *I Remember*: 66

Chapter 2 (pp. 287–305)

1. HC Select Committee on Estimates, Third Report, Session 1958–9, HC 252:122
2. P. Gordon Walker, *The Cabinet*: 150
3. ibid.: 151

Chapter 3 (pp. 306–16)

1. HC Deb., vol. 411, 14 June 1945
2. HMSO, *The Transfer of Power, 1942–7*, vol. VI, Document 4, Wavell to Pethick-Lawrence, 5 Aug. 1945
3. ibid., Document 73, Pethick-Lawrence to Wavell, 27 Aug. 1945
4. ibid., Document 147, Memo by S. of S. for India, Paper IB (45) 15
5. ibid., Document 168, India and Burma Committee, IB (45) 6th Meeting
6. ibid., Document 224, Note of Meeting
7. DO 35/1112/C 257/1/26, Minutes by Stephenson, 24 Nov. 1945, 1 and 8 Jan. 1946
8. ibid., Minute by Addison, 4 Jan. 1946
9. *The Transfer of Power*, vol. VI, Document 358, Brook to Monteath, 16 Jan. 1946
10. ibid., Document 477, Wavell to Pethick-Lawrence, 27 Feb. 1946
11. HC Deb., vol. 439, 1 July 1947
12. HC Select Committee on Estimates, Third Report, Session 1958–9, HC 252:122

Chapter 4 (pp. 317–36)

1. C. Dixon, *Memoirs*: 64
2. CPM Meeting, 1949, Final Communiqué, 27 Apr. 1949
3. Mansergh, *Survey 1939–52*: 252
4. Gordon Walker, *The Commonweath*: 183. *See also The Cabinet*: 150–2
5. Dixon, *Memoirs*: 64–5
6. Can. 10 Geo. VI, c. 15
7. 11 and 12 Geo. VI, c. 56
8. Dixon, *Memoirs*: 59
9. HC Deb., vol. 558, 1 Nov. 1956

10. ibid., vol. 472, 8 Mar. 1950
11. ibid., vol. 483, 26 Jan. 1951
12. ibid., vol. 491, 31 July 1951
13. HL Deb., vol. CLXXII, 27 June 1951
14. ibid., vol. CXCIX, 23 Oct. 1956
15. *The Times*, Letter from Clark, 12 June 1951
16. HL Deb., vol. CLXXII, 27 June 1951

Part IV

Chapter 1 (pp. 339–56)

1. Macmillan, *Riding the Storm*: 350
2. Cmnd. 2712, *Statement of Guidance* is attached to communiqué of CPM Meeting 1965, 25 June 1965
3. Crossman, *The Diaries of a Cabinet Minister*, vol. I: 253–5
4. Wilson, *The Labour Government*: 117
5. *The Economist*, 27 Dec. 1958 and 21 Dec. 1968
6. *The Times*, 2 Apr. 1964
7. HC Deb., vol. 531, 28 July 1954
8. Macmillan, *Pointing the Way*: 292
9. Cmnd. 1148, *Review of the Constitution of Rhodesia and Nyasaland 1960*
10. Sandys, *The Modern Commonwealth*, Jan. 1962
11. Macmillan, *Pointing the Way*: 300–1
12. Macmillan, *At the End of the Day*: 131 and 134
13. Wilson, *The Labour Government*: 277–87
14. Cmnd. 2713, CPM Meeting 1965: agreed memorandum on the Commonwealth Secretariat, July 1965
15. HMSO, *The Future of the Commonwealth. A British View*, London, 1963

Chapter 2 (pp. 357–73)

1. Roskill, *Hankey*, vol. III: 45
2. Macmillan, *Pointing the Way*: 467–8
3. HC Select Committee on Estimates, Third Report, Session 1958–9
4. ibid., Question 713, 7 May 1959

Chapter 3 (pp. 374–82)

1. Alport, *The Sudden Assignment*: 22–3
2. Macmillan, *Riding the Storm*: 412
3. HC Parly Papers, Third Report from the Select Committee on Estimates, 1958–9
4. Heeney, *The Things that are Caesar's*: 91–2
5. Grafftey-Smith, *Hands to Play*
6. Gerald Campbell, *Of True Experience*
7. Mallaby, *From My Level: unwritten minutes*
8. Alport, *Sudden Assignment*
9. Gore-Booth, *With Great Truth and Respect*
10. Hunt, *On the Spot*

11. MacDonald, *Down North*, Toronto, 1943
    The Birds of Brewery Creek, Toronto, 1947
    Birds in my Indian Garden, London, 1961
    Treasure of Kenya, London, 1965
    People and Places, London, 1969
    Titans and Others, London, 1972
12. CRO, *Earnscliffe*, London, 1955. Reprinted 1961

Chapter 4 (pp. 383–405)

1. Cmd. 5949, *Rhodesia–Nyasaland Report 1939*
2. Cmnd. 1148, *Review of the Constitution of Rhodesia and Nyasaland 1960*
3. Macmillan, *Pointing the Way*, diary entry, 25 Oct. 1958: 134
4. ibid., diary entry, 24 Feb. 1960:165
5. Macmillan, *At the End of the Day*:315 and 318
6. ibid.:321
7. Butler, *The Art of the Possible*:216
8. ibid.:226
9. Macmillan, *At the End of the Day*:329
10. Wilson, *The Labour Government*:180
11. *See* Wilson, *The Labour Government*; Butler, *The Art of the Possible*; also Alport, *The Sudden Assignment* and Welensky, *Welensky's 4000 Days*
12. Wilson, *The Labour Government*:196
13. ibid.: 286
14. ibid.: 198
15. ibid.:308 and 313
16. *Evening Standard*, article by Lord George-Brown, 'That Man Wilson', 19 Oct. 1976
17. Macmillan, *At the End of the Day*:7
18. Macmillan, *Pointing the Way*:317
19. Chandos, *The Memoirs of Chandos*, London, 1962:225
20. Macmillan, *At the End of the Day*:233
21. Wilson, *The Labour Government*:133–4
22. *The Times*, 7 Sept. 1965
23. ITV transcript, 1 Aug. 1971
24. Macmillan, *At the End of the Day*:259
25. Hunt, *On the Spot*:145–50

Chapter 5 (pp. 406–21)

1. HC Parly Papers, Third Report from Select Committee on Estimates, 1958–59, CRO
2. HC Deb., vol. 648, 2 Nov. 1961
3. ibid., vol. 648, 16 Nov. 1961
4. ibid., vol. 569, 6 May 1957
5. ibid., vol. 626, 4 July 1960
6. *The Times*, 3 May 1960
7. ibid., 31 Jan. 1957
8. ibid., 29 Aug. 1959
9. ibid., 18 Dec. 1959
10. ibid., 23 Nov. 1961
11. ibid., 27 and 28 May 1960
12. HC Deb., vol. 649, 21 Nov. 1961
13. ibid., vol. 632, 19 Dec. 1960
14. HC Parly Papers, Fourth Report from Select Committee on Estimates, 1959–60, Colonial Office
15. HC Deb., vol. 632, 13 Dec. 1960
16. ibid., vol. 632, 19 Dec. 1960

17. ibid., vol. 655, 15 Mar. 1962
18. ibid., vol. 701, 6 Nov. 1964
19. Cmnd. 2276, Report on Representational Services Overseas, 1962–63
20. Wilson, *The Governance of Britain*: 102
21. Gordon Walker, *The Cabinet*

Chapter 6 (pp. 422–30)

1. Cross, *Whitehall and the Commonwealth*: 62
2. Miller, 'The CRO and the Commonwealth Relations', *Int. Studies*, vol. II, no. 1:59

List of Works Cited

Books

Alport, Lord *The Sudden Assignment: being a record of services in Central Africa during the last controversial years of the Federation of Rhodesia and Nyasaland 1961–3*, London, 1968
Amery, L. S. *My Political Life* (3 vols)
   vol. I *England before the Storm 1896–1914*, London, 1953
   vol. II *War and Peace 1914–1929*, London, 1953
   vol. III *The Unforgiving Years 1929–1940*, London, 1955
Attlee, Earl *As It Happened*, London, 1954
Blaxland, Gregory *J. H. Thomas: A Life for Unity*, London, 1964
Butler, Lord *The Art of the Possible*, London, 1971
Cadogan, Sir Alexander *The Diaries of Sir Alexander Cadogan 1938–1945*, ed. David Dilkes, London, 1971
Campbell, Sir Gerald *Of True Experience*, New York, 1947
Carroll, J. T. *Ireland in the War Years 1939–45*, Newton Abbot, 1975
Casey, Lord *The Future of the Commonwealth*, London, 1963
   Personal Experience 1939–1946, London, 1962
Chadwick, St John *Newfoundland: Island into Province*, Cambridge 1967
Chatfield, Lord (Alfred Ernle Montacute Chatfield, Admiral of the Fleet) *An Autobiography: The Navy & Defence* (2 vols), London, 1942 and 1947
Churchill, W. S. *The Second World War* (6 vols), London
   I *The Gathering Storm*, 1950
   II *Their Finest Hour*, 1949
   III *The Grand Alliance*, 1950
   IV *The Hinge of Fate*, 1951
   V *Closing the Ring*, 1952
   VI *Triumph and Tragedy*, 1954
Creighton, D. *John A. Macdonald, the Old Chieftain*, Toronto, 1955
Cross, J. A. *Whitehall and the Commonwealth*, London, 1967
Crossman, Richard *The Diaries of a Cabinet Minister*, vols I and II, London, 1975 and 1976
Dixon, Sir Charles *Memoirs*. Unpublished
Eden, Anthony (The Earl of Avon) *The Memoirs of the Rt. Hon. Sir Anthony Eden* (3 vols), London
   1 *Facing the Dictators*, 1962
   2 *The Reckoning*, 1965
   3 *Full Circle*, 1960
Edwards, Cecil *Bruce of Melbourne: Man of Two Worlds*, London, 1965
Fiddes, Sir George *The Dominions and Colonial Offices*, London, 1926
Gladwyn, Lord *Memoirs*, New York, 1972

Gordon Walker, Patrick   *The Commonwealth*, London, 1962
The Cabinet, London, 1970 (2nd revised edition, 1972)
Gore-Booth, Lord   *With Great Truth and Respect*, London, 1974
Grafftey-Smith, Sir L.   *Hands to Play*, London and Boston, 1975
Hancock, W. K.   *Survey of British Commonwealth Affairs*, Parts 1 and 2, London, 1937 and 1940–2
   i: *Problems of Nationality 1918–36*
   ii: *Problems of Economic Policy 1918–39*
   Smuts: the fields of force 1919–50, Cambridge, 1968
Harkness, D.   *The Restless Dominion*, London, 1969
Hasluck, Sir P.   *Australia in the War of 1939–1945* Canberra, 1952
   Vol. I *The Government and the People 1939–1941*
   Vol. II *The Government and the People 1942–1945*
Heeney, A.   *The Things that are Caesar's*, Toronto, 1972
Home, Lord   *The Way the Wind Blows*, London, 1976
Hunt, Sir David   *On the Spot*, London, 1975
Hyam, R.   *The Failure of South African Expansion 1908–1948*, London, 1972
Ismay, Lord   *The Memoirs of General the Lord Ismay*, London, 1960
Jeffries, Sir Charles   *The Colonial Office*, London, 1956
Llewellyn Smith, H.   *The Board of Trade* (The Whitehall Series), London and New York, 1928
Lodge, T.   *Dictatorship in Newfoundland*, London, 1939
Longford, Earl of and **O'Neill**, T. P.   *Eamon de Valera*, London, 1970
MacDonald, Malcolm   *People and Places*, London, 1969
Titans and Others, London, 1972
Macmillan, H.   *Tides of Fortune 1945–55*, London, 1969
   Riding the Storm 1956–9, London, 1971
   Pointing the Way 1959–61, London, 1972
   At the End of the Day, London, 1973
Mallaby, Sir G.   *From my Level: unwritten minutes*, London, 1965
Mansergh, Nicholas   *The Commonwealth Experience*, London, 1969
   (ed.) *Documents & Speeches on British Commonwealth Affairs*, 1931–52 and 1952–62, London, 1952 and 1962
   Survey of British Commonwealth Affairs, 1931–39 and *1939–52*, London, 1952 and 1958
Massey, Vincent   *What's Past is Prologue: The Memoirs of the Right Hon. Vincent Massey, C.H.*, Toronto, 1963
Menzies, Sir Robert   *Afternoon Light*, Melbourne, 1967
Middlemas, K. and **Barnes**, J.   *Baldwin: A Biography*, London, 1969
Miller, J. D. B.   *Survey of Commonwealth Affairs. Problems of Expansion and Attrition 1953–1969*, London, 1974
Mountevans, Lord   *Adventurous Life*, London, 1946
Neatby, H. Blair   *William Lyon Mackenzie King, 1924–1932*, Toronto, 1963
Nicolson, Sir Harold   *King George V: His Life and Reign*, London, 1952
Parkinson, Sir Cosmo   *The Colonial Office from Within 1909–1945*, London, 1947
Pearson, L. B.   *The Memoirs of the Rt. Hon. Lester B. Pearson, vol. I, 1897–1948, Mike.* Toronto, 1972
Pickersgill, J. W.   *The Mackenzie King Record* (2 vols)
   vol. I *1939–1944*, Toronto, 1960
   vol. II *1944–1945*, Toronto, 1968
Pound, Reginald   *Evans of the Broke*, London, 1963
Ritchie, Charles   *The Siren Years—Undiplomatic Diaries 1937–1945*, London, 1974

Roskill, Stephen *Hankey: Man of Secrets* (3 vols), London, 1970–74
Shakespeare, Sir G. *Let Candles be Brought In*, London, 1949
Skidelsky, R. *Politicians and the Slump: The Labour Government of 1929–1931*, Harmondsworth, 1971
Strang, Lord *The Foreign Office* (The New Whitehall Series), London and New York, 1955
Swinton, Lord *I Remember*, London, 1948
Vansittart, Sir R. *The Mist Procession*, London, 1958
Watt, Sir Alan *The Evolution of Australian Foreign Policy 1938–1965*, Cambridge, 1967
 Australian Diplomat: Memoirs of Sir Alan Watt, Sydney, 1972
Welensky, Sir R. *Welensky's 4000 days: the life and death of the Federation of Rhodesia and Nyasaland*, London, 1964
Wertheimer, E. S. R. *Portrait of the Labour Party*, trans. Patrick Kirwan, London and New York, 1st edn 1929, 2nd edn 1930
Wheeler-Bennett, J. W. *King George VI His Life and Reign*, London, 1958
Wilson, Sir H. *The Labour Government 1964–1970 A Personal Record*, London, 1971
 The Governance of Britain, London, 1975
Windsor, H.R.H. the Duke of *A King's Story*, London, 1951

Articles

In addition the following articles, not always cited in the text, have been drawn upon.

University of London, Institute of Commonwealth Studies, collected seminar papers on:
  1. 'The changing role of Commonwealth economic connections', no. 8, Oct. 1967–Mar. 1968
  2. 'The Dominions between the Wars', no. 13, Oct. 1970–Mar. 1971, particularly
    David Carlton: 'The Dominions and British policy in the Abyssinian Crisis'
    Keith Middlemas: 'The Effect on Dominion Opinion of British Foreign Policy'
  3. 'Changing economic links in the Commonwealth in the 1970s', no. 14, Oct. 1970–Mar. 1971
The Journal of Imperial and Commonwealth History, vol. I no. 1, Oct. 1972, particularly,
 J. M. Lee: 'The Dissolution of the Empire Marketing Board, 1933: Reflections on a Diary'
 Rainer Tamchina: 'In Search of Common Causes: The Imperial Conference of 1937'
ibid. vol. I, no. 3, May 1973, particularly article by Norman Hillmer: 'A British High Commissioner for Canada 1927–8'
J. D. B. Miller: 'The CRO and Commonwealth Relations', *International Studies* (New Delhi), vol. II, no. 1, Bombay, July 1960
 'The Decline of Inter Se', *Canadian Institute of International Affairs*, vol. XXIV, no. 4, Autumn 1969
Leslie Monson: 'The Process of Decolonization' in *The Modernization of the British Government*, Pitman Publishing, 1975
The Economist: 'Cwthmas', 27 Dec. 1958
 'God rest ye Merry Cwthmen', 21 Dec. 1968
R. F. Holland, 'The Commonwealth in the British official mind: a study in Anglo–Dominion relations 1925–37', doctoral thesis

INDEX

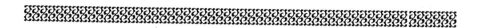

Index

472